Fourth Edition

LANGUAGE ARTS

Content and Teaching Strategies

Gail E. Tompkins

California State University, Fresno

Merrill, an imprint of Prentice Hall

Upper Saddle River, New Jersey   Columbus, Ohio

Library of Congress Cataloging-in-Publication Data

Tompkins, Gail E.
    Language arts : content and teaching strategies / Gail E.
Tompkins. — 4th ed.
      p. cm.
    Includes bibliographical references and index.
    ISBN 0-13-856907-X (hc)
    1. Language arts (Elementary)   I. Title.
LB1576.T655 1998
372.6--dc21

96-533398
CIP

Cover art: Gail E. Tompkins
Editor: Bradley J. Potthoff
Developmental Editor: Linda Scharp McElhiney
Production Editor: Patricia S. Kelly
Copyeditor: Jonathan Lawrence
Design Coordinator: Julia Zonneveld Van Hook
Text and Insert Designer: Anne Flanagan
Cover Designer: Brian Deep
Production Manager: Laura Messerly
Director of Marketing: Kevin Flanagan
Marketing Manager: Suzanne Stanton
Advertising/Marketing Coordinator: Julie Shough

This book was set in Korinna and Helvetica by The Clarinda Company and was printed and bound by Von Hoffmann Press, Inc. The cover was printed by Von Hoffmann Press, Inc.

Earlier editions © 1991 by Macmillan Publishing Company and © 1987 by Merrill Publishing Company.

Photo credits: pp. 112, 297, 425 by Brad Feinknopf, Merrill; pp. 112, 215, 297, 425, 472 by Barbara Schwartz, Merrill; pp. 129, 215, 251, 311, 362, 472, 497, 526 by Scott Cunningham, Merrill; pp. 112, 129, 215, 251, 297, 311, 362, 425, 472, 497, 526 by Anne Vega, Merrill. All other photos by Gail E. Tompkins.

Printed in the United States of America

10 9 8 7

ISBN: 0-13-856907-X

PRENTICE-HALL INTERNATIONAL (UK) LIMITED, *London*
PRENTICE-HALL OF AUSTRALIA PTY. LIMITED, *Sydney*
PRENTICE-HALL CANADA INC., *Toronto*
PRENTICE-HALL HISPANOAMERICANA, S.A., *Mexico*
PRENTICE-HALL OF INDIA PRIVATE LIMITED, *New Delhi*
PRENTICE-HALL OF JAPAN, INC., *Tokyo*
PEARSON EDUCATION ASIA PTE. LTD., *Singapore*
EDITORA PRENTICE-HALL DO BRASIL, LTDA., *Rio de Janeiro*

o Linda and John Cooke,
who are always there for me

Strategies
p. 32-33   p. 35 Skills   p. 59, 60, 61   p. 65

Preface

elping students learn to communicate effectively continues to be a great challenge, especially given the cultural and linguistic diversity of today's classrooms and the swift changes in political and technological environments. It is the intent of this new edition of *Language Arts* to be a useful resource to teachers as they accept and meet these challenges. Both preservice and inservice teachers find this text valuable enough to keep for their professional libraries. For preservice teachers who will work with students in kindergarten through eighth grade, the text provides a consistent model of instruction that helps beginning teachers control the number of instructional decisions they have to make. For inservice teachers, the text provides a rich array of strategies and ideas that experienced teachers can adapt to suit their personal instructional style.

The fourth edition of *Language Arts: Content and Teaching Strategies* is a significant revision of this popular core text designed for elementary and middle school language arts methods courses and language and literacy methods "block" courses.

Philosophy of the Text

The philosophy of the text reflects a constructivist approach to teaching and learning. The processes of reading and writing provide the foundation for the three instructional approaches presented in this book: literature focus units, reading and writing workshops, and theme cycles. These contemporary, innovative approaches to teaching share these important features:

- Establishing a community of learners
- Using "real" literature
- Involving students in meaningful, functional, and genuine activities
- Teaching skills and strategies in context
- Connecting instruction and assessment

This edition features a quilting motif—not only because it is my hobby, but because quilting is a way of looking at the language arts and understanding how they fit together.

Goal of the Text

The goal of the text is to present the content of the language arts curriculum and the most effective strategies for teaching this content. The text is organized in three parts. The first two chapters present an overview of learning and teaching language arts. The middle chapters describe the content and teaching strategies that represent research-based, best practices. The final chapter demonstrates how to create a variety of field-tested language arts units.

Did you know that there are now six language arts? In addition to **listening, talking, reading,** and **writing,** the new *Standards for the English Language Arts* (1996)* recognized the importance visual literacy plays in communication. Visual literacy is demonstrated through two modes, **viewing** and **visually representing.** Viewing, like listening and reading, is receptive. Students are viewing when they compare video versions of stories to the print versions, examine illustrations in books they are reading, and analyze charts classmates have constructed. Visually representing, like talking and writing, is productive. Students are visually representing when they create story quilts, dramatize a story, or synthesize information in a chart or diagram.

So, how does the quilting motif fit in? The six pieces in the star design on the cover represent the six language arts, and just as the red pieces of fabric fit together to form the star, the six language arts fit together to create the language arts curriculum.

Special Features in the Fourth Edition

- The processes of reading and writing provide the foundation for the three instructional approaches used in this book: **literature focus units, reading and writing workshop,** and **theme cycles.**
- **PRO-Files** at the beginning of each chapter feature actual classroom teachers and demonstrate how teachers implement the chapter information in K–8 classrooms.
- **Adapting Instruction to Meet the Needs of Every Student** is a special feature in most chapters. In this section and the accompanying figure, you will find explicit suggestions for scaffolding and modifying the learning experiences for students with special learning needs so that they can be successful.
- Information about how to teach **Minilessons** is provided in Chapter 2, and lists of topics for minilessons are included throughout the text.
- **Teacher's Notebook** pages contain practical information and teaching tips that students will want to have available when they begin their teaching careers.
- **Extension** activities help readers apply information, and many invite them to observe and interact with students in elementary and middle school

---

*Standards for the English Language Arts is a project of the National Council of Teachers of English and the International Reading Association. Copies can be ordered from either organization: NCTE, 1111 W. Kenyon Road, Urbana, IL 61801-1096; IRA, 800 Barksdale Road, P.O. Box 8139, Newark, DE 19714-8139.

classrooms. Others ask them to prepare instructional materials, consult outside readings, or examine how they use language.

New to This Edition

- This edition features a quilting motif as a way of looking at the six language arts (listening, talking, reading, writing, viewing, and visually representing), to examine how they fit together to create the language arts curriculum.
- The concepts of visual literacy—viewing and visual representation—have been added, and a variety of applications in literature focus units and theme cycles are described.
- A greater emphasis is placed on strategies and skills, the role of the reading process (particularly comprehension), and the reasons behind teaching strategies. This new edition also examines the reasons for choosing certain teaching strategies in particular situations.
- Chapter 13, "Putting It All Together," is new for this edition. In that chapter, you will learn how to develop literature focus units and theme cycles, and how to plan for and manage reading and writing workshop. Planning clusters for six field-tested focus units are also included.

Acknowledgments

Many people helped and encouraged me during the development of this text and during the revisions. My heartfelt thanks goes to each of them. First, I thank my students at California State University, Fresno, who have taught me as I taught them. Their insightful questions challenged and broadened my thinking, and their willingness to experiment with the teaching strategies that I was developing furthered my own learning.

I want to express my appreciation to the teachers who invited me into their classrooms and shared their expertise with me. In particular I want to thank the teachers spotlighted in the PRO-Files and chapter openers: Eileen Boland, Southeast Middle School, Fresno, CA; Linda Boroski, John Muir Elementary School, Fresno, CA; Kathy Brown, Jackson Elementary School, Selma, CA; Chris Carmean, Pioneer Middle School, Hanford, CA; Pat Daniel, South Rock Creek School, Norman, OK; Whitney Donnelly, Williams Ranch Elementary School, Penn Valley, CA; Josie Fierro, Wilson Elementary School, Sanger, CA; Lori Gonzalez, Garfield Elementary School, Selma, CA; Laurie Goodman, Pioneer Middle School, Hanford, CA; Sandy Harris, Anadarko Middle School, Anadarko, OK; Glenna Jarvis, Western Hills School, Lawton, OK; Terry Kasner, Sierra Elementary School, Tollhouse, CA; Diane Kirkpatrick, Wolters Elementary School, Fresno, CA; Kristi McNeal, Cooper Hills Elementary School, Clovis, CA; Carol Ochs, Jackson Elementary School, Norman, OK; Judy Reeves, Western Hills School, Lawton, OK; Albena Reinig, Thomas Oleatas Elementary School, Atwater, CA; Jeannie Santos, Cooper Middle School, Fresno, CA; Cheryl Schellenberg, Lincoln Elementary School, Dinuba, CA; Paula Schiefer, Washington School, Selma, CA; Mary Yamazaki, Truckee Elementary School, Truckee, CA; and Susan Zumwalt, Terry Elementary School, Selma, CA.

Thanks, too, to the children whose writing samples and photographs appear in the book and to the teachers and administrators who welcomed us into their schools to take photographs and collect writing samples for this edition: Juli Carson, Jefferson Elementary School, Norman, OK; Kimberly Clark, Aynesworth Elementary School, Fresno, CA; Chris Edge-Christensen, Whittier Elementary School, Lawton, OK; Susan Fields, Noble Junior High School, Noble, OK; Charlotte Fleetham, Pioneer Intermediate School, Noble, OK; Parthy Ford, Whittier Elementary School, Lawton, OK; Peggy Givens, Watonga Middle School, Watonga, OK; Garett Griebel, Chickasha, OK; Judy Hoddy, Hennessy School, Penn Valley, CA; Nancy Hutter, Tioga Elementary School, Bensenville, IL; Alison Johns, Fremont Junior High School, Fowler, CA; Judy Kenney, Jackson Elementary School, Selma, CA; Mark Mattingly, Central Junior High School, Lawton, OK; Tissie McClure, Nicoma Park Intermediate School, Nicoma Park, OK; John McCracken, Nevin Coppock School, Tipp City, OH; Teresa Miller, Hester Elementary School, Farmersville, CA; Sandra Pabst, Monroe Elementary School, Norman, OK; JoAnne Pierce, Horace Mann Elementary School, Duncan, OK; Jenny Reno, Kay Preston, Eunice Edison, Pat Blackburn, Western Hills Elementary School, Lawton, OK; Becky Selle, Bethel School, Shawnee, OK; Jo Ann Steffen, Nicoma Park Junior High School, Nicoma Park, OK; MaryBeth Webeler, Highland Elementary School, Downers Grove, IL; Sonja Weins, Ann Leavensworth Elementary School, Fresno, CA; Brenda Wilkins, Horace Mann Elementary School, Duncan, OK; and Jean Winters and Diane Lewis, Irving Middle School, Norman, OK. And, thanks, too, to the parents who welcomed me into their homes to take photographs of their children and shared their children's writing: Carole and Bill Hamilton, Martha and Rob Lamm, John and Lois McCracken, and Susan Steele.

I also want to thank my colleagues who served as reviewers for this edition: Joanne E. Bernstein, Brooklyn College, CUNY; Victoria Chou, University of Illinois-Chicago; Elaine Fowler Costas, The University of Texas at Austin; Joan B. Elliott, Indiana University of Pennsylvania; Susan I. McMahon, University of Wisconsin-Madison. I appreciate their thoughtful analyses and insights.

Finally, I want to express my sincere appreciation to Jeff Johnston and Brad Potthoff at Merrill in Columbus, Ohio. I want to thank my editor and friend, Linda Scharp McEliney, who encouraged my desire to use a quilt motif in this edition, designed the special features, and spurred me on toward impossible deadlines. Thanks to Patty Kelly, my production editor, who moved the book so expertly through the maze of production details. And, very special thanks to Jonathan Lawrence, copyeditor *extraordinaire*, who worked long and hard to make the text look the way I wanted it to look and say what I intended it to say.

Brief Contents

Contents

9 Reading and Writing Stories   343

10 Reading and Writing Information   387

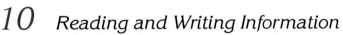

Patterns, Pieces, and Processes
A Preview of the New Edition of

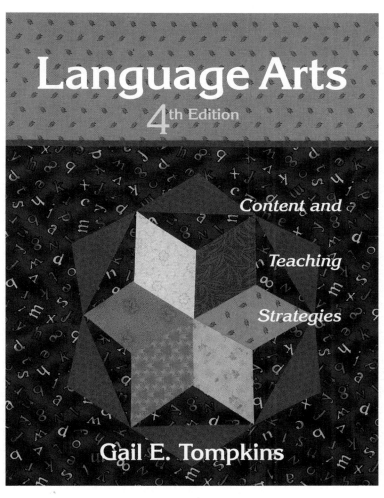

Language Arts
4th Edition

Content and

Teaching

Strategies

Gail E. Tompkins

A QUICK GLANCE will show you that I've chosen a quilting motif for the fourth edition of *Language Arts*. At first, quilting and language arts may not seem to have much in common. However, just as quilts are constructed using fabric pieces sewn into geometric patterns, language arts instruction is designed using reading, writing, and the other language arts. Quilters use a process of selecting fabrics and patterns, stitching the quilt squares together, making a quilt "sandwich," and finally quilting these layers together. Students use similar multistep, recursive processes as they use language to communicate meaning.

Do you see the six red triangles on the cover? The red triangles represent the six language arts: listening, talking, reading, writing, viewing, and visually representing. You're probably used to thinking in terms of four language arts. The two new language arts represent visual ways of constructing meaning and were recently added as part of the NCTE/IRA Standards for the English Language Arts.

You'll see other quilts inside the book. For example, each chapter begins with an illustration of a quilt square and a photograph of children with quilts they have made. Making quilts of paper or fabric is a popular classroom activity. Teachers plan quiltmaking projects for a variety of reasons—from celebrating books students have read to highlighting important information they have learned. recursive-of relating to, or constituting a procedure that can repeat itself indefinitely.

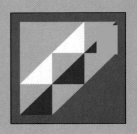

Three Approaches to Teaching

Just as there are many quilt patterns, there are a variety of ways to organize language arts instruction. This edition of *Language Arts* highlights three distinctive instructional approaches: *literature focus units, reading and writing workshops, and theme cycles.* Each of these approaches serves a different purpose. Teachers plan instruction using one or more of these approaches, sometimes alternating or combining them.

LITERATURE FOCUS UNITS are used when a teacher has a single book or several related books to share with the entire class. The shared book experience provides the context for minilessons on skills and strategies. Students respond and make personal connections to the book and create and share individual and small-group projects.

READING AND WRITING WORKSHOPS

provide students with extended opportunities for reading and writing. During reading workshop, students choose and read books that both interest them and are written at their level. Students end reading workshop by sharing the books they read with classmates. During writing workshop, students write books on self-selected topics using the writing process. Students sit in the "author's chair" to share their writings.

THEME CYCLES are interdisciplinary units in which students use the language arts as tools for learning. For example, topics for units might be deserts, weather, pioneers, or ancient Greece. During a theme cycle, students read informational books, stories, and poems; write in learning logs; view videos; and create maps and other diagrams. In addition, they research topics of special interest and present oral reports to share what they have learned.

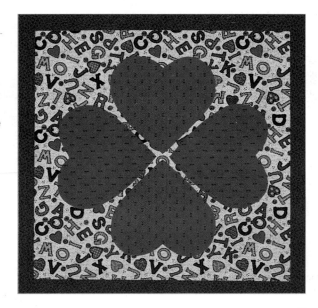

Language Processes

All six language arts are processes of communicating meaning. Listening and talking are oral processes; reading and writing are written processes; and viewing and visually representing are visual processes. In each pair, the first process is receptive and the second is productive. For example, reading is receptive in that the reader takes in symbols and creates meaning, whereas writing is productive in that writers employ symbols to create meaning.

	Oral	Written	Visual
Receptive	listening	reading	viewing
Productive	talking	writing	visually representing

IT IS IMPORTANT TO REMEMBER that a process is a systematic series of actions, not a single act. The language processes are progressive and interdependent steps that lead to comprehending and communicating meaning. The language arts processes are social, in that when students write or talk or visually represent, they have an audience in mind. It is important for students to learn and apply all six language arts processes through meaningful, functional, and genuine activities.

Content and Teaching Strategies

S imply put, *Language Arts* is about what you teach and how you teach it. Both content and teaching strategies are described and modeled in every chapter of this textbook, because both are essential for effective teaching. Examples of language arts **content** include the three types of listening, phonemic awareness, aesthetic and efferent reading, emergent literacy, the community of learners, and the elements of story structure. Examples of **teaching strategies** include grand conversations, minilessons, portfolios, story maps, word sorts, and reading logs.

F

LET'S TAKE A CLOSER LOOK at the relationship between content and teaching strategies. ***Intertextuality,*** students' ability to make connections between stories they are reading or viewing and their prior personal and literary experiences, is a good example of research-based content that needs to be taught. Researchers emphasize that students who make these connections comprehend better than those who don't. So, how do you teach intertextuality? Effective teachers choose a teaching strategy such as grand conversations, simulated journals, or Venn diagrams to help children develop the ability to make personal and literary connections.

meta·cognition

G

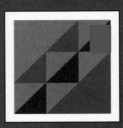

Authentic Assessment

Assessment is an integral part of teaching and learning. Effective teachers plan for assessment at the same time they plan instruction. For example, teachers identify what they are going to teach during a literature focus unit and develop a variety of authentic assessment procedures to monitor students' achievements.

Another way teachers monitor students' progress is through conferences. During conferences, they note each student's individual strengths and weaknesses and help students set goals. Teachers also use the information gained during conferences to identify topics for minilessons that can be used for individual, small-group, and whole-class instruction.

Teachers also help students create portfolios, which are systematic and meaningful collections of artifacts documenting students' language arts development. Students' work samples provide "windows" on their development. Students not only select pieces to be placed in their portfolios, but learn to establish criteria for their selections. Portfolios help students, teachers, and parents see patterns of growth from one language arts milestone to another.

Just as a quilt is pieces of fabric sewn together, the language arts "quilt" is an integration of the approaches to teaching, language processes, content and teaching strategies, and authentic assessment. Quilters know how to use the techniques of quilting to make an heirloom; effective teachers know how to create a harmonious, cohesive, instructional program to meet the needs of their students.

For more information on Merrill Education products, visit our Internet home page at http://www.smartpages.com/merrill

Special Features

About the Author

Gail E. Tompkins is a Professor at California State University, Fresno, in the Department of Literacy and Early Education, where she teaches courses in language arts, reading, and writing for preservice and inservice teachers. She directs the San Joaquin Valley Writing Project and works regularly with teachers, both by teaching model lessons in classrooms and by leading inservice workshops. Previously, Dr. Tompkins taught at Miami University in Ohio and at the University of Oklahoma, where she received the prestigious Regent's Award for Superior Teaching. She was also an elementary teacher in Manassas, Virginia, for eight years.

Several years ago Dr. Tompkins took a course in quilting offered by a local fabric store, and she's been buying fabric, piecing scraps of fabric together, and quilting ever since. For the fourth edition of *Language Arts,* Dr. Tompkins designed the cover for the text and the quilt designs featured on the first page of each chapter. Dr. Tompkins says that she has enjoyed combining her two hobbies--quilting and writing.

Dr. Tompkins is also the author of *Literacy for the 21st Century: A Balanced Approach* (Merrill/Prentice Hall, 1997), *Teaching Writing: Balancing Process and Product* (2nd ed.) (Merrill/Prentice Hall, 1994) and co-author, with Lea McGee, of *Teaching Reading With Literature* (Merrill/Prentice Hall, 1993). She has written numerous articles related to language arts that have appeared in *Language Arts, The Reading Teacher, Journal of Adolescent and Adult Literacy,* and other professional journals. She currently serves on the Review Board of *The Reading Teacher.*

> **❝** I've always loved quilts. I have several from my grandmother that I treasure, and I like sharing them with my students. It's part of America, part of our cultural heritage. Every year I find a way to work them into the language arts curriculum. **❞**
>
> **Terry Kasner**
> Second-Grade Teacher
> Sierra Elementary School

PROCEDURE

At the beginning of the school year, I always hang one of my quilts in the classroom. I tell my students about my grandmother who made the quilt and about how it was passed down to me. My students often talk about the quilts they have in their homes, too. Their parents even allow them to bring some of their quilts to school to share with us. I identify some of the quilt patterns, and we talk about the use of pattern design and color in quilts.

Then I suggest that we make paper quilts to celebrate our favorite books. We make a Cinderella quilt as part of a unit comparing various versions of the familiar folktale. My students work in small groups to make quilt squares. They draw a picture of the Cinderella character they like best in the center of the square and add a quote from the book around the outside of the square. After we arrange the squares on the wall, we make a border for the quilt. Students choose an object or design for the border that symbolizes the book. For the Cinderella quilt, they cut out shoes for the border.

My students also make individual quilts about themselves during a unit on autobiography. They cut out a large square of posterboard for their quilts. Then they cut four smaller squares to place on the quilt. In each square they draw and write information about themselves. One square is about their families, for example, and another square is about their favorite books. Other squares might focus on hobbies, pets, important events, or dreams for the future.

In the spring when we begin our pioneer unit, I focus on quilts again. I read these quilt books with my students:

The Rag Coat (Mills, 1991)

Tar Beach (Ringgold, 1991)

The Patchwork Quilt (Flournoy, 1985)

The Keeping Quilt (Polacco, 1988)

Sam Johnson and the Blue Ribbon Quilt (Ernst, 1983)

Sweet Clara and the Freedom Quilt (Hopkinson, 1993)

The Quilt (Jonas, 1984)

The Whispering Cloth: A Refugee's Story (Shea, 1995)

The Quilt Story (Johnson, 1985)

Selina and the Bear Paw Quilt (Smucker, 1996)

Some of the books I read aloud to the class. I have five or six copies of several quilt books for my students to read in small-group book clubs, and students read other books independently during reading workshop. Students look for quilt patterns in each of the books, and then they make quilt pictures in the art center using geometric shapes cut from wallpaper sample books. It seems that every year the log cabin pattern is the students' favorite.

Now we're making small quilts, approximately six inches square. Several parents volunteer to help the children choose coordinating fabrics, cut and stitch the pieces, make the quilt sandwich, and do the quilting. I think my class has a new appreciation of the work involved in making a quilt now that they are doing it themselves!

ASSESSMENT

I'm a kid-watcher and I notice how my children work together on projects. I notice which children are involved in activities, which ones suggest ideas for quilt designs, colors, and symbols, and which ones seem disinterested or unsure. All of my students are involved with quilts, and that's probably because I care so much about quilts. They're all eager to make paper quilt squares as part of literature focus units, and everyone is now busy sewing their own quilts.

ADAPTATIONS

I have thought about making quilts as part of social studies and science themes. When we study insects, for example, my students could draw pictures of their favorite insects and write facts they've learned around the outside of the quilt square. Or, when we study weather, they could write information about different kinds of weather in each square. There's a zigzag pattern that looks like lightning that students could use for a weather quilt. Perhaps bright yellow zigzag on a gray background. I think my students would like that!

REFLECTIONS

Quilts are very versatile. I've been able to work them into the second-grade curriculum in a variety of ways—reading, writing, social studies, art, and even math. At the beginning of the school year when I shared my quilt, and the children shared their family quilts, we became a classroom community. The most important thing I've accomplished, I guess, is to develop my children's awareness of our American heritage. Every one of these children will more deeply appreciate any quilts that might be passed down to them, and I can already spot two or three students who might just become quilters.

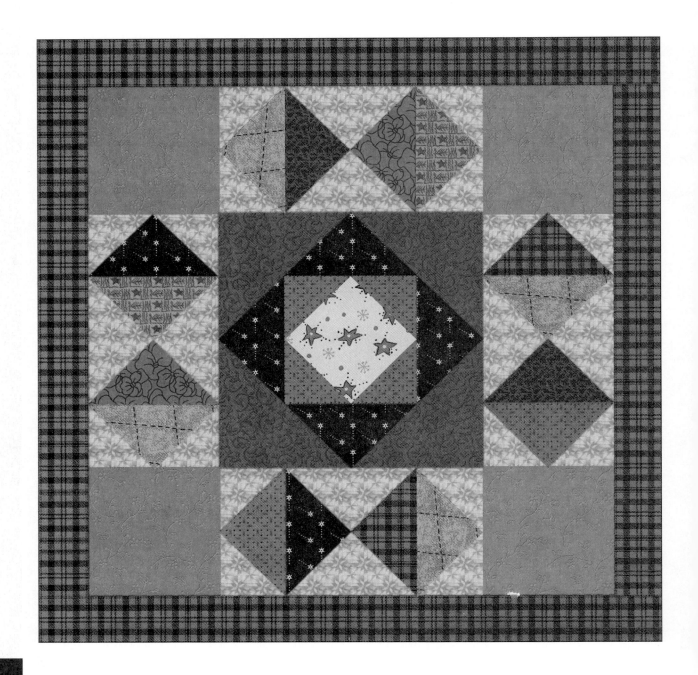

Learning and the Language Arts

Jeannie Santos and her middle school students created a quilt of their favorite books as part of their reading workshop. Mrs. Santos took photos of the students for the center of the quilt squares, and students wrote about a favorite book and chose colors for their squares in keeping with the theme of the book. The students in Mrs. Santos's classroom have a 30-minute reading workshop block each day, and students add their square to the quilt when they do a book talk to share a favorite book with classmates.

nderstanding how children learn and, particularly, how they learn language influences how we teach language arts. The instructional program should never be construed as a smorgasbord of materials and activities; instead, teachers design instruction based on what they know about how children learn. The teacher's role in the elementary classroom is changing. Teachers are now decision makers, empowered with both the obligation and the responsibility to make curricular decisions. In the language arts program, these curricular decisions have an impact on the content (information being taught) and the teaching strategies (techniques for teaching content).

My approach in this textbook incorporates both the constructivist theory of learning proposed by Jean Piaget and the sociolinguistic theory of Lev Vygotsky. As you read this chapter, think about these questions:

- How do children learn?
- What are the roles of language and culture in learning?
- What are the language arts?
- How do children learn language arts?

HOW CHILDREN LEARN

Swiss psychologist Jean Piaget (1886–1980) developed a new theory of learning that radically changed our conceptions of child development. His constructivist framework (1969) differs substantially from behavioral theories that had influenced education for decades. Piaget described learning as the modification of students' cognitive structures as they interact with and adapt to their environment. He believed that children construct their own knowledge from their experiences. Related to Piaget's theory is information-processing theory (Flavell, 1985; Siegler, 1986), which focuses on how learners use cognitive processes and think about what and how they are learning. This new view of learning requires a reexamination of the teacher's role. Instead of being primarily dispensers of knowledge, teachers provide students with reading and writing experiences and opportunities to manipulate objects such as story boards, magnetic letters, and objects in book boxes in order for students to construct their own knowledge (Pearson, 1993).

Sociolinguists emphasize the importance of language in learning and view learning as a reflection of the culture and community in which students live (Heath, 1983b; Vygotsky, 1978, 1986). According to Vygotsky, language helps to organize thought, and children use language to learn as well as to communicate and share experiences with others. Understanding that children use language for social purposes, teachers plan instructional activities that incorporate a social component, such as having students share their writing with classmates. And, because children's language and concepts of literacy reflect their cultures and home communities, teachers must respect students' language and appreciate cultural differences in their attitudes toward learning—and toward learning language arts in particular.

The Cognitive Structure

Children's knowledge is not just a collection of isolated bits of information; it is organized in the brain, and this organization becomes increasingly integrated and interrelated as their knowledge grows. The organization of knowledge is the cognitive structure, and knowledge is arranged in category systems called *schemata*. (A single category is called a *schema*.) Within the schemata are three components: categories of knowledge, the features or rules for determining what constitutes a category and what will be included in each category, and a network of interrelationships among the categories.

These schemata may be likened to a conceptual filing system in which children and adults organize and store the information derived from their past experiences. Taking this analogy further, information is filed in the brain in "file folders." As children learn, they add file folders to their filing system, and as they study a topic, that file folder becomes thicker.

As children learn, they invent new categories, and while different people have many similar categories, schemata are personalized according to individual experiences and interests. Some people, for example, may have only one general category, bugs, into which they lump their knowledge of ants, butterflies, spiders, and bees, while other people distinguish between insects and spiders and develop a category for each. Those who distinguish between insects and spiders also develop a set of rules based on the distinctive characteristics of these animals for classifying them into one category or the other. In addition to insect or spider categories, a network of interrelationships connects these categories to other categories. Networks, too, are individualized, depending on each person's unique knowledge and experiences. The category of spiders might be networked as a subcategory of arachnids, and the class relationship between scorpions and spiders might be made. Other networks, such as a connection to a poisonous animals category or a webs and nests category, could have been made. The networks that link categories, characteristics, and examples with other categories, characteristics, and examples are extremely complex.

As children adapt to their environment, they add new information about their experiences that requires them to enlarge existing categories or to construct new ones. According to Piaget (1969), two processes make this change possible. Assimilation is the cognitive process by which information from the environment is integrated into existing schemata. In contrast, accommodation is the cognitive process by which existing schemata are modified or new schemata are restructured to adapt to the environment. Through assimilation, children add new information to their picture of the world; through accommodation, they change that picture on the basis of new information.

The Process of Learning

Piaget recognized that children are naturally curious about their world and are active and motivated learners. New experiences are necessary for learning. Children experiment with the objects they encounter and try to make sense out of their experiences; that is to say, they construct their own knowledge from interactions and experiences rather than through passively receiving environmental stimulation. Oral and written language work the same way. Children interact with language just as they experiment with bicycles they ride.

Learning occurs through the process of equilibration (Piaget, 1975). When a child encounters something he or she does not understand or cannot assimilate, disequilibrium, or cognitive conflict, results. This disequilibrium typically

discrepant.
difference or
disagreement

produces confusion and agitation, feelings that impel children to seek equilibrium, or a comfortable balance with the environment. In other words, when confronted with new or discrepant information, children (as well as adults) are intrinsically motivated to try to make sense of it. If the child's schemata can accommodate the new information, then the disequilibrium caused by the new experience will motivate the child to learn. Equilibrium is thus regained at a higher developmental level. These are the steps of this process:

1. Equilibrium is disrupted by the introduction of new or discrepant information.
2. Disequilibrium occurs, and the dual processes of assimilation and accommodation function.
3. Equilibrium is attained at a higher developmental level.

The process of equilibration happens to us again and again during the course of a day. In fact, it is occurring right now as you are reading this chapter. If you are already familiar with the constructivist learning theory and have learned about Piaget in other education courses, your mental filing cabinet has been activated and you are assimilating the information you are reading into the file folder on "Piaget" or "learning theories" already in your filing cabinet. If, however, you're not familiar with constructivist learning theories, your mind is actively creating a new file folder in which to put the information you are reading.

Learning doesn't always occur when we are presented with new information, however. If the new information is too difficult and we cannot relate it to what we already know, we do not learn. This is true for both children and adults. The important implication for teachers is that new information must be puzzling, challenging, or, in Piaget's words, "moderately novel." Information that is too familiar is quickly assimilated, and information that is too unfamiliar cannot be accommodated and will not be learned.

Learning Strategies

We all have skills that we use automatically, as well as self-regulated strategies for things that we do well—driving defensively, playing volleyball, training a new pet, or maintaining classroom discipline. We apply skills we have learned unconsciously and choose among skills as we think strategically. The strategies we use in these activities are problem-solving mechanisms that involve complex thinking processes. When we are just learning how to drive a car, for example, we learn both skills and strategies. Some of the first skills we learn are how to start the engine, make left turns, and parallel park. With practice, these skills become automatic. Some of the first strategies we learn are how to pass another car and how to stay a safe distance behind the cars ahead of us. At first we have only a small repertoire of strategies, and we don't always use them effectively. That's one reason why we take lessons from a driving instructor and have a learner's permit that requires a more experienced driver to ride along with us. These seasoned drivers teach us defensive driving strategies. We learn strategies for driving on interstate highways, on slippery roads, and at night. With practice and guidance, we become more successful drivers, able to anticipate driving problems and take defensive actions.

First graders use organizing and elaborating strategies as they retell the story "I Know an Old Lady Who Swallowed a Fly."

During the elementary grades, children develop a number of learning strategies or methods for learning. Rehearsal—repeating information over and over—is one learning strategy or cognitive process that children can use to remember something. Other learning strategies include:

Predicting: anticipating what will happen

Organizing: grouping information into categories

Elaborating: expanding on the information presented

Monitoring: regulating or keeping track of progress

Information-processing theory suggests that as children grow older, their use of learning strategies improves (Flavell, 1985).

As they acquire more effective methods for learning and remembering information, children also become more aware of their own cognitive processes and better able to regulate them. Elementary students can reflect on their literacy processes and talk about themselves as readers and writers. For example, third grader Mario reports that "It's mostly after I read a book that I write" (Muhammad, 1993, p. 99), and fifth grader Hobbes reports that "the pictures in my head help me when I write stuff down 'cause then I can get ideas from my pictures" (Cleary, 1993, p. 142). Eighth grader Chandra talks about poetry: "Poetry is a fine activity, and it can get you in tune with yourself. . . . I think that my favorite person who does poetry is Maya Angelou" (Steinbergh, 1993, p. 212).

Students become more realistic about the limitations of their memories and more knowledgeable about which learning strategies are most effective in particular situations. They also become increasingly aware of what they know and don't know. The term *metacognition* refers to this knowledge children acquire about their own cognitive processes and to children's regulation of their cognitive processes to maximize learning.

Teachers play an important role in developing children's metacognitive abilities. During large-group activities, teachers introduce and model learning strategies. In small-group lessons, teachers provide guided practice, talk with children about learning strategies, and ask students to reflect on their own use of these cognitive processes. Teachers also guide students about when to use particular strategies and which strategies are more effective with various activities.

Social Contexts of Learning

Children's cognitive development is enhanced through social interaction. Russian psychologist Lev Vygotsky (1896–1934) asserted that children learn through socially meaningful interactions and that language is both social and an important facilitator of learning. Children's experiences are organized and shaped by society, but rather than merely absorbing these experiences, children negotiate and transform them as a dynamic part of culture. They learn to talk through social interactions and to read and write through interactions with literate children and adults (Dyson, 1993; Harste, 1990). Community is important for both readers and writers. Students talk about books they are reading with classmates, and they turn to classmates for feedback about their writing (Zebroski, 1994).

Through interactions with adults and collaboration with other children, children learn things they could not learn on their own. Adults guide and support children as they move from their current level of knowledge toward a more advanced level. Vygotsky (1978) described these two levels as, first, the actual developmental level, the level at which children can perform a task independently; and second, the level of potential development, the level at which children can perform a task with assistance. Children can typically do more difficult things in collaboration than they can on their own, and this is why teachers are important models for their students and why children often work with partners and in small groups.

A child's "zone of proximal development" (Vygotsky, 1978) is the range of tasks that the child can perform with guidance from others but cannot yet perform independently. Vygotsky believed that children learn best when what they are attempting to learn within this zone. He felt that children learn little by performing tasks they can already do independently—tasks at their actual developmental level—or by attempting tasks that are too difficult or beyond their zone of proximal development.

Vygotsky and Jerome Bruner (1986) both used the term *scaffold* as a metaphor to describe adults' contributions to children's learning. Scaffolds are support mechanisms that teachers, parents, or other more competent individuals provide to help children successfully perform a task within their zone of proximal development. Teachers serve as scaffolds when they model or demonstrate a procedure, guide children through a task, ask questions, break complex tasks into smaller steps, and supply pieces of information. As children gain knowledge and experience about how to perform a task, teachers gradually withdraw their support so that children make the transition from social interaction to internalized, independent functioning.

The teacher's role in guiding students' learning within the zone of proximal development includes three components, according to Dixon-Krauss (1996):

1. Teachers mediate or augment children's learning through social interaction.
2. Teachers are flexible and provide support based on feedback from the children as they are engaged in the learning task. (inc, assessment)
3. Teachers vary the amount of support from very explicit to vague, according to children's needs.

Language, according to Vygotsky, can be used for purposes other than social. Piaget (1975) described how young children engage in egocentric speech—talking aloud to themselves as they pursue activities, such as building with blocks. Vygotsky (1986) noticed that older children and adults sometimes talk to themselves while performing a difficult or frustrating task, and he noted that this talking aloud seemed to guide or direct their thinking. From these observations, Vygotsky concluded that language is a mechanism for thought and that children's egocentric speech (which he called "self-talk") gradually becomes inner speech, where children talk to themselves mentally rather than orally. Self-talk is the link between talk used for social purposes and for intellectual purposes. According to Vygotsky, children use both self-talk and inner speech to guide their learning.

Implications for Learning Language Arts

Students interact with their environment and actively construct knowledge using the processes of assimilation and accommodation. Students learn when their existing schemata are enlarged because of assimilated information and when their schemata are restructured to account for new experiences being acted on and accommodated.

As students engage in learning activities, they are faced with learning and discovering some new element in an otherwise known or familiar system of information. Students recognize or seek out the information embedded in a situation that makes sense and is moderately novel. When students are forced to contend with the novel part of the information, their schemata are disrupted, or put in a state of disequilibrium. Accommodation of the novel information causes a reorganization of the schemata, resulting in students' having more complex schemata and being able to apply more complex information than was previously possible.

Vygotsky's (1978) concept of the zone of proximal development emphasizes the importance of talk and explains how children learn through social interactions with adults. Adults use scaffolds to help children move from their current stage of development toward their potential, and teachers provide a similar type of assistance as they support students in learning language arts (Applebee & Langer, 1983).

In the lessons they prepare for their students, teachers can create optimal conditions for learning. When students do not have the schemata for predicting and interpreting the new information, teachers must help students relate what they know to what they do not know. Therefore, the new information must appear in a situation that makes sense and must be moderately novel; it must not be too difficult for students to accommodate it.

How children learn has important implications for how students learn language arts in school and how teachers teach language arts. Contributions from the constructivist and sociolinguistic learning theories include:

- Students are active participants in learning.
- Students learn by relating the new information to prior knowledge.
- Students organize their knowledge in schemata.
- Students use skills automatically and strategies consciously as they learn.
- Students learn through social interactions with classmates and the teacher.
- Teachers provide scaffolds for students.

LANGUAGE LEARNING AND CULTURE

Language is a complex system for creating meaning through socially shared conventions (Halliday, 1978). Before children enter elementary school, they learn the language of their community. They understand what community members say to them, and they share their ideas with others through that language. In an amazingly short period of 3 or 4 years, children master the exceedingly complex system of their native language, allowing them to understand sentences they have never heard before and to create sentences they have never said before. Young children are not "taught" how to talk; this knowledge about language develops tacitly, or unconsciously.

The Four Language Systems

Language is organized using four cueing systems, and together these systems make oral and written communication possible. The four language systems are:

- The phonological or sound system of language
- The syntactic or structural system of language
- The semantic or meaning system of language
- The pragmatic or social and cultural use system of language

As children learn to talk, they develop an implicit understanding of the systems, and they apply their knowledge of the four systems whenever they use words—whether for listening or talking, reading or writing, or viewing or visually representing. Students integrate information simultaneously from these four language systems in order to communicate. No one system is more important than any other one.

The Phonological System. There are approximately 44 speech sounds in English. Children learn to pronounce these sounds as they learn to talk, and they learn to associate the sounds with letters as they learn to read and write. Sounds are called phonemes, and they are represented in print with diagonal lines to differentiate them from graphemes, or letter combinations. Thus, the first letter in *mother* is written *m,* while the phoneme is written /m/; the phoneme in *soap* represented by the grapheme *oa* is written /ō/.

The phonological system is important in both oral and written language. Regional and cultural differences exist in the way people pronounce phonemes. For example, Jimmy Carter's speech is characteristic of the southeastern United States, while John F. Kennedy's is typical of New England. Similarly, the English spoken in Australia is different from American English. Children who are learning English as a second language must learn to pronounce English sounds, and sounds that are different from those in their native language are particularly difficult for children to learn. For example, Spanish does not have /th/, and children who have immigrated to the United States from Mexico and other Spanish-speaking countries have difficulty pronouncing this sound. They often substitute /d/ for /th/ because both sounds are articulated in similar ways (Nathenson-Mejia, 1989). Younger children usually learn to pronounce the difficult sounds more easily than older children and adults.

■ *For more information about phonics, see Chapter 4, "Emergent Literacy," pp. 147–154.*

Children use their knowledge of the phonological system as they learn to read and write. In a purely phonetic language, there would be a one-to-one correspondence between letters and sounds, and teaching students to sound out words would be a simple process. But English is not a purely phonetic language, since there are 26 letters and 44 sounds and many ways to combine the letters to spell some of the sounds, especially vowels. Consider these ways to spell long *e: sea, green, Pete, me,* and *people.* And sometimes the patterns used to spell long *e* don't work, as in *head* and *great.* Phonics, which describes the phoneme-grapheme correspondences and related spelling rules, is an important part of reading instruction, since students use phonics information to decode words. However, because not all words can easily be decoded, and because good readers do much more than just decode words when they read, phonics instruction cannot be an entire reading program, even through the advertisements for some commercial phonics programs claim that they are complete programs.

■ *See Chapter 12, pp. 479–484, to learn more about invented spelling.*

Students in the primary grades also use their understanding of the phonological system to create invented or temporary spellings. First graders might, for example, spell *home* as *hm* or *hom,* and second graders might spell *school* as *skule,* based on their knowledge of phoneme-grapheme relationships and the spelling patterns. As students learn more phonics and gain more experience reading and writing, their spellings become more sophisticated and finally become conventional. For students who are learning English as a second language, their spellings often reflect their pronunciations of words (Nathenson-Mejia, 1989).

The Syntactic System. The syntactic system is the structural organization of English. This system is the grammar that regulates how words are combined into sentences. The word *grammar* here means the rules governing how words are combined in sentences, not the grammar of English textbooks or the conventional etiquette of language. Children use the syntactic system as they combine words to form sentences. Word order is important in English, and English speakers must arrange words into a sequence that makes sense. Young Spanish-speaking children who are learning English as a second language, for example, learn to say "This is my red sweater," not "This is my sweater red," which is the literal translation from Spanish. Children also learn to comprehend and produce statements, questions, and other types of sentences during the preschool years.

■ *To read about teaching grammar in the elementary grades, see Chapter 12, pp. 511–527.*

Students use their knowledge of the syntactic system as they read. They anticipate that the words they are reading have been strung together into sentences. When they come to an unfamiliar word, they recognize its role in the sentence even if they don't know the terms for parts of speech. In the sentence "The horses galloped through the gate and out into the field," students may not be able to decode the word *through,* but they can easily substitute a reasonable word or phrase, such as *out of* or *past.* Many of the capitalization and punctuation rules that elementary students learn reflect the syntactic system of language. Similarly, when students learn about simple, compound, and complex sentences, they are learning about the syntactic system.

Another component of syntax is word forms. Words such as *dog* and *play* are morphemes, the smallest meaningful units in language. Words parts that change the meaning of a word are also morphemes. When the plural marker *-s* is added to *dog* to make *dogs,* for instance, or the past-tense marker *-ed* is added to *play* to make *played,* these words now have two morphemes because the inflectional endings changed the meaning of the words. The words *dog* and *play* are free morphemes because they convey meaning while standing alone. The endings *-s* and *-ed* are bound morphemes because they must be attached to a free morpheme to convey meaning. As they learn to talk, children quickly learn to combine words and word parts, such as adding *-s* to *cookie* to create a plural, and adding *-er* to *big* to indicate a comparison. They also learn to combine two or more free morphemes to form compound words. *Birthday,* for example, is a compound word created by combining two free morphemes.

■ *See Chapter 5, "Looking Closely at Words," pp. 186–190, for more information about root words and affixes.*

During the elementary grades, students learn to add affixes to words. Affixes added at the beginning of a word are prefixes, and affixes added at the end are suffixes. Both kinds of affixes are bound morphemes. For example, the prefix *un-* in *unhappy* is a bound morpheme, whereas *happy* is a free morpheme because it can stand alone as a word.

The Semantic System.   The third language system is the semantic or meaning system. Vocabulary is the key component of this system. As children learn to talk, they acquire a vocabulary that is continually increasing through the preschool years and the elementary grades. Researchers estimate that children have a vocabulary of 5,000 words by the time they enter school, and they continue to acquire 3,000 words each year during the elementary grades (Lindfors, 1987; Nagy, 1988). Considering how many words students learn each year, it is unreasonable to assume that they learn words only through formal instruction. Students learn many, many words informally through reading and through social studies, science, and other curricular areas. Students probably learn 8 to 10 words a day. A remarkable achievement!

At the same time that children are learning new words, they are also learning that many words have more than one meaning. Meaning is usually based on the context, or the surrounding words. The common word *run,* for instance, has more than 30 meanings listed in *The Random House Dictionary of the English Language* (Flexner, 1993). Read these sentences to see how the meaning of the word *run* is tied to the context in which it is used:

Will the mayor run for reelection?

The bus runs between Dallas and Houston.

The advertisement will run for three days.

Did you run in the 50-yard dash?

The plane made a bombing run.

Will you run to the store and get a loaf of bread for me?

The dogs are out in the run.

Oh, no! I got a run in my new pair of pantyhose!

■ *Chapter 5, "Looking Closely at Words," focuses on vocabulary, and check Chapter 11, pp. 433–440, for more information on wordplay.*

Children often don't have the full, adult meaning of many words; rather, they learn meanings through a process of refinement. They add "features," or layers of meaning.

Children learn other sophisticated concepts about words as well. They learn about shades of meaning—for example, the differences among these *sad* words: *unhappy, crushed, desolate, miserable, disappointed, cheerless, down,* and *grief-stricken.* They also learn about synonyms and antonyms, wordplay, and figurative language, including idioms.

The Pragmatic System.   The fourth language system is pragmatics, which deals with the social and cultural aspects of language use. People use language for many different purposes, and how they talk or write varies according to purpose and audience.

Language variety is also part of the pragmatic system. Language use varies among social classes, cultural and ethnic groups, and geographic regions. These varieties are known as dialects. School is one cultural community, and the language of school is Standard English. This register, or style, is formal—the one used in textbooks, newspapers, and magazines and by television newscasters. Other forms, including those spoken in urban ghettos, in Appalachia, and by Mexican Americans in the Southwest, are generally classified as nonstandard English. These nonstandard forms of English are alternatives in which the phonology, syntax, and semantics differ from those of Standard English, but they are neither inferior nor substandard. They reflect the communities of the speakers, and the speakers communicate as effectively as those who use Standard English in their communities. The goal is for students to add Standard English to their repertoire of language registers, not to replace their home dialect with Standard English.

As students who speak nonstandard English read texts written in Standard English, they often translate what they read into their own dialect. Sometimes this occurs when they are reading aloud. For example, a sentence that is written "They are going to school" might be read aloud this way: "They be goin' to school." Emergent or beginning readers are not usually corrected when they translate words into nonstandard dialects without changing the meaning, but older, more fluent readers should be directed to read the words as they are printed in the book.

Many trade books include dialogue written in nonstandard English. *Shiloh* (Naylor, 1991), for example, is set in West Virginia, and some of the characters speak nonstandard English. *Mirandy and Brother Wind* (McKissack, 1988) is an African-American folktale, and some of the characters speak Black English. *White Dynamite and Curly Kidd* (Martin & Archambault, 1986) is a rodeo story, rich with the vocabulary, rhyme, and sentence structure of this truly American institution. As students read these books, they learn about the richness and variety of English dialects in the United States.

The four language systems and their terminology are reviewed in Figure 1–1. Both children and adults use the four language systems as they communicate through oral and written language.

Culturally and Linguistically Diverse Students

America is a culturally pluralistic society, and our ethnic, racial, and socioeconomic diversity is increasingly being reflected in elementary classrooms. According to the 1990 Census, 27% of the population in the United States classify themselves as non-European Americans (*The World Almanac and Book of Facts 1997,* 1996, p. 377). The percentage of culturally diverse children is even higher. In California, 51% of school-age children belong to ethnic minority groups, and in New York State 40% do. Given current birthrates of minority groups and immigration patterns, it has been estimated that by the year 2000, both Hispanic-American and Asian-American populations will have grown by more than 20%. The African-American population is estimated to grow by 12%. In fact, demographers predict that by the year 2000, one in three Americans will be nonwhite, and by the middle of the twenty-first century more than half of Americans will be minorities (Bishop, 1992a). These changing demographic realities will have a significant impact on elementary classrooms, as more and more students come from linguistically and culturally diverse backgrounds. More than ever before, all of today's students will live in a global society, and they need the skills and knowledge to live harmoniously with other cultural groups.

America is a nation of immigrants, and dealing with cultural diversity is not a new responsibility for public schools; however, the magnitude of diversity is much greater now. In the past, America was viewed as a melting pot in which language and cultural differences would be assimilated or combined to form a new, truly American culture. What actually happened, though, was that the European-American culture rose to the top because it was the dominant immigrant group, and the cultures of other groups sank (Banks, 1994a). The concept of cultural pluralism has replaced assimilation. According to cultural pluralism, people have the right to retain their cultural identity within American society, and each culture contributes to and enriches the total society. This concept is an outgrowth of the Civil Rights movement of the 1960s. Other ethnic cultures were inspired by the Civil Rights movement and the pride that African Americans showed for their culture, and they have been empowered, too.

Children of diverse cultures come to school with a broad range of language and literacy experiences, even if those experiences are not the same as those of mainstream or European-American children. Minority children have already learned to communicate in at least one language, and, if they don't speak English, they want to learn English in order to make friends, learn, and communicate just like their classmates. Teachers of culturally and linguistically diverse students must implement a language arts program that is sensitive to and reflective of these students' backgrounds and needs. In fact, all teachers must be prepared to work with this ever-growing population,

Figure 1–1 *Overview of the Four Language Systems*

System	Description	Terms	Uses in the Elementary Grades
Phonological System	The sound system of English with approximately 44 sounds	• Phoneme (the smallest unit of sound) • Grapheme (the written representation of a phoneme using one or more letters)	• Pronouncing words • Detecting regional and other dialects • Decoding words when reading • Using invented spelling • Reading and writing alliterations and onomatopoeia
Syntactic System	The structural system of English that governs how words are combined into sentences	• Syntax (the structure or grammar of a sentence) • Morpheme (the smallest meaningful unit of language) • Free morpheme (a morpheme that can stand alone as a word) • Bound morpheme (a morpheme that must be attached to a free morpheme)	• Adding inflectional endings to words • Combining words to form compound words • Adding prefixes and suffixes to root words • Using capitalization and punctuation to indicate beginnings and ends of sentences • Writing simple, compound, and complex sentences • Combining sentences
Semantic System	The meaning system of English that focuses on vocabulary	• Semantics (meaning)	• Learning the meanings of words • Discovering that some words have multiple meanings • Studying synonyms, antonyms, and homonyms • Using a dictionary and thesaurus • Reading and writing comparisons (metaphors and similes)
Pragmatic System	The system of English that varies language according to social and cultural uses	• Function (the purpose for which a person uses language) • Standard English (the form of English used in textbooks and by television newscasters) • Nonstandard English (other forms of English)	• Varying language to fit specific purposes • Reading and writing dialogue in dialects • Comparing standard and nonstandard forms of English

and teachers who have no minority students in their classrooms still need to incorporate a multicultural perspective in their curriculum in order to prepare their students to interact effectively in the increasingly multicultural American society.

I take the perspective that cultural and linguistic diversity is not a problem for teachers to overcome; instead, it provides an opportunity to enhance and enrich the learning of all students. Teachers need to provide literacy experiences that reflect the multitude of backgrounds from which their students come, and multicultural literature plays an important role in filling that need (Yokota, 1993).

Bilingual Students and Students Who Speak English as a Second Language

Students whose native language is not English are referred to as English as a Second Language (ESL) students, and students who are not yet sufficiently fluent in English to perform academic tasks successfully are sometimes called English Language Learners (ELL). Children who speak their native language at home and speak English fluently at school are bilingual speakers.

Students learning English as a second language are a diverse group. Some are fluent in both English and their native language, while others know little or no English. Some learn to speak English quickly, and others learn more slowly. It often takes 4 to 7 years to become a proficient speaker of English, and the more similar the first language is to English, the easier it will be to learn English (Allen, 1991).

One conflict for bilingual students is that learning and speaking Standard English are often perceived by family and community members as a rejection of family and culture. Cultural pluralism has replaced the "melting pot" point of view, and people in minority ethnic groups are no longer as willing to give up their culture and language to join the mainstream culture. Often they choose to live and function in both cultures, with free access to their cultural patterns, switching from one culture to the other as the situation demands.

Valuing Students' Native Language. Until recently, most non-English-speaking students were submerged into English-speaking classrooms and left to "sink or swim" (Spangenberg-Urbschat & Pritchard, 1994). Unfortunately, many students sank and dropped out before graduating from high school. To better meet the needs of linguistically diverse students, teachers now value students' native language and help their students develop a high level of proficiency in their native language as well as in English as a second language. Instruction in students' native language is effective and equitable for large groups of language-minority students (Faltis, 1993).

Whether language arts instruction is in English or in students' native language, teachers can support and value students' native language (Freeman & Freeman, 1993). A list of suggestions for supporting and valuing students' native language is presented in the Teacher's Notebook on page 17. Even teachers who do not speak or write students' native language themselves can follow most of these guidelines using a foreign-language dictionary. For example, they can use a foreign-language dictionary to post signs in the classroom and encourage students to read and write books in their native lan-

Teacher's Notebook
Guidelines for Supporting and Valuing Students' Native Language

1. Use Environmental Print in Students' Native Language

Teachers post signs and other environmental print written in students' native language in the classroom. In a primary-grade classroom, posters with color words, numbers, and the days of the week should be written both in English and in students' native language. Bulletin board titles and captions on posters can also be translated in students' native language.

2. Add Native-Language Reading Materials to the Classroom Library

Teachers add books, magazines, and other reading materials written in the students' native language in the library center. Quality books for children written in a variety of languages are becoming increasingly available in the United States. Also, award-winning books of children's literature are being translated into other languages, especially Spanish and Chinese. Books such as *Where the Wild Things Are* (Sendak, 1963) have been translated for younger children, and *Tuck Everlasting* (Babbitt, 1975) for older children. Sometimes parents and other members of the community are willing to lend books written in a child's native language for the child to use in school. Or, sometimes parents can translate a book being used in class for their child.

3. Encourage Students to Write Books in Their Native Language

Language-minority students can write and publish books in their native language. They use the writing process just as English-speaking students do, and they can share their published books with classmates and place them in the classroom library.

4. Use Bilingual Tutors

Language-minority students can read and write with tutors, older students, classmates, and parents who speak their native language. Some classrooms have native-language aides who read and write with students in the native language. Other times parents or older native-speaking students come into the classroom to work with students.

5. View Native-Language Videotapes

Teachers can use videotapes of students reading and dramatizing stories in their native language. In addition, students can dramatize events in history or demonstrate how to do something in their native language. Creating and viewing these videotapes is useful for building students' proficiency in their native language.

Freeman & Freeman, 1993.

guage. The activities also help students expand their native-language proficiency, develop greater self-confidence, and value their own language.

Learning a Second Language. Learning a second language is a constructive process, just as learning a native language is, and children develop language in a predictable way through interactions with children and adults. Research suggests that second-language acquisition is similar to first-language acquisition (Spangenberg-Urbschat & Pritchard, 1994). Urzua (1980) lists three principles culled from the research:

culled = select

1. People use many similar language-learning strategies, whether they are small children learning their native language or older children or adults learning a second language.
2. Just as children learning to speak their native language move through a series of developmental stages, second-language learners move through several stages as they learn a new language.
3. First- or second-language learning takes place only when learners have the opportunity to use language for meaningful, functional, and genuine purposes.

When children and adults first arrive in the United States, they generally go through a silent period (Krashen, 1982) of several months during which they observe others communicating prior to talking or writing in English themselves. Then they begin tentatively to use language to communicate, and through listening, talking, reading, and writing, their language use becomes more cognitively and linguistically complex. The English spoken by newcomers is syntactically less complex; in addition, they enunciate words clearly, speak more slowly, and avoid using idiomatic expressions.

New English speakers use very short sentences, often with two or three key words, much like the telegraphic speech of young children. For example, a newcomer might say "No pencil" for "I don't have a pencil," or "Book table" for "The book is on the table." They may also overgeneralize and call all adults in the school "teachers." As second-language learners acquire labels for more concepts and more sophisticated syntactic structures, they progressively use longer and more complex sentences. They move out of the here-and-now, present-tense verb constructions to past and future constructions; however, many students learning English as a second language have difficulty adding the *-ed* past-tense marker to verbs, as in "Yesterday I play ball."

When parents talk with preschool children learning to speak their native language, they scaffold and extend the children's language. Parents also understand their children's special words for things. These adaptations are called "motherese." There are striking parallels between the adaptations made by people who interact effectively with ESL students and those described for motherese.

Students learning English as a second language often mix English with their native language, shifting back and forth even within sentences. This often-misunderstood phenomenon is called code-switching (Lara, 1989; Troika, 1981). Sometimes students read the text in English but mentally translate it into their native language in order to understand it. This takes a little more time than native speakers need, so teachers must allow more time for ESL students to translate teachers' and classmates' questions and comments from English into their native language and translate their ideas from their native language into English. Too often teachers assume that students have not understood or do not know the answer when they do not respond immediately. Code-switching is a special linguistic and social skill; it is not a confusion between languages or a corruption of students' native language.

After approximately 2 years, many second-language learners are fluent enough in English to carry on everyday conversations, but it can take these students as many as 5, 6, or 7 years to achieve the same level of fluency in English as their mainstream classmates (Cummins, 1989). Interestingly, Wong-Fillmore (1985) has found that ESL students learn English in class from teachers and classmates who speak fluent English rather than from their cultural peer group. Moreover, school may be the only place where students speak English!

Implications for Learning Language Arts

Children come to school with an intuitive understanding of the four language systems based on having learned to speak their native language. Listening to parents tell and read aloud stories also contributes to this knowledge. During the elementary grades, students learn more about the phonological system as they learn phonics and spelling, more about the semantic system as their vocabularies expand, more about the syntactic system through grammar instruction, and more about the pragmatic system as they learn to vary the language they use according to purpose and audience.

Think about writing and how the four language systems work together as writers express ideas through words. Writers gather and organize ideas and choose specific words and phrases to express their ideas. They use the semantic system as they choose words to express their ideas, and the syntactic system to organize the words into sentences, paragraphs, and various writing forms, such as letters, reports, and stories. The pragmatic system comes into play as writers consider their audience and purpose for writing. They decide whether to craft longer or shorter sentences, and consider the impact of informal or more formal word choices, jargon, nonstandard English, or technical vocabulary on their readers. They consider the style of their composition, and decide whether to state facts objectively, use persuasive language, or create wordplays, rhymes, or poetic images to express their ideas. As they transcribe their ideas into words and sentences, writers use their knowledge of the phonological system to spell words. Without any one of the language systems, writers would be hampered in their attempt to use language to express ideas.

Culture affects the way people think and the way they use language. In her study of three culturally different American communities, Shirley Brice Heath (1983b) found that because of different lifestyles and child-rearing practices, children come to school with radically different literacy experiences and expectations about learning. Since the American families in her study had dramatically different experiences with written language in their English-speaking homes, the diversity of experiences of children from homes where English is not the primary language would be even greater.

Children from each cultural group bring their unique backgrounds of experience to the process of learning, and they have difficulty understanding concepts outside their backgrounds of experience. This difficulty is greater for students who are learning English as a second language. Think, for example, of the different experiences and language knowledge that children of Vietnamese refugees, Native American children, and children of Russian Jewish immigrants bring to school. No matter what ethnic group they belong to or what language they speak, all students use the same cognitive and linguistic processes to learn.

Children of diverse ethnic groups have met with varying degrees of success in schools, depending on their previous cultural experiences, the expectations students and their parents have, and the expectations teachers have for them. Often a discrepancy exists between the way classrooms operate and the ways students from various ethnic groups behave (Law & Eckes, 1990). Four common cultural behaviors that differ from mainstream behaviors are:

1. *No eye contact.* In some Asian and Hispanic cultures, avoiding eye contact is polite and respectful behavior. Mainstream teachers sometimes mistakenly assume that when students avoid eye contact, they are not paying attention or are sullen and uncooperative.

2. *Cooperation.* Students from many Southeast Asian, Polynesian, and Native American cultures are taught to cooperate and help each other, and in school they often assist classmates with their work. In contrast, many mainstream students are more competitive than cooperative, and sometimes mainstream teachers view cooperating on assignments as cheating.

3. *Fear of making mistakes.* Mainstream teachers encourage students to take risks and view making mistakes as a natural part of the learning process. In some cultures, especially the Japanese culture, correctness is valued above all else, and students are taught not to guess or take risks.

4. *Informal classroom environment.* In some cultures, including European and Asian cultures, the school environment is much more formal than it is in American schools. Students from these cultures view American schools as chaotic, and they interpret the informality as permission to misbehave.

■ *For more information on grand conversations, see Chapter 8, "Sustaining Talk in the Classroom," pp. 311–314.*

Many Asian-American students have been taught to keep a social distance between the teacher and themselves. For example, out of respect to the teacher, they look down when they are spoken to and feel more comfortable remaining in their assigned seats. Literature discussions called grand conversations, as well as other informal activities, can make these students feel uncomfortable because the lack of structure appears to indicate disrespect for the teacher. Asian-American parents typically equate learning and knowledge with memorizing factual information, and they expect a great deal of homework (Cheng, 1987).

Hakuta and Garcia (1989) found that the most effective classrooms for Mexican-American students have a discourse style similar to the one they know at home. Many Mexican-American students are familiar with the give-and-take of cooperative learning, and they value working together and learning in a warm, responsive environment. These students work well in a child-centered, integrated program that is responsive to children's needs.

African-American and Native American students have special needs, too. For too long schools have neglected and failed these students. Teachers understand and build on these students' abilities, appreciate their varied backgrounds, and nurture their potential for learning (Brooks, 1985). Teachers must also take into account historical, economic, psychological, and linguistic barriers that have led to oppression and low expectations. One way to help raise children's self-esteem and build pride in their cultural groups is by incorporating literature about African Americans and Native Americans into their instructional programs. Teachers' acceptance of students' nonstandard English dialects is also important.

Language and culture have important implications for how children learn language arts in school and how teachers teach language arts. Some implications are:

- Children use the four language systems simultaneously as they communicate.
- Children from each cultural group bring their unique backgrounds of experience to the process of learning.
- Children's cultural and linguistic diversity provides an opportunity to enhance and enrich the learning of all students.

Guidelines for teaching language-minority students are presented in the Teacher's Notebook on page 22.

During a literature focus unit on Leo the Late Bloomer, *these bilingual students read and respond to the Spanish version of the story.*

Teacher's Notebook
Guidelines for Teaching Language-Minority Students

1. Provide Comprehensible Input

- Use language that is neither too hard nor too easy for students.
- Embed language in context-rich activities.
- Speak more slowly, and rarely use idioms.
- Highlight key words.
- Expand the two- and three-word sentences that students produce.

2. Create a Stress-Free Environment

- Show genuine interest in students, their language, and their culture.
- Allow students to speak and write their own language.
- Avoid forcing students to speak.
- Encourage risk-taking.
- Don't correct grammatical errors.
- Understand that diverse students are caught between two cultures.

3. Provide Opportunities to Use English

- Provide many opportunities for students to listen to and speak English and to read and write English in low-risk situations.
- Have students work together with buddies and in cooperative groups.
- Promote friendships among students.

4. Examine Your Prejudice

- Avoid stereotyping any linguistic or cultural group.
- Do not lower your expectations for certain groups of students.
- Encourage bilingualism.
- Consider your tolerance for nonstandard English and code-switching.

5. Alleviate Home-School Mismatches

- Consider the contrast between how children use language in home communities and at school.
- Smooth the transition between home and school.
- Expect students to be uncomfortable in unfamiliar activities.

6. Involve Language-Minority Parents

- Make home visits.
- Encourage parents to participate in school activities.
- Translate letters, information sheets, and memos into native languages.
- Have translators available for school meetings and conferences.
- Plan parent-child and home-school activities.

Gibbons, 1991; Faltis, 1993; Law & Eckes, 1990; Scarcella, 1990.

HOW CHILDREN LEARN LANGUAGE ARTS

Language arts instruction is changing to reflect the greater oral, written, and visual communication needs as we enter the twenty-first century (*Standards for the English Language Arts,* 1996). The Steering Committee of the Elementary Section of the National Council of Teachers of English (NCTE, 1996) has identified these characteristics of competent language users:

1. *Personal expression.* Students use language to express themselves, to make connections between their own experiences and their social world, to choose books they want to read and topics they want to write about, and to create a personal voice.
2. *Aesthetic appreciation.* Students use language aesthetically to read literature, talk with others, and enrich their lives.
3. *Collaborative exploration.* Students use language as a learning tool as they investigate concepts and issues in collaboration with classmates.
4. *Strategic language use.* Students use strategies as they create and share meaning through language.
5. *Creative communication.* Students use text forms and genres creatively as they share ideas through language.
6. *Reflective interpretation.* Students use language to organize and evaluate learning experiences, question personal and social values, and think critically.
7. *Thoughtful application.* Students use language to solve problems, persuade, and take action.

Students exemplify these characteristics of competent language users as they:

- Compare the video and book versions a same story
- Interview community resource persons with special knowledge, interests, or talents in connection with literature focus units and social studies/science theme cycles
- Examine propaganda techniques used in print advertisements and television commercials
- Assume the role of a character while reading a story, and write simulated journal entries as that character
- Use the writing process to write stories, and share the stories with classmates
- Analyze an author's writing style during an author unit, or an artist's drawing style during an illustrator unit

These activities exhibit the three characteristics of all worthwhile experiences with language. First, they use language in meaningful rather than contrived situations. Second, they are functional, or real-life, activities. And third, they are genuine rather than artificial (such as worksheets) activities, because they communicate ideas.

The Language Arts

Traditionally, language arts educators have defined the language arts as the study of the four modes of language: listening, talking, reading, and writing. Recently, however, the National Council of Teachers of English and the International Reading Association (*Standards,* 1996) proposed two additional language arts—viewing and visually representing. These new language arts reflect the growing importance of visual literacy (Ernst, 1993; Whitin, 1996b). Also, thinking is sometimes referred to as an additional language art, but, more accurately, it permeates all of the language arts.

■ *Chapter 7, "Listening to Learn," explores these concepts and suggests strategies for teaching listening.*

Listening.   Beginning at birth, a child's first contact with language is through listening. Listening instruction is often neglected in elementary classrooms because teachers feel that students have already learned how to listen and that instructional time should be devoted to reading and writing. I present an alternative view of listening and listening instruction and focus on these key concepts:

- Listening is a process of which hearing is only one part.
- Students listen differently according to their purpose.
- Students listen aesthetically to stories, efferently to learn information as part of across-the-curriculum theme cycles, and critically to persuasive appeals.
- Students use listening strategies and monitor their comprehension in order to listen more effectively.

■ *See Chapter 8, "Sustaining Talk in the Classroom," to learn more about these concepts.*

Talking.   As with listening, teachers often neglect instruction in talk during the elementary grades because they feel students already know how to talk. Recent research emphasizes the importance of talk in the learning process (Dwyer, 1991; Newkirk & McLure, 1992). For example, students use talk to respond to literature, provide feedback about classmates' writing in writing groups, and present oral reports during social studies and science theme cycles. The key concepts about talk are:

- Talk is an essential part of the language arts curriculum.
- Students use talk for both aesthetic and efferent purposes.
- Students participate in grand conversations as they respond to literature.
- Students give presentations, including oral reports and debates.
- Drama, including storytelling and role-playing, provides a valuable method of learning and a powerful way of communicating.

■ *The reading process is presented in Chapter 3, and in later chapters you will learn about teaching students to read stories (Chapter 9), reports and biographies (Chapter 10), and poems (Chapter 11).*

Reading.   Reading is a process, and students use skills and strategies in order to decode words and comprehend what they are reading. Students vary the way they read according to their purpose. They read for pleasure differently than they read to locate and remember information (Rosenblatt, 1991). The key concepts about reading are:

- Reading is a strategic process.
- The goal of reading instruction is comprehension, or meaning-making.
- Students read differently for different purposes.
- Students participate in five types of reading: independent reading, shared reading, guided reading, buddy reading, and reading aloud to students.

Writing.   Like reading, writing is a strategic process. Students use the writing process as they write stories, reports, poems, and other types of writing. Students also do informal writing, such as writing in reading logs and making clusters. As you continue reading, you will learn about these key concepts about writing:

- Writing is a process in which students cycle recursively through prewriting, drafting, revising, editing, and publishing stages.
- Students experiment with many written language forms.
- Informal writing is used to develop writing fluency and as a learning tool.
- Spelling and handwriting are tools for writers.

Viewing. Visual media include film and videos, print advertisements and commercials, photographs and book illustrations, and CD-ROM. Because visual media are commonplace in American life today, children need to learn how to comprehend them and to integrate visual knowledge with other literacy knowledge. The key concepts about viewing are:

- Viewing is an important component of literacy.
- Students view visual media for a variety of purposes.
- Viewing is much like reading, and students use comprehension strategies in both reading and viewing.
- Students use story boards to examine the illustrations in picture books.
- Students learn about propaganda techniques in order to critically analyze commercials and advertisements.

Visually Representing. Students create meaning through multiple sign systems such as video productions, hypertext and other computer programs, story quilts, and illustrations on charts, posters, and books they are writing. According to Harste, "Seeing something familiar in a new way is often a process of gaining new insights" (1993, p. 4). Projects involving visual texts are often completed as part of literature focus units and theme cycles. Key concepts about visually representing presented in this book are:

- Students consider audience, purpose, and form as they create visual texts.
- Visual texts, like writing, can be created to share information learned during literature focus units and theme cycles.

Relationships Among the Language Arts. Discussing the language arts one by one suggests a division among them, as though they could be used separately. In reality, they are used simultaneously and reciprocally. Almost any language arts activity involves more than one of the language arts. In a seminal study, researcher Walter Loban (1976) documented the language growth and development of a group of 338 students from kindergarten through 12th grade (ages 5–18). Two purposes of his longitudinal study were, first, to examine differences between students who used language effectively and those who did not, and second, to identify predictable stages of language development. Three of Loban's conclusions are especially noteworthy to our discussion of the language arts. First, he reported positive correlations among listening, talking, reading, and writing. Second, he found that students with less effective oral language abilities tended to have less effective written language abilities. And third, he found a strong relationship between students' oral language ability and their overall academic ability. Loban's study demonstrates clear relationships among the language arts and

■ *You will learn about the writing process in Chapter 3, and in later chapters you will learn how to teach students to write stories (Chapter 9), informational books (Chapter 10), and poems (Chapter 11). Information about handwriting is included in Chapter 12.*

■ *For more information about these three instructional approaches, see Chapter 2, "Teaching Language Arts," pp. 59–64, and Chapter 13, "Putting It All Together," pp. 544–576.*

emphasizes the need to teach listening and talking during the elementary grades.

Literature focus units, reading and writing workshop, and across-the-curriculum theme cycles are three ways to make language arts instruction meaningful. Students use all six language modes as they read and respond to literature in focus units. For example, as fifth graders read and respond to *Number the Stars* (Lowry, 1989), a story about friendship between a Christian girl and a Jewish girl set in Denmark during World War II, they use listening, talking, reading, writing, viewing, and visually representing in some of the ways shown in Figure 1–2. Across-the-curriculum connections are also possible given the historical setting of the story.

Similarly, students use the six language arts as they learn and share their learning in social studies and science theme cycles. As second graders learn about the desert in a theme cycle, they use the six modes to explore the concepts they are learning as well as to share what they have learned. Some of these across-the-curriculum connections for a theme on the desert are shown in Figure 1–3.

A Paradigm for Language Arts Instruction

Language arts instruction should be based on how children learn, on the impact of language and culture on learning, and on society's goals for its children's literacy development. Teachers create a community of learners in their classrooms in order to facilitate students' learning, they support students as they learn skills and strategies related to language arts, and they teach lessons that allow students to apply what they are learning in listening, talking, reading, writing, viewing, and visually representing activities.

A Community of Learners. Language arts classrooms are social settings. Together, students and their teacher create the classroom community, and the type of community they create strongly influences students' learning. Effective teachers establish a community of learners in which students are motivated to learn and are actively involved in language arts activities. Teachers and students work collaboratively and purposefully. Perhaps the most striking quality of classroom communities is the partnership that the teacher and students create. Students are a "family" in which all the members respect one another and support each other's learning. Students value culturally and linguistically diverse classmates and recognize that all students can make important contributions to the classroom (Wells & Chang-Wells, 1992).

Students and the teacher work together for the common good of the community. Consider the differences between renting and owning a home. In a classroom community, students and the teacher are joint owners of the classroom. Students assume responsibility for their own learning and behavior, work collaboratively with classmates, complete assignments, and care for the classroom. In contrast, in traditional classrooms, the classroom is the teacher's and students are simply renters for the school year. This doesn't mean that, in a classroom community, teachers abdicate their responsibility to students. Teachers retain their roles as organizer, facilitator, participant, instructor, model, manager, diagnostician, evaluator, coordinator, and communicator. These roles are often shared with students, but the ultimate responsibility remains with the teacher.

1. Listening

Students listen to *Number the Stars* as it is read aloud, and they listen to classmates' comments during literature discussions. They listen and watch as classmates dramatize events from the story and as classmates share reports of information or projects.

2. Talking

Students talk as they make predictions about what will happen in upcoming chapters and as they share their responses to the story during literature discussions. They may share the results of their research into World War II or report on the geography of Denmark and trace the trip the girls took from Copenhagen to the seacoast. Students also use talk as they dramatize story events and share projects they create after reading the story.

3. Reading

Students read *Number the Stars* aloud, with a buddy, or independently. They may reread brief excerpts from the story during discussions or read-arounds and read other books by the author, Lois Lowry, or other books about World War II and the Holocaust. Students read aloud their journal entries and quickwrites to share them with classmates. During writing groups students read aloud sequels, poems, reports, or other projects they are writing.

4. Writing

Students write their predictions about and reactions to each chapter in reading logs or keep simulated journals written from the viewpoint of one of the characters. Students write quickwrites on topics related to the story. They also make notes during presentations by the teacher about World War II and the Holocaust. Students also use the writing process as they write sequels, poems, reports, and other compositions after reading *Number the Stars*.

5. Viewing

Students observe as classmates dramatize scenes from the story. They examine large black-and-white photos of war scenes that the teacher has collected and talk about the impact of the black-and-white photos. They consider how the impact would differ if they were in color. They also watch videotapes about World War II and take notes after viewing and talk about the videotapes in grand conversations.

6. Visually Representing

Students make setting maps of Denmark and include sites mentioned in the story, and they make a story quilt to celebrate students' favorite quotes from the story. They also make open-mind portraits of the main characters. For these portraits, students draw a large picture of the character's face and cut it out. Then they cut a second piece of paper the same size and glue it on a piece of construction paper. They draw pictures and write words on this piece of paper to represent the character's thoughts. Then they staple the character's face paper on top so that it flips open to reveal the character's thoughts.

Figure 1–3   *Ways Second Graders Use the Six Language Arts in a Theme Cycle on the Desert*

1. Listening

Students listen to the teacher read books about the desert. They listen to *Mojave* (Siebert, 1988), a book-length poem about one special desert, and picture books by Byrd Baylor that depict life in the desert, including *Desert Voices* (1981). Students also listen as the teacher presents information about the desert.

2. Talking

Students talk about the desert and what they are learning in the theme cycle. After reading or listening to the teacher read a book, they participate in grand conversations in which they share their responses to the book. They also create their own riddles after listening to the teacher read the riddles in *Desert* (Hirschi, 1992). Later, students will write their riddles and add them to a desert mural they are creating.

3. Reading

Students read *Cactus Hotel* (Guiberson, 1991) in small groups and then diagram the life cycle of the cactus in their learning logs. Students read story boards the teacher has made by cutting apart two copies of *Desert Life* (Taylor, 1992) and backing the pages with cardboard and laminating them. Each page in the book presents a close-up look at a desert animal or plant, including tortoises, cacti, locusts, and scorpions. Students read and examine three of the pages and record facts in their learning logs. Also, using books from the classroom library, students read and reread other stories, informational books, and poems about deserts and desert life.

4. Writing

Students write in learning logs and make clusters, diagrams, and other charts in the logs, too. Then they use the writing process to research and write reports about the cacti and animals. They post their finished reports next to the large papier-mâché cactus hotel they create. Some students work together to write an alphabet book about deserts. Each student chooses a letter and writes one page, and then the pages are compiled and bound into a book. Other students write a cumulative book following the pattern in *Here Is the Southwestern Desert* (Dunphy, 1995). Each student prepares one page for the book, and then the pages are compiled and bound into a book.

5. Viewing

Students view videos and films about desert life, and they examine prints of several of Georgia O'Keefe's desert scenes.

6. Visually Representing

As they learn about the plants and animals that live in the desert, students take notes and draw digarams to help them remember important information. After reading *Cactus Hotel*, students make a large papier-mâché saguaro cactus and desert animals mentioned in the book. They hang their reports next to this display.

Researchers have identified ten characteristics of classroom communities (Cambourne & Turbill, 1987). These characteristics, which are described in Figure 1–4, show how the learning theories presented at the beginning of this chapter are translated into practice.

Susan Hepler writes that "the real challenge to teachers . . . is to set up the kind of classroom community where children pick their own ways to literacy and continue to learn to read" (1991, p. 179). Frank Smith (1988) calls these classrooms "literacy clubs" in which all students feel a sense of acceptance and belonging and no one is left out because he or she doesn't read or write as well as others. All students are welcomed and treated with respect, and teachers expect excellence. Donald Graves (1994) identifies five characteristics for writing classrooms: opportunities, demonstrations, choice, time, and engagement.

Figure 1–4   Ten Characteristics of Classroom Communities

1. Responsibility

Students are responsible for their learning, their behavior, and the contributions they make in the classroom. They see themselves as valued and contributing members of the classroom community. Students become more self-reliant when they make choices about the language arts activities in which they are involved.

2. Opportunities

Students have opportunities to participate in language arts activities that are meaningful, functional, and genuine. They read real books and write books for real audiences—their classmates, their parents and grandparents, and other members of their community. They rarely use workbooks or drill-and-practice sheets.

3. Engagement

Students are motivated to learn and to be actively involved in language arts activities. In a student-centered classroom, the activities are interesting, and students sometimes choose which books to read, how they will respond to a book, topics for writing, and the writing form they will use.

4. Demonstration

Students learn procedures, concepts, skills, and strategies through demonstrations—with modeling and scaffolding—that teachers provide.

5. Risk-taking

Students are encouraged to explore topics, make guesses, and take risks. Rather than having students focus on correct answers, teachers promote students' experimentation with new skills and strategies.

6. Instruction

Teachers are expert language users, and they provide instruction through minilessons on procedures, skills, strategies, and other concepts related to language arts. These minilessons are planned and taught to small groups, the whole class, or individual students so that students can apply what they are learning in meaningful literacy projects.

Figure 1–4   continued

---

7. Response

Students have opportunities to respond after reading and viewing and to share their interpretations of stories. Through writing in reading logs and participating in discussions called grand conversations, students share personal connections to the story, make predictions, ask questions, and deepen their comprehension. When they write, students share their rough drafts in writing groups to get feedback on how well they are communicating, and they celebrate their published books by sharing them with classmates and other "real" audiences.

8. Choice

Students often make choices about the language arts activities in which they are involved. They choose what books they will read and what projects they will create after reading. Students make choices within the parameters set by the teacher. When they are given the opportunity to make choices, students are often more highly motivated to do the activity, and they value their learning experience more. It is more meaningful to them.

9. Time

Students need large chunks of time to pursue language arts activities. It doesn't work well for teachers to break the classroom schedule into many small time blocks for phonics, reading, spelling, handwriting, grammar, and writing. Students need two or three hours of uninterrupted time each day for language arts instruction. It is important to minimize disruptions during the time set aside, and administrators should schedule computer, music, art, and other pull-out programs so that they do not interfere. This is especially important in the primary grades.

10. Assessment

Teachers and students work together to establish guidelines for assessment, and students monitor their own work and participate in the evaluation. Rather than imposing assessment on students, teachers share with their students the responsibility for monitoring and evaluating their progress.

Adapted from Cambourne & Turbill, 1987.

intrinsic- essential
2. actual

Motivation for Learning.   Motivation is intrinsic and internal—a driving force within us. Often students' motivation for language arts diminishes as they reach the upper grades. Penny Oldfather (1995) conducted a four-year study to examine the factors influencing students' motivation and found that when students had opportunities for authentic self-expression as part of language arts activities, they were more highly motivated. Students she interviewed reported that they were more highly motivated when they had ownership of the learning activities. Specific activities that they mentioned included opportunities to:

- express their own ideas and opinions
- choose topics for writing and books for reading
- talk about books they are reading
- share their writings with classmates
- pursue "authentic" activities—not worksheets—using the language arts

    Some students are not strongly motivated for language arts, and they adopt strategies for avoiding failure rather than strategies for making meaning. These strategies are defensive tactics (Dweck, 1986; Paris, Wasik, & Turner, 1991). Unmotivated students often give up or remain passive, uninvolved in reading and other language arts activities (Johnston & Winograd, 1985). Some students feign interest or pretend to be involved even though they are not. Others don't think language arts is important, and they choose to focus on other curricular areas—math or sports, for instance. Some students complain about feeling ill or that other students are bothering them. They place the blame on anything other than themselves.

There are other students who avoid language arts entirely. They just don't do it. Another group of students reads books that are too easy for them or writes short pieces so that they don't have to exert much effort. Even though these strategies are self-serving, students use them because they lead to short-term success. The long-term result, however, is devastating because these students fail to learn to read and write.

Language Arts Strategies and Skills. Students learn both strategies and skills through language arts instruction. Strategies are problem-solving methods or behaviors. Students develop and use both general learning strategies and specific strategies related to language arts. While there is no definitive list of language arts strategies, researchers have identified a number of strategies that capable readers and writers use (Lewin, 1992; Paris & Jacobs, 1984; Schmitt, 1990). I will focus on 12 of these strategies in this text:

tapping prior knowledge	applying fix-up strategies
predicting	revising meaning
organizing ideas	monitoring
figuring out unknown words	playing with language
visualizing	generalizing
making connections	evaluating

These strategies are described in Figure 1–5. Students often use more than one of these strategies for a language arts activity, but they rarely, if ever, use all the strategies for a single activity. Students choose the appropriate strategies to accomplish the activities in which they are engaged.

These strategies are applied in all six language arts. Consider revising meaning, for example. Probably the best-known application is in writing. Students revise meaning as they add, substitute, delete, and move information in their rough drafts. Revising meaning in visual representations works the same way. But students also revise meaning as they listen to a speaker, view a videotape, or read a book. They revise their understanding as they continue listening, viewing, or reading and get more information. And, students revise meaning while they are talking on the basis of feedback from the audience.

Skills, in contrast, are information-processing techniques that students use automatically and unconsciously as they construct meaning. Many skills focus at the word level, but some require students to attend to larger chunks of text. For example, readers use skills such as decoding unfamiliar words, noting details, and sequencing events, and writers employ skills such as forming contractions, using punctuation marks, and capitalizing people's names. Skills and strategies are not the same thing, since strategies are problem-solving tactics selected deliberately to achieve particular goals (Paris et

Figure 1–5   Language Arts Strategies

---

1. Tapping Prior Knowledge

Students think about what they already know about the topic as they listen, read, view, or write. This knowledge includes information and vocabulary about content-area topics such as whales or the solar system, as well as language arts information about authors, types of literature, and literal and figurative meanings.

2. Predicting

Students make predictions about what will happen as they read or view. These guesses are based on students' knowledge about the topic and the type of literature, or what they have read or viewed thus far. Students also make predictions as they talk, write, and visually represent. They make plans and set purposes.

3. Organizing Ideas

Students organize ideas and sequence story events when they read, write, view, or listen to stories read aloud. Students organize ideas for writing using clusters and demonstrate comprehension after reading or viewing using other graphic organizers. Students organize ideas differently depending on whether they are exploring stories, informational books, or poetry.

4. Figuring Out Unknown Words

Students figure out unknown words as they read, listen, and view. Depending on the particular situation, students choose whether to use word attack skills, context clues, or skip over a word. Writers use "sound it out" and "think it out" strategies to spell unfamiliar words.

5. Visualizing

Students draw pictures in their minds of what they are listening to, reading, or writing. Often film versions of stories are disappointing because they don't match students' visualizations.

6. Making Connections

Students relate what they are listening, reading, or viewing to their own lives and to books they have read. Similarly, students make connections between their writing or oral presentations and books they have read and experiences they have had.

---

al., 1991). The important difference between skills and strategies is how they are used.

During the elementary grades, students learn to use five types of skills. While many of the skills are oriented to reading and writing, some are used for listening, talking, viewing, and visually representing. The five types of skills are:

1. Meaning-making skills. These include summarizing, separating facts and opinions, comparing and contrasting, and recognizing literary genres and structures. Students use these skills as they create meaning using all six language arts.

2. Decoding and spelling skills. These include sounding out words, noticing word families, using root words and affixes to decode and spell

Figure 1–5   continued

7. Applying Fix-up Strategies

When students are listening, reading, viewing, writing, talking, or visually repre-senting and something doesn't make sense, they apply fix-up strategies. They may assume that things will make sense soon and continue with the activity, or they ask a question, go back or skip ahead when reading or viewing, or talk to a class-mate.

8. Revising Meaning

Students continuously revise meaning as they proceed with a language arts activ-ity. When reading, for example, students reread for more information or because something doesn't make sense, they study the illustrations, or they get ideas from classmates during discussions. Writers meet in writing groups to get feedback on their rough drafts in order to revise their writing and make it stronger. Students also get feedback when they create visual representations.

9. Monitoring

Students ask themselves questions to monitor their understanding as they partici-pate in language arts activities. They monitor their comprehension as they read, view, and listen. They recognize when comprehension breaks down and use other strategies to regain comprehension. When they give oral presentations or partici-pate in discussions, students monitor what they are saying and the reactions of classmates.

10. Playing With Language

Students notice figurative and novel uses of langauge as they listen, read, and view. When they give oral presentations and write, students incorporate interesting language in their presentations and compositions.

11. Generalizing

When students read, view, and listen, they note ideas and put them together to draw conclusions. Generalizing is important because big ideas are easier to remember than lots of details. Writers often state their big ideas at the beginning of a paragraph and then support them with facts. They want their readers to be able to make generalizations. When students give oral presentations and create visual representations, they emphasize generalizations, too.

12. Evaluating

Students make judgments about, reflect on, and value the language arts activities in which they participate. They also think about themselves as language users and reflect on what they do as listeners, talkers, readers, and writers.

words, and using abbreviations. Students use these skills as they decode words when reading and as they spell words when writing.

3. *Study skills.* These include skimming and scanning, taking notes, making clusters, and previewing a book before reading. Students use study skills during across-the-curriculum theme cycles, while reading informational books, and while collecting information to use in writing reports.

4. *Language skills.* These include identifying and inferring meanings of words, noticing idioms, dividing words into syllables, and choosing syn-

onyms. Students are continuously interacting with language as they use the language arts, and they use these skills to analyze words when they are listening and reading and to choose more precise language when they are talking and writing.

5.   Reference skills.   These include alphabetizing a list of words, using a dictionary, and reading and making graphs and other diagrams. Elementary students learn to use reference skills in order to read newspaper articles, locate information in encyclopedias and other informational books, and use library resources.

Examples of each of the five types of skills are presented in Figure 1–6. Students use these skills for various language arts activities. For example, students use some of the skills when giving an oral report and others when making a square for a class story quilt or comparing several versions of a folktale. It is unlikely that students use every skill listed in Figure 1–6 for any particular language arts activity, but capable students are familiar with most of these skills and can use them automatically whenever they are needed.

Teachers often wonder when they should teach the skills listed in Figure 1–6. School districts often prepare curriculum guides that list the skills to be taught at each grade level, and skills are usually listed on scope-and-sequence charts that accompany textbook programs. On scope-and-sequence charts, textbook makers identify the grade level at which the skill should be introduced and the grade levels at which it is practiced and tested. These resources provide guidelines, but teachers decide which skills to teach based on their students' level of development and the activities in which their students are involved.

Teachers use both direct and indirect instruction to provide information that students need to know about skills and strategies. Both types of instruction are presented in context so that students see a reason to learn them and are able to apply what they learning in meaningful ways (Calkins, 1980; Routman, 1996). When teachers model how to do something, scaffold students' use of a strategy or skill, or respond to a student's question, they are using indirect instruction. In contrast, direct instruction is planned. Teachers often teach minilessons, brief 10- to 30-minute lessons in which teachers explicitly explain a particular skill or strategy, model its use, and provide examples and opportunities for practice. Then students apply what they have learned using meaningful, functional, and genuine activities.

A Teaching Strategy.   Learning theories can be applied in designing a strategy or lesson format to be used in teaching strategies, skills, concepts, procedures, and other types of information. Piaget's concepts of assimilation and accommodation are important because they describe how children learn concepts and add information to their cognitive structures. Similarly, Vygotsky's concept of the zone of proximal development is useful because it explains that teachers can support students and assist them in learning things that they cannot learn by themselves. The following six-step teaching strategy establishes a sequence of instruction for minilessons, and it can be adapted for teaching almost any language arts procedure, concept, strategy, or skill:

Figure 1–6   Language Arts Skills

Meaning-Making Skills

Sequence
Summarize
Categorize
Classify
Identify the author's purpose
Separate facts and opinions
Note details
Draw conclusions
Identify cause and effect
Compare and contrast
Determine problem and solution
Use context clues
Notice organizational patterns of poetry, plays, business and friendly letters, stories, essays, and reports
Recognize literary genres (traditional stories, fantasies, science fiction, realistic fiction, historical fiction, biography, autobiography, and poetry)
Identify mood
Recognize persuasion and propaganda

Decoding and Spelling Skills

Sound out words using knowledge of phonics
Notice word families
Look for picture cues
Ask a classmate or the teacher
Consult a dictionary or glossary
Apply spelling rules
Write plurals
Use root words and affixes
Use structural clues
Capitalize proper nouns and adjectives
Use abbreviations

Study Skills

Adjust rate of reading
Skim
Scan
Preview
Follow directions
Make outlines and clusters
Take notes
Paraphrase

Language Skills

Choose among multiple meanings of words
Notice compound words
Use contractions
Divide words into syllables
Use possessives
Notice figurative language
Use similes and metaphors
Notice idioms and slang
Use comparatives and superlatives
Choose synonyms
Recognize antonyms
Differentiate among homonyms
Appreciate rhyme, imagery, and other poetic devices
Use punctuation marks (period, question mark, exclamation mark, quotation marks, comma, colon, semicolon, and hyphen)
Use simple, compound, and complex sentences
Use declarative, interrogative, exclamatory, and imperative sentences
Combine sentences
Recognize parts of sentences
Avoid sentence fragments
Recognize parts of speech (nouns, pronouns, verbs, adjectives, adverbs, conjunctions, prepositions, and interjections)

Reference Skills

Sort in alphabetical order
Use a glossary or dictionary
Locate etymologies in the dictionary
Use the pronunciation guide in the dictionary
Locate synonyms in a thesaurus
Locate information in an encyclopedia, atlas, or almanac
Compare information from more than one source
Use a table of contents
Use an index
Use a card catalogue
Read and make graphs, tables, and diagrams
Read and make timelines
Read newspapers and magazines
Use bibliographic forms

6 Step Teaching Strategy

*Step
by
Step*

1. **Initiating.**   Teachers introduce the strategy, skill, concept, or procedure. The initiating step includes questions, statements, examples, and activities for stimulating interest in the lesson and engaging students' participation.

2. **Structuring.**   Teachers present information and relate it to what students already know so that students can begin to overcome the cognitive conflict they experienced in the first step. To overcome cognitive conflict, students begin to enlarge or restructure an existing schema to fit the information, or they begin to develop a new schema to organize the information.

3. **Conceptualizing.**   Students experiment with and analyze the information presented in the second step in order make connections to related information. This step furthers the process of accommodation begun earlier. When the accommodation process is completed, the existing schemata have been enlarged or a new schema has been developed that fits the new information.

4. **Summarizing.**   Teachers and students review the major points of the lesson. The information and examples presented in the structuring step and the relationships established during the conceptualizing step are organized and summarized. This step allows students to make any necessary adjustments in the schema and in the new interrelationships established within their cognitive structures. For students who have not understood the information being presented, summarizing presents another opportunity to accommodate the information.

5. **Generalizing.**   Teachers present new examples or variations of the information introduced in the first step. This step is a check on students' understanding, and students demonstrate their understanding by generalizing from the first example to this new example.

6. **Applying.**   Students incorporate the information in an activity that allows them to demonstrate their knowledge by using the concept in a novel or unique way.

Students do not, of course, learn in such neat little steps. Rather, learning is a process of ebb and flow in which the assimilating and accommodating processes move back and forth as the student grasps pieces of information. Students may grasp a new concept in any of the steps of the teaching strategy; some students may not learn it at all. Teachers will plan additional lessons for the students who do not learn. Whether or not they learn depends on the closeness of the fit between their schemata and the information being presented. Information that does not in some way relate to an existing schema is almost impossible to learn. Information must be moderately novel to fit students' existing cognitive structures.

This teaching strategy will be adapted for minilessons in just about every chapter of this book. Some lessons may not lend themselves readily to this six-step sequence of instruction; for certain concepts, one or more of the steps may not be appropriate, and some adjustments may be necessary.

Two applications to illustrate how the teaching strategy can be used with almost any language arts topic are presented in Figure 1–7. The first is a minilesson on fables, brief stories that teach a lesson. Our best-known fables were compiled by Aesop, a Greek slave who lived in the sixth century B.C.,

Figure 1–7   Using the Teaching Strategy

Step	Fables Lesson	Rhyming Words Lesson
Initiating	The teacher rereads "The Hare and the Tortoise" and "The Lion and the Mouse" from Hague's *Aesop's Fables* (1985) and explains that these short stories that teach a moral are called fables.	The teacher sets out a large hat and passes out a variety of small objects, including a bat puppet, a block, a toy cat, a place mat, a fork, a plastic rat, and a toy horse. Students place the objects with rhyming names in the hat. The teacher explains that rhyming words sound the same at the end: c*at*, h*at*, m*at*, b*at*, and r*at*.
Structuring	Students and the teacher develop a chart listing the characteristics of fables. The list may include these characteristics: • Fables are short. • The characters are usually animals. • The setting is usually rural and not important to the story. • Fables involve only one event. • The moral is usually stated at the end of the story.	The teacher distributes word cards with these -*at* words written on them: *bat, cat, fat, hat, mat, pat, rat, sat, flat, chat, that,* and *splat*. Students read the words and place them in the hat. They also suggest any other -*at* words they can think of, and the teacher writes these words on word cards.
Conceptualizing	The teacher then reads one or two other fables, and the students check that their lists of the characteristics of fables are complete.	The teacher passes out white erase-boards, and students write -*at* family words as the teacher holds up objects from the hat and reads words on the word cards. Students can invent other -*at* words, such as *dat* and *zat*.
Summarizing	The teacher asks students to make a chart in their language arts notebooks explaining what a fable is. Students share their explanations and compare them to the list of characteristics.	Students brainstorm a list of words that rhyme with *hat* and write them on a chart. Students take turns circling the -*at* pattern at the end of each word.
Generalizing	Students read other fables, such as Lobel's *Fables* (1980) or Lionni's *Frederick's Fables* (1985). It is important to include some fables that state the moral implicitly rather than explicitly. Students explain why these stories are or are not fables. The teacher also points out that although these fables are based on many of the same morals that Aesop used, they were created—not retold—by Arnold Lobel and Leo Lionni.	Students create a rhyming -*at* book. They draw pictures of four rhyming words and write the words beside each picture. After students compile their books, they share them with classmates.
Applying	Students apply what they have learned when they write their own fables. Students may explicitly state the moral at the end of the story or imply it in the story.	Students apply what they have learned about rhyming words with other rhyming patterns. The teacher sets out a pan, a hen, a toy car, and a nail, and students match rhyming objects with these objects: pan: can, man, fan, tan crayon hen: pen, ten, men car: candy bar, jar, star nail: mail, pail, sail (on a boat), snail

but many other civilizations have contributed fables as well. A number of fables have been retold for children, and children's authors such as Arnold Lobel (1980) have written their own books of fables. The goal of this mini-lesson is for students to examine the genre of fables and learn the character-istics of a fable. This minilesson might be taught as part of a literature focus unit on fables in which students read and respond to fables and then tell and write some of their own. The minilesson is organized around the six steps of the teaching strategy I have presented. For the sake of clarity, other activities that would be part of this two-week unit for a fourth-grade class are not included in this plan.

The second application presented in Figure 1–7 focuses on rhyming words. This minilesson might be taught after students read Dr. Seuss's *The Cat in the Hat* (1985). The goal of this lesson is for students to create words that rhyme with *cat,* including *bat, fat, hat, mat, pat, rat,* and *sat.* Other *-at* words requiring consonant digraphs and blends include *flat, chat, splat,* and *that.* This plan is also organized around the six steps of the teaching strategy. This minilesson is a part of a two-week author study on Dr. Seuss, planned for a first-grade class.

Review

Language arts instruction should be based on theories and research about how children learn. Language and culture also have an impact on how ele-mentary students learn language arts. The goal of language arts instruction is for students to develop communicative competence in the six language arts—listening, talking, reading, writing, viewing, and visually representing. Key concepts presented in this chapter are:

1. Language arts instruction should be based on how children learn.
2. Students learn through active involvement in listening, talking, reading, writing, viewing, and visually representing activities.
3. Teachers should provide instruction within children's zone of proximal development.
4. Teachers scaffold or support children's learning.
5. Students use all four language systems: phonological, syntactic, seman-tic, and pragmatic.
6. Seven characteristics of competent language users are personal expres-sion, aesthetic appreciation, collaborative exploration, strategic language use, creative communication, reflective interpretation, and thoughtful application.
7. Students need opportunities to participate in language arts activities that are meaningful, functional, and genuine.
8. Teachers create a community of learners in their classrooms.
9. Students learn and use language arts strategies and skills.
10. A teaching strategy should include initiating, structuring, conceptualiz-ing, summarizing, generalizing, and applying components.

Extensions

1. Observe a language arts lesson being taught in an elementary classroom. Try to determine if the components of the language-learning paradigm presented in this chapter are operational in the classroom. What conclusions can you draw about students' learning?

2. Observe and tape-record several students' talk. Analyze their phonological, syntactic, semantic, and pragmatic language systems. If possible, compare primary-grade students' language with that of middle- and upper-grade students.

3. Interview an elementary teacher and ask how he or she teaches the six language arts—listening, talking, reading, writing, viewing, and visually representing. Compare the teacher's comments with the information in this chapter.

4. Observe in an elementary classroom. Has the teacher created a community of learners? If yes, how did the teacher create the community? If not, how might the teacher create such a community?

5. Observe a student participating in language arts activities. What skills and strategies from those listed in Figures 1–5 and 1–6 does this student demonstrate? What other skills and strategies should the teacher introduce to that student?

> **❝** I wanted to devise an 'authentic' test that allowed my students to 'show me' what they had learned during a science or social studies unit. I wanted my students to express their learning both visually and through writing. **❞**
>
> **Whitney Donnelly**
> *Third-Grade Teacher*
> *Williams Ranch Elementary School*

PROCEDURE

When I plan a theme cycle, I decide on several key ideas that I want my students to learn. In a science theme on the human body, for example, I want my students to learn about four systems: the skeletal systems, the digestive system, the respiratory system, and the circulatory system. Then I choose activities and assignments that focus on each key idea. At the beginning of the theme cycle, I talk with students about the theme and what they want to learn, and I introduce the key concepts so that students will know my goals for them.

Toward the end of the theme, I bring students together to talk about what they have learned. As we talk, I make a list of the key concepts on the chalkboard. Then I take each key concept and write it in the center of a cluster that I have drawn on large sheets of chart paper.

Each day, we review one of the key concepts and add information to complete the cluster on chart paper. If students don't recall one of the important ideas that I've been working on, I ask a question or two. If this prompting doesn't result in several students offering the information, I realize that I need to reteach the idea. We take several days to complete the clusters.

Next, I have students work in small groups to review the charts. Each day, I allot 30 minutes for students to review one of the charts, and students talk about the main ideas on the chart. Students also take notes using both writing and drawing. Over three or four days, students review all of the key concepts.

The next day, students do the Show Me test. Students each choose one of the key concepts to focus on. It doesn't matter which of the concepts they choose because they are all important. I give students large sheets of unlined paper, and they divide a piece of paper into two parts. On one part they draw pictures, diagrams, maps, or charts to describe the key concept and they label the drawings with key words and phrases. On the other part of the paper they describe the main ideas with words.

I take down the review clusters before my students begin the test, but I leave the word wall and all other charts, diagrams, and pictures in the classroom.

ASSESSMENT

I want my students to include at least three main ideas about the key concept they have chosen and to limit the information that they present to the key concept they have chosen. These guidelines are like a rubric. When I grade their Show Me's, I count the number of main ideas in their drawings and writings. I also check for ideas that don't fit the topic or inaccurate information. Then I grade the Show Me's this way:

A = 3 or more ideas in the draw-
     ing and labels
    3 or more ideas in the writing
    0 ideas that don't belong
B = 2 ideas in the drawing and
     labels
    2 ideas in the writing
    1 idea that doesn't belong

C = 1 idea in the drawing and no
     labels
    1 idea in the writing
    2 ideas that don't belong
D = 1 idea in drawing or writing
    3 or more ideas that don't
     belong

Matt's Show Me on the skeletal system is presented in the figure. He drew three pictures of the skeletal system, illustrating different kinds of bones, and he wrote about two functions of the skeleton—to give the body shape and to protect organs. He also pointed out that the bones, joints, and muscles work together to help a person move. Two other things that we studied about the skeletal system that Matt didn't mention were that bone marrow helps keep blood healthy and that there are 206 bones in the body. In the middle of the written

part, he included unrelated information about the functions of the heart, lungs, and brain. Matt's grade is a B on this Show Me. There are a few misspelled words and missing punctuation marks, but they do not affect the grade since they do not interfere with the information presented.

ADAPTATIONS

My students also create Show Me's at the end of a literature focus unit. We choose key concepts from the story—the theme, a character's traits, a comparison of the book and video versions, or information about the author—for the Show Me. We develop clusters and students review them in small groups. Then students draw and write about one key concept.

REFLECTIONS

Traditional tests focus on students' decontextualized knowledge of skills and low-level recall knowledge. I think teachers must design tests that are more authentic and allow students to show us what they have learned about key concepts.

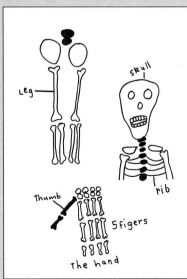

Teaching Language Arts

A s the project for a literature focus unit on *If You Give a Mouse a Cookie* (Numeroff, 1985), Diane Kirkpatrick and her first graders made a cookie quilt. Earlier, children had a cookie-tasting party and made a graph of their favorite cookies. (The class favorite, not surprisingly, was chocolate chip cookies!) On each quilt square, students drew a large picture of their favorite cookie and wrote a sentence about it around the edge of the square. One child wrote, "I think oatmeal raisin cookies are the best," and another concluded, "I like to eat yummy cookies."

anguage arts instruction should be based on how children learn. Donald Graves (1991) admonishes teachers to build a literate environment that facilitates the development of lifelong readers and writers. Certainly, the classroom environment reflects teachers' goals for their students. Classrooms with publishing centers and author's chairs, libraries filled with books, and computer banks with word-processing and hypercard programs, for example, reflect teachers' expectations for their students to effectively use all six language arts.

Teachers use three organizational approaches to involve students in meaningful, functional, and genuine language-learning activities. These three approaches are literature focus units, theme cycles, and reading and writing workshop. I recommend that teachers incorporate a combination of the three approaches in their instructional programs. No longer is it enough to teach using a language arts textbook and have students complete the worksheets and other assignments that accompany the textbook.

Assessment is also a component of the instructional program. It should be authentic and reflect how children learn. Teachers and students collaborate to document students' learning and collect artifacts in portfolios. Assigning grades is a fact of life in classrooms, and there are innovative ways to involve students in assessing their own learning and determining grades.

As you read this chapter, you will learn how to create a language-rich classroom, organize for instruction, and assess students' learning. Think about these questions as you continue reading:

- What are the components of a language-rich classroom?
- What are literature focus units?
- What are theme cycles?
- What is reading and writing workshop?
- How do teachers assess students' learning in language arts?

LANGUAGE-RICH CLASSROOMS

Elementary classrooms should be authentic language environments that encourage students to listen, talk, read and write, view, and visually represent; that is, they should be language-rich. As Susan Hepler explains, "The real challenge to teachers . . . is to set up the kind of classroom community where children pick their own ways to literacy" (1991, p. 179). The physical arrangement and materials provided in the classroom play an important role in setting the stage for language arts instruction (Morrow, 1996).

In the past, textbooks were the primary instructional material, and students sat in desks arranged in rows facing the teacher. Now a wide variety of instructional materials are available in addition to textbooks, including trade books and multimedia materials. Students' desks are more often arranged in small groups, materials are set out in centers, and classrooms are visually stimulating with signs, posters, charts, and other teacher- and student-made displays related to the literature focus units and theme cycles. These are components of a language-rich classroom:

- Desks arranged in groups to facilitate cooperative learning
- Classroom libraries stocked with a variety of reading materials

- Posted messages about the current day
- Displays of student work and projects
- A chair designated as the author's chair
- Displayed signs, labels for items, and quotations
- Posted directions for activities or use of equipment
- Abundant supply of materials for recording language, including pencils, pens, paper, journals and logs, books, and computers
- Centers for reading and writing activities
- Reference materials for literature focus units and theme cycles
- A listening center and other multimedia equipment and software
- A puppet stage or an area for presenting plays and storytelling
- Charts for recording information (e.g., sign-in charts for attendance or writing group charts)
- World-related print (e.g., newspapers, maps, and calendars)
- Reading and writing materials in young children's dramatic play centers

Figure 2–1 elaborates on these components of a language-rich classroom.

The Physical Arrangement

No one physical arrangement best represents a language-rich classroom, but the configuration of any classroom can be modified to include many of the language-rich characteristics. Student desks or tables should be grouped to encourage students to talk, share, and work cooperatively. Separate areas are needed for reading and writing, a classroom library, a listening center, centers for materials related to content-area theme cycles, and a center for dramatic activities. Kindergarten classrooms also need dramatic play centers. Some variations obviously occur at various grade levels. Older students, for example, use reference centers with materials related to the units and themes they are studying. The three diagrams in Figure 2–2 suggest ways to make the classroom design more language-rich.

■ *Dramatic play centers are discussed in Chapter 4, "Emergent Literacy," pp. 141–142.*

Centers

Teachers arrange centers in their classrooms with language arts materials, and students participate in meaningful, functional, and genuine language activities in these centers. At the library center, students select books for independent reading; at the listening center, they listen to stories; and at the writing center, they construct books. At other centers students practice language arts skills that teachers have introduced in minilessons or watch a videotape to learn about an author. Some centers, such as library and listening centers, are part of the physical arrangement of the classroom, and other centers are set up on students' desks or anywhere in the classroom that there is available space.

Library centers are stocked with trade books that are attractively displayed and available for students to peruse. These books might be from the teacher's own collection or borrowed from the school or public library. Many of the books should relate to units of study, and these should be changed periodically. Other books for students to read independently are also included in the library center. After studying library centers in classrooms, Leslie Morrow (1989) makes these recommendations:

Figure 2–1   *Characteristics of a Language-Rich Classroom*

---

1. Classroom Organization

- Desks are arranged in groups.
- The arrangement facilitates group interaction.
- Other parts of the classroom are organized into centers such as the library center, writing center, and theme center.

2. Classroom Library Center

- There are at least four times as many books as there are students in the classroom.
- Stories, informational books, and poetry are included.
- Multicultural books and other reading materials are included.
- Information about authors and illustrators is displayed.
- Some of the books were written by students.
- Books related to literature focus units and theme cycles are highlighted.
- Students monitor the center.

3. Message Center

- Schedules and announcements about the current day are posted.
- Some of the announcements are student-initiated.
- There are mailboxes and/or a message board for students to use.
- Students are encouraged to write notes to classmates.

4. Display of Student Work and Projects

- All students have work displayed in the classroom.
- Student work reflects a variety of curricular areas.
- Students' projects and other student-made displays are exhibited in the classroom.
- There is an area where students can display their own work.
- Other student work is stored in portfolios.

5. Author's Chair

- One chair in the classroom has been designated as the author's chair for students to use when sharing their writing.
- The author's chair is labeled.

6. Signs, Labels, and Quotations

- Equipment and other classroom items are labeled.
- Words, phrases, and sentences are posted in the classroom.
- Some signs, labels, and quotes are written by students.

---

1. Make the library center inviting.
2. Define the library center with shelves, carpets, benches, sofas, or other partitions.
3. Make the center large enough to accommodate five or six students comfortably at one time.
4. Use two kinds of bookshelves. Most of the collection should be shelved with the spines facing outward, but some books should be set so that the front covers are displayed.
5. Shelve books by category, and color-code books by type.

Figure 2–1 *continued*

---

7. Directions

- Directions are provided in the classroom so that students can work independently.
- Some of the directions are written by students.

8. Materials for Writing

- Pencils, pens, paper, journals, books, computers, and other materials are available for recording language.
- Students have access to these materials.

9. Places for Reading and Writing

- There are special places in the classroom for reading and writing activities.
- These areas are quiet and separated from other areas.

10. Reference Materials

- Word walls list important words related to literature focus units and theme cycles.
- Lists, clusters, pictures, charts, books, models, and other reference materials are available for content-area study.
- Artifacts and other items related to theme cycles are labeled and displayed.
- Students use these materials as they work on projects related to theme cycles.

11. Multimedia Technology

- A listening center with tapes of stories read during literature focus units is available for students to use.
- Computers with word-processing, illustration, and hypercard software, a CD-ROM, a modem, a scanner, and other related technology are available.
- Multimedia materials—such as CD-ROM, filmstrips, videotapes, and laserdics—related to literature focus units and theme cycles and the related equipment are available.
- A camcorder and VCR playback system is available for student use.

12. Dramatic Center

- A puppet stage is set up in the classroom.
- Art materials are available for making puppets and other props.
- An area in the classroom is accessible for presenting plays and telling stories.
- Props are available in the classroom.
- Primary-grade classrooms have dramatic play centers, including reading and writing materials.

---

6. Display books written by one author or related to a theme being studied, and change the displays regularly.
7. Cover the floor with a rug and furnish the area with pillows, beanbag chairs, or comfortable furniture.
8. Stock the center with at least four times as many books as there are students in the classroom.

9. Include a variety of types of reading materials, including books, newspapers, magazines, posters, and charts, in the center.
10. Display posters that encourage reading in the library center.

These recommendations are based on research in primary-grade classrooms, but they are equally appropriate for older students.

Listening centers are equipped with tape players and headphones. Students listen to cassette tapes of stories and sometimes follow along in accompanying books, if they are available. Many commercially prepared tape recordings of children's books are available, and teachers can tape-record their own reading of books so that students can reread books and listen again and again to their favorite stories. Too often teachers think of listening centers as equipment for primary-grade classrooms and do not realize their potential usefulness with older students.

Supplies of writing and art materials for students to use as they write books and respond to books they read are stored in writing centers. These materials include:

- A variety of pens, pencils, crayons, markers, and other writing and drawing instruments
- Lined and unlined paper of varied sizes and colors

KINDERGARTEN CLASSROOM

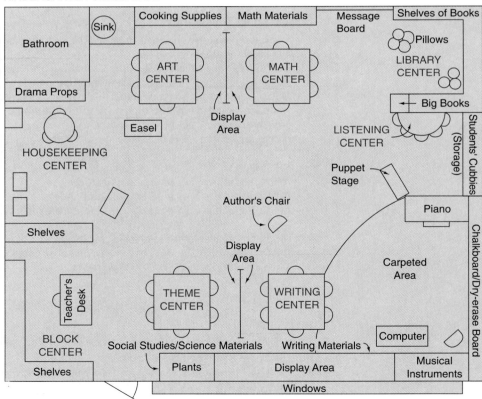

Figure 2–2   Diagrams of Language-Rich Classrooms

p.54, 56-58

- Materials for making and binding books
- Computers with word-processing, graphic, and hypercard programs and printers
- A camera and film for taking illustration photos and photos of students for their "All About the Author" pages
- Scrap art materials for illustrations and covers

In primary-grade classrooms, a table is included in the center so that students can gather to write and share their writing. In middle- and upper-grade classrooms, however, writing materials are stored on shelves or in cabinets, and students usually write at their own desks. They gather in small groups to revise their writing wherever there is space in the classroom, and they meet with the teacher at a conference table to edit their writing.

Teachers also set up centers for students to work in small groups to practice skills and explore literacy concepts. Groups of students manipulate literacy materials, such as a box of small objects for students to sort according to beginning sound, flannel-board pictures to use in retelling a story, strips of paper on which lines of poem have been written for students to sequence, or a set of magnetic letters for students to sort to spell words. Students might apply what the teacher presented at a recent minilesson. For instance, students might write group poems using the format the teacher introduced in a

THIRD-GRADE CLASSROOM

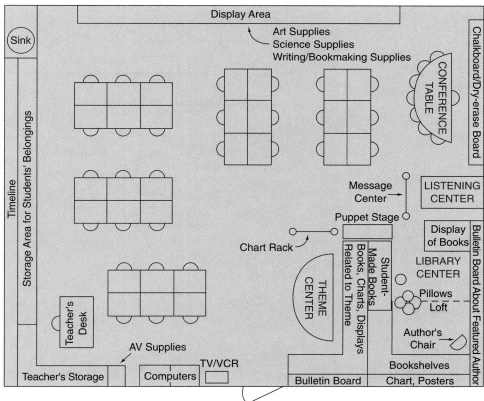

Figure 2–2   continued

minilesson, or they might compile individual books or charts of compound words using the class word list created during a minilesson. Students also participate in exploring activities related to the book the class is reading at centers. They might examine brochures, watch a video, or read an autobiography about the author of the story the class is reading, read informational books about a concept related to the story, or experiment with the artistic techniques the illustrator used in the story.

Textbooks

Textbooks are one tool for teaching language arts concepts, strategies, and skills. They are the most accessible resource and have some benefits. Textbooks provide information about language arts topics and a sequence of topics for each grade level. They present models, examples, and practice activities. Although these tools provide security for beginning teachers, there are drawbacks. The textbook's format is probably its greatest drawback, because textbooks are inappropriate for many activities. Also, the six language arts involve much more than can be contained in a single textbook. Other weaknesses are:

- Little attention to listening, talking, and viewing
- Excessive emphasis on grammar and usage skills

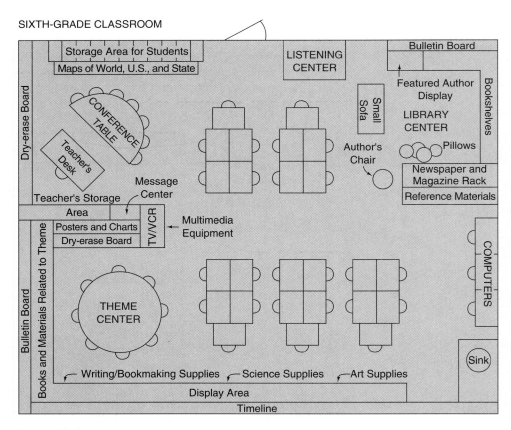

SIXTH-GRADE CLASSROOM

Figure 2–2   *continued*

- Emphasis on rote memorization of skills rather than on effective communication
- Focus on correctness rather than on experimentation with language
- Few opportunities to individualize instruction
- Difficulty in connecting textbook activities to literature focus units and across-the-curriculum theme cycles

Teachers should consider these weaknesses when they adopt language arts textbooks and make decisions about whether or not to use textbooks in their language arts programs. If teachers are going to use language arts textbooks, they should choose textbooks that exemplify these characteristics (Shanahan & Knight, 1991):

1. Center on children's own language
2. Emphasize the social uses of language
3. Integrate the six language arts
4. Recognize the developmental aspects of students' learning
5. Assist teachers in assessing students' learning
6. Develop students' creative and critical thinking
7. Respect cultural and linguistic diversity
8. Emphasize the language arts as tools for learning across the curriculum

These characteristics should permeate the textbook, not be superficially addressed in only one chapter or in isolated examples.

Teachers should never assume that textbooks are equivalent to the total language arts program, and teachers who start on the first page of the language arts textbook on the first day of school and continue page by page through the textbook fail to consider the students' language-learning needs. One of the best ways to use language arts textbooks is as a resource for mini-lessons. As part of a lesson on how to present an oral report, for example, students might create a rubric using the guidelines presented in the textbook; during a lesson on how to form plurals, students might use the information presented in the textbook to make a class chart; or students might check the examples of graphs in the textbook before making a graph to chart the plot of a story they are reading. Students can also make notes, write rules, list examples, and draw diagrams in their language arts notebooks to create their own handbook or textbook.

■ *Check Chapter 6, "Writing in Journals," pp. 233–234, for more information on language arts notebooks.*

Trade Books

Books written for children that are not textbooks are called trade books, and thousands of excellent trade books are currently available. Trade books can be categorized in several ways. The format of the book is one consideration. Trade books are formatted as either picture books or chapter books. Genre is another consideration. Stories, informational books, and poems are three general categories of genre.

Picture Books. In picture books, which are usually 32 pages long, text and illustrations combine to tell a story, present information, or illustrate a poem. The text is minimal, and the illustrations are often used to supplement the sparse text. The illustrations in many picture books are striking. Many picture books, such as *Officer Buckle and Gloria* (Rathmann, 1995), are appropriate for young children, but others, such as Eve Bunting's *Smoky Night* (1994), were written with middle-grade students in mind. Fairy tales, myths, and legends have also been retold beautifully as picture books, and new versions of these traditional tales have also been created. Examples include *The Three Little Javelinas* (Lowell, 1992), a Southwestern adaptation of "The Three Little Pigs," and *The True Story of the Three Little Pigs!* (Scieszka, 1989), the hilarious wolf's version of the story.

Many informational books, such as *Who Eats What? Food Chains and Food Webs* (Lauber, 1995), are published in picture book format. Single poems and collections of poems are also published as picture books. Longfellow's poem "Paul Revere's Ride" (1990) is a picture book with Ted Rand's brilliant illustrations on each page, and Larrick's collection of cat poems, *Cats Are Cats* (1988), is sensitively illustrated by Ed Young. The coveted Caldecott Medal, given annually for the best illustrations in a children's book published during the preceding year, has honored many picture books.

Wordless picture books are a special type of picture book. They are similar to picture books but contain no text. The story is told or the information is provided entirely through the pictures, which makes this type of book particularly useful for children who are learning English as a second language or are novice readers. Books such as *Frog Goes to Dinner* (Mayer, 1974) and Aliki's *Tabby: A Story in Pictures* (1995) are popular with primary-grade students. Other books, such as *Anno's U.S.A.* (Anno, 1983) and *The Story of a Castle* (Goodall, 1986), appeal to middle- and upper-grade students because they can be connected to social studies and science themes.

Chapter Books. Chapter books are longer story and informational books, written in chapter format, for elementary students. Most are written for middle- and upper-grade students, but Patricia Reilly Giff has written stories, including *Ronald Morgan Goes to Camp* (1995), for students reading at the second-grade level. Paula Danziger has begun a series of books written at the third-grade reading level featuring Amber Brown. The first book in the series is *Amber Brown Is Not a Crayon* (Danziger, 1994).

Chapter books for middle-grade students include *Ramona Quimby, Age 8* (Cleary, 1981) and *Bunnicula: A Rabbit-Tale of Mystery* (Howe & Howe, 1979). Two award-winning chapter books for upper-grade students are *Catherine, Called Birdy* (Cushman, 1994), set in the Middle Ages, and *The Giver* (Lowry, 1993), about a "perfect" society. Chapter books have only a few illustrations, if any, and the illustrations, usually small black-and-white sketches, do not play an integral role in the book.

Some informational books are also written in this chapter format. *The Riddle of the Rosetta Stone* (Giblin, 1990) and *Toilets, Bathtubs, Sinks, and Sewers: A History of the Bathroom* (Colman, 1994) are two examples. In informational books, illustrations (often photographs and diagrams) are used to support the text, but they are not as integral as in picture books. These chapter books usually include a table of contents, a glossary, and an index.

A number of chapter books, such as *Sarah, Plain and Tall* (MacLachlan, 1985), *The Giver* (Lowry, 1993), and *Lincoln: A Photobiography* (Freedman,

1987), have received the Newbery Medal for distinguished children's literature. In contrast to the Caldecott Medal, awarded for outstanding illustrations, the Newbery is given for distinguished prose.

Stories. Most stories for younger children, such as *Sylvester and the Magic Pebble* (Steig, 1969) and *Officer Buckle and Gloria* (Rathmann, 1995), are picture books, and many stories for older children, including Natalie Babbitt's *Tuck Everlasting* (1975) and Gary Paulsen's *Hatchet* (1987), are chapter books. There are, however, a number of picture book stories that appeal to older students, such as *Pink and Say* (Polacco, 1994) and Chris Van Allsburg's fantasies. Many stories feature multicultural characters and themes, including *Smoky Night* (Bunting, 1994), about the Los Angeles riot; *Abuela* (Dorros, 1991), a fanciful story about a Hispanic child and her grandmother; and *The Bracelet* (Uchida, 1993), about a Japanese-American family's experiences in an internment camp during World War II.

Informational Books. Informational books provide information on social studies, science, math, art, music, and other topics. Some are written in a story format, such as *The Magic School Bus Inside a Hurricane* (Cole, 1995) and *Castle* (Macaulay, 1977), while others are written in a more traditional informational style, with a table of contents, an index, and a glossary. Examples of traditional informational books are *Red-tail Angels: The Story of the Tuskegee Airmen of World War II* (McKissack & McKissack, 1995) and *Summer Ice: Life Along the Antarctic Peninsula* (McMillan, 1995). Some informational books are written for young children, with a phrase or sentence of text presented on each page along with a photograph or illustration. *Giant Sequoia Trees* (Wadsworth, 1995) is an easy-to-read description of the life cycle of this giant tree and is illustrated with color photographs on every page. In *I See Animals Hiding* (1995), Jim Arnosky explains camouflage using watercolor illustrations of wild animals in natural settings and simple sentences about animals who blend in with their environment.

Another type of informational book presents language arts concepts, including opposites, homonyms, and comparisons. One example is Burningham's *Opposites* (1985), which presents pairs of opposites (e.g., *hard* and *soft*) illustrated on each two-page spread. Alphabet books are informational books, too. Although many alphabet books are designed for very young children, others are appropriate for elementary students, such as *A for Antarctica* (Chester, 1995).

Biographies are another type of informational book. Most biographies are chapter books, such as Russell Freedman's *Eleanor Roosevelt: A Life of Discovery* (1993), but several authors have written shorter biographies that resemble picture books. Perhaps the best-known biographer for younger children is David Adler, who has written *A Picture Book of Helen Keller* (1990), *A Picture Book of Patrick Henry* (1995), and other biographies of important historical figures. Jean Fritz has written a very popular series of biographies, such as *You Want Women to Vote, Lizzie Stanton?* (1995) and *Will You Sign Here, John Hancock?* (1976). A few autobiographies have also been written for children, and books by children's authors, such as Eve Bunting's *Once Upon a Time* (1995), are popular.

Books of Poetry.   Many delightful books of poetry for children are available today. Some are collections of poems on a single topic written by one poet, such as *The Dragons Are Singing Tonight* (Prelutsky, 1993) and Fleischman's *Joyful Noise: Poems for Two Voices* (1988), which is about insects. Other collections of poetry on a single topic selected by a compiler are Hopkins's *Hand in Hand: An American History Through Poetry* (1994) and Carle's *Animals, Animals* (1989). Two excellent anthologies (collections of poems written by different poets on a variety of topics) are *The Random House Book of Poetry for Children* (Prelutsky, 1983) for younger children and *Knock at a Star: A Child's Introduction to Poetry* (Kennedy & Kennedy, 1982) for older children.

All three genres—stories, informational books, and poetry books—can be used to teach language arts or any other content area, and by using all three types students learn more about a topic than they could if they read only stories or only informational books or poems. Figure 2–3 presents three text sets (or collections) of books. One text set is for a primary-grade unit on insects, the second is for a middle-grade unit on cowboys, and the third is for an upper-grade unit on the Middle Ages. The main drawback to using trade books is that they are not sequenced and prepackaged as textbooks are, so teachers must make choices and design activities to accompany the books. Similar text sets of trade books can be collected for almost any topic.

Multimedia Technology

Computers with word-processing programs and speech synthesizers, videotape recorders and players, and other electronic media are becoming an integral part of a language-rich classroom. New multimedia equipment is replacing record players and film projectors, and software programs are expanding the ways teachers and students use the new technology. Students are often more eager to use technology than their teachers are, but the power of technology to expand our communicative competence in the twenty-first century is undeniable.

For the past thousand years, print has been the preeminent technology, but the technology of the future is digital media (Rose & Meyer, 1994). Digital information—text, sounds, images, recorded language, movie clips, and animations—can be manipulated, transformed, customized, and copied. In contrast, print is fixed, not malleable. Using digital media, students read books on the computer using CD-ROM and hypercard programs and write using word-processing programs. They view dramatizations of stories or other films on laserdisc. They create visual representations using hypercard programs and scan their drawings to add them to books they are writing on the computer. Sound has been digitized, too, and students can add their own voice to projects they create and listen to a story or other text aloud using synthetic speech on the computer. Movies and news films and videotapes have been digitized, and students can watch movie clips, listen to authors talk about the books they have written, and listen to the speeches of historical figures, such as Martin Luther King, Jr., giving his "I Have a Dream" speech. Interviews, guest speakers, dramatic productions, and oral reports can be videotaped and added to multimedia productions, too.

Computers and related technologies give students new powers and incentives (Marcus, 1990). Students use computers with word-processing programs

Figure 2–3   *Three Text Sets*

Text Set on Insects

Stories

Brinckloe, J. (1985). *Fireflies!* New York: Aladdin.

Carle, E. (1969). *The very hungry caterpillar.* New York: Philomel.

Carle, E. (1977). *The grouchy ladybug.* New York: Crowell.

Carle, E. (1990). *The very quiet cricket.* New York: Philomel.

Carle, E. (1995). *The very lonely firefly.* New York: Philomel.

Informational Books

Facklam, M. (1996). *Creepy, crawly caterpillars.* Boston: Little, Brown.

Fowler, A. (1990). *It's a good thing there are insects.* Chicago: Childrens Press.

Gibbons, G. (1989). *Monarch butterfly.* New York: Holiday House.

Godkin, C. (1995). *What about ladybugs?* New York: Sierra.

Heiligman, D. (1996). *From caterpillar to butterfly.* New York: HarperCollins.

Heller, R. (1985). *How to hide a butterfly and other insects.* New York: Grosset & Dunlap.

Micucci, C. (1995). *The life and times of the honey-bee.* New York: Ticknor.

Books of Poetry

Moses, A. (1992). *If I were an ant.* Chicago: Childrens Press.

Ryder, J. (1989). *Where butterflies grow.* New York: Lodestar.

Walton, R. (1995). *What to do when a bug climbs in your mouth: And other poems to drive you buggy.* New York: Lothrop & Lee.

Text Set on Cowboys

Stories

Antle, N. (1995). *Sam's Wild West show.* New York: Dial.

Brusca, M. C., & Wilson, T. (1995). *Three friends: A counting book/Tres amigos: Un cuento para contar.* New York: Holt.

Martin, B., Jr., & Archambault, J. (1986). *White Dynamite and Curly Kidd.* New York: Henry Holt.

Scott, A. H. (1989). *Someday rider.* New York: Clarion.

Scott, A. H. (1993). *Cowboy country.* New York: Clarion.

Van Allsburg, C. (1995). *Bad day at Riverbend.* Boston: Houghton Mifflin.

Informational Books

Christian, M. (1993). *Hats are for watering horses: Why the cowboy dressed that way.* New York: Kendrick.

Freedman, R. (1985). *Cowboys of the Wild West.* New York: Clarion.

Johnson, N. (1993). *Jack Creek cowboy.* New York: Dial.

Murdoch, D. H. (1993). *Eyewitness books: Cowboy.* New York: Knopf.

Scott, A. H. (1990). *One good horse: A cowpuncher's counting book.* New York: Greenwillow.

Winter, J. (1995). *Cowboy Charlie: The story of Charles M. Russell.* San Diego: Harcourt Brace.

Books of Poetry

Geis, J. (1992). *Where the buffalo roam.* New York: Ideals.

Grossman, B. (1993). *Cowboy Ed.* New York: HarperCollins.

Sullivan, C. (1993). *Cowboys.* New York: Rizzoli.

Text Set on the Middle Ages

Stories

Cushman, K. (1994). *Catherine, called Birdy.* New York: HarperCollins.

Cushman, K. (1995). *The midwife's apprentice.* New York: Clarion.

Mayer, M. (1987). *The pied piper of Hamelin.* New York: Macmillan.

Morpurgo, M. (1995). *Arthur, high king of Britain.* San Diego: Harcourt Brace.

Shannon, M. (1994). *Gawain and the Green Knight.* New York: Putnam.

Vaes, A. (1994). *Reynard the fox.* New York: Turner.

Informational Books

Aliki. (1983). *A medieval feast.* New York: Crowell.

Gibbons, G. (1995). *Knights in shining armor.* Boston: Little, Brown.

Howarth, S. (1993). *The Middle Ages.* New York: Viking.

Howe, J. (1995). *Knights.* New York: Orchard.

Hunt, J. (1989). *Illuminations.* New York: Bradbury Press.

Lasker, J. (1976). *Merry ever after.* New York: Viking.

Macaulay. B. (1977). *Castle.* Boston: Houghton Mifflin.

Steele, P. (1995). *Castles.* New York: Kingfisher.

Books of Poetry

Yolen, J. (1994). *Here there be unicorns.* San Diego: Harcourt Brace.

These second graders write stories on a computer during writing workshop

to write, and use drawing programs to add illustrations. These programs simplify revising and editing and eliminate the tedium of recopying compositions. Several word-processing programs, such as Bank Street Writer III, Writing Workshop, FirstWriter, Magic Slate, and Quill, have been developed especially for elementary students and are easy to use. Because of the limited number of computers available in the classroom, students often work collaboratively, talking about ideas, planning their writing project, deciding how to spell words and use writing formats, and rereading to check what they have written, When students compose collaboratively, they work longer at the computer and write longer compositions than they do with paper and pencil. Spellcheckers are useful proofreading tools that allow students to interact with their own texts in new ways.

Even first graders can use the computer to write stories (Butler & Cox, 1992; Dickinson, 1986; Phenix & Hannan, 1984). Butler and Cox note that an added benefit is that children learn keyboarding skills, including how to use the shift key, how to delete and move text, and how to break pages of text. Because changing text is easy on the computer, students show interest in revising earlier than they might when writing with paper and pencil.

Computers are also used to take young children's dictation (Grabe & Grabe, 1985; N. J. Smith, 1985). Teachers take children's dictation as they do in traditional language experience activities using a computer rather than paper and pencil. After entering the child's dictation, the child and the teacher read the text and make revisions. Next the text is printed out, and the child adds a illustration. If the child has already drawn a picture, the printout can be cut and taped onto the drawing. The computer simplifies the process of

■ *For more information about taking students' dictation, read about the language experience approach (LEA) in Chapter 4, "Emergent Literacy," pp. 167–168.*

taking children's dictation—teachers can record dictation more quickly than they can write, the dictation can be revised easily, and a clean copy of the revised text can be printed out.

Students can use modems to transmit information from their computer to another computer across telephone wires or through the Internet. One application is to create a pen pals program so that students write back and forth to students in another classroom across town or in another state. Another possibility is for students to dialogue electronically with college students enrolled in a language arts course at a local university. Students can correspond about books they are both reading. For more information about this program, see Margaret A. Moore's article "Electronic Dialoguing: An Avenue to Literacy" (1991). Other networks are becoming increasingly available so that students in classrooms across the United States can participate in interdisciplinary programs and share what they learn with each other (Mulligan & Gore, 1992). Kids Network by the National Geographic Society is one telecommunication-based program, and other programs are available on the Internet.

Hypercard is another computer application that students can use to create databases with text and graphics. The information is stored in stacks that appear as cards on separate screens. These "cards" can be arranged and accessed in different ways. Information from laserdiscs and digitized pictures and photos can be added, and students can add sounds or their own voices to their productions. Elementary students can create reports, biographies, files on favorite authors, and other types of writing projects using hypercard (J. Smith, 1991). Figure 2–4 presents a frame from an eighth grader's hypercard report on space.

Reading programs that use hypercard technology are being developed so that students can check meanings of unfamiliar words they read in dictionary

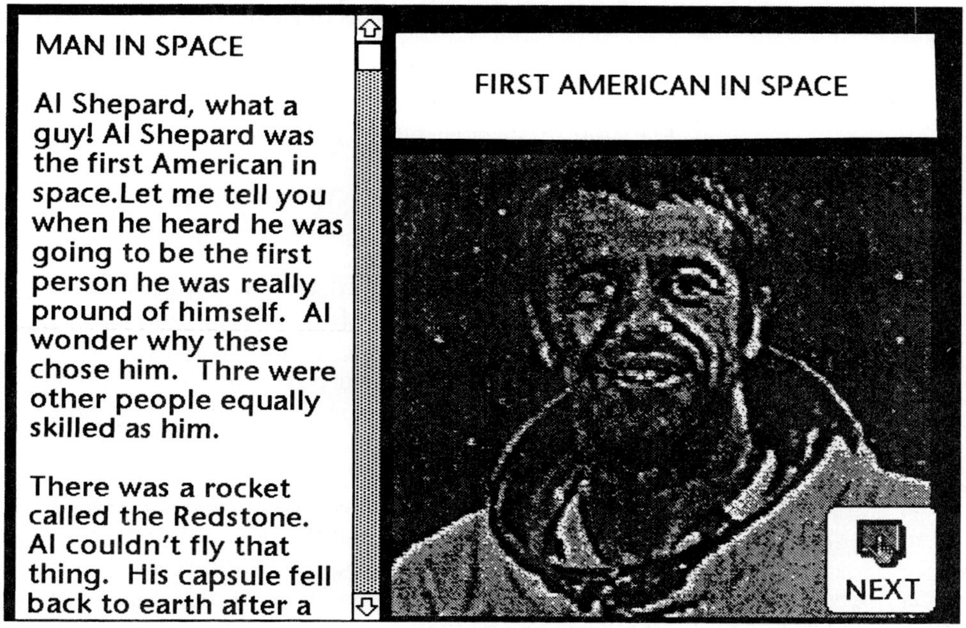

MAN IN SPACE

Al Shepard, what a guy! Al Shepard was the first American in space. Let me tell you when he heard he was going to be the first person he was really pround of himself. Al wonder why these chose him. Thre were other people equally skilled as him.

There was a rocket called the Redstone. Al couldn't fly that thing. His capsule fell back to earth after a

FIRST AMERICAN IN SPACE

NEXT

Figure 2–4   A Frame From an Upper-Grade Student's Hypercard Report

stacks and learn more about the author and literary elements in other stacks as they read a story (Anderson-Inman, Horney, Chen, & Lewin, 1994; Blanchard & Rottenberg, 1990). When students use these hypertext programs, they learn and apply special reading skills and strategies, including noticing the selection's structure or organization, engaging with the selection in order to comprehend, and making choices as they move through the selection. The format of hypertext programs offers students many options as they read. They interact with the selection as they delve more deeply into a topic or find information about an unfamiliar topic or word. In order to take advantage of hypertext capabilities, students need to understand that reading is more than a linear, once-through-the-text process.

Interactive electronic books are available on CD-ROM. These electronic books use hypertext technology to organize information and provide options for readers. Beginning readers read interactive electronic books. The text and illustrations are displayed page-by-page on the computer screen. The selection can be read aloud for students, with each word or phrase highlighted as it is read; students can read the book themselves and ask the computer to identify unfamiliar words; or students can read along with the computer to develop reading fluency. Music and sound effects accompany each program. Many electronic books include reading logs, word-identification activities, and other reading and writing activities. Scholastic's "WiggleWorks" and Broderbund's "The Living Books Framework" are two of the best-known programs, and they use trade books written by well-known children's authors such as Norman Bridwell, Mercer Mayer, and Jack Prelutsky. Electronic encyclopedias also take advantage of hypertext technology in ways that a book encyclopedia cannot. One example is Compton's Multimedia Encyclopedia (26 volumes in book format), which is totally contained on a single CD-ROM disc. Students can search an electronic encyclopedia for information on a particular topic and use hypertext capabilities to:

- Ask the computer to pronounce or define unfamiliar words
- View color photographs, diagrams, and animated illustrations
- Listen to sounds related to the topic
- View film clips
- Check related articles in the encyclopedia
- Print hard copies of the information

Because of the format and search capabilities of electronic encyclopedias, students explore topics in more depth than they can in book encyclopedias.

Laserdiscs are another exciting form of technology that elementary students and their teachers can use (Lewis, 1991). Movie versions of stories are available on laserdiscs, and they are used interactively with computers. Movies on laserdiscs are durable, and they have clear pictures and high-quality sound. Laserdiscs look like silver-colored LP records and have a massive storage capacity. Some discs have two audio tracks—the story on one track and a commentary on the second track. One of the most important features of laserdisc technology is random access. Frame numbers are used to locate specific information or start the disc at a particular episode. Other laserdiscs are available with art masterpieces, encyclopedias, news clips, and nonfiction topics such as photographic essays about landforms and animals.

Students can also use laserdiscs to add photographs, film clips, and other video information to computer projects.

Another innovative technology is captioning. Captions on videotapes and television programs that are designed for hearing-impaired adults can be used for reading practice. Students view captioned video and television programs and read along with the captions (Koskinen, Wilson, Gambrell, & Neuman, 1993). Captioned television programs provide students with opportunities for reading practice that are entertaining and self-correcting. Koskinen and her colleagues found that less fluent readers and bilingual students become more motivated readers when they use captioned television and video.

motivated

On captioned TV programs, sentences corresponding to the words spoken on the video are printed on the screen, much like the subtitles on foreign films. The captions can be seen on television sets that are equipped with special electronic TeleCaption decoders. These decoders can be purchased for less than $200 and can easily be attached to a television. All new televisions have the built-in circuitry to decode and display closed-captioned programming. Some captioned videos, such as Reading Rainbow programs, can be purchased from video stores and educational publishers. Captioned programs can be videotaped from television, but copyright laws restrict the length of time they can be saved and the number of times the tapes can be used.

New multimedia technology expands the range of language arts materials and the tools students have available for learning. The traditional language arts—listening, talking, reading, and writing—have not been abandoned, but technology provides new tools for learning and using these language arts as well as for redefining what the language arts are. The recent addition of viewing and visually representing as the fifth and sixth language arts illustrates the changes brought by technology.

Supplanting- take the place of

Technology is not just a toy for playing games or completing an electronic workbook. Teachers must find ways to use the technology to support their programs rather than supplanting their programs with technology (Lapp, Flood, & Lungren, 1995). Children are excited about technology and enthusiastic about using it. They adapt easily to using the hardware and software and use it for valuable language-learning activities. Teachers are learners too, as they learn the capabilities of the technology and find ways to incorporate technology into their instructional programs.

3 Approaches (p. 64)

INSTRUCTIONAL APPROACHES

Three approaches for teaching language arts are literature focus units, theme cycles, and reading and writing workshop. All three approaches embody the characteristics of learning described in Chapter 1 and provide opportunities for students to be involved in meaningful, functional, and genuine activities. Teachers organize their instructional programs in different ways, but students need to have opportunities to participate in all three approaches during each school year.

Teachers can organize their daily schedule to include both literature focus units and reading and writing workshop. When teachers don't have that much time available, Lewin (1992) recommends alternating teacher-led literature focus units with student-selected reading and writing workshop. Both teacher-led and student-selected instructional programs provide valuable language-learning opportunities, and neither type of program provides all the opportunities that students need. The logical solution is to use a combination of approaches. Schedules for reading and writing workshop at the second-, fifth-, and eighth-grade levels are presented in Figure 2–5.

Literature Focus Units

■ See Chapter 3, "The Reading and Writing Processes," pp. 90–105, for more information about the reading process.

In literature focus units, a unit is organized around a featured selection or several related books. Students read the featured selection using a five-step reading process in which they prepare, read, respond, explore, and extend their reading. Because students are reading together in groups or as a class, they share their interpretations of the story and become a community of readers. Four components of literature focus units are:

1. Reading books.　Students read books together as a class or in small groups. Students may read independently or together with a partner, or they may read along as the teacher reads the book aloud or guides their reading.

Figure 2–5　Schedules for Reading and Writing Workshop

Second-Grade Schedule

15 minutes	Reading aloud to students
15 minutes	Teaching a minilesson (on a reading or writing topic)
30 minutes	Reading and responding
15 minutes	Sharing
	—Later—
30 minutes	Writing
15 minutes	Sharing

This 2-hour schedule is broken into two parts. The first 75 minutes, scheduled in the morning, focuses on reading, and the second 45 minutes, scheduled after lunch, is devoted to writing.

Fifth-Grade Schedule

40 minutes	Reading and responding
20 minutes	Teaching a minilesson (on a reading or writing topic)
40 minutes	Writing
20 minutes	Sharing

This schedule is also planned for 2 hours. The minilesson separates the two independent work sessions, and during the sharing session students share books they have read, response projects they have created, and compositions they have published.

Eighth-Grade Schedule

40 minutes	Reading and responding or writing
15 minutes	Teaching a minilesson (on Mondays–Thursdays)
	Sharing (on Fridays)

The eighth-grade schedule is for 55 minutes. Because of time limitations, students alternate reading and writing workshop, minilessons are scheduled for 4 days each week, and sharing is held on Fridays.

2. Responding. Students respond to the selection to record their initial impressions of it and to develop their comprehension. Students write in reading logs and participate in discussions called grand conversations.

3. Teaching minilessons. Teachers teach minilessons on language arts procedures, concepts, strategies, and skills and connect the lesson to books students are reading or compositions they are writing (Atwell, 1987). These lessons are brief, usually lasting 10 to 30 minutes, and may be taught over a period of several days. The steps in teaching a minilesson are based on the teaching strategy presented in Chapter 1. The steps are:

a. Introduce the language arts procedure, concept, strategy, or skill.
b. Share examples of the topic using children's writing or trade books written for children.
c. Provide information about the topic and make connections to trade books or to children's writing.
d. Have students make notes about the topic on a poster to be displayed in the classroom or in their language arts notebooks. Or, practice the procedure, concept, or strategy or skill being taught.
e. Ask students to reflect or speculate on how they can use this information in their reading and writing.

The purpose of minilessons is to highlight the topic and teach it in the context of authentic literacy activities, not to isolate it or provide drill-and-practice. Worksheets are rarely used in minilessons; instead, students apply the lesson to their own language arts activities. Minilessons can be conducted with the whole class, with small groups of students who have indicated that they need to learn more about a particular topic, and with individual students. Teachers can also plan minilessons on a regular basis to introduce or review topics.

4. Creating projects. Students create projects to extend their reading. Projects may involve any of the language arts, but students usually choose the projects they create based on their interests and the opportunities the selection presents to them. For example, after reading *Jumanji* (Van Allsburg, 1981), students often choose to write sequels; and after reading *Sylvester and the Magic Pebble* (Steig, 1969), students may work together as a small group to dramatize the story, or they may choose to read other books by William Steig.

■ *To learn more about developing literature focus units, turn to Chapter 13, "Putting It All Together," pp. 544–550.*

Theme Cycles

Theme cycles are a new type of interdisciplinary unit that integrate language arts with social studies, science, math, and other curricular areas (Altwerger & Flores, 1994). They often extend across most or all of the school day, and students are involved in planning the direction for the theme. Topics for theme cycles are broad and encompass many possible directions for exploration. Possible topics include inventions, laws, wild animals, houses and homes, natural disasters, and civilizations.

Students use all of the language arts as they investigate, solve problems, and learn during theme cycles. They also use language arts to demonstrate their new learning at the end of the theme. Three types of language arts activities during theme cycles are:

Activities During Theme Cycles

■ *Chapter 13, pp. 567–571, provides more information about how to develop a theme cycle.*

1. *Keeping learning logs.* Students keep learning logs in which they write entries about new concepts they are learning, record new and interesting words, make charts and diagrams, and reflect on their learning.
2. *Reading books.* Students read informational books and magazines, stories, and poems related to the theme.
3. *Creating projects.* Students create projects to extend their learning and demonstrate their new knowledge.

Reading and Writing Workshop

Two types of workshops are reading workshop and writing workshop. Reading workshop fosters real reading of self-selected stories, poems, and informational books, and writing workshop fosters real writing for genuine purposes and authentic audiences. Teachers often use the two workshops concurrently, but if their schedule does not allow them to do so, they may alternate the two.

Many teachers fear that their students' standardized achievement test scores will decline if they implement a workshop approach in their classrooms, even though many teachers have reported either an increase in test scores or no change at all (Five, 1988; Swift, 1993). Kathleen Swift reported the results of a year-long study comparing two groups of her students. One group read basal reader stories, and the other participated in reading workshop. The workshop group showed significantly greater improvement, and Swift also reported that students participating in reading workshop showed more positive attitudes toward reading.

Reading Workshop. In reading workshop students read self-selected books independently or in small groups and respond to books by writing in reading logs and by discussing the book if a small group of students are reading the same book (Atwell, 1987; Hornsby, Sukarna, & Parry, 1986). Through reading workshop, students become more fluent readers and deepen their appreciation of books and reading. They develop lifelong reading habits, are introduced to different genres, and choose favorite authors. Most importantly, students come to think of themselves as readers (Daniels, 1994). The components of reading workshop are:

1. *Reading and responding.* Students spend 30 to 60 minutes independently reading books and other reading materials. They also keep reading logs to write responses to their reading and participate in conferences with the teacher or in small discussion groups to extend their understanding of favorite books.
2. *Sharing.* For the last 15 minutes of reading workshop, the class gathers together to share books and response projects.
3. *Teaching minilessons.* The teacher spends approximately 15 minutes teaching lessons on reading workshop procedures, literary concepts, and reading strategies and skills.

Writing Workshop. Writing workshop is a new way of implementing the writing process (Atwell, 1987; Calkins, 1994; Graves, 1983; Parry & Hornsby, 1985). Students usually write on topics they choose themselves, and they assume ownership of their learning. The classroom becomes a community of writers who write and share their writing, and students come to see themselves as writers (Samway et al., 1991). They practice writing skills and strategies and learn to choose words carefully to articulate their ideas. Perhaps most importantly, they see firsthand the power of writing to entertain, inform, and persuade.

In a writing workshop classroom, students have writing folders in which they keep all papers related to the writing project they are working on. They also keep writing notebooks in which they jot down images, impressions, dialogue, and experiences that they can build on for writing projects (Calkins, 1991). Students have access to different kinds of paper, some lined and some unlined, and various writing instruments, including pencils and red and blue pens. They also have access to the classroom library.

Students' writing grows out of favorite books. They may write a sequel to a favorite book or retell a story from a different viewpoint. Primary-grade students often use patterns from a book they have read to structure a book they are writing.

Students sit at desks or tables arranged in small groups as they write. The teacher circulates around the classroom, conferencing briefly with students, and the classroom atmosphere is free enough that students converse quietly with classmates and move around the classroom to assist classmates or share ideas. There is space for students to meet together for writing groups, and often a sign-up sheet for writing groups is posted in the classroom. A table is available for the teacher to meet with individual students or small groups for conferences, writing groups, proofreading, and minilessons.

Writing workshop is a 60- to 90-minute period scheduled each day. During this time the teacher and the students are involved in three activities:

1. Writing. Students spend 30 to 45 minutes working independently on writing projects. They move through all five stages of the writing process—prewriting, drafting, revising, editing, and publishing—at their own pace. Many times students compile their final copies to make books during writing workshop, but sometimes they attach their writing to artwork, make posters, write letters that are mailed, or perform scripts as skits or puppet shows.

2. Sharing. After reading, the class gathers together to share their new publications and make related announcements. A student who has just finished writing a puppet show script and making puppets may ask for volunteers to help perform the puppet show, which could be presented several days later during sharing time. Younger students often sit in a circle or gather together on a rug for sharing time. If an author's chair is available, each student sits in the special chair to read his or her composition. After the reading, classmates clap and offer compliments. They may also make other comments and suggestions, but the focus is on celebrating completed writing projects, not on revising the composition to make it better.

3. Teaching minilessons. During this approximately 15-minute period, teachers provide brief lessons on writing workshop procedures, literary concepts, and writing skills and strategies. They also talk about authors of children's trade books and the writing strategies and skills they use.

Sometimes teachers add a fourth component to writing workshop in which they read literature aloud to share examples of good writing with stu-

■ *To learn more about the writing process, see Chapter 3, "The Reading and Writing Processes," pp. 111–126.*

5 Stages

■ *Turn to Chapter 13, "Putting It All Together," pp. 555–566, to read more about using the workshop approach.*

dents. This activity also helps students to feel part of the community of writers. Teachers can also connect reading workshop with writing workshop.

The Teacher's Role

The teacher's role in a language arts classroom is complex and multidimensional. No longer are teachers simply providers of knowledge. Nor do teachers assign an endless series of worksheets and "busy work." Instead, teachers understand that children's literacy develops most effectively through purposeful and meaningful social contexts. These teachers create the classroom environment and a community of learners. They plan the language arts curriculum using the three instructional approaches to meet the needs of their increasingly diverse classrooms of students. Their goal is to help students develop communicative competence and to excite students about literacy.

Language arts teachers direct the life of the classroom. They are instructors, coaches, facilitators, and managers. Figure 2–6 presents a list of some of the roles teachers assume.

Establishing a Community of Learners. Teachers begin the process of establishing a community of learners when they make deliberate decisions about the kind of classroom culture they want to create (Sumara & Walker, 1991). School is "real" life for students, and they learn best when they see a purpose for learning to read and write. The social contexts that teachers create are a key. Teachers must think about their roles and the kind of language arts instruction they want in their classrooms. They must decide to have a democratic classroom where students' abilities in reading and writing develop through purposeful and meaningful literacy activities.

Teachers are more successful when they take the first two weeks of the school year to establish the classroom environment (Sumara & Walker, 1991). Teachers can't assume that students will be familiar with the procedures and routines used in language arts or that students will instinctively be cooperative, responsible, and respectful of classmates. Teachers explicitly explain classroom routines, such as how to get supplies out and put them away and how to work with classmates in a cooperative group, and set the expectation that students will adhere to the routines. Next, they demonstrate literacy procedures, including how to choose a book from the classroom library, how to provide feedback in a writing group, and how to participate in a grand conversation or discussion about a book. Third, teachers model ways of interacting with students, responding to literature, respecting classmates, and assisting classmates with reading and writing projects.

Teachers are the classroom managers or administrators. They set expectations and clearly explain to students what is expected of them and what is valued in the classroom. The classroom rules are specific and consistent, and teachers also set limits. For example, students might be allowed to talk quietly with classmates when they are working, but they are not allowed to shout across the classroom or talk when the teacher is talking or when students are making a presentation to the class. Teachers also model classroom rules themselves, as they interact with students. According to Sumara and Walker, the process of socialization at the beginning of the school year is planned, deliberate, and crucial to the success of the language arts program.

Figure 2–6   Roles Teachers Assume

Role	Description
Organizer	• Creates a language-rich environment. • Plans the language arts program. • Sets time schedules. • Develops literature focus units and theme cycles. • Schedules reading and writing workshop. • Uses the language arts as tools for learning across the curriculum.
Facilitator	• Develops a community of learners. • Stimulates students' interest in language and literacy. • Allows students to choose books to read and topics for projects. • Provides opportunities for students to use language for meaningful, functional, and genuine activities. • Invites parents to become involved in classroom activities.
Participant	• Reads and writes with students. • Learns along with students. • Asks questions and seeks answers to questions.
Instructor	• Provides information about books, authors, and illustrators. • Explains language arts procedures. • Teaches minilessons on concepts, skills, and strategies. • Provides background knowledge before reading, writing, and viewing. • Groups students flexibly for instruction.
Model	• Demonstrates procedures, skills, and strategies. • Reads aloud to students every day.
Manager	• Sets expectations and responsibilities. • Tracks students' progress during literature focus units. • Monitors students' work during reading and writing workshop. • Keeps records. • Arranges the classroom to facilitate learning. • Provides technology hardware and software to support language arts activities.
Diagnostician	• Conferences with students. • Observes students participating in language arts activities. • Assesses students' strengths and weaknesses. • Plans instruction based on students' needs.
Evaluator	• Assesses students' progress in language arts. • Helps students self-assess their learning. • Assigns grades. • Examines the effectiveness of the language arts program.
Coordinator	• Works with librarians, aides, and parent volunteers. • Works with other teachers on grade-level projects, pen pal programs, and cross-age reading programs.
Communicator	• Expects students to do their best. • Encourages students to become lifelong readers. • Communicates the language arts program to parents and administrators. • Shares language arts goals and activities with parents and the community. • Encourages parents to support the language arts program.

Not everything can be accomplished during the first two weeks, however, so teachers must continue to reinforce classroom routines and language arts procedures. One way is to have student leaders model the desired routines and behaviors and encourage other students to follow the lead. Teachers also continue to teach additional literacy procedures as students are involved in new types of activities. The classroom community evolves during the school year, but the foundation is laid during the first two weeks.

Teachers develop a predictable classroom environment with familiar routines and procedures and a set routine. Students feel comfortable, safe, and more willing to take risks and experiment in a predictable classroom environment. This is especially true for students from varied cultures, students learning English as a second language, and less capable readers and writers.

What About Teaching?   We could say that everything a teacher does during literature focus units and reading and writing workshop is teaching, and in a sense it is. If, however, we define teaching as providing information, literature-based reading teachers do two kinds of teaching. One kind is called direct instruction. In this kind of teaching, teachers provide systematic, planned lessons in which they explicitly present information, provide an opportunity for supervised practice, and then have students apply what they have learned through authentic reading and writing activities (Slaughter, 1988). Teachers often use direct instruction during minilessons in which they teach students about reading and writing procedures, skills, and strategies. Direct instruction has been associated with skill-and-drill activities, but it doesn't have to be. This kind of teaching is necessary to provide information and opportunities for students to apply what they are learning with guidance from the teacher. Some examples of direct-instruction lessons are:

- Presenting a biographical sketch of Chris Van Allsburg during a unit featuring the author and his fantasy stories
- Highlighting important vocabulary from *Sarah, Plain and Tall* (MacLachlan, 1985) on the classroom word wall
- Choosing a word from an across-the-curriculum theme and using the letters to build words (e.g., *pear, pave,* and *port* from *evaporation*) and review spelling rules
- Teaching a minilesson on pourquoi (or "why") tales before reading *Iktomi and the Boulder* (Goble, 1988)
- Demonstrating how to proofread a piece of writing to identify spelling, punctuation, and capitalization errors

The second kind of teaching is indirect teaching (Slaughter, 1988). Teachers use indirect teaching for brief on-the-spot lessons as they respond to students' questions or when students demonstrate the need to know something. These lessons take place during whole-class activities, during conferences with students, and while working with small groups. Teachers also do indirect teaching as they model reading when reading aloud to the class and as they model writing when students are writing a class collaboration. Other examples include:

- Demonstrating how to use an index when a student says he or she can't find anything about scorpions in the informational book *Desert Life* (Taylor, 1992)

- Teaching a student how to use quotation marks while editing the student's piece of writing
- Explaining what a prologue and an epilogue are during a conference with a child who is reading *Tuck Everlasting* (Babbitt, 1975)
- Explaining the spelling rule that *y* at the end of a word is usually changed to *i* before adding *-es* when a child asks how to spell *cries.*
- Showing a child how to write an innovation (new text following the same pattern) for *Dogs Don't Wear Sneakers* (Numeroff, 1993)

While direct instruction is planned, teachers seize the teachable moment for indirect instruction. Both kinds of teaching are valuable and should be included in literature-based reading programs. Sometimes teachers ask how they should balance the two types of teaching. It is important to remember that most of the instructional time is devoted to real reading and writing—perhaps as much as 70–80% (Y. M. Goodman, Watson, & Burke, 1987). Of the remaining 20–30%, probably half is spent on unplanned, indirect instruction and the other half on planned, direct instruction. Because teachable moments may not present themselves for some important language arts strategies and skills, there needs to be both planned and unplanned instruction (Baumann, 1987).

Adapting to Meet the Needs of Every Student

In every classroom some students do not learn as well as their classmates or as well as the teacher believes they can. Others do not seem to be challenged by the activities they are engaged in, or have limited proficiency in English because they are learning English as a second language. Every year classroom teachers encounter students with a variety of strengths and needs. It is important for teachers to be aware of students with special needs in their classrooms and to find ways to adapt the instructional program so that every student can be successful (Wood, 1993). A list of suggestions for adapting the language arts program to meet the needs of every student is presented in Figure 2–7.

Students With Specific Learning Disabilities. Students with specific learning disabilities have significant difficulties in learning and using one or more of the following abilities: listening, speaking, reading, writing, and math. Even though these students can have severe learning difficulties, they have average or above-average intelligence. Students with specific learning disabilities may not express themselves well, may not read fluently, and may have trouble spelling words correctly and using other written-language skills. They may exhibit poor coordination and have difficulty with handwriting. In addition, they may have low self-images, exhibit socially inappropriate behaviors, and have difficulty relating to their classmates.

Students with specific learning disabilities are capable of learning the academic content in their weak areas. They learn to compensate for their learning problems. These students are usually mainstreamed into regular education classrooms for much of the school day and are "pulled out" to a resource room for special instruction. Perhaps the most important consideration in working with these students is that the classroom and the instruction be structured.

Figure 2–7 *Adapting to Meet the Needs of Every Student*

Students With Specific Learning Disabilities

Use multisensory approaches.
Allow students to work at their own level.
Keep assignments short.
Use peer-tutors and cross-age tutors.
Connect listening and reading experiences.
Allow students to use talking rather than writing whenever possible.

Students With Mental Retardation

Focus on functional skills for independent living.
Use concrete examples.
Provide many opportunities to practice skills.
Use peer-tutors to reread familiar books.
Have students tell and dictate stories using wordless picture books.
Teach students to read and spell very high frequency words.

Students With Behavior Disorders

Closely monitor students' frustration levels.
Involve students in talk and drama activities to develop oral language fluency.
Have students work with a buddy or two to develop socialization skills.
Structure learning experiences.
Have students write their feelings and frustrations in personal journals.
Have students use art as an alternative form of communication.

Students With Language Disorders

Share books with predictable language patterns.
Use dramatic play, role-playing, and puppetry.
Have students retell familiar stories.
Have students listen to stories at the listening center.
Have students work with a buddy or two to develop socialization skills.

Students With Attention Deficit Disorder

Structure learning experiences.
Monitor students closely as they work.
Encourage students to participate in talk and drama activities.
Use a checklist to organize steps in completing an activity or project.
Provide choices for students.
Use graphic organizers for students to complete while reading or listening.

Students Who Are Learning English as a Second Language

Foster appreciation of the student's native language and culture.
Have English-speaking students serve as peer-tutors and buddies.
Teach survival words and phrases.
Show films, filmstrips, and videotapes to provide background before teaching concepts or reading books.
Teach literal and figurative meanings of idioms.
Encourage students to retell familiar stories.

Students Who Are Gifted

Encourage risk-taking and experimentation.
Provide tools for learning, including research skills and problem-solving skills.
Create a noncompetitive and individualized classroom environment.
Invite community persons with particular areas of expertise to serve as mentors.
Encourage students to use all language functions.
Have gifted students publish their writing in a variety of formats.

inclusion

Students With Mental Retardation.   Students with mental retardation have significantly subaverage intellectual functioning, along with limitations in two or more of the following areas: communicating, self-care, home living, social skills, self-direction, health and safety, functional academics, leisure, and work. Their academic performance lags 3 or 4 years behind that of other students, but they can learn to read and write. The focus of instruction should be on helping students develop the functional skills considered essential to living independently. The most valuable activities for these students are concrete, meaningful, and based on personal experience. When the pace of classroom activities is too fast, individualized instruction with peer-tutors can be provided. This individualized instruction should involve more repetition and practice than is necessary for other students.

Students With Behavior Disorders.   Students whose behavior interferes with learning are characterized as having behavior disorders. They often exhibit inappropriate behavior and feelings under normal circumstances; they may be either aggressive and disruptive or anxious and withdrawn. These students have difficulty in developing satisfactory relationships with classmates and the teacher. Often, they are unhappy or depressed, and they may develop physical symptoms or fears associated with personal or school problems. Although any student can exhibit one of these behaviors for a brief period, students with behavior disorders exhibit more than one of these behaviors to a marked degree and consistently over time. Students with behavior disorders need a structured and positive classroom environment in order to be successful. Students need to learn to control their disruptive and socially inappropriate behavior and develop interpersonal skills.

Students With Language Disorders.   Students who have grown up in an English-speaking community but have difficulty understanding or expressing language are classified as having a language disorder. Often these children talk very little, speak in childlike phrases, and lack the language to understand basic concepts. This is a very serious problem because a student's limited ability to communicate has a negative impact on learning as well as on social interaction with classmates and the teacher. It is important to note that students who speak their native language fluently and are learning English as a second language do not have a language disorder.

Students With Attention Deficit Disorder.   Students with attention deficit disorder (ADD) have great difficulty attending to tasks and activities. There is no universally accepted definition, but these students display distractibility, impulsiveness, inattention, and mood fluctuations. It is crucial that students with ADD are successful in the classroom and that teachers structure their environment to minimize their distractibility (Weaver, 1994b).

Students Who Are Learning English as a Second Language.   Many children living in the United States come from Mexican-American, Asian-American, Native American, and other linguistic and cultural communities. These students acquire their native language before they come to school, and at school they learn English. Students learn a second language in much the way they learned to speak their native language, and it takes 5 to 7 years for students to become fluent in a second language. Teachers provide a support-ive environment and use classmates as buddies for students who are learning English.

Students Who Are Gifted.   Gifted students are academically advanced, but giftedness is more than a high IQ score. Gifted students are curious, have unusually good memories, express themselves well, enjoy working indepen-dently, have a well-developed sense of humor, and are perfectionistic. How-ever, not all gifted students are high achievers. Some are underachievers who do not work up to their potential because of a lack of motivation, peer pres-sure, or fear of success. Gifted students require special adaptations to meet their needs.

My position in this text is that students with special learning needs bene-fit from the same language arts content and teaching strategies that other students do. The material in this book capitalizes on the natural ways children learn, and it can be used effectively with almost all learners, given some adaptations. Special educators continue to point out that no one way exists to teach students with special needs that is significantly different from how other students are taught. Moreover, educators recommend an integrated approach as especially valuable for learning-disabled and remedial learners (Rhodes & Dudley-Marling, 1988; Stires, 1991b) and for students learning English as a second language (Freeman & Freeman, 1992; Kucer, Silva, & Delgado-Larocco, 1995).

ASSESSING STUDENTS' LEARNING

Assessing students' learning in the language arts is a difficult task. Although it may seem fairly easy to develop and administer a criterion-referenced test, tests measure language skills rather than students' ability to use language in authentic ways. Nor do tests measure listening, talking, and viewing very well. A test on punctuation marks, for example, does not indicate students' ability to use punctuation marks correctly in their own writing. Instead, such a test typically evaluates students' ability to add punctuation marks to a set of sentences created by someone else, or to proofread and spot punctuation errors in someone else's writing. An alternative and far better approach is to examine how students use punctuation marks in their own writing.

Traditional assessment reflects outdated views of how students learn to read and write and offers an incomplete assessment of students' language abilities. Tests focus on only a few aspects of what readers do as they read, what listeners do as they listen, and what writers do as they write. Traditional assessment fails to use authentic language tasks or to help teachers find ways to help students succeed.

Assessment should resemble real language use (Valencia, Hiebert, & Afflerbach, 1994). A better approach is authentic assessment, in which teachers examine both the processes that students use as they listen, talk, read, write, view, and visually represent and the artifacts or products that stu-dents produce, such as projects and reading logs. Students, too, participate in reflecting on and self-assessing their learning. Authentic assessment has five purposes:

- To document mileposts in students' language and literacy development
- To identify students' strengths in order to plan for instruction
- To document students' language arts activities and projects
- To determine grades
- To help teachers learn more about how students become strategic readers and writers

Assessment is more than testing; it is an integral part of teaching and learning (K. S. Goodman, Goodman, & Hood, 1989). The purpose of classroom assessment is to inform and influence instruction. Through authentic assessment, teachers learn about their students, about themselves as teachers, and about the impact of the instructional program. Similarly, when students reflect on their learning and use self-assessment, they learn about themselves as learners and also about their learning. The Teacher's Notebook on page 72 presents guidelines for authentic assessment and describes how teachers use authentic assessment tools in their classrooms.

Monitoring Students' Progress

Teachers monitor students' progress as they are involved in language arts and across-the-curriculum activities during literature focus units, theme cycles, and reading and writing workshop, and they use the results of their monitoring to inform their teaching (Baskwill & Whitman, 1988; K. S. Goodman et al., 1989). Four ways to monitor students' progress are classroom observations, anecdotal notes, conferences, and checklists (Baskwill & Whitman, 1988).

Classroom Observations. Language arts teachers engage in "kid watching," a term that Yetta Goodman coined and defined as "direct and informal observation of students" (1978, p. 37). To be an effective kid watcher, teachers must understand how children develop language and must understand the role of errors in language learning. Teachers use kid watching spontaneously when they interact with children and are attentive to their behavior and comments. Other observation times should be planned when the teacher focuses on particular students and makes anecdotal notes about the students' involvement in literacy events and other language arts activities. The focus is on what students do as they use oral and written language, not on whether or not they are behaving properly or working quietly. Of course, little learning can occur in disruptive situations, but during these observations the focus is on language, not behavior.

Anecdotal Notes. Teachers write brief notes as they observe students, and the most useful notes describe specific events, report rather than evaluate, and relate the events to other information about the student (Rhodes & Nathenson-Mejia, 1992). Teachers make notes about students' performance in listening, talking, reading, writing, viewing, and visually representing activities; about the questions students ask; and about the strategies and skills they use fluently or indicate confusion about. These records document stu-

Teacher's Notebook
Guidelines for Authentic Assessment

1. *Choose Appropriate Assessment Tools*

   Teachers identify their purpose for assessment and choose an appropriate assessment tool. To judge students' spelling development, for example, teachers examine students' spelling in books they write and their use of proofreading, as well as students' performance on spelling tests.

2. *Use a Variety of Assessment Tools*

   Teachers regularly use a variety of authentic assessment tools that reflect current theories about how children learn, including anecdotal notes and reading logs.

3. *Integrate Instruction and Assessment*

   Teachers use the results of assessment to inform their teaching. They observe and conference with students as they teach and supervise students during language arts activities. When students do not understand what teachers are trying to teach, teachers need to try other instructional procedures.

4. *Keep a Positive Focus*

   Teachers focus on what students can do, not what they can't do. They should focus on how to facilitate students' development as readers, writers, and users of language.

5. *Consider Both Processes and Products*

   Teachers examine both the language processes students use and the products they create. Teachers notice the strategies students use for language activities as well as assess the quality of students' visual representations, oral reading, compositions, and other products.

6. *Consider Multiple Contexts*

   Teachers assess students' language arts development in a variety of contexts, including literature focus units, theme cycles, and reading and writing workshop. Multiple contexts are important because students often do better in one context than another.

7. *Focus on Individual Students*

   In addition to whole-class assessments, teachers make time to observe, conference with, and do other assessment procedures with individual students in order to develop clear understandings of the student's development.

8. *Teach Students to Self-Assess Their Learning*

   Self-assessment is an integral part of assessment. Students reflect on their progress in reading, writing, and the other language arts.

dents' growth and pinpoint problem areas for future minilessons and conferences. A year-long collection of records provides a comprehensive picture of a student's learning in language arts. An excerpt from a fifth-grade teacher's anecdotal notes about one student's progress during a unit on the American Revolution appears in Figure 2–8.

Several organizational schemes for anecdotal notes are possible, and teachers should use the format that is most comfortable for them. Some teachers make a card file with dividers for each child and write anecdotes on notecards. They feel comfortable jotting notes on these small cards or even carrying around a set of cards in a pocket. Other teachers divide a spiral-bound notebook into sections for each child and write anecdotes in

Figure 2–8   Anecdotal Notes About One Student's Learning During a Theme Cycle on the American Revolution

	Notes About Matthew
March 5	Matthew selected Ben Franklin as historical figure for American Revolution projects.
March 11	Matthew fascinated with information he has found about B. F. Brought several sources from home. Is completing B. F.'s lifeline with many details.
March 18	Simulated journal. Four entries in four days! Interesting how he picked up language style of the period in his journal. Volunteers to share daily. I think he enjoys the oral sharing more than the writing.
March 25	Nine simulated journal entries, all illustrated. High level of enthusiasm.
March 29	Conferenced about cluster for B. F. biography. Well-developed with five rays, many details. Matthew will work on "contributions" ray. He recognized it as the least-developed one.
April 2	Three chapters of biography drafted. Talked about "working titles" for chapters and choosing more interesting titles after writing that reflect the content of the chapters.
April 7	Drafting conference. Matthew has completed all five chapters. He and Dustin are competitive, both writing on B. F. They are reading each other's chapters and checking the accuracy of information.
April 12	Writing group. Matthew confused Declaration of Independence with the Constitution. Chapters longer and more complete since drafting conference. Compared with autobiography project, writing is more sophisticated. Longer, too. Reading is influencing writing style—e.g., "Luckily for Ben." He is still somewhat defensive about accepting suggestions except from me. He will make 3 revisions—-agreed in writing group.
April 15	Revisions: (1) eliminated "he" (substitute), (2) re-sequenced Chapter 3 (move), and (3) added sentences in Chapter 5 (add).
April 19	Proofread with Dustin. Working hard.
April 23	Editing conference—-no major problems. Discussed use of commas within sentences, capitalizing proper nouns. Matthew and Dustin more task-oriented on this project; I see more motivation and commitment.
April 29	Final copy of biography completed and shared with class.

Teacher's Notebook
Seven Types of Conferences

1. On-the-Spot Conferences

Teachers visit briefly with students at their desks to monitor some aspect of the students' work or to check on progress. These conferences are brief; the teacher may spend less than a minute at each student's desk.

2. Prereading or Prewriting Conferences

The teacher and student make plans for reading or writing at the conference. At a prereading conference, they may talk about information related to the book, difficult concepts or vocabulary words related to the reading, or the reading log the student will keep. At a prewriting conference, they may discuss possible writing topics or how to narrow a broad topic.

3. Revising Conferences

A small group of students and the teacher meet to get specific suggestions about revising their compositions. These conferences offer student writers an audience to provide feedback on how well they have communicated.

4. Book Discussion Conferences

Students and the teacher meet to discuss the book they have read. They may share reading log entries, discuss plot or characters, compare the story to others they have read, or make plans to extend their reading.

5. Editing Conferences

The teacher reviews students' proofread compositions and helps them correct spelling, punctuation, capitalization, and other mechanical errors.

6. Minilesson Conferences

The teacher meets with students to explain a procedure, strategy, or skill (e.g., writing a table of contents, using the visualization strategy when reading, or capitalizing proper nouns).

7. Assessment Conferences

The teacher meets with students after they have completed an assignment or project to talk about their growth as readers or writers. Students reflect on their competencies and set goals.

the notebook, which they keep on their desk. A third technique is to write anecdotes on small sheets of paper and clip the sheets into students' assessment folders.

Conferences.   Teachers talk with students to monitor their progress in language arts activities as well as to set goals and help students solve problems. Seven types of conferences are described in the Teacher's Notebook on page 74. Often these conferences are brief and impromptu, held at students' desks as the teacher moves around the classroom, while at other times the conferences are planned and students meet with the teacher at a designated conference table.

The teacher's role is to be listener and guide. Teachers can learn a great deal about students and their learning if they listen as students talk about their reading, writing, or other activities. When students explain a problem they are having, the teacher is often able to decide on a way to work through it. Graves (1994) suggests that teachers balance the amount of their talk with the student's talk during the conference and, at the end, reflect on what the student has taught them, what responsibilities the student can take, and whether the student understands what to do next.

Checklists.   Teachers use checklists as they observe students; as they track students' progress during literature focus units, theme cycles, and reading

Teachers monitor students' progress through conferences during writing workshop.

and writing workshop; and as they document students' use of language arts skills, strategies, procedures, and concepts. For example, when students participate in writing conferences in which they read their compositions to small groups of classmates and ask for suggestions for improving their writing, teachers can note whether students participate fully in the group, share their writing with classmates, gracefully accept suggestions about improving their writing, and make substantive changes in their writing based on some of their classmates' suggestions. Students can even help develop the checklists so that they understand what types of behavior are expected of them.

■ *Turn to Chapter 8, "Sustaining Talk in the Classroom," p. 326, to read about book talks.*

Two checklists appear in Figure 2–9. The first is a "Weekly Reading-Writing Workshop Activity Sheet" that middle-grade students might complete each week to monitor their work during reading and writing workshop. Notice that students are directed to write a letter to the teacher on the back of the

Figure 2–9   *Two Assessment Checklists*

Weekly Reading-Writing Workshop Activity Sheet			
Name_____		Week _____	
Read independently	M T W Th F	Made a cluster	M T W Th F
Wrote in a reading log	M T W Th F	Wrote a rough draft	M T W Th F
Listened to the teacher read aloud	M T W Th F	Went to a writing group	M T W Th F
Read with a classmate	M T W Th F	Made revisions	M T W Th F
Read at the listening center	M T W Th F	Proofread my own writing	M T W Th F
Had a reading confer- ence	M T W Th F	Had a writing conference	M T W Th F
Shared a book with classmates	M T W Th F	Shared my writing with classmates	M T W Th F
Other		Other	
Interesting words read this week		Spelling words needed this week	
Titles of books read		Titles of writings	
Write a letter on the back, thinking about the week and your reading and writing.			

sheet, reflecting on their work during that week. Next is a "Projects Checklist" that either the teacher or the student might use to keep track of the projects the student chooses to participate in after reading.

Implementing Portfolios in the Classroom

Portfolios are systematic and meaningful collections of artifacts documenting students' language arts learning and development over a period of time (De Fina, 1992; Graves & Sunstein, 1992; Porter & Cleland, 1995). These collections are dynamic and reflect students' day-to-day learning activities in language arts and across the curriculum. Students' work samples provide "windows" on the strategies that students employ as language users—readers, writers, listeners, viewers, and talkers.

There are many reasons why portfolio programs complement language arts instruction. The most important one is that students become more

Figure 2–9   *continued*

Projects Checklist	
Name_____	Grading Period 1 2 3 4
book jacket	plot diagram
book mark	poem
character cluster	point of view retelling
commercial or ad	portrait of character
crossword puzzle	poster
diorama	puppets
dramatization	quilt
dress as character	quotable quotes
exhibit	read other books
filmstrip	research
interview	script
letter to author	sequel
literary opposites	simulated journal
map or diagram	simulated letter
mobile	story boards
mural	story box
newspaper article	story map
open-mind portrait	travel brochure
oral reading	Venn diagram

involved in the assessment of their work and more reflective about the quality of their reading, writing, and other language use. Other benefits include:

- Students feel ownership of their work.
- Students become more responsible about their work.
- Students set goals and are motivated to work toward accomplishing them.
- Students reflect on their accomplishments.
- Students make connections between learning and assessing.
- Students' self-esteem is enhanced.
- Students recognize the connection between process and product.

In addition, portfolios eliminate the need to grade all student work. Portfolios are useful in student and parent conferences and complement the information provided in report cards.

Collecting Work in Portfolios. Portfolios are folders, large envelopes, or boxes that hold students' work. Teachers often have students label and decorate large folders and then store them in plastic crates or large cardboard boxes. Students date and label items as they place them in their portfolios, and they attach notes to the items to explain the context for the activity and why they selected a particular item for inclusion in the portfolio. Students' portfolios should be stored in the classroom in a place where they are readily accessible to students. Students review their portfolios periodically and add new pieces to them.

Students usually choose the items to place in their portfolios within the guidelines provided by the teacher. Some students submit the original piece of work; others want to keep the original, so they place a copy in the portfolio instead. In addition to the writing and art samples that can go directly into portfolios, students also record oral language and drama samples on audio- and videotapes to place in their portfolios. Large-size art and writing projects can be photographed, and the photographs placed in the portfolio. The following types of student work might be placed in a portfolio:

"All About Me" books

alphabet books

autobiographies

biographies

books

choral readings (on audiotape)

clusters

copies of letters to pen pals, businesses, and authors, along with replies received

drawings, diagrams, and charts

learning log entries

lists of books read

multimedia programs

oral reading (on audio- or videotape)

oral reports (on audio- or videotape)

poems

projects

puppets (in photographs)

puppet shows (on videotape)

quickwrites

readers theatre performances (on audio- or videotape)

reading log entries

reports

simulated journal entries

stories

timelines and lifelines

Venn diagrams comparing stories and their film versions

This variety of work samples takes into account all six language arts. Also, samples from workshops, literature focus units, and across-the-curriculum theme cycles should be included.

Not all work that is placed in a student's portfolio needs to be graded for quality. Teachers will, of course, be familiar with most pieces, but it is not necessary to correct them with a red pen. Many times, students' work is simply graded as "done" or "not done." When a piece of work is to be graded, students should choose it from the items being placed in their portfolios.

Many teachers collect students' work in folders, and they assume that portfolios are basically the same as work folders; however, the two types of collections differ in several important ways. Perhaps the most important difference is that portfolios are student-oriented, whereas work folders are usually teachers' collections. Students choose which samples will be placed in portfolios, while teachers often place all completed assignments in work folders (Clemmons, Lasse, Cooper, Areglado, & Dill, 1993). Next, portfolios focus on students' strengths, not their weaknesses. Because students choose items for portfolios, they choose samples that they feel best represent their language development. Another difference is that portfolios involve reflection (D'Aoust, 1992). Through reflection, students become aware of their strengths as readers, writers, and language users. They also use their work samples to identify the language arts skills, strategies, procedures, and concepts they already know and the ones they need to focus on.

Involving Students in Self-Assessment.   Portfolios are a useful vehicle for engaging students in self-reflection and goal setting (Clemmons et al., 1993). Students can learn to reflect on and assess their own reading and writing activities and their development as readers and writers (Stires, 1991a). Teachers begin by asking students to think about their language arts abilities in terms of contrast. For example, in reading, students identify the books they have read that they liked most and least, and ask themselves what these choices suggest about themselves as readers. They also identify what they do well in reading and what they need to improve about their reading. By making these comparisons, students begin to reflect on their language arts development.

Teachers use minilessons and conferences to talk with students about the characteristics of good listeners, good writers, good storytellers, and good viewers. In particular, they discuss:

- What good listeners do as they listen
- How to view a film or videotape
- What fluent reading is
- How to prepare to give an oral report
- Which language arts skills and strategies students use
- How students choose books for reading workshop
- How students demonstrate comprehension
- What makes a good project to extend reading
- How students decide what to write in journals
- How students adapt their writing to their audience
- How students visually represent important concepts
- How to use writing rubrics
- How to participate in a grand conversation

As students learn about what it means to be effective language users, they acquire the tools they need to reflect on and evaluate their own language development. They acquire the vocabulary to use in their reflections, terms such as "goal," "strategy," and "rubric."

Students write notes on items they choose to put into their portfolios. In these self-assessments, students explain their reasons for the selection and identify strengths and accomplishments in their work. In some classrooms, students write their reflections and other comments on index cards, while in other classrooms students design special comment sheets that they attach to the items in their portfolios. A first grader wrote this reflection to explain why she chose to make a poster about author Eric Carle and his books and include it in her portfolio: "I have a favorite author. Mr. Eric Carle. I read five of his books!" A fifth grader chose to put the reading log he wrote while reading *Shiloh* (Naylor, 1991) in his portfolio. He wrote this reflection: "I put my journal on the computer. It looks good! I used the SPELCHEK. I put in lots of details like I was him. I should of put some illustrations in the book."

Showcasing Students' Portfolios. At the end of the school year, many teachers organize "Portfolio Share Days" to celebrate students' accomplishments and to provide an opportunity for students to share their portfolios with classmates and the wider community (Porter & Cleland, 1995). Often family members, local business people and politicians, school administrators, college students, and others are invited to attend. Students and community members form small groups, and students share their portfolios, pointing out their accomplishments and strengths. This activity is especially useful in involving community members in the school and showing them the types of language arts activities in which students are involved as well as how students are becoming effective readers, writers, and language users.

These sharing days also help students accept responsibility for their own learning—especially those students who have not been as motivated as their classmates. When less-motivated students listen to their classmates talk about their work and how they have grown as readers, writers, and language users, these students often decide to work harder the next year.

Assigning Grades

Assigning grades is one of the most difficult responsibilities placed on teachers. "Grading is a fact of life," according to Donald Graves (1983, p. 93), but he adds that teachers should use grades to encourage students, not to hinder their achievement. The authentic assessment procedures described in this chapter encourage students because they document how students are using all the language arts in authentic ways. Reviewing and translating this documentation into grades is the difficult part.

Assignment Checklists.   One way for students to keep track of assignments during literature focus units and theme cycles is to use assignment checklists. Teachers create assignment checklists as they plan the unit, and then students receive a copy of the checklist at the beginning of the unit and keep it in their unit folder. Then, as they complete the assignments, they check them off, and it is easy for the teacher to make periodic checks of student progress. At the end of the unit, the teacher collects the unit folders and grades the work.

A checklist for a second-grade theme cycle on hermit crabs is presented in Figure 2–10. Eight assignments included on the checklist include both science and language arts activities. Students put a check in the boxes in the "Student's Check" column when they complete each assignment, and the teacher adds the grade in the right-hand column. Some assignments will be graded as "done" or "not done," and others will be graded for quality.

Teachers of middle- and upper-grade students often assign points to each activity in the unit checklist so that the total point value for the unit is 100 points. Activities that involve more time and effort earn more points. The second checklist in Figure 2–10 is for a fifth-grade literature focus unit on *Number the Stars* (Lowry, 1989). The point value for each activity is listed in parentheses. Students make check marks on the lines on the left side of the grading sheet, and the teacher marks the numerical grades on the right side.

Rubrics.   Teachers and students develop rubrics or scoring guides to assess students' growth as writers (Farr & Tone, 1994). Rubrics make the analysis of writing simpler and the assessment process more reliable and consistent. Rubrics may have three, four, five, or six levels, with descriptors related to ideas, organization, language, and mechanics at each level. Some rubrics are general and appropriate for almost any writing project, while others are designed for a specific writing assignment. Figure 2–11 presents two rubrics. One is a general five-level writing rubric for middle-grade students, and the other is a four-level rubric for assessing sixth graders' reports on ancient Egypt. In contrast to the general rubric, the report rubric includes specific components that students were to include in their reports.

Both teachers and students can assess writing with rubrics. They read the composition and highlight words or check statements in the rubric that best describe the composition. It is important to note that rarely are all the highlighted words or checked statements at the same level. The score is determined by examining the highlighted words or checked statements and determining which level best represents the quality of the composition.

Figure 2–10   Two Assignment Checklists

Checklist for Theme Cycle on Hermit Crabs

Name _____   Begin _____
                                           End _____

	Student's Check	Teacher's Check

1. Keep an observation log on the hermit crab ☐ ____
   on your table for 10 days.
2. Make a chart of a hermit crab and label the parts. ☐ ____
3. Make a map of the hermit crab's habitat. ☐ ____
4. Read three books about hermit crabs and ☐ ____
   do quickwrites about them.
   _____ *Hermit Crabs*
   _____ *A House for Hermit Crab*
   _____ *Is This a House for Hermit Crab?*
5. Do two science experiments and write lab reports. ☐ ____
   _____ Wet-Dry Experiment
   _____ Light-Dark Experiment
6. Write about hermit crabs. Do one: ☐ ____
   _____ *All About Hermit Crabs* book
   _____ A poem about hermit crabs
   _____ A story about hermit crabs
7. Do a project about hermit crabs. Share it. ☐ ____
8. Keep everything neatly in your hermit crab folder. ☐ ____

***Number the Stars* Grading Sheet**

Name _____   Date _____

_____ 1. Read *Number the Stars.*   _____
_____ 2. Write 5 entries in a reading log or simulated journal.   (25) _____
_____ 3. Talk about your reading in 5 grand conversations.   (25) _____
_____ 4. Make a Venn diagram to compare characters. Sum-
         marize what you learned from the diagram in an   (10)
         essay.
_____ 5. Make a cluster about one word on the word wall.   (5) _____
_____ 6. Make a square with a favorite quote for the story   (10) _____
         quilt.
_____ 7. Do a response project.   (25) _____
Total   (100) _____

Figure 2–11   *Two Rubrics*

Middle-Grade Writing Rubric
5   EXCEPTIONAL ACHIEVEMENT
• Creative and original • Clear organization • Precise word choice and figurative language • Sophisticated sentences • Essentially free of mechanical errors
4   EXCELLENT ACHIEVEMENT
• Some creativity, but more predictable than an exceptional paper • Definite organization • Good word choice but not figurative language • Varied sentences • Only a few mechanical errors
3   ADEQUATE ACHIEVEMENT
• Predictable paper • Some organization • Adequate word choice • Little variety of sentences and some run-on sentences • Some mechanical errors
2   LIMITED ACHIEVEMENT
• Brief and superficial • Lacks organization • Imprecise language • Incomplete and run-on sentences • Many mechanical errors
1   MINIMAL ACHIEVEMENT
• No ideas communicated • No organization • Inadequate word choice • Sentence fragments • Overwhelming mechanical errors

To assess students' learning systematically, teachers should use at least three evaluation approaches. Approaching an evaluation from at least three viewpoints is called triangulation. In addition to tests, teachers can use kid watching, anecdotal records, conferences, portfolios, assignment checklists, and rubrics. Using a variety of techniques enables teachers to be much more accurate in charting and assessing students' language growth.

Figure 2–11   continued

Rubric for Assessing Reports on Ancient Egypt

4   EXCELLENT REPORT

_____ Three or more chapters with titles
_____ Main idea clearly developed in each chapter
_____ Three or more illustrations
_____ Effective use of Egypt-related words in text and illustrations
_____ Very interesting to read
_____ Very few mechanical errors
_____ Table of contents

---

3   GOOD REPORT

_____ Three chapters with titles
_____ Main idea somewhat developed in each chapter
_____ Three illustrations
_____ Some Egypt-related words used
_____ Interesting to read
_____ A few mechanical errors
_____ Table of contents

---

2   AVERAGE REPORT

_____ Three chapters
_____ Main idea identified in each chapter
_____ One or two illustrations
_____ A few Egypt-related words used
_____ Some mechanical errors
_____ Sort of interesting to read
_____ Table of contents

---

1   POOR REPORT

_____ One or two chapters
_____ Information in each chapter rambles
_____ No illustrations
_____ Very few Egypt-related words used
_____ Many mechanical errors
_____ Hard to read and understand
_____ No table of contents

Review

This chapter focused on how teachers teach language arts. Creating a language-rich classroom is an important prerequisite. Teachers plan language arts instruction using three instructional approaches: literature focus units, theme cycles, and reading and writing workshop. Assessment is an integral part of instruction, and instruction should be authentic. Key points presented in this chapter include:

1. Classrooms should be authentic learning environments that encourage students to use all six language arts.
2. Textbooks should never be equivalent to the total language arts program.
3. Teachers collect three types of trade books—stories, informational books, and books of poetry—for text sets related to literature focus units and theme cycles.
4. Literature focus units include four components: reading books, responding, teaching minilessons, and creating projects.
5. Theme cycles are interdisciplinary units that integrate language arts with social studies, science, math, and other curricular areas.
6. Language arts activities during theme cycles include keeping learning logs, reading books, and creating projects.
7. Reading workshop components are reading and responding, sharing, and teaching minilessons; writing workshop components are writing, sharing, and teaching minilessons.
8. Teachers play many roles during language arts instruction, including organizer, facilitator, participant, instructor, model, manager, diagnostician, evaluator, coordinator, and communicator.
9. Students with special learning needs benefit from the same language arts program that other students do, given some adaptations.
10. Teachers use authentic assessment procedures, including observations, anecdotal notes, conferences, checklists, portfolios, and rubrics.

Extensions

1. Visit an elementary classroom and note which characteristics of a language-rich classroom it exemplifies. What might the teacher change in the classroom to incorporate other characteristics?
2. Choose one of the following categories of children's literature that were discussed in this chapter: picture books, chapter books, stories, informational books, and books of poetry. Read at least 10 books in the category and write a brief report describing the types of books within the category and annotating the books you read.
3. Create a text set of at least 10 books on a social studies or science topic taught in the elementary school similar to the text sets presented in Figure 2–3. Include stories, informational books, and books of poetry, if possible.
4. Reflect on the advantages and disadvantages of the three ways to organize for language arts instruction—literature focus units, theme cycles, and reading and writing workshops—and how you plan to organize your classroom. Write a brief paper about your reflections and your plans.
5. Interview an elementary teacher and ask about the kinds of assessment he or she uses.

PROCEDURE

Six third graders are meeting with me in a small group during our Writing Workshop. My purpose today is to touch base with these students about their new writing projects. Students are choosing their own topics and writing forms for this project. Jason eagerly tells us that he is making a joke book, and he has already begun writing and illustrating his collection of favorite jokes. He's pleased with this opportunity to pursue a hobby. Trina wants to write a fairy tale, and she shows us a cluster she has made with ideas about the story. Lance is thinking about writing a Nintendo adventure story, but he says he isn't sure how to start. Group members encourage him to begin with one of his fantastic drawings. Nikki has just read a biography about Benjamin Franklin that she shares with us. She can't decide whether she should write a retelling of this biography or write her own autobiography. The students give her suggestions, but she hasn't decided yet. Eliza wants to write a letter to Beverly Cleary, her favorite author, and as her prewriting she has made a list of the things she want to include in her letter. Derek doesn't seem to have an idea yet, but Lance and Jason offer several suggestions.

Throughout this 20-minute meeting, my students are active group members. They take turns sharing ideas for their projects and talk about how they have developed their ideas, using writing process terminology such as "rough draft" and "clustering." They are also supportive of their classmates. They listen thoughtfully and offer compliments and encouragement.

The group comes to an end with students each briefly explaining what they will do next. Those who are ready to prewrite or draft move back to their desks while I talk with Derek and Nikki, who are not sure what they want to write about. Nikki decides to try her hand at writing her autobiography, and she begins to draw a lifeline of her life. Derek decides to brainstorm a list of three possible topics and share them with me later today.

ASSESSMENT

My students use the writing process, and I confer with them during almost every stage. I want to see that they are on task. It is too easy for third graders to get sidetracked or bogged down with a problem that I or their classmates can solve.

I give my students contracts for each writing project. A copy of the contract is shown in the accompanying figure. The contract lists the steps of the writing process and the activities students will complete in each step. My students staple the contracts inside the front cover of their writing folders and check off each activity as they complete it. This how I keep track of each student and how they keep track of themselves. I ask them to confer with me several times during the writing process, and I schedule time for the conferences three afternoons a week. I think touching base is important.

ADAPTATIONS

My students spend 75 minutes each afternoon in Writing Workshop. For the first 15 minutes, I teach a minilesson, and then students work on writing projects for the next 45 minutes. During the last 15 minutes, we get together as a class to share our published books and other completed writings.

I use a similar approach for Reading Workshop during the morning. I begin by reading a book aloud to the class. Sometimes I read a picture book and sometimes I read a chapter book, a chapter or two each day. After I read, we take a few minutes to share our reactions to the book. Then my students read books they have chosen themselves. They have Reading Workshop folders and keep track of their reading by listing book titles on their reading lists and by writing entries in their reading logs. I move around the classroom, conferencing with students about their reading on a regular basis. Once or twice a month, my students create a project to extend their interpretation of a favorite book. On most days, I teach a reading-related minilesson, and students who have finished reading a book or have created a project share their books and projects during the last 15 minutes of Reading Workshop.

REFLECTIONS

I have been very pleased—maybe even amazed—at how well my third graders work in small groups and how responsible they have become. They are learning from each other and supporting each other as they learn. Cooperative learning really works! Besides conferences to touch base with students, we use conferences in this classroom when students want feedback on their writing, to teach language skills in minilessons, and to discuss authors we are studying.

Writing Workshop Contract

Name _____   Title _____

1. Prewriting
   Make a cluster.
   Conference with Mrs. Reeves.   _____
2. Drafting
   Mark it ROUGH DRAFT.   _____
   Skip lines.   _____
3. Revising
   Read your draft in writing group. _____
   Make at least 2 changes.   _____
   Conference with Mrs. Reeves.   _____
4. Editing
   Proofread carefully.   _____
   Proofread with a partner.   _____
   Conference with Mrs. Reeves.   _____
5. Publishing
   Make the final copy.   _____
   Share in the author's chair.   _____

The Reading and Writing Processes

5th GR

As part of a theme on Northwest Indians, Chris Carmean's fifth-grade class created a found poem after reading *Brother Eagle, Sister Sky: A Message From Chief Seattle* (Jeffers, 1991). After reading, students chose favorite lines, arranged them to create a found poem, and copied them on strips of construction paper. One student's poem is "You Can't":

> My father, how can you buy the sky?
> You can't, my children.
> How can you buy the wind?
> You can't, my children.
> How can you buy the water?
> You can't, my children.

I n the past 20 years there has been a significant shift in thinking about what people do as they read and write. Reading and writing are now viewed as transactive processes in which readers and writers create meaning through the lived-through experience of reading or writing (Graves, 1994; Harste, Woodward, & Burke, 1984a; Rosenblatt, 1978; Weaver, 1994a).

Both reading and writing are meaning-making processes. According to constructivist and sociolinguistic learning theories, readers create meaning through negotiation with the texts they are reading, and, similarly, writers create meaning through negotiation with the texts they are writing. Readers use their life and literature experiences and knowledge of written language as they read, and writers bring similar knowledge and experiences to writing. It is quite common for two people to read the same story and come away with different interpretations, and for two writers to write different accounts of the same event. Meaning does not exist on the pages of the book that a reader is reading or in the words of the composition that a writer is writing; instead, meaning is created through the transaction between readers and what they are reading, or between writers and what they are writing.

The reading process involves a series of stages during which readers construct interpretations—known as comprehension—as they read and then respond to the text they have read. "Text" includes all reading materials—stories, maps, newspapers, cereal boxes, textbooks, and so on—it is not limited to basal reader textbooks. The writing process is a similar recursive process involving a variety of activities as students gather and organize their ideas, draft their compositions, revise and edit the drafts, and, finally, publish their writings.

Reading and writing have long been thought of as the flip sides of a coin, as opposites: readers decoded or deciphered written language, and writers encoded or produced written language. Then researchers began to note similarities between reading and writing and talked of both of them as processes. Now reading and writing are viewed as parallel processes of meaning construction, and readers and writers use similar strategies for making meaning with text.

In this chapter you will read about the reading and writing processes and see how teachers use these processes in designing language arts instruction. As you continue reading, think about these questions:

- What are the stages in the reading process?
- What are the stages in the writing process?
- How are the two processes alike?
- How do teachers use these two processes in teaching language arts?

THE READING PROCESS

Reading is a transactive process in which a reader negotiates meaning in order to comprehend, or create an interpretation. During reading, the meaning does not go from the page to the reader. Instead, reading involves a complex negotiation between the text and the reader that is shaped by many factors: the reader's knowledge about the topic; the reader's purpose for reading;

the language community the reader belongs to, and how closely that language matches the language used in the text; the reader's culturally based expectations about reading; and the reader's expectations about reading based on his or her previous experiences (Weaver, 1994a).

Aesthetic and Efferent Reading

■ *To compare aesthetic and efferent reading with similar stances for listening, see Chapter 7, "Listening to Learn," pp. 266–268.*

Readers read for different purposes, and the way they approach the reading process varies according to their purpose. Often they read for enjoyment, but at other times they read to carry away information. When reading for enjoyment or to be entertained, readers assume an aesthetic stance and focus on the lived-through experience of reading. They concentrate on the thoughts, images, feelings, and associations evoked during reading. Readers also respond to these thoughts, images, feelings, and associations. For example, as children read Cynthia Rylant's story *The Relatives Came* (1985), they may relate the events in the book to a time when their relatives visited; as they read Diane Siebert's *Sierra* (1991), they may respond to the language of the text; or as they read *Catherine, Called Birdy* (Cushman, 1994), they may imagine themselves in Birdy's medieval world.

p. 31
Reutzel

When reading to carry away information, readers assume an efferent stance. They concentrate on the public, common referents of the words and symbols in the text. For example, as children read Patricia Lauber's *Seeing Earth From Space* (1990), with its breathtaking photographs of the earth taken by satellites, their focus is on the information in the text and illustrations, not on the experience of reading.

Almost every reading experience calls for a balance between aesthetic and efferent reading (Rosenblatt, 1978, 1991). Readers do not simply read stories and poems aesthetically and informational books efferently. As they read, readers move back and forth between the aesthetic and efferent stances. Literature, however, should be read primarily from the aesthetic stance.

During both aesthetic and efferent reading, readers move through the five stages of the reading process: preparing, reading, responding, exploring, and extending. The key features of each stage are overviewed in the Teacher's Notebook on page 92. Many of the features are characteristic of both aesthetic and efferent reading, but a few features exemplify one stance or the other.

Stage 1: Preparing

The reading process begins before readers open a book to read. The first stage is preparing. As readers prepare to read, they:

- Choose books
- Activate background knowledge
- Set purposes
- Plan for reading

Choosing Books.   Readers often begin the reading process by choosing the book they will read. Choosing an appropriate book is not easy. First of all, students need to know about themselves as readers: What types of books do

Teacher's Notebook

Key Features of the Reading Process

Stage 1: Preparing

- Choose a book.
- Activate prior knowledge.
- Connect to prior personal and literary experiences.
- Connect to theme cycles or special interests.
- Set purposes for reading.
- Make predictions.
- Preview the text.
- Consult the index to locate information.

Stage 2: Reading

- Make predictions.
- Apply skills and strategies.
- Read independently, with a buddy, using shared reading, or through guided reading, or listen to the text read aloud.
- Read the illustrations, charts, and diagrams.
- Read the entire text from beginning to end.
- Read one or more sections of the text to learn specific information.
- Take notes.

Stage 3: Responding

- Write in a reading log.
- Participate in a grand conversation.

Stage 4: Exploring

- Reread and think more deeply about the text.
- Make connections with personal experiences.
- Make connections with other literary experiences.
- Examine the author's craft.
- Identify memorable quotes.
- Learn new vocabulary words.
- Participate in minilessons.

Stage 5: Extending

- Construct projects.
- Use information in theme cycles.
- Connect with related books.
- Reflect on their interpretations.
- Value the reading experience.

PRREE

they like? Who are their favorite authors? As they become readers, students learn the answers to these questions. They can also point to books they have read and can tell about them and explain why they enjoyed reading them.

Students need to learn to choose books they can read. Ohlhausen and Jepsen (1992) developed a strategy for choosing books called the "Goldilocks Strategy." These teachers developed three categories of books—"Too Easy," "Too Hard," and "Just Right"—using "The Three Bears" folktale as their model. The books in the "Too Easy" category were books they had read before or could read fluently. "Too Hard" books were unfamiliar and confusing, and books in the "Just Right" category were interesting and had just a few unfamiliar words. The books in each category vary according to the students' reading levels. This approach was developed with a second-grade class, but the categorization scheme can work at any grade level. Figure 3–1 presents a chart about choosing books using the Goldilocks Strategy developed by a third-grade class. Sometimes teachers choose books for students, but it is important that readers have many opportunities to choose books they are interested in reading.

Figure 3–1   *A Third-Grade Chart Applying the Goldilocks Strategy*

How to Choose the Best Books for YOU

"Too Easy" Books

1. The book is short.
2. The print is big.
3. You have read the book before.
4. You know all the words in the book.
5. The book has a lot of pictures.
6. You are an expert on this topic.

"Just Right" Books

1. The book looks interesting.
2. You can decode most of the words in the book.
3. Mrs. Donnelly has read this book aloud to you.
4. You have read other books by this author.
5. There's someone to give you help if you need it.
6. You know something about this topic.

"Too Hard" Books

1. The book is long.
2. The print is small.
3. There aren't many pictures in the book.
4. There are a lot of words that you can't decode.
5. There's no one to help you read this book.
6. You don't know much about this topic.

Activating Background Knowledge. Readers activate their background knowledge or schemata about the book (or other selection) before beginning to read. The topic of the book, the title, the author, the genre, the cover illustration, a comment someone makes about the book, or something else may trigger this activation. When students are reading independently—during reading workshop, for example—they choose the books they will read and activate their background knowledge themselves. For instance, readers who love horses often choose horse books such as *Misty of Chincoteague* (Henry, 1963) to read.

At other times, such as during literature focus units, teachers teach minilessons to help students activate and build their background knowledge. They share information on a topic related to the book or introduce a book box with a collection of objects related to the book. Or, they show a video or film, tell about the author, read the first paragraph aloud, or ask students to make a prediction about the book. For instance, before reading Paula Danziger's *Amber Brown Is Not a Crayon* (1994), teachers talk about missing friends when they move away; before reading Jan Brett's *The Mitten* (1989), teachers show students a white mitten and several stuffed animals representing characters in the story—a bear, a fox, a rabbit, and an owl—and ask students whether they think these animals could fit into the mitten.

In order for readers to make meaning from the selection they are reading, their schemata must be activated. When students are preparing to read a book on an unfamiliar topic, they need to build background knowledge. By building a new schema before reading and being introduced to key vocabulary, students are more likely to be successful when they read. For example, teachers show a video on hermit crabs before reading *A House for Hermit Crab* (Carle, 1987), or before reading *The Giver* (Lowry, 1993), they build a concept of what a "perfect" society might be like by having students brainstorm a list of problems in today's society and think of possible remedies.

Another part of activating knowledge before reading is to make connections to personal experiences and to literary experiences. The more connections students make between the book they are about to read and personal experiences, the better. Students who have a hermit crab as a pet, for instance, will be better prepared to read *A House for Hermit Crab* than students who have never seen a hermit crab. Similarly, students who have read other books by Eric Carle and know about his fabulous collage illustrations will be better prepared to read *A House for Hermit Crab*.

Setting Purposes. The two overarching purposes for reading are pleasure and information. When students read for pleasure or enjoyment, they read aesthetically, to be carried into the world of the text; when they read a selection to locate and remember information or for directions about how to do something, they read efferently (Rosenblatt, 1978). Often readers use elements of both purposes as they read, but usually one purpose is more primary to the reading experience than the other. For example, when students pick up *The Sweetest Fig* (1993) or *Bad Day at Riverbend* (1995), two of the newest Chris Van Allsburg picture book fantasies, their primary purpose is enjoyment. They want to experience the story, but at the same time, they search for the white dog, a trademark that Van Allsburg includes in all of his books, and they compare these books with others of his that they have read. As they search for the white dog or make comparisons, they add efferent purposes to their primarily aesthetic reading experience.

Readers are more successful when they have a single purpose for reading the entire selection. Purpose-setting is usually directed by the teacher during literature focus units, but in reading workshop students set their own purposes because everyone is reading different self-selected books. For teacher-directed purpose-setting, teachers explain how students are expected to read and what they will do after reading. The goal of teacher-directed purpose-setting is to help students learn how to set personally relevant purposes when they are reading independently (Blanton, Wood, & Moorman, 1990). Students should always have a purpose for reading, whether they are reading aesthetically or efferently, whether reading a selection for the first time or the tenth.

When readers have a purpose for reading, comprehension of the selection they are reading is enhanced in three ways (Blanton et al., 1990). First, the purpose guides the reading process that students use. Having a purpose provides motivation and direction for reading as well as a mechanism that students use for monitoring their reading. As they monitor their reading, students ask themselves whether or not they are fulfilling their purpose. Second, purpose-setting activates a plan for teachers to use in teaching reading. They help students draw on background knowledge as they set purposes, consider strategies they might use as they read, and think about the structure of the text they are reading. Third, students are better able to sort out important from unimportant information as they read when they have a purpose for reading. Teachers direct students' attention to relevant concepts as they set purposes for reading and show them how to connect the concepts they are reading about to their background knowledge.

Planning for Reading. Students often preview the reading selection as they prepare to read. They look through the selection and check its length, the reading difficulty of the selection, and the illustrations in order to judge the general suitability of the selection for them as readers. Previewing serves an important function as students connect their background knowledge, identify their purpose for reading, and take their first look at the selection.

Teachers set the guidelines for the reading experience. They explain how the book will be read—independently, in small groups, or as a class— and set the schedule for reading. Setting the schedule is especially important when students are reading a chapter book. Often teachers and students work together to create a two- or three-week schedule for reading and responding and then write the schedule on a calendar to which students can refer.

■ *To learn more about using content-area textbooks, see Chapter 13, "Putting It All Together," pp. 570–572.*

When students are preparing to read informational books, they preview the selection by flipping through the pages and noting section headings, illustrations, diagrams, and other charts. Sometimes they examine the table of contents to see how the book is organized, or consult the index to locate specific information they want to read. They may also notice unfamiliar terminology and other words they can check in the glossary, ask a classmate or the teacher about, or look up in a dictionary. Teachers also use the SQ3R

p.572

p 571

study procedure, anticipation guides, and other teaching strategies as they introduce informational books and content-area textbooks.

Stage 2: Reading

In the second stage, students read the book or other selection. They use their knowledge of word identification, sight words, reading strategies and skills, and vocabulary while they read. Fluent readers are better able to understand what they are reading because they identify most words automatically and use decoding skills when necessary (LaBerge & Samuels, 1976). They also apply their knowledge of the structure of text as they create meaning. They continue reading as long as what they are reading fits the meaning they are constructing. When something doesn't make sense, fluent readers slow down, back up, and reread until they are making meaning again.

Students may read the entire selection or only read sections. When students are reading aesthetically, they usually read the entire selection, but when they are reading efferently, they may be searching for specific information and read only until they locate that information. Also, students may decide to put a book down if it does not capture their interest, if it is too difficult to read, or if it does not have the information they are searching for. It is unrealistic to assume that students will always read entire selections or finish reading every book they begin.

Outside of school, readers usually read silently and independently. Sometimes, however, people listen as someone else reads. Young children often sit in a parent's lap and look at the illustrations as the parent reads a picture

5ᵗʰ GR.

These fifth graders used the reading process during a literature focus unit featuring Bridge to Terabithia.

book aloud. Adults also listen to books read aloud on cassette tapes. In the classroom, teachers and students use five types of reading:

- Shared reading
- Guided reading
- Independent reading
- Buddy reading
- Reading aloud to students

Shared Reading.   Teachers use shared reading during literature focus units to introduce a book or other reading selection to students before the students read the selection with partners or individually (Pappas & Brown, 1987; Sulzby, 1985a). In this type of reading, students follow along as the teacher reads the selection aloud. Kindergarten teachers and other primary-grade teachers often use big books—enlarged versions of the selection—for shared reading (Holdaway, 1979). Students sit so that they can see the book, and they either listen to the teacher read aloud or join in and read along with the teacher. The teacher or a student points to each line of text as it is read to draw students' attention to the words, to show the direction of print on a page, and to highlight important concepts about letters, words, and sentences.

Teachers also use shared reading when students have individual copies of the reading selection. Students follow along in their copies as the teacher or another fluent reader reads aloud. This "first" reading is preparation for students so that they become familiar enough with the story line and the vocabulary that they can read the selection independently later during the literature focus unit.

When students are reading chapter books, shared reading is used as the main reading approach during the unit if students can't read the selection independently. The teacher and other fluent readers take turns reading aloud as students follow along in their copies of the selection. To ensure that all the students are following along in their copies of the book, teachers sometimes ask all students or a group of students to read aloud very softly or "mumble" along as they read aloud. Sometimes teachers read the first chapter or two of a chapter book together as a class using shared reading, and then students use other types of reading as they read the rest of the book. Only students for whom the book is too difficult continue to use shared reading and read along with the teacher.

There are several variations of shared reading (Slaughter, 1993). One is choral reading, when students divide into groups to read poems aloud. Another is readers theatre, in which students read play scripts aloud. A third type of shared reading is the listening center, where students can listen to a book read aloud as they follow along in the book. Listening centers are a good way to provide additional reading practice to help students become fluent readers.

Guided Reading.   Teachers scaffold students' reading to enable them to develop and use reading skills and strategies in guided reading (Clay, 1991; Fountas & Pinnell, 1996). This type of reading is teacher-directed and usually done in small groups with students who read at the same level or use similar reading skills and strategies.

■ *See Chapter 4, "Emergent Literacy," pp. 157–162, to read more about big books.*

■ *For more information about using shared reading with young children, see Chapter 4, pp. 155–158.*

Choral Reading pp. 445, 447

■ *See Chapter 11, "Reading and Writing Poetry," p. 447, for more information on choral reading, and Chapter 8, pp. 316–318, for more information on readers theatre.*

Selections used for guided reading should be written at students' instructional reading levels; that is, slightly beyond their ability to read the text independently or at their level of proximal development. Students usually read the selection silently, and if the selection is too difficult, shared reading might be a better approach. If the selection is too easy, then independent reading might be a better choice. Teachers often group and regroup students for guided reading so that the book that teachers select is appropriate for all students in a group. The steps in guided reading, according to Fountas and Pinnell (1996) are:

Step by Step

1. ***Choose a book.***   Teachers choose a book or other selection for the group to read based on their knowledge of students' reading levels and ability to use reading skills and strategies.

2. ***Introduce the selection.***   Teachers briefly introduce the selection by activating background knowledge, introducing characters, and setting a purpose for reading. They may also ask students to make predictions about what they think will happen in the selection.

3. ***Observe students as they read.***   Students read silently and teachers observe students as they read. Teachers notice the reading skills and strategies that students exhibit as they read and make anecdotal notes about their observations. They also note any words students ask for help with or any questions that students ask.

4. ***Provide assistance.***   If students require assistance, teachers assist them one-on-one with word identification and support their efforts to comprehend the selection, but they try not to interrupt students while they are reading.

5. ***Talk about the selection.***   Teachers encourage students to briefly share their responses to the book. Students talk about the selection, ask questions to clarify misconceptions, and relate the reading to their own lives.

6. ***Teach minilessons.***   Teachers introduce, practice, or review one or two skills or strategies after reading. Teachers may select topics for minilessons in advance or respond to students' observed needs. In these lessons, teachers ask students to return to the text to practice word-identification or comprehension skills or strategies. Teachers also have students focus their attention on elements of story structure and the language patterns used in the selection.

Guided reading is often used in literature focus units. Teachers read the featured selection with students in small groups, and teachers have opportunities to demonstrate reading strategies, clarify misconceptions as students read, point out key vocabulary words, and take advantage of many teachable moments. The small-group arrangement also gives teachers the opportunity to observe individual students as they read, monitor their comprehension, and informally assess their reading progress.

Independent Reading. When students read independently, they read silently by themselves and at their own pace (Hornsby, Sukarna, & Parry, 1986; Taylor, 1993). In order for students to read independently, the reading selections must be at their reading level. Students read the featured selection independently during literature focus units, but this is often after they have already read the selection once or twice with assistance from the teacher. They also read related books from the text set independently as part of these units.

During reading workshop, students almost always read independently. They choose the books they want to read, and they need to learn how to choose books that are written at an appropriate level of difficulty. Even young children in kindergarten can do a variation of independent reading when they look at books, creating their own text to accompany the illustrations.

Independent reading is an important part of language arts instruction because it is the most authentic type of reading. This type of reading is what most people do when they read, and this is the way students develop a love of reading and come to think of themselves as readers. The reading selection, however, must be either at an appropriate level of difficulty or very familiar so that students can read it independently. Otherwise, teachers use one of the other four types of reading to support students and make it possible for them to participate in the reading experience.

Buddy Reading. In buddy reading, students read or reread a selection with a classmate. Buddy reading is a good alternative to independent reading because students can choose books they want to read and then read at their own pace. Sometimes students read with buddies because it is an enjoyable social activity, and sometimes they read together to help each other. Often students can read selections together that neither one could read individually. By working together they are often able to figure out unfamiliar words and talk out comprehension problems.

During literature focus units, students often reread the featured selection with buddies after the teacher has presented it using shared reading. Students read and reread books from the text set this way, too. Buddy reading is used less often during reading workshop, but students might decide to read a book together, especially if it is a book they both want to read and neither could read it independently.

As teachers introduce buddy reading, they show students how to read with buddies and how to support each other as they read. Unless the teacher has explained and modeled the approach and taught students how to work collaboratively, buddy reading often deteriorates into the better reader reading aloud to the other student, and that is not the intention of this type of reading. Students need to take turns reading aloud to each other or read in unison. They often stop and help each other identify an unfamiliar word or take a minute or two at the end of each page to talk about what they have read. Buddy reading is a valuable way of providing the practice that beginning readers need to become fluent readers, and it is also an effective way to work with students with special learning needs and students who are learning English.

Reading Aloud to Students. In kindergarten through eighth grade, teachers read aloud to students for a variety of purposes each day. During literature focus units, teachers read aloud featured selections that are appropriate for students' interest level but too difficult for students to read by themselves. Teachers also read aloud the featured selection if they have only one copy of the book available. Sometimes it is also appropriate to read the featured selection aloud before distributing copies of the selection for students to read with buddies or independently. When they read aloud, teachers model what good readers do and how good readers use reading strategies. Reading aloud also provides an opportunity for teachers to model their use of reading strategies (Cochran-Smith, 1984).

During reading workshop, teachers also read aloud stories and other books to introduce students to literature they might not choose to read on their own. The reading-aloud component of reading workshop provides students with a shared social experience and an opportunity to talk about literature and reading. In addition, teachers also read aloud books related to science, social studies, and other across-the-curriculum themes.

Reading aloud to students is not the same as "round-robin" reading, in which students take turns reading paragraphs aloud as the rest of the class listens. Round-robin reading has been used for reading chapter books aloud, but it is more commonly used for reading chapters in content-area textbooks, even though there are more effective ways to teach content-area information and read textbooks.

Round-robin reading is no longer recommended, for several reasons (True, 1979). First, if students are going to read aloud, they should read fluently. When less capable readers read, their reading is often difficult to listen to and embarrassing to them personally. Less capable readers need reading practice, but performing in front of the entire class is not the most productive way for them to practice. They can read with buddies and in small groups during guided reading. Second, if the selection is appropriate for students to read aloud, they should be reading independently. Whenever the reading level of the text is appropriate for students, they should be reading independently. During round-robin reading, students often only follow along just before it is their turn to read. Third, round-robin reading is often tedious and boring, and students lose interest in reading.

The advantages and drawbacks of each type of reading are outlined in Figure 3–2.

Stage 3: Responding

During the third stage, readers respond to their reading and continue to negotiate meaning in order to deepen their comprehension. Two ways that students make tentative and exploratory comments immediately after reading are:

- Writing in reading logs
- Participating in grand conversations

Writing in Reading Logs. Students write and draw thoughts and feelings about what they have read in reading logs. Rosenblatt (1978) explains that as students write about what they have read, they unravel their thinking and, at the same time, elaborate on and clarify their responses. When students read informational books, they sometimes write in reading logs just as they do after reading stories and poems, but at other times they make notes of important information or draw charts and diagrams to use in theme cycles.

Figure 3–2   *Advantages and Disadvantages of the Five Types of Reading*

Type	Advantages	Drawbacks
Shared Reading Teacher reads aloud while students follow along using individual copies of book, a class chart, or a big book.	• Access to books students could not read themselves. • Teacher models fluent reading. • Opportunities to model reading strategies. • Students practice fluent reading. • Develops a community of readers.	• Multiple copies, a class chart, or a big book needed. • Text may not be appropriate for all students. • Students may not be interested in the text.
Guided Reading Teachers support students as they read texts at their reading levels. Students are grouped homogeneously.	• Teacher provides direction and scaffolding. • Opportunities to practice reading strategies and skills. • Students read silently. • Practice the prediction cycle.	• Multiple copies of text needed. • Teacher controls the reading experience. • Some students may not be interested in the text.
Independent Reading Students read a text independently and often choose the text themselves.	• Develops responsibility and ownership. • Self-selection of texts. • Experience is more authentic.	• Students may need assistance to read the text. • Little teacher involvement and control.
Buddy Reading Two students read or reread a text together.	• Collaboration between students. • Students assist each other. • Use to reread familiar texts. • Develops reading fluency. • Students talk and share interpretations.	• Limited teacher involvement. • Less teacher control.
Reading Aloud to Students Teacher or other fluent reader reads aloud to students.	• Access to books students could not read themselves. • Teacher models fluent reading. • Opportunities to model reading strategies. • Develops a community of readers. • Use when only one copy of text is available.	• No opportunity for students themselves to read. • Text may not be appropriate for all students. • Students may not be interested in the text. • Does not require students to take turns reading.

Students usually make reading logs by stapling together 10 to 12 sheets of paper at the beginning of a literature focus unit or reading workshop. At the beginning of a theme cycle, students make learning logs to write in during the unit. They decorate the covers in keeping with the theme of the unit, write entries related to their reading, and make notes related to what they are learning in minilessons.

Students usually choose their own topics for reading log entries, but at other times teachers offer a list of prompts for students to choose from. Students are never expected to respond to all prompts. Many teachers make a list of prompts to hang in the classroom or for students to place in their language arts notebooks. Possible prompts include:

I really don't understand . . .

I like/dislike (character) because . . .

This book reminds me of . . .

(Character) reminds me of myself because . . .

I think (character) is feeling . . .

I wonder why . . .

(Event) makes me think about the time I . . .

I like this quote because . . .

If I were (character), I'd . . .

I noticed that (the author) is . . .

I predict that . . .

These prompts are open-ended and allow students to make connections to their own lives. At other times, teachers ask a specific question to direct students' attention to some aspect of a book. For example, as upper-grade students are reading Lois Lowry's Newbery Medal book *The Giver* (1993), teachers often ask questions like these:

After Chapter 2:	Does Jonas's community seem more perfect than ours?
After Chapter 6:	What assignment do you think Jonas will get?
After Chapter 11:	Would you like to have Jonas's assignment?
After Chapter 19:	What does "release" mean?
After Chapter 23:	What happened to Jonas and Gabe?

These questions, like the prompts listed above, are open-ended and ask for students' interpretations—even the questions for Chapters 19 and 23, which may at first seem like literal questions.

Teachers monitor students' entries, often reading and responding to those entries. Because these journals are learning tools, teachers rarely correct students' spellings. They focus their responses on the students' ideas, but they expect students to spell the title of the book and the names of characters accurately. At the end of the unit, teachers review students' work and often grade the journals based on whether students completed all the entries and on the quality of the ideas in their entries.

■ *To learn more about reading logs, see Chapter 6, "Writing in Journals," pp. 229–231.*

Participating in Grand Conversations. Students also talk about the text with classmates in discussions called grand conversations or literature circles (Daniels, 1994). Peterson and Eeds (1990) explain that in this type of discussion students share their personal responses and tell what they liked about the selection. After sharing personal reactions, they shift the focus to "puzzle over what the author has written and . . . share what it is they find revealed"

(p. 61). Often students make connections between the selection and their own lives or other literature they have read. If they are reading a chapter book, they also make predictions about what will happen in the next chapter.

Martinez and Roser (1995) have researched students' grand conversations and found that students often talk about story events or characters and explore the themes of the story, while less often students delve into the author's craft to explore the way the author structured the book, the arrangement of text and illustrations on the page, or the author's use of figurative or repetitive language. The researchers call these three conversation directions experience, message, and object. They suggest that stories help to shape students' talk about books and that some books lend themselves to talk about message and others to talk about experience or object. Stories with dramatic plots or stories that present a problem that students can relate to, such as *Chrysanthemum* (Henkes, 1991), *Jeremy Thatcher, Dragon Hatcher* (Corville, 1991), and *Hatchet* (Paulsen, 1987), focus the conversation on the book as experience. Multilayered stories or books in which main characters deal with dilemmas, such as *Smoky Night* (Bunting, 1994), *Sarah, Plain and Tall* (MacLachlan, 1985), and *The Giver* (Lowry, 1993), focus the conversation on the message. Books with distinctive structures or language features, such as *Black and White* (Macaulay, 1990), *Tuesday* (Wiesner, 1991), and *Maniac Magee* (Spinelli, 1990), focus the conversation on the object.

Teachers often participate in grand conversations, but they act as interested participants, not leaders. The talk is primarily among the students, but teachers ask open-ended questions regarding things they are genuinely interested in learning more about and share information in response to questions students ask. Possible questions include (Daniels, 1994):

> Which character is most like you?
>
> What would you have done if . . . ?
>
> What did that make you think of?

In the past, many discussions have been "gentle inquisitions" during which students recited answers to factual questions teachers asked about books students were reading (Eeds & Wells, 1989). Teachers dominated the talk and asked these questions in order to determine whether or not students read the assignment; in contrast, the focus in grand conversations is on clarifying and deepening students' understanding or comprehension of the selection they have read.

Grand conversations can be held with the whole class or in small groups. Young children usually meet together as a class, while older students often prefer to talk with classmates in small groups. When students meet together as a class, there is a shared feeling of community, and the teacher can be part of the group. When students meet in small groups, students have more opportunities to participate in the discussion and share their responses, but fewer viewpoints are expressed in each group and teachers must move around, spending only a few minutes with each group. Some teachers compromise and have students begin their discussions in small groups and then come together as a class and have each group share what their group discussed.

■ *See Chapter 8, pp. 311–314, for more information about grand conversations.*

Stage 4: Exploring

During this stage, students go back into the text to explore it more analytically. They participate in some of these activities:

- Rereading the selection
- Examining the author's craft
- Focusing on new vocabulary words
- Participating in minilessons

Rereading the Selection. Through repeated readings, students reread the selection and think again about what they have read. Each time they reread, students benefit in specific ways (Yaden, 1988). They enrich their comprehension and make further connections between the selection and their own lives or between the selection and other literature they have read. Students often reread a selection several times. If the teacher used shared reading to read the selection with students in the reading stage, students might reread it with a buddy once or twice, read it with their parents, and after these experiences, read it independently.

Examining the Author's Craft. Teachers plan exploring activities to focus students' attention on the structure of the text and the literary language that authors use (Eeds & Peterson, 1995). Students notice opposites in the story, use story boards to sequence the events in the story, and make story maps to visually represent the plot, characters, and other story elements (Bromley, 1996). Another way students learn about the structure of stories is by writing books based on the selection they have read. Students write sequels, telling what happened to the chapters after the story ends. Some stories, such as *Jumanji* (Van Allsburg, 1981), end in a way that seems to invite students to create a sequel. Students also write innovations, or new versions, for the selection by following the sentence pattern. First graders often write innovations for Bill Martin, Jr.'s, *Brown Bear, Brown Bear, What Did You See?* (1983) and *Polar Bear, Polar Bear, What Did You Hear?* (1992), and older students write innovations for *Alexander and the Terrible, Horrible, No Good, Very Bad Day* (Viorst, 1977).

Teachers share information about the author of the featured selection and introduce other books by that author. Sometimes teachers have students compare several books written by a particular author. To focus on literary language, students often reread favorite excerpts in a read-around and write memorable quotes on story quilts that they create.

When students are reading picture books, they also learn about illustration and the illustrator's craft. Students can learn about the media and techniques the artist used and experiment with the media themselves. They can examine the illustrations using story boards (pages of the book cut apart and glued on tagboard cards) to find out about the illustrator's stylistic choices and think more deeply about the story (Kiefer, 1994, 1995).

Focusing on Words. Teachers and students add "important" words to word walls after reading and post these word walls in the classroom. Students refer

OfficeMax®

Get $30 Off any Neat Scanner

Bring in this coupon and get $30 off any Neat Scanner with the purchase of any Turbo Tax, Quickbooks or Quicken Software. Offer valid thru 2/1/2014.

2 4 9 0 3 0 1 1 0 1 0 5 1 4 6 1

to the word walls when they write, using these words for a variety of activities during the exploring stage. Researchers emphasize the importance of immersing students in words, teaching strategies for learning words, and personalizing word learning (Blachowicz & Fisher, 1996). Students make word clusters and posters to highlight particular words. They also make word chains, sort words, create a semantic feature analysis to analyze related words, and play word games.

Teachers choose words from word walls to use in minilessons, too. Words are used to teach phonics skills, such as beginning sounds, rhyming words, vowel patterns, *r*-controlled vowels, and syllabication (Bear, Templeton, Invernizzi, & Johnston, 1996). Other concepts such as root words and affixes, compound words, and metaphors can also be taught using examples from word walls. Teachers often teach a minilesson on a particular concept, such as the -*ly* suffix, because five or six words representing the concept are listed on the word wall.

■ *See Chapter 5, pp. 202–204, for more information on word walls and teaching vocabulary.*

Teaching Minilessons. Teachers present minilessons on reading procedures, concepts, strategies, and skills during the exploring stage. A list of topics for minilessons about the reading process is presented on page 106. In a minilesson, teachers introduce the topic and make connections between the topic and examples in the featured selection. In this way students are better able to connect the information teachers are presenting with their own reading process. Students need to learn about the process approach to reading—both aesthetic and efferent—and about ways to develop interpretations.

Stage 5: Extending

During the extending stage, readers move beyond comprehension to deepen their interpretations, reflect on their understanding, and value the reading experience. Students build on their reading, the responses they made immediately after reading, and the exploring activities as they create projects. These projects can involve reading, writing, talk and drama, viewing, visually representing, or research, and may take many forms, including murals, readers theatre scripts, oral presentations, and individual books and reports, as well as reading other books by the same author. A list of projects is presented in Figure 3–3. The wide variety of project options offers students choices and takes into account Howard Gardner's (1993) theory of multiple intelligences, that students have preferred ways of learning and showing knowledge. Usually students choose which projects they will do rather than working as a class on the same project. Sometimes, however, the class decides to work together on a project.

Teaching the Reading Process

■ *See Chapter 2, "Teaching Language Arts," for more information about creating a community of learners (pp. 44–45), arranging the classroom (pp. 45–50), and teachers' roles (pp. 64–66).*

Teachers apply the five-stage reading process in the reading lessons they teach, whether they organize instruction into literature focus units, theme cycles, or reading workshop. Successful language arts instruction doesn't just happen (Hickman, 1995). Teachers bring students together as a community of learners and teach them the procedures for various language arts activities. Each unit—literature focus unit, theme cycle, or reading workshop—requires that teachers carefully structure activities, provide appropriate books

The Reading and Writing Processes

	Procedures	Concepts	Strategies and Skills
The Reading Process	Choose books to read	The reading process	Decode words
	Use the Goldilocks Strategy	Aesthetic reading	Predict
	Listen to books read aloud	Efferent reading	Confirm
	Do shared reading	Interpretation	Visualize
	Do buddy reading		Retell
	Do guided reading		Connect to literature
	Do independent reading		Connect to life
	Respond in reading logs		Empathize
	Participate in grand conversations		Identify with characters
	Reread a book		Monitor
	Create projects		
	Participate in reading workshop		
The Writing Process	Choose a topic	The writing process	Gather ideas
	Cluster	Functions of writing	Organize ideas
	Quickwrite	Writing forms	Draft
	Participate in writing groups	Audience	Revise
	Proofread	Focus on content	Edit
	Make hardcover books	Focus on mechanics	Identify and correct spelling errors
	Write "All About the Author" pages	Proofreaders' marks	Use capital letters correctly
	Share published writing	Publish writing	Use punctuation marks correctly
			Value the composition

and other materials, and create time and space for students to work. Teachers, too, must be prepared to assume a variety of roles.

In Literature Focus Units. In literature focus units students might read a single book, such as *Bunnicula: A Rabbit-Tale of Mystery* (Howe & Howe, 1979), and as they read they will move through the five stages of the reading process. Or, they might read a collection of books on the same theme (e.g., about dogs), in the same genre (e.g., folktales), or by the same author (e.g., books by Dr. Seuss). When students read several books together, they move back and forth among the second, third, and fourth stages as they

Figure 3–3   *Projects*

Visually Representing Projects

1. Experiment with the illustration techniques (e.g., collage, watercolor, line drawing) used in a favorite book. Examine other books illustrated with the same technique.
2. Make a diagram or model using information from a book.
3. Create a collage to represent the theme of a book.
4. Design a book jacket for a book, laminate it, and place it on the book.
5. Make a story can or box. Decorate a coffee can or cardboard box using scenes from a book. Fill the can with objects and quotes related to the book.
6. Construct a shoebox or other miniature scene of an episode for a favorite book (or use a larger box to construct a diorama).
7. Make a set of story boards with one card for each episode or chapter. Include an illustration and a paragraph describing the section of the book.
8. Make a map or relief map of a book's setting or something related to the book.
9. Construct the setting of the book in the block center, or use other construction toys such as Lego's or Lincoln Logs.
10. Construct a mobile illustrating a book.
11. Make a roll-movie of a book by drawing a series of pictures on a long strip of paper. Attach ends to rollers and place in a cardboard box cut like a television set.
12. Make a comic strip to illustrate the sequence of events in a book.
13. Make a clay or soap model of a character.
14. Prepare bookmarks for a book and distribute them to classmates.
15. Prepare flannel board pictures to use in retelling the story.
16. Use or prepare illustrations of characters for pocket props to use in retelling the story.
17. Use or prepare illustrations of the events in the story for clothesline props to use in retelling the story.
18. Experiment with art techniques related to the mood of a poem.
19. Make a mural of the book.
20. Make an open-mind portrait of a character in the story.
21. Create a Venn diagram to compare the book and film versions of a story.
22. Make a chart to analyze several versions of the same story or a text set of books by one author.
23. Make a character cluster.
24. Make a character sociogram.
25. Make a plot diagram of the book.
26. Make a plot profile of the book.
27. Make a sketch-to-stretch poster.

Writing Projects

28. Write a review of a favorite book for a class review file.
29. Write a postcard or letter about a book to a classmate, friend, or pen pal.
30. Dictate or write another episode or sequel for a book.
31. Create a newspaper with news stories and advertisements based on characters and episodes from a book.
32. Make a five-senses cluster about the book.
33. Write and mail a letter to a favorite author (or participate in a class collaboration letter).
34. Write a simulated letter from one book character to another.
35. Copy five "quotable quotes" from a book and list them on a poster.
36. Make a scrapbook about the book. Label all items in the scrapbook and write a short description of the most interesting ones.

Figure 3–3 *continued*

37. Write a poem related to the book. Some types of poems to choose from are acrostic, concrete poem, color poem, "I wish" poem, "I am" poem, haiku, or found poem.
38. Write a lifeline related to the book, the era, the character, or the author.
39. Write a business letter to a company or organization requesting information on a topic related to the book.
40. Keep a simulated journal from the perspective of one character from the book.
41. Write a dictionary defining specialized vocabulary in a book.
42. Write the story from another point of view (e.g., write the story of *The Little Red Hen* from the perspective of the lazy characters).
43. Make a class collaboration book. Each child dictates or writes one page.
44. Write a letter to a famous person from a character in a book.
45. Create an alphabet book on a topic related to the book.
46. Make a cube with information about the book or a related topic.

Reading Projects

47. Read another book by the same author.
48. Read another book by the same illustrator.
49. Read another book on the same theme.
50. Read another book in the same genre.
51. Read another book about the same character.
52. Read and compare two versions of the same story.
53. Read a biography about the author or illustrator of the book.

Viewing Projects

54. View a television, film, or video version of the book.
55. Compare the illustrations in several versions of the same book. Multiple versions of folktales and other traditional stories are available for children.
56. Analyze the illustrator's craft.
57. Choose a piece of art (e.g., painting or sculpture) that represents the book and share the art with the class.

Talk and Drama Projects

58. Tape-record a book or an excerpt from it to place in the listening center.
59. Read a poem that complements the book aloud to the class. Place a copy of the poem in the book.
60. Give a readers theatre presentation of a book.
61. Create a song about a book or choose a tune for a poem and sing the song for the class.
62. Write a script and present a play about a book.
63. Make puppets and use them in retelling a book.
64. Dress as a character from the book and answer questions from classmates about the character.
65. Write and present a rap about the book.
66. Videotape a commercial for a book.

Research Projects

67. Interview someone in the community who is knowledgeable about a topic related to the book.
68. Research the author or illustrator of the book and compile information in a chart or summary. Post the chart or summary in the library center.
69. Research a topic related to the book. Present the information in an oral or written report.

read, respond to, and explore each book before moving on to the extending stage.

Figure 3–4 shows one way to organize a literature focus unit on *Bunnicula: A Rabbit-Tale of Mystery*. In this unit, sixth graders work through all five stages of the reading process. The teacher uses a book box with a stuffed rabbit dressed like a vampire, plastic vegetables that have been painted white, and a children's version of the "Dracula" story. They use shared reading to read the chapter book; then they respond to their reading and participate in exploration activities. The teacher presents minilessons on homophones (e.g., *steak–stake*) and portmanteau words (*bunny + dracula = Bunnicula; smoke + fog = smog*), and shares information about the author, James Howe. Students also construct projects to extend their study of the book.

In Theme Cycles.   Teachers often coordinate the books students are reading with what they are studying during theme cycles. For example, during a theme cycle on insects in a second-grade classroom, students might read *It's a Good Thing There Are Insects* (Fowler, 1990) at the beginning of the theme. Students move through all five stages of the reading process. First they read the easy-to-read informational book using shared reading; then they read it a second time with reading buddies; and the third time they read it independently. During the grand conversation held after students read the book the first time, they brainstorm a list of reasons why it's a good thing there are insects. Later they can write their own books about insects. Teacher can also use this book to teach minilessons about the differences between stories and informational books. *It's a Good Thing There Are Insects* is a good example of an informational book because the illustrations are photos and a glossary and an index are included in the book.

Later in the theme cycle the teacher might pair two books about ladybugs for the students to read: *The Grouchy Ladybug* (Carle, 1986), a repetitive story about an unfriendly ladybug who is looking for a fight, and *Ladybug* (Watts, 1987), an informational book with one line of large-size type on each page for students to read and additional information in smaller-size type that students or the teacher can read. If the teacher has enough copies of each book for half the class, the students divide into two groups. One group reads one book and the other group reads the other book; then the two groups trade books. As the students read these two books, the teacher has many opportunities to continue comparing stories and informational books. After reading, students might talk about which book they liked best, and they work on projects to extend their understanding of ladybugs and other insects.

In Reading Workshop.   In Chapter 2, I outlined the three components of reading workshop: reading and responding, sharing, and minilessons. In reading workshop students focus on the prereading, reading, and responding stages of the reading process, but the remaining stages are also involved. Students choose books (often using the "Goldilocks Strategy"), activate background knowledge, and make plans as they begin to read (stage 1). Next they read the book independently (stage 2). After reading, they may write in reading logs and talk about the books they are reading in conferences with the teacher (stage 3). Sometimes students read three or four books and then

Stage 1: Preparing

The teacher shares a book box of objects related to the book with students. Objects include a stuffed rabbit dressed in a vampire costume, plastic vegetables that have been painted white and marked with two small pinpricks, and a children's version of the "Dracula" story. The teacher shares the objects, and students make predictions about the book.

Stage 2: Reading

The teacher uses the shared reading approach to read the chapter book. Each student has a copy of the book and follows along as the teacher reads the book aloud. One or two chapters are read aloud each day.

Stage 3: Responding

After reading a chapter or two, students write responses in reading logs and share these logs with classmates. Students also participate in grand conversations and make connections between the story and their own lives and other experiences with literature.

Stage 4: Exploring

Students write interesting and important words from the book on a word wall (chart paper hanging on the wall) and use the words in a variety of vocabulary activities, including word sorts. The teacher shares information about the author, James Howe, and a text set of other books by the author. The teacher teaches several minilessons on characterization and the meaning-making strategy of identifying with a character. The teacher asks students to choose the character they identify with the most (Harold the dog, Chester the cat, or Bunnicula the rabbit) and explain why they chose that character. Students make an open-mind portrait of one character. Other minilessons include portmanteau words (e.g., bunny + dracula = Bunnicula) and homonyms.

Stage 5: Extending

Students each choose a project from a list of choices posted in the classroom. A number of students choose to read one of the sequels and other stories about Bunnicula: *Howliday Inn* (1982), *The Celery Stalks at Midnight* (1983), *Nighty-Nightmare* (1987), *Return to Howliday Inn* (1992), *Scared Silly* (1989), *The Fright Before Christmas* (1989), and *Hot Fudge* (1990). Other students choose these projects:

- Write a letter to author James Howe.
- Perform a play about an episode of the book.
- Make a book box and place five items related to the book with explanations in the box.
- Write a sequel to the book.
- Make a tabletop display of the Monroes' house.
- Research Dracula and vampires.

choose one book for a project (stage 5). Students also talk about the books they read during sharing time and share their completed projects with classmates (stages 3 and 5). In reading workshop, teachers also teach minilessons, and during these lessons students learn reading concepts, procedures, strategies, and skills (stage 4).

Adapting to Meet the Needs of Every Student. Reading process activities are flexible and can be adapted to help every student become a more successful reader. For students with limited experiences or for those who are learning English as a second language, more time should be spent in the preparing stage. During reading, teachers often read books aloud or use shared reading when working with students who are not yet fluent readers. Many easy-to-read stories and informational books that are well written and enticing to students are currently available, so it is possible to have several books at different reading levels on almost any topic. During the responding stage, students can draw rather than write their responses in reading logs, and grand conversations take on an even greater importance for students who need to clarify misconceptions about their reading. Students can reread the text with a buddy during the exploring stage. The fifth stage is important for all students, and many students who find reading difficult are very successful in creating art projects and dramatic productions. Suggestions for adapting the reading process to meet the needs of every student are presented on page 112.

THE WRITING PROCESS

The focus in the writing process is on what students think and do as they write. The five stages are prewriting, drafting, revising, editing, and publishing, and the key features of each stage are shown in the Teacher's Notebook on page 113. The labeling and numbering of the stages does not mean, however, that the writing process is a linear series of neatly packaged categories. Research has shown that the process involves recurring cycles, and labeling is only an aid to identifying and discussing writing activities (Graves, 1994; Perl, 1994). In the classroom the stages merge and recur as students write.

Stage 1: Prewriting

Prewriting is the getting-ready-to-write stage. The traditional notion that writers have a topic completely thought out and ready to flow onto the page is ridiculous. If writers wait for ideas to fully develop, they may wait forever. Instead, writers begin tentatively—talking, reading, writing—to discover what they know and decide what direction they want to take (Flower & Hayes, 1994). Prewriting has probably been the most neglected stage in the writing process; however, it is as crucial to writers as a warm-up is to athletes. Murray (1982) believes that at least 70% of writing time should be spent in prewriting. During the prewriting stage, students:

- Choose a topic
- Consider purpose, form, and audience
- Generate and organize ideas for writing

Adapting
The Reading Process
To Meet the Needs of Every Student

Stage 1: Preparing

- Spend more time activating background knowledge.
- Use concrete experiences, multimedia presentations, and photos.
- Introduce important vocabulary related to the topic, but not necessarily the vocabulary in the text.

Stage 2: Reading

- Read books aloud.
- Use shared reading or buddy reading.
- Have students listen to the book at the listening center.
- Use easy-to-read or predictable books on the same topic.
- Break the reading time into smaller chunks.
- Provide more challenging alternative texts.

Stage 3: Responding

- Have students draw responses instead of writing in reading logs.
- Take time in grand conversations to clarify misconceptions.

Stage 4: Exploring

- Role-play important events in the book.
- Reread the text with a buddy.
- Teach minilessons to individual students and small groups of students.

Stage 5: Extending

- Encourage students to create art projects.
- Encourage students to produce dramatic productions.
- Set out clear expectations about the projects students develop.
- Encourage students to pursue projects that they are interested in and that challenge them.

Choosing a Topic. Choosing a topic for writing can be a stumbling block for students who have become dependent on teachers to supply topics. For years teachers have supplied topics by suggesting gimmicky story starters and relieving students of the "burden" of topic selection. Often, these "creative" topics stymied students, who were forced to write on topics they knew little about or had no interest in. Graves (1976) calls this "writing welfare." Instead, students need to choose their own writing topics.

Some students complain that they do not know what to write about, but teachers can help them brainstorm a list of three, four, or five topics and then identify the one topic they are most interested in and know the most

Teacher's Notebook
Key Features of the Writing Process

Stage 1: Prewriting

- Students write on topics based on their own experiences.
- Students engage in rehearsal activities before writing.
- Students identify the audience to whom they will write.
- Students identify the function of the writing activity.
- Students choose an appropriate form for their compositions based on audience and purpose.

Stage 2: Drafting

- Students write a rough draft.
- Students emphasize content rather than mechanics.

Stage 3: Revising

- Students reread their own writing.
- Students share their writing in writing groups.
- Students participate constructively in discussions about classmates' writing.
- Students make changes in their compositions to reflect the reactions and comments of both teacher and classmates.
- Between the first and final drafts, students make substantive rather than only minor changes.

Stage 4: Editing

- Students proofread their own compositions.
- Students help proofread classmates' compositions.
- Students increasingly identify and correct their own mechanical errors.
- Students meet with the teacher for a final editing.

Stage 5: Publishing

- Students publish their writing in an appropriate form.
- Students share their finished writing with an appropriate audience.

PDREP

about. Students who feel they cannot generate any writing topics are often surprised that they have so many options. Then, through prewriting activities, students talk, draw, read, and even write to develop information about their topics.

Asking students to choose their own topics for writing doesn't mean that teachers never give writing assignments; teachers do provide general guidelines. Sometimes they may specify the writing form, and at other times they may establish the function, but students should choose their own specific content.

Considering Purpose. As students prepare to write, they need to think about their purpose for writing. Are they writing to entertain? To inform? To persuade? Understanding the purpose of a piece of writing is important because it influences other decisions students make about audience and form.

Considering Audience. Students may write primarily for themselves—to express and clarify their ideas and feelings—or they may write for others. Possible audiences include classmates, younger children, parents, foster grandparents, children's authors, and pen pals. Other audiences are more distant and less well known. For example, students write letters to businesses to request information, write articles for the local newspaper, and compose stories and poems for publication in literary magazines.

Children's writing is influenced by their sense of audience. Britton, Burgess, Martin, McLeod, and Rosen define *sense of audience* as "the manner in which the writer expresses a relationship with the reader in respect to the writer's understanding" (1975, pp. 65–66). Students adapt their writing to fit their audience just as they vary their speech to meet the needs of the people who are listening to them.

Considering Form. One of the most important considerations is the form the writing will take: A story? A letter? A poem? A journal entry? Writing activities could be handled in any one of these ways. As part of a theme cycle on hermit crabs, for instance, students might write a story about a hermit crab, draw a picture and label body parts, explain how hermit crabs obtain shells to live in, write poems about the crustacean, or keep a log of observations about the pet hermit crabs in the classroom. There is an almost endless variety of forms that children's writing may take. A list of these forms is presented in the Teacher's Notebook on page 115. Students need to experiment with a wide variety of writing forms and explore the potential of these functions and formats.

Through reading and writing, students develop a strong sense of these forms and how they are structured. Langer (1985) found that by third grade, students responded in distinctly different ways to story- and report-writing assignments; they organized the writing differently and included varied kinds of information and elaboration. Similarly, Hidi and Hildyard (1983) found that elementary students could differentiate between stories and persuasive essays. Because children are clarifying the distinctions between various writing forms during the elementary grades, it is important that teachers use the correct terminology and not label all children's writing "stories."

Teacher's Notebook
Writing Forms

acrostics
advertisements
"All About . . ." books
"All About the Author"
alphabet books
announcements
anthologies
apologies
applications
autobiographies
awards
bibliographies
biographies
book jackets
books
brochures
captions
cartoons
catalogues
certificates
character sketches
charts
cinquain poems
clusters
comics
comparisons
complaints
computer programs
concrete poems
crossword puzzles
cubes
definitions
descriptions
diagrams
dialogue
dialogue journals

diamante poems
dictionaries
directions
double-entry journals
editorials
essays
evaluations
explanations
fables
fairy tales
folktales
formula poems
found poems
greeting cards
haiku poems
hink-pinks
"I am" poems
instructions
interviews
invitations
jokes
lab reports
learning logs
letters
lifelines
limericks
lists
lyrics
maps
menus
mysteries
myths
newspapers
notes
obituaries
oral histories

personal narratives
postcards
posters
puzzles
questionnaires
questions
quickwrites
reading logs
recipes
reflections
reports
reviews
riddles
schedules
scripts
sentences
signs
simulated journals
stories
story boards
study guides
tall tales
telegrams
telephone directories
thank-you notes
thumbnail sketches
timelines
tongue twisters
valentines
Venn diagrams
word-finds
wordless picture books
word posters
word walls

Decisions about purpose, audience, and form influence each other. For example, if the function is to entertain, an appropriate form might be a story, poem, or script, and these three forms look very different on a piece of paper. Whereas a story is written in the traditional block format, scripts and poems have unique page arrangements. Scripts are written with the character's name and a colon, and the dialogue is set off. Action and dialogue, rather than description, carry the story line in a script. In contrast, poems have unique formatting considerations, and each word and phrase is chosen to convey a maximum amount of information.

Gathering and Organizing Ideas. Students engage in activities to gather and organize ideas for writing. Graves (1994) calls what writers do to prepare for writing "rehearsal" activities. Through these activities, students activate background knowledge and make plans for writing. Rehearsal activities take many forms, including:

1. **Drawing.** Drawing is the way young children gather and organize ideas for writing. Primary-grade teachers notice that students often draw before they write, and, thinking that the children are eating dessert before the meat and vegetables, the teachers insist that they write first. But many young children cannot because they don't know what to write until they see what they draw (Dyson, 1986).

2. **Clustering.** Students make clusters—weblike diagrams—in which they write the topic in a center circle and draw out rays for each main idea (Rico, 1983). Then they add details and other information on rays drawn out from each main idea. Through clustering, students organize their ideas for writing. Clustering is a better prewriting strategy than outlining because it is nonlinear.

3. **Talking.** Students talk with their classmates to share ideas about possible writing topics, try out ways to express an idea, and ask questions. Too often teachers don't recognize the power of talk as a prewriting activity. When students who cannot talk about a topic, it is unlikely that they will be able to write about it.

4. **Reading.** Students gather ideas for writing and investigate the structure of various written forms through reading. They may retell a favorite story in writing, write new adventures for favorite story characters, or experiment with repetition, onomatopoeia, or another poetic device used in a poem they have read. Informational books also provide raw material for writing. For example, if students are studying polar bears, they read to gather information about the animal, its habitat, and its predators, which they may use in writing a report.

5. **Role-playing.** Children discover and shape ideas they will use in their writing through role-playing. During theme cycles and after reading stories, students can reenact events to bring an experience to life. Heathcote (Wagner, 1983) suggests that teachers choose a dramatic focus or a particular critical moment for students to reenact. For example, after reading *Sarah, Plain and Tall* (MacLachlan, 1985), children might reenact the day Sarah took the wagon to town. This is a critical moment: Does Sarah like them and their prairie home well enough to stay?

■ *To read more about quickwriting, see Chapter 6, "Writing in Journals," pp. 243–244.*

6. *Quickwriting.* Students do a quickwrite to brainstorm ideas or explore a topic. Through this informal writing activity, they gather and organize ideas they will be able to use as they draft their compositions.

Stage 2: Drafting

Students write and refine their compositions through a series of drafts. During the drafting stage, students focus on getting their ideas down on paper. Because writers do not begin writing with their compositions already composed in their minds, students begin with tentative ideas developed through prewriting activities. The drafting stage is the time to pour out ideas, with little concern about spelling, punctuation, and other mechanical aspects of writing.

When students write their rough drafts, they write on every other line to leave space for revisions (Lane, 1993). They use arrows to move sections of text, cross-outs to delete sections, and scissors and tape to cut apart and rearrange text just as adult writers do. They write on only one side of a sheet of paper so that it can be cut apart or rearranged. As word processors become more available in elementary classrooms, revising, with all its shifting and deleting text, will be much easier. However, for students who handwrite their compositions, the wide spacing is crucial. Teachers might make small *x*'s on every other line of students' papers as a reminder to skip lines as they draft their compositions.

Students label their drafts by writing "Rough Draft" in ink at the top of the paper or by stamping them with a ROUGH DRAFT stamp. This label indicates to the writer, other students, parents, and administrators that the composition is a draft in which the emphasis is on content, not mechanics. It also explains why the teacher has not graded the paper or marked mechanical errors.

During drafting, students may need to modify their earlier decisions about purpose, audience, and, especially, the form their writing will take. For example, a composition that began as a story may be transformed into a report, a letter, or a poem if the new format allows the student to communicate more effectively. The process of modifying earlier decisions continues into the revising stage.

As students write rough drafts, it is important not to emphasize correct spelling and neatness. In fact, pointing out mechanical errors during the drafting stage sends students a message that mechanical correctness is more important than content (Sommers, 1994). Later, during editing, students can clean up mechanical errors and put their composition into a neat, final form.

Stage 3: Revising

During the revising stage, writers refine ideas in their compositions. Students often break the writing process cycle as soon as they complete a rough draft, believing that once they have jotted down their ideas, the writing task is complete. Experienced writers, however, know that they must turn to others for reactions and revise on the basis of these comments (Sommers, 1994). Revision is not just polishing; it is meeting the needs of readers by adding, substituting, deleting, and rearranging material. The word "revision" means "seeing again," and in this stage writers see their compositions again with the help of their classmates and teacher. Activities in the revising stage are:

- Rereading the rough draft
- Sharing the rough draft in a writing group
- Revising on the basis of feedback
- Conferencing with the teacher

Rereading the Rough Draft.   After finishing the rough draft, writers need to distance themselves from the draft for a day or two, then reread it from a fresh perspective, as a reader might. As they reread, students make changes—adding, substituting, deleting, and moving—and place question marks by sections that need work. It is these trouble spots that students ask for help with in their writing groups.

Sharing in Writing Groups.   Students meet in writing groups to share their compositions with classmates. Because writing must meet the needs of readers, feedback is crucial. Mohr (1984) identifies four general functions of writing groups: to offer the writer choices; to provide the writer with group members' responses, feelings, and thoughts; to show different possibilities in revising; and to speed up revising. Writing groups provide a scaffold in which teachers and classmates talk about plans and strategies for writing and revising (Calkins, 1994).

Writing groups can form spontaneously when several students have completed drafts and are ready to share their compositions, or they can be formal groupings with identified leaders. In some classrooms writing groups form when four or five students finish writing their rough drafts. Students gather around a conference table or in a corner of the classroom. They take turns reading their rough drafts aloud, and classmates in the group listen and respond, offering compliments and suggestions for revision (Gere & Abbott, 1985). Sometimes the teacher joins the writing group, but if the teacher is involved in something else, students work independently.

In other classrooms the writing groups are established. Students get together when all students in the group have completed their rough drafts and are ready to share their writing. Sometimes the teacher participates in these groups, providing feedback along with the students. At other times the writing groups can function independently. Four or five students are assigned to each group, and a list of groups and their members is posted in the classroom. The teacher puts a star by one student's name, and that student serves as group leader. The leader changes every quarter.

In writing groups students share their writing through these activities:

Step by Step

1. **The writer reads.**   Students take turns reading their compositions aloud to the group. All the students listen politely, thinking about compliments and suggestions they will make after the writer finishes reading. Only the writer looks at the composition, because when classmates and teacher look at it, they quickly notice and comment on mechanical errors, even though the emphasis during revising is on content. Listening to the writing read aloud keeps the focus on content.

2. ***Listeners offer compliments.*** Next, writing group members say what they liked about the writing. These positive comments should be specific, focusing on strengths, rather than the often heard "I liked it" or "It was good." Even though these are positive comments, they do not provide effective feedback. When teachers introduce revision, they should model appropriate responses because students may not know how to offer specific and meaningful comments. Teachers and students can brainstorm a list of appropriate comments and post it in the classroom for students to refer to. Comments may focus on organization, leads, word choice, voice, sequence, dialogue, theme, and so on. Possible comments are:

I like the part where . . .

I'd like to know more about . . .

I like the way you described . . .

Your writing made me feel . . .

I like the order you used in your writing because . . .

3. ***The writer asks questions.*** After a round of positive comments, writers ask for assistance with trouble spots they identified earlier when rereading their writing, or they may ask questions that reflect more general concerns about how well they are communicating. Admitting that they need help from their classmates is a major step in students' learning to revise. Possible questions to classmates are:

What do you want to know more about?

Is there a part that I should throw away?

What details can I add?

What do you think the best part of my writing is?

Are there some words I need to change?

4. ***Listeners offer suggestions.*** Members of the writing group ask questions about things that were unclear to them, and they make suggestions about how to revise the composition. Almost any writer resists constructive criticism, and it is especially difficult for elementary students to appreciate suggestions. It is important to teach students what kinds of comments and suggestions are acceptable so that they will word what they say in helpful rather than hurtful ways. Possible comments and suggestions that students can offer are:

I got confused in the part about . . .

Do you need a closing?

Could you add more about . . . ?

I wonder if your paragraphs are in the right order because . . .

Could you combine some sentences?

5. ***The process is repeated.*** The first four steps are repeated for each student's composition. This is the appropriate time for teachers to provide input as well. They should react to the piece of writing as any other listener would—not error-hunting with red pen in hand (Sommers, 1994). In fact, most teachers prefer to listen to students read their compositions aloud, since teachers may become frustrated by the numerous misspelled words and nearly illegible handwriting common in rough drafts if they read them themselves.

6. **Writers plan for revision.**   At the end of the writing group session, all students make a commitment to revise their writing based on the comments and suggestions of the group members. The final decisions on what to revise always rest with the writers themselves, but with the understanding that their rough drafts are not perfect comes the realization that some revision will be necessary. When students verbalize their planned revisions, they are more likely to complete the revision stage. Some students also make notes for themselves about their revision plans. After the group disbands, students make the revisions.

Making Revisions.   Students make four types of changes: additions, substitutions, deletions, and moves (Faigley & Witte, 1981). As they revise, students might add words, substitute sentences, delete paragraphs, and move phrases. Students often use a blue or red pen to cross out, draw arrows, and write in the space left between the double-spaced lines of their rough drafts so that revisions will show clearly. That way teachers can examine the types of revisions students make by examining their revised rough drafts. Revisions are another gauge of students' growth as writers.

Conferencing With the Teacher.   Sometimes teachers participate in writing groups and provide revision suggestions along with students. Other teachers conference individually with students about their rough drafts. The teacher's role during conferences is to help students make choices and define directions for revision. Barry Lane (1993) offers these suggestions for talking with students about their papers:

- Have students come to a conference prepared to begin talking about their concerns. Students should talk first in a conference.
- Ask questions rather than give answers. Ask students what is working well for them, what problems they are having, and what questions they have.
- React to students' writing as a reader, not as a teacher. Offer compliments first; give suggestions later.
- Keep the conference short and recognize that not all problem areas or concerns can be discussed.
- Limit the number of revision suggestions and make all suggestions specific.
- Have students meet in writing groups before they conference with the teacher. Then students can share the feedback they received from classmates.
- To conclude the conference, ask students to identify the revisions they plan to make.
- Take notes during conferences and summarize students' revision plans. These notes are a record of the conference, and the revision plans can be used in assessing students' revisions.

It is time-consuming to meet with every student, but many teachers believe it is worth the time (Calkins, 1994; Graves, 1994). In a short five-minute conference, teachers listen to students talk about their writing processes, guide students as they make revision plans, and offer feedback during the writing process when it is most usable.

Stage 4: Editing

Editing is putting the piece of writing into its final form. Until this stage the focus has been primarily on the content of students' writing. Once the focus changes to mechanics, students polish their writing by correcting misspellings and other mechanical errors. The goal here is to make the writing "optimally readable" (Smith, 1982). Writers who write for readers understand that if their compositions are not readable, they have written in vain because their ideas will never be read.

Mechanics are the commonly accepted conventions of written Standard English. They include capitalization, punctuation, spelling, sentence structure, usage, and formatting considerations specific to poems, scripts, letters, and other writing forms. The use of these commonly accepted conventions is a courtesy to those who will read the composition.

Mechanical skills are best taught during the editing stage, not through workbook exercises. When editing a composition that will be shared with a genuine audience, students are more interested in using mechanical skills correctly so that they can communicate effectively. In a study of two third-grade classes, Calkins (1980) found that the students in the class who learned punctuation marks as a part of editing could define or explain more marks than the students in the other class who were taught punctuation skills in a traditional manner, with instruction and practice exercises on each punctuation mark. In other words, the results of this research, as well as other studies (Graves, 1994; Routman, 1996; Weaver, 1996), suggest that students learn mechanical skills better as part of the writing process than through practice exercises.

Students move through three activities in the editing stage:

- Getting distance from the composition
- Proofreading to locate errors
- Correcting errors

Getting Distance.   Students are more efficient editors if they set the composition aside for a few days before beginning to edit. After working so closely with a piece of writing during drafting and revising, they are too familiar with it to be able to locate many mechanical errors. With the distance gained by waiting a few days, children are better able to approach editing with a fresh perspective and gather the enthusiasm necessary to finish the writing process by making the paper optimally readable.

Proofreading.   Students proofread their compositions to locate and mark possible errors. Proofreading is a unique type of reading in which students read slowly, word by word, hunting for errors rather than reading quickly for meaning (M. King, 1985). Concentrating on mechanics is difficult because our natural inclination is to read for meaning. Even experienced proofreaders often find themselves reading for meaning and thus overlooking errors that do not inhibit meaning. It is important, therefore, to take time to explain proofreading and demonstrate how it differs from regular reading.

To demonstrate proofreading, a teacher copies a piece of student writing on the chalkboard or displays it on an overhead projector. The teacher reads it several times, each time hunting for a particular type of error. During each reading, the teacher reads the composition slowly, softly pronouncing each word and touching the word with a pencil or pen to focus attention on it. The teacher marks possible errors as they are located.

Errors are marked or corrected with special proofreaders' marks. Students enjoy using these marks, the same ones that adult authors and editors use. Proofreaders' marks that elementary students can learn to use in editing their writing are presented in Figure 3–5. Editing checklists help students focus on particular types of error. Teachers can develop checklists with two to six items appropriate for the grade level. A first-grade checklist, for example, might include only two items—perhaps one about capital letters at the beginning of sentences and a second about periods at the end of sentences. In contrast, a middle-grade checklist might include items such as using commas in a series, indenting paragraphs, capitalizing proper nouns, and spelling homonyms correctly. Teachers can revise the checklist during the school year to focus attention on skills that have recently been taught.

A sample third-grade editing checklist is presented in Figure 3–6. First, students proofread their own compositions, searching for errors in each category on the checklist; after proofreading, they check off each item. Then, after completing the checklist, students sign their names and trade checklists and compositions. Now they become editors and complete each other's checklist. Having both writer and editor sign the checklist helps them to take the activity seriously.

Figure 3–5   *Proofreaders' Marks*

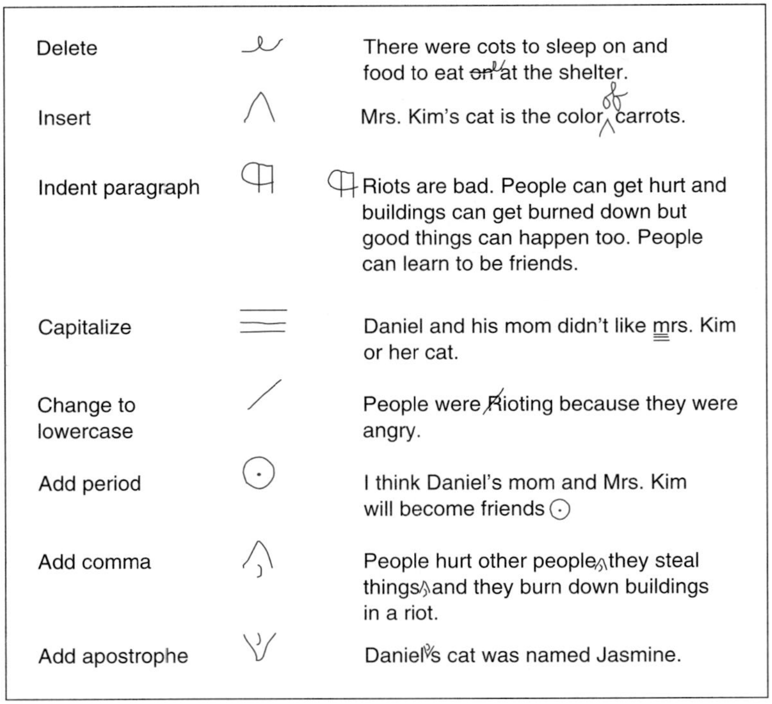

Delete		There were cots to sleep on and food to eat on at the shelter.
Insert	∧	Mrs. Kim's cat is the color carrots.
Indent paragraph	⊕	Riots are bad. People can get hurt and buildings can get burned down but good things can happen too. People can learn to be friends.
Capitalize	≡	Daniel and his mom didn't like mrs. Kim or her cat.
Change to lowercase	/	People were Rioting because they were angry.
Add period	⊙	I think Daniel's mom and Mrs. Kim will become friends ⊙
Add comma	⋏	People hurt other people they steal things and they burn down buildings in a riot.
Add apostrophe	⋎	Daniel's cat was named Jasmine.

Correcting Errors. After students proofread their compositions and locate the errors, they correct the errors individually or with an editor's assistance. Some errors are easy to correct, some require use of a dictionary, and others involve instruction from the teacher. It is unrealistic to expect students to locate and correct every mechanical error in their compositions. Not even published books are error-free! Once in a while students may change a correct spelling or punctuation mark and make it incorrect, but they correct far more errors than they create.

Editing can end after students and their editors correct as many mechanical errors as possible, or after students meet with the teacher in a conference for a final editing. When mechanical correctness is crucial, this conference is important. Teachers proofread the composition with the student, and they identify and make the remaining corrections together, or the teacher makes check marks in the margin to note errors for the student to correct independently.

Stage 5: Publishing

In this stage students bring their compositions to life by publishing them or sharing them orally with an appropriate audience. When they share their writing with real audiences of classmates, other students, parents, and the community, students come to think of themselves as authors. In this stage students:

- Make books
- Share their writing

Figure 3–6   A Third-Grade Editing Checklist

Editing Checklist

Author   Editor

1. I have circled the words that might be misspelled.

2. I have checked that all sentences begin with capital letters.

3. I have checked that all sentences end with punctuation marks.

4. I have checked that all proper nouns begin with a capital letter.

Signatures:

Author: _____   *Editor:* _____

Making Books.   One of the most popular ways for children to publish their writing is by making books (L. King & Stovall, 1992). Simple booklets can be made by folding a sheet of paper into quarters, like a greeting card. Students write the title on the front and use the three remaining sides for their compositions. They can also construct booklets by stapling sheets of writing paper together and adding construction paper covers. Sheets of wallpaper cut from old sample books also make sturdy covers. These stapled booklets can be cut into various shapes, too. Students can make more sophisticated books by covering cardboard covers with contact paper, wallpaper samples, or cloth. Pages are sewn or stapled together, and the first and last pages (endpapers) are glued to the cardboard covers to hold the book together. Directions for making one type of hardcover book are shown in Figure 3–7.

Sharing Writing.   Students read their writing to classmates or share it with larger audiences through hardcover books placed in the class or school library, plays performed for classmates, or letters sent to authors, businesses, and other correspondents. Other ways to share children's writing are:

- Read the writing aloud in class
- Submit the piece to writing contests
- Display the writing as a mobile
- Contribute to a class anthology
- Contribute to the local newspaper
- Make a shape book
- Record the writing on a cassette tape
- Submit it to a literary magazine
- Read it at a school assembly
- Share at a read-aloud party
- Share with parents and siblings
- Produce a videotape of it
- Display poetry on a "poet-tree"
- Send it to a pen pal
- Make a hardbound book
- Produce it as a roller movie
- Display it on a bulletin board
- Make a filmstrip of it
- Make a big book
- Design a poster about the writing
- Read it to foster grandparents
- Share it as a puppet show
- Display it at a public event
- Read it to children in other classes

Through this sharing, students communicate with genuine audiences who respond to their writing in meaningful ways.

Sharing writing is a social activity that helps children develop sensitivity to audiences and confidence in themselves as authors. Dyson (1985) advises that teachers consider the social interpretations of sharing—students' behavior, teacher's behavior, and interaction between students and teacher—within the classroom context. Individual students interpret sharing differently. More than just providing the opportunity for students to share writing, teachers

Figure 3–7 *Directions for Making Hardcover Books*

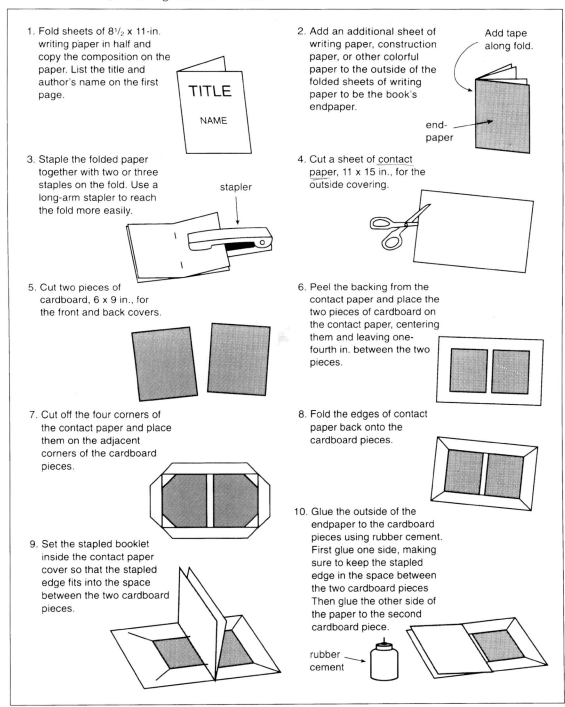

1. Fold sheets of 8½ x 11-in. writing paper in half and copy the composition on the paper. List the title and author's name on the first page.

   TITLE
   NAME

2. Add an additional sheet of writing paper, construction paper, or other colorful paper to the outside of the folded sheets of writing paper to be the book's endpaper.

   Add tape along fold.

   end-paper

3. Staple the folded paper together with two or three staples on the fold. Use a long-arm stapler to reach the fold more easily.

   stapler

4. Cut a sheet of contact paper, 11 x 15 in., for the outside covering.

5. Cut two pieces of cardboard, 6 x 9 in., for the front and back covers.

6. Peel the backing from the contact paper and place the two pieces of cardboard on the contact paper, centering them and leaving one-fourth in. between the two pieces.

7. Cut off the four corners of the contact paper and place them on the adjacent corners of the cardboard pieces.

8. Fold the edges of contact paper back onto the cardboard pieces.

9. Set the stapled booklet inside the contact paper cover so that the stapled edge fits into the space between the two cardboard pieces.

10. Glue the outside of the endpaper to the cardboard pieces using rubber cement. First glue one side, making sure to keep the stapled edge in the space between the two cardboard pieces Then glue the other side of the paper to the second cardboard piece.

    rubber cement

need to teach students how to respond to their classmates. Teachers themselves serve as a model for responding to students' writing without dominating the sharing.

Teaching the Writing Process

Students learn to use the writing process as they write compositions in literature focus units and theme cycles and as they participate in writing workshop. Learning to use the writing process is more important than any particular writing projects students might be involved in, because the writing process is a tool. Students need many opportunities to learn to use the writing process. Teachers model the writing process by writing class collaborations, and they teach minilessons on the procedures, concepts, and strategies and skills that writers use.

Writing Class Collaborations.   One way to introduce the writing process is to write a collaborative or group composition. The teacher models the writing process and provides an opportunity for students to practice the process approach to writing in a supportive environment. As students and the teacher write a composition together, they move through the five stages of the writing process just as writers do when they work independently. The teacher demonstrates the strategies that writers use and clarifies misconceptions during the group composition, and students offer ideas for writing as well as suggestions for tackling common writing problems.

The teacher begins by introducing the idea of writing a group composition and by reviewing the project. Students dictate a rough draft, which the teacher records on the chalkboard or on chart paper. The teacher notes any misunderstandings students have about the writing assignment or process and, when necessary, reviews concepts and offers suggestions. Then the teacher and students read the composition and identify ways to revise it. Some parts of the composition will need reworking, and other parts may be deleted or moved. More specific words will be substituted for less specific ones, and redundant words and sentences will be deleted. Students may also want to add new parts to the composition. After making the necessary content changes, students proofread the composition, checking for mechanical errors, for paragraph breaks, and for sentences to combine. They correct errors and make changes. Then the teacher or a student copies the completed composition on chart paper or on a sheet of notebook paper. Copies can be made and given to each student.

Collaborative compositions are an essential part of many writing experiences, especially when students are learning to use the writing process or a new writing form. Group compositions serve as a "dry run" during which students' questions and misconceptions can be clarified.

Minilessons on the Writing Process.   Students need to learn how to move through the five stages of the writing process, how to gather and organize ideas for writing, how to participate in writing groups, how to proofread, and how to share their writing. Teachers teach these procedures, concepts, and strategies and skills during minilessons. Minilessons can be taught as part of class collaborations, during literature focus units and theme cycles, and in writing workshop. Topics for minilessons on the writing process are listed on page 106. Many teachers use the editing stage as a time to informally assess students' spelling, capitalization, punctuation, and other mechanical skills and to give minilessons on a skill that a student or several students are having trouble with. The teacher notes which students are having difficulty with a particular skill—paragraphing, capitalizing proper nouns, or using the apostrophe in possessives, for example—and conducts an impromptu minilesson using the students' writing as the basis of the lesson. In this brief, 5-minute lesson, the teacher reviews the particular skill, and students practice the skill as they correct their own writing and help to correct their classmates' writing. This procedure individualizes instruction and teaches the skill when learning it matters and is relevant to students.

■ *Turn to Chapter 2, "Teaching Language Arts," pp. 66–67, for more information on minilessons.*

In Literature Focus Units. Students use the writing process as they create projects during the extending stage of the reading process. Sometimes the class works together to write a class collaboration; sometimes students work in small groups on the same writing project; and at other times students work on a variety of writing projects. Here are three examples:

- After reading Freeman's teddy bear story *Corduroy* (1968), a class of first graders worked together to write a retelling of the story, which they published as a big book.
- During an author unit on Chris Van Allsburg, fifth graders each chose an illustration from *The Mysteries of Harris Burdick* (1984) and wrote a description or story about it.
- As part of a unit on point of view, seventh-grade students rewrote familiar folktales from the viewpoint of one character after reading *The True Story of the Three Little Pigs!* (Scieszka, 1989), which is told from the wolf's viewpoint.

Students sit in the author's chair to share writing with classmates.

In each of these projects, students used the writing process and moved through all five stages as they drafted, revised, edited, and published their compositions.

In Theme Cycles.   Teachers often plan writing projects in connection with theme cycles. Sometimes all students in the classroom work together on a single project, such as making an alphabet book about the ocean as part of a theme on the oceans, or writing a collection of animal poems to put with the animal sculptures they made in art. In these cases, teachers review the writing form in a minilesson, and students work through the stages of the writing process together.

At other times, however, students choose projects and work independently. For example, during a theme cycle on pioneers, students might choose different types of projects, including:

- Write a simulated journal from the viewpoint of a pioneer.
- Write a story about a pioneer family.
- Write an informational book about covered wagons.
- Write poems about life on the Oregon Trail.
- Write an explanation to accompany a relief map of the pioneer trails across the United States.
- Make a timeline for the westward expansion, with notes about important dates and events.
- Write an essay comparing pioneers in the 1800s with immigrants coming to America today.
- Make posters about pioneer legends (e.g., Johnny Appleseed, Pecos Bill, and Paul Bunyan).

For each of these projects, students use the writing process to develop their compositions. They meet in writing groups to share their rough drafts and revise their pieces using feedback from classmates. They also edit their compositions to identify and correct as many mechanical errors as possible. Then they make final copies of their compositions and share them with classmates or other audiences.

In Writing Workshop.   In Chapter 2, I described the three components of writing workshop: writing, sharing, and minilessons. Students move through the stages of the writing process during the writing time. It would be convenient if the writing process equated to prewriting on Monday, drafting on Tuesday, revising on Wednesday, editing on Thursday, and publishing on Friday, but it does not. Writers move back and forth through the stages as they develop, refine, and polish their compositions, and they participate in some activities, such as revising, throughout the writing process (Flower & Hayes, 1994). A special sharing time is set aside for students to share their published writing projects with classmates. Sharing is a social experience, and when students share their writing with real audiences, they feel the satisfaction of a job well done.

Adapting to Meet the Needs of Every Student.   Teachers adapt the activities involved in each stage of the writing process to make writing a successful experience for all students. Teachers often shorten the writing process to

Adapting
The Writing Process
To Meet the Needs of Every Student

Stage 1: Prewriting

- Use drawing as a rehearsal activity.
- Have students "talk out" their compositions before beginning to write.
- Draw a cluster for students, using the ideas and words they suggest.

Stage 2: Drafting

- Have students dictate their rough drafts.
- Mark students' papers so that they write on every other line.
- Reassure students that spelling and other mechanical skills are not important in this stage.

Stage 3: Revising

- Participate in writing groups with students.
- Focus on compliments rather than on suggestions for revisions when students begin writing groups.
- Expect students to make only one or two revisions at first.

Stage 4: Editing

- Teach students how to proofread.
- Have students mark possible errors; then correct errors with them.
- Have students identify and correct errors on the first page of their compositions; then correct remaining errors for students.

Stage 5: Publishing

- Use a word processor for final copies.
- Handwrite the final copy for students.
- Provide opportunities for students to share their writing with a trusted group of classmates.
- Do not correct any remaining errors on the final copy.

■ *See Chapter 4, "Emergent Literacy," pp. 174–175, for more information on how to adapt the writing process for young children.*

three stages—prewriting, drafting, and publishing—for young children and for students with few successful writing experiences. Then, as students become more fluent writers and develop audience awareness, teachers add the revising and editing stages.

Teachers can develop checklists with activities for each stage of the writing process listed so that students with short attention spans or students who have trouble completing an assignment can stay on task. Other suggestions for adapting each stage are listed above.

Responding to Student Writing. The teacher's role should not be restricted to that of evaluator. Again and again researchers report that although teachers are the most common audience for student writing, they are also one of the worst audiences, because they read with a red pen in hand. Teachers should instead read their students' writing for information, for enjoyment, and for all the other purposes that other readers do. Much of students' writing does not need to be assessed; it should simply be shared with the teacher as a "trusted adult" (Martin, D'Arcy, Newton, & Parker, 1976).

When children use a process approach to writing, there is less chance they will plagiarize because they will have developed their compositions step-by-step—from prewriting and drafting to revising and editing. Nonetheless, at some time or other most teachers fear that a composition they are reading is not the student's own work. Jackson, Tway, and Frager (1987) cite several reasons why children might plagiarize. First, some students may simply internalize a piece of writing through repeated readings so that, months or years later, they do not realize that it is not their own work. Second, some students may plagiarize because of competition to succeed. Third, some students plagiarize by accident, not realizing the consequences of their actions. A final reason some students plagiarize is that they have not been taught to write by means of a process approach, so they may not know how to synthesize information for a report from published sources. The two best ways to avoid having students copy work from another source and pass it off as their own are to teach the writing process and to have students write at school rather than at home. Students who work at school and move through the various writing process activities know how to complete the writing project.

■ *See Chapter 10, "Reading and Writing Information," pp. 399–408, to read about how to teach students to write reports so that they won't plagiarize.*

CONNECTIONS BETWEEN READING AND WRITING

Reading and writing are both meaning-making processes, and readers and writers are involved in many similar activities. It is important that teachers plan literacy activities so that students can connect reading and writing.

Comparing the Two Processes

The reading and writing processes have comparable activities at each stage (Butler & Turbill, 1984). In both reading and writing the goal is to construct meaning, and, as shown in Figure 3–8, reading and writing activities at each stage are similar. For example, notice the similarities between the activities listed for responding and revising—the third stage in reading and writing, respectively. Fitzgerald (1989) analyzed these two activities and concluded that they draw on similar processes of author-reader-text interactions. Similar analyses can be made for other activities, as well.

Tierney (1983) explains that reading and writing are multidimensional and involve concurrent, complex transactions between writers, between writers as readers, between readers, and between readers as writers. Writers participate in several types of reading activities. They read other authors' works to obtain ideas and to learn about the structure of stories, but they also read and reread their own work in order to problem-solve, discover, monitor, and clarify. The quality of these reading experiences seems closely tied to success in writing. "Readers as writers" is a newer idea, but readers are involved in many of the same activities that writers use—generating ideas, organizing,

Figure 3–8   *A Comparison of the Reading and Writing Processes*

	What Readers Do	**What Writers Do**
Stage 1	*Preparing*	*Prewriting*
	Readers use knowledge about	Writers use knowledge about
	• the topic • reading • literature • language systems	• the topic • writing • literature • language systems
	Readers' expectations are cued by	Writers' expectations are cued by
	• previous reading/writing experiences • format of the text • purpose for reading • audience for reading	• previous reading/writing experiences • format of the text • purpose for writing • audience for writing
	Readers make predictions.	Writers gather and organize ideas.
Stage 2	*Reading*	*Drafting*
	Readers	Writers
	• use word identification strategies • use meaning-making strategies • monitor reading • create meaning	• use transcription strategies • use meaning-making strategies • monitor writing • create meaning
Stage 3	*Responding*	*Revising*
	Readers	Writers
	• respond to the text • interpret meaning • clarify misunderstandings • expand ideas	• respond to the text • interpret meaning • clarify misunderstandings • expand ideas
Stage 4	*Exploring*	*Editing*
	Readers	Writers
	• examine the impact of words and literary language • explore structural elements • compare the text to others	• identify and correct mechanical errors • review paragraph and sentence structure
Stage 5	*Extending*	*Publishing*
	Readers	Writers
	• go beyond the text to extend their interpretations • share projects with classmates • reflect on the reading process • make connections to life and literature • value the piece of literature • feel success • want to read again	• produce the finished copy of their compositions • share their compositions with genuine audiences • reflect on the writing process • value the composition • feel success • want to write again

Adapted from Butler & Turbill, 1984.

monitoring, problem solving, and revising. Smith (1982) believes that reading influences writing skills because readers unconsciously "read like writers":

> To read like a writer we engage with the author in what the author is writing. We can anticipate what the author will say, so that the author is in effect writing on our behalf, not showing how something is done but doing it with us. . . . Bit by bit, one thing at a time, but enormous numbers of things over the passage of time, the learner learns through reading like a writer to write like a writer. (pp. 563–564)

Also, both reading and writing are recursive, cycling back through various parts of the process; and, just as writers compose text, readers compose their meaning.

Classroom Connections

Teachers can help students appreciate the similarities between reading and writing in many ways. Tierney explains: "What we need are reading teachers who act as if their students were developing writers and writing teachers who act as if their students were readers" (1983, p. 151). These are some ways to point out the relationships between reading and writing:

- Help writers assume alternative points of view as potential readers.
- Help readers consider the writer's purpose and viewpoint.
- Point out that reading is much like composing, so that students will view reading as a process, much like the writing process.
- Talk with students about the similarities between the reading and writing processes.
- Talk with students about reading and writing strategies.

■ *To review the 12 reading and writing strategies, see Chapter 1, "Language and the Language Arts," pp. 31–33.*

Readers and writers use similar strategies for constructing meaning as they interact with print. As readers, we use a variety of problem-solving strategies to make decisions about an author's meaning and to construct meaning for ourselves. As writers, we also use problem-solving strategies to decide what our readers need as we construct meaning for them and for ourselves. Comparing reading to writing, Tierney and Pearson (1983) described reading as a composing process because readers compose and refine meaning through reading much as writers do.

There are practical benefits of connecting reading and writing. Reading contributes to students' writing development, and writing contributes to students' reading development. Shanahan (1988) has outlined seven instructional principles for relating reading and writing so that students develop a clear concept of literacy:

1. Involve students in reading and writing experiences every day.
2. Introduce reading and writing processes in kindergarten.
3. Plan instruction that reflects the developmental nature of the reading-writing relationship.
4. Make the reading-writing connection explicit to students.
5. Emphasize both the processes and the products of reading and writing.
6. Emphasize the purposes for which students use reading and writing.
7. Teach reading and writing through meaningful, functional, and genuine literacy experiences.

Review

Reading and writing are similar processes of constructing meaning. Teachers organize reading and writing instruction using the five stages of the reading and writing processes. Students learn to use the reading and writing processes through literature focus units, theme cycles, and reading and writing workshop. The key concepts presented in this chapter are:

1. Students use aesthetic reading when they read for enjoyment and efferent reading when they read for information.
2. The five stages of the reading process are preparing, reading, responding, exploring, and extending.
3. Students use the Goldilocks Strategy to choose books at their reading level.
4. Five ways to read a selection are shared reading, guided reading, independent reading, buddy reading, and listening as it is read aloud.
5. Students use the reading process during literature focus units, theme cycles, and reading workshop.
6. The five stages of the writing process are prewriting, drafting, revising, editing, and publishing.
7. Purpose, form, and audience are three considerations that influence students' compositions.
8. Students use the writing process as they write during literature focus units, theme cycles, and writing workshop.
9. Teachers present minilessons on procedures, concepts, skills, and strategies in the reading and writing processes.
10. The goal of both reading and writing is to construct meaning, and both processes have comparable activities at each stage.

Extensions

1. Observe students using the reading process in an elementary classroom. In what types of preparing, reading, responding, exploring, and extending activities are they involved?
2. Observe students using the writing process in an elementary classroom. In what types of prewriting, drafting, revising, editing, and publishing activities are they involved?
3. Plan a literature focus unit or theme cycle and include a variety of activities on the reading and writing processes.
4. Sit in on a writing group in which students share their writing and ask classmates for feedback in revising their compositions. Make a list of the students' questions and comments. What conclusions can you draw about their interactions with each other?
5. Reflect on your own reading and writing processes. What stages do you use? How do you vary your reading when you read aesthetically and efferently? Do you write single-draft papers, or do you write a series of drafts and refine them? Do you ask friends to read and react to your writing or to help you proofread your writing?
6. Read Shanahan's (1988) article, "The Reading-Writing Relationship: Seven Instructional Principles." Think about how you will implement these principles in your classroom, and share your thoughts in a brief paper.

PROCEDURE

For interactive writing, I use a large white board and a class set of small white boards, marking pens, and eraser cloths. My students write on the small boards as we work together to write on the large boards. I also use an alphabet chart and a pointer. The children sit on the floor in the circle area, facing the large board.

Each morning the children take turns sharing their personal news with the class. This is how I begin. Then I choose one child's news for interactive writing. We repeat the sentence several times and break it into separate words. Next, we focus on the first word, and stretch it out to hear the sounds. I model the stretching this way: I make my hands into fists and extend my arms out in front of me with my fists touching. Then as I say the words, I move my arms apart to demonstrate the "stretching." For the word *playing*, for example, I say *p-l-ay-ed*. For longer words, we clap the syllables. After we segment the word, a child tells me the letter or letters that represent the first sound, and that child comes forward and writes the letters on the large board. I use a contrasting-color pen to add silent letters or unusual spelling patterns because we spell all words correctly even if children don't hear the sounds. I also point out sight words such as *the, you,* and *are.* We read each new word after it is written and reread the sentence. One child who is the "spacer" comes up to the larger board to mark a two-finger space between words. I also emphasize capitalizing the first word in a sentence and adding punctuation marks.

At the beginning of the year, I keep the sentences very short because interactive writing can be quite time-consuming, and I choose children to write sounds that they have in their own names. And students usually write just one sound. Now, I often have students write entire words on the large board so the writing goes much more quickly and we can write two or three sentences instead of just one. I also notice that I do much less writing. I believe it is important that all children get to "share the pen" in a meaningful way.

Each Friday, we publish a class newspaper with our daily news. Each day the child whose news is written on the white board copies the news onto our newspaper and adds a small picture. A copy of our newspaper is shown in the figure. I make the copies on Friday, and the children take them home to share with their families.

ASSESSMENT

My students write on small individual boards during interactive writing, and I can see their growing awareness of written language. Some children follow along, writing each letter and word on their small boards as they are written on the large board. But at the beginning of the year, many children don't follow along and make random scribbles or draw pictures. Soon I notice that they make some of the letters, and then I see the first several words written accurately. Slowly, children's attention spans grow and they keep up with the group. And as children learn more about segmenting sounds in words and phoneme-grapheme correspondences, they begin volunteering to come forward to write in front of the class. I'm already noticing that seven or eight students write entire sentences correctly on their small boards without waiting to see it written on the large board.

ADAPTATIONS

I also use interactive writing to write responses to stories. I have a tablet of chart paper labeled "Our Listening Log," and we write responses after I read aloud books. I quickly write the title of the book at the top of the page, and then using the procedure I have described, my students write a sentence or two about the story. For example, after reading *Officer Buckle and Gloria* (Rathmann, 1995), they wanted to write: "Officer Buckle and Gloria make a good team. They teach safety rules." Then one or two children drew a picture beside the writing on the page.

We also make charts with information during theme cycles. During a unit on machines, for example, we wrote these facts about wheels:

> A wheel is a machine.
>
> Cars, bikes, and rollerblades have wheels.
>
> Wheels make work easier because it is easier to roll along than to walk.

REFLECTION

Interactive writing has really changed the way I teach. I focus more on moving students to conventional spelling and I see that my first graders are able to spell conventionally much sooner. They also become aware of grammar and editing skills. Stretching words and listening for individual sounds has become an important part of my instructional program.

Room Two Daily News

Weekend Edition

12/9 Week	Monday	Tuesday	Wednesday	Thursday	Friday	Weather News

Monday	Jace played soccer on Saturday!	
Tuesday	Wenston got a new bike.	
Wednesday	codYs got new shoes.	
Thursday	Chad got his Christmas tree out.	
Friday	Tonight Emily is going to spend the night. Kayia friend	

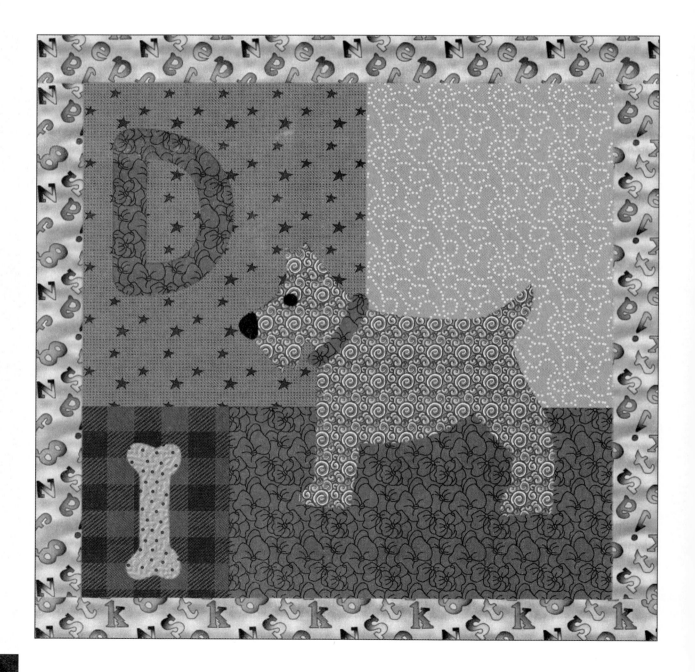

Emergent Literacy

First graders in Cheryl Schellenberg's classroom made name quilts. Children each made a series of paper squares to spell their names. In each square, they printed a letter and glued pictures and small objects representing words beginning with that letter. Then they added buttons, ribbons, and other decorations. Children made the quilts as part of a review of the letters of the alphabet at the beginning of the school year, and the quilts hung in the classroom for several months so that the first graders could refer to them as they learned consonant and vowel sounds.

s there a magic age when a child becomes a reader and a writer? Researchers used to think that at the age of 6 most children were ready to learn to read and write. We now know that children begin the process of becoming literate gradually during the preschool years. Very young children notice signs, logos, and other environmental print. Who hasn't observed children making scribbles on paper as they try to "write"? As children are read to, they learn how to hold a book and turn pages, and they observe how the text is read. Children come to kindergarten and first grade with sophisticated knowledge about written language and experiences with reading and writing.

The process of becoming literate begins well before the elementary grades and continues into adulthood, if not throughout life. It used to be that 5-year-old children came to kindergarten to be "readied" for reading and writing instruction, which would formally begin in first grade. The implication was that there was a point in children's development when it was time to begin teaching them to read and write. For those not ready, a variety of "readiness" activities would prepare them for reading and writing. Since the 1970s this view has been discredited by teachers' and researchers' observations (Clay, 1991). The children themselves demonstrated that they could recognize signs and other environmental print, retell stories, scribble letters, invent printlike writing, and listen to stories read aloud to them. Some children even taught themselves to read.

This new perspective on how children become literate—that is, how they learn to read and write—is known as emergent literacy. New Zealand educator Marie Clay is credited with coining the term. Studies from 1966 on have shaped the current outlook (Clay, 1967; Durkin, 1966; Holdaway, 1979; Taylor, 1983; Teale, 1982; Teale & Sulzby, 1989). Now, researchers are looking at literacy learning from the child's point of view. The age range has been extended to include children as young as 12 or 14 months of age who listen to stories being read aloud, notice labels and signs in their environment, and experiment with pencils. The concept of literacy has been broadened to include the cultural and social aspects of language learning, and children's experiences with and understanding of written language—both reading and writing—are included as part of emergent literacy.

Teale and Sulzby (1989) paint a portrait of young children as literacy learners with these characteristics:

- Children begin to learn to read and write very early in life.
- Young children learn the functions of literacy through observing and participating in real-life settings in which reading and writing are used.
- Young children's reading and writing abilities develop concurrently and interrelatedly through experiences in reading and writing.
- Young children learn through active involvement with literacy materials, by constructing their understanding of reading and writing.

Teale and Sulzby describe young children as active learners who construct their own knowledge about reading and writing with the assistance of parents and other literate persons. These caregivers help by demonstrating literacy as they read and write, by supplying materials, and by structuring opportunities for children to be involved in reading and writing. The environment is positive, with children experiencing reading and writing in many facets of their everyday lives and observing others who are engaged in literacy activities.

As you read this chapter, think about these questions:

- How do teachers foster children's interest in literacy?
- How do young children develop as readers and writers?
- What teaching strategies do teacher use in teaching reading and writing?

FOSTERING YOUNG CHILDREN'S INTEREST IN LITERACY

Children's introduction to written language begins before they come to school. Parents and other caregivers read to young children, and the children observe adults reading. They learn to read signs and other environmental print in their community. Children experiment with writing and have parents write for them. They also observe adults writing. When young children come to kindergarten, their knowledge about written language expands quickly as they participate in meaningful, functional, and genuine experiences with reading and writing.

Students also grow in their ability to stand back and reflect on language. The ability to talk about concepts of language is called metalinguistics (Yaden & Templeton, 1986), and children's ability to think metalinguistically is developed by their experiences with reading and writing (Templeton & Spivey, 1980).

Concepts About Written Language

Through experiences in their homes and communities, young children learn that print carries meaning and that reading and writing are used for a variety of purposes. They read menus in restaurants to know what foods are being served, write and receive letters to communicate with friends and relatives, and read (and listen to) stories for enjoyment. Children also learn as they observe parents and teachers using written language for all these purposes.

Children's understanding about the purposes of reading and writing reflects how written language is used in their community. While reading and writing are part of daily life for almost every family, families use written language for different purposes in different communities (Heath, 1983b). It is important to realize that children have a wide range of literacy experiences in both middle- and working-class families, even though those experiences might be different (Taylor, 1983; Taylor & Dorsey-Gaines, 1987). In some communities written language is used mainly as a tool for practical purposes such as paying bills, and in some communities reading and writing are also used for leisure-time activities. In other communities written language serves even wider functions, such as debating social and political issues.

Teachers demonstrate the purposes of written language and provide opportunities for students to experiment with reading and writing in these ways:

- Posting signs in the classroom
- Making a list of classroom rules
- Using literacy materials in dramatic play centers
- Writing notes to students in the class
- Exchanging messages with classmates
- Reading and writing stories
- Making posters about favorite books
- Labeling classroom items

- Drawing and writing in journals
- Writing morning messages
- Recording questions and information on charts
- Writing notes to parents
- Reading and writing letters to pen pals
- Reading and writing charts and maps

Concept of a Word.   Children's understanding of the concept of a "word" is an important part of becoming literate. Young children have only vague notions of language terms, such as *word, letter, sound,* and *sentence,* that teachers use in talking about reading and writing (Downing, 1971–1972). Researchers have found that young children move through several levels of awareness and understanding about this terminology during the primary grades (Downing & Oliver, 1973–1974).

Preschoolers equate words with the objects the words represent. As they are introduced to reading and writing experiences, children begin to differentiate between objects and words, and finally they come to appreciate that words have meanings of their own. Templeton (1980) explains children's development with these two examples:

> When asked if "dog" were a word, a four-year-old acquaintance of mine jumped up from the floor, began barking ferociously, and charged through the house, alternatively panting and woofing. Confronted with the same question, an eight-year-old friend responded "of course 'dog' is a word," and went on to explain how the spelling represented spoken sounds and how the word *dog* stood for a particular type of animal. (p. 454)

Several researchers have investigated children's understanding of a word as a unit of language. Papandropoulou and Sinclair (1974) identified four stages of word consciousness. At the first level, young children do not differentiate between words and things. At the next level, children describe words as labels for things. They consider words that stand for objects as words, but do not classify articles and prepositions as words because words such as *the* and *with* cannot be represented with objects. At the third level, children understand that words carry meaning and that stories are built from words. At the fourth level, more fluent readers and writers describe words as autonomous elements having meanings of their own with definite semantic and syntactic relationships. Children might say, "You make words with letters." Also, at this level children understand that words have different appearances—they can be spoken, listened to, read, and written.

Environmental Print.   In reading, children move from recognizing environmental print to reading decontextualized words in books. Young children begin reading by recognizing logos on fast-food restaurants, department stores, grocery stores, and commonly used household items within familiar contexts (Harste, Woodward, & Burke, 1984b). They recognize the golden arches of McDonald's and say "McDonald's," but when they are shown the word *McDonald's* written on a sheet of paper without the familiar sign and restaurant setting, they cannot read the word. Researchers have found that young emergent readers depend on context to read familiar words and memorized texts (Dyson, 1984; Sulzby, 1985b). Slowly, children develop relationships linking form and meaning as they learn concepts about written language and gain more experience reading and writing.

When children begin writing, they use scribbles or single letters to represent complex ideas (Clay, 1991; Schickedanz, 1990). As they learn about letter names and phoneme-grapheme correspondences, they use one, two, or three letters to stand for a word. At first they run their writing together, but they slowly learn to segment words and leave spaces between words. They sometimes add dots or lines as markers between words, or they draw circles around words. They also move from capitalizing words randomly to using a capital letter at the beginning of a sentence and to mark proper nouns. Similarly, children move from using periods at the end of each line of writing to marking the ends of sentences with periods. Then they learn about other end-of-sentence markers and, finally, punctuation marks that are embedded in sentences.

Dramatic Play Centers.   Young children learn about the functions of reading and writing as they use written language in their play. As they construct block buildings, children write signs and tape them on the buildings; as they play doctor, they write prescriptions on slips of paper; and as they play teacher, they read stories aloud to friends who are pretending to be students or to doll and stuffed-animal "students." Young children use these activities to reenact familiar, everyday activities and to pretend to be someone or something else. Through these dramatic play activities, children use reading and writing for a variety of functions.

Housekeeping centers are probably the most common play centers in primary classrooms, but these centers can be transformed into a grocery store,

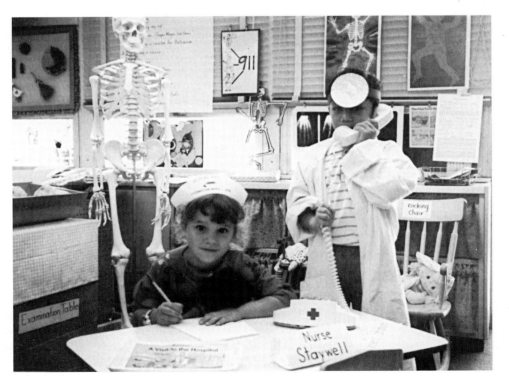

Kindergartners use reading and writing in this doctor's office dramatic play center.

■ To learn more
about the power of
drama as a learning
tool, see Chapter 8,
"Sustaining Talk in the
Classroom," pp.
330–331.

a post office, or a medical center by changing the props. Materials for reading and writing are included in each of these play centers. Food packages, price stickers, and money are props in grocery store centers; letters, stamps, and mailboxes in post office centers; and appointment books, prescription pads, and folders for patient records in medical centers. A variety of dramatic play centers can be set up in classrooms to coordinate with units and theme cycles. Ideas for five dramatic play centers are offered in Figure 4–1. Each center includes authentic literacy materials that children can experiment with and use to learn more about the functions of written language.

Concepts About the Alphabet

Young children also develop concepts about the alphabet and how letters are used to represent phonemes. Children use this phonics knowledge to decode unfamiliar words as they read and to create spellings for words as they write.

Figure 4–1   *Five Literacy Play Centers*

Post Office Center

mailboxes	wrapping paper	package seals
envelopes	tape	address labels
stamps (stickers)	packages	cash register
pens	scale	money

Hairdresser Center

hair rollers	towel	curling iron (cordless)
brush and comb	posters of hair styles	ribbons, barrettes, clips
mirror	wig and wig stand	appointment book
empty shampoo bottle	hairdryer (cordless)	open/closed sign

Restaurant Center

tablecloth	napkins	apron for waitress
dishes	menus	vests for waiter
glasses	tray	hat and apron for chef
silverware	order pad and pencil	

Medical Center

appointment books	stethoscope	folders (for patient
white shirt/jacket	thermometer	records)
medical bag	tweezers	prescription bottles
hypodermic syringe	bandages	and labels
(play)	prescription pad	walkie-talkie

Grocery Store Center

grocery cart	price stickers	marking pen
food packages	cash register	cents-off coupons
plastic fruit and	money	advertisements
artificial foods	grocery bags	

■ *Turn back to Chapter 1, "Learning and Language Arts," pp. 10–15, to review the four language systems.*

Too often it is assumed that phonics instruction is the most important component of the reading program for young children, but phonics is only one of the four language systems. Emergent readers and writers use all four language systems as well as their knowledge about written language concepts as they read and write.

The Alphabetic Principle.   The one-to-one correspondence between the phonemes (or sounds) and graphemes (or letters), such that each letter consistently represents one sound, is known as the alphabetic principle. In phonetic languages, there is a one-to-one correspondence; however, English is not a purely phonetic language. The 26 letters represent approximately 44 phonemes, and three letters—*c, q,* and *x*—are superfluous because they do not represent unique phonemes. The letter *c,* for example, can represent either /k/ as in *cat* or /s/ as in *city,* and it can be joined with *h* for the digraph /ch/. To further complicate matters, there are more than 500 spellings to represent the 44 phonemes. Consonants are more consistent and predictable than vowels. Long *e,* for instance, is spelled 14 different ways in common words (Horn, 1957).

Researchers estimate that words are spelled phonetically approximately half the time (Hanna, Hanna, Hodges, & Rudorf, 1966). The nonphonetic spellings of many words reflect morphological information. The word *sign,* for instance, is a shortened form of *signature,* and the spelling shows this relationship. Spelling the word phonetically (e.g., *sine*) might seem simpler, but the phonetic spelling lacks semantic information (Venezky, 1970).

Letter Names.   The most basic information that children learn about the alphabet is how to identify and form the letters in handwriting. They notice letters in environmental print and they often learn to sing the ABC song. By the time children enter kindergarten, they can usually recognize some letters, especially those in their own names, in names of family members and pets, and in common words in their homes and communities. Children can also write some of these familiar letters.

Young children associate letters with meaningful contexts—names, signs, T-shirts, and cereal boxes. Baghban (1984) notes that the letter *M* was the first letter her daughter noticed. She pointed to *M* in the word *K Mart* and called it "McDonald's." Even though the child confused a store and a restaurant, this account demonstrates how young children make associations with letters. Research suggests that children do not learn alphabet letter names in any particular order or by isolating letters from meaningful written language. McGee and Richgels (1996) conclude that learning letters of the alphabet requires many, many experiences with meaningful written language.

Children become aware that words are composed of letters by reading environmental print and also by seeing their own name and the names of family members written. Even when children know the names of several letters and use mock letters as well as real letters in their writing, they have different concepts about letters. For example, Anne Haas Dyson reports that 5-year-old Dexter said, "N spell my grandmama" when his grandmother's name was Hele*n* (1984, p. 262). This child's comment about letters shows that emergent readers do not have the same concepts about letters that more accomplished readers have.

Being able to name the letters of the alphabet is a good predictor of beginning reading achievement, even though knowing the names of the letters does not directly affect a child's ability to read (Adams, 1990). A more likely explanation for this relationship between letter knowledge and reading is that children who have been actively involved in reading and writing activities before entering first grade know the names of the letters, and they are more likely to emerge quickly into reading. Simply teaching children to name the letters without the accompanying reading and writing experiences does not have this effect.

Phonemic Awareness.   Phonemic awareness is children's basic understanding that speech is composed of a series of individual sounds, and it provides the foundation for phonics (Yopp, 1992). When children can choose a duck as the animal that begins with /d/ from a collection of toy animals, identify *duck* and *luck* as two words in a song that rhyme, or blend the sounds /d/, /ŭ/, and /k/ to pronounce *duck,* they are phonemically aware. (Note that the emphasis is on the sounds of spoken words, not reading letters or pronouncing letter names.) Developing phonemic awareness enables children to use sound-symbol correspondences to read and spell words. Phonemic awareness is not sounding out words for reading, nor is it using spelling patterns to write words; rather, it is the foundation for phonics.

Understanding that words are composed of smaller units—phonemes—is a significant achievement for young children because phonemes are abstract language units. Phonemes carry no meaning, and children think of words according to their meanings, not their linguistic characteristics (Griffith & Olson, 1992). When children think about *ducks,* for example, they think of animals covered with feathers that swim in ponds, fly through the air, and make noises we describe as "quacks." They don't think of *duck* as a word with three phonemes or four graphemes, as a word beginning with /d/ and rhyming with *luck.* Phonemic awareness requires that children treat speech as an object and that they shift their attention away from the meaning of words to the linguistic features of speech. This focus on phonemes is even more complicated because phonemes are not discrete units in speech. Often they are blended or slurred together in speech. Think about the blended initial sound in *tree* and the ending sound in *eating.*

Children develop phonemic awareness in two ways. They learn through a language-rich environment as they sing songs, play with words, chant rhymes, and listen to parents and teachers read wordplay books to them (Griffith & Olson, 1992). Yopp (1995) recommends that teachers read books with wordplay aloud and encourage students to talk about the books' language. Teachers ask questions and make comments, such as "Did you notice how _____ and _____ rhyme?" and "This book is fun because of all the words beginning with the /m/ sound." Once students are very familiar with the book, they can create new verses or make other variations. Books such as *Jamberry* (Degen, 1983) and *The Baby Uggs Are Hatching* (Prelutsky, 1982) stimulate children to experiment with sounds, create nonsense words, and become enthusiastic about reading. When teachers read books with alliterative or assonant patterns, such as *Faint Frogs Feeling Feverish and Other Terrifically Tantalizing Tongue Twisters* (Obligado, 1983), children attend to the smaller units of language.

Teachers also teach lessons to help students understand that their speech is composed of sounds (Ball & Blachman, 1991; Lundberg, Frost, & Petersen, 1988). The goal of phonemic awareness activities is to break down and manipulate spoken words. Students who have developed phonemic awareness can manipulate spoken language in these five ways:

- Match words by sounds
- Isolate a sound in a word
- Blend individual sound to form a word
- Substitute sounds in a word
- Segment a word into its constituent sounds (Yopp, 1992)

Teachers teach minilessons focusing on each of these tasks using familiar songs with improvised lyrics, riddles and guessing games, and wordplay books. These activities should be playful and gamelike, and they should be connected to literature focus units and theme cycles whenever possible. Five types of activities are:

1. Sound matching. Children choose one of several words beginning with a particular sound or say a word that begins with a particular sound (Yopp, 1992). For these games, teachers use familiar objects (e.g., feather, toothbrush, book) and toys (e.g., small plastic animals, toy trucks, artificial fruits and vegetables) as well as pictures of familiar objects. Children also identify rhyming words as part of sound-matching activities. Students name a word that rhymes with a given word and they identify rhyming words from familiar songs and stories. As children listen to parents and teachers read Dr. Seuss books such as *Hop on Pop* (1963) and other wordplay books, students refine their understanding of rhyme.

2. Sound isolation. Students are given a word and are asked to identify the sounds at the beginning, middle, or end of the word. Yopp (1992) created new verses to the tune of "Old MacDonald Had a Farm":

> What's the sound that starts these words:
> Chicken, chin and cheek?
> (wait for response)
> /ch/ is the sound that starts these words:
> Chicken, chin, and cheek.
> With a /ch/, /ch/ here, and a /ch/, /ch/ there,
> Here a /ch/, there a /ch/ everywhere a /ch/, /ch/.
> /ch/ is the sound that starts these words:
> Chicken, chin, and cheek. (p. 700)

Teachers change the question at the beginning of the verse to focus on medial and final sounds. For example:

> What's the sound in the middle of these words?
> Whale, game, and rain. (p. 700)

And for final sounds:

> What's the sound at the end of these words?
> Leaf, cough, and beef. (p. 700)

Teachers can also set out a tray of objects and ask students to chose the one object that doesn't belong because it doesn't begin with the sound. For example, from a tray with a toy pig, a puppet, a teddy bear, and a pen, the teddy bear doesn't belong.

3. Sound blending. Children blend sounds in order to combine them to form a word. For example, children blend the sounds /d/, /ŭ/, and /k/ to form the word *duck*. Teachers can play the "What am I thinking of?" guessing game with children by identifying several characteristics of the item and then saying the name of the item, articulating each of the sounds separately (Yopp, 1992). Then children blend the sounds together and identify the word using both the phonological and semantic information that the teacher provided. For example:

> We're studying about the pond and I am thinking of an animal that lives in the pond when it is young. When it is an adult, it can live on land and it is called a /f/, /r/, /o/, /g/. What is it?

The children blend the sounds together to pronounce the word *frog*. In this example, the teacher connects the game with a thematic unit, thereby making the game more meaningful for students.

4. Sound addition or substitution. Students play with words and create nonsense words as they add or substitute sounds in words in songs they sing or in books that are read aloud to them. Teachers read wordplay books such as Hutchins's *Don't Forget the Bacon!* (1976), in which a boy leaves for the store with a mental list of four items to buy. As he walks, he repeats his list, substituting words each time. "A cake for tea" changes to "a cape for me" and then to "a rake for leaves." Children suggest other substitutions, such as "a pail for maple sugar trees."

Students can substitute sounds in refrains of songs (Yopp, 1992). For example, students can change the "Ee-igh, ee-igh, oh!" refrain in "Old Mac-Donald Had a Farm" to "Bee-bigh, bee-bigh, boh!" to focus on the initial /b/ sound. Teachers can choose one sound, such as /sh/, and have children substitute this sound for the beginning sound in their names and in words for items in the classroom. For example, *Jimmy* becomes *Shimmy, José* becomes *Shosé,* and *the clock* becomes *the shock.*

5. Segmentation. One of the more difficult phonemic awareness activities is segmentation, in which children isolate the sounds in a spoken word (Yopp, 1988). An introductory segmentation activity is to draw out the beginning sound in words. Children enjoy exaggerating the initial sound in their own names and other familiar words. Children can pick up objects or pictures of objects and identify the initial sound. A child who picks up a toy tiger says, "This is a tiger and it starts with /t/."

From that beginning, children move to identifying all the sounds in a word. Using a toy tiger again, the child would say, "This is a tiger, /t/, /i/, /g/, /er/." Yopp (1992) suggests singing a song to the tune of "Twinkle, Twinkle, Little Star" in which children segment entire words. Here is one example:

> Listen, listen
> To my word
> Then tell me all the sounds you heard: coat
> (slowly)
> /k/ is one sound

> /o/ is two
> /t/ is last in coat
> It's true. (p. 702)

After several repetitions of the verse segmenting other words, the song ends this way:

> Thanks for listening
> To my words
> And telling all the sounds you heard! (p. 702)

Teachers also use Elkonin boxes teach students to segment words. This activity comes from the work of Russian psychologist D. B. Elkonin (Clay, 1985). As shown in Figure 4–2, the teacher shows an object or picture of an object and draws a series of boxes, with one box for each sound in the name of the object or picture. Then the teacher or a child moves a marker into each box as the sound is pronounced. Children can move small markers onto cards on their desks, or the teacher can draw the boxes on the chalkboard and use tape or small magnets to hold the larger markers in place. Elkonin boxes can also be used for spelling activities. When a child is trying to spell a word, such as *duck,* the teacher can draw three boxes, do the segmenting activity, and then have the child write the letters representing each sound. Spelling boxes for *duck* and other words with two, three, and four sounds are also shown in Figure 4–2.

In all of these activities, students are engaged in experimenting with oral language. Students do not usually read or write letters and words during phonemic awareness activities, because the focus is on speech. However, once children begin reading and writing, these activities reinforce the segmentation and blending activities they have learned. The phonemic awareness activities stimulate children's interest in language and provide valuable experiences with books and words. Effective teachers recognize the importance of building this foundation before children begin reading and writing.

The relationship between phonemic awareness and learning to read is extremely important, and researchers have concluded that at least some level of phonemic awareness is a prerequisite for learning to read (Tunmer & Nesdale, 1985). In fact, phonemic awareness seems to be both a prerequisite for and a consequence of learning to read (Stanovich, 1980; Perfitti, Beck, Bell, & Hughes, 1987). As they become phonemically aware, children recognize that speech can be segmented into smaller units, and this knowledge is very useful when children learn about sound-symbol correspondences and spelling patterns.

Moreover, phonemic awareness has been shown to be the most powerful predictor of later reading achievement (Juel, Griffith, & Gough, 1986; Lomax & McGee, 1987; Tunmer & Nesdale, 1985). In a study comparing children's progress in learning to read in whole-language and traditional reading instruction, Klesius, Griffith, and Zielonka (1991) found that children who began first grade with strong phonemic awareness did well regardless of the kind of reading instruction they received. And neither type of instruction was better for children who were low in phonemic awareness at the beginning of first grade.

Phonics.   Phonics is the set of relationships between phonology (the sounds in speech) and orthography (the spelling patterns of written language).

Figure 4–2   How to Use Elkonin Boxes for Segmentation Activities

1. The teacher shows students an object or the picture of an object, such as a duck, a bed, a game, a bee, a cup, or a cat.

2. The teacher prepares a diagram with a series of boxes, corresponding to the number of sounds heard in the name of the object. For example, the teacher draws three boxes side by side to represent the three sounds heard in the word *duck*. The teacher can draw the boxes on the chalkboard or on small cards for each child to use. The teacher also prepares markers to place on the boxes.

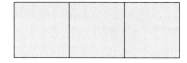

3. The teacher or students say the word slowly and move markers onto the boxes as each sound is pronounced.

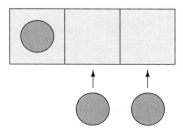

4. Elkonin boxes can also be used when spelling words. The teacher draws a series of boxes corresponding to the number of sounds heard in the word, and then the child and teacher pronounce the word, pointing to each box or sliding markers into each box. Then the child writes the letters representing each sound or spelling pattern in the boxes.

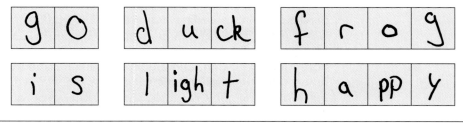

Sounds are spelled in different ways. There are several reasons for this variety. One reason is that the sounds, especially vowels, vary according to their location in a word (e.g., *go–got*). Adjacent letters often influence how letters are pronounced (e.g., *bed–bead*), as do vowel markers such as the final *e* (e.g., *bit–bite*) (Shefelbine, 1995).

Phonics is a very controversial topic. Ken Goodman called it "the most widely misunderstood aspect" of reading instruction (1993, p. 1). Some parents and politicians, as well as even a few teachers, believe that most of the educational ills in America could be solved if children were taught to read using phonics. A few people still argue that phonics is a complete reading program, but that view ignores what we know about the interrelatedness of the four cueing systems. Reading is a complex process, and the phonological system works in conjunction with the semantic, syntactic, and pragmatic systems, not in isolation.

The controversy now centers on how to teach phonics. Marilyn Adams (1990), in her landmark review of the research on phonics instruction, recommended that phonics be taught within a balanced approach that integrates instruction in reading skills and strategies with meaningful opportunities for reading and writing. She emphasized that phonics instruction should focus on the most useful information for identifying words and that it be systematic, intensive, and completed by the third grade.

Teachers teach sound-symbol correspondences, how to blend sounds together to decode words and segment sounds for spelling, and the most useful phonics generalizations or "rules." Phonics concepts build on phonemic awareness. The most important concepts that primary-grade students learn are:

1.   Consonants.   Letters are classified as either consonants or vowels. The consonants are *b, c, d, f, g, h, j, k, l, m, n, p, q, r, s, t, v, w, x, y,* and *z.* Most consonants represent a single sound consistently, but there are some exceptions. *C,* for example, does not represent a sound of its own. When it is followed by *a, o,* or *u,* it is pronounced /k/ (e.g., *castle, coffee, cut*) and when it is followed by *e, i,* or *y,* it is pronounced /s/ (e.g., *cell, city, cycle*). *G* represents two sounds, as the word *garage* illustrates. It is usually pronounced /g/ (e.g., *glass, go, green, guppy*), but when *g* is followed by *e* or *i,* it is pronounced /j/, as in *giant. X* is also pronounced differently according to its location in a word. When *x* is at the beginning of a word, it is often pronounced /z/, as in *xylophone,* but sometimes the letter name is used, as in *x-ray.* At the end of a word, *x* is pronounced /ks/, as in *box.*

The letters *w* and *y* are particularly interesting. At the beginning of a word or a syllable they are consonants (e.g., *wind, yard*), but when they are in the middle or at the end they are vowels (e.g., *saw, flown, day, by*).

Two kinds of combination consonants are blends and digraphs. Consonant blends are two or three consonants that appear next to each other in words, and their individual sounds are "blended" together, such as *grass, belt,* and *spring.* Consonant digraphs are letter combinations that represent single sounds. The four most common are *ch* as in *chair* and *each, sh* as in *shell* and *wish, th* as in *father* and *both,* and *wh* as in *whale.* Another consonant digraph is *ph,* as in *graph* and *photo.*

2.   Vowels.   The remaining five letters—*a, e, i, o,* and *u*—represent vowels, and *w* and *y* are vowels when used in the middle and at the end of syllables and words. Vowels represent several sounds. The most common are short and long vowels. The short-vowel sounds are /ă/ as in *cat*, /ĕ/ as in *bed*, /ĭ/ as in *win*, /ŏ/ as in *hot*, and /ŭ/ as in *cup*. The long-vowel sounds are the same as the letter names, and they are illustrated in the words *make, feet, bike, coal,* and *mule*. Long vowels are usually spelled with two vowels, except when *y* is used at the end of a word.

When *y* is a vowel at the end of a word, it is pronounced as long *e* or long *i*, depending on the length of the word. In one-syllable words such as *by* and *try,* the *y* is pronounced as long *i,* but in longer words such as *baby* and *happy,* the *y* is pronounced as long *e.*

When the letter *r* follows one or more vowels in a word, it influences the pronunciation of the vowel sound, as in *car, air, are, ear, bear, first, for, more, murder,* and *pure.* Vowel sounds are more complicated than consonant sounds, and there are additional vowel combinations representing other sounds. These vowel combinations often represent more than one sound and are used in only a few words:

> *au* as in *laugh* and *caught*
>
> *aw* as in *saw*
>
> *ew* as in *sew* and *few*
>
> *oi* as in *oil*
>
> *oo* as in *cook* and *moon*
>
> *ou* as in *about* and *through*
>
> *ow* as in *now*
>
> *oy* as in *toy*

3. Rimes and rhymes. One-syllable words and syllables in longer words can be divided into two parts, the onset and the rime. The onset is the consonant sound, if any, that precedes the vowel, and the rime is the vowel and any consonant sounds that follow it. For example, in *show, sh* is the onset and *ow* is the rime, and in *ball, b* is the onset and *all* is the rime. For *at* and *up,* there is no onset; the entire word is the rime. Research has shown that children make more errors decoding and spelling final consonants than initial consonants and that they make more errors on vowels than on consonants (Treiman, 1985). These problem areas correspond to rimes, and educators now speculate that onsets and rimes could provide the key to unlocking phonemic awareness.

Children can focus their attention on a rime, such as *ay,* and create rhyming words, including *bay, day, lay, may, ray, say,* and *way.* These words can be read and spelled by analogy because the vowel sounds are consistent in rimes. Wylie and Durrell (1970) identified 37 rimes that can be used to produce nearly 500 words that primary-grade students read and write. These rimes and some common words using them are presented in the Teacher's Notebook on page 151.

4. Blending into words. Readers "blend" or combine the sounds in order to decode words. Even though children may identify the sounds in a word one by one, they must be able to blend them together into a word. For example, in order to read the short-vowel word *best,* children identify /b/, /ĕ/,

Teacher's Notebook

37 Rimes and Some Common Words Using Them

phonograms

-ack	black, pack, quack, stack
-ail	mail, nail, sail, tail
-ain	brain, chain, plain, rain
-ake	cake, shake, take, wake
-ale	male, sale, tale, whale
-ame	came, flame, game, name
-an	can, man, pan, than
-ank	bank, drank, sank, thank
-ap	cap, clap, map, slap
-ash	cash, dash, flash, trash
-at	bat, cat, rat, that
-ate	gate, hate, late, plate
-aw	claw, draw, jaw, saw
-ay	day, play, say, way
-eat	beat, heat, meat, wheat
-ell	bell, sell, shell, well
-est	best, chest, nest, west
-ice	ice, mice, nice, rice
-ick	brick, pick, sick, thick
-ide	bride, hide, ride, side
-ight	bright, fight, light, might
-ill	fill, hill, kill, will
-in	chin, grin, pin, win
-ine	fine, line, mine, nine
-ing	king, sing, thing, wing
-ink	pink, sink, think, wink
-ip	drip, hip, lip, ship
-ir	fir, sir, stir
-ock	block, clock, knock, sock
-oke	choke, joke, poke, woke
-op	chop, drop, hop, shop
-ore	chore, more, shore, store
-or	for, or
-uck	duck, luck, suck, truck
-ug	bug, drug, hug, rug
-ump	bump, dump, hump, lump
-unk	bunk, dunk, junk, sunk

/s/, and /t/ and then combine them to form the word. For long-vowel words, children must identify the vowel pattern as well as the surrounding letters. In *lake*, for example, children identify /l/, /ā/, and /k/ and recognize that the *e* at the end of the word is silent and marks the preceding vowel as long. Shefelbine (1995) emphasized the importance of blending, and suggested that students who have difficulty decoding words usually know the sound-symbol correspondences but they cannot blend the sounds together into recognizable words. The ability to blend sounds together into words is part of phonemic awareness, and students have not had practice blending speech sounds into words are likely to have trouble blending sounds into words in order to identify unfamiliar written words.

5. Phonics generalizations.   Because English does not have a one-to-one correspondence between sounds and letters, both linguists and educators have tried to create rules or generalizations to clarify English spelling patterns. One rule is that *q* is followed by *u* and pronounced /kw/ (e.g., *queen, quick,* and *earthquake*). There are very few, if any, exceptions to this rule. Another generalization that has few exceptions relates to *r*-controlled vowels: *r* influences the preceding vowel so that the sound that is neither long nor short (e.g., *car, market, birth,* and *four*). There are exceptions, however, and one example is *fire*.

Many generalizations aren't very useful because there are more exceptions to the rule than words that conform (Clymer, 1996). A good example is this long-vowel rule: When there are two vowels side by side, the long-vowel sound of the first one is pronounced and the second is silent. Teachers sometimes call this the "when two vowels go walking, the first one does the talking" rule. Examples of words conforming to this rule are *meat, soap,* and *each.* There are many more exceptions, however, including *food, said, head, chief, bread, look, soup, does, too, again,* and *believe.*

Only a few phonics generalizations have a high degree of utility for readers. The generalizations that work most of the time are the ones that students should learn, because they are the most useful (Adams, 1990). Eight high-utility generalizations are listed in the Teacher's Notebook on page 153. Even though these rules are fairly reliable, very few of them approach 100% utility. The *r*-controlled vowel rule mentioned above has been calculated to be useful in 78% of words in which the letter *r* follows the vowel (Adams, 1990). Other commonly taught, useful rules have even lower percentages of utility. The CVC pattern rule—which says that when a one-syllable word has only one vowel and the vowel comes between two consonants, it is usually short, as in *bat, land,* and *cup*—is estimated to work 62% of the time. Exceptions include *told, fall, fork,* and *birth.* The CVCe pattern rule—which says when there are two vowels in a one-syllable word and one vowel is an *e* at the end of the word, the first vowel is long and the final *e* is silent—is estimated to work in 63% of CVCe words. Examples of conforming words are *came, hole,* and *pipe,* and two very common exceptions are *have* and *love.*

Students learn phonics as a natural part of reading and writing activities, and teachers also teach minilessons about phonics directly and systematically as part of literature focus units and reading workshop. Teachers often explain phonics concepts as they engage children in authentic liter-

Teacher's Notebook
The Most Useful Phonics Generalizations

Pattern	Description	Examples	
1. Two sounds of *c*	The letter *c* can be pronounced as /k/ or /s/. When *c* is followed by *a, o,* or *u,* it is pronounced /k/—the hard *c* sound. When *c* is followed by *e, i,* or *y,* it is pronounced /s/—the soft *c* sound.	cat cough cut	cent city cycle
2. Two sounds of *g*	The sound associated with the letter *g* depends on the letter following it. When *g* is followed by *a, o,* or *u,* it is pronounced as /g/—the hard *g* sound. When *g* is followed by *e, i,* or *y,* it is usually pronounced /j/—the soft *g* sound. Exceptions include *get* and *give.*	gate go guess	gentle giant gypsy
3. CVC pattern	When a one-syllable word has only one vowel and the vowel comes between two consonants, it is usually short. One exception is *told.*	bat cup land	
4. Final *e* or CVCe pattern	When there are two vowels in a one-syllable word and one of them is an *e* at the end of the word, the first vowel is long and the final *e* is silent. Two exceptions are *have* and *love.*	home safe cute	
5. CV pattern	When a vowel follows a consonant in a one-syllable word, the vowel is long. Exceptions include *the, to,* and *do.*	go be	
6. *R*-controlled vowels	Vowels that are followed by the letter *r* are overpowered and are neither short nor long. One exception is *fire.*	car for birthday	
7. *-igh*	When *gh* follows *i,* the *i* is long and the *gh* is silent. One exception is *neighbor.*	high night	
8. *Kn-* and *wr-*	In words beginning with *kn-* and *wr-,* the first letter is not pronounced.	knee write	

Adapted from Clymer, 1996.

acy activities using children's names, titles of books, and environmental print in the classroom. During these teachable moments, teachers answer students' questions about words, model using phonics knowledge to decode and spell words, and have students share the strategies they use for reading and writing (Mills, O'Keefe, & Stephens, 1992). For example, as part of a literature focus unit on *The Very Hungry Caterpillar* (Carle, 1969), teachers might point out that *Very* begins with *v* but that not many words start with *v*. Children might mention other *v* words, such as *valentine*. Teachers also demonstrate how to apply phonics information as they read big books with the class and do interactive writing. As they read and spell words, teachers break words apart into sounds and apply phonics rules and generalizations.

Teachers also present short lessons on specific high-utility phonics concepts, skills, and generalizations as part of a systematic program. According to Shefelbine, the program should be "systematic and thorough enough to enable most students to become independent and fluent readers; yet still efficient and streamlined" (1995, p. 2). Phonics instruction is always tied to reading and writing because without meaningful reading and writing activities, children see little reason to learn phonics (Freppon & Dahl, 1991).

YOUNG CHILDREN EMERGE INTO READING

Children move through three stages as they learn to read: emergent reading, beginning reading, and fluent reading (Juel, 1991). In emergent reading, also known as the selective-cue stage, children gain an understanding of the communicative purpose of print. They notice environmental print, dictate stories for the teacher to record, and reread predictable books after they have memorized the pattern. From this foundation, children move into the beginning reading stage, also known as the spelling-sound stage. In this stage, children learn phoneme-grapheme correspondences and begin to decode words. In the third stage, children have learned how to read. They recognize most words automatically and can decode unfamiliar words quickly. They are fluent readers and concentrate their cognitive energy on comprehension.

Primary-grade teachers organize language arts instruction into literature focus units and reading and writing workshop—the same two instructional approaches that teachers of middle- and upper-grade students use—but they make special adaptations to accommodate young children's developing literacy abilities. Even though they cannot read independently and write conventionally, kindergartners, first graders, and second graders need to listen to books read aloud and read them aloud with classmates through shared reading and other approaches.

Besides literature focus units, children need opportunities to read some books themselves—independently. Young children often begin by reading books with predictable refrains and repetition of events and then move on to easy-to-read books to practice decoding and to develop reading fluency. Through a multifaceted language arts program of literature, daily reading and writing experiences, and instruction in phonics, skills, and strategies, young children develop into fluent readers and writers.

Adapting Literature Focus Units for Emergent Readers

Kindergarten, first-grade, and second-grade teachers plan and teach literature focus units using quality books of children's literature, including *Officer Buckle and Gloria* (Rathmann, 1995), *Pigs Will Be Pigs* (Axelrod, 1994), and *If You Give a Mouse a Cookie* (Numeroff, 1985). Teachers use the same five-stage reading process for teaching literature focus units in kindergarten and the primary grades, even though they adapt the stages to make them developmentally appropriate for young children. Teachers involve students in hands-on activities, use shared reading and other teaching strategies, and include minilessons on phonics. Figure 4–3 presents an outline for a literature focus unit on Laura Numeroff's *If You Give a Mouse a Cookie.*

■ *To review the five-stage reading process, see Chapter 3, "The Reading and Writing Processes," pp. 90–105.*

Shared Reading.   In shared reading, teachers read a book aloud as children follow along in individual books or look at an enlarged version of a picture book, called a big book. Teachers use this approach to share with students the enjoyment of high-quality literature when students cannot read the books independently (Holdaway, 1979). Through shared reading, teachers also demonstrate how print works, provide opportunities for students to use the prediction strategy, and increase children's confidence in their ability to read. Shared reading is often used with emergent readers. However, teachers also use shared reading with older students who cannot read the shared book independently. The steps in shared reading are:

Step by Step

1. *Introduce the book.*   Teachers introduce the book by activating children's prior knowledge about the topic or by presenting new information on a topic related to the book, and then by showing the cover of the book and reading the title and author. Then children make predictions about the book. The purpose of these introductory activities is to involve children in the reading activity and to build their anticipation.

2. *Read the book.*   The teacher reads the book aloud while children follow along in individual copies of the book or on a big book positioned on a chart rack beside the teacher. The teacher models fluent reading and uses a dramatic style to keep the children's attention. Teachers encourage children to chime in on words they can predict and for phrases, sentences, and refrains that are repeated. Periodically, teachers stop to ask students to make predictions about the story or to redirect their attention to the text.

3. *Respond to the book.*   Children respond to the book by drawing and writing in reading logs and by sharing their responses in a grand conversation. Whenever children read books, enjoyment is the first and foremost goal. Afterwards, they use the book to learn more about written language.

4. *Reread the book.*   Children and the teacher read the book again together in a group, and children reread the book independently or with partners. Children need to read the book several times in order to become comfortable with the text. They may also reread the book at the listening center.

5. *Teach minilessons.*   Teachers use the book as the basis for minilessons to explore letters, words, and sentences in the text. Minilessons may also focus on

1. **Preparing**

   - The teacher brings in several types of cookies for children to sample. Students talk about their favorite cookies, and they create a graph and chart their favorite cookies.
   - The teacher introduces the book using a big book version of the story.
   - The teacher shares a book box of objects mentioned in the story (cookie, glass of milk, straw, napkin, mirror, scissors, broom, etc.), and children talk about how some of the items might be used in the story.
   - Students and the teacher begin the word wall with *cookie* and *mouse.*

2. **Reading**

   - The teacher reads the big book version of *If You Give a Mouse a Cookie* using shared reading.
   - The teacher rereads the book, and students join in reading and use echo reading to repeat each sentence after the teacher reads it.

3. **Responding**

   - The students and teacher participate in a grand conversation about the book.
   - Students dramatize the story using objects in the book box.
   - Students draw pictures in reading logs and add words (using invented spelling) to record their reactions to the book.

4. **Exploring**

   - Students and teacher add interesting and important words to the word wall.
   - Students buddy-read small-size versions of the book with partners and reread the book independently.
   - The teacher teaches minilessons on the /m/ sound or other phonemic awareness or phonics concepts.
   - The teacher explains the concept of a circle story, and students sequence picture cards of the events in the story to make a circle diagram.
   - The teacher presents a minilesson about the author, Laura Numeroff, and reads other books by the author.
   - Students make word posters of words on the word wall.
   - The teacher teaches a minilesson on irregular plurals (e.g., *mouse–mice, child–children*).
   - The teacher sets up centers for students to sort objects related to the phonics lesson, listen to *If You Give a Moose a Muffin* (Numeroff, 1991), write books about cookies, and use cards to sequence story events.

5. **Extending**

   - Students write their own versions of the story or original circle stories.
   - Students create other projects.
   - Students share their complete projects from the author's chair.

Circle
stories

156

rhyme, word-identification strategies, and reading procedures, strategies, and skills.

6. **Create projects.** Students extend their understanding of the book through other reading activities and through talk, drama, and writing projects.

Predictable Books. The stories and other books that teachers use for shared reading with young children often have repeated words and sentences, rhyme, or other patterns. Books that use these patterns are known as predictable books. They are a valuable tool for emergent readers because the repeated words and sentences, patterns, and sequence enable children to predict the next sentence or episode in the story or other book (Heald-Taylor, 1987; Tompkins & Webeler, 1983). Four characteristics of predictable books are:

1. *Repetition.* In some books, phrases and sentences are repeated over and over. Examples include *I Went Walking* (Williams, 1989), *Barnyard Banter* (Fleming, 1994), and *Polar Bear, Polar Bear, What Do You Hear?* (Martin, 1992). Sometimes each episode or section of the text ends with the same words or a refrain, and in other books the same statement or question is repeated. For example, in *The Little Red Hen* (Galdone, 1973), the animals repeat "Not I" when the Little Red Hen asks them to help her plant the seeds, harvest the wheat, and bake the bread. After their refusals to help, the hen each time says, "Then I will."

2. *Cumulative sequence.* In some books, phrases or sentences are repeated and expanded in each episode. In *The Gingerbread Boy* (Galdone, 1975), for instance, the Gingerbread Boy repeats and expands his boast as he meets each character on his run away from the Little Old Man and the Little Old Woman. Other examples include *Jack's Garden* (Cole, 1995) and *Jump, Frog, Jump* (Kalan, 1995).

3. *Rhyme and rhythm.* Rhyme and rhythm are important devices in some books. The sentences have a strong beat, and rhyme is used at the end of each line or in another poetic scheme. Also, some books have an internal rhyme within lines rather than at the end of lines. Books in this category include Dr. Seuss's *Hop on Pop* (1963), *Skip to My Lou* (Westcott, 1989), and *Sailaway Home* (Degen, 1996).

4. *Sequential patterns.* Some books use a familiar sequence—such as months of the year, days of the week, numbers 1 to 10, or letters of the alphabet—to structure the text. For example, *The Very Hungry Caterpillar* (Carle, 1969) combines number and day-of-the-week sequences as the caterpillar eats through an amazing array of foods. Laura Numeroff's *If You Give a Mouse a Cookie* (1985) and *If You Give a Moose a Muffin* (1991) are two other examples.

A list of predictable books illustrating each of these patterns is presented in Figure 4–4.

Big Books. Teachers use enlarged picture books called big books in shared reading, most commonly with primary-grade students. In this technique, developed in New Zealand, teachers use an enlarged picture book placed on

Figure 4–4   *Books With Predictable Patterns*

Repetitive Sentences

Bennett, J. (1985). *Teeny tiny*. New York: Putnam.

Carle, E. (1973). *Have you seen my cat?* New York: Philomel.

Carle, E. (1984). *The very busy spider*. New York: Philomel.

Carle, E. (1990). *The very quiet cricket*. New York: Philomel.

Carle, E. (1995). *The very lonely firefly*. New York: Philomel.

Cauley, L. B. (1982). *The cock, the mouse, and the little red hen*. New York: Putnam.

Cohen, C. L. (1996). *Where's the fly?* New York: Greenwillow.

Fleming, D. (1994). *Barnyard banter*. New York: Henry Holt.

Galdone, P. (1973). *The little red hen*. New York: Seabury.

Guarino, D. (1989). *Is your mama a llama?* New York: Scholastic.

Hill, E. (1980). *Where's Spot?* New York: Putnam.

Hutchins, P. (1972). *Good-night, owl!* New York: Macmillan.

Hutchins, P. (1986). *The doorbell rang*. New York: Morrow.

Kovalski, M. (1987). *The wheels on the bus*. Boston: Little, Brown.

Lyon, G. E. (1989). *Together*. New York: Orchard.

Martin, B., Jr. (1983). *Brown bear, brown bear, what do you see?* New York: Holt, Rinehart & Winston.

Martin, B., Jr. (1992). *Polar bear, polar bear, what do you hear?* New York: Holt, Rinehart & Winston.

Peek, M. (1981). *Roll over!* Boston: Houghton Mifflin.

Peek, M. (1985). *Mary wore her red dress*. New York: Clarion.

Rosen, M. (1989). *We're going on a bear hunt*. New York: Macmillan.

Souhami, J. (1996). *Old MacDonald*. New York: Orchard.

Viorst, J. (1972). *Alexander and the terrible, horrible, no good, very bad day*. New York: Atheneum.

Weiss, N. (1987). *If you're happy and you know it*. New York: Greenwillow.

Weiss, N. (1989). *Where does the brown bear go?* New York: Viking.

Westcott, N. B. (1988). *The lady with the alligator purse*. Boston: Little, Brown.

Williams, S. (1989). *I went walking*. San Diego: Harcourt Brace Jovanovich.

Repetitive Sentences in a Cumulative Structure

Bolton, F. (1986). *The greedy goat*. New York: Scholastic.

Brett, J. (1989). *The mitten*. New York: Putnam.

Cole, H. (1995). *Jack's garden*. New York: Greenwillow.

Fox, H. (1986). *Hattie and the fox*. New York: Bradbury.

Galdone, P. (1975). *The gingerbread boy*. New York: Seabury.

Kalan, R. (1995). *Jump, frog, jump!* New York: Greenwillow.

Thomas, S. M. (1995). *Putting the world to sleep*. Boston: Houghton Mifflin.

West, C. (1996). *"I don't care!" said the bear*. Cambridge, MA: Candlewick.

Westcott, N. B. (1980). *I know an old lady who swallowed a fly*. Boston: Little, Brown.

Westcott, N. B. (1990). *There's a hole in the bucket*. New York: HarperCollins.

Zemach, M. (1983). *The little red hen*. New York: Farrar, Straus & Giroux.

Rhyme and Rhythm

Brown, M. (1987). *Play rhymes*. New York: Dutton.

de Paola, T. (1985). *Hey diddle diddle and other Mother Goose rhymes*. New York: Putnam.

Sendak, M. (1962). *Chicken soup with rice*. New York: Harper & Row.

Seuss, Dr. (1963). *Hop on Pop*. New York: Random House.

Seuss, Dr. (1988). *Green eggs and ham*. New York: Random House.

Westcott, N. B. (1989). *Skip to my Lou*. Boston: Little, Brown.

Sequential Patterns

Carle, E. (1969). *The very hungry caterpillar*. Cleveland: Collins-World.

Carle, E. (1987). *A house for a hermit crab*. Saxonville, MA: Picture Book Studio.

Galdone, P. (1986). *Over in the meadow*. New York: Simon & Schuster.

Keats, E. J. (1973). *Over in the meadow*. New York: Scholastic.

Mack, S. (1974). *10 bears in my bed*. New York: Pantheon.

Martin, B., Jr. (1970). *Monday, Monday, I like Monday*. New York: Holt, Rinehart & Winston.

Numeroff, L. J. (1985). *If you give a mouse a cookie*. New York: HarperCollins.

Numeroff, L. J. (1991). *If you give a moose a muffin*. New York: HarperCollins.

Sendak, M. (1975). *Seven little monsters*. New York: Harper & Row.

Wood, A. (1984). *The napping house*. San Diego: Harcourt Brace Jovanovich.

an easel or chart rack where all children can see it; the teacher reads the big book with small groups of children or with the whole class (Holdaway, 1979). Trachtenburg and Ferruggia (1989) used big books with their class of transitional first graders and found that making and reading big books dramatically improved children's reading scores on standardized achievement tests. The teachers reported that children's self-concepts as readers were decidedly improved as well.

Many popular picture books, including *Tar Beach* (Ringgold, 1991), *How Much Is a Million?* (Schwartz, 1994), *Wilfred Gordon McDonald Partridge* (Fox, 1988), *The Mitten* (Brett, 1989), *Rosie's Walk* (Hutchins, 1987), and *Eating the Alphabet: Fruits and Vegetables From A to Z* (Ehlert, 1994), are available in big book editions. Teachers can also make big books themselves by printing the text of a picture book on large sheets of posterboard and adding illustrations. The steps in making a big book are shown in Figure 4–5.

Almost any type of picture book can be turned into a big book, but predictable books, nursery rhymes, songs, and poems are most popular. Heald-Taylor (1987) lists these types of big books that teachers can make:

- Replica book—an exact copy of a picture book
- Newly illustrated book—a familiar book with new illustrations
- Adapted book—a new version of a familiar picture book
- Original book—an original book composed by students or the teacher

With the big book on a chart stand or an easel, the teacher reads it aloud, pointing to every word. Before long, students join in the reading. Then the teacher rereads the book, inviting students to help with the reading. The next

First graders make a class big book to retell the story of Corduroy.

Figure 4–5   Steps in Constructing a Big Book

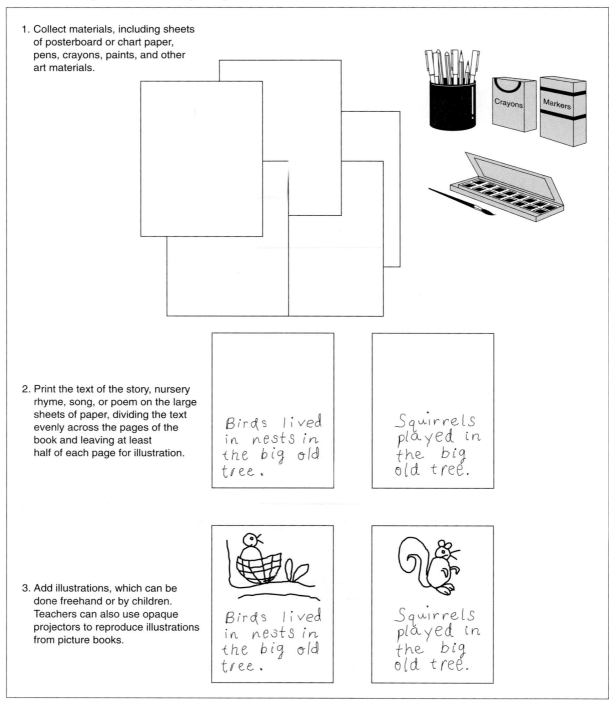

1. Collect materials, including sheets of posterboard or chart paper, pens, crayons, paints, and other art materials.

2. Print the text of the story, nursery rhyme, song, or poem on the large sheets of paper, dividing the text evenly across the pages of the book and leaving at least half of each page for illustration.

Birds lived in nests in the big old tree.

Squirrels played in the big old tree.

3. Add illustrations, which can be done freehand or by children. Teachers can also use opaque projectors to reproduce illustrations from picture books.

Birds lived in nests in the big old tree.

Squirrels played in the big old tree.

Figure 4–5   *continued*

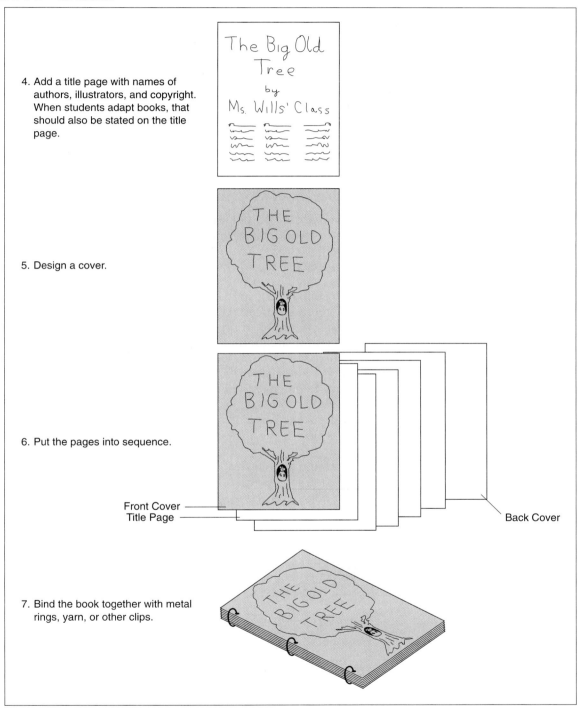

4. Add a title page with names of authors, illustrators, and copyright. When students adapt books, that should also be stated on the title page.

5. Design a cover.

6. Put the pages into sequence.

Front Cover
Title Page

Back Cover

7. Bind the book together with metal rings, yarn, or other clips.

time the book is read, the teacher reads to the point that the text becomes predictable, such as the last word of a sentence or the beginning of a refrain, and the students supply the missing text. Having students supply missing text is important because it leads to independent reading. Once students have become familiar with the text, they read the big book independently.

Students can also make big books of favorite stories. First, students choose a familiar story and write or dictate a retelling of it. Next they divide the text page by page and prepare illustrations. They write the text on large sheets of posterboard and add the illustrations. They make the title page and cover, and then they compile the pages. Teachers can use the book with young children just as they would use commercially produced big books and big books they made themselves.

Adapting Reading Workshop for Emergent Readers

Even emergent readers can participate in reading workshop. Like all students, young children need opportunities to look at books, reread favorite stories, and explore new texts. Young children read and reread many predictable books and read easy-to-read books with decodable words and familiar sight words, such as *Commander Toad in Space* (Yolen, 1980), *Mine's the Best* (Bonsall, 1996), and *The Josefina Story Quilt* (Coerr, 1986). As they read and reread books, children gain valuable experience with books, develop concepts about print, and practice decoding words. Providing daily opportunities for children to practice reading and rereading books they have chosen themselves is an essential part of literacy development.

Kindergartners and other children who are not yet reading can "look" at books, too. Teachers begin by demonstrating how to look at both familiar and unfamiliar books. For familiar books, teachers demonstrate how to think about the book, and perhaps how to remember the title, characters, or plot. Then teachers model how to turn the pages and think aloud about the story, re-creating it in their minds. For unfamiliar books, teachers show children how to carefully examine the illustrations and create a probable text for the books. Without this training, young children often flip through a book without looking at each page and developing an appreciation for the book.

Reading workshop is often used in conjunction with literature focus units, but some first- and second-grade teachers alternate the two. Once children are able to read and reread predictable texts and decode some words in order to read easy-to-read books, they can use reading workshop. First and second graders can read independently for 20 to 30 minutes and participate in minilessons and sharing, as older students do.

Other Teaching Strategies

Two other teaching strategies that teachers use with young children are assisted reading and the language experience approach. These teaching strategies are more personal, based on children's own experience and language, and they more closely approximate the literacy activities that go on at home. They are both useful for older nonreaders, too.

Assisted Reading.   Assisted reading extends the familiar routine of parents reading to their children (Hoskisson, 1975a, 1975b). In this approach, a child and a teacher (or another fluent reader) sit together to read a book. As the teacher reads aloud, the child listens and looks at the illustrations in the book. Gradually the child assumes more and more of the reading until the child is doing most of the reading and the teacher fills in the difficult words. The three stages in assisted reading are:

1. *Reading to children.* Teachers read to children and have them repeat each phrase or sentence. At first most children's attention will not be on the lines of print as they repeat the words. They may be looking around the room or at the pictures in the book. To direct their attention to the lines of print, the teacher points to the words on each line as they are read. This allows children to see that lines of print are read from left to right, not randomly. Many different books are read and reread during this stage. Rereading is important because the visual images of the words must be seen and read many times to ensure their recognition in other books. Later, one repetition of a word may be sufficient for subsequent recognition of the word in context.

2. *Shared reading.* When children begin to notice that some words occur repeatedly from book to book, they enter the second stage of assisted reading. In this stage the teacher reads and children repeat or echo the words; however, the teacher does not read the words the children seem to recognize. The teacher omits those words, and children fill them in. The fluency, or flow, of the reading should not be interrupted. If fluency is not maintained during this stage, children will not grasp the meaning of the passage, because the syntactic and semantic cues that come from a smooth flow of language will not be evident to them.

3. *Becoming independent readers.* The transition to the third stage occurs when children begin to ask the teacher to let them read the words themselves. Stage three may be initiated in this manner by the child, or it may be introduced by the teacher. When children know enough words to do the initial reading themselves, they read and the teacher willingly supplies any unknown words. It is important to assist children so that the fluency of the reading is not disrupted. In this stage, children do the major portion of the reading, but they tire more easily because they are struggling to use all the information they have acquired about written language. Children at this stage need constant encouragement; they must not feel a sense of frustration, because moving to independent reading is a gradual process.

Figure 4–6 presents a list of easy-to-read books that are written at approximately the second-grade level. These books include humorous stories such as *Amelia Bedelia* (Parish, 1963), *Buffalo Bill and the Pony Express* (Coerr, 1995) and other historical stories, and informational books such as *It Could Still Be Water* (Fowler, 1992). These books are a transition between picture books and chapter books, and they have more text on each page, even though they are sized more like a chapter book than a picture book and most pages include a picture. Young children who are developing confidence as readers enjoy reading these books, as do older students who are less successful readers.

Teachers use assisted reading whenever they read with individual children during reading workshop and literature focus units. They sense the child's familiarity with the book and his or her comfort level, and then they support

Figure 4–6   Easy-to-Read Books

Stories

Benchley, N. (1979). *Running owl the hunter.* New York: Harper & Row.

Blume, J. (1971). *Freckle juice.* New York: Dell.

Blume, J. (1981). *The one in the middle is the green kangaroo.* New York: Dell.

Brown, M. (1984). *There's no place like home.* New York: Parents Magazine Press.

Calmenson, S. (1994). *Merigold and Grandma on the town.* New York: HarperCollins.

Delton, J. (1992). *Lights, action, land-ho!* New York: Dell. (And other books in the series)

Eastman, P. D. (1960). *Are you my mother?* New York: Random House.

Giff, P. R. (1984). *The beast in Ms. Rooney's room.* NY: Dell. (And other books by this author)

Krensky, S. (1994). *Lionel in the winter.* New York: Dial.

Lewison, W. C. (1992). *"Buzz," said the bee.* New York: Scholastic.

Lobel, A. (1970). *Frog and Toad are friends.* New York: Harper & Row. (And other books in the Frog and Toad series)

Marzollo, J., & Marzollo, C. (1987). *Jed and the space bandits.* New York: Dial.

Parish, P. (1963). *Amelia Bedelia.* New York: Harper & Row. (And other books in the series)

Pomerantz, C. (1993). *The ouside dog.* New York: HarperCollins.

Rylant, C. (1995). *Mr. Putter and Tabby pick the pears.* Orlando, FL: Harcourt Brace. (And other books by this author)

Schwartz, A. (1982). *There is a carrot in my ear and other noodle tales.* New York: Harper & Row.

Schwartz, A. (1984). *In a dark, dark room.* New York: Scholastic.

Sharmat, M. W. (1995). *Nate the Great and the tardy tortoise.* New York: Dell.

Smith, J. (1991). *But no elephants.* New York: Parents Magazine Press.

Van Leeuwen, J. (1995). *Oliver and Amanda and the big snow.* New York: Dial.

Yolen, J. (1980). *Commander Toad in space.* New York: Coward-McCann. (And other books in the Commander Toad series)

Ziefert, H. (1983). *Small potatoes club.* New York: Dell. (And other books in the series)

Poetry

Hopkins, L. B. (1984). *Surprises.* New York: Harper & Row.

Hopkins, L. B. (1995). *Blast off! Poems about space.* New York: HarperCollins.

Biographies

Adler, D. A. (1989). *A picture book of Abraham Lincoln.* New York: Holiday House. (And other biographies by the author)

Coerr, E. (1995). *Buffalo Bill and the Pony Express.* New York: HarperCollins.

Krensky, S. (1991). *Christopher Columbus.* New York: Random House.

History

Benchley, N. (1969). *Sam the minuteman.* New York: Harper & Row.

Benchley, N. (1977). *George the drummer boy.* New York: Harper & Row.

Brenner, B. (1978). *Wagon wheels.* New York: Harper & Row.

Byars, B. (1994). *The Golly sisters ride again.* New York: HarperCollins.

Coerr, E. (1988). *Chang's paper pony.* New York: Harper & Row.

Coerr, E. (1986). *The Josefina story quilt.* New York: Harper & Row.

Greeson, J. (1991). *An American army of two.* Minneapolis: Carolrhoda.

Monjo, F. N. (1970). *The drinking gourd.* New York: Harper & Row.

Roop, P., & Roop, C. (1985). *Keep the lights burning, Abbie.* Minneapolis: Carolrhoda.

Roop, P., & Roop, C. (1986). *Buttons for General Washington.* Minneapolis: Carolrhoda.

Schulz, W. A. (1991). *Wil and Ory.* Minneapolis: Carolrhoda.

Wetterer, M. K. (1990). *Kate Shelley and the midnight express.* Minneapolis: Carolrhoda.

Science

Brown, M. (1984). *There's no place like home.* New York: Parents Magazine Press.

Cole, J. (1986). *Hungry, hungry sharks.* Chicago: Random House.

Fowler, A. (1990). *It could still be a bird.* Chicago: Childrens Press. (And other books in the series)

Fowler, A. (1990). *It's a good thing there are insects.* Chicago: Childrens Press.

Parish, P. (1974). *Dinosaur time.* New York: Harper & Row.

Smith, M. (1991). *A snake mistake.* New York: HarperCollins.

Ziefert, H. (1991). *Bob and Shirley: A tale of two lobsters.* New York: HarperCollins.

the child by doing most of the reading or supplying only the words the child does not seem to know. Parents, aides, and cross-age reading buddies also need to understand the three stages of assisted reading and learn how to use assisted reading to support young children as they emerge into reading.

One way to use assisted reading in a kindergarten or first-grade classroom is with cross-age reading buddies. A class of upper-grade students can be paired with a class of primary-grade children, and the students become reading buddies. Older students read books aloud to younger children, and they also read with the children using assisted reading. The effectiveness of cross-age tutoring is supported by research, and teachers report that students' reading fluency increases and their attitudes toward school and learning become more positive (Caserta-Henry, 1996; Labbo & Teale, 1990; Morrice & Simmons, 1991).

Teachers arranging a buddy reading program decide when the students will get together, how long each session will last, and what the reading schedule will be. Primary-grade teachers explain the program to their students and talk about activities the buddies will be doing together. Primary-grade students may want to draw pictures in advance to give to their buddies. Upper-grade teachers teach a series of minilessons about how to work with young children, how to read aloud and encourage children to make predictions, how to use assisted reading, how to select books to appeal to younger children, and how to help them respond to books. Then older students choose books to read aloud and practice reading them until they can read the books fluently.

At the first meeting, the students pair off, get acquainted, and read together. They also talk about the books they have read and perhaps write in special reading logs. Buddies also may want to go to the library and choose the books they will read at the next session.

There are significant social benefits to cross-age tutoring programs. Children get acquainted with other children that they might otherwise not meet, and they learn how to work with older or younger children. As they talk about books they have read, they share personal experiences and interpretations. They also talk about reading strategies, how to choose books, and their favorite authors or illustration styles. Sometimes reading buddies write notes back and forth, or the two classrooms plan holiday celebrations together, and these activities strengthen the social connections between the children.

A second way to encourage more one-on-one reading is to involve parents in the literacy program by using traveling bags of books. Teachers collect text sets of three, four, or five books on various topics for children to take home and read with their parents (Reutzel & Fawson, 1990). For example, teachers might collect copies of *The Gingerbread Boy* (Galdone, 1975), *Flossie and the Fox* (McKissack, 1986), *Red Fox Dances* (Baron, 1996), and *Rosie's Walk* (Hutchins, 1968) for a traveling bag of fox stories. Then children and their parents read one or more of the books and draw or write a response to the books they have read in the reading log that accompanies the books in the traveling bag. Children keep the bag at home for several days and then return it to school so that another child can borrow it. Text sets for ten traveling bags are listed in Figure 4–7. Many of these text sets include combinations of stories, informational books, and poems. Teachers can also add small toys, stuffed animals, audiotapes of one of the books, or other related objects to the bags.

Check the PRO-File at the beginning of Chapter 9 to learn more about how to use traveling bags of books.

Figure 4–7 <u>Text Sets</u> *for Traveling Bags of Books*

Books About Airplanes

Barton, R. (1982). *Airport.* New York: Harper & Row.

Maynard, C. (1995). *Airplane.* New York: Dorling Kindersley.

McPhail, D. (1987). *First flight.* Boston: Little, Brown.

Ziegler, S. (1988). *A visit to the airport.* Chicago: Childrens Press.

Books About Dogs

Barracca, D., & Barracca, S. (1990). *The adventures of taxi dog.* New York: Dial.

Bridwell, N. (1963). *Clifford the big red dog.* New York: Greenwillow.

Cole, J. (1991). *My puppy is born.* New York: Morrow.

Reiser, L. (1992). *Any kind of dog.* New York: Greenwillow.

Books by Ezra Jack Keats

Keats, E. J. (1962). *The snowy day.* New York: Viking.

Keats, E. J. (1964). *Whistle for Willie.* New York: Viking.

Keats, E. J. (1967). *Peter's chair.* New York: Harper & Row.

Keats, E. J. (1969). *Goggles.* New York: Macmillan.

Keats, E. J. (1970). *Hi cat!* New York: Macmillan.

Books About Frogs and Toads

Lobel, A. (1970). *Frog and Toad are friends.* New York: Harper & Row.

Mayer, M. (1974). *Frog goes to dinner.* New York: Dial.

Pallotta, J. (1990). *The frog alphabet book: And other awesome amphibians.* Watertown, MA: Charlesbridge.

Watts, B. (1991). *Frog.* New York: Lodestar.

Yolen, J. (1980). *Commander Toad in space.* New York: Coward-McCann.

Books About Mice

Cauley, L. B. (1984). *The city mouse and the country mouse.* New York: Putnam.

Henkes, K. (1991). *Chrysanthemum.* New York: Greenwillow.

Lionni, L. (1969). *Alexander and the wind-up mouse.* New York: Pantheon.

Lobel, A. (1977). *Mouse soup.* New York: Harper & Row.

Numeroff, L. J. (1985). *If you give a mouse a cookie.* New York: Harper & Row.

Books About Numbers

Aker, S. (1990). *What comes in 2's, 3's, & 4's?* New York: Simon & Schuster.

Bang, M. (1983). *Ten, nine, eight.* New York: Greenwillow.

Giganti, P., Jr. (1992). *Each orange had 8 slices: A counting book.* New York: Greenwillow.

Tafuri, N. (1986). *Who's counting?* New York: Greenwillow.

Books About Plants

Bunting, E. (1994). *Flower garden.* San Diego: Harcourt Brace.

Ehlert, L. (1987). *Growing vegetable soup.* San Diego: Harcourt Brace Jovanovich.

Ford, M. (1995). *Sunflower.* New York: Greenwillow.

Lobel, A. (1990). *Alison's zinnia.* New York: Greenwillow.

Books About Rain

Branley, F. M. (1985). *Flash, crash, rumble, and roll.* New York: Harper & Row.

Polacco, P. (1990). *Thunder cake.* New York: Philomel.

Shulevitz, U. (1969). *Rain rain rivers.* New York: Farrar, Straus & Giroux.

Spier, P. (1982). *Rain.* New York: Doubleday.

Books About the Three Bears

Cauley, L. B. (1981). *Goldilocks and the three bears.* New York: Putnam.

Galdone, P. (1972). *The three bears.* New York: Clarion Books.

Tolhurst, M. (1990). *Somebody and the three Blairs.* New York: Orchard Books.

Turkle, B. (1976). *Deep in the forest.* New York: Dutton.

Books About Trucks

Crews, D. (1980). *Truck.* New York: Greenwillow.

Llewellyn, C. (1995). *Truck.* New York: Dorling Kindersley.

Rockwell, A. (1984). *Trucks.* New York: Dutton.

Rotner, S. (1995). *Wheels around.* Boston: Houghton Mifflin.

Siebert, D. (1984). *Truck song.* New York: Harper & Row.

Teachers often introduce traveling bags at a special parents' meeting or an open house get-together and explain how parents use assisted reading to read with their children. It is important that parents understand that their children may not be familiar with the books and that children are not expected to be able to read them independently. Teachers also talk about the responses children and parents write in the reading log and show sample entries from the previous year.

+ p. 172

Language Experience Approach. The language experience approach (LEA) is based on children's language and experiences (Ashton-Warner, 1965; Stauffer, 1970). In this approach, children dictate words and sentences about their experiences, and the teacher takes down the dictation for the children. The text they develop becomes the reading material. Because the language comes from the children themselves, and because the content is based on their experiences, they are usually able to read the text easily. Reading and writing are connected as students are actively involved in reading what they have written. The steps are:

end of 4th

Step by Step

1. ***Provide an experience.*** A meaningful experience is identified to serve as the stimulus for the writing. For group writing, it can be an experience shared in school, a book read aloud, a field trip, or some other experience—such as having a pet or playing in the snow—that all children are familiar with. For individual writing, the stimulus can be any experience that is important for the particular child.

2. ***Talk about the experience.*** Students and teacher discuss the experience prior to writing. The purpose of the talk is to generate words and review the experience so that the children's dictation will be more interesting and complete. Teachers often begin with an open-ended question, such as, "What are you going to write about?" As children talk about their experiences, they clarify and organize ideas, use more specific vocabulary, and extend their understanding.

3. ***Record the dictation.*** Teachers write down the child's dictation. Texts for individual children are written on sheets of writing paper or in small booklets, and group texts are written on chart paper. Teachers print neatly, spell words correctly, and preserve students' language as much as possible. It is a great temptation to change the child's language to the teacher's own, in either word choice or grammar, but editing should be kept to a minimum so that children do not get the impression that their language is inferior or inadequate.

   For individual texts, teachers continue to take the child's dictation and write until the child finishes or hesitates. If the child hesitates, the teacher rereads what has been written and encourages the child to continue. For group texts, children take turns dictating sentences, and after writing each sentence, the teacher rereads it.

   As children become familiar with dictating to the teacher, they learn to pace their dictation to the teacher's writing speed. At first, children dictate as they think of ideas, but with experience, they watch as the teacher writes and supply the text word by word.

4. **Read the text.**   After the text has been dictated, the teacher reads it aloud, pointing to each word. This reading reminds children of the content of the text and demonstrates how to read it aloud with appropriate intonation. Then children join in the reading. After reading group texts together, individual children can take turns rereading. Group texts can also be copied so that each child has a copy to read independently.

The language experience approach is an effective way to help children emerge into reading. Even students who have not been successful with other types of reading activities can read what they have dictated. There is a drawback, however: teachers provide a "perfect" model when they take children's dictation—they write neatly and spell all words correctly. After language experience activities, some young children are not eager to do their own writing, because they prefer their teacher's "perfect" writing to their own childlike writing. To avoid this problem, teachers have young children do their own writing in personal journals and other writing activities at the same time they are participating in language experience activities. In this way, children learn that sometimes they do their own writing and at other times the teacher takes their dictation.

YOUNG CHILDREN EMERGE INTO WRITING

Many young children become writers before entering kindergarten; others are introduced to writing during their first year of school (Harste et al., 1984b; Temple, Nathan, Burris, & Temple, 1988). Young children's writing development follows a pattern similar to their reading development: emergent writing, beginning writing, and fluent writing. In the first stage, emergent writing, children make scribbles to represent writing. At first the scribbles may appear randomly on a page, but with experience children line up the letters or scribbles from left to right and from top to bottom. Children also begin to "read," or tell what their writing says. The next stage is beginning writing, and it marks children's growing awareness of the alphabetic principle. Children use invented spelling to represent words, and as they learn more about phoneme-grapheme correspondences, their writing approximates conventional spelling. The third stage is fluent writing, when children use conventional spelling and other conventions of written language, including capital letters and punctuation marks.

Opportunities for writing begin on the first day of kindergarten and continue on a daily basis throughout the primary grades, regardless of whether children have already learned to read or write letters and words. Children often begin using a combination of art and scribbles or letterlike forms to express themselves. Their writing moves toward conventional forms as they apply concepts they are learning about written language.

Four samples of young children's writing are shown in Figure 4–8. The first sample is a kindergartner's letter to the Great Pumpkin. The child wrote using scribbles, much like cursive, and followed the left-to-right, top-to-bot-

Figure 4–8   Four Samples of Young Children's Writing

To: The Great Pumpkin
From: melissa

I ♥ U
ALL

No one
evur sae
a rel dinsur.

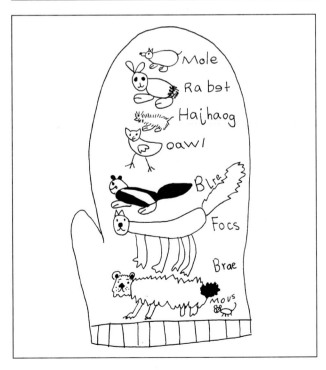

Mole
Rabət
Hajhaog
oawl
Blr
Focs
Brae
mous

oraNge
SdriBare
appie
pizza
Brfedaykа

tom orientation. The Great Pumpkin's comment, "I love you all," can be deciphered. The second sample is a page from a first grader's dinosaur book. The text reads, "No one ever saw a real dinosaur." The third sample is from a first grader's reading log. The child used invented spelling to list the animal characters that appear in *The Mitten* (Brett, 1989). The fifth animal from the top is a badger. The fourth sample is also a list. A kindergartner wrote this list of favorite foods as part of a literature focus unit on *The Very Hungry Caterpillar* (Carle, 1969). The list reads, "orange, strawberry, apple, pizza, birthday cake."

Introducing Young Children to Writing

Teachers help children emerge into writing as they show them how to use kid writing, model adult writing for children, teach minilessons about written language, and involve them in writing activities. It is important to contrast teachers' writing—adult writing—with the "kid" writing that children can do.

Kid Writing.   Kid writing takes many different forms. It can be scribbles or a collection of random marks on paper. Sometimes children are imitating adults' cursive writing as they scribble. Children can string together letters that have no phoneme-grapheme correspondences, or they can use one or two letters to represent entire words. Children with more experience with written language can invent spellings that represent more sound features of words, and they can apply spelling rules. A child's progressive spellings of "Abbie is my dog. I love her very much" over a period of eighteen months are presented in Figure 4–9. The child moves from using scribbles to single letters to represent words (top two entries), to spelling phonetically and misapplying a few spelling rules (third and fourth entries). Note that in the fourth example, the child is experimenting with using periods to mark spaces between words.

Kid writing is important for young children to understand because it gives them permission to experiment with written language when they draw and write. Too often children assume that they should write and spell like adults do, and they cannot. Without this ability, children do not want to write, or they ask teachers to spell every word or copy text out of books or from charts. Kid writing offers students several strategies for writing and gives them permission to invent spellings that reflect their knowledge of written language.

Young children's writing grows out of talking and drawing. As they begin to write, their writing is literally their talk written down, and children can usually express in writing the ideas they talk about. At the same time, children's letterlike marks develop from their drawing. With experience, children differentiate between drawing and writing. Some kindergarten teachers explain to children that they should use crayons when they draw and use pencils when they write. Teachers can also differentiate where on a page children write and draw. The writing might go at the top or bottom of a page, or children can use paper with space for drawing at the top and lines for writing at the bottom.

Reutzel + Cooter, Jr.

pp 68 - 78
Scribbing +
Drawing Stage

Prephonemic
Stage

Early Phonemic
Stage

Letter-Name
Stage

Transitional
Stage
(p. 481-482)

Figure 4–9   *A Five-Year-Old's Kid Writing*

Scribble Writing

One-Letter Labeling

A   DoᴏΘ

Invented Spelling Without Spacing

AZMIOOGİLRETS

More Sophisticated Invented Spelling With Spacing

ABe.iSMi. doG.I.(w hr. Vre ms.

Invented Spelling With Application of Rules

Abie is my dog. I love hur vrey mus.

Sign-In Sheets.   Teachers use sign-in sheets to provide opportunities for children to practice writing their names for genuine purposes. To take attendance, they can set out a piece of paper each day with writing instruments, and children write their names as they arrive in the classroom (Harste et al., 1984b). These sign-in sheets document children's learning to print their names and their understanding of concepts about written language.

Bobbi Fisher (1991), a kindergarten teacher, uses other sign-in procedures. She makes a T-chart with a question written at the top of the chart and two answer columns, and the children write their names in the answer columns in response to the question. For example, after she brought a green pumpkin to class, she wrote, "Will this pumpkin turn orange?" Students answered the question by writing their names in the Yes column or the No column.

Turn to Chapter 5, p. 193, and Chapter 7, p. 279, to see examples of T-charts.

Kindergartners learn about the alphabetic principle as they collect classmates' autographs at the writing center.

Teachers can develop other types of sign-in charts that ask students to make choices or offer opinions. For example, students can choose favorite books during an author study, or they can report information during a theme cycle on nutrition, such as what they eat for breakfast. Other first- and second-grade teachers have sign-up sheets for students to make books, work at a computer, or air a problem during a class meeting.

Interactive Writing.   Teachers use interactive writing to model adult or conventional writing (Button, Johnson, & Furgerson, 1996; Pinnell & McCarrier, 1994). In this teaching strategy, children and the teacher collaborate on constructing the text to be written. Teachers reinforce concepts about written language, provide opportunities to create texts, and focus students' attention on individual words and sounds within words. This teaching strategy grew out of the language experience approach, and conventional writing is used so that everyone can read the completed text.

Topics for interactive writing can come from stories the class has read, classroom news, and information learned during theme cycles. Children take turns holding the marking pen and doing the writing themselves. They usually sit in a circle on the carpet and write the text that they construct on chart paper that is displayed on an easel. While individual students take turns writing at the easel, other students are writing on small chalkboards or whiteboards in their laps. The steps are:

*Step
by
Step*

1. **Construct the text.** Children and the teacher choose the topic and brainstorm ideas for the text. Children suggest sentences to write, and the group reaches consensus on each sentence.

2. **Identify the words in the first sentence.** The teacher repeats the first sentence and asks students to identify or "count" the words in the sentence on their fingers as they repeat the sentence, articulating each word distinctly.

3. **Write the sentence.** Children take turns coming to the easel to write the letters (or words) in the sentence. Depending on the children's experience with writing, children either take turns writing each letter in a word or write entire words. The teacher and children "stretch" out each word and say the word slowly to notice beginning, middle, and ending sounds. As the sentence is written, teachers ask questions and provide information to focus children's attention on concepts about written language, phoneme-grapheme correspondences, spelling rules, and other conventions of print, depending on children's level of literacy development. Children and the teacher watch as children write letters and words, and the teacher helps children correct misformed letters, incorrect letters, inadequate spacing between words, forgotten punctuation marks, and other errors.

4. **Read the sentence.** After students write each sentence, the class reads what has been written and prepares to write the next sentence.

5. **Repeat steps.** Children and the teacher repeat steps 2, 3, and 4 for each sentence.

6. **Reread the completed text.** Children and the teacher reread the completed text, and individual children take turns reading sentences.

Interactive writing can be used for many types of writing projects, including lists, clusters and other diagrams, collaborative books, classroom newspapers, stories, and poems.

Minilessons About Reading and Writing. Teachers teach minilessons about written language concepts and other reading and writing topics to young children in kindergarten and the primary grades. Children learn about how reading and writing are used to convey messages and how children behave as readers and writers. A list of these topics is presented on page 174; these minilessons can be taught during reading workshop and literature focus units and through other activities.

Adapting Writing Workshop for Emergent Writers

■ *To review the five stages of the writing process, read Chapter 3, "The Reading and Writing Process," pp. 111–126.*

Young children gain valuable writing experience through writing workshop. Kindergartners and first graders often work at a writing center with the teacher or an aide, making books and working on other writing projects. For these emergent writers, teachers often abbreviate the revising and editing stages of the writing process. At first children's revising is limited to reading the text to themselves or to the teacher to check that they have written all that they want to say. Revising becomes more formal as children learn about

MINI LESSONS

Emergent Literacy

Procedures	Concepts	Strategies and Skills
Hold a book correctly	Purposes for reading	Locate familiar words and signs
Turn pages correctly	Purposes for writing	Sing ABC song to identify a letter
Separate words into onsets and rimes	Direction of print	Identify letter names
Behave like a reader	A word	Match upper- and lowercase letters
Point at words as they are read	Uppercase letters	Notice letters in words
Match each word as it is read aloud with the word on the page	Lowercase letters	Identify phoneme-grapheme correspondences
	Alphabetic principle	"Stretch" words
Do assisted reading	Rhyming words	Read environmental print
Do buddy reading	Repetition of words, phrases, and sentences	Look at words as text is read aloud
Do shared reading	Big books	Match printed words with words read aloud
Dictate language experience stories	Audience awareness	Make predictions
Do interactive writing	The author's chair	Notice repetition
Behave like a writer	Kid writing	Notice rhyme patterns
Write name on sign-in sheets	Adult spelling	Notice sequential patterns
Use writing in play activities	Invented spelling	Identify familiar words
Exchange messages with classmates		Use scribbles and random letters for writing
Share writing in the author's chair		Write own name
		Copy familiar words and environmental print
		Space between words
		Use capital letters to begin sentences
		Use punctuation marks to end sentences
		Use invented spelling
		Use sentence patterns for writing

audience and want to "add more" or "fix" their writing to make it appeal to their classmates. Some emergent writers ignore editing altogether, and as soon as they have dashed off their drafts they are ready to publish or share their writing. However, others change a spelling, fix a poorly written letter, or add a period to the end of the text as they read over their writings. When children begin writing, teachers accept their writing as it is written and focus on the message. As children gain experience with writing, teachers encourage them to "fix" one or two errors. Guidelines for adapting the writing process for emergent writers are presented in the Teacher's Notebook on page 175.

Teacher's Notebook
Guidelines for Using the Writing Process With Emergent Writers

Prewriting

Prewriting is as important to young children as it is to other writers. Children write about topics they know well and have the vocabulary to express ideas about. Topics include personal experiences, classroom activities, stories students have listened to read aloud or have read independently, and theme cycle topics. Children use drawing to gather and organize ideas before writing. Children often talk about the topic or dramatize it before beginning to write.

Drafting

Young children usually write single-draft compositions. They add words to accompany drawings they have already made. The emphasis is on expressing ideas, not on handwriting skills or conventional spelling. Often children write in small booklets of paper, and they write equally well on lined or unlined paper.

Revising

Teachers play down this stage until children have learned the importance of revising to meet the needs of their readers. At first children reread their writings to see that they have included everything they wanted to say, and they make very few changes. As they recognize the importance of audience, they begin to make changes to make their writing clearer and add more information to make their writing more complete.

Editing

Like revising, this stage is deemphasized until children have learned conventional spellings for some words and have gained control over rules for capitalizing words and adding punctuation marks. To introduce editing, teachers help children make one or two corrections by erasing the error and writing the correction in pencil on the child's writing. Teachers do not circle errors on a child's paper with a red pen. As children become more fluent writers, teachers help them make more corrections.

Publishing

Children read their writings to their classmates and share their drawings. Through sharing, children develop a concept of audience and learn new ways of writing from their classmates. Kindergartners and first graders usually do not recopy their writings, but sometimes the teacher or an assistant types the final copy, changing the child's writing into conventional form. When adults recopy children's writing, however, they send a strong message that the children's writing is inadequate, unless there is a good reason for converting the kid writing to adult writing.

PDREP

Writing Centers.   Writing centers can be set up in kindergarten classrooms so that children have a special place where they can go to write. The center should be located at a table with chairs, and a box of supplies—including pencils, crayons, a date stamp, different kinds of paper, journal notebooks, a stapler, blank books, notepaper, and envelopes—should be stored nearby. The alphabet, printed in upper- and lowercase letters, should be available on the table for children to refer to as they write. In addition, there should be a crate for children to file their work in. They can also share their completed writings by sending them to classmates or sharing them in the author's chair.

When children come to the writing center, they draw and write in journals, compile books, and write messages to classmates. Teachers should be available to encourage and assist children at the center. They can observe children as they invent spellings and can provide information about letters, words, and sentences as needed. If the teacher cannot be at the writing center, perhaps an aide, a parent volunteer, or an upper-grade student can assist.

The Author's Chair.   In primary-grade classrooms, a special chair should be designated as the author's chair (Graves & Hansen, 1983). This chair might be a rocking chair, a lawn chair with a padded seat, a wooden stool, or a director's chair, and it should be labeled "Author's Chair." Children and the teacher sit in the chair to share books they have read and other books they have written, and this is the only time anyone sits in the chair.

When teachers sit in the chair to read books aloud to children, they name the author of the book and tell a little something about the author, if they can. In this way, children gain an awareness of authors, the people who write books. Children also sit in the author's chair to share books and other compositions they have written. Sitting in the special author's chair helps children gradually realize that they are authors. Graves and Hansen describe children's growing awareness of authors and of themselves as authors in three phases:

1. *Authors write books.* After hearing many books read to them and reading books themselves, children develop the concept that authors are the people who write books.
2. *I am an author.* Sharing the books they have written with classmates from the author's chair helps children view themselves as authors.
3. *If I wrote this published book now, I wouldn't write it this way.* Children learn that they have options when they write, and this awareness grows after they have experimented with various writing functions, forms, and audiences. When children reach this phase, they are more receptive to the idea of revising.

When children share their writings, one child sits in the author's chair and a group of children sit on the floor or in chairs in front of the author's chair (Karelitz, 1993). The child sitting in the author's chair reads the book or other piece of writing aloud and shows the accompanying illustrations. Then children who want to make a comment raise their hands, and the author chooses several children to ask questions, give compliments, and make comments. Then the author chooses another child to share and takes a seat in the audience.

Review

Emergent literacy is the new perspective on how children learn to read and write. Young children learn concepts about written language as they experiment with reading and writing, and teachers demonstrate reading and writing through assisted reading, shared reading, interactive writing, and other teaching strategies. Children emerge into writing as they learn to use graphic symbols to represent their thoughts, and they refine their kid writing as they learn about phoneme-grapheme correspondences. The key concepts presented in this chapter are:

1. Emergent literacy, the concept that young children move into reading and writing through experiences with written language, has replaced the traditional "readiness" approach.
2. As children learn about words, they move from recognizing environmental print to reading decontextualized words in books.
3. Children use phonics as well as information from the other three language systems as they learn to read.
4. Both reading and writing development have three stages: emergent, beginning, and fluent.
5. Three ways to read books with young children are assisted reading, shared reading, and language experience.
6. Emergent readers read predictable books, big books, and easy-to-read books.
7. Children are introduced to writing as they watch their parents and teachers write and as they experiment with writing.
8. Children use kid writing to experiment with written language concepts and invented spelling.
9. Young children begin writing books and other compositions using an abbreviated form of the writing process that emphasizes prewriting, drafting, and publishing.
10. Young children learn about audience as they share their writing from the author's chair.

Extensions

1. Observe in a kindergarten or first-grade classroom to see how children are learning concepts about written language. Examine reading materials available in the classroom, including predictable books and big books, and opportunities for writing, such as sign-in sheets, dramatic play and writing centers, a message center, and an author's chair.
2. Establish and monitor a buddy reading program between a primary-grade class and an upper-grade class.
3. Collect books and other materials for two traveling bags of books, and share them with a group of first and second graders.
4. Plan a literature focus unit using a big book, and teach the unit in a kindergarten, first-grade, or second-grade classroom.
5. Construct a big book version of a predictable book, or compose a big book for a favorite story with a group of young children.
6. Create a dramatic play center that incorporates authentic reading and writing materials, and observe as children use the materials for a week or two.
7. Set up a writing center in a kindergarten classroom, and work with children for several weeks. Keep track of the types of writing that children engage in and note their growth as writers.

> **66** I don't teach vocabulary—at least not in the traditional way. Instead, my students are immersed in words through the books we read and the themes we are studying. I know it sounds corny, but my students learn words because they are living them. **99**

Carol Ochs
Fifth-Grade Teacher
Jackson Elementary School

PROCEDURE

Before I start a new literature focus unit, I read the books and highlight words that my students may need help with or that I might want to use in vocabulary lessons. This gets me ready to teach. Then I hang a long sheet of butcher paper in the classroom—often from the ceiling to the floor. I call it a "word wall." As we read, I point out some important words, my students spot others, and we write these words on the word wall. I usually ask students to write the words themselves because I want them to be involved in the activity. I also have them keep a reading log—a notebook with about 20 pages in it. They keep a list of words on one page in the log. Many of the words come from our word wall, but students also choose other words as they read.

Right now we're into a unit on children's author Chris Van Allsburg. In *The Garden of Abdul Gasazi* (1979), I highlighted these words: *sinking* (teeth into . . .), *bolted*, *shadowed*, *bruised*, *detest*, *blurted*, *awesome*, and *incredible*. I explain most of the words informally as we come to them, and we add them to our word wall. The one word that I've decided to teach more formally is *incredible*. To prepare, I look the word up in an unabridged dictionary, check its meaning and etymology, and make a list of related words. then I decide how to present the lesson. For *incredible*, I start with the words *credit* and *credit card* because they are familiar. Then I make a cluster with the root word *cred-* in the middle as shown in the accompanying figure. I draw out *credit, credit card*, and then add *incredible* from the story and a few other related words. My students are amazed because they don't see a relationship among the words until we start talking about them. Then a light comes on! For the students who need to be challenged, I add the words *credulity* and *credulous* and talk about their meanings.

ASSESSMENT

I want my students to "own" these words. I use the words when I talk to students and notice when they use the words. I do give tests to check their knowledge of some words, but, more importantly, I check to see if students apply the words in their writing. Sometimes I ask students to highlight vocabulary words in their reading log entries or in their reading log entries or in their stories and reports. That's when I know my students "own" the words.

ADAPTATIONS

I love using literature as the basis of my language arts program, but I feel an added responsibility to make the books we read accessible to my less able readers. I use a variety of strategies to ensure that every student in my classroom is successful. Five of my strategies are:

1. *Previewing the book.* Sometimes I preview the book with my less able readers the day before I introduce it to the class. I introduce the title of the book and allow these students to look through the book to get the gist of the story. If

the story is available on tape, I encourage these students to listen to it at the listening center. I also preteach any essential vocabulary, such as the names of the characters.

2. *Rereading the book.* I encourage my less able readers to reread the story with a buddy or at the listening center. This added practice allows these students to read more fluently and to better understand the story.

3. *Sequencing the book with story boards.* I prepare a set of story boards by cutting apart two extra copies of the book, backing each page with cardboard, and laminating them. Then I pass out the story boards, one to each student. We read the cards, sequence them, and examine the important vocabulary. I pass out little sticky-backed notes and ask students to choose one or two words from the word wall that relate to the

picture or text on a story board and write the word or words on the sticky-backed notes. Then students share their story boards and the word or words they have selected.

4. *Writing in reading logs.* During a vocabulary minilesson, I ask my less able readers to choose a word from the word wall and write it in their reading logs. Then they draw a picture of the word and use it in a sentence to describe their picture or in a question about their picture. As a change-of-pace activity, sometimes we write riddles about the words.

5. *Sorting words.* I divide a sheet of paper into 20–24 boxes and write a word in each box. Students cut the boxes apart, sort the words into categories, and glue them onto a large sheet of paper. The categories that students choose aren't so important, but through this activity, students read and talk about words.

REFLECTIONS

I don't have my students look up vocabulary words in the dictionary and copy the definitions into their reading logs. I tried it and it doesn't work. I have also tried having students use the words in sentences, and that doesn't work either. Instead, we use the words every day—several times a day—but we use them as we talk and write about the story and go beyond the story.

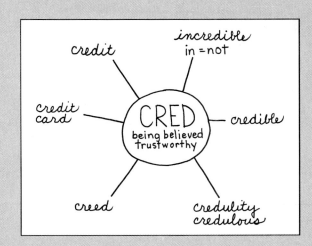

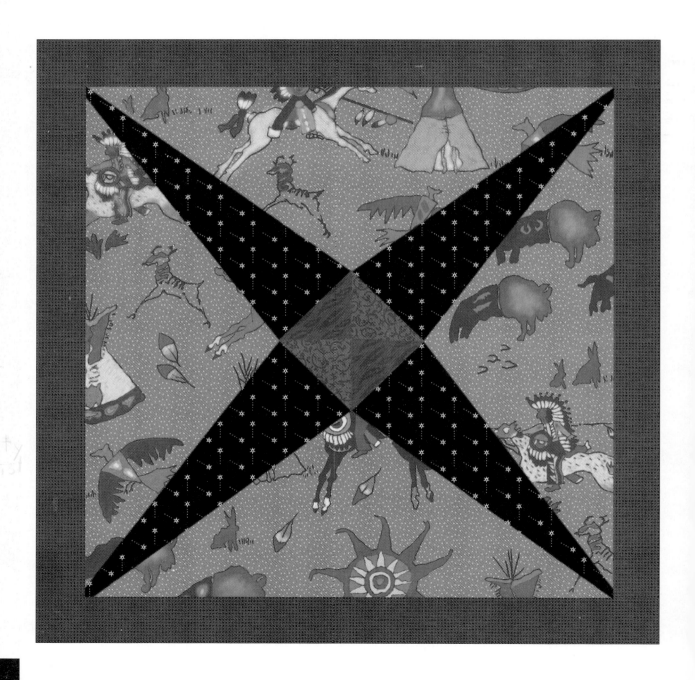

Looking Closely at Words

As the culminating project for a theme cycle on American Indians, one group of students in Eileen Boland's eighth-grade class made an alphabet quilt about Plains Indians. Students compiled a list of words related to Indians beginning with each letter of the alphabet and then chose one word beginning with each letter to illustrate on a quilt square. Students designed their squares on sheets of paper cut to the same size as the cloth quilt squares. Then they used a variety of pens to draw and color the cloth squares.

ark Twain said, "The difference between the right word and the almost right word is the difference between *lightning* and the *lightning bug.*" Learning about words and how to choose the right one to express the meaning you intend is what vocabulary is all about. Vocabulary is not decoding or word identification; rather, the focus is on meaning. Choosing the best word to express meaning is important to all language users. When we listen and read, we must understand the meaning that someone else intends, and when we talk and write, we must choose exactly the right word so that our audience will understand our message.

Words are the meaning-bearing units of language. Of the three-quarters of a million words in English, most people use only about 20,000, and most of the words we commonly use come from a body of approximately 5,000 to 7,000 words (Klein, 1988). Our personal ownership of words is quite limited. We have overlapping but separate listening, talking, reading, and writing vocabularies. Most of us may, for example, recognize a word such as *obfuscate* when listening or reading, but fewer of us would use the word in talking or writing. Our reading and listening vocabularies are more extensive than our talking and writing vocabularies, for many reasons. We may fear mispronouncing or misspelling a word, or we may fear what our friends will think if we use the word in conversation. The words we use mark us in a number of ways: by our word choice, by our pronunciation, and by the way we string the words together into sentences.

As you read this chapter, think about how students use their knowledge of words in reading and writing. Ask yourself these questions:

- How can teachers teach students about the development of the English language and word histories?
- What types of words do elementary students learn about?
- How do teachers focus on words during literature focus units and theme cycles?

HISTORY OF THE ENGLISH LANGUAGE*

Understanding the history of English and how words entered the language contributes greatly to understanding words and their meanings. English is a historic language, and this fact accounts for word meanings and some spelling inconsistencies. English has a variety of words for a single concept, and the history of English in general and the etymology of the words in particular explain apparent duplications. Consider these words related to *water: aquatic, hydrant, aquamarine, waterfall, hydroelectric, watercress, watery, aquarium, waterproof, hydraulic, aqualung,* and *hydrogen,* to name a few. These words have one of three root words that each mean water: *water* is English, of course, while *aqua* is Latin and *hydro* is Greek. The root word that is used depends on the people who created the word, the purpose of the word, and when the word entered English.

The development of the English language is divided into three periods: Old English, Middle English, and Modern English. The beginning and end of

etymology - history of a word

---

*This section is adapted from Tompkins & Yaden, 1986.

each period is marked by a significant event, such as an invasion or an invention.

Old English (A.D. 450–1100)

The recorded history of the English language begins in A.D. 449, when Germanic tribes, including the Angles and Saxons, invaded Britain. The invaders pushed the original inhabitants, the Celts, to the northern and western corners of the island. This annexation is romanticized in the King Arthur legends. Arthur is believed to have been a Celtic military leader who fought bravely against the German invaders.

The English language began as an intermingling of the dialects spoken by the Angles, Saxons, and other Germanic tribes in Britain. Many people assume that English is based on Latin, but it has Germanic roots and was brought to Britain by these invaders. Although 85% of Old English words are no longer used, many everyday words remain (e.g., *child, foot, hand, house, man, mother, old,* and *sun*). In contrast to Modern English, Old English had few loan words (words borrowed from other languages and incorporated into English) and had a highly developed inflectional system for indicating number, gender, and verb tense. The Anglo-Saxons added affixes to existing words, including *be-, for-, -ly, -dom,* and *-hood.* They also invented vividly descriptive compound words. The Old English word for *music,* for example, was "ear-sport," *world* was "age of man," and *folly* was "wanwit." The folk epic *Beowulf,* the great literary work of the period, illustrates the poetic use of words; for instance, the sea is described as a "whale-path" and a "swan's road."

Foreign words also made their way into the predominantly Germanic word stock. The borrowed words came from two main sources: Romans and Vikings. A number of words were borrowed from Latin and incorporated into English. Contact between the Roman soldiers and traders and the Germanic tribes on the Continent, before they had invaded England, contributed some words, including *cheese, copper, mile, street,* and *wine.* The missionaries who reintroduced Christianity to Britain in 597 also brought with them a number of religious words (e.g., *angel, candle, hymn*).

In 787, the Vikings from Denmark and other areas of Scandinavia began a series of raids against English villages, and for the next three centuries they attacked, conquered, and occupied much of England. Their influence was so great that the Danish king Canute ruled England during the first part of the 11th century. The Vikings' contributions to the English language were significant. They provided the pronouns *they, their, them;* introduced the /g/ and /k/ sounds (e.g., *get, kid*); contributed most of our *sk-* words (e.g., *skin, sky*) and some of our *sc-* words (e.g., *scalp, score*); and enriched our vocabulary with more than 500 everyday words, including *husband* and *window.*

In Old English some consonant combinations were pronounced that are not heard today, including the /k/ in words like *knee.* The letter *f* represented both /f/ and /v/, resulting in the Modern English spelling pattern of *wolf* and *wolves.* The pronunciation of the vowel sounds was very different, too; for example, the Old English *stan* (*a = a* in *father*) has become our word *stone.*

The structure, spelling, and pronunciation of Old English were significantly different from those of Modern English—so much so that we would not be able to read an Old English text or understand someone speaking Old English. It was a highly inflected language with many different word endings, and the arrangement of words in sentences was different, too, with verbs often placed at the end of sentences. In many ways, Old English was more like Modern German than Modern English.

Middle English (1100–1500)

An event occurred in 1066 that changed the course of the English language and ushered in the Middle English period: the Norman Conquest. In that year William the Conqueror crossed the English Channel from the French province of Normandy and defeated the English king, Harold, at the Battle of Hastings. William claimed the English throne and established a French court in London. This event had far-reaching consequences. For nearly 300 years French was the official language in England, spoken by the nobility and upper classes, although the lower classes continued to speak English. By 1300 the use of French had declined, and before the end of the 14th century English was restored as the official language. Chaucer's *Canterbury Tales,* written in the late 1300s, provides evidence that English was also replacing French as the preferred written language. Political, social, and economic changes contributed to this reversal.

The Middle English period was one of tremendous change. A large portion of the Old English vocabulary was lost as 10,000 French words were added to the language, reflecting the Norman impact on English life and society (Baugh & Cable, 1978). They included military words (e.g., *soldier, victory*), political words (e.g., *government, princess*), medical words (e.g., *physician, surgeon*), and words related to the arts (e.g., *comedy, music, poet*). Many of the new loan words duplicated Old English words. Typically, one word was eventually lost; if both words remained in the language, they developed slightly different meanings. Often it was the Old English word that disappeared. For example, the words *hardy* (Old English) and *cordial* (French) were originally synonyms, both meaning "from the heart." In time they differentiated and now express different meanings.

Most of the French loan words were derived from Latin. In addition, a few Latin words (e.g., *individual, polite*) passed directly into English during this period. In contrast to the French loan words, Latin borrowings were more sophisticated words, used more often in writing than in speech. Also, several words (e.g., *dock, freight*) were borrowed from the Dutch during the Middle English period as a result of trade with the Low Countries.

During this period there was a significant reduction in the use of inflections or word endings. Many irregular verbs were lost, and others developed regular past and past-participle forms (e.g., *climb, talk*), although Modern English still retains some irregular verbs (e.g., *sing, fly*) that contribute to our usage problems. By 1000, *-s* had become the accepted plural marker, although the Old English plural form *-en* was used in some words; this artifact remains in a few plurals, such as *children*.

Modern English (1500–Present)

The Modern English period is characterized by the development of the printing press and the tremendous upswing in exploration, colonization, and trade with countries around the world. The introduction of the printing press in England by William Caxton marks the beginning of the Modern English period. The printing press was a powerful force in standardizing English spelling, as well as a practical means for providing increasing numbers of people with books. Until the invention of the printing press, English spelling kept pace with pronunciation, but the printing press served to standardize and fix spelling, and the lag between pronunciation and spelling began to widen. The tremendous increase in travel to many different parts of the world resulted in a wide borrowing of words from more than 50 languages. Borrowings include *alcohol* (Arabic), *chocolate* (Spanish), *cookie* (Dutch), *czar* (Russian), *hallelujah* (Hebrew), *hurricane* (Spanish), *kindergarten* (German), *smorgasbord* (Swedish), *tycoon* (Chinese), and *violin* (Italian).

Many Latin and Greek words were added to English during the Renaissance to increase the language's prestige; for example, *congratulate, democracy,* and *education* came from Latin, and *catastrophe, encyclopedia,* and *thermometer* came from Greek. Many modern Latin and Greek borrowings are scientific words (e.g., *aspirin, vaccinate*), and some of the very recently borrowed forms (e.g., *criterion, focus*) have retained their native plural forms, adding confusion about how to spell these forms in English. Also, some recent loan words from French have retained their native spellings and pronunciations, such as *hors d'oeuvre* and *cul-de-sac.*

Although vocabulary expansion has been great during the Modern English period, there have also been extensive sound changes. The short vowels have remained relatively stable, but there was a striking change in the pronunciation of long vowels. This change, known as the Great Vowel Shift, has been characterized as "the most revolutionary and far-reaching sound change during the history of the language" (Alexander, 1962, p. 114). The change was gradual, occurring during the 1500s. Because spelling had become fixed before the shift, the vowel letter symbols no longer corresponded to the sounds. To illustrate the change, the word *name* had two syllables and rhymed with *comma* during the Middle English period, but during the Great Vowel Shift, the pronunciation of *name* shifted to rhyme with *game* (Hook, 1975).

The Modern English period brought changes in syntax, particularly the disappearance of double negatives and double comparatives and superlatives. Eliminations came about slowly; for instance, Shakespeare still wrote, "the most unkindest cut of all." Also, the practice of using *-er* or *-est* to form comparatives and superlatives in shorter words and *more* or *most* with longer words was not standardized until after Shakespeare's time.

Learning About Word Histories

The best source of information about word histories is an unabridged dictionary, which provides basic etymological information about words: the language the word was borrowed from, the form of the word in that language or the representation of the word in our alphabet, and the original meaning of the word. Etymologies are enclosed in square brackets and may appear at the beginning or the end of an entry. They are written in an abbreviated form to save space, using abbreviations for language names such as *Ar* for *Arabic* and *L for Latin.* We will look at three etymologies for words derived from very different sources: *king, kimono,* and *thermometer.* Each etymology is from *The Random House Dictionary of the English Language* (Flexner, 1993); we

extrapolation-
to infer 2, to project
extend, or expand

will translate and elaborate each etymology using a process I call "extrapola-tion." First, let's look at *king:*

> *king* [bef. 900; ME, OE *cyng*]
>
> *Extrapolation:* The word *king* is an Old English word originally spelled *cyng*. It was used in English before the year 900. In the Middle Eng-lish period the spelling changed to its current form.

Next let's consider *kimono:*

> *kimono* [1885–1890; < Japn: clothing, garb, equiv. to *ki* wear + *mono* thing]
>
> *Extrapolation:* Our word *kimono* comes from Japenese, and it entered English between 1885 and 1890. *Kimono* means "clothing" or "garb," and it is equivalent to the Japanese words *ki,* meaning "wear," and *mono,* meaning "thing."

Finally, we will examine *thermometer:*

> *thermometer* [1615–1625; thermo < Gr *thermos,* hot + meter < *metron,* measure]
>
> *Extrapolation:* The first recorded use of the word *thermometer* in En-glish was between 1615 and 1625. Our word was created from two Greek words meaning "hot" and "measure."

Figure 5–1 lists books about the history of English that are appropriate for elementary students. The books include fascinating stories about how words grew and changed because of historical events and linguistic accidents.

WORDS AND THEIR MEANINGS

Students begin kindergarten with approximately 5,000 words in their vocab-ularies, and their vocabularies grow at a rate of about 3,000 words a year (Nagy & Herman, 1985). Through literature focus units and theme cycles, students experiment with words and concepts, and their knowledge of words and meanings grows. Young children assume that every word has only one meaning, and words that sound alike, such as *son* and *sun,* are confusing to them. Through continuing experiences with language, students become more sophisticated about words and their literal and figurative meanings. During the elementary grades, students learn about words and word parts, words that mean the same as and the opposite of other words, words that sound alike, words with multiple meanings, the figurative language of idioms, and how words have been borrowed from languages around the world. They also learn about how words are created and have fun playing with words (Tomp-kins, 1994).

Root Words and Affixes

A root word is a morpheme, the basic part of a word to which affixes are added. Many words are developed from a single root word; for example, the Latin word *portare* ("to carry") is the source of at least nine Modern English words: *deport, export, import, port, portable, porter, report, support,* and *trans-*

Figure 5–1 *Books About the History of English for Elementary Students*

Adelson, L. (1972). *Dandelions don't bite: The story of words.* New York: Pantheon. (M–U)

Arnold, O. (1979). *What's in a name: Famous brand names.* New York: Messner. (U)

Asimov, I. (1961). *Words from myths.* Boston: Houghton Mifflin. (U)

Asimov, I. (1968). *Words from history.* Boston: Houghton Mifflin. (U)

Collis, H. (1987). *101 American English idioms.* Lincolnwood, IL: Passport. (M–U)

Conrad, P. (1995). *Animal lingo.* New York: HarperCollins. (P–M)

Fakih, K. O. (1995). *Off the clock: A lexicon of time words and expressions.* New York: Ticknor. (M–U)

Fletcher, C. (1973). *One hundred keys: Names across the land.* Nashville, TN: Abingdon Press. (M–U)

Graham-Barber, L. (1995). *A chartreuse leotard in a magenta limousine: And other words named after people and places.* New York: Hyperion. (M–U)

Greenfeld, H. (1978). *Sumer is icumen in: Our ever-changing language.* New York: Crown Books. (U)

Hazen, B. S. (1979). *Last, first, middle and nick: All about names.* Englewood Cliffs, NJ: Prentice-Hall. (M–U)

Kaye, C. B. (1985). *Word works: Why the alphabet is a kid's best friend.* Boston: Little, Brown. (M–U)

Kraske, R. (1975). *The story of the dictionary.* New York: Harcourt Brace Jovanovich. (P–M)

McCrum, R., Cran, I., & MacNeil, R. (1986). *The story of English.* New York: Viking Press. (U)

Meltzer, M. (1984). *A book about names.* New York: Crowell. (M–U)

Pizer, V. (1976). *Ink., Ark., and all that: How American places got their names.* New York: Putnam. (M–U)

Pizer, V. (1981). *Take my word for it.* New York: Dodd, Mead. (M–U)

Sanders, E. (1995). *What's your name? From Ariel to Zoe.* New York: Holiday. (P–M)

Sarnoff, J., & Ruffins, R. (1981). *Words: A book about the origins of everyday words and phrases.* New York: Scribner. (M–U)

Sorel, N. (1970). *Word people.* New York: American Heritage. (M–U)

Sperling, S. (1979). *Poplollies and bellibones: A celebration of lost words.* New York: Penguin. (U)

Steckler, A. (1979). *101 words and how they began.* Garden City, NY: Doubleday. (P–M–U)

Steckler, A. (1981). *101 more words and how they began.* Garden City, NY: Doubleday. (P–M–U)

Terban, M. (1983). *In a pickle and other funny idioms.* Boston: Houghton Mifflin. (M–U)

Weiss, A. E. (1980). *What's that you said: How words change.* New York: Harcourt Brace Jovanovich. (U)

Wolk, A. (1980). *Everyday words from names of people and places.* New York: Elsevier/Nelson. (M–U)

P = primary grades (K–2); M = middle grades (3–5); U = upper grades (6–8).

portation. Latin is one source of English root words, and Greek and Old English are two other sources.

Some root words are whole words, and others are parts of words. Some root words have become free morphemes and can be used as separate words, but others cannot. For instance, the word *act* comes from the Latin word *actus,* meaning "doing." English uses part of the word and treats it as a root word that can be used independently or in combination with affixes, as in *actor, activate, react,* and *enact.* In the words *alias, alien, unalienable,* and *alienate,* the root word *ali* comes from the Latin word *alius,* meaning "other"; it is not used as an independent root word in English. A list of root words appears in the Teacher's Notebook on page 188. Students can compile lists of words developed from these root words, and they can draw root word clusters to illustrate the relationship of the root word to the words developed from it. Figure 5–2 shows a root word cluster for the Greek root *graph,* meaning "to write." Recognizing basic elements from word to word helps students cut down on the amount of memorizing necessary to learn meanings and spellings.

Teacher's Notebook

Root Words

ann/enn (year): anniversary, annual, biennial, centennial, perennial
ast (star): aster, asterisk, astrology, astronaut, astronomy
auto (self): autobiography, automatic, automobile
bio (life): biography, biology, autobiography, biodegradable
cent (hundred): cent, centennial, centigrade, centipede, century
circ (around): circle, circular, circus, circumspect
corp (body): corporal, corporation, corps
cycl (wheel): bicycle, cycle, cyclist, cyclone, tricycle
dict (speak): contradict, dictate, dictator, predict verdict
geo (earth): geography, geology, geometry
gram (letter): diagram, grammar, monogram, telegram
graph (write): biography, graphic, paragraph, phonograph, stenographer
grat (pleasing, thankful): congratulate, grateful, gratitude
jus/jud/jur (law, right): injury, judge, justice
man (hand): manacle, manual, manufacture, manuscript
mand (order): command, demand, mandate, remand
mar (sea): aquamarine, marine, maritime, submarine
meter (measure): barometer, centimeter, diameter, speedometer, thermometer
min (small): miniature, minimize, minor, minute
mort (death): immortal, mortal, mortality, mortician, post-mortem
ped/pod (foot): pedal, pedestrian, podiatry, tripod
phon (sound): earphone, microphone, phonics, phonograph, saxophone, symphony
photo (light): photograph, photographer, photosensitive, photosynthesis
quer/ques/quis (seek): query, question, inquisitive
rupt (break): abrupt, bankrupt, interrupt, rupture
scope (see): horoscope, kaleidoscope, microscope, periscope, telescope
struct (build): construction, indestructible, instruct
tele (far): telecast, telegram, telegraph, telephone, telescope, telethon, television
terr (land): terrace, terrain, terrarium, territory
tract (pull, drag): attraction, subtract, tractor
vict/vinc (conquer): convince, convict, evict, victor, victory
vis (see): television, visa, vision, visual
viv/vit (live): survive vitamin, vivid
volv (roll): involve, revolutionary, revolver

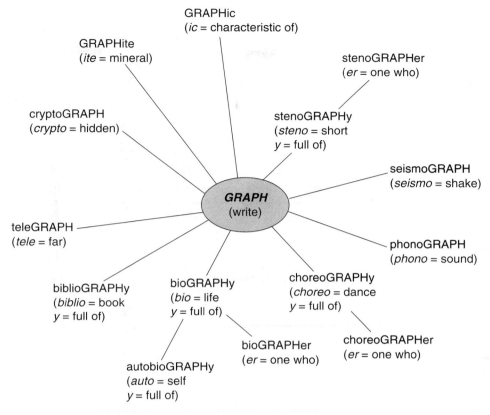

Figure 5–2   *A Cluster for the Root Word* Graph

Affixes are bound morphemes that are added to words and root words. Affixes can be prefixes or suffixes. Prefixes are added to the beginning of words, such as *re-* in *reread,* and suffixes are added to the ends of words, such as *-ing* in *singing* and *-er* in *player.* Like root words, affixes come from Old English, Latin, and Greek. They often change a word's meaning, such as adding *un-* to *happy* to form *unhappy.* Sometimes they change the part of speech, too. For example, when *-ion* is added to *attract* to form *attraction,* the verb *attract* becomes a noun.

When an affix is "peeled off" or removed from a word, the remaining word is usually a real word. For example, when the prefix *pre-* is removed from *preview,* the word *view* can stand alone; and when the suffix *-able* is removed from *lovable,* the word *love* can stand alone (when the final *e* is added, anyway). Some words include letter sequences that might be affixes, but because the remaining word cannot stand alone, they are not affixes. For example, the *in-* at the beginning of *include* is not a prefix because *clude* is not a word, and the *-ic* at the end of *magic* is not a suffix because *mag* cannot stand alone as a word. Sometimes, however, the root word cannot stand alone. One example is *legible.* The *-ible* is a suffix and *leg-* is the root word even though it cannot stand alone.

Students make charts to highlight the English, Latin, and Greek roots for "star" words.

Some affixes have more than one form. For example, the prefixes *il-, im-,* and *ir-* are forms of the prefix *in-,* with the meanings of "in," "into," and "on"; these prefixes are used with verbs and nouns. The prefixes *il-, im-, ir-,* and *ig-* are also forms of the prefix *in-,* with the meaning "not"; these prefixes are used with adjectives. Both *in-* prefixes are borrowed from Latin. The prefix *a-* and its alternate form *an-* are borrowed from Greek and also mean "not." The alternate form is used when the word it is being added to begins with a vowel. Similarly, some suffixes have alternate forms; for example, the suffix *-ible* is an alternate form of *-able.* The alternate form is used with words such as *legible* whose root words cannot stand alone.

A list of prefixes and suffixes is presented in the Teacher's Notebook on page 191. White, Sowell, and Yanagihara (1989) researched affixes and identified those that are most commonly used in English words; these are marked with an asterisk in the Teacher's Notebook. White and his colleagues recommend that the commonly used affixes be taught to middle- and upper-grade students because of their usefulness. Some of the most commonly used prefixes can be confusing because they have more than one meaning. The prefix *in-,* for instance, can mean either "not" or "again," and *un-* can mean "not" or it can reverse the meaning of the word (e.g., *tie–untie*).

Synonyms and Antonyms

Synonyms are words that have the same or nearly the same meanings as other words. English has so many synonyms because so many words have been borrowed from other languages. Synonyms are useful because they pro-

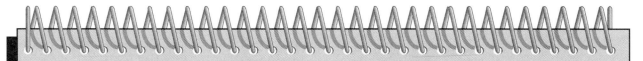

Teacher's Notebook
Affixes

Prefixes	Suffixes

a/an- (not): atheist, anaerobic

amphi- (both): amphibian

anti- (against): antiseptic

bi- (two, twice): bifocal, biannual

contra- (against): contradict

de- (away): detract

di- (two): dioxide

***dis-** (not): disapprove

***dis-** (reversal): disinfect

ex- (out): export

hemi- (half): hemisphere

***il-/im-/in-/ir-** (not): illegible, impolite, inexpensive, irrational

***in-** (in, into): indoor

inter- (between): intermission

kilo/milli- (one thousand): kilometer, milligram

micro- (small): microfilm

***mis-** (wrong): mistake

mono- (one): monarch

multi- (many): multimillionaire

omni- (all): omnivorous

***over-** (too much): overflow

poly- (many): polygon

post- (after): postwar

pre-/pro- (before): precede, prologue

quad-/quart- (four): quadruple, quarter

re- (again): repay

***re-/retro-** (back): replace, retroactive

***sub-** (under): submarine

super- (above): supermarket

trans- (across): transport

tri- (three): triangle

***un-** (not): unhappy

***un-** (reversal): untie

* = most commonly used affixes (White, Sowell, & Yanagihara, 1989).

-able/-ible (worthy of, can be): lovable, audible

***-al/-ial** (action, process): arrival, denial

-ance/-ence (state or quality): annoyance, absence

-ant (one who): servant

-ard (one who is): coward

-ary/-ory (person, place): secretary, laboratory

-dom (state or quality): freedom

-ed (past tense): played

-ee (one who is): trustee

***-er/-or/-ar** (one who): teacher, actor, liar

-er/-or (action): robber

-ern (direction): northern

-et/-ette (small): booklet, dinette

-ful (full of): hopeful

-hood (state or quality): childhood

-ic (characterized by): angelic

-icle/-ucle (small): particle, molecule

-ify (to make): simplify

-ing (participle): eating, building

-ish (like): reddish

-ism (doctrine of): communism

-less (without): hopeless

-ling (young): duckling

-logy (the study of): zoology

***-ly** (in the manner of): slowly

-ment (state or quality): enjoyment

***-ness** (state or quality): kindness

-s/-es (plural): cats, boxes

-ship (state, or art or skill): friendship, seamanship

***-sion/-tion** (state or quality): tension, attraction

-ster (one who): gangster

-ure (state or quality): failure

-ward (direction): homeward

***-y** (full of): sleepy

vide options, allowing us to express ourselves with more exactness. Think of all the different synonyms for the word *cold: cool, chilly, frigid, icy, frosty,* and *freezing,* for example. Each word has a different shade of meaning: *cool* means moderately cold; *chilly* is uncomfortably cold; *frigid* is intensely cold; *icy* means very cold; *frosty* means covered with frost; and *freezing* is so cold that water changes into ice. Our language would be limited if we could only say that we were cold.

The largest number of synonyms entered English during the Norman occupation of Britain. Compare these pairs of synonyms: *end–finish, clothing–garments, forgive–pardon, buy–purchase, deadly–mortal.* The first word in each pair comes from Old English; the second was borrowed from the Normans. The Old English words are more basic words, and the French loan words are more sophisticated. Perhaps that is why both words in each pair have survived—they express slightly different meanings. Other pairs of synonyms come from different languages. For example, in the pair *comfortable* and *cozy, comfortable* is a Latin loan word, whereas *cozy* is probably of Scandinavian origin.

Students can check a dictionary or thesaurus to locate synonyms for words. When seventh graders were reading *The Giver* (Lowry, 1993), they discussed Lowry's use of the word *release* (meaning *kill*). Students divided into small groups to examine a list of synonyms for *kill* from a thesaurus and choose those words that seemed to fit with Lois Lowry's meaning of *release.* Later, students made T-charts in their reading logs and wrote appropriate synonyms in the "yes" column and inappropriate synonyms in the "no" column. One student's T-chart is shown in Figure 5–3.

Antonyms are words that express opposite meanings. Antonyms for *loud* include *soft, subdued, quiet, silent, inaudible, sedate, somber, dull,* and *colorless.* These words express shades of meaning just as synonyms do, and some opposites are more appropriate for one meaning of *loud* than for another. When *loud* means *gaudy,* for instance, appropriate opposites might be *somber, dull,* or *colorless.*

Two important reference books for examining the meanings of words are dictionaries and thesauri. Both list synonyms and antonyms, but dictionaries also explain the shades of meaning among related words. The American Heritage series of dictionaries for students, beginning with *The American Heritage Picture Dictionary* (1989) for kindergartners and first graders, is my favorite. *The American Heritage Children's Dictionary* (1994) and *The American Heritage Student Dictionary* (1994) have boxes with etymological information about interesting words spread throughout the dictionaries. An easy-to-use thesaurus for elementary students is *A First Thesaurus* (Wittels & Greisman, 1985), which includes more than 2,000 entry words. Synonyms are printed in black type for each entry word, and the antonyms follow in red type. Other thesauri, including several small paperback editions, are also available for middle school students. These and other reference books are annotated in Figure 5–4.

Homonyms

Homonyms, words that have sound and spelling similarities, are divided into three categories: homophones, homographs, and homographic homophones. Homophones are words that sound alike but are spelled differently. Most

Figure 5–3   A Student's T-Chart of Synonyms for "Release"

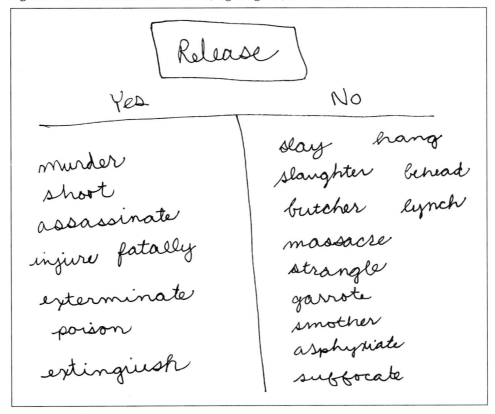

homophones developed from entirely different root words, and it is only by accident that they have come to sound alike; for example, the homophones *right* and *write* entered English before the year 900 and were pronounced differently. *Right* was spelled *reht* or *riht* in Old English; during the Middle English period the spelling was changed by French scribes to the current spelling. The verb *write* was spelled *writan* in Old English and *writen* in Middle English. *Write* is an irregular verb, suggesting its Old English heritage, and the silent *w* was pronounced hundreds of years ago. In contrast, a few words were derived from the same root words, such as *flea–flee, flower–flour, stationary–stationery,* and *metal–medal–mettle,* and the similar spellings have been retained to demonstrate the semantic relationships.

Homographs are words that are spelled the same but pronounced differently. Examples of homographs are *bow, close, lead, minute, record, read,* and *wind. Bow* is a homograph that has three unrelated meanings. The verb form, meaning "to bend in respect," was spelled *bugan* in Old English; the noun form, meaning "a gathering of ribbon" or "a weapon for propelling an arrow," is of Old English origin and was spelled *boga.* The other noun form of *bow,* meaning "forward end of a ship," did not enter English until the 1600s from German.

Homographic homophones are words that are both spelled and pronounced alike, such as *bark, bat, bill, box, fair, fly, hide, jet, mine, pen, ring,*

Figure 5–4   *Reference Books for Elementary Students*

Dictionaries

The American Heritage children's dictionary. (1994). Boston: Houghton Mifflin. (M) This volume includes 37,000 entries and 800 color illustrations. Information on word histories and vocabulary-building notes are included in special boxes. An eight-page thesaurus is included in the back of the book.

The American Heritage first dictionary. (1994). Boston: Houghton Mifflin. (P) More than 1,800 entries and 650 color illustrations are included in this dictionary. A definition and sample sentence are provided for each entry.

The American Heritage picture dictionary. (1989). Boston: Houghton Mifflin. (P) The 900 entries are arranged alphabetically and used in a sentence. More than 650 entries are accompanied by color illustrations.

The American Heritage student dictionary. (1994). Boston: Houghton Mifflin. (U) Over 65,000 entries and 2,000 photos and illustrations are included in this dictionary. Plus, biographical references, usage notes, word histories, and synonyms are listed. Word-building information is presented in boxes.

Goldman, J. L. (1996). *Webster's new world student's dictionary* (rev. ed.). New York: Macmillan. (M–U) This dictionary includes more than 50,000 entries, along with pronunciation guides, information about word origins, synonyms, and some black-and-white illustrations.

Levey, J. S. (1990). *Macmillan first dictionary.* New York: Simon & Schuster. (P) More than 2,000 entries and 550 color photographs and illustrations are included in this dictionary designed for young children. For each entry, the word is defined and used in a sentence. The dictionary is arranged in a single column on a page. Special sections focus on how words came to be, confusing words, numbers, measurements, and money.

Levey, J. S. (1990). *Macmillan picture wordbook.* New York: Macmillan. (P) This picture book is arranged in 30 themes ranging from outer space to homes. The 900 word labels are arranged on the full-color illustrations; there are no definitions or sentences. A table of contents and index are included.

McIlwain, J. (1994). *The DK children's illustrated dictionary.* London: Dorling Kindersley. (P) This dictionary has 5,000 main entries and 7,000 related words accompanied by 2,500 color photographs and illustrations. In each entry, the part of speech is identified, multiple meanings are listed, and sample sentences are provided. A pronunciation guide and antonyms are provided as needed. The entries are arranged in four columns on each page.

Neufeldt, V. (1991). *Webster's new world children's dictionary.* New York: Macmillan. (M) More than 33,000 entries, 700 idiomatic phrases, and nearly 700 drawings, photographs, and maps are included in this book. Information is also presented about word histories, synonyms, affixes, usage guidelines, and spelling tips.

Scholastic children's dictionary. (1996). New York: Scholastic. (M) Approximately 13,000 words are included in this dictionary with color illustrations and colorful page decorations. Guide words, pronunciation guides, and attractively designed boxes with information about synonyms, affixes, and word histories are included.

Thesauri

The American heritage student thesaurus. (1994). Boston: Houghton Mifflin. (M–U) Two hundred entries are included in this book. Each entry is defined, the part of speech is identified, and synonyms are listed and used in sentences. More than 800 synonyms are listed in the book. Antonyms are also included for many entries. Both the synonyms and antonyms are indexed at the back of the book.

Beal, G. (1996). *The Kingfisher illustrated pocket thesaurus.* New York: Kingfisher. (U) In this pocket-size paperback book, over 5,000 entries with sample sentences are presented. Antonyms are marked with a star, which is somewhat confusing.

Bellamy, J. (1996). *The Webster's children's thesaurus.* New York: Barnes and Noble. (M–U) More than 6,000 entries are included in this thesaurus. For each entry, synonyms and antonyms are listed, and there are a few two-color illustrations.

The Harcourt Brace student thesaurus. (1991). San Diego: Harcourt Brace. (M–U) Over 800 entries with more than 3,500 synonyms are listed. There are 150 color illustrations. For each entry, the part of speech is listed, definitions and synonyms are provided, and sample sentences are presented. Antonyms are listed for appropriate entries.

Roget's student thesaurus (Rev. ed.). (1994). New York: HarperCollins. (M–U) Over 4,000 synonyms with sample sentences are listed in this book. The pronunciation guide is listed in the index.

Wittels, H., & Greisman, J. (1985). *A first thesaurus.* Racine, WI: Western Publishing Company. (M) More than 2,000 entries are listed, with the main words printed in bold type. Synonyms are printed in regular type and antonyms in red. Some black-and-white illustrations are also included.

cudgel - club

row, spell, toast, and *yard.* Some are related words; others are linguistic accidents. The different meanings of *toast,* for example, came from the same Latin source word, *torrere,* meaning "to parch or bake." The derivation of the noun *toast* as heated and browned slices of bread is obvious; however, the relationship between the source word and *toast* as a verb, "drinking to someone's honor or health," is not immediately apparent. The connection is that toasted, spiced bread flavored the drinks used in making toasts. In contrast, *bat* is a linguistic accident: *bat* as a cudgel comes from the Old English word *batt;* the verb *to bat* is derived from the Old French word *batre;* and the nocturnal *bat* derives its name from an unknown Viking word and was spelled *bakke* in Middle English. Not only do the three forms of *bat* have unrelated etymologies, but they were borrowed from three different languages!

There are many books of homonyms for children, including Gwynne's *The King Who Rained* (1970), *A Chocolate Moose for Dinner* (1976), *The Sixteen Hand Horse* (1980), and *A Little Pigeon Toad* (1988); Maestro's *What's a Frank Frank?* (1984); and Terban's *Hey, Hay! A Wagonful of Funny Homonym Riddles* (1991). Elementary students enjoy reading these books and making their own word books. Figure 5–5 shows a page from a second grader's homophone book.

Multiple Meanings

Many words have more than one meaning. The word *bank,* for example, may refer to a piled-up mass of snow or clouds, the slope of land beside a lake or river, the slope of a road on a turn, the lateral tilting of an airplane in a turn, to cover a fire with ashes for slow burning, a business establishment that receives and lends money, a container in which money is saved, a supply for use in emergencies (e.g., blood bank), a place for storage (e.g., computer's memory bank), to count on, similar things arranged in a row (e.g., a bank of elevators), or to arrange things in a row. You may be surprised that there are at least 12 meanings for the common word *bank.* Why does this happen? The meanings of *bank* just listed come from three different sources. The first five meanings come from a Viking word, and they are related because they all deal with something slanted or making a slanted motion. The next five meanings come from the Italian word *banca,* a money changer's table. All these meanings deal with financial banking except for the tenth meaning, to count

Figure 5–5   A Page From a Second Grader's Homophone Book

on, which requires a bit more thought. We use the saying "to bank on" figuratively to mean "to depend on," but it began more literally from the actual counting of money on a table. The last two meanings come from the Old French word *banc,* meaning "bench." Words acquired multiple meanings as society became more complex and finer shades of meaning were necessary; for example, the meanings of *bank* as an emergency supply and a storage place are fairly new. As with many words with multiple meanings, it is a linguistic accident that three original words from three languages, with related meanings, came to be spelled the same way.

Students can create posters with word clusters to show multiple meanings of words (Bromley, 1996). Figure 5–6 shows a cluster with ten meanings of the word *hot* sketched from a poster made by three seventh graders. The students drew rays and wrote the meanings, listed examples, and drew illustrations.

Words assume additional meanings when an affix is added or when they are combined with another word, or compounded. Consider the word *fire*

Figure 5–6   *Seventh Graders' Poster of 10 Meanings for* Hot

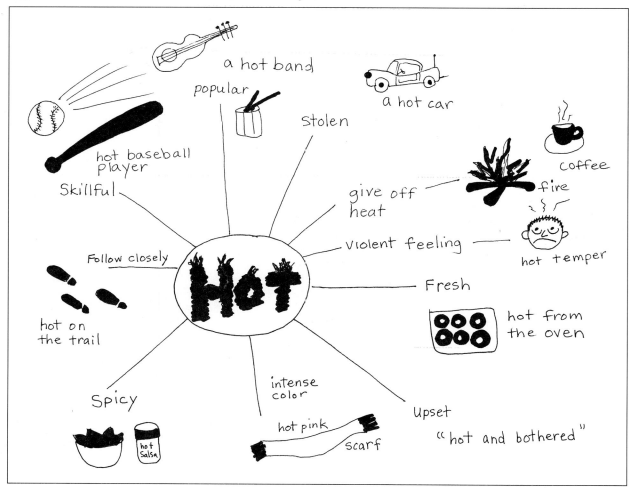

and the variety of words and phrases that incorporate *fire: fire hydrant, fire-bomb, fireproof, fireplace, firearm, fire drill, under fire, set the world on fire, fire away,* and *open fire.* Students can compile a list of words or make a booklet illustrating the words; Figure 5–7 lists more than 80 *down* words that a sixth-grade class compiled. Other common words with many variations include *short, key, water, book, rain, shoe, head, make, walk, cat,* and *side.*

Idioms and Metaphors

Many words have both literal and figurative meanings. Literal meanings are the explicit, dictionary meanings, and figurative meanings are metaphorical or use figures of speech. For example, to describe winter as the coldest season of the year is literal, but to say that winter has icy breath is figurative. Two types of figurative language are idioms and metaphors.

Idioms are groups of words, such as "spill the beans," that have a special meaning. Idioms can be confusing to students because they must be interpreted figuratively rather than literally. "Spill the beans" dates back to ancient Greece. Cox (1980) explains that at that time many Greek men belonged to secret clubs, and when someone wanted to join the club, the members took a vote to decide whether or not to admit him. They wanted the vote to remain secret, so they voted by each placing a white or brown bean in a special jar. A white bean indicated a yes vote, and a brown bean was a no vote. The club leader would then count the beans, and if all the beans were white, the person was admitted to the club. The vote was kept secret to avoid hurting the

Figure 5–7   *A Sixth-Grade Class's Collaboration List*

	"Down" Words		
downtown	climb down	reach down	downward
touchdown	down payment	write down	hunt down
get down	sit down	settle down	knock down
chow down	throw down	down it	breakdown
shake down	cut down	goose down	sundown
squat down	downhill	hop down	fall down
showdown	low down	hands down	tear down
lie down	slow down	downfall	turn down
quiet down	down right	close down	push down
shut down	beam down	run down	downstairs
shot down	downy	pin down	look down
cool down	downer	come down	inside down
crackdown	downslope	slam down	zip down
countdown	kickdown	slap down	pour down
pass down	stare down	hoe down	down pour
pass me down	boogy down	lock down	tape down
burn down	put down	water down	downgrade
downbeat	wrestle down	downturn	downstream
down to earth	flop down	stuff down	mow down
shimmey down	hung down	downcast	downhearted
downtrodden	chase down	hurl down	beat down

person's feelings in case the members voted not to admit him to the club. Sometimes during the voting one member would accidentally (or not so accidentally) knock the jar over, spilling the beans, and the vote would no longer be a secret. The Greeks turned this real happening into a saying that we still use today. Another idiom with a different history but a similar meaning is "let the cat out of the bag."

There are hundreds of idioms in English, and we use them every day to create word pictures that make language more colorful. Some examples are "out in left field," "a skeleton in the closet," "stick your neck out," "a chip off the old block," and "don't cry over spilled milk." Some of these idioms are new, and others are hundreds or thousands of years old; some are American in origin, and others come from around the world.

Four excellent books of idioms for students are *Put Your Foot in Your Mouth and Other Silly Sayings* (Cox, 1980), *Punching the Clock: Funny Action Idioms* (Terban, 1990), and *In a Pickle and Other Funny Idioms* (Terban, 1983). Because idioms are figurative sayings, many children—and especially those who are learning English as a second language—have difficulty learning them. It is crucial that children move beyond the literal meanings, thus learning flexibility in using language. One way for students to learn flexibility is to create idiom posters, as illustrated in Figure 5–8.

Metaphors and similes compare something to something else. A simile is a comparison signaled by the use of *like* or *as:* "The crowd was as rowdy as a bunch of marauding monkeys" and "In the moonlight the dead tree looked like a skeleton" are two examples. In contrast, a metaphor compares two

Figure 5–8   A Fourth Grader's Idiom Poster

things by implying that one is something else, without using *like* or *as*. "The children were frisky puppies playing in the yard" is an example. Metaphors are a stronger comparison, as these examples show:

> The two old men crossed the street as slowly as snails.
> The two old men were snails crossing the street.

> In the moonlight, the dead tree looked like a skeleton.
> In the moonlight, the dead tree was a skeleton.

Differentiating between the terms *simile* and *metaphor* is less important than understanding the meaning of comparisons in books students are reading and having students use comparisons to make their writing more vivid.

Students begin by learning traditional comparisons such as "happy as a clam" and "high as a kite," and then they learn to notice and invent fresh, unexpected comparisons. To introduce traditional comparisons to primary-grade students, teachers use Audrey Wood's *Quick as a Cricket* (1982). Middle- and upper-grade students locate comparisons in books they are reading and invent their own as they write poems, stories, and other types of writing.

Borrowed Words

The most common way of expanding vocabulary is to borrow words from other languages. This practice, which dates from Old English times, continues to the present day. Perhaps as many as 75% of our words have been borrowed from other languages and incorporated into English. Word borrowing has occurred during every period of language development, beginning when the Angles and Saxons borrowed over 400 words from the Romans. During the eighth and ninth centuries, the Vikings contributed approximately 900 words. The Norman conquerors introduced thousands of French words into English, reflecting every aspect of life: *adventure, fork, juggler,* and *quilt.* Later, during the Renaissance, when scholars translated Greek and Latin classics into English, they borrowed many words from Latin and Greek to enrich the language, including *chaos, encyclopedia, pneumonia,* and *skeleton.* More recently, words from at least 50 languages have been added to English through exploration, colonization, and trade. These are some of the loan words from other languages (Tompkins & Yaden, 1986, p. 31):

African (many languages): *banjo, cola, gumbo, safari, zombie*
Arabic: *alcohol, apricot, assassin, magazine*
Australian/New Zealand (aboriginal): *kangaroo, kiwi*
Celtic: *walnut*
Chinese: *chop suey, kowtow, tea, wok*
Czech: *pistol, robot*
Dutch: *caboose, easel, pickle, waffle*
Eskimo: *igloo, parka*
Finnish: *sauna*
French: *ballet, beige, chauffeur*
German: *kindergarten, poodle, pretzel, waltz*
Greek: *atom, cyclone, hydrogen*
Hawaiian: *aloha, hula, lei, luau*

Hebrew: *cherub, kosher, rabbi*
Hindi: *dungaree, juggernaut, jungle, shampoo*
Hungarian: *goulash, paprika*
Icelandic: *geyser*
Irish: *bog, leprechaun, shamrock, slogan*
Italian: *broccoli, carnival, macaroni, opera, pizza*
Japanese: *honcho, judo, kimono, origami*
Persian: *bazaar, divan, khaki, shawl*
Polish: *mazurka, polka*
Portuguese: *cobra, coconut, molasses*
Russian: *czar, sputnik, steppe, troika, vodka*
Scandinavian: *egg, fiord, husband, ski, sky*
Scottish: *clan, golf, slogan*
Spanish: *alligator, guitar, mosquito, potato*
Turkish: *caviar, horde, khan, kiosk, yogurt*
Yiddish: *bagel, chutzpah, pastrami*

Native Americans have also contributed a number of words to English. The early American colonists encountered many unfamiliar animals, plants, foods, and aspects of Indian life in America. They borrowed the Native American terms for these objects or events and tried to spell them phonetically. Native American loan words include *chipmunk, hickory, moccasin, moose, muskrat, opossum, papoose, powwow, raccoon, skunk, toboggan, tomahawk,* and *tepee.*

Other Sources of New Words

New words continually appear in English, many of them created to describe new inventions and scientific projects. Some of the newest words come from computer science and the space program. They are created in a variety of ways, including compounding, coining, and clipping.

Compounding means combining two existing words to create a new word. *Friendship* and *childhood* are two words that the Anglo-Saxons compounded more than a thousand years ago. Recent compoundings include *latchkey kids* and *software.* Compound words usually progress through three stages: they begin as separate words (e.g., *ice cream*), then are hyphenated (e.g., *baby-sit*), and finally are written as one word (e.g., *splashdown*). There are many exceptions to this rule, such as the compound words *post office* and *high school,* which have remained separate words. Other compound words use Greek and Latin elements, such as *stethoscope* and *television.*

Creative people have always coined new words. Lewis Carroll, author of *Alice in Wonderland* and *Through the Looking Glass,* is perhaps the best-known inventor of words. He called his new words portmanteau words (borrowing from the British word for a suitcase that opens into two halves) because they were created by blending two words into one. His most famous example, *chortle,* a blend of *snort* and *chuckle,* is from the poem "Jabberwocky." Other examples of blended words include *brunch* (*breakfast* + *lunch*), *electrocute* (*electric* + *execute*), *guesstimate* (*guess* + *estimate*), and *smog* (*smoke* + *fog*).

Two other types of coined words are trademarks and acronyms. Examples of well-known trademarks and brand names include Kleenex, Coca-Cola,

Xerox, and nylon. *Nylon,* for instance, was invented by scientists working in New York and London; they named their product by combining *ny,* the abbreviation for *New York,* with *lon,* the first three letters of *London.* Acronyms, words formed by combining the initial letters of several words, include *radar, laser,* and *scuba. Scuba,* for example, was formed by combining the initial letters of *self-contained underwater breathing apparatus.*

Clipping is a process of shortening existing words. For example, *bomb* is the shortened form of *bombard,* and *zoo* comes from *zoological park.* Most clipped words are only one syllable and are used in informal conversation. Although it is unlikely that your students will create new words that will eventually appear in the dictionary, they do create words to add pizzazz to their writing, and some words become part of the everyday jargon in a classroom.

Authors also create new words in their stories, and students should be alert to the possibility of finding a created word when they read or listen to stories. The Howes (1979) created *Bunnicula* to name their spooky young rabbit (*bunny* + dra*cula*), and Chris Van Allsburg (1981) invented the word *Jumanji* to name his adventure game.

TEACHING STUDENTS ABOUT WORDS

Students' vocabularies grow at an astonishing rate—about 3,000 words a year, or roughly 7 to 10 new words every day (Nagy & Herman, 1985). By the time students finish high school, their vocabularies reach 40,000 words. In order to learn words at such an astonishing rate, it seems obvious that students learn words both in school and outside of school. Television has a significant impact on children's vocabularies, too. Teachers often assume that students learn words primarily through the lessons they teach, but students actually learn the meanings of many more words through independent reading and writing projects than through instruction. In fact, encouraging students to read is probably the most important way teachers promote vocabulary growth (Nagy, 1988). Repeated exposure to words is crucial because students need to see and use a new word many times before it becomes a part of their ownership dictionaries—words they understand and use competently.

Not all the words students learn are equally hard or easy to learn; the degree of difficulty depends on what the student already knows about the word. Graves (1985) identifies four possible situations for unfamiliar words:

easiest
1. *Sight word.* Students recognize the word, know what it means when they hear someone say it, and can use it orally, but they don't recognize its written form.
2. *New word.* Students have a concept related to the word, but they are not familiar with the word, either orally or in written form.

most difficult
3. *New concept.* Students have little or no background knowledge about the concept underlying the word, and they don't recognize the word itself.
4. *New meaning.* Students know the word, but they are unfamiliar with the way the word is used and its meaning in this situation.

New sight words are probably the easiest words for students to learn because they already use the word orally; the most difficult category of words is the one involving new concepts because students must both learn the concept and attach the word label.

Vocabulary instruction has a place in literature focus units and theme cycles. Minilessons and other word-study activities focus on words from books students are reading. The most successful activities are meaningful to students and involve students in manipulating words from books they are reading or words related to science and social studies themes they are studying. Teachers also present minilessons to teach students how to figure out the meaning of unfamiliar words (Blachowicz & Lee, 1991). In traditional classrooms, the most common vocabulary activities involve listing new words on the chalkboard and directing students to write the words and copy the definitions from a dictionary or use the words in sentences. These activities are not effective and are no longer recommended.

Word Walls

The most important way to focus students' attention on words is to write key words on word wall charts and post them in the classroom. Teachers hang blank word walls, made from large sheets of butcher paper, in the classroom at the beginning of literature focus units and theme cycles. Students and the teacher use the word wall to write down interesting, confusing, and important words from books they are reading during literature focus units and as they learn concepts during theme cycles. Usually students choose the words to write on the word wall during the exploring stage of the reading process, and they may even do the writing themselves. Teachers add any key words that students have not chosen. Words are added to the word wall as they come up in books students are reading or during a theme cycle, not in advance; also, separate charts are used for each unit.

Teachers choose the most important words from books to teach. Important words include words that are essential to understanding the text, words that may confuse students, and words students will use as they read other books. As teachers choose words for word walls and other vocabulary activities, they consider the book being read as well as the instructional context. For example, during a literature focus unit on Amy Axelrod's *Pigs Will Be Pigs* (1994), a story about a family of pigs who hunt for money around their house in order to go to a restaurant for dinner, a second-grade class listed these words on their word wall:

■ *To review information about the exploring stage of the reading process, turn back to Chapter 3, "The Reading and Writing Processes," pp. 104–105.*

Mr. Pig	Mrs. Pig	refrigerator
empty	grocery shopping	B.J.
Dave	Mike	piglets
bank	money	wallet
dollar	hunt for money	two-dollar bill
shiny dimes	penny collection	bedroom
closets and drawers	lucky	searched
jewelry box	nickels	penny–pennies
quarter	two hundred	downstairs
upstairs	pocketbooks	fifty-cent piece
four	ten	seventeen
on a roll	laundry room	wet five-dollar bill
kitchen cupboards	pantry	basement

Students list "important" words from books they are reading on word walls.

twenty-dollar bill	toolbox	It's time to eat!
favorite restaurant	Enchanted Enchilada	waitress
hungry	jalapeños	menu
nacho chips	enchiladas	chimichangas
salad bar	sopaipillas	frijoles refritos
burritos	taco salad	chef's special
paid the bill	stuffed	going to explode
bellyaches	home, sweet home	cozy house

These words include the names of characters, rooms in the pigs' home where they search for money, amounts of money, and foods on the menu at the Mexican restaurant. They were chosen because they are important to the story, and the teacher chose to focus on the money-related words and tie in a math unit on counting money.

During a unit on Martin Luther King, Jr., seventh graders listed these words on their word wall:

1929–1968	Baptist minister	eloquent
target of violence	Atlanta, Georgia	federal holiday
discrimination	slavery	integration
segregation	protest	sit-in
1964 Nobel Peace Prize	Jim Crow laws	civil rights
boycott	Negro	prejudice
"I Have a Dream" speech	Montgomery, Alabama	March on Washington

Birmingham jail	Selma march	Lincoln Memorial
poverty	racism	riots–rioting
nonviolence	activist	assassinated
martyr	Rosa Parks	Klu Klux Klan
separate but equal	NAACP	James Earl Ray
Memphis, Tennessee	Coretta Scott King	1968 Civil Rights Act

These words highlight key events in the activist's life and the Civil Rights movement.

Even though all of these words and perhaps more will be added to the word wall, not all will be directly taught to students. As they plan, teachers create lists of words that they anticipate will be written on word walls during the unit. They try to identify which words will be sight words for their students and which words represent new concepts, new words, and new meanings for their students. From this list, teachers chose the key words—the ones that are critical to understanding the book or the theme—and these are the words that teachers plan to highlight or include in minilessons. They also choose any words that must be introduced before reading. According to Vygotsky's notion of a "zone of proximal development," teachers need to be alert to individual students and what words they are learning so that they can provide instruction when students are most interested in learning more about a word.

Identifying some words on the word wall as key words doesn't mean that the other words are unimportant. Students have many opportunities to use all the word wall words as they write and talk about what they are reading and studying. For example, students often use the word wall to locate a specific word they want to use to make a point during a discussion or to check the spelling of a word they are writing in a reading log or in a report. Teachers also use the words listed on the word wall for word-study activities.

Word-Study Activities

Word-study activities provide students with opportunities to explore the meaning of words listed on word walls, other words related to books they are reading, and words they are learning during social studies or science theme cycles. Through these activities, students explore the word meanings and make associations among words. None of these activities require students to simply write words and their definitions or to use the words in sentences or a contrived story. Here are eight types of activities:

1. Word posters.   Students choose a word from the word wall and write it on a small poster. Then they draw and color a picture to illustrate the word. They may also want to use the word in a sentence.

2. Word clusters.   Students choose a word to write in the center circle of a cluster. Then they draw rays, write information about the word, and make connections between the word and the literature focus unit or theme cycle. Figure 5–9 shows three types of word clusters. First graders made the first cluster after reading *The Adventures of Taxi Dog* (Barracca & Barracca, 1990). The second is a cluster that third graders made after reading *Sugaring Time* by Kathryn Lasky (1983). For the third cluster, seventh graders considered the definition of *reminiscent,* its history or etymology, its part of speech, other related forms, its word parts, and its synonyms.

Figure 5–9   *Three Word Clusters*

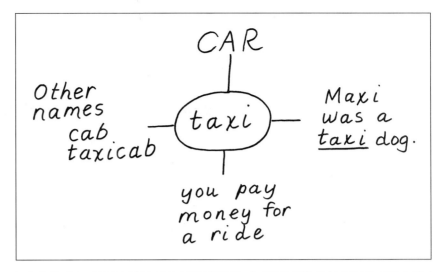

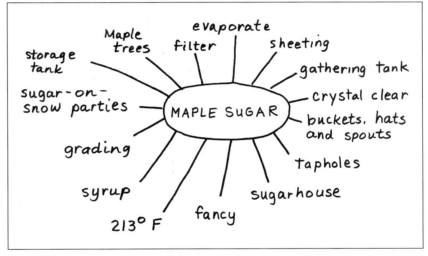

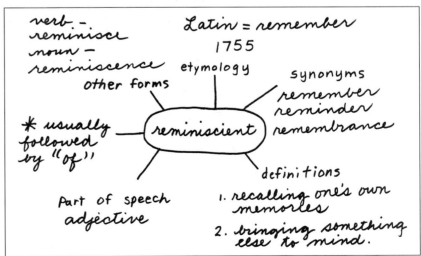

3.   *Dramatizing words*.   Students choose a word from the word wall and dramatize it for classmates to guess. Teachers might also want to choose a word from the word wall for a "word of the day."

4.   *Word sorts*.   Students sort a collection of words taken from the word wall into two or more categories (Bear, Templeton, Invernizzi, & Johnston, 1996). Usually students choose which categories they will use for the sort, but sometimes the teacher chooses. For example, words from a story might be sorted by character, or words from a theme on machines might be sorted as to whether or not they are machines or according to type of machine. The words can be written on cards, and then students sort a pack of word cards into piles. Or, students can cut apart a list of words, sort the words into categories, and then paste each group on a sheet of paper. Figure 5–10 shows a word sort done by a small group of fifth graders during a theme on the colonies. Students choose the three categories—New England Colonies, Middle Colonies, and Southern Colonies—and sorted word cards for each category. Then they glued the word cards onto a large sheet of paper.

Figure 5–10   *A Word Sort on the American Colonies*

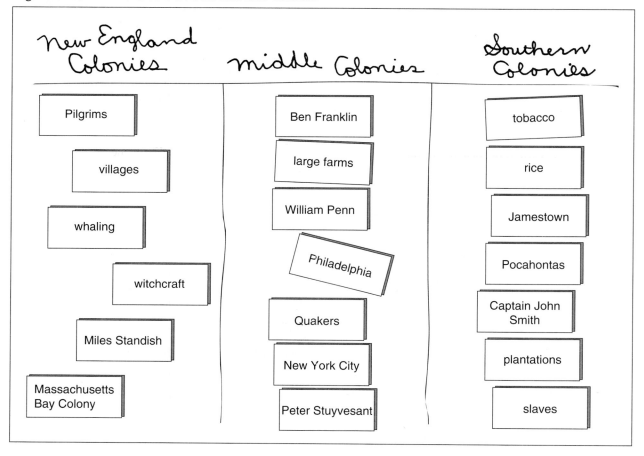

5. Books about words. A variety of books for children that are collections of words or explain words related to particular concepts have been published. *Zin! Zin! Zin! A Violin* (Moss, 1995), for instance, explains words for groups of musicians (e.g., *solo, duo, trio, quartet*), and Ruth Heller introduces *batch, school, fleet, bevy,* and *flock* in *A Cache of Jewels and Other Collective Nouns* (1987). Marvin Terban, the author of more than a dozen books about words, explains *hocus-pocus, razzmatazz, hodgepodge, knickknack,* and 103 other words in *Superdupers! Really Funny Real Words* (1989). These and other books about words are listed in Figure 5–11.

Teachers often connect books about words with literature focus units and theme cycles. For example, as part of a theme cycle on birds, teachers might use Lois Ehlert's *Feathers for Lunch* (1990), which provides detailed information about and drawings of 12 backyard birds, or during a literature focus unit on *Chrysanthemum* (Henkes, 1991), a story about a girl who didn't like being named for a flower, teachers might use *Alison's Zinnia* (Lobel, 1990) or

Figure 5–11   *Books About Words*

Browne, P. (1996). *A gaggle of geese: The collective names of the animal kingdom.* New York: Atheneum. (M)

Dewan, T. (1992). *Inside the whale and other animals.* London: Dorling Kindersley. (M–U)

Dewey, A. (1995). *Naming colors.* New York: HarperCollins. (M)

Ehlert, L. (1989). *Eating the alphabet: Fruits and vegetables from A to Z.* Orlando, FL: Harcourt Brace. (P–M)

Ehlert, L. (1990). *Feathers for lunch.* Orlando, FL: Harcourt Brace. (P–M)

Feder, J. (1995). *Table, chair, bear: A book in many languages.* New York: Ticknor. (P–M)

Gibbons, G. (1990). *Weather words and what they mean.* New York: Holiday House. (P–M)

Graham-Barber, L. (1995). *A chartreuse leotard in a magenta limousine: And other words named after people and places.* New York: Hyperion. (M–U)

Heller, R. (1983). *The reason for a flower.* New York: Sandcastle. (See other books in the series by this author.) (M)

Heller, R. (1987). *A cache of jewels and other collective nouns.* New York: Grosset & Dunlap. (M–U)

Hepworth, C. (1992). *Antics! An alphabetical anthology.* New York: Putnam. (M–U)

Hubbard, W. (1990). *C is for curious: An ABC of feelings.* San Francisco: Chronicle Books. (P–M)

Hunt, J. (1989). *Illuminations.* New York: Bradbury. (M–U)

Lobel, A. (1990). *Alison's zinnia.* New York: Greenwillow. (M)

Maestro, B., & Maestro, G. (1989). *Taxi: A book of city words.* New York: Clarion. (P–M)

Magee, D., & Newman, R. (1990). *All aboard ABC.* New York: Puffin. (P)

McMillan, B. (1989). *Super, super, superwords.* New York: Lothrop, Lee & Shepard. (P)

Moss, L. (1995). *Zin! Zin! Zin! A violin.* New York: Simon & Schuster. (P–M)

Most, B. (1980). *There's an ant in Anthony.* New York: Morrow. (P–M)

Most, B. (1991). *A dinosaur named after me.* Orlando, FL: Harcourt Brace. (P–M)

Onyefulu, I. (1993). *A is for Africa.* New York: Cobblehill Books. (M)

Pallotta, J. (1994). *The desert alphabet book.* Watertown, MA: Charlesbridge. (See other alphabet books by the same author.) (M–U)

Parker, N. W., & Wright, J. R. (1987). *Bugs.* New York: Greenwillow. (M)

Parker, N. W., & Wright, J. R. (1990). *Frogs, toads, lizards, and salamanders.* New York: Greenwillow. (M)

Rockwell, A. (1986). *Things that go.* New York: Dutton. (P)

Rotner, S. (1996). *Action alphabet.* New York: Atheneum. (P–M)

Terban, M. (1988). *Guppies in tuxedos: Funny eponyms.* New York: Clarion. (M–U)

Terban, M. (1989). *Superdupers! Really funny real words.* New York: Clarion. (M–U)

Terban, M. (1993). *It figures! Fun figures of speech.* New York: Clarion. (M)

Trucks. (1991). London: Dorling Kindersley. (P)

Wildsmith, B. (1967). *Birds.* Oxford, England: Oxford University Press. (M–U)

The Flower Alphabet Book (Pallotta, 1988) for a minilesson on the names of various flowers. Also, during minilessons on language concepts, teachers might use other books about words. For a minilesson on comparative and superlative forms, teachers might share *Super, Super, Superwords* (McMillan, 1989), or they might use *Action Alphabet* (Rotner, 1996) for a minilesson on verbs. After students read these books, they can make their class collaboration or individual books about words.

6. Tea party. Teachers prepare a set of cards with text (sentences or paragraphs) from a story or informational book students are reading. At least one "important" word from the word wall is included in each excerpt, and the word is highlighted. Students have a "tea party" and read the cards to classmates. They also talk about the highlighted word and its meaning. Sometimes teachers write the definition of the word or a synonym on the back of the card.

7. Word chains. Students choose a word from the word wall and then identify three or four words to sequence before or after the word to make a chain. For example, the word *tadpole* can be chained this way: *egg, tadpole, frog;* and the word *aggravate* can be chained like this: *irritate, bother, aggravate, annoy.* Students can draw and write their chains on a sheet of paper, or they can make a construction paper chain and write the words on each link.

8. Semantic feature analysis. Students select a group of related words, such as different kinds of birds, and then make a grid or chart to classify them according to distinguishing characteristics. A semantic feature analysis on birds is presented in Figure 5–12. This activity reinforces students' organization of knowledge and related words into schemata (Pittelman, Heimlich, Berglund, & French, 1991).

Minilessons on Word Meanings

The goal of vocabulary instruction is for students to learn new words, but traditional approaches, such as assigning students to look up the definitions of a list of words in a dictionary, often fail to produce in-depth understanding (Nagy, 1988). Carr and Wixon (1986) provide four guidelines for effective instruction:

* Students relate new words to their background knowledge.
* Students acquire ownership-level word knowledge.
* Students are actively involved in learning new words.
* Students develop strategies for learning new words independently.

The teaching strategy presented Chapter 1 embodies these guidelines of effective vocabulary instruction, and it can be used to teach minilessons on strategies for unlocking word meanings, on specific key words and groups of related words, or on a lexical concept such as idioms, prefixes, or homonyms. The steps are:

■ *Turn back to Chapter 1, "Learning and the Language Arts," pp. 34–38, to review the teaching strategy.*

Step by Step

1. **Introduce the topic.** Teachers introduce a word-identification strategy, a key word or group of related words, or a lexical concept. During the brief introduction, teachers connect the topic to students' background knowledge and share examples from books students are reading or from a theme cycle.

2. **Present information related to the topic.** Teachers demonstrate how to use the strategy, present information related to the key word or group of words, or

do a shell

	hatches from eggs	has feathers	has wings	can fly	can swim	migrates	is a bird of prey	is extinct
bluejay	✓	✓	✓	✓	○	○	○	○
owl	✓	✓	✓	✓	○	○	✓	○
roadrunner								
eagle								
pelican								
hummingbird								
quail								
ostrich								
dodo								
robin								
penguin								
chicken								
duck								
seagull								
peacock								
flamingo								

Code: ✓ = yes

○ = no

? = don't know

Figure 5–12   A Semantic Feature Analysis on Birds

morphological—study of the form and structure

share examples of the lexical concept. Teachers begin with examples from students' own writing or books they are reading. They also invite students to suggest other information or examples.

3. **Apply word knowledge.**   Teachers involve students in an activity to bring together all the information—semantic, morphological, and contextual—presented earlier. Students might sort words, make word clusters or word chains, or locate additional examples of the word or lexical concept in books they are reading or in pieces they have written.

4. **Review the topic.**   Students and the teacher review the strategy, the key word or words, or the lexical concept. Students can add the words to vocabulary notebooks or make a poster to review the strategy or lexical concept they have learned.

5. **Provide meaningful opportunities to use the topic.**   Students use the strategy, key words, or lexical concept in meaningful ways in projects and through writing, talking, and reading.

Students need to know about the English language, words and their meanings, and strategies to figure out the meanings of words independently. Students in the elementary grades learn about multiple meanings as well as about root words and affixes; homonyms, synonyms, and antonyms; and figurative meanings of words, such as idioms. A list of topics for minilessons on words is presented on page 211. Two minilessons using the steps described above are outlined in Figure 5–13. One minilesson focuses on three root words meaning "water," and the other focuses on idioms.

In Literature Focus Units

■ *See Chapter 13, "Putting It All Together," pp. 544–550, for information on planning literature focus units.*

2nd grade

As students read books during literature focus units, they learn many new words; many they learn incidentally, others through minilessons and word-study activities. As teachers prepare to read books with students, they think about which words they will teach and how they will teach them. A few word-study activities take place during the responding stage of the reading process as students ask about particular words. Students use the words as they respond to their reading in grand conversations and in reading logs. Later, during the exploring stage, students focus on specific words as they write the words on the word wall and participate in other activities and minilessons.

A second-grade class participated in these word-study activities during a week-long literature focus unit on *Tacky the Penguin* (Lester, 1988), a story about a penguin who doesn't fit in with his sleek and graceful companions but whose odd behavior comes in handy when hunters come. On Monday, after reading the book using shared reading, students and the teacher wrote these words on a word wall:

Tacky	graceful divers	penguin splashy
cannonballs	icy	pretty songs
companions	"Sunrise on the Iceberg"	an odd bird

Words

Procedures	Concepts	Strategies and Skills
Choose words for word walls	History of English	Use phonics to pronounce a word
Extrapolate the etymology	Root words	Use structural analysis to iden-
"Peel off" affixes	Affixes	tify a word
Make a word poster	Prefixes	Use context clues to identify a
Make a word cluster	Suffixes	word
Do a word sort	Synonyms	Consider shades of meaning in
Make a word chain	Antonyms	selecting a word
Do a semantic feature analysis	Homophones	Use a thesaurus to choose a
Locate a word in a dictionary	Homographs	better word
Locate a word in a thesaurus	Homographic homophones	Use a dictionary to identify a
Assess use of words in a litera- ture focus unit	Multiple meanings of words Idioms	word Avoid trite language
Assess use of words in a theme cycle	Literal meanings Figurative meanings	Consider multiple meanings of words
	Borrowed words	
	Compound words	
	Coined words	
	Clipped words	
	Invented words	
	Sniglets	

Goodly	distance	Lovely
hunters	Angel	maps and traps
Neatly	rocks and locks	Perfect
rough and tough	quietly	growly voices
politely	fright	get rich
hearty slap on the back	"What's happening?"	loud

Students referred to the words on the word wall as they wrote entries in their reading logs and talked about the story. During the grand conversation, the teacher focused on the word *odd* and asked why Tacky was called an *odd* bird. Together the class compiled this list of *odd* words: *unusual, uncommon, different, rare, weird, funny, unique, strange,* and *like numbers 1, 3, and 5.*

On Tuesday, the students reviewed the words on the word wall before rereading the story using buddy reading. The next day the teacher taught a minilesson on how to do a word sort, and students used word cards to sort words from the story into three categories: words about Tacky, words about the other penguins, and words about the hunters. On Thursday, students worked in small groups to cut apart a list of the words from the story, sort them into the three categories, and paste the words in each group on a sheet

Figure 5–13   *Two Minilessons*

Three Root Words for *Water*

This minilesson is designed for sixth graders who are familiar with the concept of root words and have studied ancient Greece and ancient Rome. The teacher teaches this minilesson over two days, and students work together as a class for some activities and in small groups for other activities.

1. Present a List of Words

The teacher writes this list of *water* words on the chalkboard and reads it to students: *water, aquamarine, aquatic, hydrant, hydraulic, hyroelectric, waterfall, waterworks, watercress, watery, aquarium, waterproof, aqualung,* and *hydrogen.* The teacher explains that the words are related to water, but some have an English root while others have a Latin or Greek root.

2. Sort the Words

Working in small groups, students sort the words into three categories: English *water* root words, Latin *aqua* root words, and Greek *hydro* root words. They write the sorted list of words on a chart and also talk about the meanings of the words.

3. Locate Additional Words

Students check dictionaries and other resources for additional *water* words, including *hydrofoil, aquarium, waterproof, watermelon, water lily, aquanaut, aquafarm, waterbed,* and *water heater.* They add these words to the sorted list.

4. Repeat With Other Word Families

Students locate and sort words representing other word families such as *star* (*stell* [L] and *ast* [Gr]), *sound* (*sono* [L] and *phon* [Gr]), *people* (*pop* [L] and *demo* [Gr]), *time* (*temp* [L] and *chrono* [Gr]), and *tooth* (*dent* [L] and *dont* [Gr]).

---

of paper. The teacher also taught minilessons on peeling off the *-ly* suffix and on rhyming words using words from the word wall.

Many students used words from the word wall and applied what they had learned in minilessons through the projects they prepared. One student wrote a poem about Tacky being an "odd bird" and included many of the words from the *odd* list in the poem. Two students worked together on a book about the penguins in the story, featuring one penguin on each page, and drew a box around the *-ly* suffix in several penguins' names. Other students made posters about the penguins in Antarctica, created new versions for Tacky's song, and wrote books of rhyming words. As they shared their completed projects with classmates at the end of the literature focus unit, word wall words and the lexical concepts introduced in the minilessons were again reinforced.

In Theme Cycles

Teachers plan many of the same types of word-study activities in theme cycles that they do for literature focus units. The goal of these activities is to help students expand their knowledge of vocabulary related to the theme.

Figure 5–13   *continued*

Idioms

This minilesson is planned for second graders or students who are learning English as a second language and do not understand that English phrases can have figurative meanings. This minilesson will take place over several days.

1. Compare Meanings

Teachers explain that some phrases in English have two meanings. These phrases are called "idioms." For example: "get up on the wrong side of the bed" (wake up in a bad mood), "rain cats and dogs" (rain hard), "fishy" (suspicious), "stick your neck out" (take a risk), "pull someone's leg (fool someone), "play it by ear" (improvise), and "kick the bucket" (die).

2. Dramatize the Meanings

Teachers and students dramatize the two meanings of each idiom and talk about how the idioms are used in sentences.

3. Explain Reason for Idioms

Teachers explain that many idioms can be traced back to their literal meanings and share interesting stories from *Put Your Foot in Your Mouth and Other Silly Sayings* (Cox, 1980), *Punching the Clock: Funny Action Idioms* (Terban, 1990), and *In a Pickle and Other Funny Idioms* (Terban, (1983).

4. Make Idiom Posters

Students make posters comparing the literal and figurative meanings of an idiom.

5. Share Posters

Students share their posters with classmates.

During a theme cycle on flight, a fifth-grade class added these words to their word wall:

airplanes	birds	U.S. Air Force
aeronautics	wings	engines
flightless birds	ostriches	penguins
lift	air pressure	gravity
Leonardo da Vinci	Concorde	Daedalus
balloons	gliders	Orville & Wilbur Wright
aviation	crop dusters	Kitty Hawk, N.C.
drag	thrust	cruising
pilot	altitude	propellers
take-off	airflow	airborne
curved surface	pitch	roll
yaw	elevator	rudder
ailerons	throttle	flapping
gliding	soaring	thermal winds
cruising speed	25–35 mph	30,000 feet high
gulls	chimney swifts	pheasants and quail
hover	fly backwards	hummingbirds

Teachers present minilessons on how to unlock word meanings using words from books students are reading in literature focus units.

■ *For more informa-
tion on planning
theme cycles, see
Chapter 13, "Putting It
All Together," pp.
567– 571.*

During the theme cycle, students made word posters and word clusters on some of the words and completed a semantic feature analysis comparing flight words about birds with flight words about airplanes. Students used words from the word wall as they wrote in learning logs, made posters explaining how flight is possible, wrote poems and picture books about flight, and sorted flight-related words.

Adapting to Meet the Needs of Every Student

Because learning about words is an important part of language arts, it is crucial that teachers find ways to help every student use the words they are learning. Having a word wall in every literature focus unit and across-the-curriculum theme cycle is probably the most important way to focus students' attention on words. Teachers also need to provide a variety of word-study activities to meet the needs of every student. A list of suggestions for adapting vocabulary instruction is presented on page 215. These suggestions focus on using vocabulary in meaningful, functional, and genuine ways.

Assessing Students' Use of Words

Teachers assess students' use of words related to literature focus units and across-the-curriculum themes in a variety of ways. They listen while students talk during the theme, examine students' writing and projects, and ask students to talk or write about the theme and what they have learned. Here are some specific strategies to determine whether students have learned and are applying new words:

Adapting
Vocabulary Instruction
To Meet the Needs of Every Student

1. Highlight Key Words on Word Walls

Teachers might highlight words on word walls by writing them with colored pens. Also, they can add pictures to illustrate the words.

2. Sort Words

The word-sorting activity is very useful for students who need additional opportunities to categorize words or learn relationships among words. After reading a story, students can sort words according to characters, or during a theme cycle they can sort words according to key concepts.

3. Teach Idioms

Students who are learning English as a second language may need to learn about idioms and separate their literal and figurative meanings. Students can dramatize or draw pictures of the two meanings of idioms.

4. Learn Multiple Meanings of Words

Students can draw diagrams to show multiple meanings of words. For example, students can draw a diagram to chart two meanings of *watch:*

$$watch \diagdown \begin{array}{l} \text{to look at something} \\ \text{a small clock on your wrist} \end{array}$$

Students can add drawings to the diagram or use the word in sentences.

5. Introduce New Concepts

Some students may need assistance in developing a concept before learning related words. Teachers need to anticipate how difficult a word might be for students and provide opportunities involving hands-on experiences, dramatic activities, or pictures.

- Check reading logs, learning logs, or simulated journals for words related to the unit or theme.
- Use these words in a conference and note the student's response.
- Listen for vocabulary when students give an oral report.
- Ask students to make a cluster or do a quickwrite about the theme or unit or about specific words.
- Ask students to brainstorm a list of words and phrases about the theme or unit.
- Check students' reports, biographies, poems, stories, or other writings for unit- or theme-related words.

- Check students' projects for these words.
- Ask students to write a letter to you, telling what they have learned in the unit or theme.

Teachers can also give tests on the vocabulary words, but this is probably the least effective approach because a correct answer on a test does not indicate whether students have ownership of a word or whether they are applying it in meaningful and genuine ways.

Review

Learning about words is an important part of language arts. Few words have only one meaning, and students in the elementary grades learn about multiple meanings as well as about root words and affixes; homonyms, synonyms, and antonyms; and figurative meanings of words, such as idioms and metaphors. The best measure of students' learning of words is their ability to use the words in meaningful, functional, and genuine activities. The key points in this chapter are:

1. English is a historic language, and its diverse origins account for word meanings and some spelling inconsistencies.
2. The fact that students' vocabularies grow at a rate of about 3,000 words a year suggests that students learn many words incidentally.
3. Students use their knowledge of root words and affixes to unlock the meaning of unfamiliar words.
4. Many words have more than one meaning, and students learn additional word meanings through literature focus units and theme cycles.
5. Idioms and metaphors can be confusing to students because they must be interpreted figuratively rather than literally.
6. Reading and writing are the most important ways students learn vocabulary.
7. Students need to use a word many times in order to learn it well.
8. All words are not equally difficult or easy to learn; the degree of difficulty depends on what the student already knows about the word.
9. Students use reference books, including dictionaries and thesauri, to learn about words.
10. Word-study activities include word walls, word posters, word clusters, word sorts, word chains, and semantic feature analysis.

Extensions

1. Learn more about the history of English by reading one or more of the books listed in Figure 5–1.
2. Choose a literature focus unit or theme cycle for a particular grade level and identify a list of possible words for the word wall. Which words do you think will be sight words, new words, new concepts, or new meanings for students?

3. Observe in an elementary classroom and note how vocabulary is taught both formally and informally. Or, interview an elementary teacher and ask how he or she teaches vocabulary. Compare the teacher's answers with the information presented in this chapter.

4. Plan and teach a series of minilessons on vocabulary. Refer to the chart of minilesson topics on page 211 to choose a topic.
5. Think back to the discussion on language-rich classrooms in Chapter 2 and brainstorm a list of 10 ways to facilitate students' incidental learning of vocabulary through the classroom environment

> **❝** We write every day, and then the boys and girls share their journals in our circle. Sharing is the most important part of writing in my classroom. **❞**
>
> **Glenna Jarvis**
> *First-Grade Teacher*
> *Western Hills Elementary School*

PROCEDURE

My 6-year-old children write in journals—one kind or another—every day. Sometimes they write about anything they want to. I usually start with these free-choice or personal journals at the beginning of the school year. Later, they write in reading logs about the stories we are reading and in learning logs about what they are learning about in social studies or science.

This week the boys and girls are writing in bear-shaped booklets that I made to go along with our literature focus unit on *Corduroy* (Freeman, 1968) and its sequel, *A Pocket of Corduroy* (Freeman, 1972). Yesterday I read *A Pocket of Corduroy,* and we made a chart of things my students would keep in their pockets. After we read a story, my children write in their reading logs. I see the ideas from the books about *Corduroy* and other bear books I've read to them appear again and again in the children's writing. The cover and one page from Melissa's reading log are presented in the accompanying figure. Melissa writes:

 I love Corduroy. I would choose him to be my very own bear.

Each morning as the children finish writing in their journals, they leave their desks and come to sit on the carpet in our circle area. The first child to finish usually sits in our author's chair and gets to be the first one to share. As they share, boys and girls read or tell about their journal entries and then show them to the audience. Children in the audience raise their hands to offer comments and compliments. I always let the child who is sharing choose the children to offer comments and compliments. After three or four children have given compliments, the child who is sitting in the author's chair chooses the next boy or girl to share.

Sharing moves really quickly; the entire class can share in about 20 minutes, so I usually encourage everyone to share. If I'm pressed for time, I sometimes have half the children share in the morning and postpone the rest of sharing until afternoon. I've also tried having only five or six children share each day, but I prefer to have everyone be a part of the sharing every day so that I know what every child is doing and what is happening in his or her life.

ASSESSMENT

Observing the boys and girls as they share is probably the most important thing I do. I notice what topics they choose to write about, how they use drawing and writing to convey their message, and the confidence they have as they share their journals. I also look to see how they act when they are in the audience, the types of comments and compliments they offer, and how they respond to their classmates' journals. I participate in sharing every day, and I watch and listen. I try to take a few minutes each day to write anecdotal notes on index cards that I keep for each student in the class.

ADAPTATIONS

I encourage my children to communicate in their journals, whether they draw or write or use a combination of the two. I think that by making time to share each day, I am emphasizing the communicative function of writing. My children do different things in their journals. Some only draw pictures, and others use a combination of drawing and writing. At the beginning of the school year, only a few children are writing, but I model "kid writing" and show them how to use a letter or two to represent an entire word. I also teach mini-lessons about sound-symbol cor-respondences, handwriting skills, using capital letters and periods, and writing sentences. Their writing matures as they learn more about written language. I realize that writing is a developmental process, as I value my children's journal entries as evidence of their development.

REFLECTIONS

My students are first graders, and I try hard to tailor my program to meet their needs. Journal writing is the perfect activity for these students, because they are applying what they are learning about reading and literature, letters of the alphabet, and writing within a socialized and cooperative group setting.

Writing in Journals

Students in Laurie Goodman's eighth-grade class made a stained-glass "quilt" after reading *Catherine, Called Birdy* (Cushman, 1994), a Newbery Honor Book written as a diary. Students used black construction paper and colorful tissue paper to create a stained-glass effect. The quilt was hung on the large windows in the classroom to create a medieval mood. Students added diamante poems to the bottom of the quilt squares. Here is one student's poem:

> *Birdy*
> *Wild,   Clever*
> *Scheming, Complaining, Intriguing*
> *Tomboy, Adventure, Lady, Seamstress*
> *Hardworking, Approving, Trusting*
> *Docile, Accomplished*
> *Catherine*

ll kinds of people—artists, scientists, dancers, politicians, writers, assassins, and children—keep journals (Mallon, 1984). People usually record in their journals the everyday events of their lives and the issues that concern them. These journals, typically written in notebook form, are personal records, not intended for public display. Other journals might be termed "working" journals, in which writers record observations and other information to use for another purpose; for example, farmers might record weather or crop data, or gardeners the blooming cycle of their plants.

The journals of some public figures have survived for hundreds of years and provide a fascinating glimpse of their authors and the times in which they lived. For example, the Renaissance genius Leonardo da Vinci recorded his daily activities, dreams, and plans for his painting and engineering projects in more than 40 notebooks. In the 1700s, Puritan theologian Jonathan Edwards documented his spiritual life in his journal. In the late 1700s, American explorers Meriwether Lewis and George Rogers Clark kept a journal of their travels across the North American continent, more for geographical than personal use. In the nineteenth century, the American writer Henry David Thoreau filled 39 notebooks with his essays. French author Victor Hugo carried a small pocket notebook to record ideas as they came to him—even at inopportune moments such as while talking with friends. American author F. Scott Fitzgerald filled his notebooks with snippets of overheard conversations, many of which he later used in *The Great Gatsby* and other novels. Anne Frank, who wrote while in hiding from the Nazis during World War II, is the best-known child diarist.

As you continue reading about the journals that elementary students use and how to incorporate journal writing in your language arts program, think about these questions:

- What types of journals do elementary students use?
- How do students use journals as tools for learning in language arts and across the curriculum?
- How do teachers introduce journal-writing activities?
- What other informal writing activities do students use journals for?

TYPES OF JOURNALS

Elementary students use journals for a variety of purposes, just as adults do. Seven types of journals are described in the Teacher's Notebook on page 223. In each type of journal the focus is on the writer, and the writing is personal and private. Students' writing is spontaneous and loosely organized, and it often contains mechanical errors because students are focusing on thinking, not on spelling, capitalization, and punctuation. James Britton and his colleagues (1975) compare this type of writing to a written conversation, and that conversation may be with oneself or with trusted readers who are interested in the writer. Some of the purposes for journal writing are to:

- Record experiences
- Stimulate interest in a topic
- Explore thinking

Teacher's Notebook
Types of Journals

Personal Journals

Students write about events in their own lives and other topics of special interest in personal journals. These journals are the most private type. Teachers respond as interested readers, often asking questions and offering comments about their own lives.

Dialogue Journals

Dialogue journals are similar to personal journals except that they are written to be shared with the teacher or a classmate. The person who receives the journal reads the entry and responds to it. These journals are like a written conversation.

Reading Logs

Students respond to stories, poems, and informational books they are reading in reading logs. They write and draw entries after reading, record key vocabulary words, make charts and other diagrams, and write memorable quotes.

Double-Entry Journals

Students divide each page of their journals into two columns and write different types of information in each column. Sometimes they write quotes from a story in one column and add reactions to the quotes in the other, or write predictions in one column and what actually happened in the story in the other.

Language Arts Notebooks

Students take notes, write rules and examples, draw diagrams, and write lists of other useful information about language arts in these notebooks. Students use these notebooks during minilessons and refer to the information during literature focus units and reading and writing workshop.

Learning Logs

Students write in learning logs as part of social studies and science theme cycles and math units. They write quickwrites, draw diagrams, take notes, and write vocabulary words.

Simulated Journals

Students assume the role of a book character or a historical personality and write journal entries from that person's viewpoint. Students include details from the story or historical period in their entries.

- Personalize learning
- Develop interpretations
- Wonder, predict, and hypothesize
- Engage the imagination
- Ask questions
- Activate prior knowledge
- Assume the role of another person
- Share experiences with trusted readers

Toby Fulwiler (1985b) shared excerpts from his daughter Megan's third-grade journal in *Language Arts,* demonstrating how she used writing for many of these functions. Later when she was a teenager, Megan Fulwiler (1986) reflected on her journal-writing experiences and her reasons for writing. Most importantly, Megan described her journal as an extension of her mind that she used to work out her feelings, ask questions and find answers, and write down and organize her thoughts. She noted that as time passed, her entries grew more personal and became a record of her growing up.

As with Megan, journal writing gives students valuable writing practice. They gain fluency and confidence that they can write. They can also experiment with writing conventions that must be considered in more public writing. If they decide to make an entry "public," students can later revise and edit their writing.

Personal Journals

Students often keep personal journals in which they recount events in their lives and write about topics of their choosing. Students choose to write about a variety of topics and explore their feelings in these entries. It is normal for students to misspell a few words in their entries; when students write in personal journals, the emphasis is on what they say, not how correctly they write.

It is often helpful to develop a list of possible journal-writing topics on a chart in the classroom or on sheets of paper for students to clip inside their journal notebooks. Students choose their own topics for personal journals. Although they can write about almost anything, some students will complain that they don't know what to write about, so a list of topics gives them a crutch. Figure 6–1 shows a list of possible journal-writing topics developed by a class of fourth and fifth graders. Students can add topics to their lists throughout the year, which may include more than 100 topics by the end of the school year. Referring students to the list or asking them to brainstorm a list of topics encourages them to become more independent writers and discourages them from relying too heavily on teachers for writing topics.

Privacy becomes an important issue as students grow older. Most young children are willing to share what they have written, but by third or fourth grade, students grow less willing to read their journal entries aloud to the class, although they are usually willing to share the entries with a trusted teacher. Teachers must be scrupulous about respecting students' privacy and not insist that they share their writing when they are unwilling to do so. It is also important to talk with students about respecting each other's privacy and not reading each other's journals. To protect students' privacy, many teachers keep personal journals on an out-of-the-way shelf when they are not in use.

Figure 6–1   *Fourth and Fifth Graders' List of Possible Writing Topics*

Things to Write About in Personal Journals

my favorite place in town	if I had three wishes
boyfriends/girlfriends	my teacher
things that make me happy or sad	TV shows I watch
music	my favorite holiday
an imaginary planet	if I were stranded on an island
cars	what I want to be when I grow up
magazines I like to read	private thoughts
what if snow were hot	how to be a superhero
dreams I have	dinosaurs
cartoons	my mom/my dad
places I've been	my friends
favorite movies	my next vacation
rock stars	love
if I were a movie/rock star	if I were an animal or something else
poems	books I've read
pets	favorite things to do
football	my hobbies
astronauts	if I were a skydiver
the president	when I get a car
jokes	if I had a lot of money
motorcycles	dolls
things that happen in my school	if I were rich
current events	wrestling and other sports
things I do on weekends	favorite colors
a soap opera with daily episodes	questions answered with "never"

or ANYTHING else I want to write about

When students share personal information with teachers through their journals, a second issue arises. Sometimes teachers learn details about students' problems and family life that they do not know how to deal with. Entries about child abuse, suicide, or drug use may be the child's way of asking for help. While teachers are not counselors, they do have a legal obligation to protect their students and report possible problems to appropriate school personnel. Occasionally a student invents a personal problem in a journal entry as an attention-getting tactic; however, asking the student about the entry or having a school counselor do so will help to ensure that the student's safety is fully considered.

Dialogue Journals

Students converse in writing with the teacher or with a classmate through dialogue journals (Bode, 1989; Gambrell, 1985; Staton, 1980, 1987). These journals are interactive and conversational in tone. Most importantly, dialogue journals are an authentic writing activity and provide the opportunity for real communication between students or between a student and the teacher. Students write informally about something of interest, a concern, about a book they are reading, or about what they are learning in a theme cycle. Students choose their own topics and usually control the direction the writing takes.

Children write and draw about their experiences in personal journals.

When teachers or classmates respond to students' entries, they answer as they would in an oral conversation. They react to students' comments, ask questions, and offer suggestions. Staton (1987) offers these suggests for teachers who are responding to students' writing and continuing the dialogue:

1. Acknowledge students' ideas and encourage them to continue to write about their interests.
2. Support students by complimenting them about behavior and schoolwork.
3. Provide new information about topics, so that students will want to read your responses.
4. Write less than the students do.
5. Avoid unspecific comments like "good idea" or "very interesting."
6. Ask few questions; instead, encourage students to ask you questions.

Teachers' responses do not need to be lengthy; a sentence or two is often enough. Even so, it is time-consuming to respond to 25, 30, or more journal entries every day. As an alternative, many teachers read and respond to students' journal entries on a rotating basis. They might respond to one group of students one week and another group the next week.

In this fifth grader's dialogue journal, Daniel shares the events and problems in his life with his teacher, and she responds sympathetically. Daniel writes:

Over spring break I went down to my grandma's house and played basketball in their backyard and while we were there we went to see some of my uncles who are all Indians. Out of my whole family down there they are all Indians except Grandpa Russell.

And Daniel's teacher responds:

> *What a fun spring break! That is so interesting to have Indians in your family. I think I might have some Indian ancestors too. Do you still plan to go to Padre Island for the summer?*

The next day Daniel writes:

> *My family and I plan to go to Padre Island in June and I imagine we will stay there for quite a while. I think the funnest part will probably be swimming or camping or something like that. When we get there my mom says we will probably stay in a nice motel.*

Daniel's teacher responds:

> *That really sounds like a fun vacation. I think swimming is the most fun, too. Who will go with you?*

Daniel continues to talk about his family, now focusing on the problems he and his family are facing:

> *Well, my mom and dad are divorced so that is why I am going to court to testify on Tuesday but my mom, me, and my sister and brother are all going and that kind of makes me sad because a couple of years ago when my mom and dad were together we used to go a lot of places like camping and hiking but now after what happened we hardly go anywhere.*

His teacher responds:

> *I am so sorry your family is having problems. It sounds as if your mom and dad are having problems with each other, but they both love you and want to be with you. Be sure to keep talking to them about how you feel.*

Daniel replies:

> *I wish my mom and dad did not have problems because I would have a lot more fun and get to go and do a lot more things together, but since my mom and dad are divorced I have to take turns spending time with both of them.*

His teacher offers a suggestion:

> *I'm sure that is hard. Trevor and Carla have parents who are divorced, too. Maybe you could talk to them. It might help.*

This journal is not a series of teacher questions and student answers; instead, the student and teacher are having a dialogue, or conversation, and the interchange is built on mutual trust and respect.

Dialogue journals can be effective in dealing with students who have behavior problems or other types of difficulties in school (Staton, 1980). The teacher and student write back and forth about the problem and identify ways to solve it. In later entries the student reflects on his or her progress toward solving the problem. The teacher responds to the student's message, asks clarifying questions, or offers sympathy and praise.

Kreeft (1984) believes that the greatest value of dialogue journals is that they bridge the gap between talking and writing; they are written conversations. As the journal excerpts between Daniel and his teacher show, a second value is the strong bond that develops between student and teacher through their writing back and forth.

Dialogue journals are especially effective in promoting the writing development of children who are learning English as a second language. Researchers have found that these students are more successful writers when they choose their own topics for writing and when their teachers contribute to the dialogue with requests for a reply, statements, and other comments (Peyton & Seyoum, 1989; Reyes, 1991). Not surprisingly, researchers found that students wrote more when teachers requested a reply than when teachers made comments that did not require a response. Also, when a student was particularly interested in a topic, it was less important what the teacher did, and when the teacher and the student were both interested in a topic, the topic seemed to take over as they shared and built on each other's writing. Reyes also found that bilingual students were much more successful in writing dialogue journal entries than in writing in response to books they had read.

Students use dialogue journals to write to classmates or the teacher about books they are reading (Barone, 1990; Dekker, 1991; Nash, 1995). In these journal entries, students write about the books they are reading, compare the books to others by the same author or other authors they have read, and offer opinions about the book and whether a classmate or the teacher might enjoy reading it. They also write about their book-selection strategies and their reading behavior.

■ *To learn more about reading workshop, see Chapter 3, "The Reading and Writing Processes," pp. 109–111.*

This approach is especially effective in reading workshop classrooms when students are reading different books. Students are often paired and write back-and-forth to their reading buddies. This activity provides the socialization that independent reading does not. Depending on whether students are reading relatively short picture books or longer chapter books, they can write dialogue journal entries every other day or once a week, and then classmates write back.

Fourth graders wrote these entries to classmates and their teacher about informational books they were reading during reading workshop:

✏ *Dear Adam,*
I'm reading the coolest book. It's about snakes and it's called A Snake's Body *[Cole, 1981]. Look at the pictures on pages 34, 35, 36, 37, 38, 39, 40, 41, and 42 to see how a python strangles and eats a chick. It's awesome.*
  Your Friend, Todd

✏ *Dear Mrs. Parker,*
I just finished reading The Magic School Bus Inside the Human Body *[Cole, 1989]. I think you would like it, too, because it's about a teacher named Ms. Frizzle and she's sort of magic. She takes her kids on a field trip and Ms. Frizzle drives the school bus inside a human body. The book takes a long time to read because it has lots of cartoons and extra things to read and look at. I'd say it was one of the best books I've ever read. I think everyone in our class should read it. What do you think?*
  Love, Ali

✏ *Trevor,*
The book I'm reading is A Wall of Names *[Donnelly, 1991]. It's ok, if you want to know about the Vietnam wall memorial. I picked this book because my Gramps was in that war and last summer we went to Washington, D.C. on vacation and I got to see the wall. It's shiny and black and all the names of the soldiers that died fighting in it are written on the wall. Have you ever heard of it?*
  From your friend, David

Before the students began writing dialogue journal entries, the teacher taught a minilesson about how to format their entries, about how to capitalize and underline book titles, and about the importance of asking questions in their entries so that respondents could answer them in their replies. In their entries most students incorporated what they had learned in the minilesson.

Reading Logs

Students write in reading logs about the stories and other books they are reading or listening to the teacher read aloud during literature focus units and reading workshop. Rather than simply summarize their reading, students relate their reading to their own lives or to other literature they have read. Students may also list interesting or unfamiliar words, jot down memorable quotes, and take notes about characters, plot, or other story elements; but the primary purpose of these journals is for students to think about the book, connect literature to their lives, and develop their own interpretations. These journals go by a variety of names, including literature response journals (Hancock, 1992), literature journals (Five, 1986), and reading journals (Wollman-Bonilla, 1989); but no matter what they are called, their purpose remains the same.

Teachers and researchers (Barone, 1990; Dekker, 1991; Hancock, 1992) have examined students' reading log entries and have identified these categories of response:

- Questions related to understanding the text
- Interaction with characters
- Empathy with characters
- Prediction and validation
- Personal experiences
- Personal feelings and opinions
- Simple and elaborate evaluations
- Philosophical reflections
- Retellings and summaries

Seventh graders' reading log entries about *The Giver* (Lowry, 1993) are shown in Figure 6–2. In these entries, students react to the book, make predictions, deepen their understanding of the story, ask questions, assume the role of the main character, and value the story.

When students begin writing entries in reading logs, their first entries are often retellings and plot summaries, but as students gain experience reading and responding to literature, their entries become more interpretive and personal. Teachers can model writing "I think" reactions, share student entries that are interpretive, and respond to students' entries by asking questions.

Teachers and researchers have examined students' responses and noticed patterns in their reading log entries. Hancock (1992, 1993) identified these eight categories:

1. *Monitoring understanding.* Students get to know the characters and explain how the story is making sense to them. These responses usually occur at the beginning of a book.
2. *Making inferences.* Students share their insights into the feelings and motives of a character. They often begin their comments with "I think."

Figure 6–2   Entries From Seventh Graders' Reading Logs About The Giver

I think the book *The Giver* is very scary because when you do something wrong you get released from the community. I think it would be terrible to be pushed out of your community and leave your family. Your family would be ashamed and embarrassed. It is like you are dead.

I don't think I could handle being a friend of Jonas's. In other words NO I would not like to be a friend of his. There would be too much pain involved and most of the time I wouldn't see Jonas.

The part that hooked me was when the book said Jonas took his pills and did not have feelings about Fiona.

As I'm reading I'm wondering if they get married at twelve because they get jobs at twelve.

Something that surprised me so far in the story was when Lily said she wanted to be a birthmother. Lily's mom became mad and said three years, three births, and then you're a laborer. Being a birthmother is not a good job at least after the three years. I hope that doesn't happen to Lily but I don't know what other job she should have.

So far I think that the story is really sad. The story is sad because everyone has sameness except Jonas and the Giver. Jonas and the Giver are the only ones who can see color because of the memories. The story is also sad because no one has feelings.

Why didn't Jonas use the fire in his favorite memory to stay warmer on his long journey through the rain, and snow, and the terrible coldness? Also, why didn't the author explain more about the things that are between the lines so the reader could really grasp them?

Well, I can't really make a prediction of what is going to happen because I already read the book. If I hadn't read ahead my prediction would be that Jonas would get drowned in the river because he couldn't handle the pain.

I think Jonas will confront his father. He won't ever forget what he saw his father do and it is wrong. Just wrong, wrong, wrong. If my father ever did that to an innocent little baby I would never forgive him. It's like abortion. I would confront him and tell him that I know. I will always know and so will God.

I don't exactly understand what happens at the end. It sounds like they froze to death. I think they died but I wish they found freedom and happiness. It is very sad.

The ending is cool. Jonas and Gabe come back to the community but now it is changed. There are colors and the people have feelings. They believe in God and it is Christmas.

At first I thought it would be good to have a perfect community. There would be no gangs and no crime and no sickness. but there is a lesson in this story. Now I think you can't have a perfect community. Even though we have bad things in our community we have love and other emotions and we can make choices.

3. *Making, validating, or invalidating predictions.* Students speculate about what will happen later in the story and also confirm or deny predictions they made previously.
4. *Expressing wonder or confusion.* Students reflect on the way the story is developing. They ask "I wonder why" questions and write about confusions.
5. *Character interaction.* Students show that they are personally involved with a character, sometimes writing "If I were _____, I would . . ." They express empathy and share related experiences from their own lives. Also, they may give advice to the character.
6. *Character assessment.* Students judge a character's actions and often use evaluative terms such as "nice" or "dumb."
7. *Story involvement.* Students reveal their involvement in the story as they express satisfaction with how the story is developing. They may comment on their desire to continue reading or use terms such as "disgusting," "weird," or "awesome" to react to sensory aspects of the story.
8. *Literary criticism.* Students offer "I liked/I didn't like" opinions and praise or condemn an author's style. Sometimes students compare the book with others they have read or compare the author with other authors with whom they are familiar.

The first four categories are personal meaning-making options in which students make inferences about characters, offer predictions, ask questions, or discuss confusions. The next three categories focus on character and plot development. Students are more involved with the story, and they offer reactions to the characters and events of the story. The last category is literary evaluation, in which students evaluate books and reflect on their own literary tastes.

These categories can extend the possibilities of response by introducing teachers and students to a wide variety of response options. Hancock (1992, 1993) recommends that teachers begin by assessing the kinds of responses students are currently making. They can read students' reading logs, categorize the entries, tally the categories, and make an assessment. Often students use only a few types of responses, not the wide range that is available. Teachers can teach minilessons and model types of responses that students aren't using, and they can ask questions when they read journals to prompt students to think in new ways about the story they are reading.

Double-Entry Journals

For double-entry journals, students divide each entry into two parts (Barone, 1990; Berthoff, 1981). Often, students divide their journal pages into two columns; in the left column they write quotes from the story or other book they are reading, and in the right column they relate each quote to their own life and to literature they have read. Through this type of journal, students become more engaged in what they are reading, note sentences that have personal connections, and become more sensitive to the author's language.

Students in a fifth-grade class kept a double-entry journal as they read C. S. Lewis's classic *The Lion, the Witch and the Wardrobe* (1950). After they read each chapter, they reviewed the chapter and selected one, two, or three brief quotes. They wrote these excerpts in the left column of their journals, and they wrote reactions beside each quote in the right column. Excerpts from a fifth grader's journal are presented in Figure 6–3. This student's responses indicate that she is engaged in the story and is connecting the story to her own life as well as to another story she has read.

Double-entry journals can be used in several other ways. Instead of recording quotes from the book, students can write "Reading Notes" in the left column and then add "Reactions" in the right column. In the left column students write about the events they read about in the chapter. Then in the right column they make personal connections to the events.

As an alternative, students can use the heading "Reading Notes" for one column and "Discussion Notes" for the second column. Students write reading notes as they read or immediately after reading. Later, after discussing the story or chapter of a longer book, students add discussion notes. As with other types of double-entry journals, it is in the second column that students make more interpretive comments.

Younger students can use the double-entry format for a prediction journal (Macon, Bewell, & Vogt, 1991). They label the left column "Predictions" and the right column "What Happened." In the left column they write or draw a picture of what they predict will happen in the story or chapter before read-

Figure 6–3   *Excerpts from a Fifth Grader's Double-Entry Journal about* The Lion, the Witch and the Wardrobe

In the Text	**My Response**
Chapter 1	
I tell you this is the sort of house where no one is going to mind what we do.	I remember the time that I went to Beaumont, Texas to stay with my aunt. My aunt's house was very we large. She had a piano and she let us play it. She told us what we could do whatever we wanted to.
Chapter 5	
"How do you know?" he asked, "that your sister's story is not true?"	It reminds me of when I was little and I had an imaginary place. I would go there in my mind. I made up all kinds of make-believe stories about myself in this imaginary place. One time I told my big brother about my imaginary place. He laughed at me and told me I was silly. But it didn't bother me because nobody can stop me from thinking what I want.
Chapter 15	
Still they could see the shape of the great lion lying dead in his bonds.	When Aslan died I thought about when my Uncle Carl died.
They're nibbling at the cords.	This reminds me of the story where the lion lets the mouse go and the mouse helps the lion.

ing it. Then, after reading, they draw or write what actually happened in the right column.

Language Arts Notebooks

Language arts notebooks are a specialized type of journal in which students record a variety of information about language arts. Often students use these notebooks to take notes about procedures, concepts, strategies, and skills during minilessons. Procedure entries include the steps in giving a book talk, participating in a grand conversation, and proofreading a paper. Concept entries include information on authors and genres, contractions, homophones, parts of speech, plot diagrams, affixes, poetic formulas, and types of sentences. Strategy entries include explanations of visualization or connecting to personal experience, and student reflections about how they use the strategy during language arts activities. Skill entries include charts about forming plurals, using quotations in writing dialogue, alphabetizing a list of words, and skimming a content-area textbook.

By recording this information in a notebook, students create a permanent reference book to use during language arts activities. Teachers of upper-grade students often have students divide their language arts notebooks into several sections, and students add information to sections on authors, words, spelling, parts of speech, sentences, strategies, poetry, stories, and study skills.

Four entries from sixth graders' language arts notebooks are shown in Figure 6–4. The first page lists the steps in writing a summary; the second page lists the two parts of a sentence, with sample sentences from Naylor's award-winning *Shiloh* (1991); the third page compares *dessert* and *desert*, two easily confused spellings; and the fourth page lists prepositions that describe locations.

Learning Logs

Students write entries in learning logs to record or react to what they are learning in math, science, social studies, or other content areas. Fulwiler explains: "When people write about something they learn it better" (1987, p. 9). As students write in these journals, they reflect on their learning, discover gaps in their knowledge, and explore relationships between what they are learning and their past experiences.

Learning Logs in Math. Students use learning logs to write about what they are learning in math (Salem, 1982). They record explanations and examples of concepts presented in class, and react to the mathematical concepts they are learning and any problems they may be having. Some upper-grade teachers allow students the last 5 minutes of math class to summarize the day's lesson and react to it in their learning logs (Schubert, 1987). Through these activities, students practice taking notes, writing descriptions and directions, and using other writing skills. They also learn how to reflect on and evaluate their own learning (Stanford, 1988).

Figure 6–5 presents an entry from a sixth grader's learning log in which she describes how to change improper fractions. Notice that after she describes the steps in sequence, she includes a review of the six steps.

Figure 6–4   Four Excerpts From Sixth Graders' Language Arts Notebooks

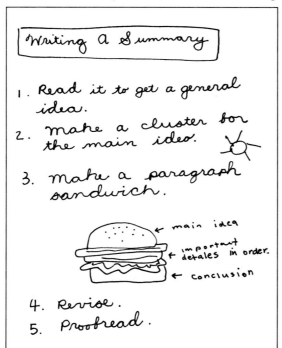

Writing a Summary

1. Read it to get a general idea.
2. make a cluster for the main idea.
3. make a paragraph sandwich.

← main idea
← important detailes in order.
← conclusion

4. Revise.
5. Proofread.

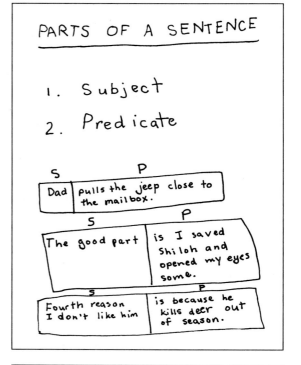

PARTS OF A SENTENCE

1. Subject
2. Predicate

S	P
Dad	pulls the jeep close to the mailbox.

S	P
The good part	is I saved Shiloh and opened my eyes some.

S	P
Fourth reason I don't like him	is because he kills deer out of season.

1 S OR 2 SS ?

de[ss]ert

de[s]e rt

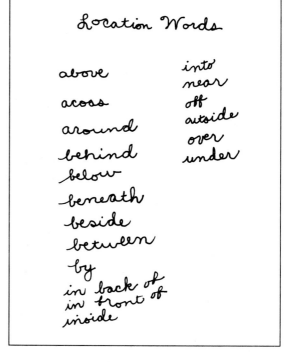

Location Words

above   into
acoss   near
around   off
behind   outside
below   over
beneath   under
beside
between
by
in back of
in front of
inside

Figure 6–5   *A Sixth Grader's Math Learning Log Entry*

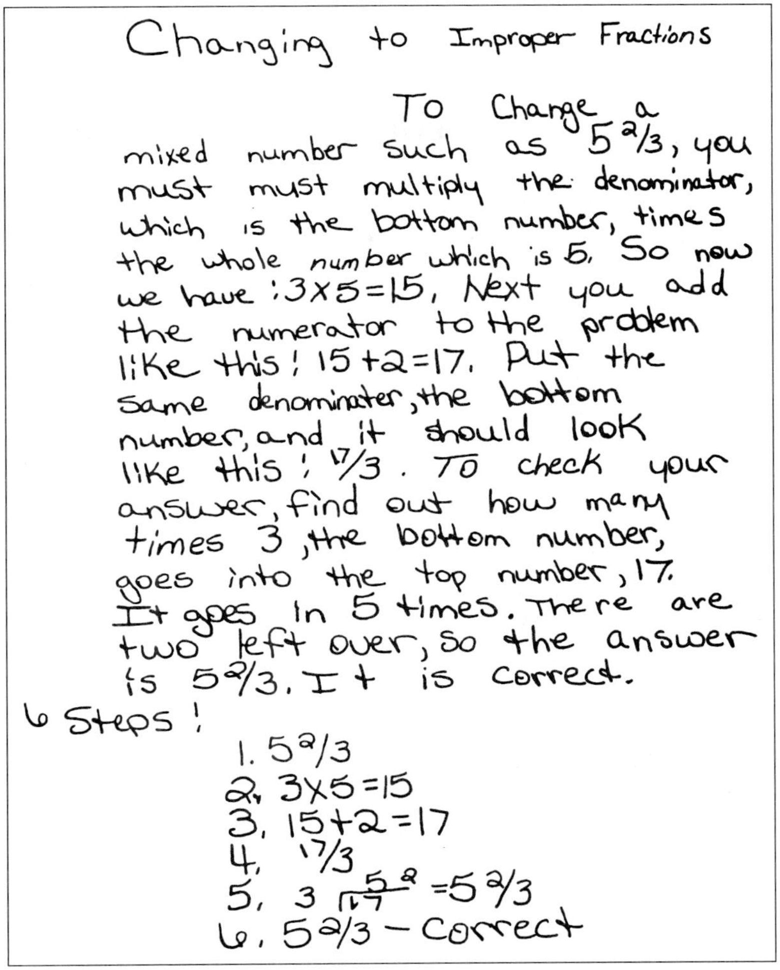

Changing to Improper Fractions

To Change a mixed number such as $5\frac{2}{3}$, you must must multiply the denominator, which is the bottom number, times the whole number which is 5. So now we have : $3 \times 5 = 15$, Next you add the numerator to the problem like this! $15 + 2 = 17$. Put the same denominator, the bottom number, and it should look like this! $\frac{17}{3}$. To check your answer, find out how many times 3, the bottom number, goes into the top number, 17. It goes in 5 times. There are two left over, so the answer is $5\frac{2}{3}$. It is correct.

6 Steps!

1. $5\frac{2}{3}$
2. $3 \times 5 = 15$
3. $15 + 2 = 17$
4. $\frac{17}{3}$
5. $3\overline{)17} = 5\frac{2}{3}$
6. $5\frac{2}{3}$ – correct

In addition to these benefits to students, teachers use learning logs to informally assess students' learning. Through students' math entries, teachers can assess what students already know about a topic before teaching, discover what students are learning, and check on confusions and misconceptions. Teachers can also use the entries to monitor students' attitudes toward math and assess their learning of a concept after teaching (McGonegal, 1987). Sometimes teachers simply read these entries, and at other times the learning logs become dialogue journals as teachers respond to students by clarifying misconceptions and offering encouragement.

Learning Logs in Science.   Science-related learning logs can take several different forms. One type is an observation log in which students make daily entries to track the growth of plants or animals. For instance, a second-grade class observed caterpillars as they changed from caterpillars to chrysalides to butterflies over a period of 4 to 6 weeks. Students each kept a log with daily entries, in which they were to describe the changes they observed using words describing shape, color, size, and other properties. Two pages from a second grader's log documenting the caterpillars' growth and change are presented in Figure 6–6. A second type of learning log is one in which students make entries during a theme cycle. Students may take notes during presentations by the teacher or after reading, after viewing films, or at the end of each class period. Sometimes students make entries in list form, sometimes in clusters, charts, or maps, and at other times in paragraphs.

Learning Logs in Social Studies.   Students often keep learning logs as part of theme cycles in social studies. In their logs, students write in response to stories and informational books, note interesting words related to the theme, create timelines, and draw diagrams, charts, and maps. For example, as part of a theme cycle on the Civil War for eighth graders, students might include the following in their learning logs:

* Informal quickwrites about the causes of the war and other topics related to the war
* A list of words related to the theme
* A chart of major battles in the war

Figure 6–6   *Two Entries From a Second Grader's Science Log on Caterpillars*

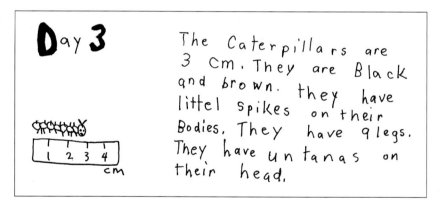

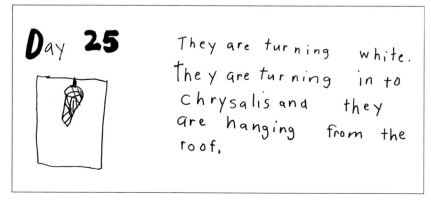

These primary-grade students write in their learning logs about the salamander they are observing.

- A Venn diagram comparing the Northern and Southern viewpoints
- A timeline showing events related to the war
- A map of the United States at the time of the war with battle locations marked
- Notes after viewing several films about the Civil War era
- A list of favorite quotes from Lincoln's "Gettysburg Address"
- Their responses to chapter books such as *Charley Skedaddle* (Beatty, 1987), *Brady* (Fritz, 1987), *Across Five Aprils* (Hunt, 1987), or *The 290* (O'Dell, 1976)

Through these learning log activities, students explore concepts they are learning and record information they want to remember about the Civil War.

Simulated Journals

Some children's books, such as *Catherine, Called Birdy* (Cushman, 1994) and *Stranded at Plimoth Plantation, 1626* (Bowen, 1994), are written as journals, and the authors assumed the role of a character and wrote from the character's point of view. I call these books simulated journals. They are rich with historical details and feature examples of both words and phrasing of the period. At the end of the book, authors often include information about how they researched the period and explanations about the liberties they took with the character, setting, or events that are recorded. Scholastic Books is creating a new series of historical journals appropriate for fourth- through eighth-grade students. The books published thus far include *A Journey to the New World: The Diary of Remember Patience Whipple* (Lasky, 1996), *The Winter of Red Snow: The Revolutionary War Diary of Abigail Jane Stewart* (Gregory, 1996), *A Picture of Freedom: The Diary of Clotee, a Slave Girl* (McKissack, 1997), and *When Will This Cruel War Be Over? The Civil War Diary of Emma Simpson* (Denenberg, 1996). These books each provide a glimpse into history from a young girl's perspective, and they are handsomely bound to look like an old journal. The paper is heavy and rough cut around the edges, and a ribbon page marker is bound into the book.

Elementary students, too can write simulated journals. They can assume the role of another person and write from that person's viewpoint. They can assume the role of a historical figure when they read biographies or as part of social studies theme cycles (Tompkins, 1995). As they read stories, students can assume the role of a character in the story. In this way students gain insight into other people's lives and into historical events. A look at a series of diary entries written by a fifth grader who has assumed the role of Betsy Ross shows how she carefully chose the dates for each entry and wove in factual information:

✎   *May 15, 1773*
Dear Diary,
This morning at 5:00 I had to wake up my husband John to get up for work but he wouldn't wake up. I immediately called the doc. He came over as fast as he could. He asked me to leave the room so I did. An hour later he came out and told me he had passed away. I am so sad. I don't know what to do.

✎   *June 16, 1776*
Dear Diary,
Today General Washington visited me about making a flag. I was so surprised. Me making a flag! I have made flags for the navy, but this is too much. But I said yes. He showed me a pattern of the flag he wanted. He also wanted six-pointed stars but I talked him into having five-pointed stars.

✎   *July 8, 1776*
Dear Diary,
Today in front of Carpenter Hall the Declaration of Independence was read by Tom Jefferson. Well, I will tell you the whole story. I heard some yelling and shouting about liberty and everyone was gathering around Carpenter Hall. So I went to my next door neighbors to ask what was happening but Mistress Peters didn't know either so we both went down to Carpenter Hall. We saw firecrackers and heard a bell and the Declaration of Independence was being read aloud. When I heard this I knew a new country was born.

✎   *June 14, 1777*
Dear Diary,
Today was a happy but scary day. Today the flag I made was adopted by Congress. I thought for sure that if England found out that a new flag was taking the old one's place something bad would happen. But I'm happy because I am the maker of the first American flag and I'm only 25 years old!

Students can use simulated journals in two ways. They can use them as a tool for learning or as a project. When students use simulated journals as a tool for learning, they write the entries as they are reading a book in order to get to know the character better, or during the theme cycle as they are learning about the historical period. In these entries, students are exploring concepts and making connections between what they are learning and what they already know. These journal entries are less polished than when students write a simulated journal as a project. Students might choose to write a simulated journal as a culminating project for a literature focus unit or a theme cycle. As a project, students plan out their journals carefully, choose important dates, and use the writing process to draft, revise, edit, and publish their journals.

One variation of simulated journals is simulated letters (Roop, 1995). Students assume the role of a book character or historical figure, as they do for simulated journals, but students write a letter—not a journal entry—to another character in the book or to another historical figure. Students can exchange letters with classmates or the teacher and write replies.

■ *To read more about writing simulated letters, turn to Chapter 10 "Reading and Writing Information," p. 415.*

Young Children's Journals

■ *To read about invented spelling, turn to Chapter 12, "Language Tools: Spelling, Handwriting, and Grammar," pp. 479–484, and to learn more about how young children emerge into writing, see Chapter 4, "Emergent Literacy," pp. 168–176.*

Young children can write in journals by drawing, or they can use a combination of drawing and writing (Hipple, 1985; McGee & Richgels, 1996; Nathan, 1987). Children may write scribbles, random letters and numbers, simple captions, or extended texts using invented spelling. Their invented spellings often seem bizarre by adult standards, but they are reasonable in terms of children's knowledge of phoneme-grapheme correspondences and spelling patterns. Other children want parents and teachers to take their dictation and write the text. After the text has been written, children can usually read it immediately, and they retain recognition of the words for several days.

Young children usually begin writing in personal or dialogue journals and then expand their repertoire of journal forms to include reading logs and learning logs. Four kindergartners' journal entries are presented in Figure 6–7. The top two entries are from personal journals, and the bottom two are from reading logs. In the top left entry this 5-year-old focuses on the illustration, drawing a detailed picture of a football game (note that the player in the middle right position has the ball); he adds five letters for the text so that his entry will have some writing. In the top right entry the kindergartner writes, "I spent the night at my dad's house." The child wrote the entry on the bottom left after listening to his teacher read *The Three Billy Goats Gruff* (Stevens, 1987) and then acting out the story. As he shared his entry with classmates, he read the text this way: "You are a mean bad troll." The kindergartner wrote the entry on the bottom right after listening to the teacher read *The Jolly Postman, or Other People's Letters* (Ahlberg & Ahlberg, 1986). This child drew a picture of the three bears receiving a letter from Goldilocks. She labeled the mom, dad, and baby bear in the picture and wrote, "I [am] sorry I ate your porridge."

Through a variety of forms and purposes, journal writing helps elementary students discover the power of writing to record information and explore ideas. Students usually cherish their journals and are amazed by the amount of writing they contain.

Figure 6–7   *Entries From Young Children's Journals*

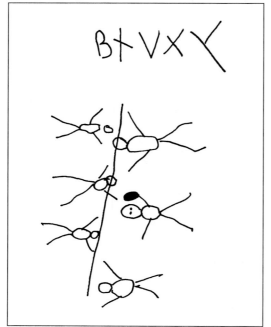

TEACHING STUDENTS TO WRITE IN JOURNALS

Journals are typically written in notebooks. Spiral-bound notebooks are useful for long-term personal and dialogue journals and language arts notebooks, while small booklets of paper stapled together are more often used for reading logs, learning logs, and simulated journals that are used for one literature focus unit or theme cycle. Most teachers prefer to keep the journals in the classroom so that they will be available for students to write in each day, but students might write in journals at home as well.

Students usually write at a particular time each day. Many teachers have students make personal or dialogue journal entries while they take attendance or immediately after recess. Language arts notebooks are often used during minilessons to record information about topics such as poetic forms or quotation marks. Entries are made in reading logs during literature focus units and reading workshop. Learning logs and simulated journals can be written in as part of math class or social studies or science theme cycles.

Introducing Students to Journal Writing

Teachers introduce students to journal writing using minilessons in which they explain the purpose of the journal-writing activity and the procedures for gathering ideas, writing the entry, and sharing it with classmates. Teachers often model the procedure by writing a sample entry on the chalkboard or on chart paper as students observe. This sample demonstrates that the writing is to be informal, with ideas emphasized over correctness. Then students make their own first entries, and several read their entries aloud. Through this sharing, students who are still unclear about the activity have additional models on which to base their own writing.

Similar procedural minilessons are used to introduce each type of journal. Whereas all journals are informal writing activities, the purpose of the journal, the information included in the entries, and the viewpoint of the writer vary according to the type of journal.

Journal writing can also be introduced with examples from literature. Characters in children's literature, such as Harriet in *Harriet the Spy* (Fitzhugh, 1964), Leigh in *Dear Mr. Henshaw* (Cleary, 1983), and Birdy in *Catherine, Called Birdy* (Cushman, 1994), keep journals in which they record events in their lives, their ideas, and their dreams. A list of books in which characters and historical personalities keep journals is presented in Figure 6–8. In these books the characters demonstrate the process of journal writing and illustrate both the pleasures and the difficulties of keeping a journal.

Sustaining Journal Writing

Students write in journals on a regular schedule, usually daily. After they know how to write the appropriate type of entry, they can write independently. While some children prefer to write private journals, others will volunteer to read their journal entries aloud each day no matter what type of journal they are writing. Young children share their picture journal entries and talk about them. If the sharing becomes too time-consuming, students can share in small groups or with partners. Then, after everyone has had a chance to

Figure 6–8   Books in Which Characters and Historical Personalities Keep Journals

Altman, S. (1995). *My worst days diary.* New York: Bantam. (P)

Anderson, J. (1987). *Joshua's westward journey.* New York: Morrow. (M)

Blos, J. (1979). *A gathering of days: A New England girl's journal, 1830–1832.* New York: Scribner. (U)

Bowen, G. (1994). *Stranded at Plimoth plantation, 1626.* New York: HarperCollins. (M–U)

Cartlidge, M. (1994). *A mouse's diary.* New York: Dutton. (P)

Cleary, B. (1983). *Dear Mr. Henshaw.* New York: Morrow. (M)

Cleary, B. (1991). *Strider.* New York: Morrow. (M)

Conrad, P. (1991). *Pedro's journal: A voyage with Christopher Columbus (August 3, 1492–February 14, 1493).* Honedale, PA: Boyds Mills Press. (M–U)

Creech, S. (1995). *Absolutely normal chaos.* New York: HarperCollins. (U)

Cummings, P. (1992). *Petey Moroni's Camp Runamok diary.* New York: Bradbury. (P)

Cushman, K. (1994). *Catherine, called Birdy.* New York: Clarion. (U)

Denenberg, B. (1996). *When will this cruel war be over? The Civil War diary of Emma Simpson.* New York: Scholastic. (M–U)

Ducey, J. S. (1995). *The bittersweet time.* New York: Eerdmans. (M–U)

Filipovic, Z. (1994). *Zlata's diary: A child's life in Sarajevo.* New York: Viking. (U)

Fitzhugh, L. (1964). *Harriet the spy.* New York: Harper & Row. (M)

Frank, A. (1987). *Anne Frank: The diary of a young girl.* Philadelphia: Washington Square. (U)

George, J. C. (1959). *My side of the mountain.* New York: Dutton. (M–U)

Gregory, K. (1996). *The winter of red snow: The Revolutionary War diary of Abigail Jane Stewart.* New York: Scholastic. (M–U)

Harvey, B. (1986). *My prairie year: Based on the diary of Elenore Plaisted.* New York: Holiday House. (M)

Harvey, B. (1988). *Cassie's journey: Going west in the 1860s.* New York: Holiday House. (M)

Hest, A. (1995). *The private notebook of Katie Roberts, age 11.* Cambridge, MA: Candlewick Press. (M–U)

Johnson, D. (1994). *Seminole diary: Remembrances of a slave.* New York: Macmillan. (M)

Kalman, E. (1995). *Tchaikovsky discovers America.* New York: Orchard. (M–U)

Krupinski, L. (1995). *Bluewater journal: The voyage of the Sea Tiger.* New York: HarperCollins. (M–U)

Lasky, K. (1996). *A journey to the new world: The diary of Remember Patience Whipple.* New York: Scholastic. (M–U)

Leslie, C. W. (1991). *Nature all year long.* New York: Greenwillow. (M)

Lyon, G. E. (1994). *Here and then.* New York: Orchard. (M–U)

McKissack, P. C. (1997). *A picture of freedom: The diary of Clotee, a slave girl.* New York: Scholastic, (M–U)

Morpurgo, M. (1995). *The wreck of the Zanzibar.* New York: Viking. (M–U).

Moss, M. (1995). *Amelia's notebook.* New York: Tricycle. (P–M)

Roop, P., & Roop, C. (Eds.). (1990). *I Colombus: My journal, 1492–1493.* New York: Avon Books. (M–U)

Roop, P., & Roop, C. (1993). *Off the map: The journals of Lewis and Clark.* New York: Walker. (M–U)

Roth, S. L. (1990). *Marco Polo: His notebook.* New York: Doubleday. (U)

Ruby, L. (1994). *Steal away home.* New York: Macmillan. (U)

Thaxter, C. (1992). *Celia's island journal.* Boston: Little, Brown. (P–M)

Thesman, J. (1993). *Molly Donnelly.* Boston: Houghton Mifflin. (U)

Vasil, R. (1994). *Ever after.* New York: Orchard. (U)

Van Allsburg, C. (1991). *The wretched stone.* Boston: Houghton Mifflin. (M–U)

Whiteley, P. (1994). *Only Opal: The diary of a young girl.* New York: Philomel. (P–M)

Williams, V. B. (1981). *Three days on a river in a red canoe.* New York: Greenwillow. (P–M)

P = primary grades (K–2); M = middle grades (3–5); U = upper grades (6–8).

M I N I L E S S O N S

Journal Writing

Procedures	Concepts	Strategies and Skills
Write a journal entry	Kinds of journals	Choose a topic
Share entries	Uses of journals	Generate ideas
Give feedback about class-mates' entries	Values of writing in journals	Organize ideas
Respond in dialogue journals	Informal versus polished writing	Focus on ideas
Write in language arts note-books	Personal journals	Compare
Write reading log entries	Dialogue journals	Interpret
Write double-entry journals	Language arts notebooks	Predict
Use logs in math	Reading logs	Describe
Write science observation logs	Double-entry journals	Analyze
Use logs in theme cycles	Learning logs	Report
Write simulated journals	Simulated journals	Value
Quickwrite or quickdraw	Qualities of a good entry	Reflect on
Cluster	Respecting classmates' privacy	Incorporate key vocabulary
Make charts and diagrams		Assume another viewpoint
Do a sketch-to-stretch illustra-tion		
Cube a topic		

share, several students can be selected to share with the entire class. Teachers and classmates may offer compliments about the topic, word choice, humor, and so on.

Students may write in personal journals throughout the school year, or they may alternate other types of journals, starting and stopping with particular literature focus units and social studies and science theme cycles. Sometimes students seem to lose interest in personal journals. If this happens, many teachers find it useful to put the personal journals away and try another type of journal.

Minilessons. Teachers teach minilessons on procedures, concepts, and strategies and skills about writing in journals. A list of minilesson topics is presented above. Minilessons are especially important when students are learning a new type of journal or when they are having difficulty with a particular procedure or strategy, such as changing point of view for simulated journals or writing in two columns in double-entry journals. Four strategies that students often use when writing in journals—quickwriting, clustering, sketch-to-stretch, and cubing—are described in the following sections.

Quickwriting. Quickwriting is a strategy students use as they write in journals or do other types of impromptu writing. Students reflect on what they know about a topic, ramble on paper, generate words and ideas, and make connections among the ideas. Students write about a topic for 5 to 10 minutes, letting their thoughts flow from their minds to their pens without focusing on mechanics or revisions. This strategy, originally called "freewriting" and popularized by Peter Elbow (1973), is a way to help students focus on content rather than mechanics. Even by second or third grade, students have learned that many teachers emphasize correct spelling and careful handwriting more than the content of a composition. Elbow explains that focusing on mechanics makes writing "dead" because it doesn't allow students' natural voices to come through.

■ See Chapter 5, "Looking Closely at Words," pp. 202–204, for information about word walls.

During a theme cycle on the solar system, fourth graders each chose a word from the word wall (a list of vocabulary words hanging in the classroom) to quickwrite about in their learning logs. This is one student's quickwrite on Mars:

Mars is known as the red planet. Mars is Earth's neighbor. Mars is a lot like Earth. On Mars one day lasts 24 hours. It is the fourth planet in the solar system. Mars may have life forms. Two Viking ships landed on Mars. Mars has a dusty and rocky surface. The Viking ships found no life forms. Mars' surface shows signs of water long ago. Mars has no water now. Mars has no rings.

Another student wrote about the sun:

The sun is an important star. It gives the planets light. The sun is a hot ball of gas. Even though it appears large, it really isn't. It's pretty small. The sun's light takes time to travel to the planets so when you see light it's really from a different time. The closer the planet is to the sun the quicker the light reaches it. The sun has spots where gas has cooled. These are called sun spots. Sun spots look like black dots. The sun is the center of the universe.

These quickwrites, which took 10 minutes for students to draft, provide both a good way of checking on what students are learning and an opportunity to clarify misconceptions. After students write, they usually share their quickwrites in small groups, and then one student in each group shares with the class. Sharing also takes about 10 minutes, and the entire activity can be completed in approximately 20 minutes.

Before starting a new unit of study, teachers might ask students to quickwrite on the new topic to check their knowledge about the topic, to relate personal experiences about it, and to stimulate interest. For example, students can participate in the following quickwrites in connection with current events, literature, social studies, and science themes:

- Before discussing a current events topic, quickwrite on freedom or a geographic location.
- Before reading *The Giver* (Lowry, 1993), quickwrite about creating a perfect community.
- Before studying the Oregon Trail, quickwrite on a trip students have taken.
- Before studying reptiles, quickwrite on snakes.
- Before studying nutrition, quickwrite on junk food.

After completing the theme, students quickwrite again on the topic, applying what they have learned. Then they compare the two quickwrites as one measure of what they have learned.

■ *For an example of a cluster story, turn to Chapter 9, "Reading and Writing Stories," p. 347.*

Clustering. Clustering is a strategy students use to gather and organize information they are learning in a learning log or on a chart or poster or to analyze the structure of a story (Bromley, 1996; Rico, 1983). Students also use clustering to organize ideas before beginning to write a composition. Clusters are weblike diagrams with the topic or nuclear word written in a circle centered on a sheet of paper. Main ideas are written on rays drawn out from the circle, and branches with details and examples are added to complete each main idea.

Two clusters are presented in Figure 6–9. The top cluster was developed by a sixth-grade teacher during a theme cycle on birds. The purpose of the cluster was to assist students in categorizing birds such as cardinals, penguins, vultures, chickens, and ducks. As the class talked about the categories, students wrote the names of examples beside each category to complete the cluster. Later in the theme cycle, students each chose one bird to research, and then they presented the results of their research in cluster form. The bottom cluster presents the results of one student's research on bald eagles. The information in the cluster is divided into four categories: life, hunters, symbol, and body; other, more general, information is listed at the top of the figure.

Sketch-to-Stretch. Sketch-to-stretch (Harste, Short, & Burke, 1988) is a visually representing activity that moves students beyond literal comprehension to think more deeply about the characters, theme, and other elements of story structure and the author's craft in a story they are reading. Students work in small groups to draw pictures or diagrams to represent what the story

Students work together to draw a diagram to visually represent concepts they are learning.

Figure 6–9   Two Clusters About Birds

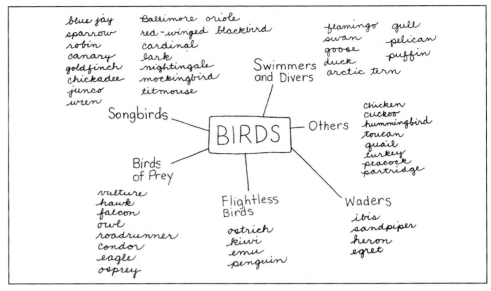

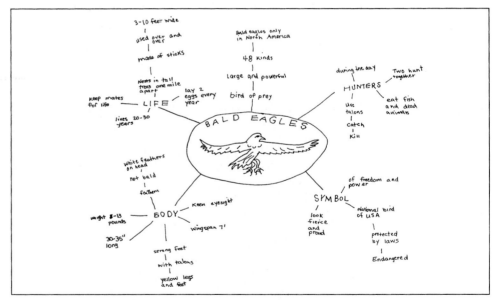

means to them, not pictures of their favorite character or episode. In their sketches, students use lines, shapes, colors, symbols, and words to express their interpretations and feelings. Since students work in a social setting with the support of classmates, they share ideas with each other, extend their understanding, and generate new insights. Students make sketch-to-stretch drawings in reading logs, learning logs, or on posters. The steps in sketch-to-stretch are:

*Step
by
Step*

1. ***Read and respond to a story.***   Students read a story or several chapters of a longer book and respond to the story in a grand conversation about literature or in reading logs.

2. ***Talk about the themes in the story and ways to symbolize meanings.***
Teachers remind students that there are many ways to represent the meaning of an experience, and that students can use lines, colors, shapes, symbols, and words to visually represent what a story means to them. Students and the teacher talk about possible meanings and ways they might visually represent these meanings.

3. ***Have students draw sketches.***   Students work in small groups to draw sketches that reflect what the story means to them. Emphasize that students should focus on the meaning of the story, not their favorite episode, and that there is no single correct interpretation of the story.

4. ***Have students share their sketches with classmates.***   Students meet in small groups to share their sketches and talk about the symbols they used. Encourage classmates to study each student's sketch and tell what they think the student is trying to convey.

5. ***Have some students share with the class.***   Each group chooses one sketch from their group to share with the class.

6. ***Revise sketches and make final copies.***   Some students will want to revise and add to their sketches based on feedback they received and ideas from classmates. Also, students make final copies if the sketches are being used as projects (Whitin, 1994, 1996a).

Students need many opportunities to experiment with this activity before they move beyond drawing pictures of the story and are able to think symbolically. It is helpful to introduce this teaching strategy through a minilesson and draw several sketches together as a class before students do their own sketches. By drawing several sketches, students learn that there is no single correct interpretation, and teachers help students focus on the interpretation rather than on their artistic talents (Ernst, 1993).

Figure 6–10 presents two sketch-to-stretch drawings. The first one is a first grader's representation for the award-winning *Officer Buckle and Gloria* (Rathmann, 1995), the story of a police officer who is jealous of the attention his dog, Gloria, gets. In this drawing, the student emphasizes the importance of working together as a team. The second sketch-to-stretch drawing was done by a fourth grader in response to Eve Bunting's *Smoky Night* (1994), a Caldecott Medal book about the riots in Los Angeles. This student used the bold lettering, fire triangles, and smoke swirls from the book's illustrations in his sketch-to-stretch poster about hope growing out of adversity.

In a year-long study of two seventh-grade language arts classes, Whitin (1996a) found that students' use of sketching helped deepen their understanding of theme, conflict, and character relationships in the novels they read. Students explored new avenues of expression, such as using color to

Figure 6-10   *Two Sketch-to-Stretch Drawings*

signify meaning and pie charts to signify feelings. Whitin warned that some upper-grade students viewed this strategy as an easy form of response and suggested that teachers clarify this misconception early in the school year. Whitin also had her students write reflections to accompany the sketches.

Cubing.   Cubing is a useful procedure for across-the-curriculum theme cycles, and middle- and upper-grade students can cube topics such as Antarctica, the United States Constitution, tigers or other endangered animals, the Underground Railroad, and the Nile River. In cubing, students explore a topic they have studied from six dimensions or viewpoints (Neeld, 1986). The name *cubing* comes from the fact that cubes have six sides and students example the topic from six perspectives in this teaching strategy. These six dimensions are:

1. Describe the topic, including its colors, shapes, and sizes.
2. Compare the topic to something else. Consider how it is similar to or different from this other thing.
3. Associate the topic to something else and explain why the topic makes you think of this other thing.

4. Analyze the topic and tell how it is made or what it is composed of.

5. Apply the topic and tell how it can be used or what can be done with it.

6. Argue for or against the topic. Take a stand and list reasons to support it.

Cubing involves the following steps:

Step by Step

1. ***Choose a topic.*** Students and the teacher choose a topic related to a social studies or science theme. It is important that students are already familiar with the topic.

2. ***Examine the topic from each perspective.*** Students divide into six small groups, and each group examines the topic from one of the perspectives.

3. ***Quickwrite on each perspective.*** Students spend 5 to 10 minutes thinking about the perspective, brainstorming a list of possible ideas, and doing a quick-write or quickdraw based on the ideas.

4. ***Share quickwrites with the class.*** Students read their quickwrites to the class, and students react to the ideas and novel connections students have made. If desired, students can later revise, edit, and then make a final copy of their quickwrites to use in the next step.

5. ***Construct the cube.*** Students attach the quickwrites or quickdraws to a box or construct a cube using cardboard in order to display the cube in the class-room.

What is especially valuable about cubing is that students think about and apply the information they have been learning about a topic in new ways as they analyze, associate, and consider the other perspectives. Figure 6–11 presents a cubing written in small groups of fifth graders as a review at the end of an across-the-curriculum theme on the American Revolution.

Adapting to Meet the Needs of Every Student

Journals can easily be adapted to meet the needs of every student. Students who have not had a lot of experience with journals may be more successful in writing personal or dialogue journals in which they focus on experiences from their own lives rather than on literature they are reading or on across-the-curriculum theme cycles. Research suggests that students learning English as a second language are more successful using dialogue journals than other types.

For students who have difficulty writing, spelling, or expressing them-selves in English, two alternatives are drawing illustrations and dictating entries to the teacher or a cross-age tutor. Some students may benefit from talking about their reactions to stories before writing in reading logs, or from talking about topics for quickwrites before writing in learning logs. No matter what type of journals students are writing, it is important to help them focus on their ideas and the interpretations they are expressing, not on mechanical correctness. A list of suggestions for adapting journal-writing activities to meet the needs of every student is presented on page 251.

Figure 6–11   Cubing on the American Revolution

Describe	The American Revolution was fought from 1775 to 1783 between Britain's Lobster Backs and the young American patriots. From the first major battle of Bunker Hill in 1775 to the battle of Yorktown in 1781, there were many hardships and deaths. The brave Americans continued on in spite of Britain's better supplied army because they wanted freedom, justice, and independence from King George.
Compare	The American Revolution and the Civil War were alike in many ways. They were both fought on American soil. Both wars were fought for people's rights and freedoms. With families fighting against families, these wars were very emotional. The winning side of each war had commanding generals who became presidents of the United States: George Washington and Ulysses S. Grant. The soldiers in the wars rallied to the song "Yankee Doodle."
Associate	We celebrate the American Revolution on the 4th of July with fireworks and parades. Fireworks are spectacular things for spectacular days! Rockets shoot into the air like cannonballs! Great big booms and sparkles fall from the sky as people celebrate! Parades remind us of soldiers marching into battle led by flutes, drums, and flags! The 4th of July is a celebration of history.
Analyze	The American Revolution began when King George taxed the colonists too much and did not ask them if they wanted to pay or not. In five years, the Stamp Act, the Townsend Act, the Quartering Act, and the Intolerable Acts were forced on the colonists. This money was to pay for the French and Indian War. This made the colonists angry. One time the colonists dressed up like Indians and threw tea into Boston Harbor. King George kept on pushing until the colonists revolted and started a war.
Apply	The most important outcome of the American Revolution was the beginning of our 200-year-old country. We enjoy the freedom of speech, religion, and the press. The Constitution grants us a lot of other freedoms, too. This living document has given us the opportunity to be anything we want to be.
Argue For	If we had not fought and won the American Revolution, there would be no United States of America. We would not have the right to speak our minds. We might all have to go to the same church. We would not have freedom or equality. There would be no Liberty Bell or Statue of Liberty. Although war is scary, painful, and violent, if we had the chance to go back, we would go and fight with all our might. We would rather do math problems all day than be ruled by a king.

Assessing Students' Journal Entries

Students can write in journals independently with little or no sharing with the teacher, or they can make daily entries that the teacher monitors or reads regularly. Typically, students are accustomed to having teachers read all or most of their writing, but the quantity of writing students produce in journals

Adapting Journal Writing To Meet the Needs of Every Student

1. Draw Journal Entries

Students can draw their thoughts and ideas in journal entries instead of writing them, or they can draw pictures before writing. What is important is that students explore their thoughts and feelings or record important information they are learning.

2. Talk Before Writing

Students can talk about topics to generate and narrow ideas before beginning to write. As they talk, students find the words and sentences to express their ideas, and they use these words and expand them as they write.

3. Dictate Entries

Teachers or cross-age tutors can take students' dictation and write the entries for students. Then students reread their dictation with the teacher's or cross-age tutor's assistance. They can also pick key words and phrases from the dictated text and use the words to label drawings.

4. Share in Small Groups

Sharing is an important part of writing, but some students may not feel comfortable sharing with the whole class. These students may prefer sharing their journal entries with a partner or in small groups, which are less threatening than large groups.

5. Focus on Ideas

Students focus on ideas, not mechanical correctness, as they write journal entries because they use journal writing to develop writing fluency and explore the ideas they are learning. Similarly, when teachers assess students' entries, they should consider whether or not students have developed their ideas and not correct their mechanical errors.

is often too great for teachers to keep up with. Some teachers try to read all entries; others read selected entries and monitor remaining entries; still others rarely check students' journals. The three management approaches can be termed private journals, monitored journals, and shared journals. When students write private journals, they write primarily for themselves, and sharing with classmates or the teacher is voluntary—the teacher does not read the journals unless invited to. When students write monitored journals, they write primarily for themselves, but the teacher monitors the writing to ensure that entries are being made regularly. The teacher simply checks that entries have been made and does not read the entries unless they are specially marked "Read me." Students write shared journals primarily for the teacher; the teacher regularly reads all entries, except those marked "private," and offers encouragement and suggestions.

Many teachers have concerns about how to grade journal entries. Because the writing is usually not revised and edited, teachers should not grade the quality of the entries. One option is to give points for each entry made, especially in personal journals. However, some teachers grade the content in learning logs and simulated journals because they can check to see if the entries include particular pieces of information. For example, if students were writing simulated journals about the Crusades, they could be asked to include five pieces of historically accurate information in their entries. (It is helpful to ask students to identify the five pieces of information by underlining and numbering them.) Rough-draft journal entries should not be graded for mechanical correctness. Students need to complete the writing process and revise and edit their entries if they are to be graded for mechanical correctness.

Figure 6–12 presents two first graders' reading log entries written after they listened to *Sam, Bangs, and Moonshine* (Ness, 1966) read aloud. This Caldecott Medal story is about a girl named Sam (for Samantha) who has a cat named Bangs. Sam tells "moonshine" about a make-believe baby kangaroo to her friend Thomas. The results are almost disastrous. The two reading logs illustrate the problems in grading students' journal entries. In her entry, Andi draws a picture of Bangs and the baby kangaroo and writes, "If you lie you will get in big trouble and you will hurt your friends." She has thoughtfully and accurately described the theme of the story. In his entry, Julio writes from the point of view of Thomas. His picture is of the make-believe kanga-

Figure 6–12 *Two First Graders' Reading Log Entries About* Sam, Bangs, and Moonshine

roo, and the text originally read, "He is lying to me. He don't have a kangaroo." After he shared his entry with classmates and they mentioned that Sam was a girl, not a boy, Julio changed the *he* to *she* and added the picture of Sam. Julio writes two sentences and spells all words correctly; Andi, on the other hand, uses invented spelling and punctuates her text as one sentence.

Which reading log entry is better? Which deserves a higher grade? It is very difficult to make these types of judgments, and such decisions are probably unnecessary. In both entries students have explored the story through illustrations and text, and both entries are remarkable in one way or another: I particularly like Andi's articulation of the theme and Julio's viewpoint and his ability to make revisions that reflect the feedback he received from classmates. Andi and Julio's teacher marked the two entries the same way. They each received a check in the gradebook for a reading log entry that was completed and met these two requirements: first, the entry contains both an illustration and some writing; and second, the entry contains information about the story.

Review

Journals are an important learning tool that students at all grade levels can use effectively. Students use journal writing to share events in their lives and record what they are learning in literature focus units and theme cycles. The key concepts presented in this chapter are:

1. Students write in seven kinds of journals: personal journals, dialogue journals, reading logs, double-entry journals, language arts notebooks, learning logs, and simulated journals.
2. Dialogue journals are especially useful for students learning English as a second language.
3. Reading logs, double-entry journals, and simulated journals are often used during literature focus units.
4. Learning logs and simulated journals are used for across-the-curriculum theme cycles.
5. Even young children can draw and write in personal journals and reading logs.
6. Teachers teach minilessons about how to write in journals.
7. Students often share entries with classmates, although personal journal entries are usually private.
8. Four strategies that students use as they write in journals are quickwriting, clustering, sketch-to-stretch, and cubing.
9. Teachers monitor students' writing in journals by reading selected entries, not by correcting misspelled words and other mechanical errors.
10. The focus in journal writing is on developing writing fluency and using writing as a tool for learning.

Extensions

1. Have elementary students keep reading logs as they read and respond to a chapter book. Or, experiment with one of the other types of journals with elementary students.

2. Using dialogue journals, write back and forth with three students who are having difficulty in your classroom. Continue for several weeks. Use this opportunity to get to know these students better and make the activity a positive experience for students. What changes do you see in students' entries and your own over the period?

3. Keep a personal journal in which you record experiences and feelings, or keep a double-entry journal in which you reflect on the material in this book as well as your teaching experiences for the remainder of the school term.

4. Have a small group of students write a quickwrite or make a cluster as part of a social studies or science theme cycle. Then examine these papers to determine which concepts students are learning, as well as any misconceptions they may have.

5. Read two of the books listed in Figure 6–8 in which characters or historical personalities keep journals, and share the books with classmates.

6. Plan and teach a minilesson on a language arts topic to a small group of students, and have the students make notes in their language arts notebooks.

> **"** I want every child in my class to be a reader, but some of them haven't had many experiences with books. To compensate, I have my children take books home every week to read with their parents. **"**
>
> **Mary Yamazaki**
> *Bilingual Kindergarten Teacher*
> *Truckee Elementary School*

PROCEDURE

I began a book bag project in my classroom several years ago. My aide and I bought the cloth, and together we sewed 40 book bags with handles. Next we collected two or three related books to put into each bag. We have book bags about dinosaurs, trucks, dogs, "The Three Bears," colors, and other topics.

The three books in the book bag about colors, for example, are *Mary Wore Her Red Dress* (Peek, 1985), Dr. Seuss's *Green Eggs and Ham* (1988), and *Color Zoo* (Ehlert, 1989). Some of the bags have books written in English, and others have books written in Spanish. It's taken us a while to collect enough books, and most of them are paperbacks that I've bought inexpensively through book clubs. The PTA gave us some money for books, too. I also put a reading log notebook—20 sheets of paper stapled together with a construction paper cover that has been laminated—in each bag

and a pencil. Children write their names and the date in the reading log after their parents have read the books in the book bag to them. The children are also invited to add a picture or write comments. Parents, too, are encouraged to draw pictures and write comments in the log.

I introduce the book bag project at our Back-to-School Night program and explain how parents should read the books with their children. I emphasize that parents are not expected to teach their children to read and that they should not expect their children to read the books independently. I demonstrate how to read with a child so that it is a pleasurable experience, and how to talk with the child about the book after reading without asking a long series of comprehension questions. I also demonstrate how to write in a reading log with a child. My aide translates my comments for the Spanish-speaking parents. I also include a one-page list of guidelines in each book bag. The guidelines are printed in English on one side and in Spanish on the other. The English version of this list is shown in the accompanying figure.

Then my kindergartners begin taking book bags home once a week. On Friday the children select the book bag they want to take home with them. They check out the bag using a cardfile system. An index card is in each bag, and children take the card out of the bag and sign it. Then they place the card on our checkout chart. The chart has a pocket for each child, and the child puts the card in the pocket with his or her name on it. The children keep the book bags at home over the weekend and the first part of the next week. I have them bring the bags back to school on Wednesday. The children take the checkout card out of the chart and put it back in the book bag. Then on Thursday my aide and I check the bags and get them ready to go home again on Friday.

ASSESSMENT

I use a checkout system to keep track of the book bags, and I talk informally with the children about the books and the reading activities that go on at home. I try to take a look at the reading logs and read the entries the children have made, but I do it very informally. I don't assign grades or anything like that. What is important to me is that my children are being read to on a regular basis at home and that it is a positive experience for both the children and their parents.

ADAPTATIONS

Book bags wouldn't work without the parents' cooperation and assistance. I've found that my parents are very enthusiastic and want to read with their children. I've wondered what I would do if parents weren't interested in or capable of reading with their children. I've thought about using wordless books such as *Pancakes for Breakfast* (de Paola, 1978) and *Picnic* (McCully, 1984). I've also wondered about using small, battery-operated audiotape players so that my children and their parents could listen to the book read aloud together. So far I haven't had to adapt my program, but I would if it were necessary.

REFLECTIONS

Teaching and learning go on at school and at home. I couldn't possibly do the job alone. I need parents to work with me, and I think that my children's parents appreciate the opportunity. They take good care of the book bags at home and almost always remember to return them to school on Wednesdays. Many of my children's families come from cultures where school and home were kept separate, but when you show them how you want them to work with their children, they are very responsible.

Guidelines for Reading Book Bag Books

1. Plan a special, 10-minute period several times a week for reading with your child.
2. Read one of the books in the book bag. Ask your child to choose which book to read.
3. Have your child sit in your lap or next to you, and invite him or her to hold the book and turn the pages as you read.
4. Make this reading experience a pleasant one. It is not a reading lesson, and your child should not be quizzed on reading skills.
5. Begin by reading aloud the title and the name of the author. Then read to your child or encourage your child to read along with you if the book is a familiar one. Do not expect your child to read the book independently!
6. After reading, talk to your child about the book. You might ask one of these questions:

   What part of the book did you like best?
   Did you like the book? Why?
   What did the book make you think of?

7. Choose another book from the book bag the next day and repeat steps 1–6.
8. After reading the books, help your child write his or her name in the Reading Log that is in the book bag. Your child may also draw a picture or write a message, if he or she is interested in doing so.
9. Return the book bag on Wednesday.

Listening to Learn

The kindergartners and first graders in Linda Boroski's class created several small fox quilts after reading *Rosie's Walk* (Hutchins, 1968), the story of a hen who outwits a fox who is following her. After reading the book, students asked many questions about foxes, and Mrs. Borowski read aloud several books to provide some answers. The children decided to make a fox quilt to share what they had learned. Pictures of a fox were cut from fabric and glued to each quilt square. The children wrote or dictated a sentence about foxes to accompany their pictures.

istening has been called the "neglected language art" for almost 50 years because it is rarely taught in elementary classrooms. Students are admonished to listen, but few teachers teach students how to improve their listening strategies and skills. It has been assumed that children come to school already knowing how to listen. Also, some teachers feel that it is more important to spend the limited instructional time available on reading and writing instruction. Despite these concerns about teaching listening in the elementary grades, most teachers agree that students need to know how to listen because it is the most used language art.

Listening is the first language mode that children acquire, and it provides the basis for the other language arts (Lundsteen, 1979). Infants use listening to begin the process of learning to comprehend and produce language. From the beginning of their lives, children listen to sounds in their immediate environment, attend to speech sounds, and construct their knowledge of oral language. Listening is also important in learning to read. Children are introduced to written language by listening to stories that parents and other caregivers read to them. When children are read to, they begin to see the connection between what they hear and what they see on the printed page and gain an understanding of stories. The processes of reading and listening and the strategies and skills used during both reading and listening are similar in many ways (Sticht & James, 1984).

Listening is "the most used and perhaps the most important of the language (and learning) arts" (Devine, 1982, p. 1). Researchers have found that children and adults spend as much time listening as they do in reading, writing, and talking combined (Rankin, 1926; Werner, 1975; Wilt, 1950). Figure 7–1 illustrates the amount of time we communicate in these language modes. Both children and adults spend approximately 50% of their communication time listening. Language researcher Walter Loban has described the importance of listening this way: "We listen a book a day, we speak a book a week, we read a book a month, and we write a book a year" (cited in Erickson, 1985, p. 13).

Despite the importance of listening in our lives, listening has remained the "orphan" language art for nearly half a century (Anderson, 1949). Little time has been devoted to listening instruction in most classrooms, and teach-

Figure 7–1   Percentage of Communication Time in Each Language Mode

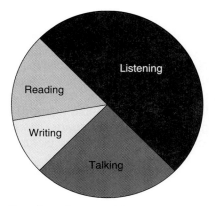

Data from Rankin, 1926; Werner, 1975; Wilt, 1950.

ers often complain that they do not know how to teach listening (Devine, 1978; Landry, 1969; Strother, 1987).

As you continue reading, you will learn about different kinds of listening, how to teach listening, and ways to incorporate listening instruction into the language arts curriculum. Keep these points in mind as you read:

• What is the listening process?
• How do students listen aesthetically?
• How do students listen efferently?
• What is critical listening?
• How is listening taught as part of literature focus units, theme cycles, and reading and writing workshop?

THE LISTENING PROCESS

Listening is elusive because it occurs internally. Lundsteen (1979) describes listening as the "most mysterious" language process. In fact, teachers often do not know whether listening has occurred until they ask students to apply what they have listened to through discussions, projects, and other assignments. Even then, there is no guarantee that the students' responses indicate that they have listened, because they may have known the material before listening or may have learned it from someone else at about the same time.

Listening is a complex, multistep process "by which spoken language is converted to meaning in the mind" (Lundsteen, 1979, p. 1). As this definition suggests, listening is more than just hearing, even though children and adults often use the terms *hearing* and *listening* synonymously. Rather, hearing is an integral component, but only one component, of the listening process. The crucial part is thinking, or converting to meaning what one has heard.

Steps in the Listening Process

The listening process involves three steps: receiving, attending, and assigning meaning (Wolvin & Coakley, 1985). In the first step, listeners receive the aural stimuli or the combined aural and visual stimuli presented by the speaker. Next, listeners focus on selected stimuli while ignoring other, distracting, stimuli. Because so many stimuli surround students in the classroom, they must attend to the speaker's message, focusing on the most important information in that message. In the third step, listeners assign meaning to, or understand, the speaker's message. Listeners assign meaning using assimilation and accommodation to fit the message into their existing cognitive structures or to create new structures if necessary. Responding or reacting to the message is not considered part of the listening process; the response occurs afterward, and it sets another communication process into action in which the listener becomes the message sender.

The second step of Wolvin and Coakley's listening process model may be called the "paying attention" component. Elementary teachers spend a great deal of instructional time reminding students to pay attention; unfortunately, however, children often do not understand the admonition. When asked to explain what "paying attention" means, some children equate it with physical

■ *For more information about Piaget's equilibration process, refer back to Chapter 1, pp. 5–6.*

behaviors such as not kicking their feet, or cleaning off their desks. Learning to attend to the speaker's message is especially important because researchers have learned that students can listen to 250 words per minute—two to three times the normal rate of talking (Foulke, 1968). This differential allows listeners time to tune in and out as well as to become distracted during listening.

Furthermore, the intensity of students' need to attend to the speaker's message varies with the purpose for listening. Some types of listening require more attentiveness than others. Effective listeners, for example, listen differently to directions on how to reach a friend's home than they do to a poem or story being read aloud.

Purposes for Listening

Why do we listen? Students often answer that question by explaining that they listen to learn or to avoid punishment. It is unfortunate that some students have such a vague and limited view of the purposes for listening. Wolvin and Coakley (1979, 1985) delineate five broad types of listening:

- Discriminative listening
- Aesthetic listening
- Efferent listening
- Critical listening
- Therapeutic listening

■ *See Chapter 9, "Reading and Writing Stories," pp. 363–367, for more information about Louise Rosenblatt's reader-response theories.*

I have applied Louise Rosenblatt's (1985b, 1991) terms *aesthetic reading,* meaning "reading for pleasure," and *efferent reading,* meaning "reading to carry away information," for two of the listening categories. These terms can be applied because reading and listening are similar language modes, except that one is written and the other is oral.

Discriminative Listening. People use discriminative listening to distinguish sounds and to develop a sensitivity to nonverbal communication. Teaching discriminative listening involves one sort of activity in the primary grades and a different activity for older students. Having kindergartners listen to tape-recorded animal sounds and common household noises is one discriminative listening activity. Most children are able to discriminate among sounds by the time they reach age 5 or 6. Primary-grade students also use discriminative listening as they develop phonemic awareness, the ability to blend and segment the sounds in spoken words. Older students use discriminative listening to sound out spellings of words and divide words into syllables.

■ *For more information on phonemic awareness, check Chapter 4, "Emergent Literacy," pp. 144–147.*

Students at all levels also learn to "listen" to the nonverbal messages that people communicate. Young children quickly recognize the unspoken message when a parent's expression changes from a smile to a frown or when a teacher expresses puzzlement. Older students learn the meanings of more sophisticated forms of body language, such as folding your arms over your chest, and the ways that teachers emphasize that something they are teaching is important, such as writing it on the chalkboard, raising eyebrows, speaking more loudly, or repeating it.

When teachers read aloud books such as Dr. Seuss's *Fox in Socks* (1965) and Nancy Shaw's *Sheep Out to Eat* (1992) (and other books in the series about the cavorting sheep), they provide opportunities for young children to develop their discriminative listening abilities. Middle- and upper-grade students develop more sophisticated knowledge about the sounds of language when they read *Zin! Zin! Zin! A Violin* (Moss, 1995) and *Lots of Limericks* (Livingston, 1991).

Aesthetic Listening.   People listen aesthetically to a speaker or reader when they listen for enjoyment. Listening to someone read stories aloud or recite poems is a pleasurable activity. Teachers encourage children's aesthetic listening by reading aloud and teaching students how to visualize characters and episodes and notice figurative language. Viewing videotape versions of stories and listening to classmates converse or talk about literature they have read or which they have listened to someone else read aloud are other examples of aesthetic listening.

As students listen to the teacher read aloud well-crafted stories such as *Charlotte's Web* (White, 1980), *Thunder Cake* (Polacco, 1990), and *The Giver* (Lowry, 1993), they engage with the text and step into the secondary world of the story. In *Charlotte's Web,* they feel the unlikely friendship between Charlotte and Wilbur. In *Thunder Cake,* they understand the granddaughter's fear of thunderstorms and the urgency with which she and her grandmother collect the ingredients and prepare the thundercake. And in *The Giver,* students share Jonas's outrage at his community and escape with him.

Students also listen aesthetically as teachers read poems aloud, such as *Welcome to the Green House* (Yolen, 1993), a book-length poem about the rain forest, or *Sierra* (Siebert, 1991), a book-length poem about the California mountains. Another way to share poems and stories is through readers theatre presentations. In readers theatre, students read aloud play scripts dramatically. One script for second and third graders is *I Am the Dog/I Am the Cat* (Hall, 1994), in which one child assumes the perspective of the dog and a second child becomes the cat.

■ *See Chapter 8 "Sustaining Talk in the Classroom," pp. 316–318, to read more about readers theatre.*

Efferent Listening.   People listen efferently to understand a message, and this is the type of listening required in many instructional activities, particularly in theme cycles. Students determine the speaker's purpose, identify the main ideas, and then organize the information they are listening to in order to remember it. Elementary students usually receive little instruction in efferent listening; rather, teachers assume that students simply know how to listen. Note-taking is typically the one efferent listening strategy taught in the elementary grades.

Students often use efferent listening as they listen to teachers read aloud books or view video versions of books as part of social studies and science theme cycles. Students learn how plants and animals coexist in the desert as they listen to the teacher read *Cactus Hotel* (Guiberson, 1991), learn about the mummification process in *Mummies Made in Egypt* (Aliki, 1979), and find out how a volcanic island is formed in *Surtsey: The Newest Place on Earth* (Lasky, 1996). Even though these three books are informational books, students don't necessarily listen to informational books efferently. As students are reading about the mummification process in *Mummies Made in Egypt,* for example, they often travel back in time and imagine themselves in ancient Egypt—living in the secondary world of the book. Louise Rosenblatt (1991) explains that aesthetic and efferent reading represent two ends of a continuum and that students rarely use one type of reading or the other exclusively. The same is true of listening.

Critical Listening.   People listen critically to evaluate a message. Critical listening is an extension of efferent listening. As in efferent listening, listeners seek to understand a message, but they must filter the message to detect propaganda devices, persuasive language, and emotional appeals. Critical listening is used when people listen to debates, commercials, political speeches, and other arguments.

When students listen to teachers read aloud stories such as *The True Story of the Three Little Pigs!* (Scieszka, 1989) and *Nothing But the Truth* (Avi, 1991), they critically analyze the characters' claims, and when they read informational books such as *Antarctica* (Cowcher, 1990) and biographies such as *My Hiroshima* (Morimoto, 1987), they evaluate the authors' warnings about destroying the environment and nuclear war.

Therapeutic Listening.   In therapeutic listening, people listen to allow a speaker to talk through a problem. Children, as well as adults, serve as sympathetic listeners for friends and family members. Although this type of listening is important, it is less appropriate for elementary students, so we will not discuss it in this chapter.

Students rarely use these types of listening in isolation. As students listen to stories such as *Catherine, Called Birdy* (Cushman, 1994), set in the Middle Ages, or *The Bracelet* (Uchida, 1993), set in World War II, for instance, they often use several types of listening simultaneously. They step back into history and imagine they are Birdy or Emi and feel what the characters feel as they listen aesthetically. They use efferent listening as they think about geographic locations, historical events, kings and other historical figures, and other information that authors have carefully researched and included in the story. They use discriminative listening as they notice rhyme, alliteration, and other types of wordplay. Critical listening plays a role, too, as students consider the author's viewpoint, assess emotional appeals, and think about the theme. The five types of listening are reviewed in Figure 7–2.

Teaching Listening Strategies

Activities involving listening go on in every elementary classroom. Students listen to the teacher give directions and instruction, to tape-recorded stories at listening centers, to classmates during discussions, and to someone reading stories and poetry aloud. Since listening plays a significant role in these and other classroom activities, listening is not neglected. However, although these activities provide opportunities for students to practice listening strategies and skills they already possess, they do not teach students how to become more effective listeners.

■ *For more information on strategies, turn to Chapter 1, "Learning and the Language Arts," pp. 31–34.*

Language arts educators have repeatedly cited the need to teach listening strategies (Brent & Anderson, 1993; Devine, 1978; Lundsteen, 1979; Pearson & Fielding, 1982; Wolvin & Coakley, 1985). Most of what has traditionally been called "listening instruction" has been merely practice. When students listen to a story at a listening center and then answer questions

Figure 7–2 *Overview of the Five Types of Listening*

Types	Characteristics	Examples
Discriminative	Distinguish among sounds	Participate in phonemic awareness activities Notice rhyming words in poems and songs Recognize alliteration and onomatopoeia Experiment with tongue twisters
Aesthetic	Listen for pleasure or enjoyment	Listen to stories and poems read aloud View video versions of stories Listen to stories at a listening center Watch students perform a play or readers theatre reading Participate in grand conversations Participate in tea party activities
Efferent	Listen to understand a message	Listen to informational books read aloud or at a listening center Listen to oral reports View informational videos Listen to book talks Participate in writing groups Listen during minilessons Listen to students share projects
Critical	Evaluate messages	Listen to debates and political speeches View commercials and other advertisements Evaluate themes and arguments in books read aloud
Therapeutic	Listen sympathetically	Very few language arts activities focus on this type of listening, even though children use therapeutic listening when they listen to a friend talk out a problem.

about it, for example, teachers assume that the students know how to listen and that they will be able to answer the questions. However, a listening center activity is practice, not instruction!

Rather than have more practice opportunities, students need to learn to vary how they listen to fit the purpose for listening, and they need to develop specific strategies to use when listening (Brent & Anderson, 1993; Jalongo, 1991). Many less capable listeners have only one approach to listening, no matter what the purpose. They listen as hard as they can and try to remember everything. This strategy is destined to fail for at least two reasons: first, trying to remember everything places an impossible demand on short-term memory; and second, many items in a message are not important enough to remember. Other students equate listening with intelligence, assuming that they are poor listeners because they "just aren't smart enough." Kucer (1991) urges teachers to talk with students about their understanding of strategies because he found that students' interpretations often don't match those of the teacher, as these listening examples point out.

AESTHETIC LISTENING

Louise Rosenblatt (1978, 1983, 1991) coined the term *aesthetic reading* to describe one stance readers take. During aesthetic reading, readers are concerned with the experience they are living through and with their relationship with the literature they are reading. The focus is on their experience during reading, not on the information they will carry away from the experience. The term *aesthetic listening* can be used to describe the type of listening children and adults do as they listen to storytellers tell stories, poets recite poems, actors perform a play, singers sing songs, readers read stories aloud, and as they view films and videotape versions of stories. The focus of this type of listening is on the lived-through experience and the connections the listeners are making to the literature they are listening to. More traditional names for aesthetic listening are appreciative listening and listening for pleasure.

Teachers often take aesthetic listening for granted and assume that students are experienced listeners and know how to listen to literature. Teachers should not take this for granted; it is important to explain to students that they listen differently for various purposes. For aesthetic listening, students focus on the experience of the literature—forming mental images, predicting what will happen next, appreciating the beauty of the language, and making connections to other experiences or other literature. Students do not concen-

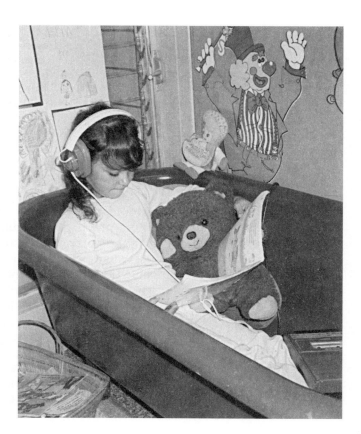

This student listens aesthetically to a favorite story.

trate on remembering specific information; instead, they listen for the emotional impact.

Strategies for Aesthetic Listening

Students use many of the same strategies for aesthetic listening that they use for reading and writing (Pinnell & Jaggar, 1991). Six strategies that are especially important for aesthetic listening are:

1. Predicting. As students listen to a story read aloud or view a puppet show, they are predicting or making guesses about what will happen next in the story. Then they revise their predictions as they continue listening to and/or viewing the story. When they read aloud, teachers help students develop the predicting strategy by asking them what they think will happen in the story before reading and stopping several times while reading to have students predict again.

2. Visualizing. Students create an image or picture in their minds while listening to a story that has strong visual images, details, or descriptive words. Students practice this strategy by closing their eyes and trying to draw mental pictures while they listen to a story, and then reproducing these pictures on paper after reading.

3. Making connections. Students make personal connections between the story they are listening to and experiences in their own lives. Students might share these connections in reading log entries and in grand conversations after reading. They also make connections between the story they are listening to and other stories they have listened to read aloud, stories they have read themselves, or films they have viewed. Students make connections between the story they are listening to and another story with the same theme, or a character or episode in this story and a character or episode in another story. Teachers help students use this strategy by asking them to talk about any connections they are making as the story is discussed or by having them make entries in their reading logs. These literary connections are known as intertextuality.

■ *To read more about intertextuality, turn to Chapter 9, "Reading and Writing Stories," pp. 364–366.*

4. Revising meaning. Students begin to formulate meaning as soon as they see the cover of the book and hear the title of the story. As students listen to the story read aloud, their comprehension or understanding of the story expands and deepens. Comprehension doesn't happen all at once, but in layers as students listen to the story. Sometimes students misunderstand a word or phrase, don't understand a character's motivations, or miss some important information when they are distracted, and their understanding of the story goes awry. As they continue to listen, students realize that what they are listening to doesn't make sense, and they make corrections.

5. Playing with language. As they are listening, students should be sensitive to the author's choice of language, to the way sentences are phrased, and to the author's use of comparisons or wordplay. Children take over the language they hear and make it part of their own (Cullinan, 1987). Teachers comment on examples of powerful and beautiful language as they are reading or after reading, and students can collect examples in their reading logs, on charts, or in story quilts.

■ *See Chapter 9,
"Reading and Writing
Stories," pp. 345–358,
to learn more about
the elements of story
structure.*

6. *Organizing ideas.* As they listen to a story read aloud or view a film or video version of a story, students apply their knowledge of plot, characters, setting, theme, and point of view in order to anticipate what will happen next and how the problem introduced in the beginning of the story will be resolved at the end. They also apply their knowledge of various genres (e.g., fantasy, historical fiction, contemporary realistic fiction) in order to understand stories they are listening to.

Students also use these strategies as they listen aesthetically to poems or informational books read aloud. They create mental images and make connections between what they are listening to and their own lives and other literature they know. Instead of using story structure to help them organize what they are listening to, they use their knowledge about how poetry or informational books are organized. Similarly, as they think about the powerful figurative language of poems, they consider the impact that alliteration and metaphors have on listeners. When listening to informational books, they think about how the author's use of factual information, examples, diagrams, and photographs helps students to create mental images.

Since reading and listening involve many of the same strategies, teachers can teach strategies through listening and then have students use the strategies during reading (Pearson & Fielding, 1982). As they read aloud, teachers model how to use these strategies, and after listening students can reflect on how they used the strategies. It is easier for students to focus on strategy use during listening than during reading because students don't have to decode written words when listening.

Reading Aloud to Students

Sharing stories, poems, and informational books orally with students is a wonderful way to develop an appreciation of literature, model fluent reading, encourage interest in reading, and create a community of learners in the classroom. Reading stories to children is an important component in most kindergarten and first-grade classrooms. Unfortunately, teachers often think they need to read to children only until they learn to read for themselves; however, reading aloud and sharing the excitement of books, language, and reading should remain an important part of the language arts program at all grade levels.

A common complaint is that there is not enough time in the school day to read to children, but reading a story or a chapter of a longer story aloud can take as little as 10 or 15 minutes a day. Many educators, such as Jim Trelease (1995), point out the necessity of finding time to read aloud so as to take advantage of the many benefits:

• Stimulating children's interest in books and in reading
• Broadening children's reading interests and developing their taste for quality literature
• Introducing children to the sounds of written language and expanding their vocabulary and sentence patterns
• Sharing with children books that are "too good to miss"
• Allowing children to listen to books that would be too difficult for them to read on their own or books that are "hard to get into"
• Expanding children's background of experiences

- Introducing children to concepts about written language, different genres of literature, poetry, and elements of story structure
- Providing a pleasurable, shared experience
- Modeling to children that adults read and enjoy reading, to increase the likelihood that children will become lifelong readers

Guidelines for choosing literature to read aloud are simple: choose books that you like and which you think will appeal to your students. Trelease (1995) suggests four additional criteria of good read-aloud books. They should be fast-paced to hook children's interest as quickly as possible; contain well-developed characters; include easy-to-read dialogue; and keep long descriptive passages to a minimum. There are a number of annotated guidebooks to help teachers select books for reading aloud as well as for independent reading. Figure 7–3 lists these guides as well as journals and other resources teachers can use to select books to read aloud.

Books that have received awards or other acclaim from teachers, librarians, and children make good choices. Two of the most prestigious awards are the Caldecott Medal and the Newbery Medal. Lists of outstanding books are prepared annually by professional groups such as the National Council of Teachers of English and the National Council of Teachers of Social Studies. In many states children read and vote on books to receive recognition, such as the Buckeye Book Award in Ohio and the Sequoia Book Award in Oklahoma. The International Reading Association sponsors a Children's Choices competition in which children read and select their favorite books and a similar Teachers' Choices competition; lists of these books are published annually in *The Reading Teacher.*

Figure 7–3 *Guides for Choosing Literature to Read Aloud to Students*

Books

Bishop, R. S. (Ed.). (1994). *A multicultural booklist for grades K–8.* Urbana, IL: National Council of Teachers of English.

Jensen, J. M., & Roser, N. L. (1993). *Adventuring with books: A booklist for pre-K–grade 6* (10th ed.). Urbana, IL: National Council of Teachers of English.

Kids' favorite books. (1992). Newark, DE: International Reading Association.

Nilsen, A. P. (Ed.). (1991). *Your reading: A booklist for junior high and middle school students* (8th ed.). Urbana, IL: National Council of Teachers of English.

Recommended readings in literature: Kindergarten through grade eight (Rev. ed.). (1996). Sacramento: California State Department of Education.

Samuels, B. G., & Beers, G. K. (Eds.). (1995). *Your reading: An annotated booklist for middle school and junior high* (10th ed.). Urbana, IL: National Council of Teachers of English.

Teens' favorite books. (1992). Newark, DE: International Reading Association.

Trelease, J. (1995). *The new read-aloud handbook* (4th ed.). New York: Penguin.

Webb, C. A. (Ed.). (1993). *Your reading: A booklist for junior high and middle school students* (9th ed.). Urbana, IL: National Council of Teachers of English.

Journals and Newsletters

Book Links. American Library Association, 50 E. Huron Street, Chicago, IL 60611–2795.

CBC Features. The Children's Book Council, 67 Irving Place, New York, NY 10003.

The Horn Book. Park Square Building, 31 St. James Avenue, Boston, MA 02116.

Language Arts. National Council of Teachers of English, 1111 Kenyon Road, Urbana, IL 61801.

The New Advocate. Christopher-Gordon Publishers, P.O. Box 809, Needham Heights, MA 02194.

The Reading Teacher. International Reading Association, P.O. Box 8139, Newark, DE 19711.

Teachers in many primary-grade classrooms read one story aloud as part of a literature focus unit and later during the day read informational books aloud as part of social studies or science theme cycles. Poems, too, are read aloud in connection with content-area themes. It is not unusual for primary-grade students to listen to their teacher read aloud three or more stories and other books during the school day. If children are read to only once a day, they will listen to fewer than 200 books during the school year, and this is not enough! More than 40,000 books are available for children, and reading stories and other books aloud is an important way to share more of this literature with children. Students in middle and upper grades should also read and listen to chapter books and poems read aloud as part of literature or author units, along with reading and listening to informational books, magazines, and newspaper articles in content-area units.

Students—especially kindergartners and primary-grade students—often beg to have a familiar book reread. Although it is important to share a wide variety of books with children, researchers have found that children benefit in specific ways from repeated readings (Yaden, 1988). Through repetition, students gain control over the parts of a story and are better able to synthesize those parts into a whole. The quality of children's responses to a repeated story changes (Beaver, 1982), and children become more independent users of the classroom library center (Martinez & Teale, 1988).

Martinez and Roser (1985) examined young children's responses to stories and found that as stories become increasingly familiar, students' responses indicate a greater depth of understanding. They found that children talked almost twice as much about familiar books that had been reread many times as they did about unfamiliar books that had been read only once or twice. The form and focus of children's talk changed, too. While children tended to ask questions about unfamiliar stories, they made comments about familiar stories. Children's talk about unfamiliar stories focused on characters; the focus changed to details and word meanings when they talked about familiar stories. The researchers also found that children's comments after repeated readings were more probing and more specific, suggesting that they had greater insight into the story. Researchers investigating the value of repeated readings have focused mainly on preschool and primary-grade students, but rereading favorite stories may have similar benefits for older students as well.

Other Oral Presentation Modes

Stories, poems, and informational books can be shared with students through storytelling, puppet shows, readers theatre, and plays, and these oral presentation modes will be discussed in Chapter 8. Students also listen to (and sometimes view) multimedia presentations on audiotapes, videotapes, CD-ROM, and film versions of books.

Students often view high-quality videos of children's literature as part of literature focus units and theme cycles, and it is important that teachers take advantage of the unique capabilities of this technology (Green, 1989). Teachers use videos in connection with books children are reading or books they are listening to the teacher read aloud. Teachers decide whether students view the video before or after reading, or how much of the video they watch, depending on the students' needs and interests. Students with limited background knowledge often benefit from viewing before reading or listening to the book read aloud, but for other students, watching a video before reading would curtail their interest in reading the book.

Students often make comparisons between the book and video versions of a story and choose the one they like better. Interestingly, less capable students who don't visualize the story in their minds often prefer the video version, while more capable readers often prefer the book version because the video doesn't meet their expectations. They can also examine some of the conventions used in video productions, such as narration, music and sound effects, the visual representation of characters and the setting, the camera's perspective, and any changes from the book version. Guidelines for using videos in the classroom are listed in the Teacher's Notebook on page 272.

Teaching Aesthetic Listening

Teachers use the same five-stage reading process when reading aloud to students that they use when students do the reading themselves. As teachers read aloud, they provide opportunities for students to listen aesthetically and know the lived-through experience of aesthetic listening. Students also learn how to use the aesthetic listening strategies.

Steps in Reading Aloud to Students.   Sometimes teachers simply pick up a book and start reading aloud to students, but for the most meaningful experience, teachers use the five-stage reading process described in Chapter 3, even though one or more stages might be abbreviated. It is crucial that teachers help students activate their background knowledge before reading and provide opportunities for students to respond to the book after reading (Pinnell & Jaggar, 1991).

Step by Step

1. **Prepare to share the story.**   Teachers activate background knowledge or provide necessary concepts or experiences so that students can understand the story. The teacher may also set the purpose for listening.

2. **Read aloud to students.**   Teachers read the story aloud to students or play an audiotape of the story. One procedure teachers can use to read the story aloud is the Directed Listening-Thinking Approach (DLTA), in which the teacher asks students to make predictions about the story and then listen to confirm or reject their predictions. The DLTA procedure is described in Figure 7–4.

3. **Capture an initial response.**   Immediately after reading, students reflect on the story (or a chapter of a longer book) by talking about the story or writing in a reading log. In these initial responses, students focus on voicing their personal feelings, making connections to their own lives, articulating questions and confusions, and identifying favorite characters, events, and quotations. Students need an opportunity to talk about a story after reading. They may talk about the book with a partner, in small groups, or with the entire class. The focus is on interpreting the story, not answering the teacher's questions about the story.

    Students also capture initial responses to a story by writing entries in a reading log. Primary-grade students keep a reading log by writing the title and author of the story and drawing a picture related to the story. They can also add

Teacher's Notebook
Guidelines for Using Videos in the Classroom

1. Preview the Video

Before showing the video to students, teachers make sure it is suitable for them to view. It may be necessary to skip some portions due to excessive length of unsuitable content when showing the video to students.

2. Plan How to Use the Video

Students who have little background knowledge on the topic or students for whom the sentence structure or vocabulary is difficult may benefit from viewing the video before reading or listening to the book read aloud.

3. Set the Purpose

Teachers explain the purpose for viewing the video and explain whether students should use primarily aesthetic, efferent, or critical listening.

4. Use the Pause Function

Teachers stop the video periodically in order for students to make predictions, reflect on their use of a listening strategy, talk about the video, or compare the book and video versions. When students are listening to an informational video, they often stop periodically to take notes.

5. Re-view the Video

Consider showing the video more than once because re-viewing is as beneficial as rereading. Teachers can use the rewind function to show particular scenes twice while students are viewing, or teachers can show the video without interruption the first time and then play it a second time.

6. Vary the Procedure Used to Show Videos

Teachers sometimes show the beginning of the story on the videotape and then read aloud the entire book. Afterwards, students view the entire video. Or teachers can alternate reading and viewing chapters of a longer book.

7. Compare the Author's and Camera's Views

Students can examine the impact of the narration, music and sound effects, the visual representation of the characters and setting, and camera angles.

8. Respond to the Video

Provide opportunities for students to respond to videos after viewing. Students can respond by participating in grand conversations and writing in reading logs.

Figure 7–4   *The Directed Listening-Thinking Approach*

The Directed Listening-Thinking Approach (DLTA) is based on the Directed Reading-Thinking Activity, a procedure developed by Russell Stauffer (1975). In DLTA the teacher reads the story or other piece of literature aloud to students, who are actively listening by making predictions and listening to confirm their predictions. After reading, students discuss their predictions and give reasons to support them. The three steps are:

1. Prepare to Read

Teachers provide necessary information related to the story or the author, thereby stimulating students' interest in the story. Teachers might discuss the topic or theme, show pictures, or share objects related to the story to draw on prior knowledge or to create new experiences. For example, teachers might talk about students' favorite games before reading Van Allsburg's jungle adventure game, *Jumanji* (1981). Then the teacher shows students the cover of the book and reads the title and asks them to make a prediction about the story using questions like these:

- What do you think a story with a title like this might be about?
- What do you think might happen in this story?
- Does this picture give you any ideas about what might happen in this story?

If necessary, the teacher reads the first paragraph or two to provide more information for students to use in making their predictions. After a brief discussion in which all students commit themselves to one or another of the alternatives presented, the teacher asks these questions:

- Which of these ideas do you think would be the likely one?
- Why do you think that idea is a good one?

2. Read Aloud to Students

After students set their purposes for listening, the teacher reads part of the story aloud and then asks students to confirm or reject their predictions by answering questions such as the following:

- What do you think now?
- What do you think will happen next?
- What would happen if . . . ?

The teacher continues reading the story aloud, stopping at several key points to repeat this step.

3. Reflect on Students' Predictions

Students talk about the story, expressing their feelings and making connections to their own lives and experiences with literature. Then students reflect on the predictions they made as they listened to the story being read aloud, and they provide reasons to support their predictions. Teachers ask these questions to help students think about their predictions:

- What predictions did you make?
- What in the story made you think of that prediction?
- What in the story supports that idea?

DLTA is useful only when students are reading or listening to an unfamilar story so that the prediction actively involves them in the story. This strategy can be used both when students are listening to the teacher read literature aloud and when they are doing the reading themselves.

a few words or a sentence. During an author unit on Eve Bunting, for instance, third graders, after listening to each story, record the title on a page in their reading logs and write a response telling what they liked about the story or what it made them think of. Figure 7–5 presents three entries from a third grader's read-

Figure 7–5 *Three Entries from a Third Grader's Reading Log*

<u>Fly Away Home</u> by Eve Bunting

This book was so sad I stareted crying. Its sad to be homeless but Andrew has a lot of hope and hes going to get out just like the bird. Hes going to get a home again. I think everone shold have a home to live in.

<u>A Day's Work</u> by Eve Bunting

I liked this book alot. Francesco said his Abuelo was a fine gardner but he didn't know what to do. But they got to keep the jobs because they were honest. Weeds and flowers can look the same if your not a gardner.

<u>The Blue And The Gray</u> by Eve Bunting

War is very sad. And the Civil War was brother agenst brother. People hate each other and solders fight and die. I think they shold always put a marker to show where they died. "I think the Angels wept." That means war is so very very very sad. I hope I am never in a war.

ing log written during an author study on Eve Bunting. Older students write an entry after each chapter. After drawing and writing, students often share their reading logs with classmates, and this sharing provides another opportunity for classmates to listen aesthetically.

4. **Explore the story.**   Students explore the text by examining the vocabulary, collecting notable language samples, learning about story structure and authors, and participating in other word-study activities. Teachers also teach minilessons related to aesthetic listening. This stage is often abbreviated when teachers are reading aloud stories for enjoyment, as they often do after lunch or at the end of the day. Even so, teachers often need to clarify difficult words, discuss the structure of the story, or share information about the author or topics related to the book.

5. **Extend the response.**   Students expand their responses through reading, writing, talk, drama, research, and other projects. Students choose projects they are interested in pursuing to extend their enjoyment and interpretation of a book. These projects include making puppets to use in retelling a favorite story, writing letters to authors, creating a mobile for a favorite story, and reading other books by the same author or on a similar theme, to name only a few possibilities.

■ *For a list of projects, turn to Chapter 3, "The Reading and Writing Processes," pp. 107–108.*

Teaching Minilessons About Aesthetic Listening.   Teachers present minilessons during the preparing and exploring stages of the reading process using the instructional model presented in Chapter 1. The steps for teaching minilessons on aesthetic listening strategies are:

Step by Step

1. *Introduce the strategy.*   Explain the listening strategy, the way it is used, and the types of listening activities for which it is most effective. Develop a chart with the students to list the characteristics or steps of the strategy. For example, after introducing visualizing, you can list the following steps in creating a mind picture on a chart:

   • Close your eyes.
   • Draw a picture of a scene or character in your mind.
   • Listen for details and add them to your picture.
   • Add colors to your mind picture.

2. *Demonstrate the strategy.*   Demonstrate the strategy as you read a story aloud or as students listen to an audiotape of a story. Stop the presentation periodically to talk aloud about what you are doing or how you are using the strategy. After completing the activity, discuss your use of the strategy with students. For example, you might demonstrate how to create mind pictures of the characters and story events while reading aloud the first four or five chapters of Judy Blume's *Tales of a Fourth Grade Nothing* (1972).

3. *Practice the strategy.*   Provide students with opportunities to practice the strategy as you read aloud several other stories. Stop reading periodically to ask students to describe how they are using the strategy to listen aesthetically. For example, you might provide opportunities for students to practice creating mind pictures as they continue listening to the last five or six chapters of *Tales of a*

Fourth Grade Nothing. Children especially enjoy creating mind pictures about the last chapter, when Peter finds out that his little brother Fudge ate his turtle, Dribble.

4. **Review the strategy.**   After using an aesthetic listening strategy, have a student summarize the strategy and explain how he or she used it. Students can also write in their language arts notebooks about how they used what they have learned, or they can draw pictures. For example, after listening to the last chapter of *Tales of a Fourth Grade Nothing* read aloud, one fourth grader explained his visualization strategy:

✏️ *I made a picture in my mind of how upset Peter was that Fudge ate his turtle. He was crazy for wanting to find his turtle and mad at his brother and because no one cared about his turtle, only about his brother. He's been running and looking all over for his turtle. His face was red because he was crazy mad and he was yelling at Fudge and at his mom. He was crying, too, and wiping at his eyes because his turtle was eaten. Then I had a new picture in my mind when Peter got the big box—but with no wrapping paper or a bow—with a puppy in it from his dad at the end. He was calm but not really happy. He was still sad about his turtle being dead. He had a smart look on his face because he knew it had to be a puppy and he thought to name him Turtle so he wouldn't forget. I see him holding the black and white dog and that dog is licking him all over his face. Now he's going to start giggling and giggling and he's happy.*

5. **Apply the strategy.**   After students develop a repertoire of the aesthetic listening strategies, they practice the strategies as they listen to stories and other types of literature read aloud.

Teachers also teach minilessons to introduce, practice, and review procedures, concepts, and skills related to aesthetic listening. See page 277 for a list of topics for minilessons on aesthetic listening and the other types of listening. The teaching strategy discussed in the previous section can be taught as a series of minilessons, or minilessons can be taught when teachers are reading stories aloud or as part of literature focus units.

For example, during a literature focus unit on *The Sign of the Beaver* (Speare, 1983), a historical fiction set in the Maine wilderness in 1768, teachers might review the visualizing strategy and ask fifth graders to create a mind picture image of the cabin Matt and his father built in the wilderness. Then students might recall their mental images as they design and construct a tabletop diorama of the cabin. Another possibility is that teachers use a series of minilessons to teach students about literature discussions and how to listen to and build on their classmates' reactions. Or, through a discussion or in reading log entries, students might practice the strategy of connecting to personal experience by thinking about what they would do in Matt's position of having to stay behind at the cabin while his father walks back to Massachusetts to bring the rest of the family to the new homestead. As another alternative, a teacher might introduce the connecting-to-literature strategy and ask students to compare *The Sign of the Beaver* to another survival story, such as *Hatchet* (Paulsen, 1987). After listening to both stories read aloud, students might work in small groups to draw Venn diagrams to compare and contrast the stories.

Listening

	Procedures	Concepts	Strategies and Skills
Aesthetic Listening	Listen to a story read aloud Respond to classmates' comments Listen to a poem read aloud Write a response in a reading log Choose favorite quotations from a story Work on projects	Aesthetic listening Difference between aesthetic and efferent listening Concept of story	Predict Confirm Visualize Connect to personal experiences Connect to other stories Notice the power and beauty of language Apply knowledge of text structure
Efferent Listening	Take notes Do note-taking/note-making Use graphic organizers	The listening process Efferent listening Organizational patterns of informational texts	Categorize ideas Generalize Monitor Ask questions of the speaker Ask self questions Note cue words Get clues from the speaker
Critical Listening	Write advertisements Make storyboards Film commercials	Critical listening Three types of persuasion Propaganda Persuasion compared to propaganda Deceptive language Propaganda devices	Evaluate the message Determine the speaker's purpose Recognize appeals Recognize deceptive language Identify propaganda devices

Assessing Students' Aesthetic Listening

Students need to learn how to listen aesthetically so that they can engage more fully in the lived-through experience of literature. Teachers assess whether or not students are listening aesthetically in several ways. First of all, they can listen to the comments students make during grand conversations and read entries in students' reading logs to see if they are:

• Making predictions
• Visualizing
• Connecting to personal experience and to literature
• Revising meaning

- Playing with language from the story
- Applying knowledge of story structure

Teachers can also convert the list of aesthetic listening procedures, concepts, and strategies and skills presented in the list of minilessons on page 277 into a checklist and keep track of each topic as it is introduced, practiced, and reviewed.

EFFERENT LISTENING

Efferent listening is practical listening to understand a message. The term *efferent,* first applied to language arts by Louise Rosenblatt (1978, 1983), means "to carry away." It is the most common type of listening students do in school. For example, a fifth-grade teacher who discusses the causes of the American Revolution, a first-grade teacher who explains how to dial 911 in an emergency, and an eighth-grade teacher who discusses the greenhouse effect are all providing information for students to relate to what they already know and remember. Students use efferent listening to identify and remember important pieces of information.

Whether or not students comprehend and remember the message is determined by many factors. Some of these factors are operative before listening, others during and after. First, students need a background of knowledge about the content they are listening to. They must be able to relate what they are about to hear to what they already know, and speakers can help provide some of these links. Second, as they listen, students use a strategy to help them remember. They organize and "chunk" the information they receive, and they may want to take notes to help them remember. Then, after listening, students should somehow apply what they have heard so that there is a reason to remember the information.

Strategies for Efferent Listening

Students use a variety of strategies as they listen efferently; some of the strategies are the same as for reading and writing, and others are unique to efferent listening. The purpose of each strategy is to help students organize and remember the information they are listening to. Six strategies elementary students use for efferent listening are:

1. Organizing ideas. Informational presentations are usually organized in special ways called expository text structures. The five most common patterns are description, sequence, comparison, cause and effect, and problem and solution. Students learn to recognize these patterns and use them to understand and remember a speaker's message more easily. Speakers often use certain words to signal the organizational structures they are following. Signal words include *first, second, third, next, in contrast,* and *in summary.* Students can learn to attend to these signals to identify the organizational pattern the speaker is using.

■ *To learn more about the expository text structures, see Chapter 10, "Reading and Writing Information," pp. 392–396.*

Students often use graphic organizers to visualize the organization of oral presentations, informational videos, or informational books (Yopp & Yopp, 1996). When students listen to a presentation comparing amphibians and

Figure 7–6 *A Sixth Grader's T-Chart Comparing Amphibians and Reptiles*

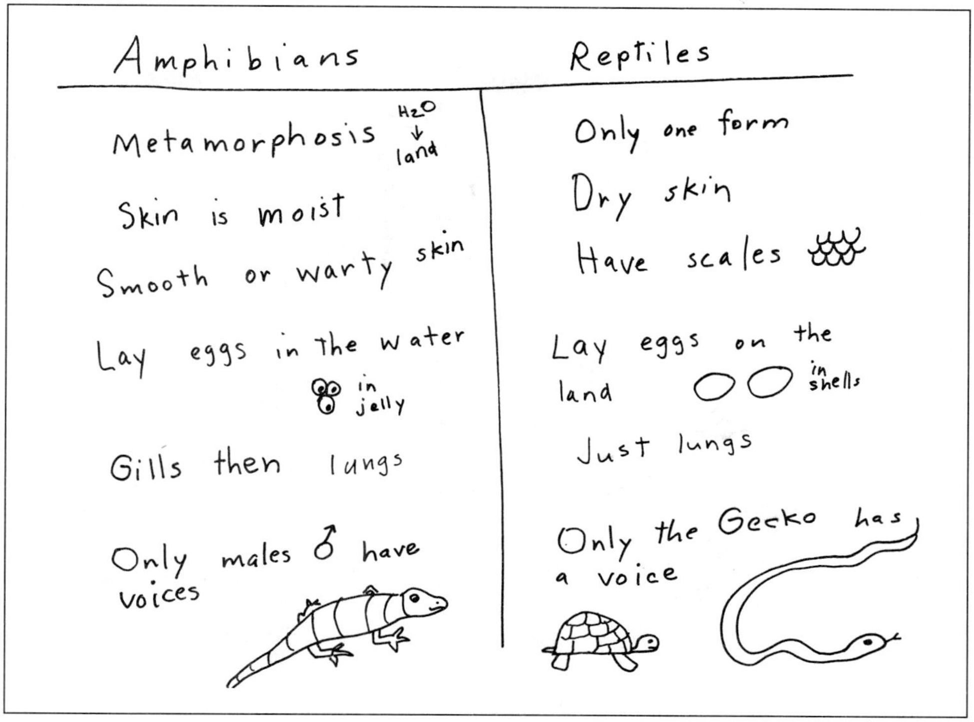

reptiles, for example, students make <u>T-charts or Venn diagrams to organize the information</u>. Students can draw a two-column T chart, labeling one column "Amphibians" and the other "Reptiles." Then students write notes in the columns while they listen to the presentation or immediately after listening. A sixth grader's <u>T-chart comparing amphibians and reptiles</u> is shown in Figure 7–6.

When students are listening to a presentation or an informational book that contains information on more than two or three categories, they can make a cluster diagram, write each category on a ray, and then add descriptive information. For example, when students are listening to a presentation on simple machines, they can make a cluster with a five rays, one for each type of simple machines. Then students add words and drawings to take notes about each type of simple machines. A fifth grader's cluster is shown in Figure 7–7.

2. Generalizing. Speakers present several main ideas and many details during oral presentations, and students need to learn to generalize or focus on the main ideas. Otherwise, they try to remember everything and quickly feel overwhelmed. Once students can identify the main ideas, they can then chunk the details to the main idea.

When teachers introduce the generalizing strategy, they ask students to listen for two or three main ideas. They write these ideas on the chalkboard and draw boxes around them. Then, as they give an oral presentation, teachers ask students to raise their hands when they hear the first main idea stated.

Figure 7–7   *A Cluster Diagram on Simple Machines*

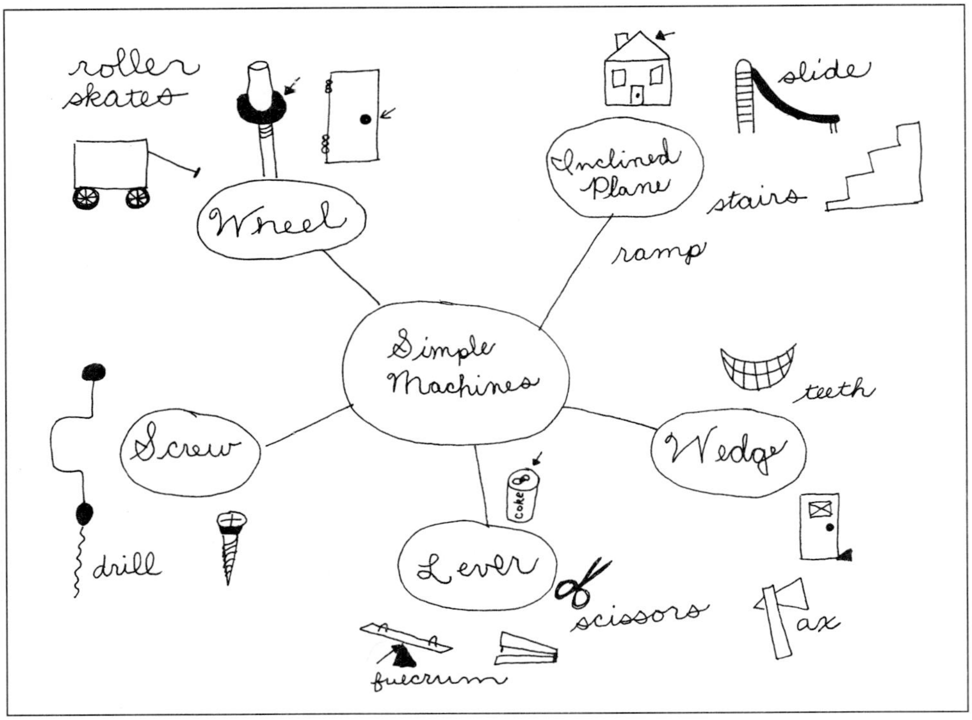

Students again raise their hands when they hear the second main idea, and again for the third main idea. Once students gain practice in detecting already-stated main ideas, teachers give a very brief presentation with one main idea and ask students to identify the main idea. Once students can identify the main idea, teachers give longer oral presentations and ask students to identify two or three main ideas. A fifth-grade teacher might make these points when giving an oral presentation on simple machines:

1. There are five kinds of simple machines.
2. Simple machines are combined in specialized machines.
3. Machines make work easier.
4. Almost everything we do involves machines.

Once students can identify the main ideas during an oral presentation, they can chunk details to the main ideas. This hierarchical organization is the most economical way to remember information, and students need to understand that they can remember more information when they use the generalization strategy.

3. Note-taking.   Note-taking helps students become more active listeners. Devine describes note-taking as "responding-with-pen-in-hand" (1981, p. 156). Students' interest in note-taking begins with the realization that they cannot store unlimited amounts of information in their minds; they need some kind of external storage system. Many listening strategies require listeners to make written notes about what they are hearing. Note-taking is often thought of as a listing or an outline, but notes can also be written in clusters and other diagrams.

■ *See Chapter 6, "Writing in Journals," pp. 231–233, for other examples of double-entry journals written in two columns.*

Teachers introduce note-taking by taking notes with the class on the chalkboard. During an oral presentation, the teacher stops periodically, asks students to identify what important information was presented, and lists their responses on the chalkboard. Teachers often begin by writing notes in a list format, but the notes can also be written in outline or cluster formats. Similarly, the teacher can use key words, phrases, or sentences in recording notes. After an introduction to various note-taking strategies, students develop personal note-taking systems in which they write notes in their own words and use a consistent format.

Upper-grade students might try a special kind of note-taking in which they divide their papers into two columns, labeling the left column "Take Notes" and the right column "Make Notes." They take notes in the left column, but more importantly, they think about the notes, make connections, and personalize the notes in the right column (Berthoff, 1981). Students can use this strategy when listening to oral presentations as well as when reading a content-area textbook or an informational book. Students need to stop periodically and reflect on the notes they have taken. The right column should be more extensive than the left one. A sample note-taking and note-making sheet is presented in Figure 7–8. In this figure a sixth grader is taking notes as she reads about illegal drugs.

Children's awareness of note-taking as a strategy "to help you remember what you are listening to" begins in the primary grades. Teachers begin demonstrating the usefulness of note-taking on the chalkboard or on charts with kindergartners and first graders. Second and third graders then begin taking notes in their learning logs as a part of social studies and science classes.

Outlining is a useful note-taking strategy, but it has gained a bad reputation from misuse in secondary and college English and content-area classes (Devine, 1981). It may be preferable to use print materials to introduce outlining, because oral presentations are often less structured than print materials, and students must discover the speaker's plan in order to outline. Teachers who want to teach outlining through oral presentations, however, should begin with a simple organization of perhaps three main ideas with two subordinate ideas for each main idea. Teachers can also give students a partial outline to complete during an oral presentation.

The information students should include in the notes they take depends on their purpose for listening. Thus, it is essential that students understand the purpose for listening before they begin to take notes. Some listening tasks require noting main ideas or details; others require noting sequence, cause and effect, or comparisons.

Students can take notes from informational books they are reading and from reference materials; however, taking notes from a speaker is an equally important strategy. When they are taking notes from a speaker, students cannot control the speed at which information is presented. They usually cannot listen more than once to a speaker in order to complete their notes, and the structure of oral presentations is often not as formal as that of printed materials. Students need to become aware of these differences so that they can adapt their note-taking system to the presentation mode.

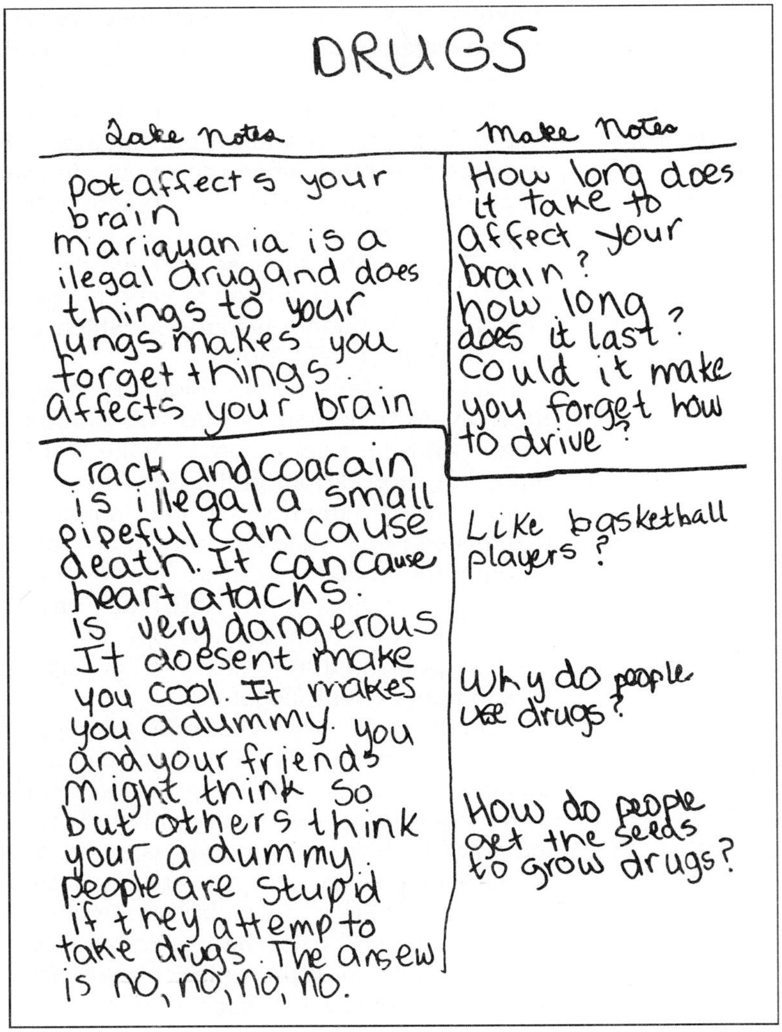

Figure 7–8   *A Fifth Grader's Note-Taking and Note-Making Sheet*

DRUGS

Take notes	Make Notes
pot affects your brain mariquania is a ilegal drug and does things to your lungs makes you forget things. affects your brain	How long does it take to affect your brain? how long? does it last? Could it make you forget how to drive?
Crack and coacain is illegal a small pipeful can cause death. It can cause heart atachs. is very dangerous It doesent make you cool. It makes you a dummy. you and your friends might think so but others think your a dummy. people are stupid if they attempt to take drugs. The ansew is no, no, no, no.	Like basketball players? Why do people use drugs? How do people get the seeds to grow drugs?

4.   Monitoring.   Students monitor their listening to make sure they are understanding. Monitoring is important so that students know when they are not listening successfully, when a listening strategy is not working, or when they need to ask a question. Students can use these self-questions to monitor their understanding while they are listening:

- Why am I listening to this message?
- Do I know what _____ means?
- Does this information make sense to me?

5.   Applying fix-up strategies.   When students are listening and something doesn't make sense, they must take action in order to resolve the problem. Otherwise, they are likely to become confused and frustrated. Often students ask a question to clarify information or eliminate confusion. Although asking questions can disturb other students and may interrupt the speaker's train of thought, students should usually be allowed to ask questions because confusion inhibits their listening and learning.

Asking questions is only one fix-up strategy. Other ways to fix comprehension problems include:

- Continue listening because the speaker may clarify, summarize, or review the point
- Check any visual displays the speaker has presented
- Make connections to what the listener already knows about the topic
- Write down questions to ask later

Students need to learn how to manage comprehension problems during listening rather than becoming confused and frustrated. When readers don't understand something, they often turn back a page or two and reread, but listeners can't turn back unless they are listening to an audiotape or video presentation.

6. Getting clues from the speaker. Speakers use both visual and verbal cues to convey their messages and direct their listeners' attention. Visual cues include gesturing, writing or underlining important information on the chalkboard, and changing facial expressions. Verbal cues include pausing, raising or lowering the voice, slowing down speech to stress key points, and repeating important information. Surprisingly, many students are not aware of these attention-directing behaviors, so teachers must point them out. Once students are aware of these cues, they can use them to increase their understanding of a message.

Teaching Efferent Listening

Learning to listen efferently is an important school task, and students use efferent listening as they listen to presentations as part of theme cycles. Using the efferent listening strategies helps students to more efficiently remember information and better understand the message they are listening to. Teachers need to explain the differences between aesthetic and efferent listening and teach students to use the efferent listening strategies. Teachers also teach minilessons about procedures, concepts, and strategies and skills related to efferent listening. Then students use what they have learned about efferent listening as part of theme cycles and other across-the-curriculum learning.

Teaching Minilessons About Efferent Listening. Teachers teach minilessons to introduce, practice, and review procedures, concepts, and strategies and skills related to efferent listening. The list of topics for minilessons presented on page 277 includes topics related to efferent listening. The teaching strategy discussed in the previous section on aesthetic listening can be used to teach minilessons on efferent listening.

Students need to learn to select appropriate strategies for specific listening purposes. The choice depends on both the listener's and the speaker's purpose. Although students must decide which strategy to use before they begin to listen, they need to continue to monitor their selection during and after listening. Students can generate a list of questions to guide their selection of strategies and monitor their effectiveness. Asking themselves questions like these before listening will help them select a listening strategy:

• What is the speaker's purpose?
• What is my purpose for listening?
• What am I going to do with what I listen to?
• Will I need to take notes?
• Which strategies could I use?
• Which strategy will I select?

These are possible questions to use during listening:

• Is my strategy still working?
• Am I organizing the information effectively?
• Is the speaker giving me cues about the organization of the message?
• Is the speaker giving me nonverbal cues, such as gestures and facial expressions?
• Is the speaker's voice giving me other cues?

These questions are appropriate after listening:

• Do I have questions for the speaker?
• Is any part of the message unclear?
• Are my notes complete?
• Did I make a good choice of strategies? Why or why not? (Tompkins, Friend, & Smith, 1987, p. 39)

Presenting Information as Part of Theme Cycles.   During theme cycles, students use efferent listening in order to remember the important information that teachers present. Students need to understand the differences between aesthetic and efferent listening and know how to use the efferent listening strategies to help them generalize key concepts and chunk information. The way teachers present information often determines whether or not students understand the presentation. The three steps in giving a presentation of information are:

*Step
by
Step*

1. ***Build students' background knowledge.***   Before beginning the presentation, teachers make sure that students have the necessary background knowledge; then, when teachers present the new information, they link it to students' background knowledge. Teachers explain the purposes of the listening activity and review one or more strategies students can use to facilitate their understanding. They may also draw a graphic organizer on the chalkboard or give students copies to use in taking notes.

2. ***Present the information.***   While the students listen, teachers can draw graphic organizers on the chalkboard and add key words to help students organize the information being presented. This information can also be the basis for the notes students take either as they are listening or immediately after they have listened.

Teachers can also pass out sheets with skeleton notes that students complete while they are listening or after they have listened.

Teachers use both visual and verbal cues—writing notes on the chalkboard, repeating key concepts, raising their voices to highlight conclusions—to direct students' attention to the important information being presented. As teachers draw the presentation to a close, they summarize the important points or draw conclusions.

3. Provide application opportunities. After students listen to the presentation, teachers provide opportunities to apply the new information in a meaningful way.

As part of a theme cycle on rivers, for example, a sixth-grade teacher might give a presentation on the Mississippi River. First, the teacher builds background knowledge by locating the river on a large map of the United States and then asking students to trace the river from its source in Minnesota to its mouth in the Gulf of Mexico on their smaller, individual maps. Then the teacher explains that he will talk about four topics related to the Mississippi: uses, boats, floods, and plant and animal life. Students divide a sheet of paper into four sections to take notes as each topic is discussed.

Then the teacher gives the first part of the presentation, talking briefly about how the river is used as an inland waterway. He writes *corn, coal, steel,* and *oil* on the chalkboard as he describes the northbound and southbound commercial traffic on the Mississippi. Then he stops for students to take notes using the key words he has written. He also asks students to monitor their listening, think about what he has said, and ask themselves if they have understood. Then the teacher repeats this process as he talks briefly about the other three topics.

After this presentation, students review their notes with a classmate and add any important information they have not included. Later during the theme cycle, students will divide into small groups to teach their classmates about other rivers of the world using the same procedure.

Reading Aloud Informational Books. Teachers read aloud informational books during theme cycles. Informational books have the power to intrigue and excite students, and students use a combination of efferent and aesthetic listening because informational books provide both a literary and a learning experience (Vardell & Copeland, 1992). High-quality informational books such as *Welcome to the Green House* (Yolen, 1993), *Wolves* (Simon, 1992), *Buffalo Hunt* (Freedman, 1988), *A River Ran Wild* (Cherry, 1992), and *Cleopatra* (Stanley & Vennema, 1994) cover a wide range of topics. When teachers read aloud informational books they often think about the instructional value of the books, but the books captivate students' imaginations while they are learning.

Many different types of informational books can be shared with students. Some informational books incorporate a story frame, such as *The Magic School Bus in the Time of the Dinosaurs* (Cole, 1994) and others in the Magic School Bus series. Other informational books are written in rhyme. Ruth Heller's science books including *The Reason for a Flower* (1983) and her books about words such as *Up, Up and Away: A Book about Adverbs* (1991)

■ *For more information about informational books, see Chapter 10, "Reading and Writing Information," pp. 389–392.*

are stunning. Biographies are another type of informational book, and they can be integrated into history theme cycles. Teachers also read aloud autobiographies of children's book authors such as *Firetalking* by Patricia Polacco (1994) and *A Letter From Phoenix Farm* by Jane Yolen (1992) in connection with author units.

There are many reasons to read aloud informational books (Vardell, 1996). Students learn content-area knowledge and specialized vocabulary. Teachers introduce students to books they might not tackle on their own, and students often read books independently that have been read aloud to them. Students also learn about the genre of informational books and use the format when writing their own books.

Teachers use the reading process introduced in Chapter 3 and discussed earlier in this chapter to share informational books with students. Even though teachers often abbreviate some of the stages, it is important that teachers activate students' background knowledge and set a purpose before reading. When teachers set a purpose, students know how to focus their attention as they listen. Often teachers read an informational book twice. During the first reading, students often listen aesthetically and are immersed in the experience. Then during the second reading, they focus their attention on the main ideas or important information. Teachers also use informational books to teach the efferent listening strategies. Guidelines for using informational books are listed in the Teacher's Notebook on page 287.

After reading, students need to be able to talk about the book. They share interesting information, ask questions, clarify confusions, and respond to the listening experience. Teachers often have students complete graphic organizers, write in learning logs, and apply what they have learned. Students apply what they have learned as they create projects, including posters, oral reports, and found poems. Students can also write their own informational books and create information quilts, like story quilts but with facts they have learned written and illustrated on each square. During a theme cycle on penguins, a class of first graders made an information quilt about penguins, and one square is shown in Figure 7–9. Before making the quilt, students listened to the teacher read aloud several informational books on penguins and wrote facts that they learned on a class chart. Students referred to the chart when they made their quilt.

Assessing Students' Efferent Listening

■ *Turn back to the PRO-File before Chapter 2, pp. 40–41, to read how one teacher uses "show-me's" to assess students' learning.*

Teachers often use objective tests to measure students' efferent listening. For example, if teachers have provided information about the causes of the American Revolution, how to dial 911 for an emergency, or the greenhouse effect, they can check the students' understanding of the information and infer whether or not students listened. Teachers should also assess students' listening more directly. Specifically, they should check how well students understand efferent listening procedures, strategies, and skills and how they apply them in listening activities. Asking students to reflect on and talk about the strategies they use and what they do before, during, and after listening provides insights into children's thinking in a way that objective tests cannot.

Teacher's Notebook
Guidelines for Reading Aloud Informational Books

1. Choose High-Quality Books

Teachers choose high-quality informational books for theme cycle text sets. Books should have visual appeal and relevance to the theme cycle or other unit.

2. Share a Variety of Informational Books

Teachers read aloud storylike nonfiction, books with rhyming texts, alphabet and counting books, and biographies.

3. Use the Reading Process

While some stages may be abbreviated, teachers activate background knowledge, set purposes for listening, and provide opportunities for students to apply what they have learned.

4. Read Books Aloud More Than Once

During the first reading, students may use primarily aesthetic listening, and then during the second reading, students focus on remembering information.

5. Teach Efferent Listening Strategies

Teachers model and teach note-taking and other efferent listening strategies when reading aloud informational books.

6. Use Graphic Organizers

Teachers either give students copies of a chart to complete while they listen or draw a diagram on the chalkboard to organize students' thinking before reading.

7. Set Up a Listening Center

Teachers use listening centers so that students can listen to the informational book a second or third time. Listening centers can also be used instead of reading aloud to students.

8. Plan Oral Performances

Teachers and students adapt informational books for readers theatre performances, choral reading, puppet shows, and other presentations.

Figure 7–9 *A Square for a First-Grade Information Quilt on Penguins*

Penguens like to eat lots of fish.

CRITICAL LISTENING

Students—even those in the primary grades—need to develop critical listening skills because they are exposed to many types of persuasion and propaganda. Interpreting books and films requires critical thinking and listening. And social studies and science lessons on topics such as pollution, political candidates, and drugs demand that students listen and think critically.

Television commercials are another form of persuasion and source of propaganda, and because many commercials are directed at children, it is essential that they listen critically and learn to judge the advertising claims. For example, do the jogging shoes actually help you to run faster? Will the breakfast cereal make you a better football player? Will a particular toy make you a more popular child?

Persuasion and Propaganda

There are three basic ways to persuade people. The first is by reason. People seek logical conclusions, whether from absolute facts or from strong possibilities; for example, people can be persuaded to practice more healthful living as the result of medical research. It is necessary, of course, to distinguish between reasonable arguments and unreasonable appeals. To suggest that diet pills will bring about extraordinary weight loss is an unreasonable appeal.

A second means of persuasion is an appeal to character. We can be persuaded by what another person recommends if we trust that person. Trust comes from personal knowledge or the reputation of the person who is trying to persuade. We must always question whether we can believe the persuader. We can believe what scientists say about the dangers of nuclear waste, but can we believe what a sports personality says about the effectiveness of a particular sports shoe?

The third way to persuade people is by appealing to their emotions. Emotional appeals can be as strong as intellectual appeals. We have strong feelings and concern for ourselves and other people and animals. Fear, a need for peer acceptance, and a desire for freedom of expression are all strong feelings that influence our opinions and beliefs.

Any of the three types of appeals can be used to try to persuade someone. For example, when a child tries to persuade her parents that her bedtime should be delayed by 30 minutes, she might argue that neighbors allow their children to stay up later—an appeal to character. It is an appeal to reason when the argument focuses on the amount of sleep a 10-year-old needs. And when the child announces that she has the earliest bedtime of anyone in her class and it makes her feel like a baby, the appeal is to emotion. The same three appeals apply to in-school persuasion. To persuade classmates to read a particular book in a book report "commercial," a student might argue that they should read the book because it is short and interesting (reason); because it is hilarious and they'll laugh (emotion); or because it is the most popular book in the second grade and everyone else is reading it (character).

Children need to learn to become critical consumers of advertisements (Lutz, 1989; Rudasill, 1986; Tutolo, 1981). Advertisers use appeals to reason, character, and emotion just as other persuaders do to promote products, ideas, and services; however, advertisers may also use propaganda to influence our beliefs and actions. Propaganda suggests something shady or underhanded. Like persuasion, propaganda is designed to influence people's beliefs and actions, but propagandists may use certain techniques to distort, conceal, and exaggerate. Two of these techniques are deceptive language and propaganda devices.

People seeking to influence us often use words that evoke a variety of responses. They claim that something is "improved," "more natural," or "50% better"—loaded words and phrases that are deceptive because they are suggestive. When a product is advertised as 50% better, for example, consumers need to ask, "50% better than what?" Advertisements rarely answer that question.

Doublespeak is another type of deceptive language characterized as evasive, euphemistic, confusing, and self-contradictory. It is language that "pretends to communicate but really does not" (Lutz, 1991, p. 17). Lutz cites a number of kinds of doublespeak, and elementary students can easily understand two kinds: euphemisms and inflated language. Euphemisms are words or phrases (e.g., "passed away") that are used to avoid a harsh or distasteful reality, often out of concern for someone's feelings rather than to deceive. Inflated language includes words intended to make the ordinary seem extraordinary. Thus, car mechanics become "automotive internists," and used cars become "pre-owned" or "experienced" cars. Examples of deceptive language are listed in Figure 7–10. Children need to learn that people sometimes use words that only pretend to communicate; sometimes they use words to intentionally misrepresent, as when someone advertises a vinyl wallet as "genuine imitation leather" or a ring with a glass stone as a "faux diamond." Children need to be able to interpret deceptive language and to avoid using it themselves.

To sell products, advertisers use propaganda devices such as testimonials, the bandwagon effect, and rewards. Nine devices that elementary students can learn to identify are listed in Figure 7–11. Students can listen to commercials to find examples of each propaganda device and discuss the effect the device has on them. They can also investigate to see how the same devices vary in commercials directed toward youngsters, teenagers, and adults. For instance, a snack food commercial with a sticker or toy in the package will appeal to a youngster, and a videotape recorder advertisement offering a factory rebate will appeal to an adult. The propaganda device for both ads is the same: a reward! Propaganda devices can be used to sell ideas as well as products. Public service announcements about smoking or wearing seat belts, as well as political advertisements, endorsements, and speeches, use these devices.

Figure 7–10   Examples of Deceptive Language

Loaded Words	**Doublespeak**
best buy	bathroom tissue (toilet paper)
better than	civil disorder (riot)
carefree	correctional facility (jail, prison)
discount	dentures (false teeth)
easier	disadvantaged (poor)
extra strong	encore telecast (rerun)
fortified	funeral director (undertaker)
fresh	genuine imitation leather (vinyl)
guaranteed	inner city (slum, ghetto)
improved	memorial park (cemetery)
longer lasting	mobile home (house trailer)
lowest	nervous wetness (sweat)
maximum	occasional irregularity (constipation)
more natural	passed away (died)
more powerful	people expressways (sidewalks)
new/newer	personal preservation flotation device (life preserver)
plus	pre-owned or experienced (used)
stronger	pupil station (student's desk)
ultra	senior citizen (old person)
virtually	terminal living (dying)

Source: Lutz, 1989.

Figure 7–11 *Propaganda Devices*

---

1. Glittering Generality

Generalities such as "motherhood," "justice," and "The American Way" are used to enhance the quality of a product or the character of a political figure. Propagandists select a generality (such as motherhood or patriotism) so attractive that listeners do not challenge the speaker's real point.

2. Testimonial

To convince people to purchase a product, an advertiser associates it with a popular personality such as an athlete or film star. For example, "Bozo Cereal must be good because Joe Footballstar eats it every morning." Listeners consider whether the person offering the testimonial has the expertise to judge the quality of the product.

3. Transfer

Persuaders try to transfer the prestige of a person or object to another person or object that will then be accepted. A film star, for example, is shown using Super Soap, and viewers are to believe that they can have youthful skin if they use this soap. Likewise, politicians appear with famous athletes or entertainers so that the luster of the stars will rub off on them.

4. Name-calling

Advertisers try to pin a bad label on something they want listeners to dislike. In a discussion of health insurance, for example, an opponent may call the sponsor of a bill a socialist. Whether or not the sponsor is a socialist does not matter to the name-caller; the purpose is to cause unpleasant associations to rub off on the victim. Listeners consider the effect the label has on the product.

5. Card Stacking

Persuaders often choose only items that favor one side of an issue. Unfavorable facts are ignored. To be objective, listeners seek information about other viewpoints.

6. Bandwagon

This technique appeals to people's need to be a part of a group. Advertisers claim that everyone is using this product and you should, too. For example, "More physicians recommend this pill than any other." Listeners ask: Does everyone really use this product? What is it better than?

7. Snob Appeal

Persuaders use snob appeal to attract the attention people who want to be part of an exclusive group. Advertisements for expensive clothes, cosmetics, and gourmet foods often use this technique. Listeners consider whether the product is of high quality or merely has an expensive nametag.

8. Rewards

Advertisers often offer rewards for buying their products. For example, cereal products offer toys, and adults are lured by this device, too. Free gifts, rebates from manufacturers, and low-cost financing are being offered with expensive items. Listeners consider the value of rewards and how they increase the product's cost.

Techniques 1–5 adapted from Devine, 1982, pp. 39–40.

Students listen critically while classmates present puppet show "commercials" for their favorite Beverly Cleary books.

When students locate advertisements and commercials they believe are misleading or deceptive, they can write letters of complaint to the following watchdog agencies:

Action for Children's Television
46 Austin St.
Newton, MA 02160

Federal Trade Commission
Pennsylvania Ave. at Sixth St. NW
Washington, DC 20580

Children's Advertising Review Unit
Council of Better Business Bureaus
845 Third Ave.
New York, NY 10022

Zillions Ad Complaints
256 Washington St.
Mt. Vernon, NY 10553

In their letters, students should carefully describe the advertisement and explain what bothers them about it. They should also tell where and when they saw or heard the advertisement or commercial.

Strategies for Critical Listening

Listening critically means evaluating the message, and the most important strategy for critical listening is evaluating (Lundsteen, 1979). Students use the evaluating strategy to determine and judge the author's message. Students consider a variety of points simultaneously:

- What is the speaker or author's purpose?
- Is there an intellectual appeal?
- Is there a character appeal?

- Is there an emotional appeal?
- Are illustrations persuasive?
- Are propaganda devices being used?
- Are deceptive words or inflated language used?

As students listen to books read aloud, view commercials and advertisements, and listen to speakers, they need to ask themselves these questions in order to critically evaluate the message.

Students also use efferent listening strategies during critical listening because critical listening is an extension of efferent listening. They organize ideas, generalize main ideas, and monitor their understanding of the presentation. With this foundation, students evaluate the message.

Teaching Critical Listening

The steps in teaching students to be critical listeners are similar to the steps in teaching aesthetic and efferent listening strategies. In this teaching strategy students view commercials to examine propaganda devices and persuasive language. Later they can create their own commercials and advertisements. The steps are:

Step by Step

1. **Introduce commercials.**   Talk about commercials and ask students about familiar commercials. Videotape some commercials and view them with students. Discuss the purpose of each commercial. Use these questions about commercials to probe students' thinking about persuasion and propaganda:

   - What is the speaker's purpose?
   - What are the speaker's credentials?
   - Is there evidence of bias?
   - Does the speaker use deceptive language?
   - Does the speaker make sweeping generalizations or unsupported inferences?
   - Do opinions predominate the talk?
   - Does the speaker use any propaganda devices?
   - Do you accept the message? (Devine, 1982, pp. 41–42)

2. **Explain deceptive language.**   Present the terms *persuasion* and *propaganda*. Introduce the propaganda devices and view the commercials again to look for examples of each device. Introduce loaded words and doublespeak, and view the commercials a third time to look for examples of deceptive language.

3. **Analyze deceptive language.**   Have students work in small groups to critique a commercial as to the types of persuasion, propaganda devices, and deceptive language. Students might also want to test the claims made in the commercial.

4. **Review concepts.**   Review the concepts about persuasion, propaganda devices, and deceptive language introduced in the first three steps. It may be helpful for students to make charts about these concepts.

5. **Provide practice.**   Present a new set of videotaped commercials for students to critique. Ask them to identify persuasion, propaganda devices, and deceptive language in the commercials.

6. **Create commercials.**   Have students apply what they have learned about persuasion, propaganda devices, and deceptive language by creating their own

products and writing and producing their own commercials to advertise them. Possible products include breakfast cereals, toys, beauty and diet products, and sports equipment. Students might also create homework and house-sitting services to advertise, or they can choose community or environmental issues to campaign for or against. An excerpt from a story board for a commercial created by a group of fifth graders appears in Figure 7–12. As the students present the commercials, classmates act as critical listeners to detect persuasion, propaganda devices, loaded words, and doublespeak.

Using Advertisements.   Students can use the same procedures and activities with advertisements they collect from magazines and product packages. Have children collect advertisements and display them on a bulletin board. Written advertisements also use deceptive language and propaganda devices. Students examine advertisements and then decide how the writer is trying to

Figure 7–12   An Excerpt From Fifth Graders' Story Board for Their "Dream Date" Commercial

persuade them to purchase the product. They can also compare the amount of text to the amount of pictures. Students often notice that toy advertisements feature large, colorful pictures and that cosmetic advertisements feature pictures of beautiful women, whereas advertisements for medicines devote more space to text. They also point out sports stars and entertainment personalities in many advertisements. Even primary-grade students recognize intellectual, character, and emotional appeals in these advertisements.

Students often apply what they have learned about persuasion in advertisements they create. Students can create advertisements as part of literature focus units, reading workshop, and theme cycles. Figure 7–13 shows the "Wanted" poster that a second grader made after reading *Sylvester and the Magic Pebble* (Steig, 1969), the story of a donkey who is lost after he is magically turned into a stone. Before students made these posters, the teacher taught a minilesson about persuasion and shared examples of advertisements with the students. With this introduction, students decided to feature large pictures of the donkey, emotional appeals, reward offers, and their telephone numbers. Students can also make advertisements about their favorite books as part of reading workshop, and make recycling, anti-drug, and safe-driving advertisements during theme cycles.

Teaching Minilessons About Critical Listening. Teachers also teach minilessons to introduce, practice, and review procedures, concepts, and strate-

Figure 7–13 *A Second Grader's "Wanted" Poster*

gies and skills related to critical listening. See page 277 for a list of topics for minilessons on critical listening. These topics can be taught when students are studying commercials or writing advertisements as part of a social studies or science theme cycle, or they can be taught as minilessons during reading and writing workshop.

Using Trade Books to Teach Critical Listening. A variety of stories, informational books, and poetry encourage critical thinking. When teachers read aloud stories such as *The Giver* (Lowry, 1993) and *The True Story of the Three Little Pigs!* (Scieszka, 1989), students use both aesthetic and critical listening. They use critical listening to evaluate the theme of *The Giver* and to determine whether the wolf's story is believable. When students listen to informational books such as *Antarctica* (Cowcher, 1990) and *Encounter* (Yolen, 1992), they confront important ecological and social issues. The books provide information about the issues, and classmates share their ideas during discussions. Through these activities, students think more deeply about controversial issues and challenge and expand their own beliefs. Even some books of poetry stimulate critical listening. *Sierra* (Siebert, 1991), for example, a book-length poem about this western mountain range, ends with a warning about the threat people pose to the environment. A list of these and other books that encourage critical listening (and thinking) is presented in Figure 7–14.

Adapting to Meet the Needs of Every Student. Because listening is the language mode used most often, it is especially important that all students be effective listeners. Too often teachers simply admonish students to listen or assume that students are listening because they are sitting quietly. To become effective listeners, students need to learn how to vary the way they listen for different purposes and how to use the listening strategies presented in this

Figure 7–14   Books That Encourage Critical Listening

Avi. (1991). *Nothing but the truth.* New York: Orchard. (U)

Cohen, B. (1983). *Molly's pilgrim.* New York: Lothrop, Lee & Shepard. (M)

Cowcher, H. (1990). *Antarctica.* New York: Farrar, Straus & Giroux. (P–M)

Jeffers. S. (1991). *Brother eagle, sister sky.* New York: Dial. (M)

Knight, M. B. (1993). *Who belongs here? An American story.* Gardiner, ME: Tilbury House. (M)

Lowry, L. (1993). *The giver.* Boston: Houghton Mifflin. (U)

Morimoto, J. (1987). *My Hiroshima.* New York: Puffin. (M)

Naylor, P. R. (1991). *Shiloh.* New York: Macmillan. (M–U)

Ringgold, F. (1996). *My dream of Martin Luther King.* New York: Crown. (M)

Scieszka, J. (1989). *The true story of the three little pigs!* New York: Viking. (P–M)

Siebert, D. (1991). *Sierra.* New York: HarperCollins. (M–U)

Turner, A. (1987). *Nettie's trip south.* New York: Macmillan. (M)

Van Allsburg, C. (1986). *The stranger.* Boston: Houghton Mifflin. (M)

Williams, S. A. (1992). *Working cotton.* Orlando, FL: Harcourt Brace. (P–M)

Yolen, J. (1992). *Encounter.* Orlando, FL: Harcourt Brace. (M)

Zolotow, C. (1972). *William's doll.* New York: Harper & Row. (P)

P = primary grades (K–2); M = middle grades (3–5); U = upper grades (6–8).

Adapting Listening Instruction To Meet the Needs of Every Student

1. Identify a Purpose for Listening

Whenever students listen to an oral presentation, they need a specific purpose for listening. By identifying the purpose for listening, students understand why they are listening and know what they will be expected to do after listening.

2. Use the Directed Listening-Thinking Approach

The Directed Listening-Thinking Approach is a good way to introduce the aesthetic listening strategies. Many teachers use DLTA whenever they read aloud to actively involve their students in listening.

3. Teach Students to Take Notes

Many students have difficulty identifying the key concepts in order to take useful notes. Teachers demonstrate note-taking by writing notes on chart paper as they give oral presentations, and afterwards they talk about why some points were more important than others.

4. Teach Students to Monitor Their Listening

Too often students view listening as something that happens automatically, and they don't realize that listeners are actively involved in the listening process. It is important for students to learn to monitor themselves as they listen and to ask themselves if they are understanding what they are listening to and whether or not the listening strategies they are using are working.

5. Make the Listening Process Visible

Listening is an invisible process, but students can make it more visible by talking, drawing, and writing about what they do when they listen. Encourage students to think about how they vary the way they listen for different purposes and to think about the strategies they use.

chapter. See above for a list of ways to adapt listening instruction to meet the needs of all students.

Assessing Students' Critical Listening

After teaching about persuasion and propaganda, teachers can assess students' knowledge of critical listening by having them view and critique commercials, advertisements, and other oral presentations. They can note the critical listening procedures, strategies, and skills their students use. A second way to assess students' understanding of critical listening is to have them develop their own commercials and advertisements. Critical listening goes beyond one unit, however, and is something that teachers should return to again and again during the school year.

Review

Listening is the most basic and most used of the language modes. Despite its importance, listening instruction has been neglected in elementary classrooms. Students vary the way they listen for different purposes, and they use different procedures, strategies, and skills for each type of listening. The key concepts presented in this chapter are:

1. Listening is the neglected language art because it is rarely taught; instead, teachers admonish students to listen or merely provide practice activities.
2. Listening is a three-step process: receiving, attending, and assigning meaning.
3. There are five types of listening: discriminative, aesthetic, efferent, critical, and therapeutic.
4. Students listen aesthetically as teachers read stories aloud and while viewing puppet shows, plays, and video versions of stories.
5. The Directed Listening-Thinking Approach (DLTA) is one way to actively involve students in aesthetic listening.
6. During theme cycles, students use efferent listening to remember information and use critical listening to evaluate a message.
7. Students need to learn to use listening strategies to enhance their listening abilities.
8. Teachers introduce listening strategies during minilessons and then provide opportunities for students to use the strategies during literature focus units and theme cycles.
9. Students need to learn to listen critically because they are exposed to many types of persuasion and propaganda.
10. Students apply what they learn about persuasion and propaganda as they create commercials and advertisements.

Extensions

1. Visit a classroom and observe how listening is taught or practiced. Consider how practice activities might be changed into instructional activities.
2. Interview primary-, middle-, and upper-grade students about strategies they use while listening. Ask questions such as these:

   - What is listening?
   - Why do people listen? Why else?
   - What do you do while you are listening?
   - What do you do to help you remember what you are listening to?

   - Do you always listen in the same way, or do you listen differently to stories read aloud and to information your teacher is telling you?
   - How do you know what is important in the message you are listening to?
   - What is the hardest thing about listening?
   - Are you a good listener? Why? Why not?

   Compare students' responses across grade levels. Are older students more aware of the listening process than younger students are? Can older students identify a greater variety of listening strategies than younger students can?

3. Plan and teach a minilesson on one of the aesthetic listening strategies and on one of the efferent listening strategies discussed in this chapter. Reflect on the lessons and on the differences between aesthetic and efferent listening.

4. Using the Directed Listening-Thinking Approach presented in Figure 7–4, read a story with a group of students. Notice the students' interest in the story and the types of predictions they make.

5. Become a pen pal with several students and correspond about the books their teacher is reading aloud to them. As you write to the students, ask them about their listening process and invite them to share their reactions to the story with you.

6. Using the teaching strategy presented in the section on critical listening, teach a lesson about commercials or advertisements.

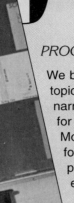

PRO-File
Sixth-Grade Debaters

> 66 Debates are one way I encourage my students to become independent thinkers and to see another point of view. 99

Pat Daniel
Sixth-Grade Teacher
South Rock Creek School

PROCEDURE

We brainstorm possible debate topics, and the class votes to narrow our list: more sports for students, the Lock Ness Monster, soft drink machines for students, and women for president. My students enjoy defending answers, presenting logical reasons, or sharing their creative thought processes. I capitalize on the fact that they are entering a developmental stage ripe for questioning authority. Debates provide a supportive, appropriate environment for testing their ideas. Careful preparation allows students to build sound arguments and build confidence in expressing their opinions.

Students select the topic they want to debate. They divide into "pro" and "con" teams of three or four members each. Some groups have to choose numbers to form the teams; consequently, some students debate against the way they believe. The groups prepare for the debate by interviewing students, administrators, parents, and teachers; researching information in the library; and developing charts to present the data they collect. I provide in-class time for the students to prepare. We talk about how to present information and how to be persuasive.

One debate is held each day. Each debate takes about 20 minutes, so all debates can be held within a week's time. Students arrange a podium in the front of the classroom; the podium divides the pro and con teams. Students hang their charts and other visuals on the wall behind the podium for easy reference. Another student is chosen as moderator, who opens and closes the debate. The moderator states the question in debate format, for example, "Should there be more sports for students at South Rock Creek School?" The first member of the pro team presents a prepared statement, referring to notecards. These remarks are followed by a response from the con team. Students alternate until each student has spoken once. Then comes the rebuttal—a time that students really need to think on their feet. The rebuttal is more freewheeling. I allow it to continue as long as someone has something to say—usually about 10 minutes. Students have learned that comments such as "out of the ball park" or "you're wrong" are not polite. They quickly learn to substitute facts for emotional responses. The moderator closes with a statement such as "That concludes our debate."

ASSESSMENT

The students develop a list of criteria that the judges—three community members—use in assessing each student's performance in the debate and deciding the "winning" team. The winning team is the one that earns more overall points. The checklist for assessing one debate is shown in the accompanying figure.

ADAPTATIONS

My students have participated in debates on topics of special interest to them—issues in their lives and questions related to our theme cycles. A number of my students have suggested that we plan a debate on a topic related to a book we have read. For example, after reading *Tuck Everlasting* (Babbitt, 1975), we could debate whether people should live forever. Three other books that many of my students read that lend themselves to debates are *The Midnight Fox* (Byars, 1968), *Shiloh* (Naylor, 1991), and *Nothing But the Truth* (Avi, 1991). My students have strong feelings about the issues raised in these books, and now they understand that a debate provides a forum for thinking about important issues.

REFLECTIONS

I believe in using talk in my classroom. My students regularly work in small groups and give book talks, but debates are something special. My students learn to take a stand and to marshal facts to support their position. They also learn about the power of language to solve real problems in their lives.

DEBATE RUBRIC

Resolved: There should be more sports for students at South Rock Creek School.

Rating Code:

1–5; 5 = highest, 1 = lowest

	Appearance	Delivery	Factual information	Keeping to the point	Persuasiveness	Teamwork	Participation in rebuttal	Total
Pro								
Sundee Aday	——	——	——	——	——	——	——	——
James Zientek	——	——	——	——	——	——	——	——
Jeremy Bailey	——	——	——	——	——	——	——	——
							Total	——
Con								
Melody Brooks	——	——	——	——	——	——	——	——
Whitney Lawson	——	——	——	——	——	——	——	——
Darth Taylor	——	——	——	——	——	——	——	——
							Total	——

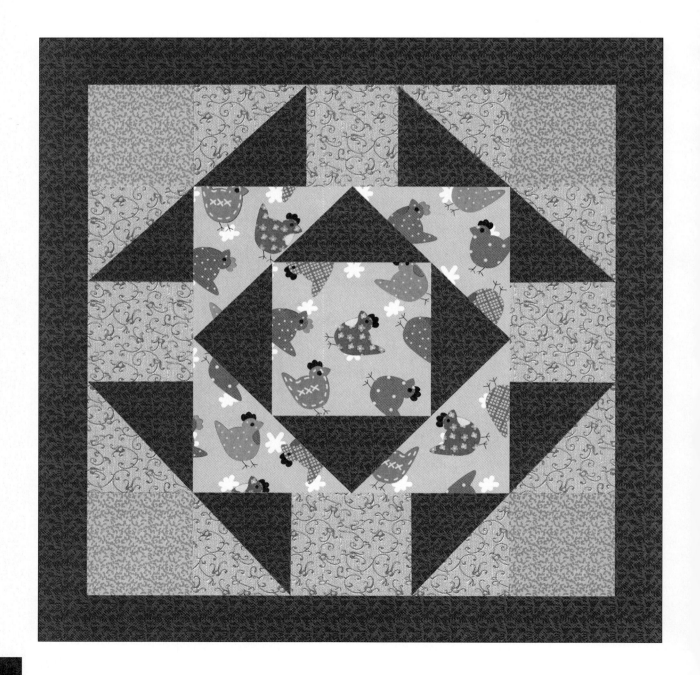

Sustaining Talk in the Classroom

Tea party has become a popular activity in Lori Gonzales's third-grade classroom. She gives each student a card with a page from a picture book or a paragraph from a chapter book that students are reading for the activity. Students move around the classroom during the "tea party" and read their cards to classmates. Sometimes students trade cards with classmates, and sometimes they keep the same card through the party. During this tea party, students are reading excerpts from books about quilts, including *The Patchwork Quilt* (Flournoy, 1985). The quilt square on the opposite page is a design called "Tea Party."

alk is the primary expressive language mode. Both children and adults use it more frequently than writing, and children learn to talk before they learn to read and write. Talk is also the communication mode that all peoples around the world develop. Of the nearly 3,000 languages spoken today, only a fraction of them—fewer than 200—have developed written forms.

When they come to school, most children are fluent oral language users. They have had four or five years of extensive practice talking and listening. Because students have acquired basic oral language competencies, teachers often assume that they don't need to emphasize talk in the elementary school curriculum. Research shows, however, that students benefit from participating in talk activities throughout the school day and that talk is a necessary ingredient for learning (Cazden, 1988; Heath, 1983a; Wells & Chang-Wells, 1992).

Heath (1983a) questioned the value of talk in elementary classrooms and concluded that children's talk is an essential part of language arts and is necessary for academic success in all content areas. Quiet classrooms have been considered the most conducive to learning, but research now suggests that talk is a necessary ingredient for learning. Shuy (1987) says talk is often thwarted in elementary classrooms because of large class size and the mistaken assumption that silence facilitates learning. Teachers must make an extra effort to provide opportunities for socialization and talk.

As you continue reading, you will learn ways to encourage talk in your classroom. Think about these questions as you read:

- Why is talk important in the learning process?
- How do students learn to conduct conversations in the classroom?
- What types of aesthetic talk activities are appropriate for elementary students?
- What types of efferent talk activities are appropriate for elementary students?
- What types of dramatic activities are appropriate for elementary students?

CONVERSATIONS

Brief, informal conversations are common occurrences in the social environment of school. Students converse with classmates as they work on a mural as part of a theme cycle, as they sort books in the class library center, and after they listen to a story at the listening center. In these brief conversations, students use talk for different purposes (Wilkinson, 1984). They try to control the behavior of classmates, maintain social relationships, convey information, and share personal experiences and opinions. Teachers use spare minutes before class begins or while conferencing with students for similar conversations with students. The purpose of these conversations is socialization, and they are essential to creating a climate of trust in the classroom.

Other conversations serve instructional purposes. Students meet in small groups to react to literature they have read, respond to each other's writing, work on projects, and explore concepts they are learning in literature focus units and theme cycles. Students use talk for both aesthetic and efferent purposes, and the most important feature of small-group conversations is that they promote thinking. Teachers take students' ideas seriously, and Nystrand,

■ *To read more about
aesthetic and efferent
stances, turn back to
Chapter 3, "The
Reading and Writing
Processes," p. 91.*

Gamoran, and Heck (1993) point out that students are validated as thinkers, not just "rememberers," in these conversations. As students work in groups, they become engaged in the learning process and feel ownership of the knowledge they produce.

Researchers have compared the effectiveness of small-group conversations with other instructional approaches, and they have found that students' learning is enhanced when students relate what they are learning to their own experiences—especially when they do so in their own words (Wittrock & Alesandrini, 1990). Similarly, Pressley (1992) reported that students' learning was promoted when they had opportunities to elaborate on ideas through talk.

Students use talk to work out problems, accomplish a goal, or generate an interpretation or new knowledge in small-group conversations. These conversations can be used at all grade levels, kindergarten through eighth grade. Kindergartners might work together in a small group to experiment with objects and sort them according to whether or not they float. Middle-grade students might work in a small group to plan a dramatization of a story they have read.

Students' talk is spontaneous and reflects their thinking. Group members extend and expand on each other's comments as the conversation grows. They disagree, ask questions, and seek clarification for comments they do not understand. In the conversation, students' talk determines the direction of the activity because students are not hunting for predetermined correct answers. For example, in a small-group conversation during a theme cycle on weather, students might brainstorm a list of ways weather has an impact on their lives, but they would not talk about weather in order to recall the four types of clouds they had studied. Characteristics of small-group conversations are listed in Figure 8–1.

Figure 8–1   Characteristics of Small-Group Conversations

1. Each group has three to six members. These groups may be permanent, or they may be established for specific activities. It is important that group members be a cohesive group and be courteous to and supportive of each other. Students in established groups often choose names for their groups.
2. The purpose of the small-group conversation or work session is to develop interpretations and create knowledge.
3. Students' talk is meaningful, functional, and genuine. They use talk to solve problems and discover answers to authentic questions—questions that require interpretation and critical thinking.
4. The teacher clearly defines the goal of the group work and outlines the activities to be completed. Activities should require cooperation and collaboration and could not be done as effectively through independent work.
5. Group members have assigned jobs. Sometimes students keep the same jobs over a period of time, and at other times specific jobs are identified for a particular purpose.
6. Students use strategies to begin the conversation, keep it moving forward and on task, and end it.
7. Students feel ownership of and responsibility for the activities they are involved in and the projects they create.

Adapted from Cintorino, 1993; Nystrand, Gamoran, & Heck, 1993; Shafer, 1993.

Teachers play an important role in planning activities for small-group conversations. The activities and projects should be interesting to students, and teachers should ask authentic questions—questions without obvious answers—that require students to interpret or think critically. As students work in small groups, teachers assist groups and make suggestions as they are needed, but they do not impose their ideas on students. Teachers are confident of students' ability to create knowledge, are respectful of their ideas, and take their comments and questions seriously.

Guidelines for Conducting Conversations

Students learn and refine their strategies and skills for socializing and conversing with classmates as they participate in small-group conversations (Cintorino, 1993). Students learn how to begin the conversation, take turns, keep the conversation moving forward, support comments and questions that group members make, deal with conflicts, and bring the conversation to a close. And, they learn how powerful talk is in making meaning and creating knowledge.

Beginning the Conversation.   To begin the conversation, a student volunteers or someone is appointed. Sometimes teachers provide an authentic question to be discussed. Then the teacher or a student begins the conversation by repeating or reading the question, and a group member offers a response or subdivides the question into manageable parts. If students have written quickwrites or journal entries, one student might begin by reading his or her writing aloud to the group.

Keeping the Conversation Going.   Students take turns making comments and asking questions, and they support the other group members and elaborate on and expand their comments. The tone is exploratory, and throughout the conversation the group is progressing toward a common goal (Cintorino, 1993). The goal may be creating a project, developing an interpretation to a book the group has read, or responding to a question the teacher has asked. From time to time the conversation slows down and there may be a few minutes of silence (Sorenson, 1993). Then a group member asks a question or makes a comment that sends the conversation in a new direction.

Students are courteous, and they receive group members' comments attentively and respectfully. Students support one another in groups. Perhaps the most important way they do this is by calling each other by name. They also cultivate a climate of trust in the group by expressing agreement, sharing feelings, voicing approval, and referring to comments that group members made earlier.

Conflict in small-group conversations is inevitable, but students need to learn how to deal with it so that it doesn't get out of control. Students need to accept that they will have differing viewpoints and interpretations and learn to respect each other's ideas and make compromises. Cintorino (1993) reported that her eighth graders used humor to defuse disagreements in small-group conversations.

Ending the Conversation. At the end of a conversation, students reach consensus, conclude that they have explored all dimensions of a question, or complete a project. Sometimes students have a product from the conversation. Sometimes this may be a brainstormed list or a collection of notes, while at other times it may be a product or project students have created. Group members may be responsible for collecting and storing materials they have used or for reporting on the group's work.

Types of Conversations

Students participate in many types of small-group conversations, and they use talk for both aesthetic and efferent purposes. Ten examples are to:

- Analyze propaganda in commercials and advertisements
- Compare characters in book and video versions of a story
- Brainstorm questions for an interview
- Design a mural or bulletin board display
- Assess the effectiveness of a cross-age tutoring program
- Share writing in writing groups and get feedback from classmates about how to revise rough drafts
- Write a script for a puppet show, design puppets, and plan for the puppet show performance
- Discuss reactions and develop comprehension as students read a chapter book
- Make a cluster or other graphic organizer about information presented in a video
- Plan a storytelling project

Students participate in a grand conversation about The Giver.

These examples create situations where students have opportunities to talk with classmates and to listen, to argue, and to agree. The activities and projects are authentic and integrate talking with listening, reading, and writing. Students do not hunt for correct answers; they talk to develop interpretations and create knowledge.

Teaching Students to Talk in Small Groups

For small-group conversations to be successful, teachers need to create a climate of trust in their classrooms. Teachers do this by demonstrating to students that they trust them and their ability to learn. Similarly, students learn to socialize with classmates and to trust each other as they work together in small groups. For primary- and middle-grade students, reading Diane Stanley's *The Conversation Club* (1983) is a good way to introduce the climate of trust and to explain the roles of speakers and listeners during conversations.

Sorenson (1993) begins the school year by telling her eighth-grade students that they will participate in a different type of discussion in her classroom. She hangs a sign in the classroom that says "Teach Each Other," and she tells them that it is a quote from one of her students about why this different kind of discussion works. The students learn that what they say is just as important as what the teacher says and that through conversations, students are teaching each other.

The teacher models working in small groups and discusses how students can begin conversations, sustain them, and bring them to a close. Together the teacher and students summarize what they have learned and develop guidelines for small-group conversations. The teacher observes students as they work in small groups and teaches minilessons on needed procedures, concepts, and strategies and skills.

Teaching Minilessons on Talk

Even though most children come to school speaking fluently, they need to learn new ways to use talk. Small-group conversations provide one of these new ways. Teachers are wrong to assume that because students know how to talk, they know how to work in small groups, tell stories, participate in debates, and use talk in other ways. Teachers need to explain and demonstrate various types of talk and teach minilessons on procedures, concepts, and strategies and skills for different types of talk. A list of minilesson topics on talk is presented on page 309. Teachers use the procedure developed in Chapter 1 for these minilessons so that students are introduced to the topic and have opportunities to use talk in meaningful ways.

■ *See Chapter 1, "Learning and the Language Arts," pp. 34–38, to review the teaching strategy on which these minilessons are based.*

Adapting to Meet the Needs of Every Student

Talk is a useful learning tool, and it is important that activities be adapted so that every student can use talk. Small-group conversations and the other talk activities discussed in this chapter can be adapted in many ways to meet students' needs. Perhaps the most basic way to meet the needs of students who are uncomfortable speaking in a large group, or who are hesitant to speak because they are learning English as a second language or have other lan-

Talk

	Procedures	Concepts	Strategies and Skills
Conversations	Begin a conversation Take turns Expand or extend a classmate's comment Sustain a conversation Deal with conflicts End a conversation	Small-group conversations Climate of trust Roles of speakers and listeners	Share ideas and feelings Refer to previous comments Call group members by name Look at classmates Ask questions Extend and expand classmates' comments Seek clarification
Aesthetic Talk	Participate in literature conversations Choose a story to tell Prepare and tell a story Make props Select a script for readers theatre	Aesthetic talk Storytelling Readers theatre Parts of a script	Include the beginning, middle, and end Incorporate interesting or repeated phrases Use dialogue Use props Use facial expressions or gestures
Efferent Talk	Participate in theme cycle conversations Do a show-and-tell presentation Prepare and present an oral report Do a book talk and/or a book review Conduct an interview Participate in a debate	Efferent talk Theme cycle conversations Facts and opinions Guidelines for speakers and listeners Persuasion	Present information Vary points of view Support opinions Ask clarifying questions Choose a topic Gather information Organize information Use visuals Rehearse Speak loudly Use notecards Look at the audience
Dramatic Activities	Role-play Participate in a dramatic production Participate in a puppet show Make puppets Write scripts Make a story board	Narrator Types of puppets Scripts Dramatic conventions Story boards	Assume the role of a character Create dialogue for a character Interpret a character Sequence events Explore themes and issues

guage disabilities, is to have them work in a small, comfortable group and to keep the language use informal. It is much easier to work in a small group to accomplish a project than to give an oral report in front of the class or participate in a debate.

Drama is a powerful way of knowing, and many students benefit from dramatizing stories they have read and events they are learning about in theme cycles to understand them better. Also, many students are more comfortable talking in front of a group when they have a puppet on their hand than when they are standing in front of a group by themselves. These and other ways to adapt talk activities to meet the needs of every student are presented on page 311.

Assessing Students' Talk

Students' talk can be assessed, although it rarely is in elementary classrooms. However, because students and their parents often value what can be assessed, it is important to assess talk, and all of the types of talk discussed in this chapter can be assessed. In small-group conversations, teachers can simply note whether or not students are contributing members of their groups, or they can observe students' behavior and assess how students contribute to their groups. Teachers can "listen in" on students' conversations to learn about their language competencies and their abilities to work in small groups. Teachers of primary-grade students might assess whether students:

- Contribute to the conversation
- Share ideas and feelings
- Are courteous
- Listen carefully to classmates' comments
- Call group members by name
- Look at classmates when talking to them

Middle- and upper-grade students learn more sophisticated procedures, strategies, and skills, and in addition to the six behaviors listed above, teachers of older students might assess whether students:

- Volunteer to begin the conversation
- Perform their assigned jobs in the group
- Extend and expand classmates' comments
- Ask questions and seek clarifications
- Invite other group members to contribute
- Stay on task
- Take turns
- Deal with conflict within the group
- Help to end the conversation
- Assume a leadership role in the group

Teachers can use these items to create a self-assessment checklist so that students can assess their own contributions to small-group conversations. It is important that students know what is expected of them during conversations and that they reflect on their behavior and contributions.

Adapting Talk Activities To Meet the Needs of Every Student

1. Include All Students in Conversations

Conversations have social as well as instructional purposes. As students learn ways to talk with classmates—how to ask questions, share information, and keep the conversation moving—they build a sense of community and a climate of trust.

2. Use Smaller Groups

Some students may feel more comfortable working in small groups of classmates they know well or in the same cultural group. These students might be more successful in small-group conversations, or they might be more articulate in giving book talks to a small group than to the whole class.

3. Give Group Presentations

Instead of preparing oral presentations individually, students can work in pairs or small groups to interview, tell stories, and give oral reports and book talks. When students work with a partner or in a small group, they share the responsibility and the talking. Students also learn important socialization skills and develop friendships.

4. Use Manipulatives

Many students find it easier to talk in front of a group when they are talking about an object they are holding. Young children bring objects for show-and-tell, and students can make charts and posters to use in oral reports.

5. Create Drama Projects

Drama is a powerful mode for students who have difficulty using written language. Students can use dramatic activities, such as role-playing and puppet shows, as projects for literature focus units and in theme cycles.

AESTHETIC TALK

Aesthetic talk, like aesthetic listening, deals with the lived-through experience of literature and creating interpretations. Students use aesthetic talk in discussing literature, telling stories, and participating in readers theatre.

Conversations About Literature

In order to dig deeper into a story and develop their interpretations, students talk about literature they are reading. These conversations are often called grand conversations (Eeds & Wells, 1989; Peterson & Eeds, 1990) or litera-

LC. pp. 311-314, 102, + p. 559, 561

Literature Circles

ture circles (Daniels, 1994). Students voice their opinions and support their views with examples from the literature. Through these conversations, students take responsibility for learning. They talk about what puzzles them, what they find interesting, their personal connections to the story, and connections they see between this story and others they have read. Students also encourage their classmates to contribute to the discussion. Teachers often sit in on conversations about literature as a participant, not as a judge; the talk is primarily among the students.

Literature conversations can be held with the whole class or in small groups. Young children usually meet together as a class, while older students often talk in small groups. When students meet together as a class, there is a shared feeling of community, and the teacher can be a part of the group. Young children usually meet together as a class, and older students meet together when they are learning literature conversation procedures or when they are listening to the teacher read a book aloud to the class. Students meet in small groups when they are reading different books and when they want to have more opportunities to talk. When the entire class meets together, students have only a few opportunities to talk, but when they meet in small groups they have many, many more opportunities to share their interpretations.

quoted →

Steps in Literature Conversations.   Literature conversations often have two parts. The first part is open-ended: students talk about their reactions to the book, and the direction of the conversation is determined by students' comments. Teachers do participate, however, and share their responses, ask questions, and provide information. In the second part the teacher focuses students' attention on one or two aspects of the book that they did not talk about in the first part of the conversation. The steps are:

*Step
by
Step*

1. **Meet in groups.**   Students meet together as a class or in small groups to talk about a book or a section of a book. When students meet together as a class, they sit in a circle in order to see each other; when they meet in a small group, they sit close together so that they can talk without disturbing their classmates.

2. **Share responses.**   Students share their reactions to the book. To begin the conversation, a student or the teacher asks, "Who would like to begin? What did you think of the story? Who would like to share a reaction?" As students share their responses, they comment on the events in the story, on the literary elements, or on the author's language, and they might make connections to their own lives and to other literature they have read. Each student participates and may build on classmates' comments and ask for clarifications. In order that everyone may participate, teachers often ask students to make no more than three comments until everyone has spoken at least once. Students may refer to the book or read a short piece to make a point, but there is no round-robin reading. Usually students don't raise their hands and are not called on by the teacher or a group leader. Instead, students take turns and speak when no else is speaking, much like adults do when they talk with friends. Pauses and brief silences may occur, and when students indicate that they have run out of things to say, the discussion may end or continue on to the next part.

3. Ask questions. Teachers ask open-ended questions to focus students' attention on one or two aspects of the book that have been missed. Four possible directions are:

- *Focus on illustrations.* After reading *El Chino* (Say, 1990), teachers might ask, "Did you like the illustrations in *El Chino*? How did the illustrations change during the book? Why do you think Allen Say did that?"
- *Focus on authors.* During a literature focus unit on Chris Van Allsburg, teachers might say, "This is the third book we've read by Chris Van Allsburg. What is so special about his books? Why do we like his books so much? Is there something they all share?"
- *Focus on comparison.* Teachers ask students to make a comparison: "How did this book compare with _____? Did you like the book or the film version better? Why? Which of Beverly Cleary's characters is your favorite?"
- *Focus on literary elements, stylistic devices, and/or genres.* After reading *Johnny Appleseed* (Kellogg, 1988) and *Swamp Angel* (Isaacs, 1994), teachers might ask, "Is *Johnny Appleseed* a legend? Is *Swamp Angel* a legend? What are the characteristics of legends? Which of these characteristics did you notice in these two books? What was the theme of the books? How did the authors tell us the theme?"

After the literature conversation, students often write (or draw) in their reading logs, or write again if they wrote before the literature conversation. Then they continue reading the book if they have read only part of it. Both participating in literature conversations and writing entries in reading logs help students think about and respond to what they have read.

It is not necessary to have questions for conversations about literature, but teachers or students can develop questions. The most useful questions cannot be answered with yes or no, and they require students to give personal opinions. After reading *Amber Brown Is Not a Crayon* (Danziger, 1994), a group of third graders wrote their own questions, and the group spent the first few minutes of group time considering the questions and deciding which ones to actually use. Their questions included:

3rd

- Why do you think Amber and Justin are best friends?
- Do you think Mr. Cohn is sort of like Ms. Frizzle [in the Magic School Bus series]?
- Do you think Mr. Cohn is a good teacher?
- Did you know from the beginning that Justin was going to move away?
- How can best friends fight and still be best friends?
- Is Justin happy or sad about moving to Alabama?
- Why is Amber so mean to Justin?
- What do you think will happen to Amber and Justin after he moves away?
- Can they still be best friends after Justin moves away?

Benefits of Conversations About Literature. From their observational study of fifth and sixth graders conducting conversations about literature, Eeds and Wells (1989) found that, through talk, students extend their individual interpretations of their reading and even create a better understanding of it. Stu-

M. Eeds + D. Wells

dents talk about their understanding of the story and can change their opinions after listening to classmates' alternative views. They share personal stories related to their reading in poignant ways that trigger other students to identify with them. Students also gain insights about how authors use the elements of story structure to develop their message.

An additional benefit of literature conversations is that when students talk in depth about literature, their writing shows the same level of interpretation (Sorenson, 1993). Students seem to be more successful in literature conversations if they have written in journals first, and they are more successful in writing journal entries if they have participated in literature conversations first.

Storytelling

The ancient art of storytelling is a valuable instructional tool. Teachers share literature with their students using storytelling techniques, and students tell stories, too. Storytelling is entertaining and stimulates children's imaginations. It expands their language abilities, and it helps them internalize the characteristics of stories and develop interpretations of stories (Morrow, 1985).

Steps in Telling Stories.   Students learn how to tell stories as they listen to their teachers tell stories. They notice that teachers change their voices for dialogue and emphasize repetitive phrases. They also watch teachers use puppets and other props. Modeling is very important, but teachers also teach mini-lessons to explain the storytelling procedure. Storytelling involves four steps:

Step by Step

1. ***Choose a story.***   Traditional stories, such as folktales, are often chosen for storytelling activities; however, any type of literature can be used. The most important considerations in choosing a story are that you like the story, know it well, and want to tell it. Morrow (1979) lists other considerations:

   - The story has a simple, well-rounded plot.
   - The story has a clear beginning, middle, and end.
   - The story has an underlying theme.
   - The story has a small number of well-defined characters.
   - The story contains dialogue.
   - The story uses repetition.
   - The story uses colorful language or "catch phrases."

   Figure 8–2 lists stories that contain many of these characteristics.

   Children can also create and tell stories to accompany wordless picture books. For example, Tomie de Paola's *Pancakes for Breakfast* (1978) is the charming story of a little old woman who tries to cook pancakes for breakfast but runs into a series of problems as she tries to assemble the ingredients. In the end, her neighbors invite her to their home for pancakes. The repetition of events in this story makes it easy for primary-grade children to tell.

2. ***Prepare to tell the story.***   Students plan and rehearse a familiar story before telling it. It is not necessary to memorize a story to tell it effectively. Kingore (1982) recommends that students choose a familiar story that they really like, and that they reread the story once or twice to review details about characters and to place major events in proper sequence. Then students choose interesting or repeated phrases from the story to enliven the language of their retelling and

Figure 8–2 *Stories for Storytelling Activities*

Aardema, V. (1975). *Why mosquitoes buzz in people's ears.* New York: Dial. (M–U)

Ada, A. F. (1995). *Mediopollito/Half-chicken.* New York: Doubleday. (P–M)

Brett, J. (1989). *The mitten.* New York: Putnam. (P–M)

Carle, E. (1970). *The very hungry caterpillar.* Cleveland: Collins-World. (P)

Fox, M. (1986). *Hattie and the fox.* New York: Bradbury Press. (P–M)

Gag, W. (1956). *Millions of cats.* New York: Coward McCann. (P)

Galdone, P. (1973). *The three billy goats Gruff.* Boston: Houghton Mifflin. (P)

Hamilton, V. (1995). *Her stories: African American folktales, fairy tales, and true tales.* New York: Blue Sky. (M–U)

Hastings, S. (1985). *Sir Gawain and the loathly lady.* New York: Mulberry. (U)

Kasza, K. (1987). *The wolf's chicken stew.* New York: Putnam. (P–M)

Lionni, L. (1969). *Alexander and the wind-up mouse.* New York: Pantheon. (M)

Mahy, M. (1990). *The seven Chinese brothers.* New York: Scholastic. (M)

Martin, B., Jr., & Archambault, J. (1985). *The ghost-eye tree.* New York: Holt, Rinehart & Winston. (M–U)

Mayer, M. (1978). *Beauty and the beast.* New York: Macmillan. (U)

Mayer, M. (1987). *There's an alligator under my bed.* New York: Dial. (P–M)

Meddaugh, S. (1995). *Hog-eye.* Boston: Houghton Mifflin. (M)

Numeroff, L. J. (1985). *If you give a mouse a cookie.* New York: Harper & Row. (P–M–U)

Polacco, P. (1988). *Rechenka's eggs.* New York: Philomel. (M)

Slobodkina, E. (1947). *Caps for sale.* New York: Scott. (P)

Wood, A. (1984). *The napping house.* San Diego: Harcourt Brace Jovanovich. (P)

Xiong, B. (1989). *Nine-in-one Grr! Grr!* San Francisco: Children's Book Press. (M)

Young, E. (1995). *Donkey trouble.* New York: Atheneum. (P–M)

Zemach, M. (1976). *It could always be worse.* New York: Farrar, Straus & Giroux. (P–M–U)

Ziefert, H. (1995). *The teeny-tiny woman.* New York: Viking. (P–M)

P = primary grades (K–2); M = middle grades (3–5); U = upper grades (6–8).

consider how to vary their speaking voice to make the story more interesting for listeners. Students also plan simple props or gestures to accompany the story. Then they prepare a brief introduction that relates the story to the audience's experiences. Students rehearse the story several times, incorporating phrases to enliven the story, varying their speaking voices, and using props or gestures. This process can be abbreviated when very young children tell stories. They choose a story they already know well and make props to guide the telling.

3. Add props. Three types of props that add variety and interest to stories are:

- *Flannel-board pictures.* Students place drawings or pictures cut from books and backed with flannel on the flannel board as the story is told.
- *Puppets.* Students use puppets they have made or commercially available puppets representing the main characters to tell a story with dialogue.
- *Small objects.* Students use stuffed animals to represent animal characters, or use other small objects to represent important things in the story being told. For instance, to retell *The Mitten* (Brett, 1989), students can use a white mitten and pictures of the animals that squeeze into the mitten in telling the story, or they can use a Ukrainian painted egg when telling *Rechenka's Eggs* (Polacco, 1988).

■ *For more information on making puppets, see pp. 333–335 in this chapter.*

4. Tell the story. Students tell the stories they have prepared to small groups of classmates or to younger children. Teachers may want to divide the audience into small groups so that more students can tell stories at one time.

Assessing Students' Storytelling Activities.   Teachers can assess both the process students use to tell stories and the quality of the storytelling production, but the process of developing interpretations is far more important than the quality of the storytelling. Teachers check that students move through the steps of planning and rehearsing the story before telling it, and that they:

- Introduce the story to the audience
- Include the beginning, middle, and end of the story
- Incorporate interesting or repeated phrases in their story
- Add dialogue
- Vary their voices for more interest
- Use props or gestures

As students gain experience telling stories, they become more comfortable in front of an audience and learn ways to "play" to their audience.

Readers Theatre

Readers theatre is "a formalized dramatic presentation of a script by a group of readers" (Busching, 1981, p. 330). Each student assumes a role and reads the character's lines in the script. The reader's responsibility is to interpret a story without using much action. Students may stand or sit, but they must carry the whole communication of the plot, characterization, mood, and theme by using their voices, gestures, and facial expressions.

Steps in Readers Theatre Performances.   Readers theatre avoids many of the restrictions inherent in theatrical productions. Students do not memorize their parts, and elaborate props, costumes, and backdrops are not needed. Neither do students spend long, tedious hours rehearsing the performance. Three steps in developing readers theatre performances are:

Step by Step

1. **Select a script.**   Quality play scripts exhibit the same characteristics as other types of fine literature. Five essential characteristics are an interesting story, a well-paced plot, recognizable and believable characters, plausible language, and a distinct style (Manna, 1984). The arrangement of the text on the page is also an important consideration when selecting or preparing a script. There should be a clear distinction between stage directions and dialogue through adequate spacing and variation in the print types and colors. This distinction is especially important for students who are not familiar with script format.

   Very few quality scripts are available for elementary students, so students usually prepare their own scripts from books they have read. Laughlin and Latrobe (1989) suggest that students begin by reading the book and thinking about its theme, characters, and plot. Next, students choose a scene or scenes to script, and they make copies of the scene and use felt-tip pens to highlight the dialogue. They then adapt the scene by adding narrators' lines to bridge gaps, set the scene, and summarize. Students assume roles and read the script aloud, revising and experimenting with new text until they are satisfied with the script.

Figure 8–3   *Stories That Can Be Scripted for Readers Theatre*

Babbitt, N. (1975). *Tuck everlasting.* New York: Farrar, Straus & Giroux. (U)

Blume, J. (1972). *Tales of a fourth grade nothing.* New York: Dutton. (M)

Byars, B. (1968). *The midnight fox.* New York: Viking. (M–U)

Cleary, B. (1973). *Ramona and her father.* New York: Morrow. (M)

Coerr, E. (1977). *Sadako and the thousand paper cranes.* New York: Putnam. (M)

Danziger, P. (1994). *Amber Brown is not a crayon.* New York: Putnam. (M)

Fleischman, S. (1986). *The whipping boy.* New York: Greenwillow. (M–U)

Gilson, J. (1983). *Thirteen ways to sink a sub.* New York: Lothrop, Lee & Shepard. (U)

Howe, D., & Howe, J. (1979). *Bunnicula: A rabbit-tale of mystery.* New York: Atheneum. (M–U)

Hurwitz, J. (1995). *Elisa in the middle.* New York: Morrow. (M)

King-Smith, D. (1988). *Martin's mice.* New York: Crown. (M–U)

Lewis, C. S. (1950). *The lion, the witch and the wardrobe.* New York: Macmillan. (M–U)

Lobel, A. (1970). *Frog and Toad are friends.* New York: Harper & Row. (P)

Lowry, L. (1989). *Number the stars.* Boston: Houghton Mifflin. (M–U)

MacLachlan, P. (1985). *Sarah, plain and tall.* New York: Harper & Row. (M)

Mathis, S. B. (1975). *The hundred penny box.* New York: Viking. (M)

McBratney, S. (1995). *Guess how much I love you.* Cambridge, MA: Candlewick. (P)

Milne, A. A. (1974). *Winnie-the-Pooh.* New York: Dutton. (P–M)

Naylor, P. R. (1991). *Shiloh.* New York: Atheneum. (M–U)

Sebestyen, O. (1979). *Words by heart.* Boston: Little, Brown. (U)

The final version is typed, duplicated, and stapled into pamphlets. Some recommended stories are presented in Figure 8–3.

2. **Rehearse the performance.**   To begin, students choose the parts they will read. One student is needed for each character, plus one for a narrator if the script calls for one. Students read through the script once or twice, then stop to discuss the story. Busching (1981) recommends using questions to probe students' understanding. Through this discussion, students gain a clearer understanding of the story and decide how to interpret their characters.

After students decide how to use their voices, gestures, and facial expressions to interpret the characters, they should read the script one or two more times, striving for accurate pronunciation, strong voice projection, and appropriate inflection. Obviously, less rehearsal is needed for an informal, in-class performance than for a more formal production; nevertheless, interpretations should always be developed as fully as possible.

3. **Stage the performance.**   Readers theatre can be performed on a stage or in a corner of the classroom. Students stand or sit in a row and read their lines in the script. They stay in position throughout the performance or enter and leave according to the characters' appearances "on stage." If readers are sitting, they may stand to read their lines; if they are standing, they may step forward to read. The emphasis is not on production quality; rather, it is on the interpretive quality of the readers' voices and expressions. Costumes and props are unnecessary; however, adding a few enhances interest and enjoyment, as long as they do not interfere with the interpretive quality of the reading.

Assessing Students' Performances.   Students work in small groups to plan and rehearse their readers theatre performances. Teachers can assess students' work in small groups as well as their interpretation of the story during the performances. The focus is on students' interpretation of the text, and teachers need to assess students' understanding of the story and the characters they performed. Teachers may want to ask students to explain how they portrayed their character and how this interpretation influenced the way they read their part.

EFFERENT TALK

Students use efferent talk to inform and persuade. They use efferent talk in conversations during theme cycles. They also use four other types of efferent talk: show-and-tell, oral reports, interviews, and debates. These activities are more formal, and students prepare and rehearse their talks before giving them in front of an audience.

Conversations During Theme Cycles

Conversations are an important part of theme cycles. Students talk about concepts they are learning and about issues such as pollution, immigration, nuclear energy, and human rights. These conversations can take place when students meet in small groups or together as a class. In contrast to literature conversations, in which students use primarily aesthetic talk to create and deepen their interpretations, students use primarily efferent talk to create knowledge and understand relationships among concepts they are learning. Students gather information for the conversation through giving or listening to oral presentations, reading informational books and newspapers, and watching television news reports, videos, and films. As they participate in conversations—offering information, considering other points of view, searching for additional information to support opinions, and listening to alternative viewpoints—students learn social skills as well as content-area information.

Questioning Strategies.   Teachers often use questions to initiate conversations during theme cycles, and the questions teachers ask go beyond knowledge-level thinking (with single correct answers) to authentic questions in which students analyze and synthesize information and make connections to their own lives. Here are some examples for a theme cycle on pioneers:

- As part of a conversation introducing a theme cycle on pioneers, teachers ask if there are pioneers today. After students conclude that there are, teachers ask where modern-day pioneers go, what they do, and why they are pioneers.
- After making a list of the reasons why people moved west, teachers ask students which reason seems most important to them.
- After sharing a map of the westward trails that pioneers traveled, teachers ask students to choose a destination and plan their travel along one of the trails.
- Together as a class, students brainstorm a list of the possessions pioneers carried with them, and then students work in small groups to choose the

five most important possessions for pioneers traveling to and settling in particular areas.

Wilen (1986) reviewed the research about questioning strategies and offers these suggestions:

- Ask carefully planned questions to organize and direct the lesson.
- Ask clearly phrased questions rather than vaguely worded or multiple questions.
- Sequence questions to move from factual-level questions to higher-level questions that require critical thinking.
- Ask questions to follow up on students' responses.

Teachers need to allow students sufficient time to think about questions and plan their responses. Sometimes the most effective way to do this is to have students talk about the question in small groups and then report back to the class. It is important to encourage wide participation and interaction among students and to draw in students who do not volunteer contributions. Seating students in a circle is one technique, and having students work in small groups is another. Other ways to promote student involvement are to have students create questions, lead the conversation, and follow up on ideas developed during the conversation. The emphasis in these conversations is on creating knowledge and making connections with information students are learning. Students also use persuasive language as they argue their viewpoints and try to persuade classmates of the importance of the points they make and the issues they discuss.

K-W-L Charts. K-W-L charts are a good way to help students take an active role in talking about what they are learning in theme cycles (Ogle, 1986, 1989). The letters *K, W,* and *L* stand for "What We *K*now," "What We *W*ant to Learn," and "What We *L*earned." Teachers use these charts at the beginning of theme cycles to help students think about what they will study and to encourage them to ask questions to direct their learning during the theme.

To begin, the teacher asks students to brainstorm what they know about a topic. Then the teacher records the information in the "K" column—"What We Know"—on a class chart, as shown in the Teacher's Notebook on page 320. As students suggest information and as confusion arises, the teacher adds questions in the "W" column—"What We Want to Learn." Students also suggest questions they would like to explore during the theme. Brainstorming information in the "K" column helps students activate prior knowledge, and developing questions in the "W" column provides students with specific purposes for learning.

Next, students look for ways to categorize the information they brainstormed, and they will also use the categories to organize information they are reading or learning from a video presentation. For example, second graders making a K-W-L chart on penguins might identify these categories: what they look like, where they live, how they move, and what their families are like. Older students might use categories such as appearance, habitat, diet, and enemies.

After this, students participate in activities related to the theme, looking for new information and for answers to questions in the "W" column. Later,

Teacher's Notebook

A K-W-L Chart

K What We Know	W What We Want to Learn	L What We Learned

Categories of information we expect to use

A.

B.

C.

D.

Ogle, 1986, p. 565.

students reflect on what they have learned and complete the "L" column—"What We Learned." The K-W-L chart helps prepare students to learn, and it helps them organize their learning, clarify their misconceptions, and appreciate their learning.

Teachers can make class K-W-L charts on chart paper or a bulletin board. Class charts are best for primary-grade students or for older students who have not made K-W-L charts before. Older students can also work in small groups to make charts on chart paper, or they can make individual K-W-L charts. Students make individual K-W-L charts by folding a sheet of paper in half vertically. Then students cut three flaps and label them *K, W,* and *L* as shown in the top drawing in Figure 8–4. Students flip up the flaps to write on the chart as shown in the lower picture in Figure 8–4.

Show-and-Tell

Daily sharing time is a familiar ritual in many kindergarten and primary-grade classrooms. Children bring favorite objects to school and talk about them. This is a nice bridge between home and school, and show-and-tell is a good introduction to speaking in front of a group.

Figure 8–4   A Middle-Grade Student's K-W-L Chart on Spiders

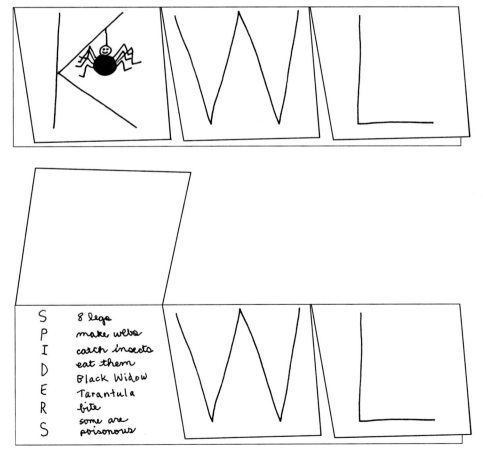

Guidelines for Speakers and Listeners.   If sharing time becomes repetitive, children can lose interest, so teachers must play an active role to make sharing a worthwhile activity. Teachers can discuss the roles and responsibilities of both speakers and listeners. A second-grade class developed the list of responsibilities for speakers and listeners shown in Figure 8–5. This list, with minor variations, has been used with students in upper grades as well.

Some children need prompting even if they have been advised to plan in advance to say two or three things about the object they have brought to school. It is tempting for teachers to speed things up by asking questions and, without realizing it, to answer their own questions, especially for a very quiet child. Show-and-tell could go like this:

Teacher:	Jerry, what did you bring today?
Jerry:	(Holds up a stuffed bear.)
Teacher:	Is that a teddy bear?
Jerry:	Yeah.
Teacher:	Is it new?
Jerry:	(Shakes head yes.)
Teacher:	Can you tell us about your bear?
Jerry:	(Silence.)
Teacher:	Jerry, why don't you walk around and show your bear to everyone?

Jerry needed prompting, but the teacher in this example dominated the conversation and Jerry said only one word—"Yeah." Two strategies may help. First, talk with children like Jerry and help them plan something to say. Second, invite listeners to ask the speakers questions using the "5 Ws plus one" questions (who, what, where, when, why, and how).

Classmates are the audience for show-and-tell activities, but often teachers become the focus (Cazden, 1988). To avoid this, teachers join the audi-

Figure 8–5   *A Second-Grade Class List of Responsibilities of Talkers and Listeners*

Our Rules for Show-and-Tell

What a Speaker Does

Brings something interesting to talk about.

Brings the same thing *only* one time.

Thinks of three things to say about it.

Speaks loudly so everyone can hear.

Passes what he or she brought around so everyone can see it.

What Listeners Do

Be interested.

Pay attention.

Listen.

Ask a question.

Say something nice.

---

ence rather than direct the activity. They also limit their comments and allow the student who is sharing to assume responsibility for the activity and the discussion that follows. Students can ask three or four classmates for comments and then choose which student will share next. It is difficult for teachers to share control of their classrooms, but young students are capable of handling the activity themselves.

Assessing Show-and-Tell Presentations. Students can discuss the effectiveness of their presentations using the guidelines in Figure 8–5. These guidelines can be converted into a checklist that both speakers and listeners can complete for each presentation. Through the checklists and discussion, students learn to give interesting presentations and gain confidence in speaking in front of a group.

Show-and-tell can evolve into an informal type of oral report for middle-grade students. When this method is used effectively, older students gain valuable practice talking in an informal and nonthreatening situation. For example, to begin a sharing activity, students can talk about a collection of sharks' teeth, a program from an Ice Capades show, a recently found snakeskin, or snapshots of a vacation at Yellowstone National Park. Such show-and-tell presentations can lead to informal dramatics, reading, and writing activities. One student may act out dances recalled from the Ice Capades show; another student may point out the location of Yellowstone National Park on a map or check an almanac for more information about the park. A third student may write about the prized collection of sharks' teeth and how they were collected. Experience plus oral rehearsal helps students gear up for other language activities.

Oral Reports

Learning how to prepare and present an oral report is an important efferent talk activity for middle- and upper-grade students. But students are often simply assigned to give an oral report without any guidance about how to prepare and give one. Too many students simply copy the report verbatim from an encyclopedia and then read it aloud. The result is that students learn to fear speaking in front of a group rather than build confidence in their oral language abilities.

I will focus on the steps in teaching students how to prepare and present two types of oral reports. The first type includes reports on social studies or science topics, such as Native Americans, the solar system, or Canada. The second type includes book talks and reviews of television shows and films. Oral reports have genuine language functions—to inform or to persuade—and they are often done as projects during theme cycles.

Reports of Information. Students prepare and give reports about topics they are studying in social studies and science. Giving a report orally helps students to learn about topics in specific content areas as well as to develop their speaking abilities. Students need more than just an assignment to prepare a report for presentation on a particular date; they need to learn how to prepare and present research reports. The four steps in preparing reports are choosing a topic, gathering and organizing information, creating visuals, and giving the presentation.

Students present oral reports to share what they learn during theme cycles.

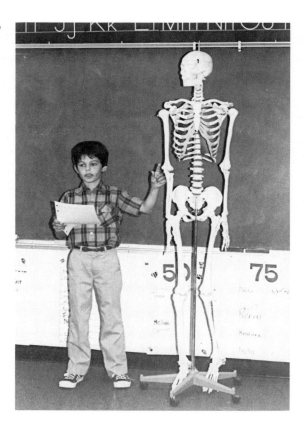

Step by Step

1. ***Choose a topic.*** The class begins by choosing a topic for the reports. For example, if a second-grade class is studying the human body, each student might select a different part of the body for a report. After students have chosen their topics, they need to inventory, or think over, what they know about the topic and decide what they need to learn about it. They can learn to focus on the key points for their reports in several ways. One strategy is to create a cluster with the topic written and circled in the center of a piece of paper; the key points are drawn out from the topic like rays from the sun. Then students write the details on rays drawn from each main idea.

   Another strategy is a data chart, where the teacher provides a chart listing three or more key points to guide students as they gather information for their reports (McKenzie, 1979). Figure 8–6 shows a cluster and a data chart for a report on the human body. A third strategy is brainstorming ideas for possible key points by asking questions about the topic prefaced with the "5 Ws plus one" question words (who, what, where, when, why, and how). The number and complexity of the key points depend on the students' ages or levels of experience.

2. ***Gather and organize information.*** Students gather information using a variety of reference materials, including, but not limited to, informational books, magazines, newspapers, encyclopedias, almanacs, and atlases. Encyclopedias are a

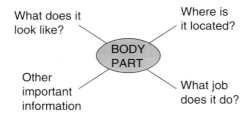

HUMAN BODY REPORT DATA CHART				
Source of information	What does it look like?	Where is it located?	What job does it do?	Other important information

Figure 8–6   *A Cluster and a Data Chart for a Report on the Human Body*

valuable resource, but they are only one possible source, and other reference materials must be available. In addition to print sources, students can view filmstrips, films, and videotapes and can interview people in the community who have special expertise on the topic.

The preliminary organization—deciding on the key points—completed in the first step gives direction for gathering the information. Now students review the information they have gathered and decide how best to present it so that the report will be both interesting and well organized. Students can transfer the "notes" they want to use for their reports from the cluster or data chart onto notecards. Only key words—not sentences or paragraphs—should be written on the cards.

3. **Create visuals.**   Students may develop visuals such as charts, diagrams, maps, pictures, models, and timelines. For example, the second graders who gave reports on parts of the body made drawings and clay models of the parts and used a large skeleton hanging in the classroom to show the location of the organ in the body. Visuals provide a "crutch" for the speaker and add an element of interest for the listeners.

4. **Give the presentation.**   The final step is to rehearse and then give the presentation. Students can rehearse several times by reviewing key points and reading over their notecards. They should not, however, read the report verbatim from the notecards. Students might want to choose a particularly interesting fact to begin the presentation.

Before the presentations begin, teachers teach minilessons on the characteristics of successful presentations. For instance, speakers should talk loudly enough for all to hear, look at the audience, keep to the key points, refer to notecards for important facts, and use the visuals they have prepared.

Students are usually the audience for the oral reports, and members of the audience have responsibilities. They should be attentive, listen to the speaker, ask questions, and applaud the speaker. Usually students give presentations to the whole class, but it is possible to divide the class into groups so that students can present reports in each group simultaneously.

Book Talks and Other Reviews.   Students give oral reports to review books they have read or television shows and films they have viewed. These book talks and reviews are one type of project students create in literature focus units, reading workshop, and theme cycles. The steps in preparing and presenting reviews are similar to those for reports of information:

Step by Step

1. *Gather information.*   Students select information for the report, including a brief summary of the selection and bibliographic information; comparisons to other selections (e.g., with similar themes, written by the same author, starring the same actor); strengths and weaknesses; and opinions and conclusions. They also choose a brief excerpt from the book to read or an excerpt from a videotape to show.

2. *Organize information.*   Students record and organize the information on a cluster and then copy key words onto notecards.

3. *Create visuals.*   Students locate or create props to show during the review. Students may show the book in a book talk or show an advertisement for the film. Or, they may collect a box or bag of objects related to the book to show during the presentation.

4. *Give the presentation.*   Students briefly rehearse the review, and then they give the presentation, referring to the notecards but not reading them, and sharing the props.

Assessing Students' Oral Reports.   Teachers can assess students' oral reports according to the steps students move through in developing their reports as well as the presentations of their reports in front of the class. Students can also assess their own presentations, considering each of the four steps involved in developing the oral report. These points might be used in developing an assessment checklist:

- Did you choose a narrow topic?
- Did you collect and organize information on a cluster or a data chart?
- Did you prepare a chart or other visual to use in the presentation?
- Did you rehearse the presentation?

Students can also reflect on the presentation itself and can respond to questions such as:

- Did you present the report as you planned?
- Did you speak loudly enough to be heard?
- Did you look at the audience?
- Did you use your visuals?
- Did you make your key points?
- How did the audience respond to your presentation?
- What are you most pleased with about your presentation?
- What will you change or do differently when you give another report?

Interviews

Almost all children see interviews on television news programs and are familiar with the interviewing techniques reporters use. Interviewing is an exciting language arts activity that helps students refine questioning skills and use oral and written language for authentic purposes (Haley-James & Hobson, 1980).

Interviewing is an important language tool that can be integrated effectively in literature focus units and theme cycles. As part of a theme cycle on school, for example, a class of first graders invited the local high school principal to visit their class to be interviewed. The principal, who had been blinded several years earlier, brought his guide dog with him. The children asked him questions about how visually impaired people manage everyday tasks, as well as how he performed his job as a principal. They also asked questions about his guide dog. After the interview, students drew pictures and wrote summaries of the interview. One first grader's report is shown in Figure 8–7.

Or, during a literature focus unit on *Number the Stars* (Lowry, 1989), fifth graders can interview grandparents and great-grandparents about their memories of World War II. After reading excerpts from Studs Terkel's book *Working* (1974), a class of eighth graders interviewed people in the community to learn about their jobs. To begin, students brainstormed a list of 25 questions they might ask people about their jobs. Then they interviewed people they had selected and shared the answers with the class. Afterwards, students wrote reports of their interviews, either in first person, as Terkel did, or in third person (Bowser, 1993). Students worked in small groups several times during this project. They brainstormed questions before the interviews in small groups, and they met again in small groups to revise and edit their compositions. The papers were both informative and insightful, as this excerpt from one student's report about being a real estate agent shows:

> Long and unpredictable hours are what she hates most about her job. You never know how much time you'll be spending with a customer. . . . She does not have close friends at work because the business is so competitive. (Bowser, 1993, p. 40)

One way to introduce interviewing is to watch interviews conducted on a television newscast and discuss what the purpose of the interview is, what a reporter does before and after an interview, and what types of questions are asked. Interviewers use a variety of questions, some to elicit facts and others to probe for feelings and opinions, but all questions are open-ended. Rarely do interviewers ask questions that require only a yes or no answer.

*Figure 8–7   A First Grader's
Interview Report*

Steps in Conducting Interviews.   Interviewing involves far more than simply conducting the actual interview. There are three steps in the interview process: planning the interview, conducting the interview, and sharing the results.

*Step
by
Step*

1. ***Plan the interview.***   In the planning step, students arrange for the interview and brainstorm questions to ask the person being interviewed. From this list, students choose which questions they will ask, making sure to avoid questions that require only yes or no answers. Students often write the questions on notecards. Then they sequence the cards in a reasonable order.

2. ***Conduct the interview.***   The second step is conducting the actual interview. Students greet the person being interviewed and conduct the interview by asking questions they have prepared in advance. They take notes or tape-record the answers. They ask follow-up questions about points that are not clear, and if the answer to one question brings up another question that has not been written down, students ask it anyway. Students are polite and respectful of the answers and opinions of the person being interviewed. At the end of the interview, students thank the person for participating in the interview.

3. ***Share the results.***   Students share the results of the interview in one of several ways. They may present an oral report, write a report or newspaper article, or make a poster.

Assessing Students' Interviews.   Teachers assess students' interviews by checking that they followed the three steps of the interview process and by examining the quality of their final products. Similarly, students can assess their own use of the interview process and their reports, much like they assess other types of efferent talk projects.

Debates

Debates are useful when the whole class is excited about an issue and most or all of the students have taken supporting or opposing positions. As they participate in debates, students learn to use language to persuade their class-mates and to articulate their viewpoints. Two types of debates are impromptu debates and formal debates.

Impromptu Debates.   The class decides on an issue, clarifies it, and identi-fies positions that support or oppose the issue. Then students who wish to speak in favor of the issue move to the side of the room designated for sup-porters, and students who wish to speak against the issue move to the other side. Class members who have not formulated a position sit in the middle of the room.

A podium is set up in the front of the classroom, and the teacher initiates the debate by asking a student from the supporting side to state that position on the issue. After this opening statement, the opposing side makes a state-ment. From this point, students take turns going to the podium and speaking in support of or in opposition to the issue. Students who wish to participate go to the side of the room for the position they support and wait in line for their opportunity to speak. After hearing arguments, students may change their minds and move to the opposite side of the room; if they are no longer certain what side they are on, they take a seat in the middle.

Students who have just made a statement are often asked a question before a student for the other side makes a return statement. Sixth graders who used this informal debate procedure in their social studies class enjoyed the experience and furthered their abilities to express themselves effectively.

Formal Debates.   A more formal type of debate is appropriate for students in the upper-elementary grades. Debates take the form of arguments between opposing sides of a proposition. A proposition is a debate subject that can be discussed from opposing points of view, such as the following:

Resolved, that students should have a role in setting standards of behavior in classes and in disciplining those students who disrupt classes.

After the proposition has been determined, teams of three or four students are designated to support the proposition (the affirmative team) or oppose it (the negative team).

Depending on the number of members on each team, the debate pro-ceeds in this order:

1. The first student from the affirmative team makes a statement.
2. The first student from the negative team makes a statement.
3. The second student from the affirmative team makes a statement.
4. The second student from the negative team makes a statement.
5. The third student from the affirmative team makes a rebuttal statement.

6. The third student from the negative team makes a rebuttal statement.
7. The fourth student from the affirmative team makes a rebuttal statement.
8. The fourth student from the negative team makes a rebuttal statement.

Sometimes three or four statements are made by each team before beginning to make rebuttal statements rather than just two for each team (steps 1–4), as in the list above. Normally there are as many rebuttal statements as there are statements about the position, but teachers may vary the procedure to fit the class and their purposes.

Students can also choose judges to determine the winning team and decide the criteria for judging. They brainstorm questions that will form the basis for their criteria and then develop a rubric. Questions similar to the following might initiate the brainstorming sessions:

- Did the speakers communicate their ideas to the listeners?
- Was a mastery of information evident in the presentations and rebuttals?
- Was there evidence that the speakers knew the topic well?
- Was the team courteous?
- Did the team work cooperatively?
- Did the second speaker on each team pick up and extend the statement of the first team member?

■ *See the debate rubric in the PRO-File at the beginning of this chapter on pp. 300–301.*

DRAMATIC ACTIVITIES

Drama provides a medium for students to use language, both verbal and nonverbal, in a meaningful context. Drama is not only a powerful form of communication but also a valuable way of knowing. When children participate in dramatic activities, they interact with classmates, share experiences, and explore their own understanding. According to Dorothy Heathcote, a highly acclaimed British drama teacher, drama "cracks the code" so that the message can be understood (Wagner, 1976). Drama has this power because it involves both logical, left-brain thinking and creative, right-brain thinking; because it requires active experience (the basic, and first, way of learning); and because it integrates the language arts. Recent research confirms that drama has a positive effect on both students' oral language development and their literacy learning (Kardash & Wright, 1987; Wagner, 1988). Drama is often neglected, however, because some consider it a nonessential part of the language arts curriculum.

Many dramatic activities that elementary students participate in are informal and spontaneous. Others involve some rehearsal and are presented for an audience. The most formal dramatic activities are theatrical productions, which are polished performances of a play produced on a stage and before a large audience. They require extensive rehearsal and are quite formal. Because the purpose of theatrical productions is a polished presentation, they are audience-centered rather than child-centered. Rather than encourage students to be spontaneous and improvisational, they require that students memorize lines. They are not recommended for students in elementary grades unless students write the scripts themselves.

Again and again, educators caution that drama activities should be informal during the elementary years (Stewig, 1983; Wagner, 1976). The one exception is the case when students write their own play and puppet show scripts and want to perform them.

Role-Playing

Students assume the role of another person as they act out stories or reenact historical events. Through role-playing, students step into someone else's shoes and view the world from another perspective. Role-playing activities are usually informal. Students assume roles and then act out the drama as the teacher narrates or guides the dramatization.

In Literature Focus Units. Students role-play stories during literature focus units. These activities can be done during the responding, exploring, and extending stages. Teachers often use role-playing as they are reading a story with students to emphasize key points in the story, to clarify misunderstandings, or to deepen students' comprehension. For example, a key point in *Johnny Tremain* (Forbes, 1970) for a role-playing activity occurs when Johnny tragically burns his hand. This moment is important because of the event's ramifications through the rest of the story. Another key point for role-playing occurs when Johnny has given up hope and lies among the graves on Copp's Hill. Because students enjoy the role-playing activity, they often ask to role-play the part about the Boston Tea Party—because it is fun, not because they do not understand.

After reading, students often act out folktales and other stories told in picture books using both dialogue and body movements. Teachers use role-playing to review and sequence the events in the story and to develop students' concept of story. Folktales such as *The Gingerbread Boy* (Galdone, 1975) and *If You Give a Mouse a Cookie* (Numeroff, 1985) are good for younger children to dramatize because they are repetitive. Middle- and upper-grade students act out favorite scenes from longer stories such as *Shiloh* (Naylor, 1991), *Nightjohn* (Paulsen, 1993), and *The Giver* (Lowry, 1993). Students can also read biographies such as *The Life and Death of Crazy Horse* (Freedman, 1996) and *Mandela: From the Life of the South African Statesman* (Cooper, 1996) and dramatize events from these people's lives.

Students also use role-playing to create dramatic productions of a favorite story as a project. Students follow approximately the same steps they do in storytelling. They choose roles in the story, reread the story, identify key parts to include in the dramatization, collect simple props, and rehearse the story several times. Then they present the story to their classmates.

In Theme Cycles. Role-playing in theme cycles is designed to help students gain insights about how to handle real-life problems and understand historical and current events (Nelson, 1988). Students assume the role of another person—not roles in a story, but rather the roles people play in society—and reenact events they are studying.

Heathcote has developed an innovative approach to role-playing to help students experience and better understand historical events (Wagner, 1976). Through a process she calls "funneling," Heathcote chooses a dramatic focus from a general topic (e.g., ancient Rome, the Civil War, the Pilgrims). She begins by thinking of all the aspects of the general topic and then decides on a dramatic focus—a particular critical moment. For example, using the topic of the Pilgrims, one possible focus is the night of December 20, 1620, eleven weeks after the Pilgrims set sail from England on the *Mayflower* and the night before the ship reached Plymouth.

The improvisation begins when students assume roles; the teacher becomes a character, too. As they begin to role-play the event, questions draw students' attention to certain features and probe their understanding. Questions about the Pilgrims might include:

- Where are you?
- After 11 weeks sailing the Atlantic Ocean, what do you think will happen?
- How are you feeling?
- Why did you leave England?
- What kind of life do you dream of in the new land?
- Can you survive in this cold winter weather?

These questions also provide information by reminding students of the time of year, the problems they are having, and the length of the voyage.

Sometimes Heathcote stops students in the middle of role-playing and asks them to write what they are thinking and feeling. As part of the Pilgrim improvisation, students might be asked to write an entry in their simulated journals for December 20, 1620. An example of a simulated journal entry written by a fourth-grade "Pilgrim" is shown in Figure 8–8. After the writing activity, students continue role-playing.

■ *For more informa-tion on simulated journals, see Chapter 6, "Writing in Jour-nals," pp. 237–239.*

Heathcote uses drama to begin study on a topic rather than as a culmi-nating activity in which students apply all they have learned, because she believes that role-playing experiences stimulate children's curiosity and make them want to read books and learn more about a historical or current event. Whether you use role-playing as an introduction or as a conclusion, it is a valuable activity because students become immersed in the event. By reliv-ing it, they are learning far more than mere facts.

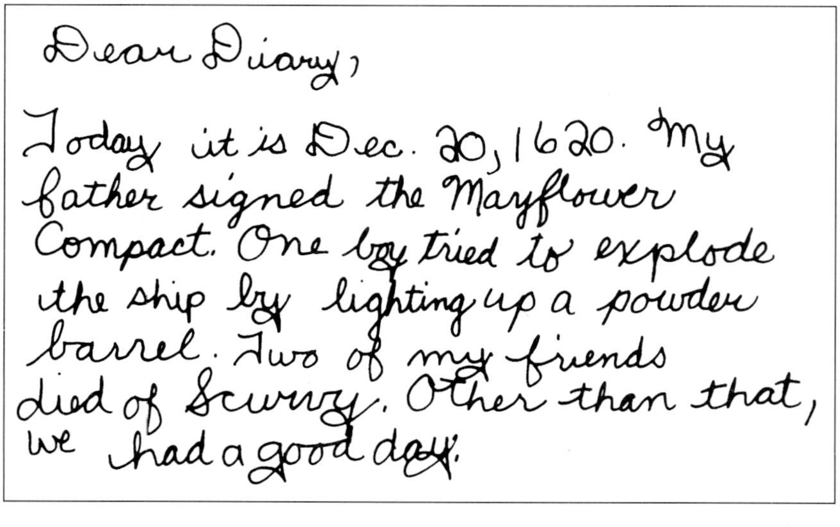

Figure 8–8   A Fourth-Grade Pil-grim's Simulated Journal Entry

Dear Diary,

Today it is Dec. 20, 1620. My father signed the Mayflower Compact. One boy tried to explode the ship by lighting up a powder barrel. Two of my friends died of Scurvy. Other than that, we had a good day.

Puppets and Other Props

Students create characters with puppets. A second grader pulls a green sock on one hand and a brown sock on the other hand, and with these socks that simply have buttons sewed on for eyes, the characters of Frog and Toad from Arnold Lobel's award-winning books *Frog and Toad Are Friends* (1970) and *Frog and Toad Together* (1972) come to life. The student talks in the voices of the two characters and involves the characters in events from the stories. While adults often feel self-conscious with puppets, children do not.

Children can create puppet shows with commercially manufactured puppets, or they can construct their own. When children create their own puppets, the only limitations are their imaginations, their ability to construct things, and the materials at hand. Puppets can be especially useful with shy students. Puppets can be used not only in all types of drama activities but also as a novel way to introduce a language skill, such as quotation marks. Teachers can use puppets to improvise a dialogue and then record it using quotation marks.

Simple puppets provide children with the opportunity to develop both creative and dramatic ability. The simpler the puppet, the more is left to the imagination of the audience and the puppeteer. Constructing elaborate puppets is beyond the resources of both teachers and students. The type of puppets the students make, however, depends on how they will be used. Students can construct puppets using all sorts of scrap materials. I will describe how to make eight types of hand and finger puppets; the puppets are illustrated in Figure 8–9.

1. Stick puppets. Stick puppets are versatile and perhaps the easiest to make. Sticks, tongue depressors, dowels, and straws can be used. The rest of the puppet that is attached to the stick is constructed from papier-mâché, Styrofoam balls, pictures students have drawn, or pictures cut from magazines and mounted on cardboard. Students draw or paint the features on the materials they have selected for the head and body. Some puppets may need only a head; others may also need a body. Making stick puppets provides an opportunity to combine art and drama.

2. Paper bag puppets. This is another simple puppet to make. The paper bags should be the right size to fit students' hands. Paper lunch bags are a convenient size, although smaller bags are better for kindergartners. What characters they portray and what emphasis the students give the size of the character are the determining factors, however. Students place the puppet's mouth at the fold of the paper bag. Then they paint on faces and clothes, add yarn for hair, and attach arms and legs. Students should choose ways to decorate their bag puppets to match the characters they develop.

3. Cylinder puppets. Cylinder puppets are made from cardboard tubes from bathroom tissue, paper towels, and aluminum foil. The diameter and length of the cylinder determine the size of the puppet. The cylinders can be painted, and various appendages and clothing can be attached. Again, the character's role should determine how the puppet is costumed. Students insert their fingers in the bottom of the cylinder to manipulate the puppet.

Figure 8–9   *Types of Puppets Students Can Make*

Stick Puppet   Paper Bag Puppet   Cylinder Puppet

Sock Puppet   Styrofoam Puppet   Paper Plate Puppet

Finger Puppet
(with tabs)

Finger puppet
(from glove finger)

Cloth Puppet

4. Sock puppets. Sock puppets are quite versatile. A sock can be used as is, with button eyes, yarn hair, pipe-cleaner antennae, and other features added. The sock can also be cut at the toe to create a mouth, and whatever else is needed to give the impression of the character can be added.

5. Cup puppets. Even primary-grade students can make puppets from Styrofoam cups. They glue facial features, hair, wings, and other decorations on the cup. Pipe cleaners, toothpicks, and Q-tips tipped with glitter can easily be attached to Styrofoam cups. Then sticks or heavy-duty straws are attached to the inside of the cup as the handle.

6. Paper plate puppets. Paper plates can be used for face puppets as well as for masks. Students add junk materials to decorate the puppets, then tape sticks or rulers to the back of the plates as handles.

Students use puppets and stuffed animals to retell the repetitive story of The Mitten.

7. Finger puppets. Students can make several different types of finger puppets. For one type, students draw, color, and cut out small figures, then add tabs to either side of the figure and tape the tabs together to fit around the finger. Larger puppets can be taped to fit around the hand. For a second type of finger puppet, students cut the finger section from a glove and add decoration. The pointed part that separates the compartments of an egg carton can also be used for a finger puppet.

8. Cloth puppets. If parents are available to assist with the sewing, students can make cloth puppets. Two pieces of cloth are sewn together on all sides except the bottom; then students personalize the puppets using scraps of fabric, lace, yarn, and other materials.

After students have created their puppets, they can perform the puppet show almost anywhere. They can make a stage from an empty appliance packing crate or an empty television cabinet. They can also drape blankets or cloths in front of classroom tables and desks. They might also turn a table on its side. There may be other classroom objects your students can use as makeshift stages.

Scriptwriting and Theatrical Productions

Scripts are a unique written language form that elementary students need opportunities to explore. Scriptwriting often grows out of role-playing and storytelling. Soon students recognize the need to write notes when they prepare for plays, puppet shows, readers theatre, and other dramatic productions. This need provides the impetus for introducing students to the unique dramatic conventions and for encouraging them to write scripts to present as theatrical productions.

Writing Play Scripts.   Once students want to write scripts, they will recognize the need to add the structures unique to dramatic writing to their repertoire of written language conventions. Students begin by examining scripts. It is especially effective to have students compare narrative and script versions of the same story; for example, Richard George has adapted two of Roald Dahl's fantastic stories, *Charlie and the Chocolate Factory* (1976) and *James and the Giant Peach* (1982), into scripts.

Then students discuss their observations and compile a list of the unique characteristics of scripts. An upper-grade class compiled this list of unique dramatic conventions:

1. Scripts are divided into acts and scenes.
2. Scripts have these parts:
   a. a list of characters (or cast)
   b. the setting at the beginning of each act or scene
   c. stage directions written in parentheses
   d. dialogue
3. The dialogue carries the action.
4. Descriptions and other information are set apart in the setting or in stage directions.
5. Stage directions give actors important information about how to act and how to feel.
6. The dialogue is written in a special way:
   Character's Name: Dialogue.
7. Sometimes a narrator is used to quickly fill in parts of the story.

The next step is to have students apply what they have learned about scripts by writing a class collaboration or group script. With the whole class, develop a script by adapting a familiar story. As the script is being written, refer to the chart of dramatic conventions and ask students to check that they are using these conventions. Collaborative writing affords unique teaching opportunities and needed practice for students before they must write individually. After the script is completed, have students read it using readers theatre procedures, or produce it as a puppet show or play.

Once students are aware of the dramatic conventions and have participated in writing a class collaboration script, they can write scripts individually or in small groups. Students often adapt familiar stories for their first scripts; later, they will want to create original scripts. An excerpt from "The Lonely Troll," a script written by a team of five upper-grade students, appears in Figure 8–10 as an example of the type of scripts older students can compose.

Figure 8–10 *An Excerpt From a Script Written by Upper-Grade Students*

The Lonely Troll

NARRATOR: Once upon a time, in a far, far away land, there was a troll named Pippin who lived all alone in his little corner of the woods. The troll hated all the creatures of the woods and was very lonely because he didn't have anyone to talk to since he scared everyone away. One day, a dwarf named Sam wandered into Pippin's yard and . . .

PIPPIN: Grrr. What are you doing here?

SAM: Ahhhhh! A troll! Please don't eat me!

PIPPIN: Why shouldn't I?

SAM: (Begging) Look, I'm all skin and bones. I won't make a good meal.

PIPPIN: You look fat enough for me. (Turns to audience) Do you think I should eat him? (Sam jumps off stage and hides in the audience.)

PIPPIN: Where did he go? (Pippin jumps off stage and looks for Sam. When he finds Sam, he takes him back on stage, laughing; then he ties Sam up.) Ha, ha, ha. Boy, that sure did tire me out. (Yawn) I'll take a nap. Then I'll eat him later. (Pippin falls asleep. Lights dim. Sam escapes and runs behind a tree. Lights return, and Pippin wakens.)

PIPPIN: (To audience) Where's my breakfast? (Sam peeps out from behind a tree and cautions the audience to be quiet.) Huh? Did someone say he was behind that tree? (Points to tree. Pippin walks around. Sam kicks him in the rear. Pippin falls and is knocked out.)

SAM: I must get out of here, and warn the queen about this short, small, mean, ugly troll. (Sam leaves. Curtains close.)

NARRATOR: So Sam went to tell Queen Muffy about the troll. Meanwhile, in the forest, Pippin awakens, and decides to set a trap for Sam. (Open curtains to forest scene, showing Pippin making a box trap.)

PIPPIN: Ha, ha, ha! That stupid dwarf will come back here looking for me. When he sees this ring, he'll take it. Then, I'll trap him! Ha, ha, ha, ha. (Pippin hides.)

NARRATOR: The dwarf finally reaches Queen Muffy's castle and hurries to tell her his story.

SAM: (Open curtains to Queen Muffy sitting on a throne, eating. Sam rushes in, out of breath.) I have some very important news for you. There's . . .

QUEEN: I don't have time for you.

SAM: But, I . . .

QUEEN: Come, come. Don't bother me with small things.

SAM: There's an ugly old . . .

QUEEN: You're wasting my time.

SAM: I just wanted to warn you, there's a big, ugly, mean . . .

QUEEN: Hurry up.

SAM: . . . man-eating . . .

QUEEN: This had better be important.

SAM: (Angry, he yells) THERE'S A TROLL IN THE FOREST!!!

QUEEN: Who cares if there's a . . . a . . . (Screams) A TROLL!!!

SAM: That's what I've been saying. A troll—in the forest.

QUEEN: Then I must send out my faithful knight . . . Sir Skippy . . . to kill him. I shall offer a reward. (Queen exits.)

Although most of the scripts they write are narrative, students can also create biographical scripts about famous people or informational scripts about science or social studies topics.

Producing Video Scripts.   Students use a similar approach in writing scripts that will be videotaped, but they must now consider the visual component of the film as well as the written script. They often compose their scripts on story boards, which focus their attention on the camera's view and how the story they are creating will be filmed (Cox, 1985). Story boards—sheets of paper divided into three sections—are used to sketch in scenes. Students place a series of three or four large squares in a row down the center of the paper, with space for dialogue and narration on the left and shooting directions on the right. Cox compares story boards to road maps because they provide directions for filming the script. The scene renderings and the shooting directions help students tie the dialogue to the visual images that will appear on the videotape. Figure 8–11 shows a sample story board form with an excerpt from a fourth-grade class collaboration script.

The script can be produced several different ways—as a live-action play, as a puppet show, or through animation. After writing the script on the story boards or transferring a previously written script to story boards, students collect or construct the properties they will need to produce the script. As with other types of drama, the properties do not need to be extensive or elaborate—a simple backdrop and costumes will suffice. Students should also print the title and credits on large posters to appear at the beginning of the film. After several rehearsals, the students film the script using a video camera.

Figure 8–11   An Excerpt From a Class Collaboration Story Board Script

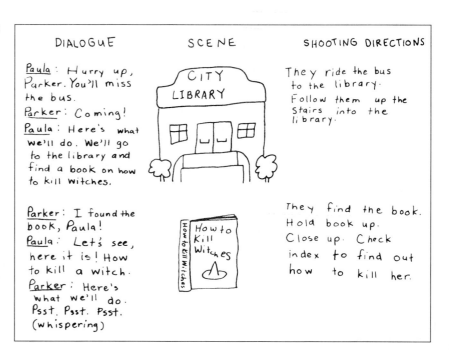

Review

Teachers sustain talk in the elementary classroom because talk has definite benefits for elementary students. Too often teachers assume that students already know how to talk, so they concentrate on reading and writing. The four types of talk activities—conversations, aesthetic talk, efferent talk, and dramatic activities—are important for developing children's talk, and they also complement students' written language development. The key points in this chapter include:

1. Talk is a necessary ingredient for learning.
2. Students talk in informal conversations as part of literature focus units and theme cycles.
3. Students participate in many types of small-group conversations, and they use talk for both aesthetic and efferent purposes.
4. In conversations about literature, students use aesthetic talk to respond to a book and develop interpretations.
5. In storytelling and readers theatre activities, students use aesthetic talk to present stories.
6. K-W-L charts are a good way to help students talk about what they are learning in a theme cycle.
7. In show-and-tell, oral reports, interviews, and debates, students use efferent talk to inform and persuade listeners.
8. Drama is not only a powerful form of communication but also a valuable way of knowing.
9. Students use role-playing and puppets to learn and share their learning in literature focus units and theme cycles.
10. In connection with literature focus units and theme cycles, students can write scripts that they present as a play or on videotape.

Extensions

1. Read Stanley's *The Conversation Club* (1983) to a group of primary-grade students to introduce conversation activities. Then organize a conversation club with the students and plan several activities with the group.
2. Teach students how to participate in conversations about literature. Then, as you read a chapter book or a collection of picture books with a group of students, have the students participate in a series of literature conversations. Observe students as they talk about the book, and notice how they interact with their classmates as well as how they develop their interpretations.
3. Plan and conduct a debate with a group of upper-grade students. Help them choose a topic from current events, school and community issues, or a theme cycle.
4. Plan and direct a role-playing activity with a group of students in conjunction with a theme cycle. Following the guidelines in this chapter, integrate a writing activity with the role-playing (e.g., by having students keep a journal or write a letter).
5. Assist a small group of middle- or upper-grade students as they prepare to tell stories to a class of primary-grade students. Help students use the procedure discussed in this chapter.
6. Introduce scriptwriting to a group of middle- or upper-grade students by having them compile a list of the unique dramatic conventions used in scriptwriting. Then write a class collaboration script by adapting a familiar folktale.

PROCEDURE

My class is reading *The Sign of the Beaver* (Speare, 1983). I have copies for each student, and we're reading it together in groups—two or three short chapters each day. Each group has a leader, and when I want to share something about a chapter, I give the information to the leader, who shares it with the group. I move from group to group to keep tabs on their progress, but the groups operate without me.

Students read silently or with a buddy and then write in their reading logs. In the entries, they write reactions and questions to use in the literature conversation. After everyone in the group finishes, the leader starts the conversation by asking a question or by asking a student to read his or her reading log entry. Students take turns talking about the chapter and sharing their ideas, comments, and questions. I take a few minutes at the end of the conversation to bring the class together so that each group can share something or make a pre-diction about what will happen in the story.

I'm focusing on one element of story structure—character—in this story. Students are examining how Mrs. Speare develops Matt's character. Before beginning the story, I told the students a bit about Matt, the 12-year-old main character. I asked them to write in their reading logs and predict what they thought this boy living in the Maine wilderness in 1769 would be like and what might happen to him in the story. Every two or three days we talk again about Matt and how Mrs. Speare has unveiled more about this character through appearance, action, dialogue, and monologue. Students add new information to the character cluster chart hanging on the wall. The cluster has Matt's name in the middle and rays for "What he looks like," "What he does," "What he says," and "What he thinks."

After reading 10 chapters, my students were surprised to find that Mrs. Speare tells about Matt primarily through his actions. The only fact students have learned about his appearance is that he wore boots, until his disastrous attempt to get honey from a beehive, and now he wears Indian moccasins.

Afterwards, we will think about the character traits that were revealed through Matt's actions. For example, Matt exhibited carelessness when he didn't close the cabin door, and he lacked common sense when he tried to get some honey from the beehive. Not all Matt's actions suggest negative traits, though. He showed resourcefulness when he learned to trap, and determination when he waited for his family. My goal is for the students to understand that Matt, like everyone else, is a combination of character traits, some good and some bad.

Also, each student will do a project related to the book. We've started a list of activities to choose from: read informational books about Maine, write a poem about Matt, make a map of the area in Maine where the story takes place, research Indians of the New England area, read another book by Mrs. Speare, write a sequel about life after Matt's parents arrive, and so on.

ASSESSMENT

I use a checklist of the assignments to monitor the students' work. I pass out the checklist at the beginning of the unit, and students keep the checklist in their unit folders along with their reading log, book, and other materials. Students check off each assignment as it is completed. Later, as I review the work, I assign points and total them for the unit grade. A copy of the checklist is shown in the accompanying figure.

ADAPTATIONS

This year most of my students can read *The Sign of the Beaver* independently or with the assistance of a classmate. Other years, I've had more students who needed help. I've tried several approaches to make the book more accessible for these students. My most successful approach is to have a sixth grader read along with each group. This student can supply words that students don't know or read aloud to the group, if necessary. I've also tape-recorded the book for students to listen to at the listening center.

REFLECTIONS

I'm learning how to make connections between the different areas of the curriculum, and through *The Sign of the Beaver* I'm connecting language arts and social studies. The students learn more and enjoy it more. It makes so much sense—I just wonder why I didn't think of it sooner.

Literature Focus Unit Checklist for *The Sign of the Beaver*

Name _____

	Points	Score
1. Read *The Sign of the Beaver* with your group.	20	_____
2. Work cooperatively with your group.	5	_____
3. Share your ideas in literature conversations.	5	_____
4. Write at least eight entries in your reading log.	20	_____
5. Do a character activity:	10	_____
_____ Open-mind portrait		
_____ Venn diagram of Matt and Attean		
_____ Character quilt		
6. Do a project.	20	_____
7. Share the project.	10	_____
8. Write a letter to me about your learning and work in this unit.	10	_____
TOTAL		_____

7th Gr.

S eventh graders in Laurie Goodman's class created this quilt using the "Hole in the Barn Door" pattern after reading *The Giver* (Lowry, 1993). Students chose monochromatic colors to reflect the sameness of the community and a bright color in the center for Elsewhere. Students wrote poems for the center of each square. Here is a five-senses poem about a memory that the Giver gave to Jonas:

> *Smells like death,*
> *Looks like a bloody slaughter,*
> *Sounds like a cry for help,*
> *Fells like a sharp throbbing pain,*
> *Tastes like salty tears,*
> *Must be the memory of war.*

S tories give meaning to the human experience, and they are a powerful way of knowing and learning. Preschool children listen to family members tell and read stories aloud, and they have developed an understanding or concept about stories by the time they come to school. Students use and refine this knowledge as they read and write stories during the elementary grades. Many educators, including Jerome Bruner (1986), recommend using stories as a way into literacy.

Primary-grade students read and respond to stories such as *Mole's Hill* (Ehlert, 1994), *Where the Wild Things Are* (Sendak, 1962), and *Abuela* (Dorros, 1991), and older students read and respond to *Charlotte's Web* (White, 1952), *The Giver* (Lowry, 1993), and *The Lion, the Witch and the Wardrobe* (Lewis, 1981). Sometimes teachers call all literature that students read and write "stories," but stories are a particular type. They have specific structural elements, including characters and plot.

Students tell and write stories about events in their lives, such as a birthday party, a fishing trip, or a car accident; retell familiar stories, including "The Gingerbread Man"; and write sequels for stories such as *Jumanji* (Van Allsburg, 1981). The stories that students write reflect the stories they have read. De Ford (1981) and Eckhoff (1983) found that when primary-grade students read stories in basal reading textbooks, the stories they write reflect the short, choppy linguistic style of the readers, but when students read stories in trade books, their writing reflects the more sophisticated language structures and literary style of the trade books. Dressel (1990) also found that the quality of fifth graders' writing was dependent on the quality of the stories they read or listened to someone else read aloud, regardless of the students' reading levels.

As you read this chapter, think about these questions:

- How do students develop a concept of story?
- How does students' knowledge of stories affect comprehension?
- How do teachers teach students about story structure?
- How do students read and write stories during literature focus units, theme cycles, and reading and writing workshop?

DEVELOPING STUDENTS' CONCEPT OF STORY

Young children have a rudimentary awareness about what makes a story. Knowledge about stories is called a concept of story. Children's concept of story includes information about the elements of story structure, such as characters, plot, and setting, as well as information about the conventions authors use. This knowledge is usually intuitive; that is, children are not conscious of what they know. Golden describes children's concept of story as "a mental representation of story structure, essentially an outline of the basic story elements and their organization" (1984, p. 578).

Researchers have documented that children's concept of story begins in the preschool years, and that children as young as two years old have a rudimentary sense of story (Applebee, 1978; Pitcher & Prelinger, 1963). Children acquire this concept of story gradually, by listening to stories read to them, by reading stories themselves, and by telling and writing stories. Not surprisingly, older children have a better understanding of story structure than do younger children. Similarly, the stories older children tell and write are increasingly more complex; the plot structures are more tightly organized, and the characters are more fully developed. Yet, Applebee found that by the time children begin kindergarten, they have already developed a basic concept of what a story is, and these expectations guide them in responding to stories and telling their own stories. He found, for example, that kindergartners could use three story markers: "Once upon a time . . ." to begin a story; the past tense in telling a story; and formal endings such as "The End" or ". . . and they lived happily ever after."

Students' concept of story plays an important role in interpreting stories they read (Mandler & Johnson, 1977; Rumelhart, 1975; Stein & Glenn, 1979), and it is just as important in writing (Golden, 1984). Students continue to grow in their understanding of stories through reading and writing experiences (Golden, Meiners, & Lewis, 1992). As they respond to and explore stories they are reading and writing, students learn about elements of story structure and genre, or categories of stories. Golden and her colleagues say that story meaning is dynamic, growing continuously in the reader's mind.

Elements of Story Structure

Stories have unique structural elements that distinguish them from other forms of writing. In fact, the structure of stories is quite complex—plot, characters, setting, and other elements interact with each other to produce a story. Authors manipulate the elements to make their stories complex and interesting. I will focus on five elements of story structure—plot, characters, setting, point of view, and theme—and will illustrate each element with familiar and award-winning trade books.

Plot.   The sequence of events involving characters in conflict situations is the plot. It is based on the goals of one or more characters and the processes they go through to attain these goals (Lukens, 1995). The main characters want to achieve a goal, and other characters are introduced to oppose the main characters or prevent them from being successful. The story events are put in motion by characters as they attempt to overcome conflict, reach their goals, and solve their problems.

The most basic aspect of plot is the division of the main events of a story into three parts—beginning, middle, and end. Upper-grade students may substitute the terms *introduction, development* or *complication,* and *resolution.* In *The Tale of Peter Rabbit* (Potter, 1902), for instance, one can easily pick out the three story parts: as the story begins, Mrs. Rabbit sends her children out to play after warning them not to go into Mr. McGregor's garden; in the middle, Peter goes to Mr. McGregor's garden and is almost caught; then Peter finds his way out of the garden and gets home safely—the end of the story. Students can cluster the beginning-middle-end of a story using words or pictures, as the cluster for *The Tale of Peter Rabbit* in Figure 9–1 shows.

Specific types of information are included in each of the three story parts. In the beginning, the author introduces the characters, describes the setting, and presents a problem. Together, the characters, setting, and events develop the plot and sustain the theme throughout the story. In the middle, the author adds to events presented in the beginning, with each event preparing readers for what will follow. Conflict heightens as the characters face roadblocks that

Students use their knowledge of story structure as they sequence story boards made from two copies of a picture book.

What keeps you interested?

keep them from solving their problems. Seeing how the characters tackle these problems adds suspense to keep readers interested. In the end, the author reconciles all that has happened in the story, and readers learn whether or not the characters' struggles are successful.

Conflict is the tension or opposition between forces in the plot, and it is what interests readers enough to continue reading the story. Conflict usually occurs (Lukens, 1995):

- Between a character and nature
- Between a character and society
- Between characters
- Within a character

Conflict between a character and nature occurs in stories in which severe weather plays an important role, such as *Brave Irene* (Steig, 1986), in which Irene endures a snowstorm to deliver a package, and in stories set in isolated geographic locations, such as *Hatchet* (Paulsen, 1987), in which thirteen-year-old Brian struggles to survive after an airplane crash in the Canadian wilderness. In some stories a character's activities and beliefs differ from those of other members of the society, and the differences cause conflict between that character and the local society. One example of this type of conflict is *The Witch of Blackbird Pond* (Speare, 1958), in which Kit Tyler is accused of being a witch because she continues activities in a New England Puritan community that were acceptable in the Caribbean community where she grew up but which are not acceptable in her new home.

Figure 9–1   *A Beginning-Middle-End Cluster for* The Tale of Peter Rabbit

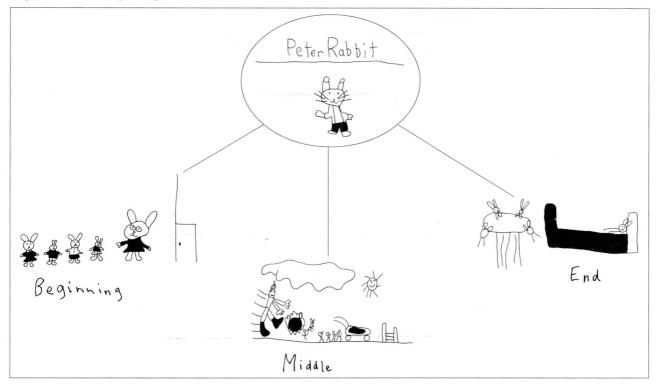

Conflict between characters is a common type of conflict in children's literature. In *Don't Fidget a Feather!* (Silverman, 1994), for example, a duck and a gander challenge each other in a series of contests. Another example is *Catherine, Called Birdy* (Cushman, 1994). In this story, set in 1290, high-spirited Birdy outwits her father and finds a husband who pleases her. The fourth type of conflict is conflict within a character, and stories such as *Ira Sleeps Over* (Waber, 1972) and *Chrysanthemum* (Henkes, 1991) are examples. In *Ira Sleeps Over,* 6-year-old Ira must decide whether to take his teddy bear with him when he goes next door to spend the night with a friend, and in *Chrysanthemum,* classmates tease a young mouse named Chrysanthemum about her name and she wishes she had a more common name. Chrysanthemum learns to appreciate her name with the support of an understanding teacher. Figure 9–2 lists stories representing the four conflict situations.

The plot is developed through conflict that is introduced in the beginning of a story, expanded in the middle, and finally resolved at the end. Plot development involves four components:

1. *A problem.* A problem that introduces conflict is presented at the beginning of a story.
2. *Roadblocks.* In the middle of the story, characters face roadblocks in attempting to solve the problem.
3. *The high point.* The high point in the action occurs when the problem is about to be solved. This high point separates the middle and end of the story.

Figure 9–2   Stories That Illustrate the Four Types of Conflict

---

Conflict Between a Character and Nature

Bunting, E. (1991). *Fly away home.* New York: Clarion. (P–M)

George, J. C. (1972). *Julie of the wolves.* New York: Harper & Row. (M–U)

MacLachlan, P. (1994). *Skylark.* New York: HarperCollins. (M)

O'Dell, S. (1960). *Island of the blue dolphins.* Boston: Houghton Mifflin. (M–U)

Paulsen, G. (1987). *Hatchet.* New York: Bradbury Press. (M–U)

Polacco, P. (1990). *Thundercake.* New York: Philomel. (P–M)

Sperry, A. (1968). *Call it courage.* New York: Macmillan. (U)

Steig, W. (1986). *Brave Irene.* New York: Farrar, Straus & Giroux. (P–M)

Conflict Between a Character and Society

Bunting, E. (1995). *Dandelions.* Orlando, FL: Harcourt Brace. (M)

Lowry, L. (1989). *Number the stars.* New York: Atheneum. (M–U)

Lowry, L. (1993). *The giver.* Boston: Houghton Mifflin. (U)

Nixon, J. L. (1987). *A family apart.* New York: Bantam. (M–U)

O'Brien, R. C. (1971). *Mrs. Frisby and the rats of NIMH.* New York: Atheneum. (M)

Polacco, P. (1994). *Pink and Say.* New York: Philomel. (M–U)

Speare, E. G. (1958). *The witch of Blackbird Pond.* Boston: Houghton Mifflin. (M–U)

Uchida, Y. (1993). *The bracelet.* New York: Philomel. (P–M)

Conflict Between Characters

Blume, J. (1972). *Tales of a fourth grade nothing.* New York: Dutton. (M)

Cohen, B. (1983). *Molly's pilgrim.* New York: Lothrop, Lee & Shepard. (M)

Cushman, K. (1994). *Catherine, called Birdy.* New York: HarperCollins. (U)

Ehlert, L. (1994). *Mole's hill.* Orlando, FL: Harcourt Brace. (P)

Naylor, P. R. (1991). *Shiloh.* New York: Atheneum. (M–U)

Paterson, K. (1994). *Flip-flop girl.* New York: Lodestar. (U)

Rathmann, P. (1995). *Officer Buckle and Gloria.* New York: Putnam. (P)

Silverman, E. (1994). *Don't fidget a feather!* New York: Simon & Schuster. (P)

Zelinsky, P. O. (1986). *Rumpelstiltskin.* New York: Dutton. (P–M)

Conflict Within a Character

Bauer, M. D. (1986). *On my honor.* Boston: Houghton Mifflin. (M–U)

Baylor, B. (1994). *The table where the rich people sit.* New York: Scribners. (P–M)

Byars, B. (1970). *The summer of the swans.* New York: Viking. (M)

Henkes, K. (1991). *Chrysanthemum.* New York: Greenwillow. (P)

Jeram, A. (1995). *Contrary Mary.* Cambridge, MA: Candlewick. (P)

Mead, A. (1995). *Junebug.* New York: Farrar, Straus & Giroux. (U)

Waber, B. (1972). *Ira sleeps over.* Boston: Houghton Mifflin. (P)

P = primary grades (K–2); M = middle grades (3–5); U = upper grades (6–8).

4. *Solution.* The problem is solved and the roadblocks are overcome at the end of the story.

The problem is introduced at the beginning of the story, and the main character is faced with trying to solve it. The problem determines the conflict. The problem in *The Ugly Duckling* (Mayer, 1987) is that the big, gray duckling does not fit in with the other ducklings, and conflict develops between the ugly duckling and the other ducks. This is an example of conflict between characters.

After the problem has been introduced, authors use conflict to throw roadblocks in the way of an easy solution. As characters remove one roadblock, the author devises another to further thwart the characters. Postponing the solution by introducing roadblocks is the core of plot development. Stories may contain any number of roadblocks, but many children's stories contain three, four, or five.

In *The Ugly Duckling,* the first conflict comes in the yard when the ducks, the other animals, and even the woman who feeds the ducks make fun of the main character. The conflict is so great that the duckling goes out into the world. Next, conflict comes from the wild ducks and other animals who scorn him, too. Third, the duckling spends a miserable, cold winter in the marsh.

The high point of the action occurs when the solution of the problem hangs in the balance. Tension is high, and readers continue reading to learn whether the main characters solve the problem. With *The Ugly Duckling,* readers are relieved that the duckling has survived the winter, but tension continues because he is still an outcast. Then he flies to a pond and sees three beautiful swans. He flies near to them even though he expects to be scorned.

As the story ends, the problem is solved and the goal is achieved. When he joins the other swans at the garden pond, they welcome him. He sees his reflection in the water and realizes that he is no longer an ugly duckling. Children come to feed the swans and praise the new swan's beauty. The newly arrived swan is happy at last!

Another way to examine plot is for students to make a chart called a plot profile to track the tension or excitement in a story (Johnson & Louis, 1987). Figure 9–3 presents a plot profile for *Stone Fox* (Gardiner, 1980), a story about a boy who wins a dogsled race to save his grandfather's farm. A class of fourth graders met in small groups to talk about each chapter, and after these discussions the whole class came together to decide how to mark the chart. At the end of the story, students analyzed the chart and rationalized the tension dips in Chapters 3 and 7. They decided that the story would be too stressful without these dips. Also, students were upset about the abrupt ending to the story and wished the story had continued a chapter or two longer so that their tension would have been reduced.

Characters.   Characters, the people or personified animals who are involved in the story, are often the most important element of story structure because many stories are centered on a character or group of characters. In *Catherine, Called Birdy* (Cushman, 1994), for example, the story focuses on Birdy and her determination to outwit her father and not be married off to a revolting, shaggy-bearded suitor.

Usually, one or two well-rounded characters and several supporting characters are involved in a story. Fully developed main characters have many character traits, both good and bad—that is to say, they have all the characteristics of real people. Knowing and inferring a character's traits is an important part of reading. Through character traits we get to know a character well, and the character seems to come alive. Figure 9–4 presents a list of stories with fully developed main characters. Supporting characters may be individualized, but they will be portrayed much less vividly than the main character. The extent to which supporting characters are developed depends on the author's purpose and the needs of the story.

Birdy is the main character in *Catherine, Called Birdy,* and readers get to know her as a real person. Although she is shaped by the culture of medieval England, she challenges the traditional role of "a fine lady" and is determined

Figure 9–3   A Plot Profile for Stone Fox

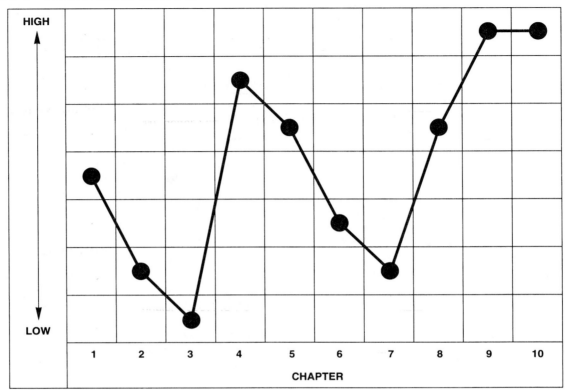

to marry someone she cares for, not some rich lord of her father's choosing. Through Birdy's journal entries, readers learn about her activities at the manor, how she helps her mother care for sick and injured people, and her beliefs and superstitions. Readers view events in the story through her eyes and sense her wit as she recounts her daily activities. In contrast, the author tells us little about the supporting characters in the story: Birdy's parents, her brothers, the servants, and the peasants who live and work on her father's lands.

Characters are developed in four ways—appearance, action, dialogue, and monologue. Authors present the characters to involve readers in the story's experiences. Similarly, readers notice these four types of information as they read in order to understand the characters.

Authors generally provide some physical description of the characters when they are introduced. Readers learn about characters by the description of their facial features, body shapes, habits of dress, mannerisms, and gestures. Little emphasis is placed on Birdy's appearance, but Birdy writes that she is unattractive. She squints because of poor eyesight and describes herself as tanned and with gray eyes. She often blackens her teeth and crosses her eyes to make herself more unattractive when her father introduces her to potential suitors.

The second way to learn about characters is through their actions, and what a character does is often the best way to know about that character. Birdy writes about picking fleas off her body, making soap and remedies for

Figure 9–4   *Stories with Fully Developed Main Characters*

Character	Story
Ramona	Cleary, B. (1981). *Ramona Quimby, age 8.* New York: Morrow. (M)
Birdy	Cushman, K. (1994). *Catherine, called Birdy.* New York: HarperCollins. (U)
Lucy	Cushman, K. (1996). *The ballad of Lucy Whipple.* New York: Clarion. (M–U)
Amber	Danziger, P. (1994). *Amber Brown is not a crayon.* New York: Putnam. (M)
Little Willy	Gardiner, J. R. (1980). *Stone Fox.* New York: Harper & Row. (M–U)
Chrysanthemum	Henkes, K. (1991). *Chrysanthemum.* New York: Greenwillow. (P)
Swamp Angel	Isaacs, A. (1994). *Swamp Angel.* New York: Dutton. (P–M)
Sarah	MacLachlan, P. (1985). *Sarah, plain and tall.* New York: Harper & Row. (M)
Marty	Naylor, P. R. (1991). *Shiloh.* New York: Atheneum. (M–U)
Karana	O'Dell, S. (1960). *Island of the blue dolphins.* Boston: Houghton Mifflin. (M–U)
Brian	Paulsen, G. (1987). *Hatchet.* New York: Viking. (U)
Babushka	Polacco, P. (1988). *Rechenka's eggs.* New York: Philomel. (P–M)
Officer Buckle	Rathmann, P. (1995). *Officer Buckle and Gloria.* New York: Putnam. (P)
Maria	Soto, G. (1993). *Too many tamales.* New York: Putnam. (P)
Matt	Speare, E. (1983). *The sign of the beaver.* Boston: Houghton Mifflin. (M–U)
Maniac	Spinelli, J. (1990). *Maniac Magee.* New York: Scholastic. (U)
Irene	Steig, W. (1986). *Brave Irene.* New York: Farrar, Straus & Giroux. (P–M)
Cassie	Taylor, M. (1976). *Roll of thunder, hear my cry.* New York: Dial. (U)
Moon Shadow	Yep, L. (1975). *Dragonwings.* New York: Harper & Row. (U)

the sick, doctoring with her mother, keeping birds as pets, traveling to a fair and to a friend's castle, and learning how to sew and embroider. She tells how she prefers being outside and how she sneaks away to visit the goat-boy and other friends who work at the manor.

Dialogue is the third way characters are developed. What characters say is important, but so is how they speak. The register of the characters' language is determined by the social situation. A character might speak less formally with friends than with respected elders or characters in positions of authority. The geographic location of the story, the historical period, and the

SES

characters' socioeconomic status also determine how characters speak. The language in Birdy's journal entries is often archaic:

> "Mayhap I could be a hermit." (p. 130)
> "I am full weary tonight . . ." (p. 131)
> "God's thumbs, he locked like my brother Robert!" (p. 132)
> "Corpus bones. I utterly loathe my life." (p. 133)

4.
monologue

Authors also provide insight into characters by revealing their thoughts, or inner dialogue. Birdy shares her innermost thoughts in her journal. Readers know how she attempts to thwart her father's plans to marry her off to a rich lord, her worries about her mother's miscarriages, her love for the goat-boy, and her guilt over meddling in Uncle George's love life.

Students can draw open-mind portraits to examine characters and reflect on story events from the character's viewpoint. These portraits have two parts: the face of the character is on one page, and the mind of the character is on the second page. The two pages are stapled together, with the "mind" page under the "face" page. An eighth grader's open-mind portrait of Birdy is shown in Figure 9–5. This student divided Birdy's mind into two parts—"hate" and "love." In each section, she drew pictures and wrote words about the people, events, and things Birdy hates and loves.

8th Gr.

Figure 9–5   *An Open-Mind Portrait of Birdy*

Setting. In some stories the setting is barely sketched, and these settings are backdrop settings. The setting in many folktales, for example, is relatively unimportant and may simply use the convention "Once upon a time . . ." to set the stage. In other stories the setting is elaborated and integral to the story's effectiveness. These settings are integral settings (Lukens, 1995). A list of stories with integral settings is shown in Figure 9–6. The setting in these stories is specific, and authors take care to ensure the authenticity of the historical period or geographic location in which the story is set. Four dimensions of setting are location, weather, time period, and time.

1.   Location is an important dimension in many stories. For example, the Boston Commons in *Make Way for Ducklings* (McCloskey, 1969) and the Alaskan North Slope in *Julie of the Wolves* (George, 1972) are integral to the stories' effectiveness. The settings are artfully described and add something unique to the story. In contrast, many stories take place in predictable settings that do not contribute to the story's effectiveness.

2.   Weather is a second dimension of setting and, like location, is crucial in some stories. A rainstorm is essential to the plot development in both *Bridge to Terabithia* (Paterson, 1977) and *Sam, Bangs, and Moonshine* (Ness, 1966). At other times weather is not mentioned because it does not affect the outcome of the story. Many stories take place on warm, sunny days. Think about the impact weather can have on a story; for example, what might have happened if a snowstorm had prevented Little Red Riding Hood from reaching her grandmother's house?

Figure 9–6   *Stories With Integral Settings*

Babbitt, N. (1975). *Tuck everlasting.* New York: Farrar, Straus & Giroux. (M–U)

Bunting, E. (1994). *Smoky night.* Orlando, FL: Harcourt Brace. (P–M)

Cauley, L. B. (1984). *The city mouse and the country mouse.* New York: Putnam. (P–M)

Choi, S. N. (1991). *Year of impossible goodbyes.* Boston: Houghton Mifflin. (U)

George, J. C. (1972). *Julie of the wolves.* New York: Harper & Row. (M–U)

Harvey, B. (1988). *Cassie's journey: Going west in the 1860s.* New York: Holiday House. (M)

Johnston, T. (1994). *Amber on the mountain.* New York: Dial. (P)

Konigsburg, E. L. (1983). *From the mixed-up files of Mrs. Basil E. Frankweiler.* New York: Atheneum. (M)

Lowry, L. (1989). *Number the stars.* Boston: Houghton Mifflin. (M–U)

MacLachlan, P. (1983). *Sarah, plain and tall.* New York: Harper & Row. (M)

McCloskey, R. (1969). *Make way for ducklings.* New York: Viking. (P)

Myers, W. D. (1988). *Scorpions.* New York: Harper & Row. (U)

Ness, E. (1966). *Sam, Bangs, and moonshine.* New York: Holt, Rinehart & Winston. (P)

Paterson, K. (1977). *Bridge to Terabithia.* New York: Crowell. (M–U)

Paulsen, G. (1987). *Hatchet.* New York: Viking. (U)

Polacco, P. (1988). *The keeping quilt.* New York: Simon & Schuster. (M)

Ringgold, F. (1991). *Tar beach.* New York: Crown. (P–M)

Say, A. (1993). *Grandfather's journey.* Boston: Houghton Mifflin. (P–M)

Speare, E. G. (1958). *The witch of Blackbird Pond.* Boston: Houghton Mifflin. (M–U)

Speare, E. G. (1983). *The sign of the beaver.* Boston: Houghton Mifflin. (M–U)

Steig, W. (1986). *Brave Irene.* New York: Farrar, Straus & Giroux. (P–M)

Torres, L. (1993). *Subway sparrow.* New York: Farrar, Straus & Giroux. (P–M)

Tregebov, R. (1993). *The big storm.* New York: Hyperion. (P)

Uchida, Y. (1993). *The bracelet.* New York: Philomel. (P–M)

Wilder, L. I. (1971). *The long winter.* New York: Harper & Row. (M)

3.   The third dimension of setting is the time period, an important element in stories set in the past or future. If *The Witch of Blackbird Pond* (Speare, 1958) and *Number the Stars* (Lowry, 1989) were set in different eras, for example, they would lose much of their impact. Today, few people would believe that Kit Tyler is a witch or that Jewish people are the focus of government persecution. In stories that take place in the future, such as *A Wrinkle in Time* (L'Engle, 1962), things are possible that are not possible today.

4   The fourth dimension, time, includes both time of day and the passage of time. Most stories ignore time of day, except for scary stories that take place after dark. In stories such as *The Ghost-Eye Tree* (Martin & Archambault, 1985), a story of two children who must walk past a scary tree at night to get a pail of milk, time is a more important dimension than in stories that take place during the day, because night makes things scarier.

Many short stories span a brief period of time, often less than a day, and sometimes less than an hour. In *Jumanji* (Van Allsburg, 1981), Peter and Judy's bizarre adventure, during which their house is overtaken by exotic jungle creatures, lasts only the several hours their parents are at the opera. Other stories, such as *Charlotte's Web* (White, 1952) and *The Ugly Duckling* (Mayer, 1987), span a long enough period for the main character to grow to maturity.

Students can draw maps to show the setting of a story. These maps may show the path a character traveled or the passage of time in a story. Figure 9–7 shows a setting map for *Number the Stars* (Lowry, 1989). In this chapter book set in Denmark during World War II, a Christian girl and her family help a Jewish family flee to safety in Sweden. The setting map shows where the families lived in Copenhagen, their trip to a fishing village in northern Denmark, and the ship they hid away on for the trip to Sweden.

Point of View.   Stories are written from a particular viewpoint, and this focus determines to a great extent readers' understanding of the characters and the events of the story. The four points of view are first-person viewpoint, omniscient viewpoint, limited omniscient viewpoint, and objective viewpoint (Lukens, 1995). Figure 9–8 presents a list of stories written from each viewpoint.

1.   The first-person viewpoint is used to tell a story through the eyes of one character using the first-person pronoun "I." In this point of view, the reader experiences the story as the narrator tells it. The narrator, usually the main character, speaks as an eyewitness to and a participant in the events. For example, in *Shiloh* (Naylor, 1991), Marty tells how he works for Judd Travers in order to buy the puppy Travers has mistreated, and in *Abuela* (Dorros, 1991) and the sequel *Isla* (Dorros, 1995), a girl describes magical flying adventures with her *abuela,* or grandmother. Many children's books are written from the first-person viewpoint, and the narrator's voice is usually very effective. One limitation is that the narrator must remain an eyewitness.

2.   In the omniscient viewpoint the author is godlike, seeing and knowing all. The author tells readers about the thought processes of each character without worrying about how the information is obtained. Most stories told from the omniscient viewpoint are chapter books, because revealing the thought processes of each character takes up space. One notable exception is *Doctor De Soto* (Steig, 1982), a picture book story about a mouse dentist who outwits a fox with a toothache. Steig lets readers know that the fox wants to eat the dentist as soon as his toothache is cured and that the mouse dentist is

Figure 9–7 A Setting Map for
Number the Stars

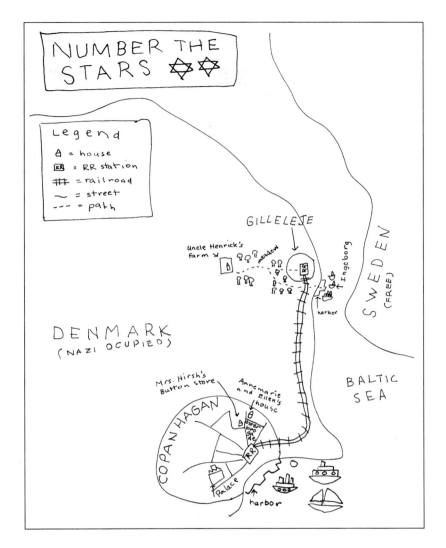

aware of the fox's thoughts and plans a clever trick. Examples of chapter books written from the omniscient viewpoint are *Tuck Everlasting* (Babbitt, 1975) and *Scorpions* (Myers, 1988).

3. The limited omniscient viewpoint is used so that readers can know the thoughts of one character. The story is told in third person, and the author concentrates on the thoughts, feelings, and significant past experiences of the main character or another important character. Many picture book and chapter book stories are told from this viewpoint. Lois Lowry uses the limited omniscient viewpoint in *The Giver* (1993). Lowry concentrates on the main character, Jonas, using his thoughts to explain Jonas's "perfect" community to readers. Later in the story, Jonas's thoughts reveal his growing dissatisfaction with the community and his decision to escape to Elsewhere with the baby Gabriel.

4. In the objective viewpoint, readers are eyewitnesses to the story and are confined to the immediate scene. They learn only what is visible and audible, without knowing what any character thinks. Many folktales, such as *Cinderella* (Galdone, 1978) and *The Little Red Hen* (Zemach, 1983), are told

Figure 9–8   *Stories Illustrating the Four Points of View*

First-Person Viewpoint

Dorros, A. (1991). *Abuela.* New York; Dutton. (P)

Howe, D., & Howe, J. (1979). *Bunnicula: A rabbit-tale of mystery.* New York: Atheneum. (M)

MacLachlan, P. (1985). *Sarah, plain and tall.* New York: Harper & Row. (M)

Naylor, P. R. (1991). *Shiloh.* New York: Atheneum. (M–U)

Say, A. (1993). *Grandfather's journey.* Boston: Houghton Mifflin. (M)

Woodruff, E. (1994). *The magnificent mummy maker.* New York: Scholastic. (M–U)

Omniscient Viewpoint

Babbitt, N. (1975). *Tuck everlasting.* New York: Farrar, Straus & Giroux. (M–U)

Grahame, K. (1961). *The wind in the willows.* New York: Scribner. (M)

Lewis, C. S. (1981). *The lion, the witch and the wardrobe.* New York: Macmillan. (M–U)

Myers, W. D. (1988). *Scorpions.* New York: Harper & Row. (U)

Steig, W. (1982). *Doctor De Soto.* New York: Farrar, Straus & Giroux. (P)

Limited Omniscient Viewpoint

Bunting, E. (1994). *A day's work.* New York: Clarion. (P–M)

Burch, R. (1966). *Queenie Peavy.* New York: Dell. (U)

Cleary, B. (1981). *Ramona Quimby, age 8.* New York: Morrow. (M)

Gardiner, J. R. (1980). *Stone Fox.* New York: Harper & Row. (M)

Lionni, L. (1969). *Alexander and the wind-up mouse.* New York: Pantheon. (P)

Lowry, L. (1993). *The giver.* Boston: Houghton Mifflin. (U)

Objective Viewpoint

Brett, J. (1987). *Goldilocks and the three bears.* New York: Putnam. (P)

Cauley, L. B. (1988). *The pancake boy.* New York: Putnam. (P)

Conrad, P. (1989). *The tub people.* New York: Harper & Row. (P–M)

Ehlert, L. (1994). *Mole's hill.* Orlando, FL: Harcourt Brace. (P)

Galdone, P. (1978). *Cinderella.* New York: McGraw-Hill. (P–M)

Zemach, M. (1983). *The little red hen.* New York: Farrar, Straus & Giroux. (P)

Multiple and Alternating Viewpoints

Avi. (1991). *Nothing but the truth: A documentary novel.* New York: Orchard. (U)

Dorris, M. (1992). *Morning girl.* New York: Hyperion. (U)

Fleischman, P. (1991). *Bull Run.* New York: Harper-Collins. (U)

Gray, N. (1988). *A country far away.* New York: Orchard. (P–M)

Laker, J. (1976). *Merry ever after.* New York: Viking. (M)

Rowland, D. (1991). *Little red riding hood/The wolf's tale.* New York: Birch Lane Press. (P–M)

---

from the objective viewpoint. Other picture book stories, such as *The Tub People* (Conrad, 1989) and *Mole's Hill* (Ehlert, 1994), are also told from this "eyewitness" viewpoint. The focus is on recounting events, not on developing the personalities of the characters.

Most teachers postpone introducing the four viewpoints until the upper grades, but younger children can experiment with point of view to understand how the author's viewpoint affects a story. One way to demonstrate point of view is to contrast *The Three Little Pigs* (Galdone, 1970), the traditional version of the story told from an objective viewpoint, with *The True Story of the Three Little Pigs!* (Scieszka, 1989), a self-serving narrative told by Mr. A. Wolf from a first-person viewpoint. In this unusual and satirical retelling, the wolf tries to explain away his bad image. Even first graders are struck by how different the two versions are and how the narrator filters the information.

Another way to demonstrate the impact of different viewpoints is for students to retell or rewrite a familiar story, such as *Little Red Riding Hood*

(Hyman, 1983), from specific points of view—through the eyes of Little Red Riding Hood; her sick, old grandmother; the hungry wolf; or the hunter. As they shift the point of view, students learn that they can change some aspects of a story but not others. To help them appreciate how these changes affect a story, have them take a story such as *The Lion, the Witch and the Wardrobe* (Lewis, 1981), which is told from the omniscient viewpoint, and retell short episodes from the viewpoints of different characters. As students shift to other points of view, they must decide what to leave out according to the new perspective.

A few stories are written from multiple viewpoints. In flip picture books, one version of the story begins at the front of the book, and then the book is flipped over for another story beginning at the back of the book. In Rowland's *Little Red Riding Hood/The Wolf's Tale* (1991), the traditional version begins on one side of the book, the wolf's version on the other. In some chapter books, such as *Bull Run* (Fleischman, 1991), alternating chapters are written from different characters' perspectives. Other stories written from multiple or alternating viewpoints are also listed in Figure 9–8.

Theme. The underlying meaning of a story is the theme, and it embodies general truths about human nature (Lehr, 1991). It usually deals with the characters' emotions and values. Themes can be stated either explicitly or implicitly. Explicit themes are stated openly and clearly in the story. Lukens (1995) uses *Charlotte's Web* to point out how one theme of friendship—the giving of oneself for a friend—is expressed as an explicit theme:

> Charlotte has encouraged, protected, and mothered Wilbur, bargained and sacrificed for him, and Wilbur, the grateful receiver, realizes that "Friendship is one of the most satisfying things in the world." And Charlotte says later, "By helping you perhaps I was trying to lift up my life a little. Anyone's life can stand a little of that." Because these quoted sentences are exact statements from the text they are called explicit themes. (p. 94)

Implicit themes are implied rather than explicitly stated in the story. They are developed as the characters attempt to overcome the obstacles that prevent them from reaching their goals. The theme emerges through the thoughts, speech, and actions of the characters as they seek to resolve their conflicts. Lukens also uses *Charlotte's Web* to illustrate implicit themes:

> Charlotte's selflessness—working late at night to finish a new word, expending her last energies for her friend—is evidence that friendship is giving oneself. Wilbur's protection of Charlotte's egg sac, his sacrifice of first turn at the slops, and his devotion to Charlotte's babies—giving without any need to stay even or to pay back—leads us to another theme: True friendship is naturally reciprocal. As the two become fond of each other, still another theme emerges: One's best friend can do no wrong. In fact, a best friend is sensational! Both Charlotte and Wilbur believe in these ideas; their experiences verify them. (p. 95)

Charlotte's Web has several friendship themes, one explicitly stated and others inferred from the text. Stories usually have more than one theme, and their themes usually cannot be articulated with a single word. Friendship is a multidimensional theme. Teachers can ask questions during conversations about literature to guide students' thinking as they work to construct a theme (Au, 1992). Students must go beyond one-word labels in describing the theme and construct their own ideas about a theme.

Sketch-to-stretch activities help students think more deeply about the theme of stories (Harste, Short, & Burke, 1988; Whitin, 1994, 1996a). As students create symbolic illustrations of books, they probe their understanding of the story and what it means to them. *The Ballad of Lucy Whipple* (Cushman, 1996), for example, is the story of a girl who reluctantly comes with her family to Lucky Diggins, California, during the 1849 Gold Rush. Even though she wants nothing more than to return home to Massachusetts, Lucy makes a new home for herself and finally becomes a "happy citizen" (p. 187) in Lucky Diggins. Figure 9–9 shows a fourth grader's sketch-to-stretch drawing about *The Ballad of Lucy Whipple* that reflects the "home" theme. Students also examine the theme as they create story quilts. As students design class quilts, the symbols, colors, and quotes that they choose reflect their understanding of theme.

■ To read more about sketch-to-stretch activities, see Chapter 6, "Writing in Journals," pp. 245–248.

Teaching Students About Stories

The most important way that students refine their concepts of story is by reading and writing stories, but teachers help students expand their concepts through minilessons that focus on particular story elements. Minilessons are usually taught during the exploring stage of the reading process, after students have had an opportunity to read and respond to a story and share their reactions.

■ See Chapter 1, "Learning and the Language Arts," pp. 34–38, for more information about the teaching strategy on which minilessons are based.

Minilessons About Stories. Teachers adapt the teaching strategy set out in Chapter 1 to teach minilessons on the elements of story structure and other procedures, concepts, and strategies and skills related to stories. The steps in teaching minilessons about stories are:

Figure 9–9   *A Fourth Grader's Sketch-to-Stretch Drawing for* The Ballad of Lucy Whipple

Step by Step

1. **Introduce the element.**   Teachers introduce the element of story structure using a chart to define and list the characteristics of the element. Figure 9–10 shows charts that can be developed for the elements. Next, students think about stories they have read recently that exemplify the element, and they talk about how these stories were organized.

2. **Analyze the element in stories.**   Students read or listen to one or more stories that illustrate the element. After reading and responding to the story, students analyze how the author used the element in the story. As students talk about the

Figure 9–10   *Charts for the Elements of Story Structure*

Chart 1

Stories

Stories have three parts:

1. A beginning
2. A middle
3. An end

Chart 2

Beginnings of Stories

Writers put these things in the beginning of a story:

1. The characters are introduced.
2. The setting is described.
3. A problem is established.
4. Readers get interested in the story.

Chart 3

Middles of Stories

Writers put these things in the middle of a story:

1. The problem gets worse.
2. Roadblocks thwart the main character.
3. More information is provided about the characters.
4. The middle is the longest part
5. Readers become engaged with the story and empathize with the characters.

Chart 4

Ends of Stories

Writers put these things in the end of a story:

1. The problem is resolved.
2. The loose ends are tied up.
3. Readers feel a release of emotions that were built up in the middle.

Chart 5

Conflict

Conflict is the problem that characters face in the story. There are four kinds of conflict:

1. Conflict between a character and nature
2. Conflict between a character and society
3. Conflict between characters
4. Conflict within a character

stories they have read, they tie their analyses to the information about the element presented in the first step. Students can also write the information from the chart in their reading logs.

3. ***Explore the story.***   Students participate in exploring activities to investigate how authors use the element in particular stories. Activities include:

- Retell a story.
- Write a retelling of a story in book format.
- Dramatize a story.

Figure 9–10   *continued*

Chart 6

Plot

Plot is the sequence of events in a story. It has four parts:

1. A Problem: The problem introduces conflict at the beginning of the story.
2. Roadblocks: Characters face roadblocks as they try to solve the problem in the middle of the story.
3. The High Point: The high point in the action occurs when the problem is about to be solved. It separates the middle and the end.
4. The Solution: The problem is solved and the roadblocks are overcome at the end of the story.

Chart 7

Setting

The setting is where and when the story takes place.

1. Location: Stories can take place anywhere.
2. Weather: Stories take place in different kinds of weather.
3. Time of Day: Stories take place during the day or at night.
4. Time Period: Stories take place in the past, at the current time, or in the future.

Chart 8

Characters

Writers develop characters in four ways:

1. Appearance: How characters look
2. Action: What characters do
3. Dialogue: What characters say
4. Monologue: What characters think

Chart 9

Theme

Theme is the underlying meaning of a story.

1. Explicit Themes: The meaning is stated clearly in the story.
2. Implicit Themes: The meaning is suggested by the characters, action, and monologue.

Chart 10

Point of View

Writers tell the story according to one of four viewpoints:

1. First-Person Viewpoint: The writer tells the story through the eyes of one character using "I."
2. Omniscient Viewpoint: The writer sees all and knows all about each character.
3. Limited Omniscient Viewpoint: The writer focuses on one character and tells that character's thoughts and feelings.
4. Objective Viewpoint: The writer focuses on the events of the story without telling what the characters are thinking and feeling.

Reading and Writing Stories

Procedures	Concepts	Strategies and Skills
Make a beginning-middle-end cluster	Concept of story	Visualize
Make a setting map	Beginning-middle-end	Predict and confirm
Make a plot profile	Plot	Engage with text
Make an open-mind portrait	Characters	Empathize with characters
Do a sketch-to-stretch drawing	Setting	Identify with characters
Design a story quilt	Theme	Write dialogue for characters
Use story boards	Point of view	Elaborate on the plot
Make a chart to compare versions of a folktale	Genre of story	Notice opposites in the story
Make a class collaboration book	Aesthetic reading	Retell the story
	Comprehension	Monitor understanding
Write an innovation on a text	Authors	Connect to one's own life
Write a sequel	Illustrators	Connect to previously read literature
Assess effectiveness of a story	Types of illustrations	Extend the story
Assess use of reading/writing strategies	Sequels	Value the story
		Evaluate the story
		Analyze the story

- Present a puppet show of a story.
- Draw clusters or other diagrams to visually represent the structure of a story.
- Make a class book of the story, with each student contributing one page.

As students participate in these activities, the teacher draws their attention to the element being studied.

4. **Review the element.** The teacher reviews the information about the element, using the charts introduced in the first step. Students explain the element in their own words, using one story they have read as an example.

A list of topics for minilessons about stories is presented above. These topics include procedures, concepts, and strategies and skills for reading and writing stories.

Adapting to Meet the Needs of Every Student. Stories are a large part of the elementary language arts program, and teachers must find ways to involve all students in successful reading and writing experiences with stories. A list of suggestions for adapting the information presented in this chapter to meet students' needs is presented on page 362. These suggestions emphasize the importance of allowing students to respond to stories before exploring them, as well as finding ways to support students as they read and write.

Adapting
Reading and Writing Stories
To Meet the Needs of Every Student

1. Read Aloud to Students

Teachers can make stories that students cannot read independently accessible by reading them aloud to students. When students listen to a story together in a small group or as a class, they become an interpretive community, and the shared experience of the story develops a strong bond among the students. Students can also listen to stories at a listening center.

2. Encourage Students to Choose Stories to Read

Teachers should schedule reading workshop on a regular basis so that students can read stories they are interested in reading or reread favorite stories. Classroom libraries should be well stocked with a wide variety of books, and teachers can give book talks to introduce students to stories and authors from which they might choose.

3. Dramatize Stories

Drama is an effective technique that students can use to understand stories they are reading and to create stories they will write. When students are reading a complex story, they can role-play important scenes in order to better understand the characters and events.

4. Write Retellings of Stories

Students can write retellings of favorite stories or retell the story from a particular character's viewpoint. Many students are more successful in writing retellings than writing original stories because they are better able to control the familiar storyline.

5. Work in Collaborative Reading and Writing Groups

Students can work together in pairs or in small groups to read and write stories. This way, students support each other as they read and write.

■ To learn more about reading logs, see Chapter 6, "Writing in Journals," pp. 229–231, and for more information on grand conversations, see Chapter 8, "Sustaining Talk in the Classroom," pp. 311–314.

Assessing Students' Concept of Story

Teachers assess students' concept of story in many ways. They observe students as they read and respond to stories. They can note whether or not students are sensitive to story elements as they talk about stories during grand conversations. Some students talk about the character who is most like them, or they compare two stories they have read. Teachers note whether students use terminology related to story elements. Do they talk about conflict, or the way a story ends? If they are talking about point of view, do they use that term? Teachers also ask questions about story elements during grand conversations and note the responses that students make. Students' reading logs also provide evidence of the same sorts of comments and reactions.

Reading Workshop pp. 109-111, 76, 162, 556, 557-559, 445

Another way that students demonstrate their understanding of story elements is by making clusters, charts, and diagrams. These activities are a natural outgrowth of students' responses to a story, not the reason why students are reading stories (Urzua, 1992). Teachers also document students' understanding of story elements by examining the stories they have written to see how they have applied their knowledge about stories.

READING STORIES

Students read stories aesthetically, and their concept of story informs and supports their reading. They read popular and award-winning stories together as a class during literature focus units, they read stories they choose themselves in reading workshop, and they read other stories as part of theme cycles. Students use the reading process to read, respond to, explore, and extend their reading. Reading stories with students is more than simply a pleasurable way to spend an hour; it is how classroom communities are created (Cairney, 1992). Reading, writing, and talking about stories are natural extensions of the relationships that students have built together. Students share stories they are reading with classmates, and they work together on projects to extend their interpretations.

Aesthetic Reading

■ *To read more about aesthetic reading, see Chapter 3, "The Reading and Writing Processes," p. 91.*

According to Louise Rosenblatt (1978), reading is a personal experience during which readers connect the story they are reading to their own lives and previous experiences with literature. The goal of aesthetic reading is comprehension, the negotiation of meaning between the reader and the text (Rosenblatt, 1978, 1985a). Readers do not search for the author's "correct" meaning; instead, they create a personal meaning for themselves. A story evokes different meanings from different readers, or even from the same reader at different times in his or her life.

Students use strategies as they deepen their comprehension. These strategies for reading and responding to stories include the following:

- *Visualizing.* Students create images or pictures of the story in their minds.
- *Predicting.* Students anticipate or make predictions about what will happen in the story. Students also think back to what they have read and consider its impact on what they are now reading.
- *Engaging.* Students become so involved in the story that they feel as though they are transported through time and space into the story.
- *Empathizing.* Students respond with their feelings as they read.
- *Identifying.* Students make connections between a character and themselves.
- *Elaborating.* Students make inferences and add information to what they read.
- *Noticing opposites.* Students note tensions or contrasts in the story.
- *Monitoring.* Students make sure that what they are reading makes sense to them.
- *Connecting to life.* Students make connections between events, characters, and other aspects of the story with their own lives.

inferences
drawing
conclusions

- *Connecting to literature.* Students make connections between the story they are reading and other stories they have read.
- *Evaluating.* Students make judgments about why they liked a story or whether it was worth reading.
- *Analyzing.* Students analyze the author's use of the elements of story structure (Corcoran, 1987; Cox & Many, 1992; Tompkins & McGee, 1993).

Teachers explain these strategies during minilessons, and students learn to use the strategies as they read aesthetically and participate in response activities.

Comprehension develops gradually. As students pick up a book by a favorite author or look at the cover of a book, they call to mind past experiences and make predictions, and the comprehension begins to form. It continues to develop as students read, respond to, and explore the story. As students discuss the story and write responses in reading logs, their comprehension deepens. Students move beyond the actual text as they work on projects, and these projects extend their comprehension further.

Students use the aesthetic stance when reading stories, as opposed to the efferent stance, which they use when reading to remember information. The stance readers take indicates the focus of their attention during reading. In her study on the effects of aesthetic and efferent stances on fourth, sixth, and eighth graders' interpretation of stories, Joyce Many (1991) found that students who read aesthetically had higher levels of comprehension.

Teachers encourage aesthetic reading and comprehension in many ways. From the stories they share with students to the minilessons they teach and the types of response and exploring activities they plan for students, teachers establish a classroom climate for aesthetic reading. A list of ways teachers can encourage comprehension in their classrooms is presented in the Teacher's Notebook on page 365.

Intertextuality. As students comprehend and create interpretations, they make connections to books they have read previously, and these connections are called intertextuality (de Beaugrande, 1980). Students use intertextuality as they respond to books they are reading by recognizing similarities between characters, plots, and themes. Students also use intertextuality as they incorporate ideas and structures from the stories they have read into the stories they are writing. Five characteristics of intertextuality are (Cairney, 1990, 1992):

1. *Individual and unique.* Students' literary experiences and the connections they make among them are different.
2. *Dependent on literary experiences.* Intertextuality is dependent on the types of books students have read, their purpose for and interest in reading, and the literary communities to which they belong.
3. *Metacognitive awareness.* Most students are aware of intertextuality and consciously make connections among texts.
4. *Links to concept of story.* Students' connections among stories are linked to their knowledge about literature.
5. *Reading-writing connections.* Students make connections between stories they read and stories they write.

The sum of students' experiences with literature—including the stories parents have read and told to young children, the books students have read

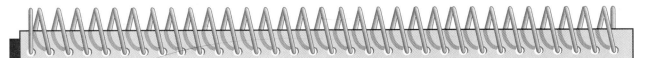

Teacher's Notebook
Ways to Enhance Comprehension

1. Encouraging Aesthetic Reading

Students learn about the aesthetic and efferent stances and the differences between them. Students are encouraged to read stories aesthetically for the lived-through experience of reading.

2. Grouping Books Into Text Sets

Students read a wide variety of literature, including stories, poems, and informational books. Often, teachers should group the literature into text sets, or students can make their own text sets.

3. Making Initial Responses

Students make initial responses to stories through grand conversations, writing in reading logs, and participating in role-playing activities.

4. Exploring the Story

Students explore the story through activities such as creating word walls, rereading the story, sequencing the events using storyboards, making diagrams, looking for opposites, and noting examples of literary style.

5. Teaching Reading Strategies

Teachers teach minilessons on reading strategies, including imaging, predicting, engaging, connecting to life and literature, valuing, and evaluating.

6. Expanding Concept of Story

Teachers teach minilessons about the elements of story structure, genre, authors and illustrators, and illustration to help students expand their concept of story.

7. Developing Intertextuality

Students make connections from the story to their own lives and to other literature they have read.

8. Creating Projects

Students extend comprehension through reading, writing, talk, drama, and research projects. It is important that students choose the projects they pursue.

or listened to the teacher read aloud, film versions they have viewed, their concepts of story and knowledge about authors and illustrators, and the books students have written—constitute their intertextual histories (Cairney, 1992). Cairney's research indicates that elementary students are aware of their past experiences with literature and use this knowledge as they read and write.

One way teachers encourage students to make intertextual ties is by grouping literature into text sets—collections of three or more books that are related in some way. Possible text sets include:

- Stories written by the same author
- Stories featuring the same character
- Stories illustrating the same theme
- Different versions of a folktale
- Stories in the same genre
- Stories and other books related to a theme cycle

As students read and discuss these books, they make connections among them. As students share the connections they are making, classmates gain insights about literature and build on classmates' ideas. Teachers can prompt students and ask them to describe commonalities among the books. Students can also make charts and other diagrams to compare authors, characters, and other aspects of stories.

Literary Opposites.   Stories are usually built around opposites or contrasts, and these literary opposites help to create excitement in a story (Temple,

<table>
<tr><td>■ *See Chapter 2, "Teaching Language Arts," pp. 54–55, for more information about text sets.*</td></tr>
</table>

Students make intertextual links as they compare different versions of the same story.

1992). *Where the Wild Things Are* (Sendak, 1962), for example, is built around the contrast between Max's bedroom and the land of the wild things. While his bedroom is safe and secure, where the wild things live is thrilling but a little scary, too. Max's mother sends him to his bedroom for misbehaving, and she is clearly in charge; but when Max becomes king of the wild things, he is in charge. In Phyllis Reynolds Naylor's *Shiloh* (1991), the main characters—Marty Preston and Judd Travers—are opposites. Marty is the "good" character who bravely works for mean-spirited Travers to buy a beagle pup that has been mistreated. Through the experience, Marty learns about human nature and about himself.

Opposites can be between settings, characters, or events in the story, and there is more than one opposite in most stories. For example, after reading Steig's *Amos and Boris* (1971), a class of third graders listed these opposites:

big	little
land animal	sea animal
helping	being helped
Amos and Boris	*The Lion and the Mouse*
life	death
forgetting	remembering
hope	hopeless
in the sea	out of the sea
hello	good-bye

Students each picked the opposite that seemed most important to them and drew pictures and wrote about them. One student's writing is shown in Figure 9–11. This was a valuable way for students to think deeply about stories and extend their comprehension of the story. Another student made a very interesting intertextual tie between Amos and Boris and *The Lion and the Mouse* (Young, 1979), pointing out that the two stories have the same theme.

In Literature Focus Units

■ *To learn how to plan a literature focus unit, see Chapter 13, "Putting It All Together," pp. 544–550.*

Teachers plan literature focus units featuring popular and award-winning stories for children and adolescents. Some literature focus units feature a single book—either a picture book or a chapter book—and others feature a text set of books. During these units students move through the five stages of the reading process as they read and respond to stories. Some of the activities in each stage are:

1. Preparing. Teachers introduce the story or stories and activate students' background knowledge.

2. Reading. Students read the story in one of several ways: they might listen to the teacher read the book aloud, read it independently or with a buddy, or read it through shared reading.

3. Responding. Students respond to the story through grand conversations, by dramatizing events from the story, and by writing in reading logs.

4. Exploring. Students participate in a variety of exploring activities to dig more deeply into the story. A list of exploring activities is presented in the Teacher's Notebook on page 369. Students also add interesting and impor-

Figure 9–11   *A Third Grader's Quickwrite about* Amos and Boris

3rd/Gr.

You might think a whale and a mouse are very, very diferent but they are not! They both have hearts full of love for there friends and minds ful of memories. They are mammales too.

tant words from the story to a word wall. Teachers often teach minilessons about story elements, aesthetic reading, comprehension, reading strategies, and other topics during this stage.

    5.   Extending.   Students do projects to extend their interpretations of the story. They share their completed projects with classmates.

2nd/Gr.

    Second graders might spend a week reading *Tacky the Penguin* (Lester, 1988), a popular story about an oddball penguin who saves all the penguins from some hunters. During the unit, students read the story several times, respond to the story, participate in a variety of exploring activities, and do projects to extend their interpretations. A week-long plan for teaching a unit on *Tacky the Penguin* is presented in Figure 9–12.

    Several different types of exploring activities are included in this plan. One type focuses on vocabulary. On Monday, students list words from the story on a word wall; the next day they reread the words and sort them according to the character they refer to; and on Thursday the teacher teaches a minilesson about peeling off the *-ly* suffix to learn the main word (root word). It's not typical to teach a lesson on derivational suffixes in second grade, but second graders notice that many of the words on the word wall have *-ly* at the end of them and often ask about the suffix. Another activity examines character. The teacher teaches a minilesson on characters on Tues-

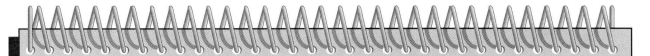

Teacher's Notebook
Activities to Explore Stories

Story Boards

The teacher cuts apart two copies of a picture book, backs each page with a sheet of posterboard, and laminates each page. Students read story boards and identify important words for the word wall, memorable quotes, and so on. Students can also create story boards for a chapter book. After reading the book, students each choose a chapter, reread it, draw a picture about it, and write a summary of it. Then the pictures and summaries are backed with posterboard and laminated.

Story Boxes

Students and the teacher collect items related to a story and place them in a box. The box cover is decorated with the title and author, pictures of scenes from the story, pictures of the characters, and memorable quotes. Making the box is a good way to focus students' attention on what is important about the story, and students can examine the items in a box prepared by students in a previous class as they talk about the story and what it means to them.

Open-Mind Portraits

In order to probe a character, students draw portraits of the character and cut around the face so that the head flips up. Next they back the page with another sheet of paper. Then they write words and draw pictures in the "open mind" behind the face that reflect the character's thoughts.

Setting Maps

Students draw setting maps to illustrate a character's journey in a story. Other types of maps are beginning-middle-end clusters, Venn diagrams to compare characters, and plot profiles. For more information about maps, see *Responses to Literature, Grades K–8* (Macon, Bewell, & Vogt, 1991).

Sketch-to-Stretch

Students make sketch-to-stretch drawings to represent the theme of a story. These drawings are not illustrations of particular events in the story, but they symbolize the story's message. After making their sketches, students share them with classmates and talk about the symbols and messages they have included in the drawings.

Story Quilts

Students create paper or cloth quilts with pictures to represent the story and memorable quotes. Students design the quilt to emphasize the theme of the book and choose colors to symbolize the story. Students work individually or in small groups to make each square, and then the squares are placed side-by-side to complete the quilt.

Figure 9–12   A Week-Long Plan for Teaching Tacky the Penguin

Monday

Talk about penguins to introduce the story.

Read the story aloud to students as they follow along in their copies of the story.

Discuss the story in a grand conversation. Ask why Tacky is called an "odd" bird. Ask if students think they are more like Tacky or more like the other penguins.

Add words that students suggest to the word wall.

Have students draw and write about the story in their reading logs.

Tuesday

Have students share their reading log entries in small groups, and have one student from each group share with the class.

Reread the words on the word wall. Pass out word cards for students to sort according to whether they relate to Tacky, to the other penguins, or to the hunters.

Have students reread the story with a buddy.

Teach a minilesson about characters and explain that authors develop characters in four ways.

Have students draw portraits of Tacky and add open minds to show what he is thinking.

Wednesday

Make a list of students' questions about penguins.

Read aloud *A Penguin Year* (Bonners, 1981) to answer many of their questions. Research answers to any remaining questions.

Discuss possible projects and begin work on projects.

Thursday

Work on projects.

Reread *Tacky the Penguin* with small groups of students.

Teach minilesson on the suffix *-ly* and how to "peel" the suffix off to find the main word. Use words from the word wall for the lesson.

Friday

Finish work on projects and share them.

Make a story quilt with pictures of Tacky and favorite quotes from the story.

Have students reflect on the unit.

day. Then students make a character cluster about Tacky and draw open-mind portraits to show what Tacky is thinking.

Genre Studies.   Genre units provide an opportunity for students to learn about a particular genre, or category, of literature. Students read stories illustrating the genre and then participate in a variety of activities to deepen their interpretations and knowledge about the genre. In these units students participate in the following activities:

• Read several stories illustrating a genre.
• Learn the characteristics of the genre.

- Respond to and explore the genre stories.
- Write or rewrite stories exemplifying the genre.

Genre studies about traditional literature, including fables, folktales, legends, and myths, are very appropriate for elementary students.

During a genre study of folktales, for example, third-grade students read folktales such as *The Little Red Hen* (Zemach, 1983), *The Mitten* (Brett, 1989), and *Little Red Riding Hood* (Hyman, 1983), and the teacher explains that these stories are folktales and that folktales are relatively short stories that originated as part of the oral tradition. The students make a list of these characteristics of folktales:

- The story is often introduced with the words "Once upon a time."
- The setting is usually generalized and could be located anywhere.
- The plot structure is simple and straightforward.
- The story usually revolves around a journey from home to perform some tasks, a journey that involves a confrontation with a monster, the miraculous change from a harsh home to a secure home, or a confrontation between a wise character and a foolish character.
- Characters are portrayed in one dimension—either good or bad, stupid or clever, or industrious or lazy.
- The ending is happy, and everyone "lives happily ever after."

Then students spend several days reading and responding to other folktales from a special display set up in the classroom. The teacher brings the class together, and they share the folktales they have read and find examples of the characteristics in the stories. Then the teacher explains that folktales have motifs—small, recurring elements—such as three wishes, a magical ring, or a character who is a trickster. Next the teacher presents this list of six common motifs, and students name a folktale illustrating each motif:

- *A long sleep or enchantment.* An example of a story with the long sleep motif is *The Sleeping Beauty* (Yolen, 1986).
- *Magical powers.* Characters in folktales often have magical powers, such as the fool's companions in *The Fool of the World and the Flying Ship* (Ransome, 1968).
- *Magical transformations.* In stories such as *Beauty and the Beast* (Mayer, 1978), characters are magically transformed from one form into another.
- *Magical objects.* Magical objects play an important role in some folktales. One example is *Aladdin and the Wonderful Lamp* (Carrick, 1989).
- *Wishes.* Characters are granted wishes but sometimes use them unwisely, as in *The Stonecutter* (Newton, 1990).
- *Trickery.* Animals and people trick each other in many folktales. For example, the wolf tricks the little girl in *Little Red Riding Hood* (Hyman, 1983).

Students spend several more days reading and rereading folktales and finding other examples of motifs.

Next, students read different versions of "Cinderella" in small groups. Then they get back together as a class to talk about their reading and make a chart to compare the versions. Later in the unit, students work on projects. Some choose to write their own versions of folktales, some make puppets and produce a play of a folktale, and others read versions of different folktales and compare them on a chart. A list of versions of "Cinderella" and other familiar folktales is presented in Figure 9–13.

Author Studies. During author studies, students read and respond to stories written by a particular author. They also learn about the author, his or her writing style, and other interesting information about the person. If possible, students write to the author or arrange to meet him or her.

One way that students learn about authors and illustrators is by reading about them. A number of biographies and autobiographies of well-known authors and illustrators, including Patricia Polacco (1994), Jean Fritz (1992), Lois Ehlert (1996), and Joanna Cole (1996), are available for elementary students. Filmstrips, videotapes, and other audiovisual materials about authors and illustrators are becoming increasingly available. In addition, upper-grade students can read articles about favorite writers. Many articles profiling authors and illustrators have been published in *Language Arts, Horn Book,* and other journals, and teachers can clip and file these articles.

In Reading Workshop

■ *To read about how to plan and teach using reading workshop, see Chapter 13, "Putting It All Together," pp. 557–559.*

Reading workshop brings "real-world" reading into the classroom. Students read and respond to stories in authentic ways, more like people do outside of school settings. They choose books they want to read. Sometimes they choose books by favorite authors, books recommended by classmates, or old favorites they want to reread. As they read, students are so engaged in reading that they often lose track of where they are and don't hear when someone calls their name. Students respond emotionally—by laughing or crying—and make connections to their own lives and other literature they have read.

Teachers encourage students to develop interpretations during all three parts of reading workshop. They teach minilessons about aesthetic reading, interpretation, and reading strategies, and they provide opportunities for students to apply what they are learning as they read and respond to stories. During the independent reading time, students move through all five stages of the reading process. They choose the stories they will read and begin the process of interpretation during the preparing step. Next, they read the story independently, with a buddy, or in a small group. After reading, they write and draw a response in a reading log and talk about the story with a small group of students or in a conference with the teacher. When students particularly enjoy a story, they extend the reading experience by working on a project. They share the story and their project during sharing time. Sharing is a social time, and when students share the stories they have read, they have the opportunity to celebrate their reading and value the story. Sharing is also important because students often choose a book based on classmates' recommendations.

Teachers often connect reading workshop with literature focus units and author studies. They may begin with a book that all students in the class read, and then move into a reading workshop so that students can read independently. For example, during a literature focus unit, students might read *Bunnicula: A Rabbit-Tale of Mystery* (Howe & Howe, 1979) together as a class and then read other books in the series in a reading workshop. Or, during a unit on folktales, students may read several folktales together as a class and

Figure 9–13   *Versions of Folktales and Related Stories*

"Cinderella"

Climo, S. (1989). *The Egyptian Cinderella.* New York: Crowell. (M)

Climo, S. (1993). *The Korean Cinderella.* New York: HarperCollins. (M)

Cole, B. (1987). *Prince Cinders.* New York: Putnam. (M)

Compton, J. (1994). *Ashpet: An Appalachian tale.* New York: Holiday. (P–M)

Ehrlich, A. (1985). *Cinderella.* New York: Dial. (P–M)

Galdone, P. (1978). *Cinderella.* New York: McGraw-Hill. (P–M)

Hooks, W. H. (1987). *Moss gown.* New York: Clarion. (M–U)

Huck, C. (1989). *Princess Furball.* New York: Greenwillow. (P–M)

Louie, A. L. (1982). *Yeh-Shen: A Cinderella story from China.* New York: Philomel. (M–U)

Martin, R. (1992). *The rough-face girl.* New York: Putnam. (M)

Munsch, R. N. (1980). *The paper bag princess.* Toronto, Canada: Annick Press. (P–M)

Pollock, P. (1996). *The turkey girl: A Zuni Cinderella story.* Boston: Little, Brown. (P–M)

Steptoe, J. (1987). *Mufaro's beautiful daughters: An African tale.* New York: Lothrop. (P–M–U)

"The Gingerbread Boy"

Asbjorsen, P. C., & Moe, J. (1980). *The runaway pancake.* New York: Larousse. (P)

Brown, M. (1972). *The bun: A tale from Russia.* New York: Harcourt Brace Jovanovich. (P)

Cauley, L. B. (1988). *The pancake boy: An old Norwegian folk tale.* New York: Putnam. (P)

Galdone, P. (1975). *The gingerbread boy.* New York: Seabury. (P)

Jarrell, R. (1964). *The gingerbread rabbit.* New York: Collier. (P–M)

Oppenheim, J. (1986). *You can't catch me!* Boston: Houghton Mifflin. (P)

Sawyer, R. (1953). *Journey cake, ho!* New York: Viking. (P–M)

Ziefert, H. (1995). *The gingerbread boy.* New York: Viking. (P)

"Goldilocks and the Three Bears"

Cauley, L. B. (1981). *Goldilocks and the three bears.* New York: Putman. (P)

Galdone, P. (1972). *The three bears.* New York: Clarion. (P)

Petach, H. (1995). *Goldilocks and three hares.* New York: Putman. (P–M)

Tolhurst, M. (1990). *Somebody and the three Blairs.* New York: Orchard. (P)

Turkle, B. (1976). *Deep in the forest.* New York: Dutton. (P)

"Little Red Riding Hood"

de Regniers, B. S. (1972). *Red Riding Hood.* New York: Atheneum. (M–U)

Emberley, M. (1990). *Ruby.* Boston: Little, Brown. (M–U)

Galdone, P. (1974). *Little Red Riding Hood.* New York: McGraw-Hill. (P–M)

Goodall, J. S. (1988). *Little Red Riding Hood.* New York: McElderry Books. (P–M–U)

Hyman, T. S. (1983). *Little Red Riding Hood.* New York: Holiday House. (P–M)

Marshall, J. (1987). *Red Riding Hood.* New York: Dial. (P–M)

Young, E. (1989). *Lon po po: A Red-Riding Hood story from China.* New York: Philomel. (M–U)

Zwerger, L. (1983). *Little Red Cap.* New York: Morrow. (M)

"The Princess and the Frog"

Berenzy, A. (1989). *A frog prince.* New York: Henry Holt. (P–M–U)

Gwynne, F. (1990). *Pondlarker.* New York: Simon & Schuster. (M–U)

Isadora, R. (1989). *The princess and the frog.* New York: Crowell. (P–M–U)

Isele, E. (1984). *The frog prince.* New York: Crowell. (P–M–U)

Scieszka, J. (1991). *The frog prince continued.* New York: Viking. (M–U)

Tarcov, E. H. (1974). *The frog prince.* New York: Scholastic. (P–M–U)

"The Three Little Pigs"

Bishop, G. (1989). *The three little pigs.* New York: Scholastic. (M)

Galdone, P. (1970). *The three little pigs.* New York: Seabury. (P)

Lowell, S. (1992). *The three little javelinas.* Flagstaff, AZ: Northland. (P–M)

Marshall, J. (1989). *The three little pigs.* New York: Dial. (P–M)

Scieszka, J. (1989). *The true story of the three little pigs!* New York: Viking. (P–M–U)

Trivizas, E. (1993). *The three little wolves and the big bad pig.* New York: McElderry Books. (P–M)

Zemach, M. (1988). *The three little pigs.* New York: Farrar, Straus & Giroux. (P)

Students read books, view videos, and learn about the author during an author study on Gary Paulsen.

then break into small groups to read other folktales. During an author unit on Tomie de Paola, Eric Carle, or Beverly Cleary, students may read one or more books together as a class and then break into small groups to read others.

In Theme Cycles

■ *For more informa-tion about how to plan theme cycles, turn to Chapter 13, "Putting It All Together," pp. 567–571.*

Students often read stories as part of theme cycles. Stories are useful be-cause they provide an additional viewpoint to that provided in informational books. They personalize history in a way that informational books cannot (Fennessey, 1995; Tunnell & Ammon, 1993). Many stories have been written to chronicle events in American history. Here is a sampling:

- Life in the Connecticut colony—*The Witch of Blackbird Pond* (Speare, 1958)
- The American Revolution—*The Fighting Ground* (Avi, 1984)
- The slave trade—*The Slave Dancer* (Fox, 1973)
- The Underground Railroad—*The House of Dies Drear* (Hamilton, 1968)
- Life in a New England mill town—*Lyddie* (Paterson, 1991)
- The California gold rush—*Chang's Paper Pony* (Coerr, 1988)
- Pioneers traveling west—*Cassie's Journey: Going West in the 1860s* (Har-vey, 1988)
- The settlement of orphans on prairie farms—*A Family Apart* (Nixon, 1987)
- Russian Jews coming to America for religious freedom—*Molly's Pilgrim* (Cohen, 1983)
- The Depression—*Drylongso* (Hamilton, 1992)
- Discrimination—*Roll of Thunder, Hear My Cry* (Taylor, 1976)
- Japanese Americans' internment during World War II—*Baseball Saved Us* (Mochizuki, 1993)
- The Vietnam conflict—*The Wall* (Bunting, 1990)

These books are <u>historical fiction</u>, and the historical settings have been described accurately; moreover, these stories introduce readers to memorable characters and present themes that transcend the historical period in which the book is set.

Students also read books in connection with <u>science themes</u>. For example, during a theme cycle on mice, a multi-age classroom of first, second, and third graders read many of these stories about mice:

[handwritten: 1st, 2nd, 3rd]

- *A Beautiful Feast for a Big King Cat* (Archambault & Martin, 1994)
- *The Town Mouse and the Country Mouse* (Cauley, 1984)
- *Chrysanthemum* (Henkes, 1991)
- *The Island of the Skog* (Kellogg, 1973)
- *Alexander and the Wind-Up Mouse* (Lionni, 1969)
- *Mouse Tales* (Lobel, 1972)
- *If You Give a Mouse a Cookie* (Numeroff, 1985)
- *Chato's Kitchen* (Soto, 1995)
- *Amos and Boris* (Steig, 1971)
- *Doctor De Soto* (Steig, 1982)
- *Do You See a Mouse?* (Waber, 1995)
- *Partners* (Waggoner, 1995)
- *The Lion and the Mouse* (Young, 1979)

Students in this classroom had two mice as classroom pets, and their curiosity about their pets set the stage for the theme. The teacher read some of the books aloud to students, and students read other books independently or with buddies during reading workshop. After reading, students talked about the stories and drew and wrote responses in their <u>mice learning logs</u>. They also did projects to extend their interpretations.

Assessing Students' Understanding of Stories

Students' interpretations are unique and personal, and having students answer comprehension questions or fill in the blanks on worksheets is not an effective assessment technique. Teachers can better assess students' interpretation in these ways (Cairney, 1990):

- Listen to students as they talk about stories during grand conversations and other literature discussions.
- Read students' entries in reading logs.
- Note students' use of reading strategies.
- Observe students' participation in exploring activities.
- Examine the projects that students do.

Teachers also ask students to reflect on their interpretations during reading conferences or in reading log entries.

WRITING STORIES

As students read and talk about literature, they learn how writers craft stories. They also draw from stories they have read as they create their own stories, intertwining several story ideas and adapting story elements to meet their own needs (Atwell, 1987; Graves, 1989; Hansen, 1987; Harste, Short, &

Burke, 1988; Harwayne, 1992). In his research about intertextuality, Cairney (1990) found that elementary students do think about stories they have read as they write, and Blackburn (1985) describes a cycle of intertextuality: students read and talk about trade books; they weave bits of the stories they have read into the stories they write; they share their compositions; and then bits of these compositions make their way into classmates' compositions. Students make intertextual links in different ways, such as:

- Use specific story ideas without copying the plot.
- Copy the plot from a story, but add new events, characters, and settings.
- Use a specific genre they have studied for a story.
- Use a character borrowed from a story read previously.
- Write a retelling of the story.
- Incorporate content from an informational book into a story.
- Combine several stories into a new story.

The first two strategies were the ones most commonly used in Cairney's study of sixth graders. It is interesting to note that the next-to-the-last strategy was used only by less capable readers, and the last one only by more capable readers.

Students incorporate what they have learned about stories when they write stories, and they use the writing process to draft and refine their stories. They write stories as part of literature focus units, during theme cycles, and in writing workshop. Stories are probably the most complex writing form that elementary students use. It is difficult—even for adults—to craft well-formed stories with plot and character development and other elements of story structure incorporated.

In Literature Focus Units

Students often write stories as part of literature focus units. These writing activities are often done as projects during the extending stage of the reading process. Students make intertextual links and write retellings of stories, new stories using patterns from stories they have read, sequels to stories they have read, and original genre stories.

Writing Retellings of Stories. Elementary students often write retellings of stories they have read and enjoyed. As they retell a story, they internalize the structure of the story and play with the language that the author used. Sometimes students work together to write a collaborative retelling, and at other times they write their own individual retellings.

Students can work together as a group to write or dictate the retelling, or they can divide the story into sections or chapters and have each student or pair of students write a small part. Then the parts are compiled. A class of first graders worked together to dictate their retelling of *Where the Wild Things Are* (Sendak, 1962), which was published as a big book:

Page 1: *Max got in trouble. He scared his dog and got sent to bed.*
Page 2: *This room turned into a jungle. It grew and grew.*
Page 3: *A boat came for Max. It was his private boat.*
Page 4: *He sailed to where the wild things lived.*
Page 5: *They made him king of all the wild things.*

Page 6:   *The wild things had a wild rumpus. They danced and hung on trees.*
Page 7:   *Max sent them to bed without any supper.*
Page 8:   *Then Max wanted to come back home. He waved good-bye and sailed home on his boat.*
Page 9:   *And his dinner was waiting for him. It was still hot from the microwave.*

■ Turn to Chapter 4, "Emergent Literacy," pp. 157–162, for more information on making a big book.

As the first graders dictated the retelling, their teacher wrote it on chart paper. Then they read over the story several times, making revisions. Next, the students divided the text into sections for each page. Then they recopied the text onto each page for the big book, drew pictures to illustrate each page, and added a cover and a title page. Students also wrote their own books, including the major points at the beginning, middle, and end of the story.

Sometimes students change the point of view in their retellings and tell the story from a particular character's viewpoint. A fourth grader wrote this retelling of "Goldilocks and the Three Bears" from Baby Bear's perspective:

One day mom got me up. I had to take a bath. I hate to take baths, but I had to. While I was taking my bath, Mom was making breakfast. When I got out of the tub breakfast was ready. But Dad got mad because his breakfast porridge was too hot to eat. So Mom said, "Let's go for a walk and let it cool." I thought, "Oh boy, we get to go for a walk!" My porridge was just right, but I could eat it later.

When we got back our front door was open. Dad thought it was an animal so he started to growl. I hate it when Dad growls. It really scares me. Anyway, there was no animal anywhere so I rushed to the table. Everybody was sitting down to eat. I said, "Someone ate my porridge." Then Dad noticed someone had tasted his porridge. He got really mad.

Then I went into the living room because I did not want to get yelled at. I noticed my rocking chair was broken. I told Dad and he got even madder.

Then I went into my bedroom. I said, "Someone has been sleeping in my bed and she's still in it." So this little girl with long blond hair raises up and starts to scream. Dad plugged his ears. She jumped up like she was scared of us and ran out of the house. We never saw that little girl again.

Writing Innovations on Texts. Many stories have a repetitive pattern or refrain, and students can use this structure to write their own stories. As part of a literature focus unit on mice, a first-grade class read *If You Give a Mouse a Cookie* (Numeroff, 1985) and talked about the circle structure of the story. The story begins with giving a mouse a cookie and ends with the mouse getting a second cookie. Then first graders wrote stories about what they would do if they were given a cookie. A student named Michelle drew the circle diagram shown in Figure 9–14 to organize her story, and then she wrote this story, which has been transcribed into conventional English spelling:

If you gave Michelle a cookie she would probably want some pop. Then she would want a napkin to clean her face. That would make her tired and she would go to bed to take a nap. Before you know it, she will be awake and she would like to take a swim in a swimming pool. Then she would watch cartoons on T.V. And she would be getting hungry again so she would probably want another cookie.

Judith Viorst's *Alexander and the Terrible, Horrible, No Good, Very Bad Day* (1977) is a more sophisticated pattern story. After reading the book, students often write about their own bad days. A fifth grader named Jacob wrote his version entitled "Jacob and the Crummy, Stupid, Very Bad Day":

Figure 9–14   A Circle Diagram for If You Give a Mouse a Cookie

One day I was riding my bike and I fell off and broke my arm and sprained my foot. I had to go to the hospital in an ambulance and get my arm set in a cast and my foot wrapped up real tight in a bandage. I knew it was going to be a crummy, stupid, very bad day. I think I'll swim to China.

Then I had to go to the dentist with my sister Melissa. My sister had no cavities, but guess who had two cavities. I knew it was going to be a crummy, stupid, very bad day. I think I'll swim to China.

My mom felt bad for me because it was such a bad day so she went and bought me a present—two Nintendo games. But my sister started fighting with me and my mom blamed me for it even though it wasn't my fault. So my mom took the games away. I wonder if there are better sisters in China?

Then I went outside and found out that someone had stolen my bike. It was gone without a trace. It really was a crummy, stupid, very bad day. Now I am going to swim to China for sure.

Writing Sequels.   Students often choose to write sequels as projects during literature focus units. For example, after reading *The Sign of the Beaver* (Speare, 1983), students often write sequels in which Matt and Attean meet again. Students write additional adventures about the boa constrictor after reading *The Day Jimmy's Boa Ate the Wash* (Noble, 1980). Many stories lend themselves to sequels, and students enjoy extending a favorite story.

Writing Genre Stories.   During some literature focus units, students read books and learn about a particular genre, such as folktales, historical fiction, myths, or fables. After learning about the genre, students try their hand at writing stories that incorporate the characteristics of the genre. After reading Gingerbread Man stories, a <u>class of kindergartners</u> dictated this story, which their teacher wrote on chart paper. Interestingly, the students asked their teacher to write the story in two columns. In the left column the teacher wrote the story, and in the right column she wrote the refrain:

The Runaway Horse

Once upon a time	*Run, run,*
there was a horse.	*as fast as you can,*
He jumped over the	*you can't catch me!*
stable gate and ran away.	
He meets a farmer.	*Run, run,*
The farmer chases him	*as fast as you can,*
but the horse runs	*you can't catch me!*
as fast as the wind.	
The horse meets a dog.	*Run, run,*
The dog chases him.	*as fast as you can,*
The horse runs	*you can't catch me!*
as fast as the wind.	
The horse meets the wolf.	*Run, run,*
The wolf chases him.	*as fast as you can,*
The horse runs	*you can't catch me!*
as fast as the wind.	
Then the horse meets a fox.	*Snip, snap, snout,*
And the fox gobbles him up.	*This tale is told out.*

A <u>seventh-grade</u> class read and examined myths and compared myths from various cultures. Then they applied what they had learned about myths in this class collaboration myth, "Suntaria and Lunaria: Rulers of the Earth," about the origin of the sun and the moon:

Long ago when gods still ruled the earth, there lived two brothers, Suntaria and Lunaria. Both brothers were wise and powerful men. People from all over the earth sought their wisdom and counsel. Each man, in his own way, was good and just, yet the two were as different as gold and coal. Suntaria was large and strong with blue eyes and brilliantly golden hair. Lunaria's hair and eyes were the blackest black.

One day Zeus, looking down from Mount Olympus, decided that Earth needed a ruler—someone to watch over his people whenever he became too tired or too busy to do his job. His eyes fell upon Suntaria and Lunaria. Both men were wise and honest. Both men would be good rulers. Which man would be the first ruler of the earth?

Zeus decided there was only one fair way to solve his problem. He sent his messenger, Postlet, down to earth with ballots instructing the mortals to vote for a king. There were only two names on the ballot—Suntaria and Lunaria.

Each mortal voted and after the ballots were placed in a secure box, Postlet returned them to Zeus. For seven years Zeus and Postlet counted and recounted the ballots. Each time they came up with the same results: 50% of the votes were for Suntaria and 50% were for Lunaria. There was only one thing Zeus could do. He declared that both men would rule over the earth.

This is how it was, and this is how it is. Suntaria still spreads his warm golden rays to rule over our days. At night he steps down from his throne, and Lunaria's dark, soft night watches and protects us while we dream.

The students incorporated the characteristics of myths in their story. First, their myth explained a phenomenon that has more recently been explained scientifically. Second, the setting is backdrop and barely sketched. Finally, the characters in their myth are heroes with supernatural powers. It is interesting to compare this myth to the sun and moon myths told by aboriginal Australians, Native Americans, Nigerians, and Polynesians collected in *Legends of the Sun and Moon* (Hadley & Hadley, 1983).

In Theme Cycles

Students also write stories as part of theme cycles. During a theme cycle on weather, for example, students might write stories set in different types of weather, or during an upper-grade theme on medieval life, students might write a story set in a castle. In these stories, students weave the information they are learning into their stories. For example, a multi-age class of middle-grade students was traveling around the world during their year-long social studies theme cycle. As they studied Hawaii, the students wrote stories and incorporated information into their stories, as this student's story shows:

My Trip to Hawaii

Today I reached Hawaii, the fiftieth state. On the way to my hotel I saw fields of sugarcane, coffee and pineapple. Then I stopped my car. There was a coconut laying in the middle of the road. I got out and got it. A coconut is a fruit that contains milk inside. However the milk does not rot.

Finally I got to my hotel. My hotel is by an extinct volcano called Diamond Head. It is the most known volcano on the islands. I was glad to be on the top of a 15 story high hotel. I wanted to go surfing in the Pacific Ocean, but I got to the part of the day that it started raining. It rains every day here. Well, I'm going to go eat a sandwich. The Hawaiian Islands were first discovered by Capt. James Cook in 1778. He named them the Sandwich Islands.

Now I'm going to go to the museum. I heard they have a travel guide today and I'm going to go. When I got there they gave me a map of where we're going to go. We're going to go to the coffee fields. Yuck! I hate coffee but I will go because Hawaii is the only state that grows coffee.

Next we're going to drive by Pearl Harbor. If you are a war lover and you are wondering how the United States got in World War 2, well, it's because the Japanese bombed Pearl Harbor in 1941. There is about 68 people on this bus and about 100 more people waiting back at the museum.

Oh and tonight I'm going to a hula dance. Tomorrow my hotel reservation expires so I better go pack so I'll be ready for the hula dance. Then I'm going to Australia.

Even though the insertion of information about Hawaii into this story is somewhat awkward, the student was proud that he could incorporate more than 10 facts in his story.

In Writing Workshop

■ *For more information about how to set up writing workshop, turn to Chapter 13, "Putting It All Together," pp. 562–566.*

Much of the writing that students do during writing workshop is stories. First graders often write single-draft stories that feature prominent illustrations and are bound into books, but older students and more experienced writers move through all five stages of the writing process as they write stories. Students apply what they have learned about the elements of story structure in their stories, and teachers often teach minilessons about the elements of story structure during writing workshop.

Many students write stories about their pets and family members. In this example, a first grader writes about her dog, Sebastian. Her story is entitled "Sebastian Goes to the Circus," and it was written in a book format with a sentence and a picture on each page:

Page 1: *Sebastian walks to the circus.*
Page 2: *It takes him a long time to get to the circus.*
Page 3: *When he gets there he can't find a man to help him.*
Page 4: *Sebastian tried to do some tricks but he couldn't.*
Page 5: *He found the Dog Trainer and he learned to do many tricks.*
Page 6: *Now he is the most famous circus dog in the world!*

Older students also write stories about themselves. A sixth grader wrote this story, "The Cave," in which he and his friends are the main characters:

> *There were five of us when we started. Now there is just me and my friend Joe. This is what happened.*
> *The five of us, me (Boris Mudlumpus), Joe Marvinson, Ted Vergille, Jerry Marvinson (Joe's brother), and Mike Gorgolo, decided to explore the old cave on the hill before they cemented up the entrance. It seemed like a great thing to do, then. But slowly, one by one, we started disappearing. Ted Vergille was a kind of fat guy who liked to crack jokes. We were laughing at one of his jokes when he suddenly he wasn't there anymore. We found him a little farther down the cave. His bones had been disjointed and his neck was broken. There were many punctures in his veins but no blood was anywhere. Someone, or something, had drained his blood and his eyes had the look that made you think he had seen horrors untold. We ran to the entrance as fast as we could, but by the time we got there, there was only me and Joe left, and the entrance had already been cemented over! We could never get out!*
> *That's the way it happened. Now we are trapped. Oh, no! It's closing in on us. Augh!!!!*
> *"George, wake up," my mother was calling. "It's time to go to school." I let out a long deep sigh. It was only a dream.*

This story can be used to make two important points. Many students include gruesome descriptions and events in their stories, and teachers must decide for themselves where to set the limit on what is acceptable in their classrooms. Also, students often use dreams as a way to escape from a story. When the story gets complicated, the main character escapes by waking up from a dream.

Students also write story retellings, sequels, and pattern stories during writing workshop. They get ideas for the stories they write as they listen to classmates share their stories and through minilessons that teachers teach about different types of stories.

Assessing the Stories Students Write

Assessing the stories students write involves far more than simply judging the quality of the finished stories. Assessment also takes into account students' knowledge of story structure as well as the activities they engage in while writing and refining their stories. Teachers consider four components in assessing students' stories: students' knowledge of the elements of story structure, their application of the elements in writing, their use of the writing process, and the quality of the finished stories.

Determining whether students learned about the element and applied what they learned in their stories is crucial in assessing students' stories. Consider the following points:

- Can the student define or identify the characteristics of the element?
- Can the student explain how the element was used in a particular story?
- Did the student apply the element in the story he or she has written?

Teachers assess students' use of the writing process by observing them as they write and asking these questions:

- Did the student write a rough draft?
- Did the student participate in a writing group?
- Did the student revise the story according to feedback received from the writing group?
- Did the student complete a revision checklist?
- Did the student proofread the story and correct as many mechanical errors as possible?
- Did the student share the story?

The quality of students' stories is difficult to measure. Students who write high-quality and interesting stories use the elements of story structure to their advantage. Their stories are creative and well organized. Ask these questions to assess the quality of children's stories:

- Is the story interesting?
- Is the story well organized?

The assessment and grading of students' stories reflects more than simply the quality of the finished product. It should reflect all four components of students' involvement with stories.

Review

During the elementary grades students learn about five elements of story structure: plot, characters, setting, point of view, and theme. Students apply this knowledge as they read and write stories. They read stories aesthetically and develop interpretations as they read and respond to stories. Students read stories as part of literature focus units, reading workshop, and theme cycles. Students use the writing process to write retellings of familiar stories, new versions of stories, sequels, and original stories during literature focus units, in theme cycles, and in writing workshop. Key concepts are:

1. Students acquire a concept of story by reading and writing stories and by learning about the elements of story structure.
2. Stories have unique structural elements that distinguish them from other forms of writing: plot, characters, setting, theme, and point of view.
3. Teachers present minilessons about the elements of story structure, and students apply what they learn as they read and write stories.
4. Students read stories aesthetically, and their concept of story informs and supports their reading.
5. The goal of aesthetic reading is comprehension, the negotiation of meaning between the reader and the text.
6. Students use strategies such as imaging, anticipating, empathizing, retelling, and connecting to personal experiences and literature as they create meanings.

7. Students read stories as part of literature focus units, reading workshop, and theme cycles.
8. Story boards, story boxes, open-mind portraits, setting maps, and story quilts are five ways to explore stories.
9. Students use intertextuality as they incorporate ideas from the stories they have read into the stories they write.
10. Students write stories as part of literature focus units, writing workshop, and theme cycles.

Extensions

1. Compile a list of books to use in teaching about story elements at the grade level you teach or plan to teach. Write a brief summary for each book, commenting specifically on the element of story structure or genre that the book exemplifies.
2. Construct a set of charts to use in teaching the elements of story structure, as shown in Figure 9–9.
3. Interview several students about their concept of story and what they think about as they read and write stories. Ask questions such as these:

   - Tell me about a story you have read that is really a good one.
   - What things do authors include in stories to make them good?
   - Do you like to read stories? Write stories?
   - Tell me about some of the stories you have written.

   - Tell me some of the things you think about while you are writing a story.
   - What do you include in stories you write to make them good?
   - What have your teachers taught you about reading and writing stories?

4. Teach a series of minilessons about reading strategies or one of the elements of story structure to a small group of students. Use the teaching strategy presented in this chapter.
5. Plan a literature focus unit on a picture book or a chapter book.
6. Collect samples of children's stories and examine them to see how students use the elements of story structure.
7. Plan an author study unit. Collect information about the author and copies of the stories the author has written.

> *I introduce my girls and boys to autobiography by having them make "Me" boxes about themselves. Anything is possible in kindergarten, and an added benefit from this project is forging strong links between home and school.* **99**
>
> **Albena Reinig**
> Kindergarten Teacher
> Thomas Oleatas Elementary School

PROCEDURE

We do our "Me" box project at the beginning of the school year. The children make their boxes at home and bring them to school to share.

These boxes are great! Not only do I introduce the concept of autobiography, but the children are sharing with classmates and speaking in front of the class. I learn a lot about my children and their families.

I bring my own Me box to share with the class. I used a shoebox, and I've written my name and decorated the outside of the box with rose-colored paper—my favorite color. Inside I have a picture of my family, a small stuffed cat like my Boots, a postcard from our vacation last year in New York City, and a small cross-stitch kit because I like to do needlework. Next, I explain that everyone is going to make a Me box, and I distribute a letter about the project for children to take home to their parents. I ask each child to make a Me box from a shoebox, a tissue box, or another container, and to deco-

rate the outside of their boxes with their names and favorite colors, pictures cut from magazines, or gift wrap. Sometimes they add glitter, stickers, or other decorations on it. They put three or four objects inside that represent people, pets, events, and other things in their lives.

I give children a week to prepare their boxes, and as they bring their Me boxes to school, they begin sharing them. Several children share each day until everyone has shared. Here is one child's sharing:

👉 *This is my Me box. My mom helped me put this Happy Birthday paper on it and you can count these candles [candles are taped on the top of the box]—1–2–3–4–5. That's how old I am. And this is my name: J–E–R–E–D. My mom she cut these name letters for me and I pasted them on my box.*

Now look inside. Here's one thing I got inside—my TeeTee. He's a tiger and I got him when I was little. I forgot where. He always sleeps on my bed. See this? He's got one of my little shirts from when I was a baby on. You can touch him but be real careful.

Now . . . this is a picture of me and Santa Claus. My mom put a four on the back. It means I was four when I got the picture made. And here's a picture of my family. It's got my mom and my dad and Josh—he's my baby brother.

And this is my Mickey Mouse. My Gramps and Nana gave it to me for my birthday because they are going to take me to Disneyland when school is out.

I explain that they need to show the outside of the box and then tell about each object or picture they have placed in the box. As they share each item, they show it to the class and tell something about it.

Then I put the boxes away in a safe place, and several times during the year we add things to the boxes. This year I am saving the hand prints and the number books we made to put in the boxes. At the end of the school year we'll write a class poem about kindergarten friends which everyone will sign, and I'll make a copy for each child. Then parents will collect boxes at our spring back-to-school night.

ASSESSMENT

My assessment is simple. I make sure that every child brings a Me box and shares it with the class. I expected to have to help one or two children who did not have assistance at home prepare their boxes at school, but it wasn't necessary. My children's parents take the project very seriously.

ADAPTATIONS

I've started making book boxes, too. In my box for *The Very Busy Spider* by Eric Carle (1984), I have a spider puppet, a spider web made of sticks and yarn, and pictures of the horse, cow, sheep, goat, pig, dog, cat, duck, rooster, and fly that I have colored, cut out, and laminated for my children to use in retelling the story. I also have boxes for informational books. In my box for *Growing Vegetable Soup* (Ehlert, 1987), I have several packages of vegetable seeds, a toy shovel and rake, plastic vegetables, and the recipe for vegetable soup.

I introduce the box when I first read the story or informational book, and then I provide opportunities for my children to look at the book again and explore the objects in the box in small groups. Of course, I remove any dangerous objects or very fragile items before setting the box out.

REFLECTIONS

Me boxes are a wonderful way to get to know my children at the beginning of the kindergarten year. My students are very proud when they share their Me boxes with us. They're sharing themselves and their families. I began using Me boxes to introduce autobiography to my students, but I've accomplished much more.

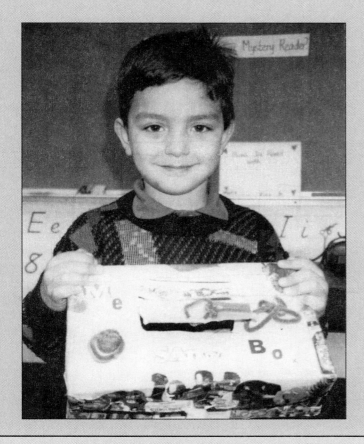

As part of a theme cycle on insects, Josie Fierro and her bilingual second graders made this quilt. Students reread the Spanish and English versions of Eric Carle's *The Very Hungry Caterpillar* (1969) and made quilt squares with a picture of a caterpillar on one side and a butterfly on the other. Students wrote about the four stages of the butterfly's life cycle—egg, caterpillar, chrysalis, and butterfly—around the edge of each square. Students chose green as one of the colors for this quilt because insects live much of their lives on plants.

t's common to hear teachers say, "I have an exciting *story* to read to you today about how whales migrate" and "What a wonderful *story* you've written, and I learned a lot about baleen whales!" These books about whales may be stories, but it is more likely that they are informational or nonfiction books, because their primary purpose is to provide information. Teachers often use the word *story* as a generic term for all books students read, thinking that *stories* is an easier term for them to understand. But it is unfair to students to do this. Stories and informational books are different genres, although they overlap. Some informational books, such as *The Magic School Bus Inside a Hurricane* (Cole, 1995), use a storylike format, but the emphasis is on providing information (Freeman & Person, 1992).

■ *To review information on aesthetic and efferent reading, turn back to Chapter 3, "The Reading and Writing Processes," p. 91.*

Teachers have assumed that constructing stories in the mind is a fundamental way of learning (Wells, 1986). Recent research, however, suggests that stories are not more basic for children to understand, and that children are able to understand informational texts as well as they do stories (Pappas, 1991, 1993). Children are interested in learning about their world—about baleen whales, how a road is built, threats to the environment of Antarctica, or Helen Keller's courage—and informational books provide this knowledge.

Students often assume the efferent stance as they read informational books to locate facts, but this is not always the case (Rosenblatt, 1978, 1991). Many times they pick up an informational book to check a fact, and then they continue reading—aesthetically, now—because they are fascinated by what they are reading. They get carried away in the book, just as they do when reading stories. At other times students read books about topics they are interested in, and they read aesthetically, engaging in the lived-through experience of reading and connecting what they are reading to their own lives and prior reading experiences.

Russell Freedman, who won the 1988 Newbery Medal for *Lincoln: A Photobiography* (1987), talks about the purpose of informational books and explains that it is not enough for an informational book to provide information: "[An informational book] must animate its subject, infuse it with life. It must create a vivid and believable world that the reader will enter willingly and leave only with reluctance. . . . It should be just as compelling as a good story" (1992, p. 3). High-quality informational books like Freedman's encourage students to read aesthetically because they engage readers and tap their curiosity. Barbara Moss advocates using informational books for read-alouds and explains that reading nonfiction trade books "has the ever widening effect of a pebble thrown into a pond" (1995, p. 122).

Students also write informational books about concepts and information they are learning during theme cycles. The informational trade books they have read serve as models for their writing, and they organize the information that they present using the same types of patterns or structures used in informational books (Freeman, 1991; Tompkins, Smith, & Hitchcock, 1987).

This chapter focuses on expository text, the type of writing used in informational books. As you continue reading, think about these questions:

- How do teachers develop students' knowledge about expository text?
- How can teachers facilitate students' reading of informational books?

- How can teachers facilitate students' writing of various types of informational writing, including reports, letters, and biographies?

DEVELOPING STUDENTS' KNOWLEDGE ABOUT INFORMATIONAL BOOKS

As students read informational books and listen to them read aloud, they learn about the world around them and many other things as well. They learn how to vary their reading, depending on their purpose. Sometimes they read informational books from beginning to end like stories, or they may use the index to locate a specific topic and then read just that section. They learn how to use an index and a table of contents, and how to read charts, graphs, maps, and diagrams. They also notice the different ways informational books are organized and how authors develop interrelationships among the pieces of information being presented.

Types of Informational Books

There is a new wave of engaging and artistic informational books being published today, and these books show increased respect for children. Peter Roop (1992) explains that for years informational books were the "ugly duckling" of children's literature, but now they have grown into a beautiful swan.

Four qualities of informational books are accuracy, organization, design, and style (Vardell, 1991). First and foremost, the facts must be current and complete. These books must be well researched, and, when appropriate, varying points of view should be presented. Stereotypes are to be avoided, and the details in both the text and the illustrations must be authentic. Second, information should be presented clearly and logically, using organizational patterns to increase the book's readability. Third, the design of the book should be eye-catching and should enhance its usability. Illustrations should complement the text, and explanations should accompany each illustration. Last, the book should be written in a lively and stimulating style so as to engage the reader's curiosity and wonder.

A wide variety of informational books are available today. Topics include the biological sciences, the physical sciences, the social sciences, the arts, and biographies. *Cactus Hotel* (Guiberson, 1991) is a fine informational book about the desert ecosystem. The author describes the life cycle of a giant saguaro cactus and its role as a home for other desert creatures. Other books—such as *Whales* (Simon, 1989), illustrated with striking full-page color photos, and *Antarctica* (Cowcher, 1990), illustrated with dramatic double-page paintings—are socially responsible and emphasize the threats that people represent to animals and the earth.

Other books present historical and geographic concepts. *Rosie the Riveter: Women Working on the Home Front in World War II* (Colman, 1995), for instance, examines the diversity of opportunities available to women during the war, and *Surrounded by Sea: Life on a New England Fishing Island* (Gibbons, 1991) describes the social life and customs of island residents throughout the four seasons. These books are exciting to read, and they provide an engaging and enriching reading experience for elementary students.

Life-stories are another type of informational books; one type of life-story is biography, and another is autobiography. Life-stories being written today are more realistic than in the past, and they present well-known personalities, warts and all. Jean Fritz's portraits of Revolutionary War figures, such as *Will You Sign Here, John Hancock?* (1976), are among the best-known, but she has also written comprehensive biographies, including *The Great Little Madison* (1989). As I mentioned earlier, another fine biography is Russell Freedman's *Lincoln: A Photobiography* (1987), which won the Newbery Medal. Authors often include notes in the back of books to explain how the details were researched and to provide additional information.

Fewer autobiographies are available to elementary students today, but more are being published each year. Autobiographies about authors and illustrators, such as *On the Bus with Joanna Cole* by Joanna Cole (1996), author of the popular series of The Magic School Bus informational books, and Lois Ehlert's *Under My Nose* (1996), are popular.

In addition to these main types of informational books, there are other, more specialized, types. Four types that elementary students read are:

1. Alphabet and counting books. While many alphabet and counting books with pictures of familiar objects are designed for young children, others provide a wealth of information on various topics. In his alphabet book

Kindergartners learn about sequence as they arrange information boards made from two copies of an informational book about the life cycle of a chicken.

Illuminations (1989), Jonathan Hunt presents detailed information about medieval life, and in *The Underwater Alphabet Book* (1991), Jerry Pallotta provides information about 26 types of fish and other sea creatures. Muriel and Tom Feelings present information about Africa in *Moja Means One: Swahili Counting Book* (1971), and Ann Herbert Scott cleverly integrates information about cowboys in *One Good Horse: A Cowpuncher's Counting Book* (1990). In some of these books new terms are introduced and illustrated, and in others the term is explained in a sentence or a paragraph.

2. Books that present information through a song or poem. In these powerful books, songs and poems are illustrated with a word, line, or stanza on each page. Together the text and illustrations provide information. In *America the Beautiful* (Bates, 1993), Neil Waldman's expressionistic illustrations highlight fourteen natural and man-made wonders, including the Great Smokies and Mesa Verde, and information about each is presented in the back of the book. Jeannette Winter's haunting illustrations underscore the dangers of the Underground Railroad in *Follow the Drinking Gourd* (1988). Diane Siebert's poem and Wendell Minor's paintings combine to present a powerful portrait in *Sierra* (1991), and Jane Yolen's poem and Laura Regan's illustrations combine to describe the lush rain forest environment in *Welcome to the Green House* (1993).

3. Books that present information within a story. Authors are devising innovative strategies for combining information with a story. Margy Burns Knight's *Who Belongs Here? An American Story* (1993), a two-part book, is a good example. One part is the story of Nary, a young Cambodian refugee who escapes to the United States after his parents are killed by the Khmer Rouge. This story is told in a picture book format, with the story text accompanying each picture. The second part of the book is information about refugees, immigration laws, and cultural diversity in America. The text for this second part is printed in a different typeface and set apart and under the story text on each page. Additional information about America as a nation of immigrants is presented at the back of the book. The two parts create a very powerful book.

Flashback is another useful technique for presenting information. In *The House on Maple Street* (Pryor, 1987), flashback is used to show all the different groups of people who have lived on the same piece of land. The text and the illustrations combine to present information, and the presentation of information is more central to the book than the story line is.

Some combination informational/story books are imaginative fantasies. The Magic School Bus series, written by Joanna Cole and illustrated by Bruce Degen, is perhaps the best-known. In *The Magic School Bus Inside a Hurricane* (Cole, 1995), for example, Ms. Frizzle and her class study weather up close as their bus survives both a hurricane and a tornado on its way to a weather station. Charts and reports with factual information and suggestions for projects are presented throughout the book. Another fantasy story with factual information is Faith Ringgold's *Aunt Harriet's Underground Railroad in the Sky* (1992). Information and a map about the Underground Railroad and a biographical sketch of Harriet Tubman are included in the back of the book.

Other authors use the story format to tell about experiences in their own lives. Sherley Anne Williams tells her own childhood story of migrant farming in *Working Cotton* (1992), and Junko Morimoto tells of her experiences in the atomic blast in *My Hiroshima* (1987). In both of these books, factual information about the topics is woven into the text.

4. Journals and letters.   Journals and letters are other types of informational books, and these artifacts provide a glimpse into historical periods and the lives of historical personalities. One example is *Off the Map: The Journals of Lewis and Clark* (Roop & Roop, 1993). Journals of pioneers are increasingly used in picture books. *The Way West: Journal of a Pioneer Woman* (Knight, 1993) describes the hardships of a woman and her family as they travel west on the Oregon Trail.

■ *For more information about journals, turn to Chapter 6, "Writing in Journals."*

Some journals and collections of letters are authentic accounts, but others are fictionalized. The Roops' *I, Columbus: My Journal 1492–1493* (1989) is an informational book with excerpts from Columbus's journal, while *Pedro's Journal: A Voyage With Christopher Columbus August 3, 1492–February 14, 1493* (Conrad, 1991) is a fictionalized account. *Marco Polo: His Notebook* (Roth, 1992) is another fictionalized account, even though it looks very authentic. The journal is well researched and based on Marco Polo's autobiography. *Nettie's Trip South* (Turner, 1987) is a fictionalized letter written by a Northern girl about her trip to antebellum Richmond. She tells about the horrors of a slave market. Even the fictionalized accounts can be used in conjunction with informational books, but teachers and students should be aware of the differences between the two types.

Expository Text Structures

Just as stories are structured using plot, characters, and the other elements of story structure, informational books are organized or patterned in particular ways called expository text structures. Five of the most common organizational patterns are description, sequence, comparison, cause and effect, and problem and solution (Meyer & Freedle, 1984; Niles, 1974). Figure 10–1 describes these patterns and presents sample passages and cue words that signal use of each pattern. The story structure patterns interact together to create the framework for the story; however, in informational books, expository text structures can be used separately.

Description.   In this organizational pattern, the writer describes a topic by listing characteristics, features, and examples. Phrases such as *for example* and *characteristics are* cue this structure. Examples of books using description include *Spiders* (Gibbons, 1992) and *Mercury* (Simon, 1993), and in these books the authors describe many facets of their topic. When students delineate any topic, such as the Mississippi River, eagles, or Alaska, they use description.

Sequence.   In this pattern, the writer lists items or events in numerical or chronological order. Cue words include *first, second, third, next, then,* and *finally.* Caroline Arnold describes the steps in creating a museum display in *Dinosaurs All Around: An Artist's View of the Prehistoric World* (1993), and David Macaulay describes how a castle was constructed in *Castle*

(1977). Students use the sequence pattern to write directions for completing a math problem, the stages in an animal's life cycle, or events in a biography.

Comparison.   In this structure, the writer explains how two or more things are alike or different. *Different, in contrast, alike, same as,* and *on the other hand* are cue words and phrases that signal this structure. In *Horns, Antlers, Fangs, and Tusks* (Rauzon, 1993), for example, the author compares animals with these distinctive types of headgear. When students compare and contrast book and video versions of a story, reptiles and amphibians, or life in ancient Greece with life in ancient Egypt, they use this organizational pattern.

Cause and Effect.   In this pattern, the writer describes one or more causes and the resulting effect or effects. *Reasons why, if . . . then, as a result, therefore,* and *because* are words and phrases that cue this structure. Explanations of why dinosaurs became extinct, the effects of pollution on the environment, or the causes of the Civil War use the cause-and-effect pattern. Betsy Maestro's *How Do Apples Grow?* (1992) and Paul Showers's *What Happens to a Hamburger?* (1985) are two informational books that exemplify the cause-and-effect structure.

Problem and Solution.   In this expository structure the writer states a problem and offers one or more solutions. In *Man and Mustang* (Ancona, 1992), the author describes the problem of wild mustangs and explains how they are rescued. A variation is the question-and-answer format, in which the writer poses a question and then answers it; one question-and-answer book is . . . *If You Traveled West in a Covered Wagon* (Levine, 1986). Cue words and phrases include *the problem is, the puzzle is, solve,* and *question . . . answer.* Students use this structure when they write about why money was invented, saving endangered animals, and building dams to stop flooding. They often use the problem-solution pattern in writing advertisements and in other persuasive writing.

These organizational patterns correspond to the traditional organization of main ideas and details within paragraphs. The main idea is embodied in the organizational pattern, and the details are the elaboration; for example, in the sample passage of the comparison pattern in Figure 10–1, the main idea is that the modern Olympic games are very different from the ancient Olympic games. The details are the specific comparisons and contrasts.

Graphic organizers can help students organize and visually represent ideas for the five organizational patterns (Piccolo, 1987; Smith & Tompkins, 1988). Students might use a cluster for description, a Venn diagram or T chart for comparison, or a series of boxes and arrows for cause and effect (Bromley, 1991; Yopp & Yopp, 1996). Diagrams of a variety of graphic organizers also appear in Figure 10–1. Most of the research on expository text structures has focused on older students' use of these patterns in reading; however, elementary students also use the patterns and cue words in their writing (Langer, 1986; Raphael, Englert, & Kirschner, 1989; Tompkins, 1994).

Figure 10–1   The Five Expository Text Structures

Pattern	Description	Cue Words	Graphic Organizer	Sample Passage
Description	The author describes a topic by listing characteristics, features, and examples.	for example characteristics are	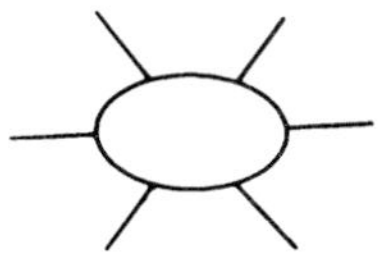	The Olympic symbol consists of five interlocking rings. The rings represent the five continents—Africa, Asia, Europe, North America, and South America—from which athletes come to compete in the games. The rings are colored black, blue, green, red, and yellow. At least one of these colors is found in the flag of every country sending athletes to compete in the Olympic games.
Sequence	The author lists items or events in numerical or chronological order.	first, second, third next then finally		The Olympic games began as athletic festivals to honor the Greek gods. The most important festival was held in the valley of Olympia to honor Zeus, the king of the gods. It was this festival that became the Olympic games in 776 B.C. These games were ended in A.D. 394 by the Roman Emperor who ruled Greece. No Olympic games were held for more than 1,500 years. Then the modern Olympics began in 1896. Almost 300 male athletes competed in the first modern Olympics. In the games held in 1900, female athletes were allowed to compete. The games have continued every four years since 1896 except during World War II, and they will most likely continue for many years to come.
Comparison	The author explains how two or more things are alike and/or how they are different.	different in contrast alike same as on the other hand	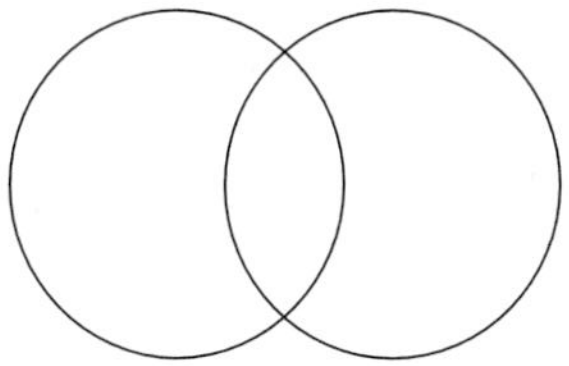	The modern Olympics is very unlike the ancient Olympic games. Individual events are different. While there were no swimming races in the ancient games, for example, there were chariot races. There were no female contestants and all athletes competed in the nude. Of course, the ancient and modern Olympics are also alike in many ways. Some events, such as the javelin and discus throws, are the same. Some people say that cheating, professionalism, and nationalism in the modern games are a disgrace to the Olympic tradition. But according to the ancient Greek writers, there were many cases of cheating, nationalism, and professionalism in their Olympics, too.

Figure 10-1   *continued*

Pattern	Description	Cue Words	Graphic Organizer	Sample Passage
Cause and Effect	The author lists one or more causes and the resulting effect or effects.	*reasons why* *if . . . then* *as a result* *therefore* *because*	Cause → Effect #1, Effect #2, Effect #3	There are several reasons why so many people attend the Olympic games or watch them on television. One reason is tradition. The name *Olympics* and the torch and flame remind people of the ancient games. People can escape the ordinariness of daily life by attending or watching the Olympics. They like to identify with someone else's individual sacrifice and accomplishment. National pride is another reason, and an athlete's or a team's hard earned victory becomes a nation's victory. There are national medal counts and people keep track of how many medals their country's athletes have won.
Problem and Solution	The author states a problems and lists one or more solutions for the problem. A variation of this pattern is the question-and-answer format in which the author poses a question and then answers it.	*problem is* *dilemma is* *puzzle is* *solved* *question . . .* *answer*	Problem → Solution	One problem with the modern Olympics is that it has become very big and expensive to operate. The city or country that hosts the games often loses a lot of money. A stadium, pools, and playing fields must be built for the athletic events and housing is needed for the athletes who come from around the world. And all of these facilities are used for only 2 weeks! In 1984, Los Angeles solved these problems by charging a fee for companies who wanted to be official sponsors of the games. Companies like McDonald's paid a lot of money to be part of the Olympics. Many buildings that were already built in the Los Angeles area were also used. The Coliseum where the 1932 games were held was used again and many colleges and universities in the area became playing and living sites.

395

Even though the expository text structures are used with informational texts, some books that are classified as stories also involve sequence, cause and effect, or one of the other expository text structures. Teachers can point out these structures or use graphic organizers to help students look more closely at the story. The popular *The Very Hungry Caterpillar* (Carle, 1969), for example, involves two sequences. Eric Carle uses sequence to show the development of the caterpillar from egg to butterfly and to list what the caterpillar ate each day. In *The Blue and the Gray* (1996), a story about the construction of a modern interracial community on the site of a Civil War battlefield, Eve Bunting contrasts the misery of the war with the harmony of the neighborhood. The Caldecott Medal book about the riots in Los Angeles, *Smoky Night* (Bunting, 1994), demonstrates cause and effect. Anger causes the riots, and the riots bring hope and understanding. Problem and solution is illustrated in *A New Coat for Anna* (Ziefert, 1986), a story set in war-torn Europe, as Anna's mother makes a series of trades to get a new coat for her daughter.

Teaching Students About Expository Text Structures

Teachers present minilessons about the five expository text structures and show students how to use the organizational patterns to improve their reading comprehension as well as to organize their writing (Flood, Lapp, & Farnan, 1986; McGee & Richgels, 1985; Piccolo, 1987). A list of minilesson topics related to expository text structures is presented on page 397.

The teaching strategy presented in Chapter 1 can be adapted for minilessons on expository text structures. The steps in the minilesson are:

Step
by
Step

1. **Introduce an organizational pattern.**   Explain the pattern and when writers use it; note cue words that signal the pattern. Then share an example of the pattern and describe the graphic organizer for that pattern.

2. **Analyze examples of the pattern in informational books, not in stories.** Figure 10–2 lists books that illustrate each of the five expository text structures. Sometimes the pattern is signaled clearly by means of titles, topic sentences, and cue words, and sometimes it is not. Students learn to identify cue words, and they talk about why writers may or may not explicitly signal the structure. They also diagram the structure using a graphic organizer.

3. **Write paragraphs using the pattern.**   The first writing activity may be a whole-class activity; later, students can write paragraphs in small groups and individually. Students choose a topic, gather information, and organize it using a graphic organizer. Next they write a rough draft of the paragraph, inserting cue words to signal the structure. They revise, edit, and write a final copy of the paragraph. Then they share the paragraphs they have written and explain how they have used the particular organizational pattern in their writing.

4. **Repeat steps 1–3 for each pattern.**   Teachers repeat the first three steps in the teaching strategy to teach each of the five expository text structures.

■ *See Chapter 7, "Listening to Learn," pp. 278–288, for more information on teaching with informational books.*

Reading and Writing Information

	Procedures	Concepts	Strategies and Skills
Expository Text Structures	Identify expository text structures in books Make graphic organizers Write paragraphs using the structures	Informational books Efferent reading Expository text structures Cue words	Vary reading according to purpose Locate information using index Identify expository text structures Note cue words Use graphic organizers
Reports	Read charts, diagrams, and maps Make K-W-L charts Collect data on clusters Collect data on data charts Write collaborative reports Write individual reports Write tables of contents Write bibliographies Compile alphabet books Assess effectiveness of report	Reports versus stories Alphabet books	Design research questions Narrow topics Gather information Organize information Take a stand Summarize Present information in charts
Letters	Write pen pal letters Write courtesy letters Write letters to authors and illustrators Write business letters Write simulated letters Assess effectiveness of letter	Friendly letter format Business letter format	Use letter format correctly Ask questions to elicit information Respond to correspondent's questions
Life-Stories	Make lifelines Make timelines Make "Me" boxes Write "All About Me" books Write autobiographies Write biographies Assess effectiveness of life-story	Life-stories Autobiographies Biographies Phase biographies Contemporary biographies Historical biographies	Choose events to write about Elaborate events Sequence events Add details Add descriptions Include information in illustrations Assume a point of view

Description

Arnosky, J. (1995). *All about owls.* New York: Scholastic. (P–M)

de Bourgoing, P. (1995). *Under the ground.* New York: Scholastic. (P)

Fowler, A. (1990). *It could still be a bird.* Chicago: Childrens Press. (P–M)

Gibbons, G. (1995). *Sea turtles.* New York: Holiday House. (P)

Patent, D. H. (1992). *Feathers.* New York: Cobblehill. (M–U)

Pringle, L. (1995). *Coral reefs: Earth's undersea treasures.* New York: Simon & Schuster. (U)

Wexler, J. (1995). *Sundew stranglers: Plants that eat insects.* New York: Dutton. (U)

Sequence

Aliki. (1992). *Milk from cow to carton.* New York: HarperCollins. (P–M)

Cole, J. (1991). *My puppy is born.* New York: Morrow. (P–M)

Gibbons, G. (1995). *Planet earth/inside out.* New York: Morrow. (M)

Matthews, D. (1995). *Arctic foxes.* New York: Simon & Schuster. (P)

Provensen, A. (1990). *The buck stops here.* New York: HarperCollins. (M–U)

Steltzer, U. (1995). *Building an igloo.* New York: Holt. (P–M)

Wadsworth, G. (1995). *Giant Sequoia trees.* Chicago: Lerner. (P–M)

Comparison

Gibbons, G. (1984). *Fire! Fire!* New York: Harper & Row. (P–M)

Lasker, J. (1976). *Merry ever after: The story of two medieval weddings.* New York: Viking. (M–U)

Markle, S. (1993). *Outside and inside trees.* New York: Bradbury Press. (M)

Munro, R. (1987). *The inside-outside book of Washington, D.C.* New York: Dutton. (M–U)

Rauzon, M. J. (1993). *Horns, antlers, fangs, and tusks.* New York: Lothrop, Lee & Shepard. (P–M)

Sewall, M. (1995). *Thunder from the clear sky.* New York: Atheneum. (M–U)

Singer, M. (1995). *A wasp is not a bee.* New York: Holt. (P)

Spier, P. (1987). *We the people.* New York: Doubleday. (M–U)

Cause and Effect

Branley, F. M. (1985). *Volcanoes.* New York: Harper & Row. (P–M)

Branley, F. M. (1986). *What makes day and night?* New York: Harper & Row. (P–M)

Casey, D. (1995). *Weather everywhere.* New York: Macmillan. (P)

Heller, R. (1983). *The reason for a flower.* New York: Grosset & Dunlap. (M)

Lauber, P. (1995). *Who eats what? Food chains and food webs.* New York: HarperCollins. (M)

Showers, P. (1985). *What happens to a hamburger?* New York: Harper & Row. (P–M)

Souza, D. M. (1994). *Northern lights.* Minneapolis: Carolrhoda. (U)

Zoehfeld, K. W. (1995). *How mountains are made.* New York: HarperCollins. (M)

Problem and Solution

Arnosky, J. (1995). *I see animals hiding.* New York: Scholastic. (P)

Colman, P. (1995). *Rosie the riveter: Women working on the home front in World War II.* New York: Drown. (U)

Geisert, B. (1995). *Haystack.* Boston: Houghton Mifflin. (P)

Heller, R. (1986). *How to hide a whippoorwill and other birds.* New York: Grosset & Dunlap. (P–M)

Johnson, S. A. (1995). *Raptor rescue! An eagle flies free.* New York: Dutton. (M)

Lauber, P. (1990). *How we learned the earth is round.* New York: Crowell. (P–M)

McMillan, B. (1995). *Night of the puffings.* Boston: Houghton Mifflin. (P–M)

Rounds, G. (1995). *Sod houses on the Great Plains.* New York: Holiday House. (M)

Combination

Aliki. (1981). *Digging up dinosaurs.* New York: Harper & Row. (M)

Carrick, C. (1993). *Whaling days.* New York: Clarion. (P–M)

Coombs, K. M. (1995). *Flush! Treating wastewater.* Minneapolis: Carolrhoda. (M–U)

George, J. C. (1995). *Everglades.* New York: HarperCollins. (M)

Guiberson, B. Z. (1991). *Cactus hotel.* New York: Henry Holt. (P–M)

Hoyt-Goldsmith, D. (1992). *Hoang Anh: A Vietnamese-American boy.* New York: Holiday House. (M)

McKissack, P., & McKissack, F. (1995). *Red-tail angels: The story of the Tuskeegee airmen of World War II.* New York: Walker. (U)

Patent, D. H. (1995). *Why mammals have fur.* New York: Cobblehill. (P)

P = primary grades (K–2); M = middle grades (3–5); U = upper grades (6–8).

5. *Choose the most appropriate pattern.* After students have learned to use the five patterns, they need to learn to choose the most appropriate pattern to communicate effectively. Students can experiment to discover the appropriateness of various patterns by writing paragraphs about one set of information using different organizational patterns. For example, information about igloos might be written as a description, as a comparison to Indian tepees, or as a solution to a housing problem in the Arctic.

Assessing Students' Use of Expository Text Structures

Teachers can assess how students use expository text structures to comprehend as they read and listen to informational books read aloud. Students should learn to recognize the structural patterns and use graphic organizers to classify information, take notes, and generalize main ideas. Teachers can monitor students as they participate in discussions about informational books and review students' learning log entries during theme cycles to assess their understanding of key concepts and their use of graphic organizers.

Teachers can also assess how well students organize information when they write paragraphs, reports, and other across-the-curriculum pieces. When students write to present information, they:

- Choose the most appropriate structure
- Develop a graphic organizer before writing
- Write a topic sentence that identifies the structure
- Use cue words to signal the structure

These four components can be used to develop a checklist or rubric to assess students' use of expository text structures.

REPORTS

Often, students are not exposed to report writing until they are faced with writing a term paper in high school, at which point they are overwhelmed with learning how to take notes on notecards, organize and write the paper, and compile a bibliography. There is no reason to postpone report writing until students reach high school. Students in the elementary grades—even in the primary grades—write both class collaboration and individual reports (Duthie, 1994; Krogness, 1987; Queenan, 1986). Early, successful experiences with informative writing teach students about content-area topics as well as how to interview, collect data, and write reports.

Young Children's Reports

Contrary to the popular assumption that young children's first writing is narrative, educators have found that kindergartners and first graders write many nonnarrative compositions in which they provide information about familiar topics, including "Signs of Fall," or directions for familiar activities, such as

"How to Feed Your Pet" (Bonin, 1988; Sowers, 1985). Many of these writings might be termed "All About . . ." books, and others are informational pieces that children dictate for the teacher to record. These two types introduce young children to informational writing.

In young children's "All About . . ." books, they write an entire booklet on a single topic. Usually one piece of information and an illustration appear on each page. A second grader wrote an "All About . . ." book, *Snowy Thoughts,* shown in Figure 10–3. It was written as part of a theme on the four seasons. Even though the student omitted some capital letters and punctuation marks and used invented spelling for a few words in his book, the information can be easily deciphered.

Young children can dictate reports to their teacher, who serves as scribe to record them. After listening to a guest speaker, viewing a film, or reading several books about a particular topic, kindergartners and first graders can dictate brief reports. A class of kindergartners compiled this book-length report on police officers:

Page 1: *Police officers help people who are in trouble. They are nice to kids. They are only mean to robbers and bad people. Police officers make people obey the laws. They give tickets to people who drive cars too fast.*

Page 2: *Men and women can be police officers. They wear blue uniforms like Officer Jerry's. But sometimes police officers wear regular clothes when they work undercover. They wear badges on their uniforms and on their hats. Officer Jerry's badge number is 3407. Police officers have guns, handcuffs, whistles, sticks, and two-way radios. They have to carry all these things.*

Page 3: *Police officers drive police cars with flashing lights and loud sirens. The cars have radios so the officers can talk to other police officers at the police station. Sometimes they ride on police motorcycles or on police horses or in police helicopters or in police boats.*

Page 4: *Police officers work at police stations. The jail for the bad people that they catch is right next door. One police officer sits at the radio to talk to the police officers who are driving their cars. The police chief works at the police station, too.*

Page 5: *Police officers are your friends. They want to help you so you shouldn't be afraid of them. You can ask them if you need some help.*

Page 6: *How We Learned about Police Officers for Our Report*

1. *We read these books:*
   Police by Ray Broekel
   What Do They Do? Policemen and Firemen by Carla Greene
2. *We interviewed Officer Jerry.*
3. *We visited the police station.*

The teacher read two books aloud to the students, and Officer Jerry visited the classroom and talked to the students about his job. The students also took a field trip to the police station. The teacher took photos of Officer Jerry, his police car, and the police station to illustrate the report. With this background, the students and the teacher together developed a cluster with these five main ideas: what police officers do, what equipment police officers have, how police officers travel, where police officers work, and police officers are your friends. The students added details to each main idea until each main idea developed into one page of the report. The background of experiences

Figure 10–3 *A Second Grader's "All About . . ." Book*

and the clustering activity prepared students to compose their report. After students completed the report, included a bibliography called "How We Learned About Police Officers for Our Report," and inserted the photographs, it was ceremoniously presented to the school library to be enjoyed by all students in the school.

Collaborative Reports

A successful first report-writing experience for middle- and upper-grade students is a class collaboration research report. Small groups of students work together to write sections of the report, which are then compiled. Students benefit from writing a group report in two ways: first, because they learn the steps in writing a research report—with the group as a scaffold or support system—before tackling individual reports; and second, because working in groups lets them share the laborious parts of the work.

A group of four fourth graders wrote a collaborative report on hermit crabs. The students sat together at one table and watched hermit crabs in a terrarium. They cared for the crustaceans for two weeks and made notes of their observations in learning logs. After this period the students were bursting with questions about the hermit crabs and were eager for answers. They wanted to know about the crabs' natural habitat, what the best habitat was for them in the classroom, how they breathed air, why they lived in "borrowed" shells, why one pincer was bigger than the other, and so on. Their teacher provided some answers and directed them to books that would provide additional information. As they collected information, they created a cluster that they taped to the table next to the terrarium. The cluster became inadequate for reporting information, so they decided to share their knowledge by writing a book titled *The Encyclopedia About Hermit Crabs*. Chapters from this book and the cluster used in gathering the information appear in Figure 10–4. The students decided to share the work of writing the book, and they chose four main ideas, one for each to write: what hermit crabs look like, how they act, where they really live, and what they eat. One student wrote each section and returned to the group to share the rough draft. The students gave each other suggestions and made revisions based on the suggestions. Next, they edited their report with the teacher and added an introduction, a conclusion, and a bibliography. Finally, they recopied their report and added illustrations in a cloth-bound book, which they read to each class in the school before adding it to the school library.

Students can organize reports in a variety of formats—formats they see used in informational books. One possibility is a question-and-answer format; another possibility is an alphabet book. A group of fourth-grade students wrote an alphabet book about the California missions with one page for each letter of the alphabet. The "U" page appears in Figure 10–5.

Individual Reports

Toby Fulwiler (1985a) recommends that students do "authentic" research in which they explore topics that interest them or hunt for answers to questions that puzzle them. When students become immersed in content-area study, questions arise that they want to explore. A fourth-grade class began a unit on birds by brainstorming questions they wanted to answer. The teacher encouraged them to search for answers in the books they had checked out of the school and community libraries and during an interview with an ornithologist from the local zoo. Once they learned the answers to their questions, the students were eager to share their new knowledge and decided to write reports and publish them as books.

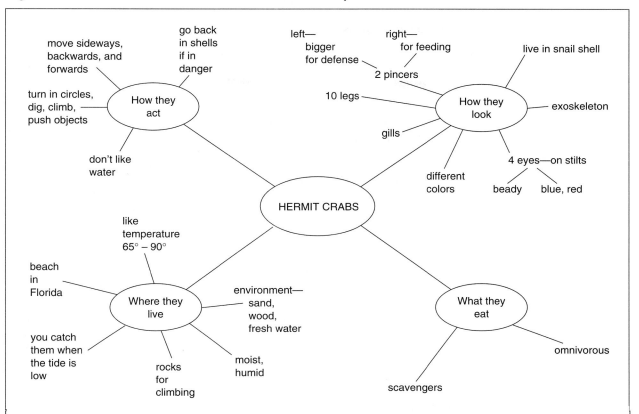

The Encyclopedia About Hermit Crabs

How They Look

Hermit crabs are very much like regular crabs but hermit crabs transfer shells. They have gills. Why? Because they are born in water and when they mature they come to land and kill snails so they can have a shell. They have two beady eyes that look like they are on stilts. Their body is a sight! Their shell looks like a rock. Really it is an exoskeleton which means the skeleton is on the outside. They have two pincers. The left one is bigger so it is used for defense. The right one is for feeding. They also have ten legs.

Where They Live

Hermit crabs live mostly on beaches in Florida where the weather is 65°–90°. They live in fresh water. They like humid weather and places that have sand, wood, and rocks (for climbing on). The best time to catch hermit crabs is a low tide.

What They Eat

Hermit crabs are omnivorous scavengers which means they eat just about anything. They even eat leftovers.

How They Act

Hermit crabs are very unusual. They go back into their shell if they think there is danger. They are funny because they walk sideways, forwards, and backwards. They can go in circles. They can also get up when they get upside down. And that's how they act.

Figure 10–5   *The "U" Page From an Alphabet Book on California Missions*

Some of the Indians thought life was UNBEARABLE at the missions. They thought this because they couldn't hunt or do the things they were used to. Once they were at the missions they couldn't leave. They were sometimes beaten if they did.

Each student's book began with a table of contents, four or five chapters, a glossary, a bibliography, and an index. An excerpt from one fourth grader's book on egrets is presented in Figure 10–6. The text was word-processed, and then the student added the illustrations.

Teaching Students to Write Reports

Students learn how to write reports through experience. As they write "All About . . ." books and collaborative reports, they learn how to search for answers to questions about a topic and then compose a report to share what they have learned. Designing questions and gathering information comprise the prewriting stage; then students draft, polish, and make final copies of their reports. Teachers also present minilessons on procedures, concepts, strategies, and skills related to report writing. See the list of minilesson topics on page 397.

Figure 10–6   *An Excerpt From a Fourth Grader's Report on Egrets.*

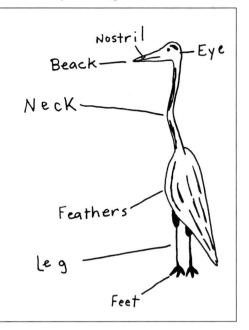

How to Recognize an Egret!

An egret is a bird with white feathers. Some egrets have black and red feathers but the egrets around Marysville are white. They have very long necks and long beaks because they stick their heads under water to catch fish. An egret can be from 20 to 41 inches tall. When they are just standing, they look like in the picture but when they are flying their wing spand can stretch to one-and-a-half feet.

Writing Class Collaboration Reports.   To apply the process approach in writing class collaboration reports, students follow six steps:

Step
by
Step

1. ***Choose a topic.***   The first step is to choose a topic, which should be something students are studying or want to study. Almost any social studies, science, or current events topic that can be subdivided into 4 to 10 parts works well for class collaboration reports. Some possible general topics are oceans, dinosaurs, the solar system, the human body, continents, life in the Middle Ages, and transportation.

    From these general topics, students choose specific topics for small groups or pairs of students to research. For a report on the continents, students choose which continent they will research; for a theme on the solar system, they choose a planet. For a theme such as dinosaurs or the Middle Ages, students may not be able to identify the specific topic they will research until they have learned more and designed research questions.

2. ***Design research questions.***   Research questions emerge as students study a topic. They brainstorm a list of questions on a chart posted in the classroom, and they add to the list as other questions arise. If they are planning a report on the human body, for example, the small groups that are studying each organ may decide to research the same three, four, or five questions: What does the organ look like? What job does the organ do? Where is the organ located in the human body? (Elementary students who research the human body often want to include a question as to whether a person can live without the organ; this interest proba-

bly reflects the current attention in the news media on organ transplants.) Students studying a theme such as the Middle Ages might brainstorm the following questions about life in that era: What did the people wear? What did they eat? What were their communities like? What kind of entertainment did people enjoy? What were their occupations? How did people protect themselves? What kinds of transportation did they use? Each small group selects one of the questions as the specific topic for its report and chooses questions related to the specific topic.

To provide a rehearsal before students research and write their section of the report, the teacher and students may work through the procedure using a research question that no one chose. Together as a class, students gather information, organize it, and write the section of the report using the drafting, revising, and editing stages of the writing process.

3. ***Gather and organize information.***   Students work in small groups or in pairs to search for answers to their research questions. The questions provide the structure for data collection, because students are seeking answers to specific questions, not just randomly writing down information. Students can use clusters or data charts to record the information they gather. The research questions are the same for each data-collection instrument. On a cluster, students add information as details to each main-idea ray; if they are working with data charts, they record information from the first source in the first row under the appropriate question, from the second source in the second row, and so on. These two instruments are effective because they organize the data collection question by question and limit the amount of information that can be gathered from any one source. Students list their sources of information for clusters and data charts on the back of the paper.

■ *See Chapter 8, "Sustaining Talk in the Classroom," p. 325, for an example of a data chart.*

Students gather information from a variety of reference materials, including trade books, textbooks, encyclopedias, magazines, films, videotapes, filmstrips, field trips, interviews, demonstrations, and observations. Teachers often require that students consult two or three different sources and that no more than one source be an encyclopedia.

Report writing has been equated with copying facts out of an encyclopedia, but even elementary students are not too young to understand what plagiarism is and why it is wrong. Even primary-grade students realize they should not "borrow" items belonging to classmates and pretend the items are theirs. Similarly, students should not "borrow" someone else's words, especially without giving credit in the composition. The format of clusters and data charts makes it easier for students to take notes without plagiarizing.

After students gather information, they read it over to check that they have answered their research questions fully and to delete unnecessary or redundant information. Next, they consider how they will sequence the information in their rough drafts. Some students tentatively number the research questions in the order they plan to use them in their composition. They also identify a piece of information that is especially interesting to use as the lead-in to the section.

4. ***Draft the sections of the report.***   Students write their report sections using the process approach to writing. They write the rough draft, skipping every other line to allow space for revising and editing. Because students are working in pairs or

in small groups, one student can be the scribe to write the draft while the other student or students in the group dictate the sentences, using information from a cluster or a data chart. Next, they share their draft with students from other small groups and revise it on the basis of feedback they receive. Last, students proofread and correct mechanical errors.

5. ***Compile the sections.*** Students compile their completed sections of the research report and, as a class, write the introduction, conclusion, and bibliography to add to the report. A list at the end of the report should identify the authors of each section. After all the parts are compiled, students read the entire report aloud to catch inconsistencies or redundant passages.

6. ***Publish the report.*** The last step in writing a class collaboration research report is to publish it. A final copy is made with all the parts of the report in the correct sequence. If the report has been written on a computer, it is easy to print out the final copy; otherwise, the report can be typed or recopied by hand. Copies are made for each student, and special bound copies can be constructed for the class or school library.

Writing Individual Reports. Writing an individual report is similar to writing a collaborative report. Students continue to design research questions, gather information to answer the questions, and compile what they have learned in a report. However, writing individually demands two significant changes: first, students narrow their topics, and second, they assume the entire responsibility for writing the report. The steps are:

Step by Step

1. ***Choose and narrow a topic.*** Students choose topics for research reports from a content area, hobbies, or other interests. After choosing a general topic, such as cats or the human body, they need to narrow the topic so that it is manageable. The broad topic of cats might be narrowed to pet cats or tigers, and the human body to one organ or system.

2. ***Design research questions.*** Students design research questions by brainstorming a list of questions in a learning log. They review the list, combine some questions, delete others, and finally arrive at four to six questions that are worthy of answering. When they begin their research, they may add new questions and delete others if they reach a dead end.

3. ***Gather and organize information.*** As in collaborative reports, students use clusters or data charts to gather and organize information. Data charts, with their rectangular spaces for writing information, serve as a transition for upper-grade students between clusters and notecards.

4. ***Draft the report.*** Students write a rough draft from the information they have gathered. Each research question can become a paragraph, section, or chapter in the report.

5. ***Revise and edit the report.***   Students meet in writing groups to share their rough drafts, and then they make revisions based on the feedback they receive from their classmates. After they revise, students use an editing checklist to proofread their reports and identify and correct mechanical errors.

6. ***Publish the report.***   Students recopy their reports in books and add bibliographic information. Research reports can also be published in several other ways—for example, as a filmstrip or video presentation, as a series of illustrated charts or dioramas, or as a dramatization.

Assessing Students' Reports

Students need to know the requirements for the research project and how they will be assessed or graded. Many teachers distribute a checklist of requirements for the project before students begin working so that the students know what is expected of them and can assume responsibility for completing each step of the assignment. The checklist for an individual report might include these observation behaviors and products:

- Choose a narrow topic.
- Identify four or five research questions.
- Use a cluster to gather information to answer the questions.
- Write a rough draft with a section or a chapter to answer each question.
- Meet in writing groups to share your report.
- Make at least three changes in your rough draft.
- Complete an editing checklist with a partner.
- Add a bibliography.
- Write the final copy of the report.
- Share the report with someone.

The checklist can be simpler or more complex depending on students' ages and experiences. Students staple the checklist to the inside cover of the folder in which they keep all the work for the project, and they check off each requirement as they complete it. A checklist enables students to monitor their own work and learn that writing is a process, not just a final product.

After completing the project, students submit their folders to the teacher for assessment. The teacher considers all the requirements on the checklist in determining a student's grade. If the checklist has 10 requirements, each requirement might be worth 10 points, and the grading can be done objectively on a 100-point scale. Thus, if the student's project is complete, the student scores 100, or a grade of A. Points can be subtracted for work that is sloppy or incomplete.

LETTERS

Letters are a way of talking to people who live too far away to visit. Audience and purpose are important considerations, but form is also important in letter writing. Although letters may be personal, they involve a genuine audience of one or more persons. Students have the opportunity not only to sharpen their writing skills through letter writing but also to increase their awareness of audience. Because letters are written to communicate with a specific and important audience, students take more care to think through what they want to say, to write legibly, and to use spelling, capitalization, and punctuation conventions correctly.

Elementary students' letters are typically classified as friendly or business letters. Formats for friendly and business letters are shown in the Teacher's Notebook on page 410. The choice of format depends on the purpose of the letter. Friendly letters might be informal, chatty letters to pen pals or thank-you notes to a television newscaster who has visited the classroom. When students write to the National Park Service requesting information about the Grand Canyon or another park or send letters to the president expressing an opinion about current events, they use the more formal, business letter style. Before students write both types of letters, they need to learn how to format them.

Friendly and business letter formats are accepted writing conventions, and most teachers simply explain the formats to students and prepare a set of charts to illustrate them. Attention to format should not suggest, however, that form is more important than content; rather, it should highlight formatting considerations of letter writing that elementary students are typically unfamiliar with.

Friendly Letters

After teachers have introduced the format for friendly letters, students need to choose a "real" someone to write to. Writing authentic letters that will be delivered is much more valuable than writing practice letters to be graded by the teacher. Children write friendly letters to classmates, friends who live out of town, relatives, and pen pals. Students may want to keep a list of addresses of people to write friendly letters to on a special page in their journals or in address booklets. In these casual letters, they share news about events in their lives and ask questions to learn more about the person they are writing to and to encourage that person to write back. Receiving mail is the real reward of letter writing!

Students use the writing process in letter writing. In the prewriting stage they decide what to include in their letters. Brainstorming and clustering are effective strategies to help students choose information to include and questions to ask. Figure 10–7 shows a cluster with four rays developed by a third-grade class for pen pal letters. As a class, the students brainstormed a list of possible topics and finally decided on the four main-idea rays (me and my family, my school, my hobbies, and questions for my pen pal). Then students completed the clusters by adding details to each main idea.

Students' rough drafts incorporated the information from one ray into the first paragraph, information from a second ray into the second paragraph, and so on, for the body of the letters. After writing their rough drafts, students met in writing groups to revise content and edit to correct mechanical errors,

Teacher's Notebook
Forms for Friendly and Business Letters

Friendly Letter Form

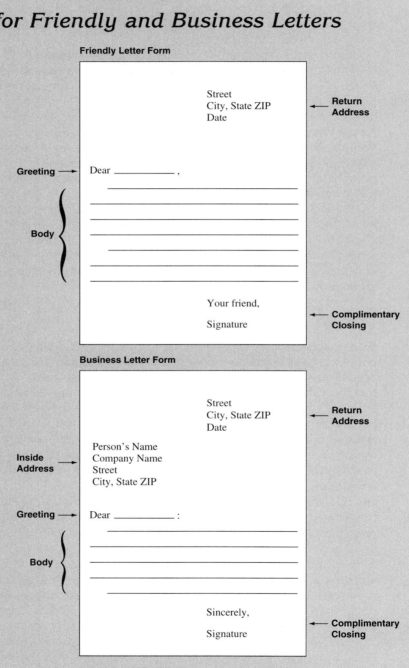

Street
City, State ZIP
Date
→ **Return Address**

Greeting → Dear _____ ,

Body {

Your friend,

Signature
← **Complimentary Closing**

Business Letter Form

Street
City, State ZIP
Date
← **Return Address**

Inside Address → Person's Name
Company Name
Street
City, State ZIP

Greeting → Dear _____ :

Body {

Sincerely,

Signature
← **Complimentary Closing**

Figure 10–7   *A Third Grader's Cluster and Pen Pal Letter*

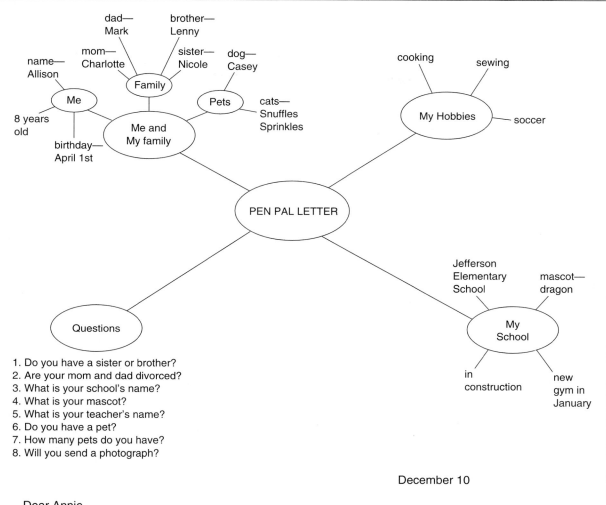

1. Do you have a sister or brother?
2. Are your mom and dad divorced?
3. What is your school's name?
4. What is your mascot?
5. What is your teacher's name?
6. Do you have a pet?
7. How many pets do you have?
8. Will you send a photograph?

December 10

Dear Annie,

I'm your pen pal now. My name is Allison and I'm 8 years old. My birthday is on April 1st.

I go to Jefferson Elementary School. Our mascot is a dragon. We are in construction because we're going to have a new gym in January.

My hobbies are soccer, sewing, and cooking. I play soccer, sewing I do in free time, and I cook dinner sometimes.

My pets are two cats and a dog. The dog's name is Casey and he's a boy. He is two years old. The cat is a girl and her name is Snuffles. She is four years old. The kitten is a girl and her name is Sprinkles. She is two months old.

My dad's name is Mark and my mom's name is Charlotte. Her birthday is the day after Mother's Day. My brother's name is Lenny. He is 13 years old. My sister's name is Nicole. She is 3 years old.

I have some questions for you. Do you have a sister or a brother? Are your mom and dad divorced? Mine aren't. What is your school's name? What is your mascot? What is your teacher's name? Do you have a pet? How many pets do you have? Will you send me a photograph of yourself?

Your friend,
Allison

first with a classmate and later with the teacher. Next, they recopied their final drafts, addressed envelopes, and mailed them. A sample letter is also presented in Figure 10–7. Comparing each paragraph of the letter with the cluster reveals that using the cluster helped the student write a well-organized and interesting letter that was packed with information.

Pen Pal Letters.   Teachers can arrange for their students to exchange letters with students in another class by contacting a teacher in a nearby school or local educational associations, or by answering advertisements in educational magazines.

Another possible arrangement is to have an elementary class become pen pals with college students in a language arts methods class. Over a semester the elementary students and preservice teachers can write back and forth to each other four, five, or six times, and perhaps can even meet each other at the end of the semester. The children have the opportunity to be pen pals with college students, and the college students have the opportunity to get to know an elementary student and examine the student's writing.

In a study by Greenlee, Hiebert, Bridge, and Winograd (1986), a class of second graders became pen pals with a class of college students who were majoring in elementary education. The researchers investigated whether having a genuine audience would influence the quality of the letters the students wrote. They compared the second graders' letters to letters written by a control group who wrote letters to imaginary audiences and received traditional teacher comments on their letters. The researchers found that the students who wrote to pen pals wrote longer and more complex letters once they received responses to their letters. The results of this study emphasize the importance of providing real audiences for student writing.

Courtesy Letters.   Invitations and thank-you notes are two other types of friendly letters that elementary students write. They may write to parents to invite them to an after-school program, to the class across the hall to invite them to visit a classroom exhibit, or to a community person to invite him or her to be interviewed as part of a content-area unit. Similarly, children write letters to thank people who have been helpful.

Letters to Authors and Illustrators.   Students write letters to favorite authors and illustrators to share their ideas and feelings about the books they have read. They ask questions about how a particular character was developed or why the illustrator used a certain art medium. Students also describe the books they have written. Here are letters from fourth graders to Eve Bunting. These letters were written at the end of an author study, after the class had read and responded to eight of her books:

Dear Eve Bunting,
*   I have read some of your books. All of them had friendship in them. My favorite book is* Smoky Night. *I think the theme is get along and respect each other. My family needs to learn to respect each other and to get along because I fight with my brother and he fights with my sister.*

How many picture books have your written? I have read eight of them. Have you ever met Chris Van Allsburg because we did an author study on him also. Why do you write your books?
    Sincerely, Jeffrey

✏ *Dear Eve Bunting,*
    I've read some of your books and I like them all. That's why I wanted to write to you. The Man Who Could Call Down Owls *appealed to me because it's not like the other books. Most of your books are realistic. My favorite sentence from the book is "They came swooping on noiseless wings."*
    I have a few questions to ask you. Are you going to write any more books that have mysteries? I like mysteries. Is the illustrator of The Man Who Could Call Down Owls *an Indian? I think he is because of the way he draws nature. Have you met Jerry Pallotta? I did when he came to our school. Have you written any chapter books? I would like to read some.*
    Your fan, Brad

Most authors and illustrators reply to children's letters when possible, and Eve Bunting answered these fourth graders' letters. However, they receive thousands of letters from children every year and cannot be pen pals with students. Beverly Cleary's award-winning book *Dear Mr. Henshaw* (1983) offers a worthwhile lesson about what students (and their teachers) can realistically expect from authors and illustrators. I suggest the following guidelines for writing to authors and illustrators:

- Follow the correct letter format with return address, greeting, body, closing, and signature.
- Use the process approach to write, revise, and edit the letter. Be sure to proofread and correct errors.
- Recopy the letter so that it will be neat and easy to read.
- Write the return address on both envelope and letter.
- Include a stamped, self-addressed envelope for a reply.
- Be polite in the letter; use the words "please" and "thank you."

Students should write genuine letters to share their thoughts and feelings about the author's writing or the illustrator's artwork, and they should write only to authors and illustrators whose work they are familiar with. In their letters, students should avoid asking personal questions, such as how much money he or she earns. They should not ask for free books, because authors/illustrators usually don't have copies of their books to give away. Students send their letters to the author/illustrator in care of the publisher (the publisher's name appears on the book's title page, and the address usually appears on the copyright page, the page following the title page). If students cannot find the complete mailing address, they can check *Books in Print* or *Literary Market Place,* reference books that are available in most public libraries.

Young Children's Letters. Young children can write individual letters, as the first grader's letter to Goldilocks in Figure 10–8 illustrates. Carrie wrote the letter after reading *The Jolly Postman, or Other People's Letters* (Ahlberg & Ahlberg, 1986), a collection of letters to nursery rhyme and storybook characters. Young children prewrite by drawing pictures before writing. A quick review of how to begin and end letters is also helpful. In contrast with older

Figure 10–8 A First Grader's
Letter to Goldilocks

children's letters, kindergartners and first graders' letters may involve only a single draft, since invented spellings and the artwork may carry much of the message.

Primary-grade students can also compose class collaboration letters. The children brainstorm ideas, which the teacher records on a large chart. After the letter is finished, children add their signatures. They might write collaborative letters to thank community persons who have visited the class, to invite another class to attend a puppet show, or to compliment a favorite author. Class collaboration letters can also serve as pen pal letters to another class.

Business Letters

Students write business letters to seek information, to complain and compliment, and to transact business. They use this more formal letter style and format (as shown in the Teacher's Notebook on page 410) to communicate with businesses, local newspapers, and governmental agencies. Students may write to businesses to order products, to ask questions, and to complain about or compliment specific products; they write letters to the editors of local newspapers and magazines to comment on articles and to express their opinions. It is important that students support their comments and opinions with facts if they hope to have their letters published. Students can also write to local, state, and national government officials to express concerns, make suggestions, or seek information.

Addresses of local elected officials are listed in the telephone directory, and addresses of state officials are available in the reference section of the public library. Here are the addresses of the president and U.S. senators and representatives:

President's name
The White House
Washington, DC 20500

Senator's name
Senate Office Building
Washington, DC 20510

Representative's name
House of Representatives Office
  Building
Washington, DC 20515

Students may also write other types of business letters to request information and free materials. Two sources of free materials are *Freebies for Kids* (Abbett, 1996) and *Free Stuff for Kids* (Lansky, 1996). These books are updated regularly and list hundreds of free or inexpensive materials that elementary students can write for. Children can also write to NASA, the National Wildlife Federation, publishers, state tourism bureaus, and other businesses to request materials.

Simulated Letters

■ *To read more about simulated journals, turn back to Chapter 6, "Writing in Journals," pp. 237–239.*

Students can also write simulated letters, in which they assume the identity of a historical or literary figure. Simulated letters are similar to simulated journals except that they are written as letters using the friendly letter form. Students can write letters as though they were Davy Crockett or another of the men defending the Alamo, or Thomas Edison, inventor of the lightbulb. Students can write from one book character to another; for example, after reading *Sarah, Plain and Tall* (MacLachlan, 1985), students can assume the persona of Sarah and write a letter to her brother William, as a third grader did in this letter:

Dear William,

> *I'm having fun here. There was a very big storm here. It was so big it looked like the sea. Sometimes I am very lonesome for home but sometimes it is very fun here in Ohio. We swam in the cow pond and I taught Caleb how to swim. They were afraid I would leave. Maggie and Matthew brought some chickens.*
> *Love, Sarah*

Even though these letters are never mailed, they are written to a specific audience. Classmates can assume the role of the person to whom the letter is addressed and respond to the letter from that point of view. Also, these letters show clearly how well students comprehend the story, and teachers can use them to monitor students' learning.

Teaching Students to Write Letters

Teachers teach a variety of minilessons so that students will know how to write letters and how the format and style of letters differs from the format and style of stories, informational books, and journals. Topics for minilessons include using the letter-writing forms, focusing on your audience, organizing information in the letter, and asking questions. Teachers also teach mini-lessons on capitalizing proper nouns, addressing an envelope, using para-graphs, and being courteous. See the list of minilesson topics on p. 397 for other topics.

Students use the process approach to write letters so that they can make their letters interesting, complete, and readable. The steps are:

Step by Step

1. ***Gather and organize information for the letter.*** Students participate in prewriting activities, such as brainstorming or clustering, to decide what informa-tion to include in their letters. If they are writing friendly letters, particularly to pen pals, they also identify several questions to include.

2. ***Review the friendly or business letter form.*** Before writing the rough drafts of their letters, students review the friendly or business letter form.

3. ***Draft the letter.*** Students write a rough draft, incorporating the information developed during prewriting and following either the friendly or the business letter style.

4. ***Revise the letter.*** Next, students meet in a writing group to share their rough drafts, receive compliments, and get feedback. They make changes based on the feedback in order to communicate more effectively.

5. ***Edit the letter.*** Students edit their letters with a partner, proofreading to identify errors and correcting as many as possible. They also make sure they have used the appropriate letter format.

6. ***Make the final copy of the letter.*** After making all the mechanical corrections, students recopy their letters and address envelopes. Teachers often review how to address an envelope during this step, too.

7. ***Mail the letter.*** The crucial last step is to mail the letters and wait for a reply.

A variety of books that include letters have been published for children. Some of these are stories with letters that children can take out of envelopes and read. *The Jolly Postman, or Other People's Letters* (Ahlberg & Ahlberg, 1986) and *Dear Peter Rabbit* (Potter, 1995) are collections of let-ters that have been published for children. Ann Turner's *Nettie's Trip South* (1987) is a book-length letter. Figure 10–9 presents a list of books that include letters that teachers can share with students as part of letter-writing activities.

Assessing Students' Letters

Traditionally, students wrote letters and turned them in for the teacher to grade. The letters were returned to the students after they were graded, but they were never mailed. Educators now recognize the importance of having an audience for student writing, and research suggests that students write better when they know that their writing will be read by someone other than the teacher. Whereas it is often necessary to assess student writing, it would be inappropriate for the teacher to put a grade on the letter if it is going to be mailed to someone. Teachers can instead develop a checklist or rubric for evaluating students' letters without marking on them.

A third-grade teacher developed the checklist in Figure 10–10, which identifies specific behaviors and measurable products. The teacher shares the checklist with students before they begin to write so that they know what is expected of them and how they will be graded. At an evaluation conference before the letters are mailed, the teacher reviews the checklist with each student. The letters are mailed without evaluative comments or grades written on them, but the completed checklist goes into students' writing folders. A grading scale can be developed from the checklist; for example, points can be awarded for each check mark in the yes column, or five check marks can be determined to equal a grade of A, four check marks a B, and so on.

Figure 10–9   *Books That Include Letters*

Ahlberg, J., & Ahlberg, A. (1986). *The jolly postman, or other people's letters.* Boston: Little, Brown. (P)

Avi. (1991). *Nothing but the truth.* New York: Orchard. (U)

Cartlidge, M. (1993). *Mouse's letters.* New York: Dutton. (P)

Cartlidge, M. (1995). *Mouse's scrapbook.* New York: Dutton. (P)

Cherry, L. (1994). *The armadillo from Amarillo.* New York: Gulliver Green. (M)

George, J. C. (1993). *Dear Rececca, winter is here.* New York: HarperCollins. (M)

Hample, S. (Comp.) (1993). *Dear Mr. President.* New York: Workman. (M)

Harrison, J. (1994). *Dear bear.* Minneapolis: Carolrhoda. (P)

Heisel, S. E. (1993). *Wrapped in a riddle.* Boston: Houghton Mifflin. (M–U)

Hesse, K. (1992). *Letters from Rifka.* New York: Holt. (U)

Jakobsen, K. (1993). *My New York.* Boston: Little, Brown. (P–M)

James, E., & Barkin, C. (1993). *Sincerely yours: How to write great letters.* New York: Clarion. (M–U)

Johnston, T. (1994). *Amber on the mountain.* New York: Dial. (P–M)

Langen, A., & Droop, C. (1994). *Letters from Felix: A little rabbit on a world tour.* New York: Abbeville Press. (M)

Lyons, M. E. (1992). *Letters from a slave girl: The story of Harriet Jacobs.* New York: Scribner. (U)

Nichol, B. (1994). *Beethoven lives upstairs.* New York: Orchard. (M–U)

Pinkney, A. D. (1994). *Dear Benjamin Banneker.* San Diego: Gulliver/Harcourt Brace. (M)

Potter, B. (1995). *Dear Peter Rabbit.* New York: Warne. (P–M)

Rabbi, N. S. (1994). *Casey over there.* San Diego: Harcourt Brace. (P–M)

Tryon, L. (1994). *Albert's Thanksgiving.* New York: Atheneum. (P)

Turner, A. (1987). *Nettie's trip south.* New York: Macmillan. (M–U)

Woodruff, E. (1994). *Dear Levi: Letters from the Overland Trail.* New York: Knopf. (M–U)

Figure 10–10   A Checklist for Assessing Students' Pen Pal Letters

Pen Pal Letter Checklist

Name _____

	Yes	No
1. Did you complete the cluster?	☐	☐
2. Did you include questions in your letter?	☐	☐
3. Did you put your letter in the friendly letter form?	☐	☐

_____ return address
_____ greeting
_____ 3 or more paragraphs
_____ closing
_____ salutation and name

	Yes	No
4. Did you write a rough draft of your letter?	☐	☐
5. Did you revise your letter with suggestions from people in your writing group?	☐	☐
6. Did you proofread your letter and correct as many errors as possible?	☐	☐

LIFE-STORIES

Elementary students enjoy sharing information about their lives and learning about the lives of well-known personalities. As they read life-stories written for young people, students examine their structure and use the books as models for their own writing. Life-stories combine expository writing with some elements of narration.

Authors use several different approaches in writing autobiographies and biographies (Fleming & McGinnis, 1985). The most common approach is historical; the writer focuses on dates and events and presents them chronologically. Many autobiographies and biographies that span the person's entire life follow this pattern. A second pattern is the sociological approach, wherein the writer describes life during a historical period, providing information about family life, food, clothing, education, economics, transportation, and so on. For instance, *Katie Henio: Navajo Sheepherder* (Thomson, 1995) is a photo documentary that provides a fascinating glimpse into life of this sheepherder in rural New Mexico.

A third approach is psychological: the writer focuses on conflicts the central figure faces. Conflicts may be with oneself, others, nature, or society. The psychological approach has many elements in common with stories and is most often used in shorter autobiographies and biographies that revolve around particular events or phases in the person's life. One example is *You Want Women to Vote, Lizzie Stanton?* (Fritz, 1995), which is about one of the leaders in the women's rights movement. This book focuses on Lizzie Stanton's role in the suffrage movement; it doesn't recount her entire life.

Autobiographies

When students write autobiographies, they relive and document their lives, usually in chronological order. They describe the memorable events that one would need to know about in order to understand them. Autobiographical writing grows out of children's personal journal entries and "All About Me" books that they write in kindergarten and first grade. Students' own experiences and memories are their primary sources of information for writing.

■ *To read more about personal journals, turn to Chapter 6, "Writing in Journals," pp. 224–225.*

"Me" Boxes.   One way for students to reflect on their own lives and identify key events is to make a "Me" box. Students can collect objects and pictures representing their families, their hobbies, events in their lives, and special accomplishments, and then write explanations or reflections to accompany each object. Then students put all the objects in a shoe box, coffee can, or other container and decorate the outside of the container.

"All About Me" Books.   Children in kindergarten and first grade often compile "All About Me" books. These first autobiographies usually list information such as the child's birthday, family members, friends, and favorite activities, with drawings as well as text. Figure 10–11 shows two pages from a first grader's "All About Me" book. To write these books, the children and the teacher first decide on a topic for each page; then, after brainstorming possible ideas for the topic, children draw a picture and write about it. Children

Figure 10–11   *Two Pages from a First Grader's "All About Me" Book*

This is me wen I'm five. I'm reading a book. MY MOM comes in and puts out my Cloths for me to wear but I didn't wat to wear them. I became very picky about my cloths my dad said.

This is my Grammy's house. I have my own room in it. Sometimes I sleep on the love seat. I like to see papa. Sometimes my papa takes me fishing. I love to go fishing. My Grammy makes me feel special.

may also need to ask their parents for information about their birth and events during their preschool years.

Biographies

Biographies are accounts of a person's life written by someone else. Writers try to make the account as accurate and authentic as possible, and to do this they consult a variety of sources of information during their research. The best source, of course, is the biography's subject, and writers can learn many things about the person through an interview. Other primary sources include diaries and letters, photographs, mementos, historical records, and recollections of people who know the person. Examples of secondary sources are books and newspaper articles written by someone other than the biographical subject.

■ *See the section on interviewing in Chapter 8, "Sustaining Talk in the Classroom," pp. 327–329.*

Biographies are categorized as historical or contemporary. Contemporary biographies are written about a living person, especially someone the writer can interview, whereas historical biographies are about persons who are no longer alive.

Contemporary Biographies.   Students write biographies about living people they know personally as well as about famous personalities. In contrast to the primary sources of information available for gathering information about local people, students may have to depend on secondary sources (e.g., books, magazines, newspapers) for information about well-known and geographically more distant persons. Sometimes, however, students can write letters to well-known personalities or perhaps arrange conference telephone calls.

■ *See Chapter 9, "Reading and Writing Stories," p. 372, for more information about author studies.*

Author studies are one type of contemporary biography unit. Students learn about authors as real people by reading autobiographies they have written, viewing videotapes and other media presentations of the authors, reading the books the author has written, and writing letters to the author. Christine Duthie (1994) recommends conducting author studies of people such as Gail Gibbons, who writes informational books. Then teachers can connect the author study with learning about expository text structures, research techniques, interviews, and other concepts related to informational books.

Historical Biographies.   Whereas biographies are based on known facts, some parts of historical biographies must necessarily be fictionalized. Dialogue and other details about daily life, for example, must often be invented after careful research of the period. In *The Double Life of Pocahontas* (Fritz, 1983), for instance, the author had to take what sketchy facts are known about Pocahontas and make some reasonable guesses to fill in the missing links. To give one example, historians know that Pocahontas was a young woman when she died in 1617, but they are unsure how old she was when John Smith and the other English settlers arrived in Virginia in 1607. Fritz chose to make her 11 years old when the settlers arrived.

When students study someone else's life in preparation for writing a biography, they need to become personally involved in the project (Zarnowski, 1988). There are several ways to engage students in biographical study, that is, to help them walk in the subject's footsteps. For contemporary biogra-

These middle-grade students plan a video interview program during which their class-mates will appear as well-know historical persons.

■ *For more information about simulated journals, turn back to Chapter 6, "Writing in Journals," pp. 237–239.*

phies, meeting and interviewing the person is the best way; for other projects, students read books about the person, view films and videos, dramatize events from the person's life, and write about the persons they are studying. An especially valuable activity is writing simulated journals, in which students assume the role of the person they are studying and write journal entries just as that person might have.

Teaching Students to Write Life-Stories

Students learn to write life-stories through a process approach. The teaching strategy is similar for writing autobiographies and biographies, but the two forms are different and should be taught separately. The steps in writing life-stories are:

Step by Step

1. **Read to learn about the format and unique conventions.** Autobiographies and biographies written for children can serve as models for the life-stories students write. Many autobiographies of scientists, entertainers, sports figures, and others are available for upper-grade students, but, unfortunately, only a few autobiographies have been written for younger children. A list of suggested autobiographies appears in Figure 10–12; some are entire-life and others are shorter-event types. When students read autobiographies, they should note which events the narrator focuses on, how the narrator presents information and feelings, and what the narrator's viewpoint is.

Figure 10–12   *Recommended Life-Stories for Elementary Students*

Autobiographies

Bunting, E. (1995). *Once upon a time.* Katonwah, NY: Richard C. Owen. (M)

Caras, R. (1994). *A world full of animals: The Roger Caras story.* New York: Chronicle Books. (U)

Cleary, B. (1995). *My own two feet: A memoir.* New York: Morrow. (U)

de Paola, T. (1989). *The art lesson.* New York: Putnam. (P)

Dewy, J. O. (1995). *Cowgirl dreams: A western childhood.* Honesdale, PA: Boyds Mill. (M–U)

Filipovic, Z. (1994). *Zlata's diary: A child's life in Sarajevo.* New York: Viking. (U)

Fritz, J. (1992). *Surprising myself.* Katonwah, NY: Richard C. Owen. (M)

Gish, L. (1988). *An actor's life for me.* New York: Viking. (U)

Goble, P. (1994). *Hau kola/Hello friend.* Katonah, NY: Richard C. Owen. (M)

Goodall, J. (1988). *My life with the chimpanzees.* New York: Simon & Schuster. (M)

Hopkins, L. B. (1992). *The writing bug.* Katonwah, NY: Richard C. Owen. (M)

Howe, J. (1994). *Playing with words.* Katonah, NY: Richard C. Owen. (M–U)

Keller, H. (1980). *The story of my life.* New York: Watermill Press. (M–U)

Nuynh, Q. N. (1982). *The land I lost: Adventures of a boy in Vietnam.* New York: Harper & Row. (M–U)

O'Kelley, M. L. (1983). *From the hills of Georgia: An autobiography in paintings.* Boston: Little, Brown. (P–M–U)

Polacco, P. (1994). *Firetalking.* Katonah, NY: Richard C. Owen. (M)

Zindel, P. (1992). *The pigman and me.* New York: HarperCollins. (M–U)

Biographies

Adler, D. A. (1992). *A picturebook of Anne Frank.* New York: Holiday House. (P)

Aliki. (1988). *The many lives of Benjamin Franklin.* New York: Simon & Schuster. (M)

Bruchac, J. (1995). *A boy called slow: The true story of Sitting Bull.* New York: Philomel. (P–M)

Freedman, R. (1987). *Lincoln: A photobiography.* New York: Clarion. (M–U)

Fritz, J. (1995). *You want women to vote, Lizzie Stanton?* New York: Putnam. (M)

Gherman, B. (1989). *Agnes de Mille: Dancing off the earth.* New York: Atheneum. (U)

Giblin, J. C. (1992). *George Washington: A picturebook biography.* New York: Scholastic. (P–M)

Golenbock, P. (1990). *Teammates.* San Diego: Harcourt Brace Jovanovich. (P–M)

Harrison, B., & Terris, D. (1992). *A twilight struggle: The life of John Fitzgerald Kennedy.* New York: Lothrop, Lee & Shepard. (M–U)

McKissack, P. C., & McKissack, F. (1992). *Soujourner Truth: Ain't I a woman?* New York: Scholastic. (M–U)

Meltzer, M. (1992). *Thomas Jefferson: The revolutionary aristocrat.* New York: Franklin Watts. (U)

Mitchell, B. (1986). *Click: A story about George Eastman.* Minneapolis: Carolrhoda Books. (M)

Stanley, D., & Vennema, P. (1992). *Bard of Avon: The story of William Shakespeare.* New York: Morrow. (M)

Stevens, B. (1992). *Frank Thompson: Her Civil War story.* New York: Macmillan. (M–U)

Thomson, P. (1995). *Katie Kenio: Navajo sheepherder.* New York: Cobblehill. (M–U)

Biographies of well-known people such as explorers, kings and queens, scientists, sports figures, artists, and movie stars, as well as "common" people who have endured hardship and shown exceptional courage, are available for elementary students to read. Figure 10–12 also lists biographies. Biographers David Adler and Jean Fritz have written many excellent biographies for primary- and middle-grade students, some of which are noted in the list, and numerous authors have written biographies for older students. Students' autobiographies and biographies from previous years are another source of books for your class to read. Students can often be persuaded to bring their prized life-stories back the following year to share with other students.

2. **Gather information for the life-story.** Students gather information about themselves or about the person they will write about in several different ways. Students are the best source of information about their own lives, but they may need to get information from parents and other family members. Parents often share information from baby books and photo albums, and older brothers and sisters can share their remembrances. Another strategy students can use to gather information for an autobiography is to collect objects that symbolize their life and hang them on a "lifeline" clothesline or put them in a life-box made from a shoe box (Fleming, 1985). They can then write briefly about each object, explaining what it is and how it relates to their lives. They can also decorate the box with words and pictures clipped from magazines to create an autobiographical collage.

■ *Review the Pro-File on pp. 384–385 to learn how one kindergarten teacher uses book boxes.*

For biographical writing, students can interview their subject, either in person or by telephone and letter. To write a historical biography, students read books to learn about the person and the time period in which he or she lived. Other sources of information are films, videotapes, and newspaper and magazine articles. Students also need to keep a record of their sources for the bibliography they will include with their biographies.

Students sequence the information they gather—about either their life or someone else's—on a lifeline or timeline. This activity helps students identify and sequence milestones and other events. They can use the information on the lifeline to identify topics for the life-story.

3. **Organize the information for the life-story.** Students select from their lifelines the topics they will write about; then they develop a cluster with each topic as a main idea. They add details from the information they have gathered; if they don't have four or five details for each topic, they can search for additional information. When students aren't sure if they have enough information, they can cluster the topic using the "5 Ws plus one" questions (who, what, where, when, why, and how) and try to answer the six questions. If they can complete the cluster, they are ready to write; if they cannot, they need to gather additional information. After developing the cluster, students decide on the sequence of topics and add an introduction and a conclusion.

4. **Draft the life-story.** Students use the information in their clusters to write their rough drafts. The main ideas become topic sentences for paragraphs, and details are expanded into sentences.

5. **Revise the life-story.** After they write the rough draft, students meet in writing groups to get feedback on their writing; then they make revisions.

6. **Edit and recopy the life-story.** Next, they edit and recopy, adding drawings, photographs, or other memorabilia. Students also add a bibliography to a biography, listing their sources of information.

7. **Publish the life-story.** Students share the final copy of their life-stories with classmates. They can also share what they have learned in other ways. They might dress up as the subject of their biography and tell the person's story, let classmates interview them, write a poem, or make a poster about the person.

Teachers choose topics for minilessons on life-stories based on the needs of their students and the opportunities provided in the reading materials and writing projects. Check the minilesson figure on page 397 for other topics. When fifth graders are reading biographies as part of a theme cycle on the American Revolution, for example, teachers might plan to teach a series of minilessons about life-stories, including these topics:

- The difference between stories and biographies
- How to make a lifeline
- Author information about Jean Fritz
- The difference between phase and life biographies
- Creating a view of life during a historical period using information in a biography
- Interpreting lessons about life from a biography
- Writing simulated journal entries as a historical personality

In these minilessons students apply the information the teacher presents in the biographies they are reading and the response projects they are involved in after reading.

Some minilessons are taught as students begin reading, others while students are reading or after they have read. A minilesson on how to make a lifeline, for example, might be taught as students are beginning to read so that they can then make lifelines about the personalities in their biographies. The lesson about creating a view of life during a historical period might be presented while students are reading so that they can begin to note descriptions in the book. Minilessons on interpreting lessons about life and writing simulated journal entries might be taught during the exploring stage of the reading process to help students develop and refine their interpretations of the biography.

Assessing Students' Life-Stories

Students need to know the requirements for their autobiography or biography project, as well as how they will be assessed or graded. A checklist for an autobiography might include the following components:

- Make a lifeline showing at least one important event for each year of your life.
- Draw a cluster showing at least three main-idea topics and at least five details for each topic.
- Write a rough draft with an introduction, three or more chapters, and a conclusion.
- Meet in a writing group to share your autobiography.
- Make at least three changes in your rough draft.
- Complete an editing checklist with a partner.
- Write a final copy with photos or drawings as illustrations.
- Compile your autobiography as a book.
- Decorate the cover.

The checklist for a biography might list the following requirements:

- Learn about the person's life from at least three sources (and no more than one encyclopedia).
- Make a lifeline listing at least 10 important events.

Adapting
Reading and Writing Information
To Meet the Needs of Every Student

1. Examine Informational Books

Informational books are organized differently than stories, and they often have unique conventions. Teachers can help students examine this genre and compare these books with stories so that they can recognize the differences.

2. Compare Aesthetic and Efferent Reading

Students read informational books efferently to locate specific information, and aesthetically for the lived-through experience of reading. Too often, less fluent readers read efferently and assume that they must read the entire book and remember everything, even when they are reading to locate a specific piece of information. These students need to learn how to assume an efferent stance to locate specific information and an aesthetic stance at other times.

3. Write "All About . . ." Books

Less experienced writers can write "All About . . ." books. In these books students write information they are learning during theme cycles or information about hobbies. Because students draw a picture and write only a sentence or two on each page, they are able to complete the project before they lose interest or become frustrated.

4. Write Authentic Letters

Teachers can arrange for students to write friendly and business letters so that students can have the experience of writing to a real audience. Receiving a reply is one of the best ways to stimulate students' interest in writing!

5. Write Collaborative Biographies

Students work together to write collaborative biographies, with each student writing one page. They identify important events in the person's life. Each student writes about one event. Then the pages are compiled for the book.

- Write at least 10 simulated journal entries as the person you are studying.
- Make a cluster with at least three main-idea topics and at least five details for each topic.
- Write a rough draft with at least three chapters and a bibliography.
- Meet in a writing group to share your biography.
- Make at least three changes in your rough draft.
- Complete an editing checklist with a partner.
- Recopy the biography.

Students keep the checklist in their project folders and check off each item as it is completed; at the end of the project, they submit the folders to be assessed or graded. Teachers can award credit for each item on the checklist, as I discussed in the section on assessing students' research reports. This approach helps students assume greater responsibility for their own learning and gives them a better understanding of why they receive a particular grade.

Adapting to Meet the Needs of Every Student

Teachers can make adaptations as students read and write informational books so that every student can be successful. A list of recommendations is presented on page 425. It is important to teach students about the genre of informational books and the unique conventions these books have to help readers—including diagrams, glossaries, and indexes. Students also need to learn about the five expository text patterns because research has shown that less fluent readers are not as conscious of them as better readers are. Informational books are available on a wide variety of topics and at a range of reading levels, so selecting reading materials to meet the needs of every student should not be too difficult.

Students can write a variety of reports, ranging from posters and "All About . . ." books to more formal individual reports. Teachers should choose a format that is appropriate for their students. For letter writing, too, students can write group letters or dictate letters. What is most important is that students write authentic letters that are mailed. Receiving a reply makes the work that goes into writing a letter worthwhile. Teachers can coordinate letter-writing activities with theme cycles, literature focus units, or pen pals.

Too often, less capable readers don't have opportunities to read life-stories, but there are many interesting picture book biographies. All students should have opportunities to read these books and to write their own autobiographies. "Me" boxes are a good alternative for young children and for other children who find it difficult to sustain writing an entire autobiography.

Review

Recent research suggests that reading and writing information may be as primary as reading and writing stories. Three types of informational texts that elementary students read and write are reports and other informational books, letters, and life-stories. Important concepts presented in this chapter include:

1. Students read informational books to learn information, and they write informational books to share information with others.
2. Students may use either efferent or aesthetic reading when reading informational books, depending on their purpose for reading.
3. Informational writing is organized into five expository text patterns: description, sequence, comparison, cause and effect, and problem and solution.
4. Students use their knowledge of expository text structures when reading and writing informational books.
5. Students write both collaborative and individual reports using the writing process.

6. Students can organize reports in a variety of formats, include posters, alphabet books, and question-and-answer books.
7. The friendly and business letters that students write should be mailed to authentic audiences.
8. Student write simulated letters in connection with literature focus units and social studies and science theme cycles.
9. Students write autobiographies about events in their own lives and write biographies about both historical and contemporary personalities.
10. Students use the writing process to write reports, letters, autobiographies, and biographies.

Extensions

1. Follow the guidelines in this chapter to write a class collaboration report with a group of elementary students on a social studies topic, such as modes of transportation, types of houses, or ancient civilizations, or on a science topic, such as the solar system, water, or the human body.

2. Choose a topic related to teaching language arts in the elementary school, such as writing in journals, aesthetic and efferent reading, the writing process, or the uses of drama. Research the topic following the guidelines in this chapter and write an "All About . . ." book or a report that you can share with the students in your university language arts class or the elementary students you teach.

3. Have students interview a community leader and then write a collaborative biography.

4. Arrange for a group of students to write friendly letters to pen pals in another school. Review the friendly letter form and how to address an envelope. Use the writing process, in which students draft, revise, and edit their letters before mailing them.

5. Have a small group of students develop a lifeline for a historical personality or other famous person, choose several events from the lifeline to write about, and compile the writings to form a biography.

6. Read one of the biographies or autobiographies listed in Figure 10–12. Then develop a lifeline or a cluster about the subject's life.

PRO-File
Seventh Graders Read and Write Poems

" My seventh graders think they don't like poetry. Then we read lots of poems by Shel Silverstein, Jack Prelutsky, and others, and the students discover that poetry can be fun! "

Sandy Harris
Seventh-Grade Teacher
Anadarko Middle School

PROCEDURE

I bring at least 50 books of poetry into the classroom. I share some of my favorites, and soon the students bring their favorites to read aloud to the class. The seventh graders invite each other to comment on the poetry they read aloud. Some of our favorite poems are listed in the accompanying figure, and I share Karla Kuskin's "Take a Word Like Cat," Mary O'Neill's "Feelings About Words," and other poems in *Inner Chimes: Poems on Poetry* (Goldstein, 1992) during the mini-lessons that I teach.

I start the school year with a unit on poetry because I can demonstrate the writing process without getting bogged down in extensive revision and editing work, as often happens with longer compositions. The experience my students have reading and sharing poetry and discussing their favorites is reflected in the comments I hear them making in writing groups.

I've taken many of my ideas from Kenneth Koch's *Rose, Where Did You Get That Red?*

(1990). One poetry writing activity my students enjoy is creating "model" poems; for example, I read William Blake's "The Tyger," and my students try their hands at writing poems in which they speak directly to an animal. Like Blake, they try to create strong images. One of my students wrote this poem in which he talks to an eagle:

Eagle, is it the color you see from the sky, or is it the movement that catches your eye?

Eagle, at what moment do you know
as you dive from the sky,
precisely when something will die?

Eagle, do you have fear
while you dive and peal,
or might your nerves be made of steel?

Eagle, what are your thoughts,
as your claws and beak
prepare the main course?

Eagle, do you know
as you perch majestically on the tree,
that you represent our country's liberty?

After drafting their poems, students refine them in writing groups; then they meet with me for editing. Finally, students recopy their poems. For this activity, I'm working with the art teacher, and my students will make papier-mâché animals to accompany their poems.

Our Favorite Books of Poetry

Dakos, K. (1990). *If you're not here, please raise your hand: Poems about school.* New York: Macmillan. (Also *Don't read this book, whatever you do! More poems about school* by the same author)

Eliot, T. S. (1967). *Old Possum's book of practical cats.* New York: Harcourt Brace Jovanovich.

Fleischman, P. (1988). *Joyful noise: Poems for two voices.* New York: Harper & Row. (Also *I am phoenix* by the same author)

Frost, R. (1988). *Birches.* New York: Henry Holt.

Janeczko, P. B. (1993). *Looking for your name: A collection of contemporary poems.* New York: Orchard.

Jones, H. (1993). *The trees stand shining: Poetry of the North American Indians.* New York: Dial.

Lobel, A. (1983). *The book of pigericks.* New York: Harper & Row.

Longfellow, H. W. (1990). *Paul Revere's ride.* New York: Dutton.

Noyes, A. (1983). *The highwayman.* New York: Lothrop, Lee & Shepard.

O'Neill, M. (1989). *Hailstones and halibut bones.* New York: Doubleday.

Prelutsky, J. (1984). *The new kid on the block.* New York: Greenwillow.

Sandburg, C. (1982). *Rainbows are made: Poems by Carl Sandburg.* San Diego: Harcourt Brace Jovanovich. (Also Sandburg's *Arithmetic* illustrated by Ted Rand)

Siebert, D. (1989). *Heartland.* New York: Crowell.

Silverstein, S. (1974). *Where the sidewalk ends.* New York: Harper & Row.

Soto, G. (1992). *Neighborhood odes.* San Diego: Harcourt Brace Jovanovich.

ASSESSMENT

Before writing these "Talk to the Animals" poems, the students and I make a checklist of the components they should include. In these poems, they were to (1) speak directly to an animal, (2) ask the animal a question in each stanza, and (3) create a strong visual image in each stanza. Almost every student is successful using this approach. I think identifying the criteria before the students begin and having them meet in writing groups make the difference. In writing groups, students check each poem against the criteria and offer suggestions to authors on how to revise their poems if they don't meet the criteria.

ADAPTATIONS

"Talking to the Animals" is only one type of poem that my students write. Other forms that I've taken from *Rose, Where Did You Get That Red?* and used are:

- Writing invitation poems following the model of Shakespeare's "Come Unto These Yellow Sands"
- Writing about a common thing from a number of perspectives following the model of Wallace Stevens's "Thirteen Ways of Looking at a Blackbird"
- Writing an apology for something you are secretly glad that you did following the model of William Carlos Williams's "This Is Just to Say"
- Writing a quiet poem following the model of D. H. Lawrence's "The White Horse"
- Writing a shape poem following the model of Guillaume Apolliaire's shape poems

REFLECTIONS

By observing the poems my students choose to share, I get a clearer idea of their preferences. By beginning from a base that is popular with the students, I can extend their appreciation to more sophisticated poetry—even Blake and Shakespeare. I begin with their choices, and before long my students—even the "jocks"—are reading poetry and enjoying it. Then when the students write poems, I use models and other formulas so they can be successful. The formulas provide the skeleton so that students can concentrate on creating images and using interesting words. I de-emphasize rhyme because it often gets in the way when my students write.

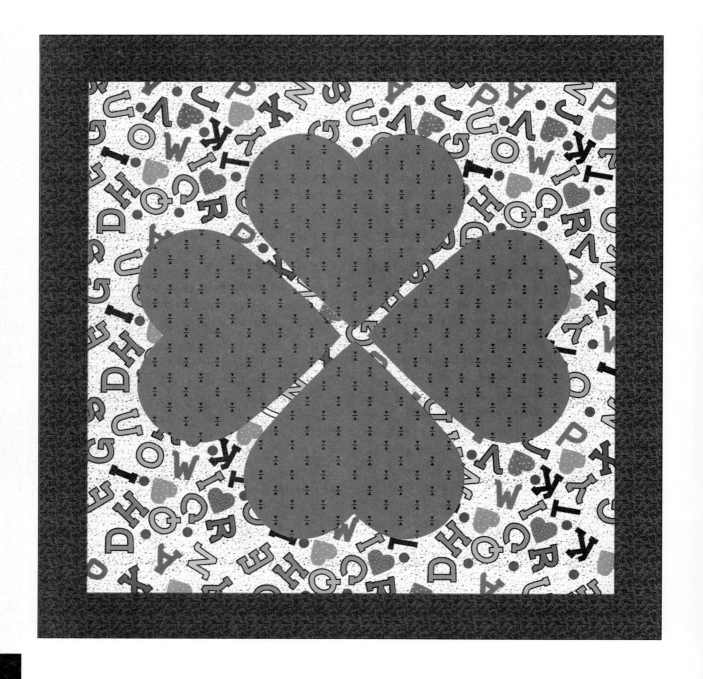

Reading and Writing Poetry

As part of a theme cycle on pioneer life, students in Susan Zumwalt's third-grade class learned to quilt. They made heart books with quilted covers. Mrs. Zumwalt told the students that quilting was close to her heart, and she invited her students to write about things that were close to their hearts in their heart books. Several children wrote about quilting. One student wrote, "I love to make quilts. With my whole heart I quilt. I sew under and over and into my heart. Quilts, you are soft and pretty. You comfort my heart."

oetry "brings sound and sense together in words and lines," according to Donald Graves, "ordering them on the page in such a way that both the writer and reader get a different view of life" (1992, p. 3). Children are natural poets, and poetry surrounds them as they chant jump-rope rhymes on the playground, clap out the rhythm of favorite poems, and dance in response to songs and their lyrics. Larrick (1991) believes that we enjoy poetry because of the physical involvement that the words evoke. Also, people play with words as they invent rhymes and ditties, create new words, and craft powerful comparisons.

No longer is poetry confined to rhyming verse about daffodils, clouds, and love. Both adult and child poets write poems on every imaginable subject—grasshoppers, fire trucks, boa constrictors, spaghetti and meatballs, Jupiter, and grandfathers. These poems tell stories, create images and moods, make us laugh or cry, develop our sense of wonder, and show us the world in a new way (Cullinan, Scala, & Schroder, 1995). The definition of poetry, too, has broadened to include songs and raps, word pictures, memories, riddles, observations, questions, odes, and rhymes.

In a recent article in *Language Arts,* Lisa Siemens (1996) describes how her primary-grade students are immersed in reading and writing poetry. She makes poetry the core of her language arts program, and her students respond enthusiastically. She shares four of her students' descriptions of poetry. One child writes:

A poem is like a big green
dragon waiting to blow
fire at the knight who
seeks the treasure. (p. 239)

Another child shares:

Poems are words
that you feel and
mumble jumble
words too,
also words that float
around in your head. (p. 239)

A third child explains:

I think poetry is when you wake up and see the sun racing above from the clouds. Poetry is when sunlight and moon shines up together. Poetry is when you go to Claude Monet's garden for the first time and everything is breathtaking. That is what I think poetry is. (p. 239)

Sometimes poems are "a garden of words . . . planted in neat rows, but then again, [they] grow wild and free," according to Nancy Cecil (1994, p. 3). Concrete poems, for example, are drawn like pictures on a page, hink-pinks are brief rhyming question-and-answer poems, and found poems are collections of words culled from other texts and arranged on a page. Other poems are written for two readers, and they are arranged in two columns to be read like a musical duet. Possible topics for poems and ways for arranging them on a page are nearly limitless.

The focus of this chapter is on involving students with wordplay and poetry. As you read this chapter, think about these questions:

- How do teachers encourage students to play with words and express ideas using figurative language?
- How do students read and respond to poems?
- What kinds of poems do students write?
- How can teachers incorporate poetry activities in literature focus units, reading and writing workshop, and theme cycles?

PLAYING WITH WORDS

Poet and teacher Georgia Heard calls language "the poet's paint" (1989, p. 65). As students experiment with words, they learn to create images, play with words, and evoke feelings. They laugh with language, experiment with rhyme, and invent new words. These activities provide students with a rich background of experiences for reading and writing poetry, and they gain confidence in choosing the "right" word to express an idea, emphasizing the sounds of words, and expressing familiar ideas with fresh comparisons. Figure 11–1 lists wordplay books that elementary students enjoy.

Laughing With Language

As children learn that words have the power to amuse, they enjoy reading, telling, and writing riddles and jokes. Linda Gibson Geller (1985) researched children's humorous language and identified two stages of riddle play that elementary students move through. Primary-grade children experiment with the riddle form and its content, and middle- and upper-grade students explore the paradoxical constructions in riddles. Riddles are written in a question-and-answer format, but young children at first may only ask questions, or ask questions and offer unrelated answers. With more experience, students both provide questions and give related answers, and their answers may be either descriptive or nonsensical. An example of a descriptive answer is *Why did the turtle go out of his shell? Because he was getting too big for it;* a nonsensical answer involving an invented word for the riddle *Why did the cat want to catch a snake?* is *Because he wanted to turn into a rattlecat* (Geller, 1981, p. 672). Many primary-grade students' riddles seem foolish by adult standards, but wordplay is an important precursor to creating true riddles.

Riddles depend on using metaphors and on manipulating words with multiple meanings or similar sounds. The Opies (1959) identified five riddle strategies used by elementary students:

1. **Using multiple referents for a noun:** What has an eye but cannot see? *A needle.*
2. **Combining literal and figurative interpretations for a single phrase:** Why did the kid throw the clock out the window? *Because he wanted to see time fly.*
3. **Shifting word boundaries to suggest another meaning:** Why did the cookie cry? *Because its mother was a wafer/away for so long.*
4. **Separating a word into syllables to suggest another meaning:** When is a door not a door? *When it's ajar/a jar.*
5. **Creating a metaphor:** What are polka dots on your face? *Pimples.*

Figure 11-1 *Wordplay Books for Elementary Students*

Agee, J. (1992). *Go hang a salami! I'm a lasagna hog! and other palindromes.* New York: Farrar Straus & Giroux. (U)

Barrett, J. (1983). *A snake is totally tail.* New York: Atheneum. (P–M)

Bayer, J. (1984). *A my name is Alice.* New York: Dial. (P–M)

Bierhorst, J. (Ed.). (1992). *Lightning inside you: And other Native American riddles.* New York: Morrow. (M–U)

Brown, M. (1983). *What do you call a dumb bunny? And other rabbit riddles, games, jokes, and cartoons.* Boston: Little, Brown. (P–M)

Cole, J. & Calmenson, S. (1995). *Yours till banana splits: 201 autograph rhymes.* New York: Morrow. (M–U)

Cox, J. A. (1980). *Put your foot in your mouth and other silly sayings.* New York: Random House. (P–M)

Degen, B. (1983). *Jamberry.* New York: Harper & Row. (P)

Degen, B. (1996). *Sailaway home.* New York: Scholastic. (P)

Eiting, M., & Folsom, M. (1980). *Q is for duck: An alphabet guessing game.* New York: Clarion. (P–M)

Esbensen, B. J. (1986). *Words with wrinkled knees.* New York: Crowell. (M–U)

Fakih, K. O. (1995). *Off the clock: A lexicon of time words and expressions.* New York: Clarion. (M)

Gwynne, F. (1970). *The king who rained.* New York: Dutton. (M–U)

Gwynne, F. (1976). *A chocolate moose for dinner.* New York: Dutton. (M–U)

Gwynne, F. (1980). *The sixteen hand horse.* New York: Prentice-Hall. (M–U)

Gwynne, F. (1988). *A little pigeon toad.* New York: Simon & Schuster. (M–U)

Hall, F., & Friends. (1985). *Sniglets for kids.* Yellow Springs, OH: Antioch. (M–U)

Hall, K., & Eisenberg, L. (1992). *Spacey riddles.* New York: Dial. (P)

Hanson, J. (1972). *Homographic homophones. Fly and fly and other words that look and sound the same but are as different in meaning as bat and bat.* Minneapolis: Lerner. (M)

Hartman, V. (1992). *Westward ho ho ho! Jokes from the wild west.* New York: Viking. (M–U)

Houget, S. R. (1983). *I unpacked my grandmother's trunk: A picture book game.* New York: Dutton. (P–M)

Juster, N. (1982). *Otter nonsense.* New York: Philomel. (P–M)

Kellogg, S. (1987). *Aster Aardvark's alphabet adventures.* New York: Morrow. (P–M)

Lewis, J. P. (1996). *Riddle-icious.* New York: Knopf. (M)

Maestro, G. (1984). *What's a frank Frank? Tasty homograph riddles.* New York: Clarion. (P–M)

McMillan, B. (1990). *One sun: A book of terse verse.* New York: Holiday House. (M)

Merriam, E. (1992). *Fighting words.* New York: Morrow. (P–M)

Most, B. (1992). *Zoodles.* San Diego: Harcourt Brace Jovanovich. (M)

Perl, L. (1988). *Don't sing before breakfast, don't sing in the moonlight.* New York: Random House. (M–U)

Rees, E. (1995). *Fast Freddie frog and other tongue twister rhymes.* Honesdale, PA: Wordsong. (P)

Schwartz, A. (1973). *Tomfoolery: Trickery and foolery with words.* Philadelphia: Lippincott. (M–U)

Schwartz, A. (1982). *The cat's elbow and other secret languages.* New York: Farrar, Straus & Giroux. (M–U)

Schwartz, A. (1992). *Busy buzzing bumblebees and other tongue twisters.* New York: HarperCollins. (P–M)

Smith, W. J., & Ra, C. (1992). *Behind the king's kitchen: A roster of rhyming riddles.* Honesdale, PA: Wordsong. (M–U)

Steig, J. (1992). *Alpha beta chowder.* New York: HarperCollins. (P–M)

Sterne, N. (1979). *Tyrannosaurus wrecks: A book of dinosaur riddles.* New York: Crowell. (M)

Terban, M. (1982). *Eight ate: A feast of homonym riddles.* New York: Clarion. (P–M)

Terban, M. (1983). *In a pickle and other funny idioms.* New York: Clarion. (M)

Terban, M. (1985). *Too hot to hoot: Funny palindrome riddles.* New York: Clarion. (M–U)

Terban, M. (1992). *Funny you should ask: How to make up jokes and riddles with wordplay.* New York: Clarion. (M–U)

Terban, M. (1995). *Time to rhyme: A rhyming dictionary.* Honesdale, PA: Wordsong. (M)

Van Allsburg, C. (1987). *The z was zapped.* Boston: Houghton Mifflin. (M)

Wilbur, R. (1995). *Runaway opposites.* San Diego: Harcourt Brace. (P)

Zalben, J. B. (1992). *Lewis Carroll's Jabberwocky.* Honesdale, PA: Boyds Mills Press. (M–U)

P = primary grades (K–2); M = middle grades (3–5); U = upper grades (6–8).

Children begin riddle play by telling familiar riddles and reading riddles written by others. Several excellent books of riddles to share with elementary students are *Tyrannosaurus Wrecks: A Book of Dinosaur Riddles* (Sterne, 1979), *What Do You Call a Dumb Bunny? And Other Rabbit Riddles, Games, Jokes, and Cartoons* (Brown, 1983), and *Eight Ate: A Feast of Homonym Riddles* (Terban, 1982). Soon children are composing their own by adapting riddles they have read; others turn jokes into riddles.

A third grader wrote this riddle using two meanings for Milky Way: *Why did the astronaut go to the Milky Way? Because he wanted a Milky Way Bar.* Terry, a fifth grader, wrote this riddle using the homophones *hair* and *hare: What is gray and jumpy and on your head? A gray hare!* The juxtaposition of words is important in many jokes and riddles.

Creating Word Pictures

In the primary grades, children learn to place words in horizontal lines from left to right and top to bottom across a sheet of paper just as the lines on this page are printed; however, they can break this pattern and create word pictures by placing words as they would draw lines in a drawing. These word pictures can be single-word pictures or a string of words or a sentence arranged in a picture.

Students use words instead of lines to draw a picture, as the *rabbit* picture in Figure 11–2 illustrates. Students first draw a picture with lines, then place a second sheet of paper over the drawing and replace all or most of the lines with repeated words. Students write descriptive words so that the arrangement, size, and intensity of the letters in the word illustrate the meaning. The word *nervous* is written concretely in Figure 11–2. Students can also write the names of objects and animals, such as *bird,* concretely, illustrating features of the named item through the style of the letters. Students can compose a descriptive phrase or sentence and write it in the shape of an object, as the ice-cream cone in Figure 11–2 illustrates. An asterisk indicates where to start reading the sentence picture.

Experimenting With Rhyme

Because of their experience with Dr. Seuss stories, finger plays, and nursery rhymes, kindergartners and first graders enjoy creating rhymes. When it comes naturally, rhyme adds a delightful quality to children's writing, but when it is equated with poetry, it can get in the way of wordplay and vivid images. The following three-line poem shows a fifth grader's effective use of rhyme:

Thoughts After a 40-Mile Bike Ride

My feet
And seat
Are beat.

A small group of first graders created their own version of *Oh, A-Hunting We Will Go* (Langstaff, 1974). After reading the book, they identified the refrain (lines 1, 2, and 5) and added their own rhyming couplets:

Oh, a-hunting we will go,   *1*
a-hunting we will go.   *2*
We'll catch a little bear
and curl his hair,
and never let him go.   *5*
Oh, a-hunting we will go,
a-hunting we will go.
We'll catch a little mole
and put him in a hole,
and never let him go.
Oh, a-hunting we will go,
a-hunting we will go.
We'll catch a little bug
and give him a big hug
and never let him go.
Oh, a-hunting we will go,
a-hunting we will go.
We'll catch a little bunny
and fill her full of honey,
and never let her go.
Oh, we'll put them in a ring
and listen to them sing
and then we'll let them go.

The first graders wrote this collaboration with the teacher taking dictation on a large chart. After the rough draft was written, students reread it, checking the rhymes and changing a word here or there. Then each student chose one stanza to copy and illustrate. The pages were collected and compiled to make

Fifth graders work together to write a new version of a rhyming book.

Figure 11–2   *Students' Word Pictures*

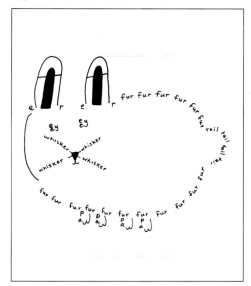

written concretely

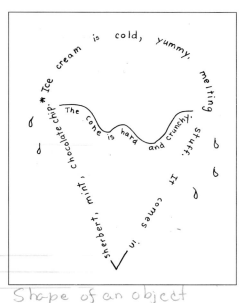

Bird written concretely through styles of letters   *Shape of an object*

a book. Students shared the book with their classmates, with each student reading his or her "own" page.

Hink-pinks are short rhymes that either take the form of an answer to a riddle or describe something. Hink-pinks are composed with 2 one-syllable rhyming words; they are called hinky-pinkies when 2 two-syllable words are used, and hinkity-pinkities with 2 three-syllable words (Geller, 1981). Two examples of these rhymes are:

Ghost	What do you call an astronaut?
White	A sky guy.
Fright	

Other Poetic Devices

Poets choose words carefully. They craft powerful images when they use unexpected comparisons, repeat sounds within a line or stanza, imitate sounds, and repeat words and phrases. These techniques are poetic devices, and as students learn about the devices they appreciate the poet's ability to manipulate the device in poems they read and apply the device in their own writing (Cullinan et al., 1995). The terminology is also helpful in response groups when students talk about poems they have read, and in writing groups so that students can compliment classmates on the use of a device or suggest that they try a particular device when they revise their writing.

Comparison.   One way to describe something is to compare it to something else. Students can compare images, feelings, and actions to other things using two types of comparisons—similes and metaphors. A simile is an explicit comparison of one thing to another—a statement that one thing is like something else. Similes are signaled by the use of *like* or *as*. In contrast, a metaphor compares two things by implying that one is something else, without using *like* or *as*. Differentiating between the two terms is less important than using comparisons to make writing more vivid; for example, children can compare anger to a thunderstorm. Using a simile, they might say, "Anger is like a thunderstorm, screaming with thunder-feelings and lightning-words." Or, as a metaphor, they might say, "Anger is a volcano, erupting with poisonous words and hot-lava actions."

Students begin by learning traditional comparisons and idioms, and they learn to avoid stale comparisons, such as "high as a kite," "butterflies in your stomach," and "light as a feather." Then they invent fresh, unexpected comparisons. A sixth grader uses a combination of expected and unexpected comparisons in this poem:

People

People are like birds
who are constantly getting their feathers ruffled.
People are like alligators
who find pleasure in evil cleverness.
People are like bees
who are always busy.
People are like penguins
who want to have fun.
People are like platypuses—
unexplainable!

Alliteration.   Alliteration is the repetition of the initial consonant sound in consecutive words or in words in close proximity. Repeating the initial sound makes poetry fun to read, and children enjoy reading and reciting alliterative verses like *A My Name is Alice* (Bayer, 1984) and *The Z Was Zapped* (Van Allsburg, 1987). After reading one of these books, children can create their own versions. A fourth-grade class created its own version of Van Allsburg's book, which they called *The Z Was Zipped*. Students divided into pairs, and each pair composed two pages for the class book. Students illustrated their letter on the front of the paper and wrote a sentence on the back to describe their illustra-

Figure 11–3   *Two Pages From* The Z Was Zipped, *a Book of Alliterations*

tion, following Van Allsburg's pattern. Two pages from the book are shown in Figure 11–3. Before reading the sentences, examine the illustrations and try to guess the sentences. These are the students' alliterative sentences:

> *The D got dunked by the duck.*
> *The T was totally terrified.*

Tongue twisters are an exaggerated type of alliteration in which every word (or almost every word) in the twister begins with the same letter. Dr. Seuss compiled an easy-to-read collection of tongue twisters for primary-grade students in *Oh Say Can You Say?* (1979). Anita Lobel's *Alison's Zinnia* (1990) and Kellogg's *Aster Aardvark's Alphabet Adventures* (1987) are two good books of tongue twisters for middle- and upper-grade students. Practice with tongue twisters and alliterative books increases children's awareness of the poetic device in poems they read and write. Few students consciously think about adding alliteration to a poem they are writing, but they get high praise in writing groups when classmates notice an alliteration and compliment the writer on it.

Onomatopoeia.   Onomatopoeia is a device in which poets use sound words to make their writing more sensory and more vivid. Sound words (e.g., *crash, slurp, varoom, me-e-e-ow*) sound like their meanings. Students can compile a list of sound words they find in stories and poems and display the list on a classroom chart or in their language arts notebooks to refer to when they write their own poems.

Spier has compiled two books of sound words; *Gobble Growl Grunt* (1971) is about animal sounds, and *Crash! Bang! Boom!* (1972) is about the sounds people and machines make. Students can use these books to select sound words for their writing. Comic strips are another good source of sound words; children collect frames from comic strips with sound words to add to a classroom chart.

In *Wishes, Lies, and Dreams* (1980), Koch recommends having children write noise poems that include a noise or sound word in each line. These first poems often sound contrived (e.g., "A dog barks bow-wow"), but the experience helps children learn to use onomatopoeia, as this poem dictated by a kindergartner illustrates:

Elephant Noses

Elephant noses
Elephant noses
Elephants have big noses
Big noses
Big noses
Elephants have big noses
through which they drink
SCHLURRP

Repetition.   Repetition of words and phrases is another device writers use to structure their writing as well as to add interest. Poe's use of the word *nevermore* in "The Raven" is one example, as is the Gingerbread Boy's boastful refrain in "The Gingerbread Boy." In this riddle a fourth grader uses a refrain effectively:

A Man

I am a little man standing all alone
In the deep, dark wood.
I am standing on one foot
In the deep, dark wood.
Tell me quickly, if you can,
What to call this little man
Standing all alone
In the deep, dark wood.
Who am I?
(Answer: a mushroom)

READING POEMS

Children grow rather naturally into poetry. The Opies (1959) have verified what we know from observing children: children have a natural affinity to verse, songs, riddles, jokes, chants, and puns. Preschoolers are introduced to poetry when their parents repeat Mother Goose rhymes, read *The House at Pooh Corner* (Milne, 1956) and the Dr. Seuss stories, and sing little songs to them. During the elementary grades, youngsters often create jump-rope rhymes and other ditties on the playground.

Types of Poems Children Read

Poems for children assume many different forms. The most common type of poetry is rhymed verse, such as Robert Louis Stevenson's "Where Go the Boats?," Vachel Lindsay's "The Little Turtle," and John Ciardi's "Mummy Slept Late and Daddy Fixed Breakfast." Poems that tell a story are narrative poems; examples are Clement Moore's "The Night Before Christmas," Robert

Browning's "The Pied Piper of Hamelin," and Henry Wadsworth Longfellow's "The Song of Hiawatha." A Japanese form, haiku, is popular in anthologies of poetry for children. Haiku is a three-line poem that contains just 17 syllables. Because of its brevity, it has been considered an appropriate form of poetry for children to read and write. Free verse has lines that don't rhyme, and rhythm is less important than in other types of poetry. Images take on greater importance in free-form verse. Langston Hughes's "Subway Rush Hour" and William Carlos Williams's "This Is Just to Say" are two examples of free verse. Other forms of poetry include limericks, a short, five-line rhymed verse form popularized by Edward Lear (1995), and concrete poems, which are arranged on the page to create a picture or an image.

Three types of poetry books are published for children. A number of picture book versions of single poems (in which each line or stanza is illustrated on a page) are available, such as *Paul Revere's Ride* (Longfellow, 1990). Other books are specialized collections of poems, either written by a single poet or related to a single theme, such as dinosaurs or Halloween. Comprehensive anthologies are the third type of poetry books for children, and they feature 50 to 500 or more poems arranged by category. One of the best anthologies is *The Random House Book of Poetry for Children* (Prelutsky, 1983). A list of poetry books including examples of each of the three types is presented in Figure 11–4.

In addition to poetry written specifically for children, some poetry written for adults can be used effectively with elementary students, especially at upper-grade levels. Apseloff (1979) explains that poems written for adults use more sophisticated language and imagery and provide children with an early introduction to poems and poets they will undoubtedly study later. For instance, elementary students will enjoy Shakespeare's "The Witches' Song" from *Macbeth* and Carl Sandburg's "Fog." A list of poems written for adults that may be appropriate with some elementary students is shown in Figure 11–5.

Children's Favorite Poems.   Children have definite preferences about which poems they like best, just as adults do. Fisher and Natarella (1982) surveyed the poetry preferences of first, second, and third graders; Terry (1974) investigated fourth, fifth, and sixth graders' preferences; and Kutiper (1985) researched seventh, eighth, and ninth graders' preferences. The results of the three studies are important for teachers to consider when they select poems. The most popular forms of poetry were limericks and narrative poems; least popular were haiku and free verse. In addition, children preferred funny poems, poems about animals, and poems about familiar experiences; they disliked poems with visual imagery and figurative language. The most important elements were rhyme, rhythm, and sound. Primary-grade students preferred traditional poetry, middle graders preferred modern poetry, and upper-grade students preferred rhyming verse. The researchers found that children in all three studies liked poetry, enjoyed listening to poetry read aloud, and could give reasons why they liked or disliked particular poems.

Researchers have also used school library circulation figures to examine children's poetry preferences. In a recent study, Kutiper and Wilson (1993) found that the humorous poetry of Shel Silverstein and Jack Prelutsky was the most popular. The three most widely circulated books were *The New Kid on the Block* (Prelutsky, 1984), *Where the Sidewalk Ends* (Silverstein, 1974),

Figure 11–4 *Collections of Poetry Written for Children*

Picture Book Versions of Single Poems

Carroll, L. (1992). (Ill. by J. B. Zalben). *Lewis Carroll's Jabberwocky.* Honesdale, PA: Wordsong. (M–U)

Frost, R. (1988). (Ill. by E. Young). *Birches.* New York: Henry Holt. (U)

Lear, E. (1986). (Ill. by L. B. Cauley). *The owl and the pussycat.* New York: Putnam. (P–M)

Longfellow, H. W. (1990). (Ill. by T. Rand). *Paul Revere's ride.* New York: Dutton. (M–U)

Moore, C. (1995). *The night before Christmas.* New York: North-South. (P–M)

Nash, O. (1995). *The tale of Custard the dragon.* Boston: Little, Brown. (P)

Noyes, A. (1981). (Ill. by C. Keeping). *The highwayman.* Oxford, England: Oxford University Press. (U)

Sandburg, C. (1993). *Arithmetic.* New York: Harcourt Brace. (P–M)

Thayer, E. L. (1988). (Ill. by P. Polacco). *Casey at the bat: A ballad of the republic, sung in the year 1888.* New York: Putnam. (M–U)

Westcott, N. B. (1988). *The lady with the alligator purse.* Boston: Little, Brown. (P)

Specialized Collections

Adoff, A. (1995). *Street music: City poems.* New York: HarperCollins. (P)

Carle, E. (1989). *Animals, animals.* New York: Philomel. (P–M)

Dickinson, E. (1978). *I'm nobody! Who are you? Poems of Emily Dickinson for children.* Owing Mills, MD: Stemmer House. (M–U)

Fleischman, P. (1985). *I am phoenix: Poems for two voices.* New York: Harper & Row. (M–U)

Fleischman, P. (1988). *Joyful noise: Poems for two voices.* New York: Harper & Row. (M–U)

Frost, R. (1982). *A swinger of birches: Poems of Robert Frost for young people.* Owing Mills, MD: Stemmer House. (U)

Glaser, I. J. (1995). *Dreams of glory: Poems starring girls.* New York: Atheneum. (M–U)

Greenfield, E. (1988). *Under the Sunday tree.* New York: Harper & Row. (M)

Hopkins, L. B. (1995). *Blast off! Poems about space.* New York: HarperCollins. (P)

Janeczko, P. B. (Sel.). (1993). *Looking for your name: A collection of contemporary poems.* New York: Orchard Books. (U)

Jones, H. (Ed.). (1993). *The trees stand shining: Poetry of the North American Indians.* New York: Dial. (M–U)

Kuskin, K. (1980). *Dogs and dragons, trees and dreams.* New York: Harper & Row. (P–M)

Lewis, J. P. (1995). *Black swan/White crow.* New York: Atheneum. (Haiku) (M–U)

Livingston, M. C. (1985). *Celebrations.* New York: Holiday House. (M)

Livingston, M. C. (1986). *Earth songs.* New York: Holiday House. (See also *Sea songs* and *Space songs*.) (M–U)

Livingston, M. C. (Sel.). (1991). *Lots of limericks.* New York: McElderry Books. (M–U)

Lobel, A. (1983). *The book of pigericks.* New York: Harper & Row. (limericks) (P–M)

McCord, D. (1974). *One at a time.* Boston: Little, Brown. (M–U)

Pomerantz, C. (1982). *If I had a paka: Poems in 11 languages.* New York: Greenwillow. (M–U)

Prelutsky, J. (1984). *The new kid on the block.* New York: Greenwillow. (P–M)

Prelutsky, J. (1989). *Poems of A. Nonny Mouse.* New York: Knopf. (P–M)

Prelutsky, J. (1990). *Something big has been here.* New York: Greenwillow. (P–M)

Prelutsky, J. (1993). *A. Nonny Mouse writes again!* New York: Knopf. (M–U)

Siebert, D. (1984). *Truck song.* New York: Harper & Row. (P–M)

Silverstein, S. (1996). *Falling up.* New York: HarperCollins. (P–M)

Yolen, J. (1990). *Bird watch: A book of poetry.* New York: Philomel. (M–U)

Comprehensive Anthologies

de Paola, T. (Compiler). (1988). *Tomie de Paola's book of poems.* New York: Putnam. (P–M)

de Regniers, B. S., Moore, E., White, M. M., & Carr, J. (Compilers). (1988). *Sing a song of popcorn: Every child's book of poems.* New York: Scholastic. (P–M–U)

Dunning, S., Leuders, E., & Smith, H. (Compilers). (1967). *Reflections on a gift of watermelon pickle, and other modern verse.* New York: Lothrop, Lee & Shepard. (U)

Kennedy, X. J. (Compiler). (1985). *The forgetful wishing well: Poems for young people.* New York: McElderry Books. (U)

Kennedy, X. J., & Kennedy, D. M. (Compilers). (1982). *Knock at a star: A child's introduction to poetry.* Boston: Little, Brown. (P–M–U)

Prelutsky, J. (Compiler). (1983). *The Random House book of poetry for children.* New York: Random House. (P–M–U)

Figure 11–5 *Adult Poems Appropriate for Elementary Students*

Poet	Poems and/or Books of Poetry
William Blake	"The Lamb," "The Tyger," "The Piper," and other selections from *Songs of Experience* and *Songs of Innocence.* Compare with Nancy Willard's *A Visit to William Blake's Inn: Poems for Innocent and Experienced Travelers* (1981).
e. e. cummings	Deborah Kogan Ray has created a picture book version of *hist whist* (1989).
Emily Dickinson	"I'm Nobody! Who Are You?," "There Is No Frigate Like a Book," and other favorite poems from *I'm Nobody! Who Are You? Poems of Emily Dickinson for Children* (1978) and *A Brighter Garden* (1990).
T. S. Eliot	Poems about cats from *Old Possum's Book of Practical Cats* (1967).
Robert Frost	"The Pasture," "Birches," "Fire and Ice," "Stopping by Woods on a Snowy Evening," and other favorites are included in *A Swinger of Birches: Poems of Robert Frost for Young People* (1982). *Stopping by Woods on a Snowy Evening,* illustrated by Susan Jeffers (1978), and *Birches* (1988) are picture book versions of individual poems.
Langston Hughes	Two new editions of Langston Hughes's poems are *The Dream Keeper and Other Poems* (1994) and *The Book of Rhythms* (1995).
Henry Wadsworth Longfellow	Ted Rand's illustrations evoke the historical moment in a picture book version of Longfellow's poem, *Paul Revere's Ride* (1990).
Carl Sandburg	Ted Rand has illustrated a stunning picture book version of *Arithmetic* (1993). Also see Lee Bennett Hopkins's collection of Sandburg's poems, *Rainbows Are Made: Poems by Carl Sandburg* (1982).
Walt Whitman	Lee Bennett Hopkins has compiled *Voyages: Poems of Walt Whitman* (1988), and Robert Sabuda has illustrated a picture book version of *I Hear America Singing* (1991).

and *A Light in the Attic* (Silverstein, 1981). In fact, 14 of the 30 most popular books used in the study were written by these two poets. Both Silverstein and Prelutsky use rhyme and rhythm effectively in their poems and write humorous narrative poems about familiar, everyday occurrences; these are the same qualities that children liked in the earlier poetry preference studies.

Poets Who Write for Children. Many poets are writing for children today, among them Arnold Adoff, Byrd Baylor, Gwendolyn Brooks, Lee Bennett Hopkins, Karla Kuskin, Lilian Moore, Mary O'Neill, Jack Prelutsky, and Shel Silverstein. Children are just as interested in learning about favorite poets as they are in learning about authors who write stories and informational books. When children view poets and other writers as real people, people whom they

During an author unit, these sixth graders read many of Jack Prelutsky's poems, including "Mean Maxine," "I'm Thankful," and "The New Kid on the Block."

For other information about poets, check Appendix B, "Resources About Authors and Illustrators."

can relate to and who enjoy the same things they do, <u>they begin to see themselves as poets</u>—a necessary criterion for successful writing. Information about poets is available in *Speaking of Poets: Interviews With Poets Who Write for Children and Young Adults* (Copeland, 1993), *Speaking of Poets 2: More Interviews With Poets Who Write for Children and Young Adults* (Copeland & Copeland, 1994), and *A Jar of Tiny Stars: Poems by <u>NCTE</u> Award-Winning Poets* (Cullinan, 1996).

Teaching Students to Read Poems

The focus in reading poems with students is on enjoyment. Students should have many, <u>many opportunities to read and listen to poems read aloud</u>, and they should learn a variety of approaches for sharing poems. Also, teachers should share poems that they especially like with students. Students are not expected to analyze poems; instead, <u>they read poems they like and share their favorite poems with classmates.</u> Students use the reading process as they read and respond to poems, and they often read poems during reading workshop and in connection with literature focus units and theme cycles.

Introducing Students to Poetry. In her poem "How to Eat a Poem," Eve Merriam (1966) provides useful advice for students who are reading poems: she says that reading a poem is like eating a piece of fruit, and she advises <u>biting right in and letting the juice run down your chin.</u> Poetry sharing does not need to be scheduled for a particular time of day. First thing in the morning or right after lunch are good times, but because poems can be shared quickly, they can be tied in with almost any activity. Often poems are coordinated with literature focus units and theme cycles.

When teachers and students read poems aloud, they enhance their reading using these four elements (Stewig, 1981):

- *Tempo*—how fast or slowly to read the lines
- *Rhythm*—which words to stress or say loudest
- *Pitch*—when to raise or lower the voice
- *Juncture*—when and how long to pause

Students experiment with these elements during minilessons and learn how to vary them to make their reading of poetry more interpretive. Students also learn that in some poems one element may be more important than another. Knowing about these elements reinforces the importance of rehearsing a poem several times before reading it aloud. During rehearsal, students experiment with tempo, rhythm, pitch, and juncture in order to read the poem effectively.

Teachers begin by reading favorite poems aloud to students and hanging charts with the poems written on them in the classroom. After doing this for several days, teachers point out a collection of poetry books in the classroom library and invite students to prepare a poem to share with the class the next day. Before long, students will be eagerly volunteering to read poems to the class. A list of guidelines for reading poems with children is presented in the Teacher's Notebook on page 446.

In Reading Workshop. Students sometimes choose collections of poetry to read during reading workshop, or teachers can plan a special poetry workshop. Some teachers devote one day a week for poetry workshop or plan a period of several weeks when all students read and respond to poems. Poetry workshop can have the same components as regular reading workshop, or poetry workshop can integrate both reading and writing workshop (Tompkins & McGee, 1993).

During a poetry workshop, the reading time is often divided into two parts. During the first part, students spend time browsing in collections of poetry and selecting poems that they want to share with classmates. Then, during the second part of reading time, students read poems aloud to partners or small groups of classmates. Because poetry is intended to be shared orally, students need to have the opportunity to read poems aloud. Students also write responses to poems they have read in reading logs and do projects to extend their poetry experience.

In Literature Focus Units. Teachers often share poems with students in conjunction with stories and other books they read aloud. For example, they might read Langston Hughes's poem "Dreams" (Prelutsky, 1983) together with *Number the Stars* (Lowry, 1989), or read Lee Bennett Hopkins's "Night Bear" (1984) before or after reading *Ira Sleeps Over* (Waber, 1972). Sometimes teachers read a poem as a preparing activity, and at other times they read it as an exploring activity. Whether a poem is used before or after reading depends on the particular story or poem and how the teacher plans to use it. Students may also locate a poem related to a story or other book and share it with the class as a project during the extending stage.

Teacher's Notebook
Guidelines for Reading Poems

1. Reading Aloud

Children and teachers read poetry aloud, not silently. Even if students are reading independently they should speak each word, albeit softly or in an undertone.

2. Expression

Teach students how to read a poem with expression, how to emphasize the rhythm and feel of the words, and where to pause.

3. Song Tunes

Children sing poems to familiar tunes such as "Twinkle, Twinkle Little Star" or "I've Been Working on the Railroad." Children experiment to find a tune that fits the line structure of the poem and then sing the poem to the tune.

4. Rehearsal

Readers rehearse poems several times before reading aloud so that they can read fluently and with expression. Encourage students to read "poetically."

5. Poetry Books

A collection of poetry books should be included in the classroom library for children to read during reading workshop and other independent reading times.

6. Memorization

Children should not be assigned to memorize a particular poem; rather, children who are interested in learning a favorite poem should be encouraged to do so and share it with class members.

7. No Analysis

Children do not analyze the meaning of a poem or its rhyme scheme; instead, they talk about poems they like and why they like them.

8. Author Units

Teachers teach author units to focus on a poet, such as Dr. Seuss, Jack Prelutsky, or Gary Soto.

Teachers can teach a unit on poetry, and during the unit students read and respond to a collection of poems. In this unit, poetry is at the center, rather than an introduction to or extension of other types of literature. Teachers choose some poems that all students will read and respond to, and students themselves select other poems.

Teachers read many poems to students, and students read other poems themselves. One way for students to read poems is using choral reading, in which students take turns reading a poem together. Students need multiple copies of the poem for choral reading, or the poem must be displayed on a chart or an overhead projector so that everyone can read it. Then students and the teacher decide how to arrange the poem for choral reading. Students may read the poem aloud together or in small groups, or individual students can read particular lines or stanzas. Four possible arrangements are (Stewig, 1981):

1. *Echo reading.* The leader reads each line, and the group repeats it.
2. *Leader and chorus reading.* The leader reads the main part of the poem, and the group reads the refrain or chorus in unison.
3. *Small-group reading.* The class divides into two or more groups, and each group reads one part of the poem.
4. *Cumulative reading.* One student or one group reads the first line or stanza, and another student or group joins in as each line or stanza is read so that a cumulative effect is created.

Choral reading makes students active participants in the poetry experience, and it helps them learn to appreciate the sounds, feelings, and magic of poetry. Two books of award-winning poems written specifically for choral reading are *I Am Phoenix* (Fleischman, 1985), a collection of poems about birds, and *Joyful Noise* (Fleischman, 1988), a collection of poems about insects. Many other poems can be used for choral reading; try, for example, Shel Silverstein's "Boa Constrictor," Karla Kuskin's "Full of the Moon," Laura E. Richards's "Eletelephony," and Eve Merriam's "Catch a Little Rhyme."

After reading, students respond to the poem they have read or listened to someone else read aloud. Sometimes the response is brief, and students talk informally about the poem, sharing connections to their own lives or expressing whether they liked it. They also might write responses in reading logs or quickwrites. At other times, students may explore the poem, choose favorite lines, or illustrate it. A list of additional ways students respond to poems is presented in the Teacher's Notebook on page 448.

One way students explore familiar poems is to sequence the lines of the poem. Teachers can copy the lines of the poem on sentence strips (long strips of chart paper), and students sequence the lines in a pocket chart or by lining up around the classroom. Or, teachers can enlarge the text of the poem using a duplicating machine and then cut the lines apart. Then students arrange the lines in order on a tray or cookie sheet and read the familiar poem. As students sequence the poem, they check a copy of the poem posted in the classroom, if necessary. For a more challenging activity, teachers can cut apart the words on each line so that students "build" the poem word by word. Through these sequencing activities, students have opportunities to practice word-identification skills and experiment with the syntactic structure of poems.

Teacher's Notebook
Ways to Respond to a Poem

1. Students read the poem aloud to classmates.
2. Students perform the poem using puppets or pantomime as a tape recording is played aloud.
3. Students write a reading log entry, discussing what the poem brings to mind or why they like it.
4. Students arrange the poem for choral reading and with classmates present it to the class.
5. Students identify a favorite line in a poem and explain why they like it, either by talking to a classmate or in a reading log entry.
6. Students draw or paint a picture of an image the poem brings to mind and write a favorite line or two from the poem on the picture. Or, students can write the favorite line on a sentence strip (long strip of chart paper). Then the line is read aloud during sharing time and added to a bulletin board of favorite lines.
7. Students make a picture book with lines or a stanza of the poem written on each page and illustrated.
8. Students make a mobile with stanzas cut apart and hung together with pictures.
9. Students "can" or "box" a poem by decorating a container and inserting a copy of the poem and two items related to the poem.
10. Students or the teacher write the poem on word cards, and then students "build" the poem, sequencing the cards in a pocket chart. Older students can enlarge a copy of the poem using a copy machine and then cut apart the words and sequence them on their desks. Sometimes students decide to arrange the words differently than the way the poet wrote them because they like their arrangement better!
11. Students read other poems written by the same author.
12. Students investigate the poet and, perhaps, write a letter to the poet.
13. Students make a cluster on a topic related to the poem.
14. Students write a poem on the same topic or following the format of the poem they have read.
15. Students dramatize the poem with a group of classmates.
16. Students make a filmstrip of the poem.
17. Students make a poster to illustrate the poem and attach a copy of the poem to it.
18. Students add the poem to a personal notebook of favorite poems.

During poetry units, students often create projects. They use drama, art, and music activities to extend their interpretations of favorite poems. For instance, students can role-play Kuskin's "I Woke Up This Morning" or construct monster puppets for the Lurpp creature in Prelutsky's "The Lurpp Is on the Loose." Students may also compile picture book versions of narrative poems with one line or stanza on each page. Students add an illustration for each page to complete the book. A page from a third-grade class book illustrating Shel Silverstein's "Hug O'War" (1974) is shown in Figure 11–6.

Some students enjoy compiling anthologies of their favorite poems. This activity often begins quite naturally when students read poems. They copy favorite poems to keep, and soon they are stapling their collections together to make books. Copying poems can also be a worthwhile handwriting activity because students are copying something meaningful to them, not just words and sentences in a workbook. In *Pass the Poetry, Please!*, poet and anthologist Lee Bennett Hopkins (1987) suggests setting up a dead tree branch or an artificial Christmas tree in the classroom as a "poetree" on which students can hang copies of their favorite poems for classmates to read and enjoy.

In Theme Cycles. Teachers often share poems in connection with theme cycles. They read poems from *Dinosaurs* (Hopkins, 1987) and *Tyrannosaurus Was a Beast* (Prelutsky, 1988) during a theme on dinosaurs, and from *Mojave* (Siebert, 1988) and *Desert Voices* (Baylor & Parnall, 1981) during a theme cycle on the desert. Text sets of books for theme cycles should include books of poetry or copies of poems written on charts whenever possible. A list of poetry collections that can be coordinated with theme cycles and holiday celebrations is presented in Figure 11–7. Including poems in theme cycles is important because poetry gives students a different perspective on social studies and science concepts.

Both teachers and students can share poems during theme cycles. Teachers read poems aloud to students, or they can duplicate copies of a poem for

Figure 11–6 *An Excerpt from, a Third-Grade Class Book Illustrating Shel Silverstein's Poem "Hug O' War"*

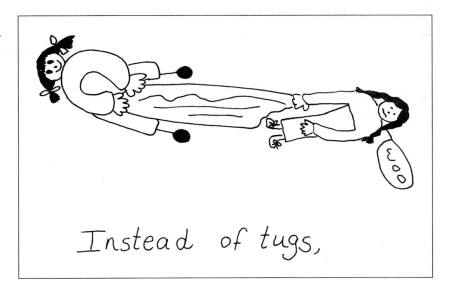

Figure 11–7 *Books of Poetry for Theme Cycles*

Amon, A. (Sel.). (1981). *The earth is sore: Native Americans on nature.* New York: Atheneum. (M–U)

Bauer, C. F. (Sel.). (1986). *Snowy day: Stories and poems.* New York: Lippincott. (See other books of weather stories and poems by the same selector.) (P–M)

Baylor, B. (1981). *Desert voices.* New York: Scribner. (P–M)

Carle, E. (Sel.). (1989). *Eric Carle's animals, animals.* New York: Philomel. (P–M)

Cassedy, S. (1993). *Zoomrimes: Poems about things that go.* New York: HarperCollins. (P)

Esbensen, B. J. (1984). *Cold stars and fireflies: Poems of the four seasons.* New York: Crowell. (U)

Fisher, A. (1983). *Rabbits, rabbits.* New York: Harper & Row. (P)

Fisher, A. (1988). *The house of a mouse.* New York: Harper & Row. (Poems about mice) (P–M)

Fleischman, P. (1985). *I am phoenix: Poems for two voices.* New York: Harper & Row. (Poems about birds) (M–U)

Fleischman, P. (1988). *Joyful noise: Poems for two voices.* New York: Harper & Row. (Poems about insects) (M–U)

Goldstein, B. S. (Sel.). (1989). *Bear in mind: A book of bear poems.* New York: Puffin. (P–M)

Goldstein, B. S. (Sel.). (1992). *What's on the menu?* New York: Viking. (Poems about food) (P–M)

Harvey, A. (Sel.). (1992). *Shades of green.* New York: Greenwillow. (Poems about ecology) (U)

Hopkins, L. B. (Sel.). (1983). *The sky is full of song.* New York: Harper & Row. (Poems about the seasons) (P–M)

Hopkins, L. B. (Sel.). (1985). *Munching: Poems about eating.* Boston: Little, Brown. (M–U)

Hopkins, L. B. (Sel.). (1987). *Dinosaurs.* San Diego: Harcourt Brace Jovanovich. (M–U)

Hopkins, L. B. (Sel.). (1987). *Click, rumble, roar: Poems about machines.* New York: Crowell. (M)

Hopkins, L. B. (Sel.). (1991). *On the farm.* Boston: Little, Brown. (P–M)

Hopkins, L. B. (Sel.). (1992). *To the zoo: Animal poems.* Boston: Little, Brown. (P–M)

Hopkins, L. B. (Sel.). (1993). *Beat the drum: Independence Day has come: Poems for the fourth of July.* Honesdale, PA: Wordsong. (See other collections of holiday poems by the same selector.) (P–M)

Hopkins, L. B. (Sel.). (1993). *Extra innings: Baseball poems.* San Diego: Harcourt Brace. (M–U)

Janeczko, P. B. (Sel.). (1984). *Strings: A gathering of family poems.* New York: Bradbury Press. (U)

Larrick, N. (Sel.). (1988). *Cats are cats.* New York: Philomel. (M–U)

Larrick, N. (Sel.). (1990). *Mice are nice.* New York: Philomel. (M)

Livingston, M. C. (1982). *Circle of seasons.* New York: Holiday House. (M–U)

Livingston, M. C. (Sel.). (1984). *Sky songs.* New York: Holiday House. (M–U)

Livingston, M. C. (1985). *Celebrations.* New York: Holiday House. (Poems about holidays) (P–M)

Livingston, M. C. (Sel.). (1986). *Earth songs.* New York: Holiday House. (M–U)

Livingston, M. C. (Sel.). (1986). *Sea songs.* New York: Holiday House. (M–U)

Livingston, M. C. (Sel.). (1987). *New Year's poems.* New York: Holiday House. (See other collections of holiday poems by the same selector.) (M–U)

Livingston, M. C. (Sel.). (1988). *Space songs.* New York: Holiday House. (M–U)

Livingston, M. C. (Sel.). (1990). *Dog poems.* New York: Holiday House. (M–U)

Livingston, M. C. (Sel.). (1990). *If the owl calls again: A collection of owl poems.* New York: McElderry Books. (U)

Livingston, M. C. (Sel.). (1992). *If you ever meet a whale.* New York: Holiday House. (P–M)

Livingston, M. C. (Sel.). (1993). *Roll along: Poems on wheels.* New York: McElderry. (M–U)

Morrison, L. (1985). *The break dance kids: Poems of sport, motion, and locomotion.* New York: Lothrop, Lee & Shepard. (U)

Morrison. L. (1995). *Slam dunk: Basketball poems.* New York: Hyperion. (M–U)

Prelutsky, J. (1977). *It's Halloween.* New York: Greenwillow. (See other books of holiday poems by the same author.) (P–M)

Prelutsky, J. (1983). *Zoo doings: Animal poems.* New York: Greenwillow. (P–M)

Prelutsky, J. (1984). *It's snowing! It's snowing!* New York: Greenwillow. (P–M)

Prelutsky, J. (1988). *Tyrannosaurus was a beast: Dinosaur poems.* New York: Greenwillow. (P–M)

Robb, L. (1995). *Snuffles and snouts.* New York: Dial. (poems about pigs) (P–M)

Sullivan, C. (1993). *Cowboys.* New York: Rizzoli. (P–M)

Turner, A. (1986). *Street talk.* Boston: Houghton Mifflin. (Poems about city life) (M–U)

Yolen, J. (1990). *Bird watch: A book of poetry.* New York: Philomel. (M–U)

Yolen, J. (1990). *Dinosaur dances.* New York: Putnam. (M)

Yolen, J. (1993). *Weather report: Poems.* Honesdale, PA: Wordsong. (M–U)

Yolen, J. (1995). *Water music: Poems for children.* Honesdale, PA: Wordsong. (M–U)

students to read, perhaps using choral reading. Then students can add these poems to their learning logs. Also, teachers can display poems related to a theme on a bulletin board or in a display. Students also can select poems to share as projects or write a favorite poem related to a theme on a poster or in a book.

Assessing Students' Experiences With Poems

Teachers assess students' experiences with poetry in several ways. They observe students as they are involved in poetry reading activities, and keep anecdotal notes of students as they read and respond to poems and share poems they like with classmates. They read students' reading logs and monitor the projects they create. Teachers can also conference with students and ask them about favorite poems and poets to assess students' interest in poetry. They also notice students' attention to how poets use wordplay and poetic devices. Students can also write reflections about their learning and work habits during the poetry activities, and these reflections provide valuable assessment information.

During poetry units, teachers prepare assessment checklists and keep track of students' reading and response activities. For example, during a 2-week poetry unit, fourth graders might be assessed on these activities:

4th grade

- Read 20 poems.
- Keep a list of the 20 poems read.
- Write in a reading log about five favorite poems.
- Participate in choral reading activities.
- Participate in minilessons about choral reading techniques, poet Jack Prelutsky, rhyme, and word pictures.
- Make a page for a class book on a favorite poem.
- Do a project about a poem.

Some people might argue that it is difficult to grade students on reading poetry, but students can earn points for these activities, and the points can be added together for a grade.

WRITING POEMS

Elementary students can have successful experiences writing poetry if they use poetic formulas. They write formula poems by beginning each line with particular words, as is the case with color poems; by counting syllables, as for haiku; or by creating word pictures, as in concrete poems. These formulas serve as scaffolds, or temporary writing frameworks, so that students focus on ideas rather than on the mechanics of writing poems (Cecil, 1994). Poetry also allows students more freedom in punctuation, capitalization, and page arrangement.

Many types of poetry do not use rhyme, and rhyme is the sticking-point for many would-be poets. In searching for a rhyming word, children often create inane verse; for example:

I see a funny little goat
Wearing a blue sailor's coat
Sitting in an old motorboat.

inane - silly or stupid

While children should not be forbidden to write rhyming poetry, rhyme should never be imposed as a criterion for acceptable poetry. Children may use rhyme when it fits naturally into their writing. When children write poetry during the elementary grades, they are searching for their own voices, and they need freedom to do that. Freed from the pressure to create rhyming poetry or from other constraints, children create sensitive word pictures, vivid images, and unique comparisons, as we see in the poems throughout this chapter.

Five types of poetic forms are formula poems, free-form poems, syllable- and word-count poems, rhymed poems, and model poems. Elementary students' poems illustrate each poetic form. Kindergartners' and first graders' poems may seem little more than lists of sentences compared to the more sophisticated poems of older students, but the range of poems effectively shows how elementary and middle-grade students grow in their ability to write poetry through these writing activities.

Formula Poems

The poetic forms may seem like recipes, but they are not intended to be followed rigidly. Rather, they provide a scaffold, organization, or skeleton for students' poems. After collecting words, images, and comparisons through brainstorming, clustering, quickwriting, or another prewriting strategy, students craft their poems, choosing words and arranging them to create a message. Meaning is always most important, and form follows the search for meaning. Perhaps a better description is that children "dig for poems" (Valentine, 1986) through words, ideas, poetic forms, rhyme, rhythm, and conventions. Poet Kenneth Koch (1980), working with students in the elementary grades, developed some simple formulas that make it easy for nearly every child to become a successful poet. These formulas call for students to begin every line the same way or to insert a particular kind of word in every line. The formulas use repetition, a stylistic device that is more effective for young poets than rhyme. Some forms may seem more like sentences than poems, but the dividing line between poetry and prose is a blurry one, and these poetry experiences help children move toward poetic expression.

"I Wish . . ." Poems.   Children begin each line of their poems with the words "I wish" and complete the line with a wish (Koch, 1980). In a second-grade class collaboration, children simply listed their wishes:

Our Wishes

I wish I had all the money in the world.
I wish I was a star fallen down from Mars.
I wish I were a butterfly.
I wish I were a teddy bear.
I wish I had a cat.
I wish I were a pink rose.
I wish it wouldn't rain today.
I wish I didn't have to wash a dish.
I wish I had a flying carpet.
I wish I could go to Disney World.
I wish school was out.
I wish I could go outside and play.

After this experience, students choose one of their wishes and expand on the idea in another poem. Brandi expanded her wish this way:

I Wish

I wish I were a teddy bear
Who sat on a beautiful bed
Who got a hug every night
By a little girl or boy
Maybe tonight I'll get my wish
And wake up on a little girl's bed
And then I'll be as happy as can be.

Color Poems. Students begin each line of their poems with a color. They can repeat the same color in each line or choose a different color (Koch, 1980). For example, a class of seventh graders writes about yellow:

Yellow

Yellow is shiny galoshes
splashing through mud puddles.
Yellow is a street lamp
beaming through a dark, black night.
Yellow is the egg yolk
bubbling in a frying pan.
Yellow is the lemon cake
that makes you pucker your lips.
Yellow is the sunset
and the warm summer breeze.
Yellow is the tingling in your mouth
after a lemon drop melts.

Students can also write more complex poems by expanding each idea into a stanza, as this poem about black illustrates:

Black

Black is a deep hole
sitting in the ground
waiting for animals
that live inside.
Black is a beautiful horse
standing on a high hill
with the wind
swirling its mane.
Black is a winter night sky
without stars
to keep it
company.
Black is a panther
creeping around a jungle
searching for
its prey.

Hailstones and Halibut Bones (O'Neill, 1989) is another source of color poems; however, O'Neill uses rhyme as a poetic device, and it is important to emphasize that students' poems need not rhyme.

Writing color poems can be coordinated with teaching young children to read and write color words. Instead of having kindergartners and first graders read worksheets and color pictures in the designated colors, students can create color poems in booklets of paper stapled together. They write and illustrate one line of the poem on each page.

Five-Senses Poems. Students write about a topic using each of the five senses. Sense poems are usually five lines long, with one line for each sense, as this poem written by a sixth grader demonstrates:

Being Heartbroken

Sounds like thunder and lightning
Looks like a carrot going through a blender
Tastes like sour milk
Feels like a splinter in your finger
Smells like a dead fish
It must be horrible!

It is often helpful to have students develop a five-senses cluster and collect ideas for each sense. Students select from the cluster the strongest or most vivid idea for each sense to use in a line of the poem.

"If I Were . . ." Poems.   Children write about how they would feel and what they would do if they were something else—a tyrannosaurus rex, a hamburger, or sunshine (Koch, 1980). They begin each poem with "If I were" and tell what it would be like to be that thing; for example, 7-year-old Robbie writes about what he would do if he were a dinosaur:

If I were a tyrannosaurus rex
I would terrorize other dinosaurs
And eat them up for supper.

In composing "If I were . . ." poems, students use personification, explore ideas and feelings, and consider the world from a different vantage point. Students can also write poems from the viewpoint of a book character. Fifth graders, for example, wrote this short poem after reading *Number the Stars* (Lowry, 1989):

If I were Annemarie,
I'd be brave.
I'd hide my friends,
and trick those Nazi soldiers.
I would lie if I had to.
If I were Annemarie,
I'd be brave.

Contrast Poems.   In contrast poems, students begin the first line of each stanza with "I used to" and the second line with "But now" (Koch, 1980). Students can use this formula to explore ways they have changed as well as how things change. Two third-grade students wrote:

I used to be a kernel
but now I am a crunchy,
tasty, buttery cloud
popped by Orville Redenbacher.

Definition Poems. In definition poems, students describe what something is or what something or someone means to them. To begin, the teacher or students identify a topic to fill in the blank, such as *anger, a friend, liberty,* or *fear;* then students start each line with ". . . is" and describe or define that thing. A group of second graders wrote the following poem as a part of their weather unit. Before discussing what causes thunder, they brainstormed a list of possible explanations for this phenomenon:

Thunder Is . . .

Thunder is someone bowling.
Thunder is a hot cloud bumping against a cold cloud.
Thunder is someone playing basketball.
Thunder is dynamite blasting.
Thunder is a brontosaurus sneezing.
Thunder is people moving their furniture.
Thunder is a giant laughing.
Thunder is elephants playing.
Thunder is an army tank.
Thunder is Bugs Bunny chewing his carrots.

Students often write powerful poems using this formula once they move beyond the cute "Happiness is . . ." and "Love is . . ." patterns.

Preposition Poems. Students begin each line of preposition poems with a preposition. This pattern often produces a delightful poetic effect. A seventh grader wrote this preposition poem about a movie superhero:

Superman

Within the city
In a phone booth
Into his clothes
Like a bird
In the sky
Through the walls
Until the crime
Among us
is defeated!

It is helpful for children to brainstorm a list of prepositions to refer to when they write preposition poems. Students may find that they need to ignore the formula for a line or two to give the content of their poems top priority, or they may mistakenly begin a line with an infinitive verb (e.g., *to say*) rather than a preposition. These forms provide a structure or skeleton for students' writing that should be adapted as necessary.

\ ə-'krös-tĭk, - 'kräs-\

Acrostic Poems. Students write acrostic poems using key words. They choose a key word and write it vertically on a sheet of paper. Then they create lines of poetry, each one beginning with a letter of the word or words they have written vertically. Students can use their names during a unit on autobiography or names of characters during a literature focus unit. For example, after reading *Officer Buckle and Gloria* (Rathmann, 1995), a small group of first graders wrote this acrostic using the dog's name, Gloria, for the key word written vertically.

Gloria
Loves to do tricks.
Officer Buckle tells safety
Rules at schools.
I wish I had
A dog like Gloria.

Another small group composed this acrostic using the same word written vertically:

Good dog Gloria
Likes to help
Officer Buckle teach safety
Rules to boys and girls.
I promise to remember
All the lessons.

Students also write acrostics using key words from social studies and science theme cycles. A sixth grader wrote about ancient Egypt:

Every
Golden treasure lies still
Young in beauty and
Precious in value beneath the earth.
The Egyptians adorned themselves in never-ending splendor.

Free-Form Poems

In free-form poems, children choose words to describe something and put the words together to express a thought or tell a story, without concern for rhyme or other arrangements. The number of words per line and the use of punctuation vary. In the following poem, an eighth grader poignantly describes his topic concisely, using only 15 well-chosen words:

Loneliness

A lifetime
Of broken dreams
And promises
Lost love
Hurt
My heart
Cries
In silence

Students can use several methods for writing free-form poems. They can select words and phrases from brainstormed lists and clusters, or they can write a paragraph and then "unwrite" it to create the poem by deleting unnecessary words. They arrange the remaining words to look like a poem.

Concrete Poems.   Students create concrete poems through art and the careful arrangement of words on a page. Words, phrases, and sentences can be written in the shape of an object, or word pictures can be inserted within poems written left to right and top to bottom. Concrete poems are extensions of the word pictures discussed earlier. Two concrete poems are shown in Figure 11–8. In "Ants," the words *ants, cake,* and *frosting* create the image of a

Figure 11–8 *Students' Concrete Poems*

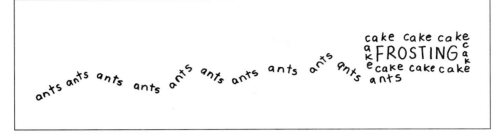

familiar picnic scene, and in "Cemetery," repetition and form create a reflection of peace. Three books of concrete poems are *Splish Splash: Poems* (Graham, 1994), *Seeing Things* (Froman, 1974), and *Walking Talking Words* (Sherman, 1980).

Found Poems. Students create poems by culling words from other sources, such as stories, songs, and newspaper articles. A third-grade class created a lengthy found poem, with a section for each chapter as they read *Sarah, Plain and Tall* (MacLachlan, 1985). This section is from Chapter 3, "The Arrival":

> *Papa drove off,*
> *New wife,*
> *New mother.*
> *Maybe? Maybe?*
>
> *Rocking on the porch,*
> *Rolling the blue marble,*
> *Back and forth,*
> *Back and forth.*
>
> *Caleb saw it too,*
> *Not smiling.*
> *We do not have the sea here.*
> *Perfect? Perfect?*

Poems for Two Voices. A unique type of free verse is poems for two voices. These poems are written in two columns, side by side, and the columns are read together by two readers. One reader (or group) reads the left column, and the other reader (or group) reads the right column. When readers both have words—either the same words or different words—written on the same line, they read them simultaneously so that the poem sounds like a musical duet.

During a theme cycle on Native Americans, students write found poems using words and phrases from books they have read.

The two best-known books of poems for two readers are Paul Fleischman's *I Am Phoenix: Poems for Two Voices* (1985), which is about birds, and the Newbery Award–winning *Joyful Noise: Poems for Two Voices* (1988), which is about insects. Students, too, can write poems for two voices, and Lorraine Wilson (1994) suggests that topics with contrasting viewpoints are the most effective.

A third-grade class wrote this poem for two voices about whales as part of their across-the-curriculum theme on the ocean:

Whales

Whales	*Whales*
dive deep	*dive deep*
into the ocean	
	then surface for air
breathing	
	through blowholes
always	*always*
swimming	*looking for food*
looking for food	*swimming*
whales	*whales*
mammals	
	look like fish
but they aren't	*but they aren't*
two groups	*two groups*
baleen whales	
	toothed whales

the humpback whale

fast swimmer
little beluga whale

all white

the blue whale

the biggest

big blue
killer whale

black and white
dangerous attacker
whales

a baleen whale
fast swimmer

a toothed whale

very unusual

a baleen whale

of all
big blue

a toothed whale
white and black
dangerous attacker
whales

Syllable- and Word-Count Poems

Haiku and other syllable- and word-count poems provide a structure that helps students succeed in writing; however, the need to adhere to these poems' formulas may restrict freedom of expression. In other words, the poetic structure may both help and hinder. The exact syllable counts force students to search for just the right words to express their ideas and feelings and provide a valuable opportunity for students to use thesauri and dictionaries.

Haiku. The most familiar syllable-counting poem is haiku (high-KOO), a Japanese poetic form consisting of 17 syllables arranged in three lines of 5, 7, and 5 syllables. Haiku poems deal with nature and present a single clear image. Haiku is a concise form, much like a telegram. A fourth grader wrote this haiku poem about a spider web she saw one morning:

> Spider web shining
> Tangled on the grass with dew
> Waiting quietly.

Books of haiku to share with students include *Black Swan/White Crow* (Lewis, 1995), *Spring: A Haiku Story* (Shannon, 1996), *Shadow Play: Night Haiku* (Harter 1994), *In a Spring Garden* (Lewis, 1965), *Cricket Songs* (Behn, 1964), and *More Cricket Songs* (Behn, 1971). The photographs and artwork in these trade books may give students ideas for illustrating their haiku poems.

Tanka. Tanka (TANK-ah) is a Japanese verse form containing 31 syllables arranged in five lines, 5-7-5-7-7. This form is similar to haiku, but with two additional lines of 7 syllables each. An eighth grader wrote this tanka poem about stars, which was published in her middle-school anthology:

> The summer dancers
> Dancing in the midnight sky,
> Waltzing and dreaming.
> Stars glistening in the night sky.
> Wish upon a shooting star.

Cinquain. A cinquain (SIN-cane) is a five-line poem containing 22 syllables in a 2-4-6-8-2 syllable pattern. Cinquain poems often describe something, but they may also tell a story. Have students ask themselves what their subject looks like, smells like, sounds like, and tastes like, and record their ideas using a five-senses cluster. The formula is as follows:

Line 1: a one-word subject with two syllables

Line 2: four syllables describing the subject

Line 3: six syllables showing action

Line 4: eight syllables expressing a feeling or an observation about the subject

Line 5: two syllables describing or renaming the subject

Here is a cinquain poem written by an upper-grade student:

Wrestling
skinny, fat
coaching, arguing, pinning
trying hard to win
tournament

If you compare this poem to the cinquain formula, you'll notice that some lines are short a syllable or two. The student bent some of the guidelines in choosing words to create a powerful image of wrestling; however, the message of the poem is always more important than adhering to the formula.

An alternate cinquain form contains five lines, but instead of following a syllable count, each line has a specified number of words. The first line contains a one-word title; the second line has two words that describe the title; the third line has three words that express action; the fourth line has four words that express feelings; and the fifth line contains a two-word synonym for the title.

Diamante. Tiedt (1970) invented the diamante (dee-ah-MAHN-tay), a seven-line contrast poem written in the shape of a diamond. This poetic form helps students apply their knowledge of opposites and parts of speech. The formula is as follows:

Line 1: one noun as the subject

Line 2: two adjectives describing the subject

Line 3: three participles (ending in *-ing*) telling about the subject

Line 4: four nouns (the first two related to the subject and the second two related to the opposite)

Line 5: three participles telling about the opposite

Line 6: two adjectives describing the opposite

Line 7: one noun that is the opposite of the subject

A third-grade class wrote this diamante poem about the stages of life:

Baby
wrinkled tiny
crying wetting sleeping
rattles diapers money house
caring working loving
smart helpful
Adult

Notice that the students created a contrast between *baby,* the subject represented by the noun in the first line, and *adult,* the opposite in the last line. This contrast gives students the opportunity to play with words and apply their understanding of opposites. The third word in the fourth line, *money,* begins the transition from *baby* to its opposite, *adult.*

Rhymed Verse Forms

middle and upper grades

Several rhymed verse forms such as limericks and clerihews can be used effectively with middle- and upper-grade students. It is important that teachers try to prevent the forms and rhyme schemes from restricting students' creative and imaginative expression.

Limericks. The limerick is a form of light verse that uses both rhyme and rhythm. The poem consists of five lines; the first, second, and fifth lines rhyme, while the third and fourth lines rhyme with each other and are shorter than the other three. The rhyme scheme is a-a-b-b-a, and a limerick is arranged this way:

Line	Rhyme
1 _____	a
2 _____	a
3 _____	b
4 _____	b
5 _____	a

8th grader

The last line often contains a funny or surprise ending, as in this limerick written by an eighth grader:

There once was a frog named Pete   a
Who did nothing but sit and eat.   a
He examined each fly   b
With so careful an eye   b
And then said, "You're dead meat."   a

Writing limericks can be a challenging assignment for many upper-grade students, but middle-grade students can also be successful with this poetic form, especially if they write a class collaboration.

Limericks are believed to have originated in the city of Limerick, Ireland, and were first popularized over a century ago by Edward Lear (1812–88). Poet X. J. Kennedy (1982) described limericks as the most popular type of poem in the English language today. Introduce students to limericks by reading aloud some of Lear's verses so that students can appreciate the rhythm of the verse. Two collections of Lear's limericks are *Daffy Down Dillies: Silly*

Limericks by Edward Lear (Lear, 1995) and *Lots of Limericks* (Livingston, 1991). Arnold Lobel has also written a book of unique pig limericks, *Pigericks* (1983). After reading Lobel's pigericks, students will want to write "birdericks" or "fishericks."

Clerihews.   Clerihews (KLER-i-hyoos), four-line rhymed verses that describe a person, are named for Edmund Clerihew Bentley (1875–1956), a British detective writer who invented the form. The formula is as follows:

Line 1:   the person's name

Line 2:   the last word rhymes with the last word in the first line

Lines 3 and 4:   the last words in these lines rhyme with each other

Clerihews can be written about anyone—historical figures, characters in stories, and even the students themselves. A sixth grader named Heather wrote this clerihew about Albert Einstein:

> *Albert Einstein*
> *His genius did shine.*
> *Of relativity and energy did he dream*
> *And scientists today hold him in high esteem.*

Model Poems

Students can model their poems on poems composed by adult poets. Koch suggested this approach in *Rose, Where Did You Get That Red?* (1990); students read a poem and write their own, using the theme expressed in the model poem. For other examples of model poems see Paul Janeczko's *Poetry from A to Z: A Guide for Young Writers* (1994) and Nancy Cecil's *For the Love of Language* (1994).

Apologies.   Using William Carlos Williams's "This Is Just to Say" as the model, children write a poem in which they apologize for something they are secretly glad they did (Koch, 1990). Middle- and upper-grade students are familiar with offering apologies and enjoy writing humorous apologies. A seventh grader, for example, wrote this apology to his dad:

> **The Truck**
>
> *Dad,*
> *I'm sorry*
> *that I took*
> *the truck*
> *out for*
> *a spin.*
> *I knew it*
> *was wrong.*
> *But . . .*
> *the exhilarating*
> *motion was*
> *AWESOME!*

Apology poems don't have to be humorous; they may be sensitive, genuine apologies, as another seventh grader's poem demonstrates:

Open Up

I didn't
open my
immature eyes
to see
the pain
within you
a death
had caused.
Forgive me,
I misunderstood
your anguished
broken heart.

Invitations.   Students write poems in which they invite someone to a magical, beautiful place full of sounds and colors and where all kinds of marvelous things happen. The model is Shakespeare's "Come Unto These Yellow Sands" (Koch, 1990). Guidelines for writing an invitation poem are that it must be an invitation to a magical place and that it must include sound or color words. The following example of an invitation poem written by a seventh grader follows these two guidelines:

The Golden Shore

Come unto the golden shore
Where days are filled with laughter,
And nights filled with whispering winds.
Where sunflowers and sun
Are filled with love.
Come take my hand
As we walk into the sun.

Prayers From the Ark.   Students write a poem or prayer from the viewpoint of an animal, following the model poems in Carmen Bernos de Gasztold's *Prayers From the Ark* (1992). Gasztold was a French nun during World War II, and in her poems she assumed the persona of the animals on Noah's ark as they prayed to God, questioning their existence and thanking God for his mercies. Children can write similar poems in which they assume the persona of an animal. A sixth grader assumes the persona of a monkey for his prayer:

Dear Lord,
I forgive you for making my face so ugly.
I thank you for giving me hands.
Thank you for placing the trees so high away
from my enemies.
I almost forgot,
Bless you for last month's big crop of bananas.

"If I Were in Charge of the World."   Students write poems in which they describe what they would do if they were in charge of the world. Judith Viorst's "If I Were in Charge of the World" (1981) is the model for this poetic form. Children are eager to share ideas about how they would change the world, as this fourth-grade class's collaborative poem illustrates:

If I Were in Charge of the World

If I were in charge of the world
School would be for one month,
Movies and videogames would be free, and
Foods would be McCalorieless at McDonalds.
Poor people would have a home,
Bubble gum would cost a penny, and
Kids would have cars to drive.
Parents wouldn't argue,
Christmas would be in July and December, and
We would never have bedtimes.
A kid would be president,
I'd meet my long lost cousin, and
Candybars would be vegetables.
I would own the mall,
People would have as much money as they wanted, and
There would be no drugs.

Teaching Students to Write Poems

As they write poems, students use what they have learned about poetry through reading poems and the information presented in minilessons on the poetic forms. They often have misconceptions that interfere with their ability to write poems. Many students think poems must rhyme, and in their search for rhymes they create inane verse. It is important that teachers help students develop a concept of poetry and what poems look like on a page as students begin writing poems.

One way to introduce students to writing poetry is to read excerpts from the first chapter of *Anastasia Krupnik* (Lowry, 1979), in which 10-year-old Anastasia, the main character, is excited when her teacher, Mrs. Westvessel, announces that the class will write poems. Anastasia works at home for eight nights to write a poem. Lowry does an excellent job of describing how poets search long and hard for words to express meaning and the delight that comes when they realize their poems are finished. Then Anastasia and her classmates bring their poems to class to read aloud. One student reads his four-line rhymed verse:

> I have a dog whose name is Spot.
> He likes to eat and drink a lot.
> When I put water in his dish,
> He laps it up just like a fish. (p. 10)

Anastasia is not impressed. She knows the child who wrote the poem has a dog named Sputnik, not Spot! But Mrs. Westvessel gives it an A and hangs it on the bulletin board. Soon it is Anastasia's turn, and she is nervous because her poem is very different. She reads her poem about tiny creatures that move about in tidepools at night:

> hush   hush   the sea-soft night is aswim
>   with wrinklesquirm creatures
>   listen (!)
> to them   move   smooth   in the moistly dark
>   here in the   whisperwarm   wet. (pp. 11–12)

Figure 11–9 *A Comparison Chart Created After Reading* Anastasia Krupnik

---

Rules About Writing Poetry

Mrs. Westvessel's Rules	*Our Rules*
1. Poems must rhyme.	1. Poems do not have to rhyme.
2. The first letter in each line must be capitalized.	2. The first letter in each line does not have to be capitalized.
3. Each line must start at the left margin.	3. Poems can take different shapes and be anywhere on a page.
4. Poems must have a certain rhythm.	4. You hear the writer's voice in a poem—-with or without rhythm.
5. Poems should be written about serious things.	5. Poems can be about anything—-serious or silly things.
6. Poems should be punctuated like other types of writing.	6. Poems can be punctuated in different ways or not be punctuated at all.
7. Poems are failures if they don't follow these rules.	7. There are no real rules for poems, and no poem is a failure.

In this free-form poem without rhyme or capital letters, Anastasia has created a marvelous picture with invented words. Regrettably, Mrs. Westvessel has an antiquated view that poems should be about only serious subjects, be composed of rhyming sentences, and use conventional capitalization and punctuation. She doesn't understand Anastasia's poem, and gives Anastasia an F because she didn't follow directions.

Although this first chapter presents a depressing picture of teachers and their lack of knowledge about poetry, it is a dramatic introduction about what poetry is and what it is not. After reading excerpts from the chapter, develop a chart with your students comparing what poetry is in Mrs. Westvessel's class and what poetry is in your class. A class of upper-grade students developed the chart in Figure 11–9. After this introduction to writing poetry, teachers teach minilessons about the poetic formulas and writing poems, and they provide opportunities for students to write poems. Students write poems during writing workshop and as part of literature focus units and theme cycles. A list of guidelines for writing poetry is shown in the Teacher's Notebook on page 466.

Poetry Minilessons.   Teachers use minilessons to teach students about the procedures, concepts, and strategies and skills for reading and writing poetry. As part of poetry writing activities, teachers teach minilessons to introduce students to particular poetic forms or to review the forms. Steps in teaching a minilesson about a poetic formula are:

*Step
by
Step*

1. ***Explain the poetic form.***   Describe the poetic form to students and explain what is included in each line or stanza. Then display a chart that describes the form, or have students write a brief description of the poetic form in their poetry notebooks.

Teacher's Notebook
Guidelines for Writing Poems

1. Concept of Poetry

Teachers explain what poetry is and what makes a good poem. Too often students assume that all poems must rhyme, are written on topics such as love and flowers, must be punctuated in a particular way, or have other restrictions.

2. Poetry Books

Books of poetry are set out in a special section of the classroom library. Students learn about poetry through reading, and some poems can serve as models for the poems students write.

3. Formulas

Students learn 5 to 10 formulas to use when they write poems so that they have a range of formulas from which to choose. At the same time, it is important that students know that they can break the formulas in order to express themselves more effectively.

4. Minilessons

Teachers present minilessons on comparison, alliteration, onomatopoeia, and repetition, and encourage students to use poetic devices other than rhyme.

5. Wordplay

Teachers encourage students to play with words, invent new words, and create word pictures as they write poems.

6. Projects

Students write poetry as part of literature focus units and theme cycles. Students can write found poems using excerpts from books, write poems about characters in stories, and write poems about topics related to themes.

7. Anthologies

Teachers and students create a class anthology of students' poems, and duplicate copies of the anthology for each student.

2. ***Share sample poems.*** Read aloud poems that are written by children and adults and which adhere to the form. Teachers can share sample poems from this chapter and poems written by students in previous years, or share poems from poetry collections written for children by adult poets. After reading and responding to each poem, students point out how the writer of each poem used the form.

3. ***Write class collaboration poems.*** Students write a class collaboration poem or poems in small groups before writing individual poems. Each student contributes a line for a class collaboration "I wish . . ." poem or a couplet for a contrast poem. To write other types of poems, such as concrete poems, students can work together by suggesting ideas and words. They dictate the poem to the teacher, who records it on the chalkboard or on chart paper. Older students work in small groups to create poems. Through collaborative poems, students review the form and gather ideas to use later in writing their own poems. The teacher should compliment students when they play with words or use poetic devices. Students also need information about how to arrange the poem on the page, how to decide about capital letters and punctuation marks, and why it may be necessary to "unwrite" and delete some words.

Teachers often simply explain several poetic forms and then allow students to choose a form and write a poem. This approach ignores the teaching component; it's back to the "assign and do" syndrome. Instead, students need to experiment with each poetic form. After these preliminary experiences, they can apply what they have learned and write poems that adhere to any of the forms they have learned during writing workshop or as part of literature focus units and theme cycles. Class collaborations are crucial because they are a practice run for children who are not sure what to do. The 5 minutes it takes to write a class collaboration poem can be the difference between success and failure for would-be poets.

Teachers teach many other poetry minilessons in addition to lessons on the poetic forms. They teach minilessons on wordplay, arranging lines of poetry for the greatest impact, punctuating poems, and how to read poems, for example. A list of topics for minilessons related to reading and writing poetry is presented on page 468.

Georgia Heard (1989) emphasizes the importance of teaching students about line breaks and white space on the page. Young children often write poems with the same page arrangement as stories, but as they gain more experience reading poems and experimenting with line breaks, they shape their poems to emphasize rhythm and rhyme, images, and poetic devices. Students learn that there are not right or wrong ways to arrange a poem on a page, but that the way the lines are broken affects both how the poem looks and how it sounds when read aloud.

In Writing Workshop. After students learn about various poetic forms, they often choose to write poems during writing workshop. They write poems about favorite topics or to express their feelings. They also experiment with forms that have been introduced during recent minilessons. Students who especially like to write poems can publish collections of their poems during

■ *To read more about reading and writing workshop, see Chapter 2, "Teaching Language Arts," pp. 62–64, and Chapter 13, "Putting It All Together," pp. 555–566.*

Reading and Writing Poetry

	Procedures	Concepts	Strategies and Skills
Wordplay	Craft riddles Create word pictures Invent words Craft tongue twisters	Wordplay Word pictures Hink-pinks Sniglets Metaphors Similes Alliteration Tongue twisters Onomatopoeia Repetition Rhyme	Rhyme Compare Use alliteration Use onomatopoeia Use repetition

Reading Poetry	Read a poem
	   interpretively
	Do choral reading
	Share poems
	Respond to poems in
	   quickwrites
	Discuss poems
	Do a project
	Compile an anthology
		Poetry
		Rhymed verse
		Narrative poems
		Free verse
		Concrete poems
		Information about poets
		Arrangements for choral
		   reading
			Vary tempo
			Emphasize rhythm
			Vary pitch
			Stress juncture

Writing Poetry	Write formula poems Write "I wish . . ." poems Write color poems Write five-senses poems Write "If I were . . ." poems Write contrast poems Write definition poems Write preposition poems Craft found poems Write free-form poems Design concrete poems Write haiku poems Write cinquain poems Write diamante poems Write limericks Write clerihews Write model poems	Poetic forms	Use poetic forms Create sensory images Paint word pictures Unwrite Use model poems Write rhymes Punctuate poems Capitalize poems Arrange poems on the page

writing workshop and share them with their classmates. This sharing often stimulates other students to write poetry.

Teachers also plan poetry workshops that incorporate components of both reading workshop and writing workshop. Students read and respond to poems during the reading workshop component, and then they write poems during the writing workshop component. One possible schedule for a 2-hour poetry workshop is:

15 minutes	The teacher leads a whole-class meeting to:
	• give a book talk on a new poetry book
	• talk about a poet
	• read several favorite poems using choral reading
	• talk about a "difficult" or "confusing" poem
30 minutes	Students read poems independently.
15 minutes	Students share poems with classmates.
15 minutes	The teacher teaches a poetry minilesson.
30 minutes	Students write poems using the writing process.
15 minutes	Students share poems they have written.

Duthie and Zimet (1992) described a similar poetry workshop for first graders that combined reading and writing. Students read poetry, and the teacher reads poetry aloud to students. Writing workshop follows reading workshop, and students also write poems. They draft poems and share them with classmates from the author's chair. Teachers also teach minilessons related to reading and writing poetry. Their minilesson topics included comparing rhyming versus nonrhyming poetry, creating invented words, introducing comprehensive anthologies and other books of poetry, arranging lines of poetry, experimenting with sound words and alliteration, inventing titles for poems, and crafting shape poems. As a culminating project, students compiled an anthology of original poems.

■ *For more information about author's chair, turn to Chapter 4 "Emergent Literacy," p. 176.*

In Literature Focus Units. Students often write poems as part of literature focus units. Sometimes they write poems together as a class during the exploring stage, and at other times they write poems individually or in small groups as projects during the extending stage. To explore the language of a book, students might write found poetry using a paragraph from a favorite book. Or students might write acrostic poems about a book title or a character's name. This acrostic poem about *Jumanji* (Van Allsburg, 1981) was written by a fourth grader:

> *J*ungle adventure game and
> f*U*n for a while.
> *M*onkeys ransacking kitchens
> *A*nd boa constrictors slithering past.
> *N*o way out until the game is done—
> *J*ust reach the city of Jumanji,
> *I* don't want to play!

Sometimes poetry writing activities are planned, and at other times they happen spontaneously. During a unit on Patricia MacLachlan's *Sarah, Plain and Tall* (1985), a third-grade class was discussing the two kinds of dunes in the story, and they wrote this free-form poem:

Dunes

Dunes of sand
on the beach.
Sarah walks on them
and watches the ocean.
Dunes of hay
beside the barn.
Papa makes them for Sarah
because she misses Maine.

In Theme Cycles.   Students also write poems as projects during theme cycles. A small group of third graders composed the following found poem after reading *Sarah Morton's Day: A Day in the Life of a Pilgrim Girl* (Waters, 1989):

This Is My Day*

Good day.
I must get up and be about my chores.
The fire is mine to tend.
I lay the table.
I muck the garden.
I pound the spices.
I draw vinegar to polish the brass.
I practice my lessons.
I feed the fire again.
I milk the goats.
I eat dinner.
I say the verses I am learning.
My father is pleased with my learning.
I fetch the water for tomorrow.
I bid my parents good night.
I say my prayers.
Fare thee well.
God be with thee.

To compose the found poem, the students collected their favorite words and sentences from the book and organized them sequentially to describe the pilgrim girl's day.

In a fourth-grade class, students often wrote cinquains as part of a theme cycle on westward movement. One student wrote this cinquain about the transcontinental railroad:

Railroads
One crazy guy's
Transcontinental dream . . .
With a golden spike it came true.
Iron horse

Other students wrote about California's gold rush. One student wrote:

---

*Tompkins & McGee, 1993, pp. 200–201.

Gold rush
Forty-niners
were sure to strike it rich.
Homesickness, pork and beans, so tired.
Panning

Adapting to Meet the Needs of Every Student

Poetry should be an important part of reading and writing, and teachers must find ways to involve all students in poetry activities. Poetry that has been written for children is available today that will evoke strong feelings and powerful images in students, and poetry writing is a valuable way for students to play with language and express themselves. As teachers plan poetry workshops and connect reading and writing poetry activities to literature focus units and theme cycles, they must find ways to adapt the activities to meet the needs of every student. A list of suggestions for adapting poetry activities to meet the needs of all students is presented on page 472.

Assessing Poems That Students Write

As teachers read, respond to, and assess the poems that students write, they need to recognize the nuggets of promise in the poems and support and build on them, instead of noticing children's lack of adult conventions (Tway, 1980). Donald Graves (1992) recommends that teachers focus on the passion and wonder in students' writing and on students' unique ability to make the common seem uncommon. Teachers can also notice the specific details, strong images, wordplay, comparisons, onomatopoeia, alliteration, and repetitions of words and lines that students incorporate in their poems.

The poetic formulas discussed in this chapter provide options for students as they experiment with ways to express their thoughts. Although children experiment with a variety of forms during the elementary grades, it is not necessary to test their knowledge of particular forms. Knowing that haiku is a Japanese poetic form composed of 17 syllables arranged in three lines will not make a child a poet. Descriptions of the forms should instead be posted in the classroom or added to language arts notebooks for students to refer to as they write.

Assessing the quality of students' poems is especially difficult, because poems are creative combinations of wordplay, poetic forms, and poetic devices. Instead of trying to give a grade for quality, teachers can assess students on other criteria:

- Has the student experimented with the poetic form presented in a minilesson?
- Has the student used the process approach in writing, revising, and editing the poem?
- Has the student used wordplay or another poetic device in the poem?

Teachers also ask students to assess their own progress in writing poems. Students choose their best efforts and poems that show promise. They can explain which writing strategies they used in particular poems and which poetic forms they used.

Adapting
Reading and Writing Poetry
To Meet the Needs of Every Student

1. Work in Groups

Have students read and write poems in small groups so that less capable readers and writers have classmates with whom to work. Students can use choral reading techniques and write collaborative poems.

2. Use Choral Reading

Use choral reading to share poems with students. As students read in groups, more capable readers support less capable readers.

3. Play With Poems

Encourage students to play or experiment with poems as they are read aloud. Students clap the rhythm or add sound effects to poems as they are read aloud. They create a refrain for a poem that does not have one, using a favorite line, the title, or a line they invent.

4. Use Songs

Songs are poems, and teachers can use songs that students are familiar with for poetry reading activities. Songs can be transcribed into stanzas and then read or sung.

5. Use Easy-to-Read Poems

Many poems are short and easy to read. Teachers who work with emergent readers and less fluent readers can collect these poems and write them on charts. Three collections of easy-to-read poems that are available as paperback books are Lee Bennett Hopkins's *Questions: Poems* (1992), *Weather* (1994), and *Blast Off! Poems About Space* (1995). These readers can also read some collections of riddles and jokes. The lines are short and easily remembered, and the structure is predictable.

Students keep copies of their poems in their writing folders or poetry booklets so that they can review and assess their own work. They may also place copies of some poems in their language arts portfolios. If a grade for quality is absolutely necessary, students should choose several of the poems in their writing folders for the teacher to evaluate.

Review

Poetry is an important part of the language arts curriculum. Elementary students participate in wordplay activities and read and write poetry as part of literature focus units, reading and writing workshop, and theme cycles. The important concepts presented in this chapter include:

1. Wordplay activities with riddles, comparisons, rhyme, and other poetic devices provide the background of experiences students need for reading and writing poetry.
2. Three types of poetry books published for children are picture book versions of single poems, specialized collections of poems, and comprehensive anthologies of poems.
3. Elementary students have definite opinions about the types of poems they like best.
4. The focus in teaching students to read and respond to poems is enjoyment.
5. Tempo, rhythm, pitch, and juncture are four elements to consider when reading poetry aloud.
6. Choral reading is an effective way for students to read poetry.
7. Students read poems during reading workshop and in connection with literature focus units and theme cycles.
8. Students can write poems successfully using poetic formulas in which they begin each line with particular words, count syllables, or create word pictures.
9. Because rhyme is a sticking point for many students, they should be encouraged to experiment with other poetic devices in their writing.
10. Students write poetry during writing workshop and as part of literature focus units and theme cycles.

Extensions

1. Invite a small group of students to study a favorite poet. Students read the poet's work and learn about his or her life. They may also want to write letters to the poet.
2. Plan and teach a 2-week poetry workshop. During the workshop, involve students with activities in reading and writing poetry, and teach minilessons on topics from the list on page 468.
3. Compile a collection of poems related to literature focus units or theme cycles that are appropriate for the grade level you teach or plan to teach.
4. Collect a group of poems for choral reading and teach a group of students to do choral reading using the four arrangements listed on page 447.
5. Plan and teach a series of lessons on wordplay to a group of elementary students.
6. Prepare a set of charts listing the formulas for poetic forms to use in teaching students to write poetry.
7. Teach a small group of students to write several types of poems, and have students compile their poems in a class anthology or in hardbound books.

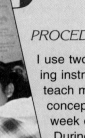

PRO-File
Eighth Graders Learn Spelling Responsibility

66 Of course I teach spelling! I used to have weekly spelling tests, but my students spelled the words correctly on the tests but continued to spell them incorrectly in their writing. Now I teach spelling through minilessons and conferences. I think it's more effective this way. 99

Eileen Boland
Eighth-Grade Language Arts Teacher
Southeast Middle School

PROCEDURE

I use two approaches for spelling instruction. First of all, I teach minilessons on spelling concepts at least once a week during the school year. During the first month of the school year, I focus on homophones (words that sound alike but are spelled differently) because many of my eighth graders still confuse *there–their–they're* and other homophones.

In each minilesson, I explain the skill, share several examples, and explain how using the skill will change their lives. For example, I might show an anonymous student paper and together we identify and correct the homophone errors. Then I distribute copies of the 25 most common homophone errors and ask students to highlight the ones used incorrectly. During a follow-up minilesson, I review the most common homophone errors and clarify any confusions students might have. Next, I ask

students to pull out a paper they are working on and proofread it, checking to see if they have made any homophone errors. For the next several weeks, I ask students to pay special attention to homophones they are spelling and to choose the correct spelling.

I know that I am reaching my students when they complain that the spellcheckers we have available in the classroom aren't much use for checking homophone errors. They explain to me that *there* might be spelled correctly but it is still wrong because it is not the correct word choice in "I gave them there lunch." I agree that eighth grade is no place for the fainthearted!

My second approach for teaching spelling is to conference with students during writing workshop. I meet with small groups of students after they have proofread and tried to correct all misspelled words in their compositions. We meet at the conference table in the classroom. I keep a basket of highlighters and red pens on the table, and I have a dictionary and thesaurus on the table for students to consult. I ask students to read their compositions aloud to me two times. During the first reading, I listen to the content of the paper and have the student use a highlighter to mark any misspelled words he or she might notice. It always amazes me how many words they catch themselves. During the second reading I highlight other misspelled words. Then I have the student use a red pen to correct as many words as possible and I help the student correct other words. I often ask students to tell me why they spelled a word as they did, and their logic often surprises me. I like the conference format. It allows me to correct misconceptions and reteach spelling rules at a teachable moment.

I make notes about each student on large index cards, and I keep the notes in a card file. I list the date of the conference, categories of spelling errors that I notice in the student's paper, examples of misspelled words, and skills that the student is now using correctly. Over the course of a semester, I can track students' spelling development using these notes.

ASSESSMENT

Since my students are in middle school, we deal with the harsh reality of report card grades. After I read students' final drafts of their papers, I count misspelled words and assign spelling grades accordingly. Students receive a grade of A if 90% or more of the words in their final papers are spelled correctly, a B for 80–89%, and so on. This grade isn't the only spelling grade my students have, but it's the most important one. I want my students to understand that writers spell correctly as a courtesy to their readers.

ADAPTATIONS

I present minilessons on each of the spelling skills that I teach. During the school year I focus on nine spelling topics plus any other topics that I notice my students need when I read their compositions. The nine topics are listed in the figure. I usually spend about one month on each of the topics, and this is the order in which I usually teach the topics.

REFLECTIONS

Teaching spelling is one of the most difficult things I do. It's not so much a matter of teaching and reteaching (even though that is important) but of making my students responsible for their own spelling accuracy.

Nine Spelling Topics I Teach in Eighth Grade

1. *Homophones.* I highlight the sound-alike words that my students confuse in their writing, such as *their–there–they're* and *to–two–too, whole–hole, its–it's, no–know,* and *threw–through.*
2. *Spelling rules.* I teach four spelling rules that work more often than they don't: the "*i* before *e* except after *c*" rule, the "doubling the final consonant" rule, the "final *e*" rule, and the "changing *y* to *i*" rule.
3. *Plurals.* I review how to form various types of plurals including plurals for nouns that end in *y, o,* and *f.*
4. *Commonly misspelled words.* I share a list of commonly misspelled words with students, and they identify the words that they misspell, such as *daily, foreign, guarantee, island, jewelry, medicine, quiet, tomorrow,* and *whether.*
5. *Multisyllabic words.* I teach students syllabication rules so that they can break long words down into syllables in order to spell them correctly.
6. *How to use a dictionary.* I teach my students how to locate words in the dictionary and about the useful information in a dictionary entry.
7. *Spelling patterns.* My students make charts of ways to spell long vowels, *r*-controlled vowels, and other sounds that can be spelled in several different ways. For example, long *a* can be spelled *a* as in *table, a-e* as in *gate, ai* as in *mail,* or *ay* as in *day.*
8. *Abbreviations.* My students review state abbreviations and other abbreviations, including Mr. and Ms., B.C. and A.D., A.M. and P.M., months of the year, and units of measurement and weight.
9. *Possessives.* I explain how to form singular and plural possessives and other uses of an apostrophe.

Sent - past and past part of send \'sent \

Send \ send \ vb

Language Tools: Spelling, Handwriting, and Grammar

des-ert \'de-zərt\ n. 1. a: arid barren land

S tudents in Whitney Donnelly's sixth-grade class reviewed confusing spelling words, including homophones and other words that have similar spellings, and made a chart of these words, including *dessert–desert, sent–scent–cent, hanger–hangar, sore–soar, died–dyed,* and *vein–vain.* They studied the words to determine why they were confusing and checked the meanings of some words in the dictionary. Students each chose a set of words to illustrate on a fabric quilt square. Later, they worked with parent volunteers to sew their squares together into small quilts to hang in the classroom or use as table covers.

dessert · n. a unually sweet course or dish \di-'zərt\

onventional spelling, neat handwriting, and Standard English grammar have been considered the <u>hallmarks of an educated person</u>. These components have been important parts of language arts instruction since the beginning of public education. <u>Today, however, more and more people are viewing spelling, handwriting, and grammar as tools for communicating through language—as means to an end, rather than the goal of education.</u>

Lucy McCormick Calkins has argued for more than 15 years that "<u>basic skills belong in context</u>" (1980, p. 567). The ability to use skills such as spelling conventionally, writing legibly, and using Standard English grammatical constructions effectively is best fostered by teaching them in the context of their use (Routman, 1996). Teachers:

- Model effective use of language tools.
- Raise expectations and hold students accountable for work done accurately and neatly.
- Teach minilessons using children's writing and excerpts from books students are reading.
- Teach students to proofread their writing.
- Encourage students to self-assess their work.
- Share research with parents about the importance of teaching the language tools in context.
- Value students' effective use of language tools.

Skills that are taught in isolation are not used as consistently or effectively as skills taught when students are using oral and written language in meaningful, functional, and genuine ways (Routman, 1996). I recommend that spelling, handwriting, grammar, and other language skills be taught as part of <u>literature focus units</u>, reading and writing workshop, and <u>theme cycles</u>.

Tompkins

As you read this chapter, think about how these three language tools can be integrated with meaningful, functional, and genuine language arts activities. Use these three additional questions to guide your reading:

- What are the components of an effective spelling program?
- How do teachers teach handwriting skills to elementary students?
- How should grammar be taught in the elementary grades?

SPELLING

arctic	consciousness	embarrass	grammar	ingenious
liquefy	marshmallow	occasion	professor	souvenir

Which of these words are spelled correctly? If you are like most people, you may be confused about the spelling of one or more of these words. <u>All of them are spelled correctly</u>, but it's easy to question the spelling of one or two words, especially if you expect pronunciation to determine spelling. <u>English is not a purely phonetic language</u>, and many words, such as *souvenir*, reflect their origins in other languages.

Spelling is a tool for writers that allows them to communicate conventionally with readers. As Graves explains: "<u>Spelling is for writing</u>. Children may achieve high scores on phonic inventories, or weekly spelling tests. But the ultimate test is what the child does under 'game conditions,' within the process of moving toward meaning" (1983, pp. 193–194). Rather than equating spelling instruction with weekly spelling tests, students need to learn to spell words conventionally so that they can communicate effectively through writing. English spelling is complex, and attempts to teach spelling through weekly lists have not been very successful. Many students spell the words correctly on the weekly test, but they continue to misspell them in their writing.

Children's Spelling Development

■ *Turn to Chapter 5, "Looking Closely at Words," pp. 185–186, for more information on the etymology of words.*

The alphabetic principle suggests a one-to-one correspondence between phonemes and graphemes, but English spelling is phonetic only about half the time. Other spellings reflect the language from which a word was borrowed. For example, *alcohol,* like most words beginning with *al-,* is an Arabic word, and *energy* is a Greek word. Other words are spelled to reflect semantic relationships, not phonological ones. The spelling of *national* and *nation* and of *grade* and *gradual* indicates related meanings even though there are vowel or consonant changes in the pronunciations of the word pairs. If English were a purely phonetic language, it would be easier to spell, but, at the same time, it would lose much of its sophistication.

■ *See Chapter 4, "Emergent Literacy," pp. 168–176, for more information about young children's writing.*

Elementary students learn to spell the phonetic elements of English as they learn about phoneme-grapheme correspondences, and they continue to refine their spelling knowledge through reading and writing. Children's spelling that reflects their growing awareness of English orthography is known as invented spelling, and during the elementary grades children move from using scribbles and single letters to represent words through a series of stages until they adopt conventional spellings.

Invented Spelling. As young children begin to write, they create unique spellings, called invented spellings, based on their knowledge of English orthography. Other names for invented spelling include temporary spelling and kid spelling. Charles Read (1975, 1986), one of the first researchers to study preschoolers' efforts to spell words, discovered that they used their knowledge of phonology to invent spellings. These children used letter names to spell words such as U (*you*) and R (*are*), and they used consonant sounds rather consistently: GRL (*girl*), TIGR (*tiger*), and NIT (*night*). The preschoolers used several unusual but phonetically based spelling patterns to represent affricates. They spelled *tr* with *chr* (e.g., CHRIBLES for *troubles*) and *dr* with *jr* (e.g., JRAGIN for *dragon*), and they substituted *d* for *t* (e.g., PREDE for *pretty*). Words with long vowels were spelled using letter names: MI (*my*), LADE (*lady*), and FEL (*feel*). The children used several ingenious strategies to spell words with short vowels. The 3-, 4-, and 5-year-olds rather consistently selected letters to represent short vowels on the basis of place of articulation in the mouth. Short *i* was represented with *e* as in FES (*fish*), short *e* with *a* as in LAFFT (*left*), and short *o* with *i* as in CLIK (*clock*). These spellings may seem odd to adults, but they are based on phonetic relationships. The children often omitted nasals within words (e.g., ED for *end*) and substituted *-eg* or *-ig* for *-ing* (e.g., CUMIG for *coming* and GOWEG for *going*). Also, they often ignored the vowel in unaccented syllables, as in AFTR (*after*) and MUTHR (*mother*).

These children developed strategies for their spellings based on their knowledge of the phonological system and of letter names, their judgments of phonetic similarities and differences, and their ability to abstract phonetic

affricates = a stop and its immediately following release into a fricative that are considered to constitute a single phoneme (as the |t| and sh| of |ch| in choose).

information from letter names. Read suggested that from among the many phonetic properties in the phonological system, children abstract away certain phonetic details and preserve others in their invented spellings.

Based on Read's seminal work, other researchers began to systematically study the development of children's spelling abilities. Henderson and other researchers (Beers & Henderson, 1977; Gentry, 1981; Templeton, 1979; Zutell, 1979) have studied the manner in which children proceed developmentally from invented spelling to conventional spelling.

Based on observations of children's spellings, researchers have identified five stages that children move through on their way to becoming conventional spellers, and at each stage they use different types of strategies. The stages are precommunicative spelling, semiphonetic spelling, phonetic spelling, transitional spelling, and conventional spelling (Gentry, 1981, 1982, 1987; Gentry & Gillet, 1993). The characteristics of each of the five stages of invented spelling are summarized in Figure 12–1.

*1. **Precommunicative spelling.*** Children string scribbles, letters, and letterlike forms together, but they do not associate the marks they make with any specific phonemes. Precommunicative spelling represents a natural, early expression of the alphabet and other concepts about writing. Children may write from left to right, right to left, top to bottom, or randomly across the page. Some precommunicative spellers have a large repertoire of letter forms to use in writing, while others repeat a small number of letters over and over. Children use both upper- and lowercase letters, but they show a distinct preference for uppercase letters. At this stage, children have not discovered how spelling works or that letters represent sounds in words. This stage is typical of preschoolers, ages 3 to 5.

*2. **Semiphonetic spelling.*** Children begin to represent phonemes in words with letters, indicating that they have a rudimentary understanding of the alphabetic principle—that a link exists between letters and sounds. Spellings are quite abbreviated, and children use only one, two, or three letters to represent an entire word. Examples of stage 2 spelling are DA (*day*), KLZ (*closed*), and SM (*swimming*). As these examples illustrate, semiphonetic spellers use a letter-name strategy to determine which letters to use to spell a word, and their spellings represent some sound features of words while ignoring other, equally important, features. Spellers at this stage include 5- and 6-year-old children.

*3. **Phonetic spelling.*** Children's understanding of the alphabetic principle is further refined in this stage. They continue to use letter names to represent sounds, but they also use consonant and vowel sounds at this stage. Examples of stage 3 spelling are LIV (*live*), DRAS (*dress*), and PEKT (*peeked*). As these examples show, children choose letters on the basis of sound alone, without considering acceptable English letter sequences (e.g., using -*t* rather than -*ed* as a past-tense marker in *peeked*). These spellings do not resemble English words, but they can be deciphered. The major achievement of this stage is that for the first time children represent *all* essential sound features in the words. Henderson (1980) explains that words are "bewilderingly homographic" at this stage because children spell on the basis of sound alone; for example, *bat, bet,* and *bait* might all be spelled BAT. Phonetic spellers are typically about 6 years old.

Figure 12–1   *Characteristics of the Stages of Invented Spelling*

Stage 1: Precommunicative Spelling *(ages 3-5)*

Child uses scribbles, letterlike forms, letters, and sometimes numbers to represent a message.

Child may write from left to right, right to left, top to bottom, or randomly on the page.

Child shows no understanding of phoneme-grapheme correspondences.

Child may repeat a few letters again and again or use most of the letters of the alphabet.

Child frequently mixes upper- and lowercase letters but shows a preference for uppercase letters.

Stage 2: Semiphonetic Spelling *(ages 5-6)*

Child becomes aware of the alphabetic principle that letters are used to represent sounds.

Child uses abbreviated one-, two-, or three-letter spelling to represent an entire word.

Child uses letter-name strategy to spell words.

Stage 3: Phonetic Spelling *(about 6)*

Child represents all essential sound features of a word in spelling.

Child develops particular spellings for long and short vowels and plural and past-tense markers.

Child chooses letters on the basis of sound without regard for English letter sequences or other conventions.

Stage 4: Transitional Spelling *7, 8, 9 year olds*

Child adheres to basic conventions of English orthography.

Child begins to use morphological and visual information in addition to phonetic information.

Child may include all appropriate letters in a word but reverse some of them.

Child uses alternate spellings for the same sound in different words, but only partially understands the conditions governing their use.

Child uses a high percentage of correctly spelled words.

Stage 5: Conventional Spelling

Child applies the basic rules of the English orthographic system.

Child extends knowledge of word structure, including the spelling of affixes, contractions, compound words, and homonyms.

Child demonstrates growing accuracy in using silent consonants and doubling consonants before adding suffixes.

Child recognizes when a word doesn't "look right" and can consider alternate spellings for the same sound.

Child learns irregular spelling patterns.

Child learns consonant and vowel alternations and other morphological structures.

Child knows how to spell a large number of words conventionally.

Adapted from Gentry, 1982a, 1982b; Gentry & Gillet, 1993.

See p. 485

4. **Transitional spelling.** Transitional spellers come close to the conventional spellings of English words. They spell many words correctly but continue to misspell words with irregular spellings. Examples of stage 4 spelling are HUOSE (*house*), TRUBAL (*trouble*), EAGUL (*eagle*), and AFTERNEWN (*afternoon*). This stage is characterized by children's growing ability to represent the features of English orthography. They include a vowel in every syllable and demonstrate knowledge of vowel patterns even though they might make a faulty decision about which marker to use. For example, *toad* is often spelled TODE when children choose the wrong vowel marker, or TAOD when the two vowels are reversed. Also, transitional spellers use common letter patterns in their spelling, such as YOUNIGHTED for *united* and HIGHCKED for *hiked*. In this stage, children use conventional alternatives for representing sounds, and although they continue to misspell words according to adult standards, transitional spelling resembles English orthography and can easily be read. As the examples show, children stop relying entirely on phonological information and begin to use visual clues and morphological information. Spellers in this stage are generally 7, 8, and 9 years old.

5. **Conventional spelling.** As the name implies, children spell most words (90% or more) conventionally (as they are spelled in the dictionary) at this stage. They have mastered the basic principles of English orthography. Children typically reach stage 5 by the age of 8 or 9. During the next 4 or 5 years, children learn to control homonyms (e.g., *road–rode*), contractions, affixes (e.g., *running*), and vowel and consonant alternations. They also learn to spell common irregularly spelled words (e.g., *school* and *they*). If the curriculum expects students to study lists of spelling words and take weekly spelling tests, they should not begin these tests until they reach the conventional stage (Gentry, 1981, 1982; Gentry & Gillet, 1993).

Teachers do many things to scaffold children's spelling development as they move through the stages of invented spelling. As children scribble, for example, teachers should encourage children to use a pencil, not a crayon, for writing, to differentiate between drawing and writing. Semiphonetic spellers notice words in their environment, and teachers help children use these familiar words to choose letters to represent the sounds in the words they are writing. During the phonetic and transitional stages, teachers provide support in other ways, including teaching students to apply phonics concepts for spelling. Figure 12–2 presents a list of guidelines for supporting young children's spelling development.

Older Students' Spelling Development. Researchers are continuing to study children's spelling development beyond age 8. Hitchcock (1989) studied children's spellings in grades 2 through 6 and classified the errors that these older, conventional-stage spellers continue to make as semiphonetic, phonetic, and transitional-stage spellings. Very few errors were categorized as semiphonetic, and these spellings seemed to serve as placeholders (Wilde, 1993), in which students used one, two, or three letters to stand for a longer word (e.g., using A to stand for *America*). More than half of their errors were classified as phonetic spellings, in which students spell words according to the way they sound or as they pronounce them (e.g., *wat* for *want, to* for *two, babes* for *babies*). That students continue to misspell words by spelling

Figure 12–2 *Ways to Support Children's Spelling Development*

Stage 1: Precommunicative Spelling

Allow the child to experiment with making and placing marks on the paper.
Suggest that the child writes with a pencil and draws with a crayon.
Model how adults write.
Point out the direction of print in books, from top-to-bottom and left-to-right across a page.
Encourage the child to notice letters in names and environmental print.
Ask the child to talk about what he or she has written.

Stage 2: Semiphonetic Spelling

Demonstrate how to say a word slowly, stretch it out, and isolate 1, 2, or 3 sounds in the word to write. (Emphasize only consonant sounds and long-vowel sounds at this stage.)
Show the child how to form letters in names and other common words.
Sing the alphabet song and name letters of the alphabet with the child.
Have the child pick out common objects beginning with particular letters and consonant sounds.
Encourage the child to read the names of classmates and look for names that begin with the same letter.
Ask the child to read what he or she has written.

Stage 3: Phonetic Spelling

Model how to write phonetically, segmenting words into beginning, middle, and ending sounds.
Use Elkonin boxes to help the child segment words into beginning, middle, and ending sounds.
Teach short and long vowels.
Have the child write rhyming words.
Teach the child how to use plural, past tense, and other word markers (e.g., *-s, -ed, -ing*).
Use "sharing the pen" interactive writing when creating class charts.

Stage 4: Transitional Spelling

Teach consonant and vowel digraphs, vowel diphthongs (e.g., *oo* in *moon, oy* in *boy*), and other spelling patterns.
Focus on silent letters in words (e.g., the final *e* in CVCE words, *gh* in *light,* and *k* in *know*).
Encourage the child to develop visualization skills in order to recognize whether or not a word "looks" right.
Help the child identify common sight words that cannot be spelled using phonics (e.g., *what, here*).
Introduce proofreading so the child can identify and correct misspelled words in compositions.

Stage 5: Conventional Spelling

Teach the child to break longer words into syllables for spelling. Introduce root words and affixes and how to build longer words using affixes.
Create class charts of spelling options (e.g., ways to spell long *o,* words that end with *-able* and *-ible* [*adaptable* and *edible*]).
Provide information about other spelling concepts (e.g., possessives, schwa, double letters).
Teach proofreading skills and encourage the child to proofread all writings.
Have the child make a personal dictionary or chart of frequently misspelled words.

them phonetically is not surprising, because teachers and parents often encourage students to sound out the spelling when children ask how to spell an unknown word. The other errors were categorized as transitional-stage spellings. Students misapplied rules about vowels, plurals, verb tenses, possessives, contractions, compound words, and affixes (e.g., *ca'nt* for *can't, alot* for *a lot, acter* for *actor,* and *huose* for *house*). Words with reversed letters and extra letters were also included in this category.

Other research has focused on the relationship between reading and spelling (Anderson, 1985). Researchers have examined the spelling strategies of poor readers in fourth through sixth grade and found that these students were likely to use a sounding-out strategy. Good readers, on the other hand, used a variety of spelling strategies, including visual information, knowledge about root words and affixes, and analogy to known words. Frith (1980) concluded that older students who are good readers and spellers make spelling errors characteristic of the transitional stage, while students who are poor readers and spellers make spelling errors characteristic of the semiphonetic and phonetic stages.

The press and concerned parent groups periodically raise concerns about invented spelling and the importance of weekly spelling tests. There seems to be a public misperception that today's children cannot spell. Researchers who are examining the types of errors students make have noted that the *number* of misspellings increases in grades 1 through 4, as students write longer compositions, but that the *percentage* of errors decreases. The percentage continues to decline in the upper grades, although some students continue to make errors (Taylor & Kidder, 1988). The Educational Testing Service (Applebee, Langer, & Mullis, 1987) reported on the frequency of spelling errors in formal writing assessments. Nine-year-olds averaged 92% correct spelling; 13-year-olds spelled 97% of words correctly; and 17-year-olds scored 98%. Stewig (1987) reported that the fourth graders in his study spelled 98–99% of words correctly. These data suggest that by fourth grade most students are conventional spellers, making fewer than 10% errors.

Analyzing Children's Spelling Development.   Teachers can analyze spelling errors in children's compositions by classifying the errors according to the five stages of spelling development. This analysis will provide information about the child's current level of spelling development and the kinds of errors the child makes. Knowing the stage of a student's spelling development helps teachers suggest the appropriate type of instruction. Children who are not yet at the conventional stage of spelling development—that is, who do not spell at least 90% of words correctly and whose errors are not mostly at the transitional level—do not benefit from formal spelling instruction. Instead, early instruction should support students' spelling development. Minilessons that are appropriate to a student's stage of development, such as learning visual and morphological strategies for a transitional speller, are much more beneficial.

A composition written by Marc, a first grader, is presented in Figure 12–3. He reverses *b* and *s,* and these two reversals make his writing more difficult to decipher. Here is a translation of Marc's composition:

Today a person at home called us and said that a bomb was in our school and made us go outside and made us wait a half of an hour and it made us waste our time on learning. The end.

Figure 12–3   *An Analysis of an Emergent Writer's Invented Spelling*

To bay a perezun at home kob
uz anb seb that a bome wuz in
or skuwl anb mab uz go at zib
anb makbe uz wat a haf uf
a awr anb it mab uz wazt or
time on loren ee ing.

THE eNb

Precommunicative	Semiphonetic	Phonetic	Transitional	Conventional
	kod	sed	peresun	today
		wus	bome	a
		or	skuwl	at
		mad	makde	home
		at sid	uf	us
		wat	loreneeing	and
		haf		that
		awr		a
		mad		in
		wast		and
		or		us
				go
				and
				us
				a
				a
				and
				it
				us
				time
				on
				the
				end
Total 0	1	11	6	23
Percent 0	2	27	15	56

Marc was writing about a traumatic event, and it was appropriate for him to use invented spelling in his composition. Primary-grade students should write using invented spelling, and correct spelling is appropriate when the composition will "go public." Prematurely differentiating between "kid" and "adult" spelling interferes with children's natural spelling development and makes them dependent on adults to supply the "adult" spelling.

Spelling can be categorized using a chart, also shown in Figure 12–3, to gauge students' spelling development and to anticipate upcoming changes in their spelling strategies. Teachers write the stages of spelling development across the top of the chart and list each word in the student's composition under one of the categories, ignoring proper nouns, capitalization errors, and poorly formed or reversed letters.

Perhaps the most interesting thing about Marc's writing is that he spelled 56% of the words correctly. Only one word, *kod* (*called*), is categorized as semiphonetic, and it is classified this way because the spelling is extremely abbreviated, with only the first and last sounds represented. The 11 words categorized as phonetic are words in which it appears that his spelling represents only the sounds heard; unpronounced letters, such as the final *e* in *made* and the *i* in *wait*, are not represented. Marc pronounces *our* as though it were a homophone for *or,* so *or* is a reasonable phonetic spelling. Homophone errors are phonological, because the child focuses on sound, not on meaning.

The words categorized as transitional exemplify a spelling strategy other than sound. In *bome* (*bomb*), for example, Marc applied the final *e* rule he recently learned, even though it isn't appropriate in this word. In time he will learn to spell the word with an unpronounced *b* and will learn that this *b* is needed because *bomb* is a newer, shortened form of *bombard,* in which the *b* in the middle of the word is pronounced. The *b* remains in *bomb* because of the etymology of the word. The word *makde* is especially interesting. Marc pronounced the word "maked," and the *de* is a reversal of letters, a common characteristic of transitional spelling. Transitional spellers often spell *girl* as *gril* and *friend* as *freind*. Marc's use of *maked,* not *made,* for the past tense of *make* is a grammatical error and unimportant in determining the stage of spelling development. *Loreneeing* (*learning*) is categorized as transitional because Marc added long-vowel markers (an *e* after *lor* and *ee* after *n*). Because the spelling is based on his pronunciation of *learning,* the long-vowel markers and the conventional spelling of the suffix *-ing* signal a transitional spelling. Categorizing spelling errors in a child's composition and computing the percentage of errors in each category is a useful tool for diagnosing the level of spelling development and deciding whether or not to begin weekly spelling tests.

From the spelling in Marc's composition, he might be classified as a phonetic speller who is moving toward the transitional stage. Marc's paper in Figure 12–3 was written in January of his first-grade year, and he is making expected progress in spelling. During the next few months he will begin to notice that his spelling doesn't look right (e.g., *sed* for *said*), and he will note visual features of words. He will apply the vowel rules he is learning more effectively, particularly the final *e* (*mad* will become *made, sid* will become *side,* and *wast* will become *waste*).

Marc is not ready for weekly spelling tests, in which he would memorize correct spellings of words, because he has not yet internalized the visual and morphological spelling strategies of the transitional stage. Also, Marc will probably self-correct the two letter reversals through daily writing experiences, as long as he is not placed under great pressure to form the letters correctly. It would be wrong to suggest, however, that Marc is not receiving spelling instruction. He is. Marc's spelling shows that he is learning consonant and vowel sounds, vowel rules, and spelling patterns.

Teaching Spelling in the Elementary Grades

Spelling instruction is more than weekly spelling tests. Too often parents and teachers equate spelling instruction with weekly spelling tests, but a comprehensive spelling program includes much more. Most importantly, it includes teaching students about English orthography, applying phonics concepts to spelling, and providing students with opportunities to read and write for meaningful, functional, and genuine purposes.

Components of the Spelling Program. A comprehensive spelling program has eight components, including reading and writing opportunities and teaching minilessons about English orthography and spelling procedures. Students learn about spelling through reading and writing and related activities.

1. Provide daily writing opportunities. Providing opportunities for students to write every day is prerequisite to any spelling program. Spelling is a writer's tool, and it is best learned through the experience of writing. Students who write daily and invent spellings for unfamiliar words move naturally toward conventional spelling. When they write, children guess at spellings using their developing knowledge of sound-symbol correspondences and spell-

Middle-grade students participate in a minilesson on how to form plurals.

ing patterns. Most of the informal writing students do each day doesn't need to be graded, and spelling errors should not be marked. Learning to spell is a lot like learning to play the piano. These daily writing opportunities are the practice sessions, not the lesson with the teacher.

When students use the writing process to develop and polish their writings, emphasis on conventional spelling belongs in the editing stage. Through the process approach, children learn to recognize spelling for what it is—a courtesy to readers. As they write, revise, edit, and share their writing with genuine audiences, students understand that they need to spell conventionally so that their audience can read their compositions.

2. Provide daily reading opportunities.   Reading plays an enormous role in students' learning to spell. As they read, students store the visual shapes of words. The ability to recall how words look helps students decide when a spelling they are writing is correct. When students decide that a word doesn't look right, they can rewrite the word several different ways until it does look right, ask the teacher or a classmate who knows the spelling, or check the spelling in a dictionary.

3. Post words on word walls.   One way to direct students' attention to words in books they are reading or in social studies and science theme cycles is through the use of word walls. Students and the teacher choose words to write on word walls, large sheets of paper hanging in the classroom. Then students refer to these word walls for word-study activities and when they are writing. Seeing the words posted on word walls, clusters, and other charts in the classroom and using them in their writing help students to learn to spell the words.

■ *To read more about word walls, turn back to Chapter 5, "Looking Closely at Words," pp. 202–204.*

Teachers also hang word walls with high-frequency words (Cunningham, 1995; Marinelli, 1996). Researchers have identified the most commonly used words and recommend that elementary students learn to spell 100 to 500 of these words because of their usefulness. The 100 most frequently used words represent more than 50% of all the words children and adults write (E. Horn, 1926)! The Teacher's Notebook on page 489 lists the 100 most frequently used words and suggests ways teachers can teach these words. Some teachers type the alphabetized word list on small cards—personal word walls—that students keep at their desks and refer to when they write (Lacey, 1994).

4. Provide opportunities for students to build words.   Students arrange and rearrange a group of letter cards to build words (Cunningham & Cunningham, 1992). Primary-grade students can use the letters *s, p, i, d, e,* and *r* to build *is, red, dip, rip, sip, side, ride,* and *ripe.* Or, with the letters *t, e, m, p, e, r, a, t, u, r,* and *e,* a class of fifth graders built these words:

1-letter words: *a*
2-letter words: *at, up*
3-letter words: *pet, are, rat, eat, ate, tap, pat*
4-letter words: *ramp, rate, pare, pear, meat, meet, team, tree*
5-letter words: *treat*
6-letter words: *temper, tamper, mature, repeat, turret*
7-letter words: *trumpet, rapture*
8-letter words: *repeater*
9-letter words: *temperate, trumpeter*

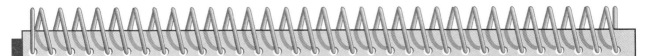

Teacher's Notebook

The 100 Most Frequently Used Words

a	did	in	out	time
about	didn't	into	over	to
after	do	is	people	too
all	don't	it	put	two
am	down	just	said	up
an	for	know	saw	us
and	from	like	school	very
are	get	little	see	was
around	got	man	she	we
as	had	me	so	well
at	have	mother	some	went
back	he	my	that	were
be	her	no	the	what
because	him	not	them	when
but	his	now	then	who
by	home	of	there	will
came	house	on	they	with
can	how	one	things	would
could	I	or	think	you
day	if	our	this	your

Ways to Use This List of Words

1. List these words on bookmarks or tagboard cards that students keep at their desks and refer to when writing.
2. Explain to students the importance of knowing how to spell these words: these 100 words are used again and again, and when students know how to spell them, they will be able to spell half of all the words they write.
3. Make a wall chart with these words and have students add other frequently used words during the school year.
4. For younger students or less capable writers, pick out the 10 or 20 words that your students use most often and make cards with these words for students to keep at their desks.
5. Use words from this list to use in minilessons to contrast "sight words" with words that can be sounded out.
6. Choose words from this list for spelling words since these words are the most frequently used, and high-frequency words should be taught before low-frequency words.
7. These words are also high-frequency reading "sight words." Use this list to develop reading fluency, too.

Students work in small groups and begin by looking for one-letter words. Then they build two-letter words and progressively longer words by arranging and rearranging the letters. Students record the words they build on a chart, in columns according to the length of the word. Teachers often introduce these activities as a whole-class lesson and then set the cards and the word list in a center for students to use again independently or in small groups. Teachers can use almost any words for word-building activities, but words related to literature focus units and theme cycles work well. The words *spider* and *temperature* were selected from science theme cycles.

5.   Teach students to proofread.   Proofreading is a special kind of reading that students use to locate misspelled words and other mechanical errors in their rough drafts. As students learn about the writing process, they are introduced to proofreading. In the editing stage, they receive more in-depth instruction about how to use proofreading to locate spelling errors and then correct these misspelled words (Wilde, 1996). Through a series of mini-lessons, students can proofread sample student papers and mark misspelled words. Then, working in pairs, students can correct the misspelled words.

Proofreading should be introduced in the primary grades. Young children and their teachers proofread class collaboration and dictated stories together, and students can be encouraged to read over their own compositions and make necessary corrections soon after they begin writing. This way students accept proofreading as a natural part of both spelling and writing. Proofreading activities are more valuable for teaching spelling than dictation activities, in which teachers dictate sentences for students to write and correctly capitalize and punctuate. Few people use dictation in their daily lives, but students use proofreading skills every time they polish a piece of writing.

■ *See Chapter 3, "The Reading and Writing Processes," pp. 121–123, to read more about proofreading and editing.*

6.   Teach students to use the dictionary.   Students need to learn how to locate the spelling of unknown words in the dictionary. Of the approximately 750,000 entry words in an unabridged dictionary, students typically learn to spell 3,000 by the end of eighth grade—leaving 747,000 words unaccounted for! Obviously, students must learn how to locate the spellings of some additional words. While it is relatively easy to find a "known" word in the dictionary, it is hard to locate an unfamiliar word, and students need to learn what to do when they don't know how to spell a word. One approach is to predict possible spellings for unknown words, then check the most probable spellings in a dictionary. This procedure involves six steps:

   a. Identify root words and affixes.
   b. Consider related words (e.g., *medicine–medical*).
   c. Determine the sounds in the word.
   d. Generate a list of possible spellings.
   e. Select the most probable alternatives.
   f. Consult a dictionary to check the correct spelling.

The fourth step, during which students develop a list of possible spellings using their knowledge of both phonology and morphology, is undoubtedly the most difficult. Phoneme-grapheme relationships may rate primary consideration in generating spelling options for some words; root words and affixes or related words may be more important in determining how other words are spelled.

7. Teach spelling options. In English there are alternate spellings for many sounds because so many words that have been borrowed from other languages retain their native spellings. There are many more options for vowel sounds than for consonants. Even so, there are four spelling options for /f/ (*f, ff, ph, gh*). Spelling options sometimes vary according to position in the word. For example, *ff* and *gh* are used to represent /f/ only at the end of a word, as in *cuff* and *laugh*. Common spelling options for phonemes are listed in Figure 12–4.

Teachers point out spelling options as they write words on word walls and when students ask about the spelling of a word. They can also use a series of minilessons to teach upper-grade students about these options. During each minilesson, students can focus on one phoneme, such as /f/ or /ar/, and as a class or small group develop a list of the various ways the sound is spelled in English, giving examples of each spelling. A sixth-grade chart on long *o* is presented in Figure 12–5.

8. Teach spelling strategies through minilessons. Students need to develop a repertoire of strategies in order to spell unfamiliar words (Laminack & Wood, 1996; Wilde, 1993). Some of these spelling strategies are:

- Invent spellings for words based on phonological, semantic, and historical knowledge of words.
- Proofread to locate and correct spelling errors.
- Locate words on word walls and other charts.
- Predict the spelling of a word by generating possible spellings and choose the best alternative.
- Apply affixes to root words.
- Spell unknown words by analogy to known words.
- Locate the spelling of unfamiliar words in a dictionary or other resource book.
- Write a string of letters as a placeholder to stand for an unfamiliar word in a rough draft.
- Ask the teacher or a classmate how to spell a word.
- Have "ownership" of a word, that is, know when the spelling of a word has been internalized.

Instead of giving the traditional "sound it out" advice when students ask how to spell an unfamiliar word, teachers should help them use a strategic approach. I suggest that teachers encourage students to "think it out." This advice reminds students that spelling involves more than phonological information and suggests a more strategic approach.

Teachers teach students about spelling procedures, concepts, and strategies and skills during minilessons. A list of topics for spelling minilessons is presented on page 494. Some of the topics are more appropriate for primary-grade students, and others are for older students.

9. Develop students' spelling conscience. The goal of spelling instruction is to help students develop what Hillerich (1977) calls a "spelling conscience"—a positive attitude toward spelling and a concern for using standard spelling. Two dimensions of a spelling conscience are understanding that standard spelling is a courtesy to readers and developing the ability to proofread to spot and correct misspellings.

Figure 12-4   *Common Spelling Options for Phonemes*

Sound	Spellings	Examples	Sound	Spellings	Examples
long a	a-e	date	short oo	oo	book
	a	angel		u	put
	ai	aid		ou	could
	ay	day		o	woman
ch	ch	church	ou	ou	out
	t(u)	picture		ow	cow
	tch	watch	s	s	sick
	ti	question		ce	office
long e	ea	each		c	city
	ee	feel		ss	class
	e	evil		se	else
	e-e	these		x(ks)	box
	ea-e	breathe	sh	ti	attention
short e	e	end		sh	she
	ea	head		ci	ancient
f	f	feel		ssi	admission
	ff	sheriff	t	t	teacher
	ph	photograph		te	definite
j	ge	strange		ed	furnished
	g	general		tt	attend
	j	job	long u	u	union
	dge	bridge		u-e	use
k	c	call		ue	value
	k	keep		ew	few
	x	expect, luxury	short u	u	ugly
	ck	black		o	company
	qu	quite, bouquet		ou	country
l	l	last	y	u	union
	ll	allow		u-e	use
	le	automobile		y	yes
m	m	man		i	onion
	me	come		ue	value
	mm	comment		ew	few
n	n	no	z	s	present
	ne	done		se	applause
long o	o	go		ze	gauze
	o-e	note	syllabic *l*	le	able
	ow	own		al	animal
	oa	load		el	cancel
short o	o	office		il	civil
	a	all	syllabic *n*	en	written
	au	author		on	lesson
	aw	saw		an	important
oi	oi	oil		in	cousin
	oy	boy		contractions	didn't
long oo	u	cruel		ain	certain
	oo	noon	*r*-controlled	er	her
	u-e	rule		ur	church
	o-e	lose		ir	first
	ue	blue		or	world
	o	to		ear	heard
	ou	group		our	courage

6th GR

Figure 12–5 *A Sixth-Grade Class Chart on Spelling Options for Long o*

Spelling	Word	Location: Initial	Location: Medial	Location: Final
o	oh, obedient	x		
	go, no, so			x
o-e	home, pole		x	
ow	own	x		
	known		x	
	blow, elbow, yellow			x
oa	oaf, oak, oat	x		
	boat, groan		x	
ew	sew			x
ol	yolk, folk		x	
oe	toe			x
ough	though			x
eau	beau			x
ou	bouquet		x	

Students in the middle and upper grades need to learn that it is unrealistic to expect readers to try to decipher numerous misspelled words. This dimension of a spelling conscience develops as students write frequently and for varied audiences. As students move from writing for themselves to writing to communicate with others, they internalize this concept. Teachers help students recognize the purpose of conventional spelling by providing meaningful writing activities directed to a variety of genuine audiences.

Weekly Spelling Tests. Many teachers question the use of spelling tests to teach spelling, since research on invented spelling suggests that spelling is best learned through reading and writing (Gentry & Gillet, 1993; Wilde, 1993). In addition, teachers complain that lists of spelling words are unrelated to the words students are reading and writing, and the 30 minutes of valuable instructional time spent each day in completing spelling textbook activities is excessive. I recommend that weekly spelling tests, when they are used, be individualized so that children learn to spell the words they need for their writing.

In an individualized approach to spelling instruction, students choose the words they will study, and many of the words they choose are words they use in their writing projects. Students study five to eight specific words during the week using a specific study strategy. This approach places more responsibility on students for their own learning, and when students have responsibility, they tend to perform better.

Teachers develop a weekly word list of 25 to 50 words of varying levels of difficulty from which students select words to study. Words for the master list are drawn from words students needed for their writing projects during the previous week, high-frequency words, and words related to literature focus

Language Tools

	Procedures	Concepts	Strategies and Skills
Spelling	Invent spellings Locate words on a word wall Locate words in a dictionary Proofread Form contractions Form plurals Use other inflectional endings Use a thesaurus Study a spelling word Assess use of spelling strategies Analyze spelling errors	Alphabetic principle "Kid" or invented spelling Homophones Root words and affixes Spelling options High-frequency words Dictionary Thesaurus Spelling conscience Phoneme-grapheme correspondences Contractions Compound words Possessives	Use placeholders Sound it out Think it out Visualize words Use analogy Apply affixes Generate possible spellings Choose probable alternatives Proofread Apply capitalization rules *sticky notes*
Handwriting	Grip a pencil Form letters Space between letters Size letters Make letters parallel Write manuscript letters Write cursive letters Make letters touch the baseline Keep letters same size Make lines steady and of even thickness Assess handwriting problems	Legible Fluent Manuscript handwriting Cursive handwriting D'Nealian handwriting Uppercase letters Lowercase letters Public and private handwriting Elements of legibility	Determine purpose of handwriting Choose manuscript or cursive Apply elements of legibility Personalize handwriting
Grammar	Identify parts of speech Classify sentence types Slot sentences Manipulate sentences Combine sentences Make concept books Assess appropriateness of usage Assess use of strategies	Grammar Usage Standard English Parts of speech Subject and predicate Simple sentences Compound sentences Complex sentences Declarative sentences Interrogative sentences Imperative sentences Exclamatory sentences	Use complete sentences Expand sentences Rearrange sentences Combine sentences Vary sentence length Consider register Proofread to locate usage errors

(handwritten in left margin) ...(t)-shən(t)/s/n 193

units and theme cycles ongoing in the classroom. Words from spelling text-books can also be added to the list, but they should never make up the entire list. The master word list can be used for minilessons during the week. Students can look for phoneme-grapheme correspondences, add words to charts of spelling options, and note root words and affixes.

On Monday the teacher administers the pretest using the master list of words, and students spell as many of the words as they can. Students correct their own pretests, and from the words they misspell, each student chooses five to eight words to study. They make two copies of their study list. Students number their spelling words using the numbers on the master list to make it easier to take the final test on Friday. Students keep one copy of the list to study, and the teacher keeps the second copy.

Researchers have found that the pretest is a critical component in learning to spell. The pretest eliminates words that students already know how to spell so that they can direct their study toward words that they don't know yet. As long ago as 1947, Ernest Horn recommended that the best way to improve students' spelling is for them to get immediate feedback by correcting their own pretests. His advice is still sound today.

Students spend approximately 5 to 10 minutes studying the words on their study lists each day during the week. Instead of "busy-work" activities, such as using their spelling words in sentences or gluing yarn in the shape of the words, research shows that it is more effective for students to use this strategy for practicing spelling words:

1. Look at the word and say it to yourself.
2. Say each letter in the word to yourself.
3. Close your eyes and spell the word to yourself.
4. Write the word, and check that you spelled it correctly.
5. Write the word again, and check that you spelled it correctly.

This strategy focuses on the whole word rather than breaking it apart into sounds or syllables. During a minilesson at the beginning of the school year, teachers explain how to use the strategy, and then they post a copy of the strategy in the classroom. In addition to this word-study strategy, sometimes students trade word lists on Wednesday or Thursday and give each other a practice test.

A final test is administered on Friday. The teacher reads the master list, and students write only those words they have practiced during the week. To make it easier to administer the test, students first list the numbers of the words they have practiced from their study lists on their test papers. Any words that students misspell should be included on their lists the following week.

This individualized approach is recommended instead of a textbook approach. Typically, textbooks are arranged in week-long units, with lists of 10 to 20 words and practice activities that often require at least 30 minutes per day to complete. Research indicates that only 60 to 75 minutes per week should be spent on spelling instruction, however, and greater periods of time do not result in increased spelling ability (Johnson, Langford, & Quorn, 1981). Moreover, many textbook activities focus on language arts skills that are not directly related to learning to spell.

The words in each unit are often grouped according to spelling patterns or phonetic generalizations, even though researchers question this approach;

Johnson et al. found that "the effectiveness of teaching spelling via phonic generalizations is highly questionable" (1981, p. 586). Students often memorize the rule or spelling pattern and score perfectly on the spelling test but later are unable to choose among spelling options in their writing. For example, after learning the *i-e* vowel rule and the *-igh* spelling pattern in isolation, students are often stumped about how to spell a word such as *light*. They have learned two spelling options for /ay/, *ie* and *-igh,* and *lite* is an option, one they often see in their environment. Instead of organizing words according to phonetic generalizations and spelling rules, we recommend that teachers teach minilessons and point out the rules as they occur when writing words on word walls.

Adapting to Meet the Needs of Every Student.   Spelling and the other language tools can be adapted to meet the needs of all students, and the single most important adaptation teachers can make is to understand the relative importance of language tools in the language arts program. Communicative competence is the goal of language arts instruction, and language tools support communication, but they do not equal it. For spelling instruction, that means encouraging students to use invented spelling so that they can communicate with others before they reach the stage of conventional spelling. Students who are learning English as a second language or who have special needs may take longer to move through the five stages of invented spelling, and their invented spelling will reflect their pronunciation of words and use of inflectional endings. For example, a child who says "I have two *cat*" or "Yesterday I *play* with my friend" usually spells words the same way. Suggestions for adapting the spelling program to meet the needs of all students are presented on page 497.

Assessing Students' Progress in Spelling.   Grades on weekly spelling tests are the traditional measure of progress in spelling, and the individualized approach to spelling instruction provides this convenient way to assess students. This method of assessing student progress is somewhat deceptive, however, because the goal of spelling instruction is not simply to spell words correctly on weekly tests but to use the words, spelled conventionally, in writing. Samples of student writing should be collected periodically to determine whether words that were spelled correctly on tests are being spelled correctly in writing projects. If students are not applying in their writing what they have learned through the weekly spelling instruction, they may not have learned to spell the words after all.

When students perform poorly on spelling tests, consider whether faulty pronunciation or poor handwriting is to blame. Ask students to pronounce words they habitually misspell to see if their pronunciation or dialect differences may be contributing to spelling problems. Students need to recognize that pronunciation does not always predict spelling. For example, in some parts of the United States, people pronounce the words *pin* and *pen* as though they were spelled with the same vowel, and sometimes we pronounce *better* as though it were spelled *bedder* and *going* as though it were spelled *goin'*. Also, ask students to spell orally the words they spell incorrectly in their writing to see whether handwriting difficulties are contributing to spelling problems. Sometimes a minilesson on how to connect two cursive letters

Adapting
Spelling Instruction
To Meet the Needs of Every Student

1. Encourage Invented Spelling

Too often poor spellers don't want to write because there are so many words they don't know how to spell. Teachers should encourage students to use invented spelling, no matter how old they are, because it allows them to write independently. Their invented spellings provide valuable insights to what students know about English orthography and what kind of instruction they need.

2. Teach High-Frequency Words

Poor spellers should learn to spell the 100 most frequently used words because of their usefulness. Knowing the 100 most frequently used words allows students to spell approximately half of all words they write correctly!

3. Teach the Think-It-Out Strategy

Poor spellers typically rely on a sound-it-out strategy to spell words, while better spellers understand that sound is only a rough guide to spelling. Teachers use minilessons to teach students how to think out and predict the spelling of unfamiliar words.

4. Read and Write Every Day

Students who are poor spellers often don't read or write very much, but they need to read and write every day in order to become better spellers.

5. Recognize That Errors Are Part of Learning

Primary-grade students who use invented spelling and older students who are poor spellers do not benefit by having teachers circle spelling errors on their papers. Instead, the teacher and student should work together to identify and correct errors on writing projects that will be published. Too much emphasis on what students misspell does not help them to spell; it teaches them that they cannot spell.

(e.g., *br*) or a reminder about the importance of legible handwriting will solve the problem.

■ *Turn to Chapter 2, "Teaching Language Arts," pp. 71–73, for more information on anecdotal notes.*

It is essential that teachers keep anecdotal information and samples of children's writing to monitor their overall progress in spelling. Teachers can examine error patterns and spelling strategies in these samples. Checking to see if students have spelled their spelling words correctly in writing samples provides one type of information, and examining writing samples for error patterns and spelling strategies provides additional information. Fewer misspellings do not necessarily indicate progress, because to learn to spell, students must experiment with spellings of unfamiliar words, which will result in errors from time to time. Students often misspell a word by misapplying

497

a newly learned spelling pattern. The word *extension* is a good example. Middle-grade students spell the word *extenshun,* then change their spelling to *extention* after they learn the suffix *-tion.* Although they are still misspelling the word, they have moved from using sound-symbol correspondences to using a spelling pattern—from a less sophisticated spelling strategy to a more sophisticated one.

Students' behavior as they proofread and edit their compositions also provides evidence of spelling development. They should become increasingly able to spot misspelled words in their compositions and locate the spelling of unknown words in a dictionary. It is easy for teachers to calculate the number of spelling errors students have identified in proofreading their compositions and to chart students' progress in learning to spot errors. Locating errors is the first step in proofreading; correcting the errors is the second step. It is fairly easy for students to correct the spelling of known words, but to correct unknown words, they must consider spelling options and predict possible spellings before they can locate the words in a dictionary. Teachers can also document students' growth in locating unfamiliar words in a dictionary by observing their behavior when they edit their compositions.

Teachers can collect writing samples to document children's spelling development. They can note primary-grade students' progression through the stages of invented spelling by analyzing writing samples in a chart such as the one in Figure 12–3 to determine a general stage of development. Teachers can adapt the checklist for students in the middle and upper grades, and students can use this chart to analyze their own spelling errors.

end of 12A

HANDWRITING

Like spelling, handwriting is a tool for writers. Graves explains: "Children win prizes for fine script, parents and teachers nod approval for a crisp, well-crafted page, a good impression is made on a job application blank . . . all important elements, but they pale next to the *substance* they carry" (1983, p. 171). Even though the message is more important than the formation of letters, handwriting is still an essential communication tool, and handwriting instruction should not be ignored. Donald Graves (1994) urges teachers to keep handwriting in perspective.

It is important to distinguish between writing and *hand*writing. Writing is the substance of a composition; handwriting is the formation of alphabetic symbols on paper. Students need to develop a legible and fluent style of handwriting so that they will be able to fully participate in all written language activities.

The goal in handwriting instruction is to help students develop legible forms to communicate effectively through writing. The two most important criteria in determining quality in handwriting are legibility (the writing can be easily and quickly read) and fluency (the writing can be easily and quickly written). Even though a few students take great pleasure in developing flawless handwriting skills, most of them feel that handwriting instruction is boring and unnecessary. It is imperative, therefore, to recognize the functional purpose of handwriting and convey to students the importance of developing legible handwriting. Writing for genuine audiences is the best way to convey the importance of legibility. A letter sent to a favorite author that is returned by the post office because the address is not decipherable or a child's published hardcover book that sits unread on the library shelf because the handwriting is illegible makes clear the importance of legibility. <u>Illegible writing means a failure to communicate—a harsh lesson for a writer!</u>

Handwriting Forms

Two forms of handwriting are currently used in elementary schools: <u>manuscript</u>, or <u>printing</u>, and cursive, or <u>connected</u> writing. These are illustrated in Figure 12–6. Typically, students in the primary grades learn and use the manuscript form; they switch to cursive handwriting in second or third grade. In the middle and upper grades, students use both handwriting forms.

Manuscript Handwriting. Until the 1920s, students learned only cursive handwriting. Marjorie Wise is credited with introducing the manuscript form for primary-grade students in 1921 (Hildreth, 1960). Manuscript handwriting is considered better for young children because they seem to lack the necessary fine motor control and eye-hand coordination for cursive handwriting. In addition, manuscript handwriting is similar to the type style in primary-level reading textbooks. <u>Only two lowercase letters, *a* and *g,* are different in typed and handwritten forms.</u> The similarity is assumed to facilitate young children's introduction to reading and writing.

Barbe and Milone (1980) suggest several additional reasons that students in the primary grades should learn manuscript before cursive handwriting. First, <u>manuscript handwriting is easier to learn.</u> Studies show that young children can copy letters and words written in the manuscript form more easily than those written in the cursive form. Also, young children can form the vertical and horizontal lines and circles of manuscript handwriting more easily than the cursive strokes. <u>Furthermore, manuscript handwriting is more legible than cursive handwriting.</u> Because it is easier to read, signs and advertisements are printed in letter forms closely approximating manuscript handwriting. Finally, people are often requested to print when completing applications and other forms. For these reasons, manuscript handwriting has become the preferred handwriting form for young children as well as a necessary handwriting skill for older children and adults.

Students' use of the manuscript form often disappears in the middle grades after they have learned cursive handwriting. It is essential that middle- and upper-grade teachers learn and use the manuscript form with their students so that it remains an option. <u>Second and third graders learn cursive handwriting, a new form, just when they are becoming proficient in the manuscript form,</u> so it is not surprising that some students want to switch back and forth between the two. The need to develop greater writing speed is often given as the reason for the quick transfer to cursive handwriting, but research does not show that one form is necessarily written more quickly than the other.

There have also been criticisms of the manuscript form. A major complaint is the reversal problem caused by some similar lowercase letters; *b* and *d* are particularly confusing. Other detractors argue that using both the manuscript and cursive forms in the elementary grades requires teaching students

500

Figure 12–6   Manuscript and Cursive Handwriting Forms

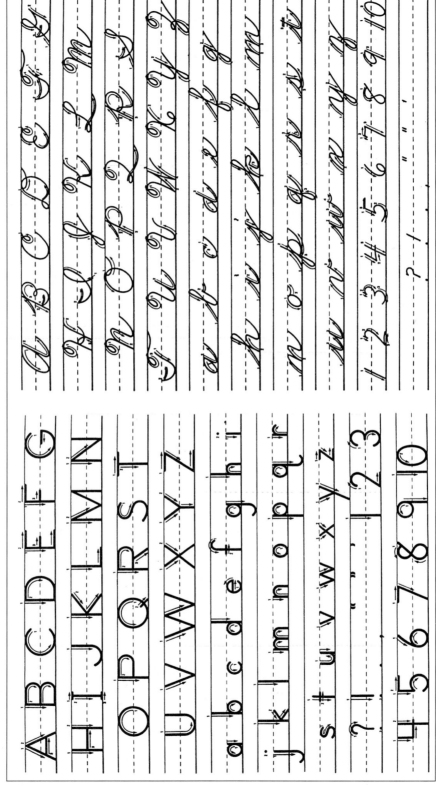

two totally different kinds of handwriting within the span of several years. They also complain that the "circle and sticks" style of manuscript handwriting requires frequent stops and starts, thus inhibiting a smooth and rhythmic flow of writing.

Cursive Handwriting. When most people think of handwriting, the cursive or connected form comes to mind. The letters in cursive handwriting are joined together to form a word with one continuous movement. Children often view cursive handwriting as the "grown-up" type. Primary-grade students often attempt to imitate this form by connecting the manuscript letters in their names and other words before they are taught how to form and join the letters. Awareness of cursive handwriting and interest in imitating it are indicators that students are ready for instruction.

D'Nealian Handwriting. D'Nealian handwriting is an innovative manuscript and cursive handwriting program developed by Donald Neal Thurber, a teacher in Michigan. The D'Nealian handwriting forms are shown in Figure 12–7. In the manuscript form, letters are slanted and formed with a continuous stroke; in the cursive form, the letters are simplified, without the flourishes of traditional cursive. Both forms were designed to increase legibility and fluency and to ease the transition from manuscript to cursive handwriting.

The purpose of the D'Nealian program was to mitigate some of the problems associated with the traditional manuscript form (Thurber, 1987). D'Nealian manuscript uses the same basic letter forms that students will need for cursive handwriting, as well as the slant and rhythm required for cursive. Another advantage of the D'Nealian style is that the transition from manuscript to cursive involves adding only connective strokes to most manuscript letters. Only five letters—*f, r, s, v,* and *z*—are shaped differently in the cursive form.

Children's Handwriting Development

During the elementary grades, children grow from using scribbles and letter-like forms in kindergarten to learning the manuscript handwriting form in the primary grades and the cursive form beginning in the middle grades. Students in the middle and upper grades use both forms interchangeably for a variety of handwriting tasks. Examples of children's handwriting from kindergarten through eighth grade are shown in Figure 12–8. The excerpts were selected from letters.

Handwriting Before First Grade. Children's handwriting grows out of their drawing activities. Young children observe words all around them in their environment: *McDonald's, Coke, STOP.* They also observe parents and teachers writing messages. From this early interest in written words and communicating through writing, preschoolers begin to write letterlike forms and scribbles. In kindergarten, children watch the teacher transcribe language experience stories, and they begin to copy their names and familiar words. Once they are familiar with some of the letters, they use invented spelling to express themselves in writing. Through this drawing-reading-writing-handwriting connection, youngsters discover that they can experiment with letters

Figure 12-7   D'Nealian Manuscript and Cursive Handwriting Forms

Source: D'Nealian is a registered trademark of Donald Neal Thurber, Copyright © 1987 by Scott, Foresman and Company.

and words and communicate through written language. Handwriting becomes the tool for this written communication.

Young children enter kindergarten with different backgrounds of handwriting experience. Some 5-year-olds have never held a pencil, and many others have written cursivelike scribbles or manuscript letterlike forms. Some

Figure 12–8   *Examples of Children's Handwriting*

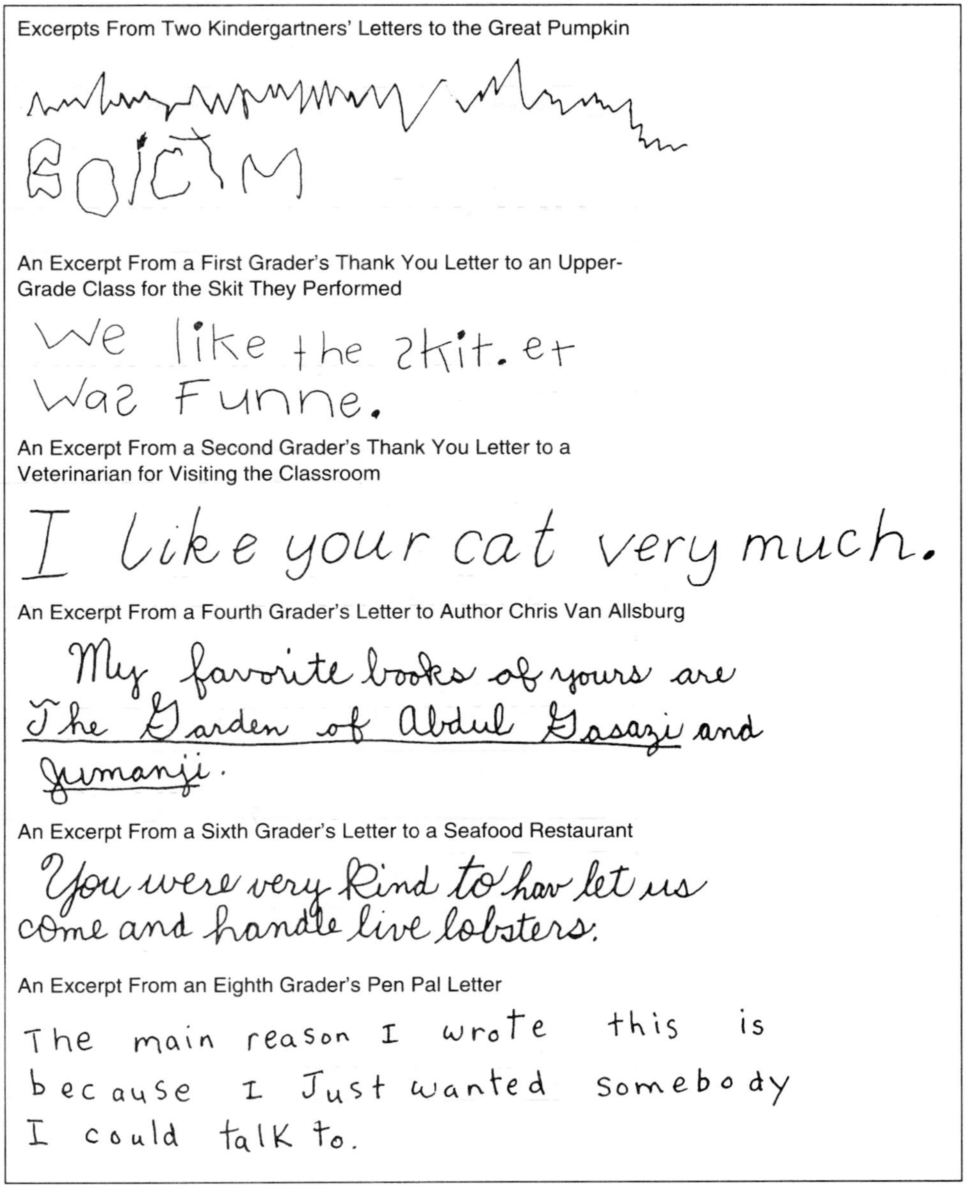

Excerpts From Two Kindergartners' Letters to the Great Pumpkin

BOICTM

An Excerpt From a First Grader's Thank You Letter to an Upper-
Grade Class for the Skit They Performed

We like the skit. et
Waz Funne.

An Excerpt From a Second Grader's Thank You Letter to a
Veterinarian for Visiting the Classroom

I Like your cat very much.

An Excerpt From a Fourth Grader's Letter to Author Chris Van Allsburg

My favorite books of yours are
The Garden of Abdul Gasazi and
Jumanji.

An Excerpt From a Sixth Grader's Letter to a Seafood Restaurant

You were very Kind to hav let us
come and handle live lobsters.

An Excerpt From an Eighth Grader's Pen Pal Letter

The main reason I wrote this is
because I Just wanted somebody
I could talk to.

preschoolers have learned to print their names and some other letters. Hand-writing in kindergarten typically includes three types of activities: stimulating children's interest in writing, developing their ability to hold writing instruments, and refining their fine motor control. Adults are influential role models in stimulating children's interest in writing. They record children's talk and write labels on signs. They can also provide paper, pencils, and pens so that children can experiment with writing. Students develop the ability to hold a pencil or other writing instrument by adults' modeling and through numerous opportunities to experiment with pencils, pens, paintbrushes, crayons, and other writing instruments.

Handwriting instruction in kindergarten usually focuses on teaching children to form upper- and lowercase letters and to print their names. Handwriting is linked with writing at all grade levels, even in kindergarten. Young children write labels, draw and write stories, keep journals, and write other messages (Klein & Schickedanz, 1980). The more they write, the greater their need becomes for instruction in handwriting. Writers need to know how to grip a pencil, form letters, and leave space between letters and words. Instruction is necessary so that students do not learn bad habits that later must be broken. Students often devise rather bizarre ways to form letters, and these bad habits can cause problems when they need to develop greater writing speed.

Handwriting in the Primary Grades.   Formal handwriting instruction begins in first grade. Students learn how to form manuscript letters and space between them, and they develop skills related to the six elements of legibility. A common handwriting activity requires students to copy short writing samples from the chalkboard, but this type of activity is not recommended. For one thing, young children have great difficulty with far-to-near copying (Lamme, 1979); a piece of writing should be placed close to the child for copying. Children can recopy their own compositions, language experience stories, and self-selected writing samples; other types of copying should be avoided. It is far better for children to create their own writing than to copy words and sentences they may not even be able to read!

Special pencils and handwriting paper are often provided for handwriting instruction. Kindergartners and first graders have commonly been given "fat" beginner pencils because it has been assumed that these pencils are easier for young children to hold; however, most children prefer to use regular-sized pencils that older students and adults use. Moreover, regular pencils have erasers! Research now indicates that beginner pencils are not better than regular-sized pencils for young children (Graham, 1992). Likewise, there is no evidence that specially shaped pencils and small writing aids that slip onto pencils to improve children's grip are effective.

Many types of paper, both lined and unlined, are used in elementary classrooms. Paper companies manufacture paper lined in a range of sizes. Typically, paper is lined at 2-inch intervals for kindergartners and at $\frac{7}{8}$- to $\frac{3}{8}$-inch intervals for older students. Lined paper for first and second graders has an added midline, often dotted, to guide students in forming lowercase letters. Sometimes a line appears below the baseline to guide placement of letters such as lowercase *g, p, q,* and *y* that have "tails" that drop below the baseline. The few research studies that have examined the value of lined paper in general and paper lined at specific intervals offer conflicting results. One study suggests that younger children's handwriting is more legible when they use unlined paper, and that older children's is better when they use lined paper (Lindsay & McLennan, 1983). Most teachers seem to prefer that students use lined paper for handwriting activities, but students easily adjust to whichever type of writing paper is available. Children often use rulers to line their paper when they are given unlined paper, and, likewise, they ignore the lines on lined paper if they interfere with their drawing or writing.

Transition to Cursive Handwriting.   Students' introduction to cursive handwriting typically occurs in the second semester of second grade or the first semester of third grade. Parents and students often attach great importance to the transition from manuscript to cursive, thus adding unnecessary pressure for the students. Beverly Cleary's *Muggie Maggie* (1990) describes the pressure one child feels. The time of transition is usually dictated by tradition rather than by sound educational theory. All students in a school or school district are usually introduced to cursive handwriting at the same time, regardless of their interest in making the change.

Some students indicate an early interest in cursive handwriting by trying to connect manuscript letters or by asking their parents to demonstrate how to write their names. Because of individual differences in motor skills and levels of interest in cursive writing, it is better to introduce some students to cursive handwriting in first or second grade while providing other students with additional time to refine their manuscript skills. These students then learn cursive handwriting in third or fourth grade.

The practice of changing to cursive handwriting only a year or two after children learn the manuscript form is receiving increasing criticism. The argument has been that students need to learn cursive handwriting as early as possible because of their increasing need for handwriting speed. Because of its continuous flow, cursive handwriting was thought to be faster to write than manuscript; however, research suggests that manuscript handwriting can be written as quickly as cursive handwriting (Jackson, 1971). The controversy over the benefits of the two forms and the best time to introduce cursive handwriting is likely to continue.

Handwriting in the Middle and Upper Grades. Students are introduced to the cursive handwriting form in second and third grades. Usually, the basic strokes that make up the letters (e.g., slant stroke, undercurve, downcurve) are taught first. Next, the lowercase letters are taught in isolation, and then the connecting strokes are introduced. Uppercase letters are taught later because they are used far less often and are more difficult to form. Which cursive letters are most difficult? The lowercase *r* is the most troublesome letter. The other lowercase letters students frequently form incorrectly are *k, p,* and *z.*

After students have learned both manuscript and cursive handwriting, they need to review both forms periodically. By this time, too, they have firmly established handwriting habits, both good and bad. At the middle- and upper-grade levels, emphasis is on helping students diagnose and correct their handwriting trouble spots so that they can develop a legible and fluent handwriting style. Older students both simplify their letter forms and also add unique flourishes to their handwriting to develop their own "trademark" styles.

Teachers often insist that students demonstrate their best handwriting every time they pick up a pencil or pen. This requirement is unrealistic; certainly there are times when handwriting is important, but at other times speed or other considerations outweigh neatness. Children need to learn to recognize two types of writing occasions—private and public. Legibility counts in public writing, but when students make notes for themselves or write a rough draft of a composition, they are doing private writing and should decide for themselves whether neatness is important.

Left-Handed Writers. Approximately 10% of the American population is left-handed, and there may be two or three left-handed students in most classrooms. Until recently teachers insisted that left-handed students use their right hands for handwriting because left-handed writers were thought to have inferior handwriting skills. Parents and teachers are more realistic now and accept children's natural tendencies for left- or right-handedness. In fact, research has shown that there is no significant difference in the quality or speed of left- and right-handed students' writing (Groff, 1963).

Most young children develop "handedness"—the preference for using either the right or the left hand for fine motor activities—before entering kindergarten or first grade. Teachers must help those few students who have not already developed handedness to choose and consistently use one hand for handwriting and other fine motor activities. Your role consists of observing the student's behavior and hand preference in play, art, writing, and playground activities. Over a period of days or weeks, observe and note which hand the child uses in activities such as building with blocks, throwing and catching balls, cutting with scissors, holding a paintbrush, manipulating clay, and pouring water or sand.

During the observation period, teachers may find that a child who has not established hand preference uses both hands interchangeably; for example, a child may first reach for several blocks with one hand and then reach for the next block with the alternate hand. During drawing activities the child will sometimes switch hands every few minutes. Consult the child's parents and ask them to observe and monitor the child's behavior at home, noting hand preferences when the child eats, brushes his or her teeth, turns on the television, opens doors, and so on. The teacher, the child, and the child's parents should then confer and—based on the results of joint observations, the handedness of family members, and the child's wishes—make a tentative decision about hand preference. At school, teacher and child will work closely together so that the child will use only the chosen hand. As long as the child continues to use both hands interchangeably, neither hand will develop the prerequisite fine motor control for handwriting, and teachers should postpone handwriting instruction until the child develops a dominant hand.

Teaching handwriting to left-handed students is not simply the reverse of teaching handwriting to right-handed students (Howell, 1978). Left-handed students have unique handwriting problems, and special adaptations of the procedures for teaching right-handed students are necessary. In fact, many of the problems that left-handed students have can be made worse by using the procedures designed for right-handed writers (Harrison, 1981). Special adjustments are necessary to allow left-handed students to write legibly, fluently, and with less fatigue.

The basic difference between right- and left-handed writing is physical orientation. Right-handed students pull their arms toward their bodies as they write, whereas left-handed writers push away. As left-handed students write, they move their left hands across what they have just written, often covering it. Many children adopt a "hook" position to avoid covering and smudging what they have written. Because of their different physical orientation, left-handed writers need to make three major types of adjustments:

1. *Holding pencils.*   Left-handed writers should hold pencils or pens an inch or more farther back from the tip than right-handed writers do. This change helps them see what they have just written and avoid smearing their writing. Left-handed writers need to work to avoid "hooking" their wrists.

Have them keep their wrists straight and elbows close to their bodies to avoid the awkward hooked position. Practicing handwriting on the chalkboard is one way to help them develop a more natural style.

2. Tilting paper. Left-handed students should tilt their writing papers slightly to the right, in contrast to right-handed students, who tilt their papers to the left. Sometimes it is helpful to place a piece of masking tape on the student's desk to indicate the proper amount of tilt.

3. Slanting letters. Whereas right-handed students are encouraged to slant their cursive letters to the right, left-handed writers often write vertically or even slant their letters slightly backward. Some handwriting programs recommend that left-handed writers slant their cursive letters slightly to the right as right-handed students do, but others advise teachers to permit any slant between vertical and 45 degrees to the left of vertical (Howell, 1978).

Teaching Handwriting in the Elementary Grades

Handwriting is best taught in separate periods of direct instruction and teacher-supervised practice. As soon as skills are taught, they should be applied in real-life writing activities. "Busy-work" assignments, such as copying sentences from the chalkboard, lack educational significance. Moreover, students may develop poor handwriting habits or learn to form letters incorrectly if they practice without direct supervision. It is much more difficult to correct bad habits and errors in letter formation than to teach handwriting correctly in the first place.

Handwriting instruction and practice periods should be brief; 15-minute periods of instruction several times a week are more effective than a single lengthy period weekly or monthly. Regular periods of handwriting instruction are necessary when teaching the manuscript form in kindergarten and first grade and the cursive form in second or third grade. In the middle and upper grades, instruction focuses on specific handwriting problems that students demonstrate and periodic reviews of both handwriting forms.

■ *To review the mini-lesson teaching strategy, turn to p. 61 in Chapter 2, "Teaching Language Arts."*

Minilessons. The teaching strategy presented in Chapter 2 can be adapted to teach minilessons on handwriting. The strategy is multisensory, with visual, auditory, and kinesthetic components, and is based on research in the field of handwriting (Askov & Greff, 1975; Furner, 1969; Hirsch & Niedermeyer, 1973). The five steps are:

Step by Step

1. *Introduce the topic.* The teacher demonstrates a specific handwriting procedure, strategy, or skill while students observe. During the demonstration, the teacher describes the steps involved in executing it.

2. *Describe the steps.* Students describe the procedure, strategy, or skill and the steps for executing it as the teacher or a classmate demonstrates it again.

3. *Review the topic.* The teacher reviews the specific handwriting procedure, strategy, or skill, summarizing the steps involved.

4. *Practice handwriting as the teacher circulates.* Students practice the procedure, strategy, or skill using pencils, pens, or other writing instruments. As they

practice, students softly repeat the steps, and the teacher circulates, providing assistance as needed.

5. **Apply handwriting in writing activities.**   Students apply the procedure, strategy, or skill they have learned in their writing. To check that they have learned it, students can review their writing over a period of several days and mark examples of correct use.

An example of applying this strategy in teaching manuscript letter formation is shown in Figure 12–9. The teacher introduces the handwriting skill and then supervises as students practice it. Research has shown the importance of the teacher's active involvement in handwriting instruction and practice. Teachers often print or write handwriting samples in advance on practice sheets. Then they distribute the sheets and ask students to practice a handwriting skill by copying the model they have written. Observing "moving" models—that is, having students watch the teacher write the handwriting sample—is of far greater value than copying models that have already been written (Wright & Wright, 1980). Moving models are possible when the teacher circulates around the classroom, stopping to demonstrate a procedure, strategy, or skill for one student and moving to assist another; circling incorrectly formed letters and marking other errors with a red pen on completed handwriting sheets is of little value. As in the writing process, the teacher's assistance is far more worthwhile while the students are writing, not after they have completed writing.

As Graves said, "Handwriting is for writing" (1983, p. 171), and for the most meaningful transfer of skills, students should be involved in writing for various purposes and for genuine audiences. Students apply their handwriting procedures, strategies, and skills whenever they write, and the best way to practice handwriting is through writing.

Adapting to Meet the Needs of Every Student.   The goal of handwriting instruction is for every student to develop legible and fluent handwriting. Students' handwriting does not need to match textbook samples, but it does need to be easy to read and quickly produced. When students are writing for genuine audiences, their handwriting is likely to be better than when they are writing for themselves. It is important that students understand and differentiate between public and private occasions for writing. For students who have difficulty with handwriting, the D'Nealian handwriting program may be more effective because the letter forms are simplified. Students with severe handwriting problems can use computers with word-processing programs to produce most of their written work. Teachers also need to adapt handwriting instruction for left-handed students.

Elements of Legibility.   In order for students to develop legible handwriting, they need to know what qualities or elements determine legibility and then analyze their own handwriting according to these elements (Hackney, 1993). The six elements of legible and fluent handwriting are:

1. *Letter formation.*   Letters are formed with specific strokes. Letters in manuscript handwriting are composed of vertical, horizontal, and slanted

■ *For other activities using sentences, turn to the "Teaching Grammar" section of this chapter, pp. 522–527.*

Figure 12–9   *Using the Teaching Strategy to Teach Letter Formation*

---

1. Introduce the Letter

Demonstrate the formation of a single letter or family of letters (e.g., the manuscript circle letters—*O, o, C, c, a, e, Q*) on the chalkboard while explaining how the letter is formed.

2. Explain How to Form the Letter

Have students describe how the letter is formed while you or a student forms the letter on the chalkboard. At first you may need to ask questions to direct students' descriptions. Possible questions include:

- How many strokes are used in making the letter?
- Which stroke comes first?
- Where do you begin the stroke?
- In which direction do you go?
- What size will the letter be?
- Where does the stroke stop?
- Which stroke comes next?

Students will quickly learn the appropriate terminology, such as *baseline, left-right, slant line, counterclockwise,* and so on, to describe how the letters are formed.

3. Review the Steps

Review the formation of the letter or letter family with students while demonstrating how to form the letter on the chalkboard.

4. Practice Writing the Letter

Have the students print the letter at the chalkboard, in sand, and with a variety of other materials such as clay, shaving cream, fingerpaint, pudding, and pipecleaners. As students form the letter, they should softly describe the formation process to themselves.

Have students practice writing the letter on paper with the accompanying verbal descriptions.

Circulate among students providing assistance and encouragement. Demonstrate and describe the correct formation of the letter as the students observe.

5. Provide Writing Activities

After the students have practiced the letter or family of letters, have them apply what they have learned in authentic writing activities. This is the crucial step!

---

math connection

lines plus circles or parts of circles. The letter *b,* for example, is composed of a vertical line and a circle, and *M* is composed of vertical and slanted lines. Cursive letters are composed of slanted lines, loops, and curved lines. The lowercase cursive letters *m* and *n,* for instance, are composed of a slant stroke, a loop, and an undercurve stroke. An additional component in cursive handwriting is the connecting stroke used to join letters.

2. Size and proportion.   During the elementary grades, students' handwriting becomes smaller, and the proportional size of uppercase to lowercase letters increases. First graders' uppercase manuscript letters are twice

D'Neilian
p. 502

Teachers provide direction during minilessons as students practice handwriting skills.

the size of lowercase letters. When second- and third-grade students first begin cursive handwriting, the proportional size of letters remains 2:1; later, the proportion increases to 3:1 for middle- and upper-grade students.

3. Spacing. Students should leave adequate space between letters in words and between words in sentences. Spacing between words in manuscript handwriting should equal one lowercase letter *o,* and spacing between sentences should equal two lowercase *o*'s. The most important aspect of spacing within words in cursive handwriting is consistency. To correctly space between words, the writer should make the beginning stroke of the new word directly below the end stroke of the preceding word. Spacing between sentences should equal one uppercase letter *O,* and the indent for a new paragraph should equal two uppercase letter *O*'s.

4. Slant. Letters should be consistently parallel. Letters in manuscript handwriting are vertical, and in the cursive form letters slant slightly to the right. To ensure the correct slant, right-handed students tilt their papers to the left, and left-handed students tilt their papers to the right.

5. Alignment. For proper alignment in both manuscript and cursive handwriting, all letters should be uniform in size and consistently touch the baseline.

6. Line quality. Students should write at a consistent speed and hold their writing instruments correctly and in a relaxed manner to make steady, unwavering lines of even thickness.

Correct letter formation and spacing receive the major focus in handwriting instruction during the elementary grades. Although the other four elements

Figure 12–10   A Checklist for Assessing Manuscript Handwriting

Handwriting Checklist

Name _____

Writing Project _____

Date _____

_____ 1. Did I form my letters correctly?
        Did I start my line letters at the top?
        Did I start my circle letters at 1:00?
        Did I join the round parts of the letters neatly?
        Did I join the slanted strokes in sharp points?
_____ 2. Did my lines touch the midline or top line neatly?
_____ 3. Did I space evenly between letters?
_____ 4. Did I leave enough space between words?
_____ 5. Did I make my letters straight up and down?
_____ 6. Did I make all my letters sit on the baseline?

usually receive less attention, they, too, are important in developing legible and fluent handwriting.

Diagnosing and Correcting Handwriting Problems.   Students use the six elements of legibility to diagnose their handwriting problems. Primary-grade students, for example, can check to see if they have formed a particular letter correctly, if the round parts of letters are joined neatly, and if slanted letters are joined in sharp points. Older students can examine a piece of handwriting to see if their letters are consistently parallel and if the letters touch the baseline consistently. A checklist for evaluating manuscript handwriting is shown in Figure 12–10. Checklists can also be developed for cursive handwriting. It is important to involve students in developing the checklists so that they appreciate the need to make their handwriting more legible.

    Another reason students need to diagnose and correct their handwriting problems is that handwriting quality influences teacher evaluation and grading. Researchers have found that teachers consistently graded papers with better handwriting higher than papers with poor handwriting, regardless of the content (Graham, 1992). Students in the elementary grades are not too young to learn that poor quality or illegible handwriting may lead to lower grades.

end of 12 B

GRAMMAR

Grammar is probably the most controversial area of language arts. Teachers, parents, and the community disagree about the content of grammar instruction, how to teach it, and when to begin teaching it. Some people believe that formal instruction in grammar is unnecessary—if not harmful—during the elementary grades; others believe that grammar instruction should be a key component of language arts instruction. Before getting into the controversy, let's clarify the terms *grammar* and *usage.* Grammar is the description of the syntax or structure of a language and prescriptions for its use (Weaver, 1996). It involves principles of word and sentence formation. In contrast, usage is correctness, or using the appropriate word or phrase in a sentence. It is the socially preferred way of using language within a dialect. *My friend, she; the man brung;* and *hisself* are examples of Standard English usage errors that elementary students sometimes make. Fraser and Hodson explain the distinction between grammar and usage this way: "Grammar is the rationale of a language; usage is its etiquette" (1978, p. 52).

Children learn the structure of the English language—its grammar—intuitively as they learn to talk; the process is an unconscious one. They have almost completed it by the time they enter kindergarten. The purpose of grammar instruction, then, is to make this intuitive knowledge about the English language explicit and to provide labels for words within sentences, parts of sentences, and types of sentences. Children speak the dialect their parents and community members speak. Dialect, whether Standard or nonstandard English, is informal and differs to some degree from the written Standard English, or "book language," that students will read and write in elementary school (Edelsky, 1989; Pooley, 1974).

Children demonstrate their knowledge of grammar when they make reading miscues (Goodman, 1965). A miscue is a departure from the words in the text, and as students read aloud they sometimes read a different word than the word printed in the text. For example, second graders sometimes substitute *dad* for *father* and *mom* for *mother* when reading "When bathtime was over, the Tub People always lined up along the edge of the bathtub—the father, the mother, the grandmother, the doctor, the policeman, the child, and the dog" in Pam Conrad's *The Tub People* (1989, n.p.). Or upper-grade students read "'Please,' he begged, 'take some of the pain'" for "'Please,' he gasped, 'take some of the pain'" when reading Lois Lowry's *The Giver* (1993, p. 118). These miscues indicate that students have an intuitive sense of grammar that they draw upon as they read. In the second-grade example, students substituted nouns for nouns, and in the upper-grade example they substituted a verb for a verb.

Applebee and his colleagues (1987) examined compositions written by 9-, 13-, and 17-year-olds as a part of the National Assessment of Educational Progress testing and were encouraged by the results. They concluded that most students made only a few grammatical errors in the compositions they wrote. The researchers examined students' sentences and categorized them as simple, compound, complex, run-on, or fragment. They found that approximately a quarter of the sentences that 9-year-olds wrote were complex, and the proportion increased to 43% for 17-year-olds. The researchers also found that the proportion of sentence fragments and run-on sentences decreased among older students, particularly between the ages of 9 and 13. Moreover, even at age 9, many students had no run-on sentences (50%) or fragments (75%) in their writing. A major conclusion of this research was that "instructional procedures that encourage students to edit their work for grammar, punctuation, and spelling as a last stage in the writing experience would seem to reflect what the best writers do" (p. 7). They also noted that everyone makes some errors, and because patterns of error differed from student to student, small-group instruction may be more effective than whole-class instruction.

Why Teach Grammar?

Teachers, parents, and the community at large cite many reasons for teaching grammar. First, using Standard English is the mark of an educated person, and students should know how to use Standard English. Many teachers feel that teaching grammar will help students understand sentence structure and form sentences to express their thoughts. Another reason is that parents expect that grammar will be taught, and teachers must meet these expectations. Other teachers explain that they teach grammar to prepare students for the next grade or for instruction in a foreign language. Others pragmatically rationalize grammar instruction because it is a part of norm-referenced achievement tests mandated by state departments of education.

Language arts textbooks have traditionally emphasized grammar; often, more than half of the pages have been devoted to drills on parts of speech, parts of sentences, and sentence types. Many teachers and parents assume that the content of a language arts textbook indicates what the curriculum should be, but it is important to separate the two so that the textbook is only one of many resources for implementing the curriculum.

Conventional wisdom is that knowledge about grammar and usage should improve students' oral language and writing, but research since the beginning of the century has not confirmed this assumption. In 1936, for example, the National Council of Teachers of English (NCTE) passed a resolution against the formal teaching of grammar, and based on their review of research conducted before 1963, Braddock, Lloyd-Jones, and Schoer concluded that "the teaching of formal grammar has a negligible or, because it usually displaces some instruction and practice in actual composition, even a harmful effect on the improvement of writing" (1963, pp. 37–38). Since then, other studies have reached the same conclusion, and the NCTE resolution has been reaffirmed again and again (Hillocks, 1987; Hillocks & Smith, 1991; Weaver, 1996).

Despite the controversy about teaching grammar and its value for elementary students, grammar is a part of the elementary language arts curriculum and will undoubtedly remain so for some time. Given this fact, it is only reasonable that grammar should be taught in the most beneficial manner possible. Researchers suggest that integrating grammar study with reading and writing produces the best results (Noguchi, 1991; Noyce & Christie, 1983). They view grammar as a tool for writers and recommend integrating grammar instruction with the revising and editing stages of the writing process.

Grammatical Concepts

The four most common types of information about grammar taught during the elementary grades are parts of speech, parts of sentences, types of sentences, and usage.

Parts of Speech. Grammarians have sorted English words into eight groups, called parts of speech: nouns, pronouns, verbs, adjectives, adverbs, prepositions, conjunctions, and interjections. Words in each group are used in essentially the same way in all sentences. Nouns and verbs are the basic building blocks of sentences, and pronouns substitute for nouns. Adjectives, adverbs, and prepositions build upon and modify the nouns and verbs. Conjunctions connect individual words or groups of words, and interjections express strong emotion or surprise.

Parts of Sentences.   A sentence is made up of one or more words to express a complete thought and, to express the thought, must have a subject and a predicate. The subject names who or what the sentence is about, and the predicate includes the verb and anything that completes or modifies it. In a simple sentence with one subject and one predicate, everything that is not part of the subject is part of the predicate.

Types of Sentences.   Sentences are classified in two ways. First, they are classified according to structure, or how they are put together. The structure of a sentence may be simple, compound, complex, or compound-complex according to the number and type of clauses. A clause consists of a subject and predicate, and there are two types of clauses. If the clause presents a complete thought and can stand alone as a sentence, it is an independent clause. If the clause in not a complete thought and cannot stand alone as a sentence, it is a dependent clause because it depends on the meaning expressed in the independent clause. A simple sentence contains only one independent clause, and a compound sentence is made up of two or more independent clauses. A complex sentence contains one independent clause and one or more dependent clauses. A compound-complex sentence contains two or more independent clauses and one or more dependent clauses.

Second, sentences are classified according to the type of message they contain. Sentences that make statements are declarative, those that ask questions are interrogative, those that make commands are imperative, and those that communicate strong emotion or surprise are exclamatory.

Usage.   Usage is the customary or "correct" way in which a language is spoken or written. Using a single negative, not a double negative, in the sentence *I don't have any money* (rather than *I ain't got no money*), or subjective pronouns, not objective pronouns, for the subject in the sentence *He and I have dirt bikes* (rather than *Him and me have dirt bikes*) are examples of Standard English usage. Ten types of usage errors that middle- and upper-grade students can learn to correct are:

*1. **Irregular verb forms.*** Students form past tense of irregular verb forms as they would a regular verb, for example, some students might use *catch + ed* to make *catched* instead of *caught,* or *swim + ed* to make *swimmed* instead of *swam.*

*2. **Past-tense forms.*** Students use present-tense or past-participle forms in place of past-tense forms, such as *I ask* for *I asked, she run* for *she ran,* or *he seen* for *he saw.*

*3. **Nonstandard verb forms.*** Students use *brung* for *brought* or *had went* for *had gone.*

*4. **Double subjects.*** Students include both a noun and a pronoun in the subject, such as *My mom she . . .*

*5. **Nonstandard pronoun forms.*** Students use nonstandard pronoun forms, such as *hisself* for *himself, them books* for *those books,* and *hisn* for *his.*

Structure
Simple
compound
complex
compound - complex

nominative · adj.
1. a: marking typically
the subject of a
verb esp. in languages
that have relatively
full inflection
3. bearing a person's
name

Gregg P. 516

* 1054
Gregg 1053
P. 232 bottom

6. Objective pronouns for the subject. Students use objective pronouns instead of subjective pronouns in the subject, such as *Me and my friend went to the store* or *Her and me want to play outside.*

7. Lack of subject-verb agreement. Students use *we was* for *we were* and *he don't* for *he doesn't.*

8. Double negatives. Students use two negatives when only one is needed, for example, *I don't got none* and *Joe don't have none.*

9. Confusing pairs of words. Some students confuse word pairs such as *learn–teach, lay–lie,* and *leave–let.* They might say *I'll learn you to read* instead of *I'll teach you to read, go lay down* instead of *go lie down,* and *leave me do it* instead of *let me do it.* Other confusing pairs include *bring–take, among–between, fewer–less, good–well, passed–past, real–really, set–sit, than–then, who–which–that, who–whom, it's–its,* and *your–you're.*

10. "I" as an objective pronoun. Students incorrectly use *I* instead of *me* as an objective pronoun. Students say or write *It's for Bill and I* instead of *It's for Bill and me* (Pooley, 1974; Weaver, 1996).

Students who speak nonstandard dialects learn Standard English forms as alternatives to the forms they already know. Rather than trying to substitute their standard forms for students' nonstandard forms, teachers can explain that Standard English is the language of school. It is the language used in books, and students can easily locate Standard English examples in books they are reading. Calling Standard English "book language" also helps to explain the importance of proofreading to identify and correct usage errors in the books that students are writing. Moreover, many Standard English usage errors are status-marking, and upper-grade students need to understand that Standard English is the language of privilege and prestige and that they can add Standard English to their repertoire of language registers.

Teaching Grammar to Elementary Students

For many years, grammar was taught using language arts textbooks. Students read rules and definitions, copied words and sentences, and marked them to apply the concepts presented in the text. This type of activity often seemed meaningless to students. A more effective approach is to connect grammar with reading and writing activities and to teach minilessons about the function of words in sentences and ways to arrange words into sentences (Cullinan, Jaggar, & Strickland, 1974; Tompkins & McGee, 1983). Guidelines for teaching grammar are listed in the Teacher's Notebook on page 516.

Connecting Grammar and Reading. Students learn many things about the structure of the English language through reading. They learn more sophisticated academic language, a more formal register than they speak, and sophisticated ways of phrasing ideas and arranging words into sentences. In *Aunt Flossie's Hats (and Crab Cakes Later)* (Howard, 1991), for example, Susan tells about a visit to her great-aunt and how she and her sister play with her great-aunt's hats: "One Sunday afternoon, I picked out a wooly winter hat, sort of green, maybe" (p. 11). This sentence is particularly rich in modifiers. The hat is wooly, it is a winter hat, and may be green—sort of.

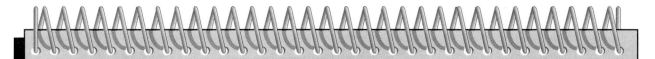

Teacher's Notebook
Guidelines for Teaching Grammar

1. Minilessons

Teachers teach minilessons on grammar and usage concepts and have students locate examples of grammar and usage concepts they are learning from books they are reading and books they are writing.

2. Concept Books

Teachers share concept books when students are studying parts of speech, and students also create their own concept books.

3. Sentence Manipulation

Students use sentences from books they are reading for grammar activities, such as sentence slotting, sentence expansion, sentence manipulation, and combining sentences.

4. Sentence Collection

Students collect favorite sentences from books they are reading and use the sentences for grammar and usage activities. One activity is copy changes.

5. Sentence Frames

Students write innovations, or new versions of books, using sentence frames or patterns in books they have read.

6. Posters

Students can make grammar posters to visually represent parts of speech, sentence types, or usage rules they are learning.

7. Proofreading

Students need to learn how to proofread so that they can locate and correct grammar and usage errors in their own writing.

8. Standard English Alternative

Teachers explain that Standard English is the language of school and is one way of speaking and writing. It is important that students understand that the purpose of grammar instruction is to expand their repertoire of language options, not to replace their home language.

Charlotte Zolotow uses a sophisticated sentence form in *This Quiet Lady* (1992). On each page, the core sentence "This girl is my mother" is expanded to chronicle the stages and events in a mother's life. The second page describes the mother when she was a girl: "This curly-haired little girl with the doll drooping from her hand is my mother" (n.p.).

Students often read sentences that are longer than the ones they speak and learn new ways to string words into sentences. In *Chrysanthemum* (Henkes, 1991), the story of a mouse named Chrysanthemum who loves her name until she starts school and is teased by her classmates, the author uses a combination of long and short sentences very effectively: "Chrysanthemum could scarcely believe her ears. She blushed. She beamed. She bloomed" (n.p.).

Students read sentences exemplifying all four sentence types in many books. One example is the Caldecott Medal–winning *Officer Buckle and Gloria* (Rathmann, 1995), the story of a police officer and his dog, Gloria. "Officer Buckle loved having a buddy" and "That night Officer Buckle watched himself on the 10 o'clock news" (n.p.) are statements, or declarative sentences. "How about Gloria?" and "Could she come?" (n.p.) are questions, or interrogative sentences. Officer Buckle's safety tips, such as "Keep your shoelaces tied" and "Do not go swimming during electrical storms!" (n.p.), are imperative sentences. The children loved Gloria and her tricks, and they cheered "Bravo!" (n.p.)—an example of an exclamation, or exclamatory sentence.

Students read simple, compound, complex, and compound-complex sentences in books. William Steig includes all of these types of sentences in his Caldecott Medal book, *Sylvester and the Magic Pebble* (1969):

Simple Sentence:	"Suddenly Mr. Duncan saw the red pebble."
Compound Sentence:	"He felt he would be a rock forever and he tried to get used to it."
Complex Sentence:	"When he was awake, he was only hopeless and unhappy."
Compound-Complex Sentence:	"If he hadn't been so frightened, he could have made the lion disappear, or he could have wished himself safe at home with his father and mother." (n.p.)

It might seem surprising, but many books for young children include complex and compound sentences. In Lois Ehlert's *Mole's Hill* (1994), for example, Fox snarls, "Where there's a mole, there's a mess" (n.p.). In Numeroff's *If You Give a Mouse a Cookie* (1985), the book begins, "If you give a mouse a cookie, he's going to ask for a glass of milk" (n.p.). It is less common to find compound sentences in books for young children, but here is one example: in Eric Carle's *The Very Quiet Cricket* (1990), children repeat the refrain "The little cricket wanted to answer, so he rubbed his wings together. But nothing happened. Not a sound" on every page. For the sake of sentence length, many authors break would-be compound sentences into two simple sentences.

Chapter books often include examples of all sentence types. On the first page of *The Giver* (Lowry, 1993), for instance, there are examples of simple, compound, and complex sentences:

Simple Sentence: "But the aircraft a year ago had been different."

Compound Sentence: "It was almost December, and Jonas was beginning to be frightened."

Complex Sentence: "Frightened was the way he had felt a year ago when an unidentified aircraft had over-flown the community twice."

And on the second page, there is an example of a compound-complex sentence: "His parents were both at work, and his little sister, Lily, was at the Childcare Center where she spent her after-school hours."

Students can pick out the subjects and predicates in these sentences. The subject in "Officer Buckle loved having a buddy" (n.p.) is "Officer Buckle," and the remainder of the simple sentence is the predicate. In "He felt he would be a rock forever and he tried to get used to it" (n.p.), a compound sentence, there are two independent clauses, and "he" is the subject of each clause. The first clause of "If you give a mouse a cookie, he's going to ask for a glass of milk" (n.p.) is a dependent clause, and the subject is "you." The second clause is an independent clause, and the subject is "he" (the mouse).

Some authors write dialogue and other text in nonstandard English that is appropriate to the characters and setting they are creating. In *Shiloh* (Naylor, 1991), for example, the story of a boy named Marty who will do anything to save a beagle puppy, Marty says, "Thinking don't cost nothing" (p. 31), and this language is appropriate for the rural setting of the book. The same is true in *Mississippi Bridge* (Taylor, 1990), which is set in the rural South during the 1930s. This story is about African Americans having to give up their seats on the bus to white people. The bus driver says "Ain't I done tole you to get off this bus?" (p. 46) and "I gots to go on this bus" (p. 47) when he forces Josias to get off the bus so that more white passengers can get on. When the bus goes over a bridge during a storm, it's one of the people who was denied a seat who jumps into the raging river to try to save the people on the bus. Jeremy, the character telling the story, runs to get help after the accident and tells his father, "The bus, it done gone off the bridge!" (p. 55). Understanding that authors (and all language users) make choices about Standard and non-standard English according to the situation in which it is used is important in helping students who speak nonstandard English become aware of Standard English options.

One way to help students focus on sentences in stories is sentence collecting (Speaker & Speaker, 1991). Students collect favorite sentences and share them with classmates. They copy their sentences on chart paper or on long strips of tagboard and post them in the classroom. Students and the teacher talk about the merits of each sentence, focus on word choice, and analyze the sentence types. Through this discussion, students gradually learn to comprehend more syntactically complex sentences. Students can cut the words in the sentences apart and rebuild them, either in the author's original order or in an order that appeals to them. These sentences can also be used in the minilessons described later in this section.

Connecting Grammar and Writing.   Not only do students notice the way the sentences are phrased in the books they read or listen to read aloud, but they also use the structures in books they are writing. Kathy Egawa (1990)

Students learn about syntactic structures as they write favorite sentence on story quilts.

1ˢᵗ GR

reports that a first grader used the structure and rhythm of Jane Yolen's *Owl Moon* (1989) in writing a book called *Salamander Sun*. *Owl Moon* begins this way: "It was late one winter night, long past my bedtime when Pa and I went owling." The child's book, written in invented spelling, begins this way: "It was lat one spring afternoon a long time after lunch when ma tact me sawlumendering" (p. 586). This first grader was not plagiarizing Yolen's book, but adapting and incorporating the structure in his own writing.

Because children's knowledge of grammar and usage is dependent on the language spoken in their homes and neighborhoods, some primary-and middle-grade students do not recognize a difference between "me and him" and "he and I." When the error is brought to their attention, they do not understand, because semantically—at a meaning level—the two versions are identical. Moreover, "me and him" sounds right to these students because they hear this construction at home. When other corrections are pointed out to middle- and upper-grade students, they repeat the correct form, shake their heads, and say that it doesn't sound right. "Real" sounds better to some than "really" because it is more familiar. An explanation that adverbs rather than adjectives modify adjectives is not useful either, even if students are familiar with the parts of speech. Correction of nonstandard English errors is perceived as a repudiation of the language spoken in children's homes rather than an explanation that written language requires a more formal language register or dialect. Jaggar (1980) recommends that teachers allow for language differences, acknowledging that everyone speaks a dialect and that one is not better or more correct than another.

■ Check Chapter 3, "The Reading and Writing Processes," pp. 121–123, for more information on the editing stage of the writing process, as well as proofreading.

■ For more information about students learning English as a second language, read Chapter 1, "Learning and the Language Arts," pp. 14–22.

■ See p. 61 in Chapter 2, "Teaching Language Arts," to review the steps in a minilesson.

A better way to deal with usage errors is to use a problem-solving approach during the editing stage of the writing process. Locating and correcting errors in students' writing is not as threatening to students as correcting their talk, because it is not as personal. Also, students can more easily accept that "book language" is a different kind of English. During editing, students are hunting for errors, trying to make their papers "optimally readable" (Smith, 1982). They recognize that it is a courtesy to readers to make their papers as correct as possible. During editing, classmates note errors and correct each other's papers, and teachers point out other errors. Sometimes teachers explain the correction (e.g., the past tense of *bring* is *brought,* not *brung*), and at other times they simply mark the correction, saying that "We usually write it this way." Some errors should be ignored, especially those made by young children and students learning English as a second language; correcting too many errors teaches students only that their language is inferior or inadequate. The goal in dealing with nonstandard English speakers is not to replace their dialects but to add Standard English to their language options.

Minilessons and Other Grammar Lessons. Teachers identify topics for grammar minilessons in two ways. The preferred way is to identify concepts by assessing students' writing and noting what types of grammar and usage errors they are making. At other times, teachers choose topics from lists of skills they are expected to teach at their grade level. The topics can be taught to the whole class or to small groups of students, but only to students who don't already know them. Atwell (1987) suggests using minilessons because of their immediate connections to reading and writing.

Teachers use the format for minilessons outlined in Chapter 2 for minilessons. Worksheets are not recommended; instead, excerpts from books students are reading or from students' own writing are used. Students can write words on cards and manipulate them into sentences, or write sentences on overhead transparencies to share with classmates. Teachers introduce a concept and its related terminology; then they provide opportunities for students to experiment with sentence construction. A variety of approaches for teaching minilessons are suggested in the following paragraphs, and topics for minilessons are suggested on page 494.

1. Parts of speech. Students work in small groups to identify words representing one part of speech or all eight parts of speech from books they are reading or from their own writing. A group of fifth graders identified the following words representing each part of speech from Van Allsburg's *The Polar Express* (1985):

- *Nouns:* train, children, Santa Claus, elves, pajamas, roller coaster, conductor, sleigh, hug, clock, Sarah
- *Pronouns:* we, they, he, it, us, you, his, I, me
- *Verbs:* filled, ate, flickered, raced, were, cheered, marched, asked, pranced, stood, shouted
- *Adjectives:* melted, white-tailed, quiet, no, first, magical, cold, dark, polar, Santa's
- *Adverbs:* soon, faster, wildly, apart, closer, alone
- *Prepositions:* in, through, over, with, of, in front of, behind, at, for, across, into

- *Conjunctions:* and, but
- *Interjections:* oh, well, now

Similarly, students can hunt for parts of sentences or sentence types in books of children's literature.

After collecting words representing one part of speech from books they are reading or from books they have written, students can create a book using some of the words they collected. Figure 12–11 shows the cover and a page from an alphabet book focusing on adjectives that second graders developed.

2. Grammar concept books. Students examine concept books that focus on one part of speech or another grammatical concept. For example, Barrett describes the essential characteristics of a variety of animals in *A Snake Is Totally Tail* (1983), and most of the descriptions include an adverb. After students read the book and identify the adverbs, they can write their own sentences, following the same pattern, and illustrate the sentences using posters, mobiles, a mural, or a class book. Useful books for teaching grammar concepts are listed in Figure 12–12.

Students in an eighth-grade class divided into small groups to read Ruth Heller's books about parts of speech, including *Up, Up and Away: A Book About Adverbs* (1991), *Behind the Mask: A Book of Prepositions* (1995), and *Merry-Go-Round: A Book About Nouns* (1990). After reading one of her books, students made a poster with information about the part of speech which they presented to the class. The students' poster for adverbs is shown

Figure 12–11　　An Excerpt From a Second-Grade Class Book on Adjectives

Figure 12–12   *Books That Illustrate Grammar Concepts*

Nouns

Heller, R. (1987). *A cache of jewels and other collective nouns.* New York: Grosset & Dunlap. (M–U)

Heller, R. (1990). *Merry-go-round: A book about nouns.* New York: Grosset & Dunlap. (M–U)

Hoban, T. (1981). *More than one.* New York: Greenwillow. (P)

MacCarthy, P. (1991). *Herds of words.* New York: Dial. (M)

Terban, M. (1986). *Your foot's on my feet! and other tricky nouns.* New York: Clarion. (M)

Wildsmith, B. (1968). *Fishes.* New York: Franklin Watts. (M)

Verbs

Beller, J. (1984). *A-B-Cing: An action alphabet.* New York: Crown. (P–M)

Burningham, J. (1986). *Cluck baa, jangle twang, slam bang, skip trip, sniff shout, wobble pop.* New York: Viking. (P–M)

Heller, R. (1988). *Kites sail high: A book about verbs.* New York: Grosset & Dunlap. (M–U)

Hoban, T. (1975). *Dig, drill, dump, fill.* New York: Greenwillow. (P)

Maestro, B., & Maestro, G. (1985). *Camping out.* New York: Crown. (P–M)

Neumeier, M., & Glasser, B. (1985). *Action alphabet.* New York: Greenwillow. (M)

Rotner, S. (1996). *Action alphabet.* New York: Atheneum. (P–M)

Schneider, R. M. (1995). *Add it, dip it, fix it: A book of verbs.* Boston: Houghton Mifflin. (M)

Shiefman, V. (1981). *M is for move.* New York: Dutton. (P–M)

Terban, M. (1984). *I think I thought and other tricky verbs.* New York: Clarion. (M)

Adjectives

Boynton, S. (1983). *A is for angry: An animal and adjective alphabet.* New York: Workman. (M–U)

Duke, K. (1983). *Guinea pig ABC.* New York: Dutton. (P)

Heller, R. (1989). *Many luscious lollipops: A book about adjectives.* New York: Grosset & Dunlap. (M–U)

Hoban, T. (1981). *A children's zoo.* New York: Greenwillow. (P)

Hubbard, W. (1990). *C is for curious: An ABC book of feelings.* San Francisco: Chronicle Books. (M)

Maestro, B., & Maestro, G. (1979). *On the go: A book of adjectives.* New York: Crown. (P–M)

McMillan, B. (1989). *Super, super, superwords.* New York: Lothrop, Lee & Shepard. (P)

Adverbs

Barrett, J. (1983). *A snake is totally tail.* New York: Atheneum. (M–U)

Heller, R. (1991). *Up, up and away: A book about adverbs.* New York: Grosset & Dunlap. (M–U)

Prepositions

Bancheck, L. (1978). *Snake in, snake out.* New York: Crowell. (P–M)

Berenstain, S., & Berenstain, J. (1968). *Inside, outside, upside, down.* New York: Random House. (M)

Berenstain, S., & Berenstain, J. (1971). *Bears in the night.* New York: Random House. (P–M)

Heller, R. (1995). *Behind the mask: A book of prepositions.* New York: Grosset & Dunlap. (M–U)

Hoban, T. (1973). *Over, under, and through and other spatial concepts.* New York: Macmillan. (P)

Hoban, T. (1991). *All about where.* New York: Greenwillow. (P)

Lillie, P. (1993). *Everything has a place.* New York: Greenwillow. (P)

P = primary grades (K–2); M = middle grades (3–5); U = upper grades (6–8).

■ *For more information on word sorts, check Chapter 5, "Looking Closely at Words" p. 206.*

in Figure 12–13. Later, students divided into small groups to do a word sort. In this activity, students cut apart a list of words and sorted them into groups according to the part of speech. All of the words had been taken from posters that students created, and students could refer to the posters if needed.

3. Sentence slotting. Students experiment with words and phrases to see how they function in sentences by filling in sentences that have slots, or blanks. Sentence slotting teaches students about several different grammatical concepts. They can experiment with parts of speech using a sentence like this:

Figure 12–13   An Eighth-Grade Poster on Adverbs

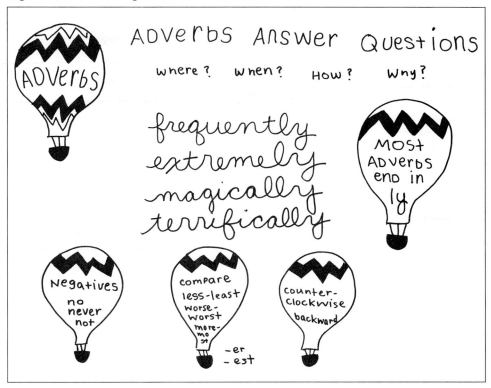

The snake slithered _____ the rock.
                    over
                    around
                    under
                    to

Students brainstorm a number of words to fill in the slot, all of which will be prepositions; adjectives, nouns, verbs, and adverbs will not make sense. This activity can be repeated to introduce or review any part of speech.

Sentence slotting also demonstrates to students that parts of speech can substitute for each other. In the following sentence, common and proper nouns as well as pronouns can be used in the slot:

_____ knew more safety tips than anyone else in Napville.
The man
Officer Buckle
He
The police officer

A similar sentence-slotting example demonstrates how phrases can function as an adverb:

The dog growled _____.
                ferociously
                with his teeth bared
                daring us to reach for his bone

In this example the adverb *ferociously* can be used in the slot, as well as prepositional and participial phrases.

Sentences with an adjective slot can be used to demonstrate that phrases function as adjectives. The goal of this activity is to demonstrate the function of words in sentences. Many sentence-slotting activities, such as the last example, also illustrate that sentences become more specific with the addition of a word or phrase. The purpose of these activities is to experiment with language; they should be done with small groups of students or the whole class, not as worksheets.

4. Sentence expansion. Students expand simple sentences, such as "A frog leaps" or "The car raced," by adding modifiers. The words and phrases with which they expand the sentence can add qualities and attributes, details, and comparisons. Using the "5 Ws plus one" (who, what, when, where, why, and how) helps students focus on expanding particular aspects of the sentence; for example:

Sentence	A frog leaps.
What kind?	green, speckled
How?	high into the air
Where?	from a half-submerged log and lands in the water with a splash
Why?	to avoid the noisy boys playing nearby
Expanded sentence	To avoid the noisy boys playing nearby, a green, speckled *frog leaps* high into the air from a half-submerged log and lands in the water with a splash.

Depending on what questions are asked and students' answers, many other expanded sentences are possible from the same basic sentence. Students enjoy working in small groups to expand a basic sentence so that they can compare their expanded version with those of the other groups. Instead of using the "5 Ws plus one" questions to expand sentences, teachers can ask older students to supply a specific part of speech or modifier at each step of expansion.

Students or the teacher can create basic sentences for expansion or take them from children's literature. Very few basic sentences appear in stories, but a basic sentence within an expanded sentence can be identified. Students enjoy comparing their expanded versions of the basic sentence with the author's. When students are familiar with the story the sentence was taken from, they can try to approximate the author's meaning. Even so, it is likely that they will go in a variety of directions, and because students' expanded sentences may vary greatly from the author's, they come to realize the power of modifiers to transform a sentence.

5. Sentence manipulation. Hudson (1980) suggests "moving language around" to help students learn about the structure of English and how to manipulate sentences. Students begin with a sentence and then apply four operations to it: They add, delete, substitute, and rearrange. With the sentence "Children play games," these manipulations are possible:

Add	Children play games at home.
	Children like to play games.
Delete	Children play.
Substitute	Adults play games.
	Children like games.
	Children play Nintendo.
Rearrange	Games are played by children.

6. Combining sentences. In sentence combining, students combine and rearrange words in sentences to make the sentences longer and more conceptually dense (Strong, 1996). The goal of sentence combining is for students to experiment with different combinations. Sentences can be joined or embedded in a variety of ways. In the following example, two sentences (S) about *Sylvester and the Magic Pebble* (Steig, 1969) are transformed or combined to create two combined sentences (C): *Relative Clauses*

"Writing" p. 292

Gregg p. 517

(S) Sylvester found a red pebble.

(S) The pebble was magic.

(C1) Sylvester found a red pebble that was magic. *Relative*

(C2) Sylvester found a magic red pebble. *Adjective transformation*

The two combined sentences illustrate embedding the adjective *magic*. The first combined sentence uses a relative clause transformation; the second uses an adjective transformation. Neither combined sentence is right or wrong; rather, they provide two options. Teachers and students can create many other sentences to combine. They can take examples from books they are reading or from their own writing, or they can create the sentences themselves on a variety of topics.

Sentence-combining activities give students opportunities to manipulate sentence structures; however, they are rather artificial. They are most effective when combined with other writing assignments. Weaver cautions that "sentence combining activities are only an adjunct to the writing program and the writing process and should never be used as substitutes for actual writing" (1979, pp. 83–84).

■ *To learn more about creating innovations, see Chapter 9, "Reading and Writing Stories," pp. 377–378.*

7. Sentence frames. Students in the primary grades often create new books or "innovations" using the structure in repetitive books. Young children create new verses for *Mary Wore Her Red Dress* (Peek, 1985) when they are studying colors, and they write their own versions of *Brown Bear, Brown Bear, What Do You See?* (Martin, 1983) and the sequel *Polar Bear, Polar Bear, What Do You Hear?* (Martin, 1992). Similarly, middle-grade students write new verses following the rhyming pattern in Laura Numeroff's *Dogs Don't Wear Sneakers* (1993) and the sequel, *Chimps Don't Wear Glasses* (1995).

A third-grade class used Numeroff's frame to write verses, and one small group composed this verse, rhyming *TV* and *bumblebee*:

3rd Gr

> Ducks don't have tea parties,
> Lions don't watch TV,
> And you won't see a salamander
> being friends with a bumblebee.

Adapting Grammar Instruction To Meet the Needs of Every Student

1. Encourage Reading and Writing

As students become more fluent readers and writers, they will acquire more Standard English syntactic forms. Teachers should provide daily reading and writing opportunities for all students, but these opportunities are especially important for students who speak nonstandard English.

2. Identify Grammar and Usage Concepts to Teach by Examining Students' Writing

Teachers analyze students' writing to identify topics for grammar minilessons. As they teach minilessons, teachers explain that Standard English is the language of books, an alternative language form, and they ask students to apply what they are learning in their writing.

3. Teach Students How to Proofread

Students learn to proofread so that they can correct many of the grammar and usage errors they make in their writing. Proofreading activities help students to focus on the words and sentences in their own writing.

4. Have Students Write Innovations on Texts

Encourage students to write innovations, or new versions of familiar patterned texts. As they use the author's sentence forms to create new versions, students practice using more complex syntactic structures than they might normally use themselves.

5. Correct Grammatical Errors on Students' Writing, Not Their Talk

Students make grammatical errors both when they talk and when they write, but because their talk is so personal, teachers are likely to damage students' self-confidence when they correct their speech. A better way to develop Standard English is to focus on students' errors in their writing.

Another group wrote this verse, rhyming *cars* and *bars:*

> Sea otters don't go to church,
> Hummingbirds never drive cars,
> And you won't see a hermit crab
> munching on candy bars.

Middle- and upper-grade students can take a favorite sentence and imitate its structure by plugging in new words. Stephen Dunning calls this procedure "copy changes" (Dunning & Stafford, 1992). For example, eighth graders chose sentences from *The Giver* (Lowry, 1993) for copy changes. The original sentence was "Dimly, from a nearly forgotten perception as blurred as the substance itself, Jonas recalled what the whiteness was" (p. 175). A student created this sentence using the sentence frame: "Softly, from a corner of the barn as cozy and warm as the kitchen, the baby kitten mewed to its mother."

Adapting to Meet the Needs of Every Student. The goal of grammar instruction is to increase students' ability to structure and manipulate sentences and to expand their repertoire of sentence patterns. Teaching grammar is a controversial issue, and it is especially so for students whose native language is not English or for students who speak a nonstandard form of English. The best way to encourage students' language development and the acquisition of Standard English is to encourage students to talk without fear of embarrassment for being corrected. Teachers and classmates model Standard English through their talk, and students also learn Standard English syntactic patterns in the books they read. Teachers can deal with nonstandard English in older students' compositions during the editing stage of the writing process.

Students with limited language fluency especially benefit from creating innovations on repetitive books so that they can expand their repertoire of sentence forms and lengthen the sentences they speak and write. Building and manipulating sentences are other useful activities to help these students increase their ability to use a variety of sentence types. A list of suggestions on adapting grammar instruction to meet the needs of every students is presented on page 526.

Assessing Students' Knowledge About Grammar. The best gauge of students' knowledge of grammar is how they arrange words into sentences as part of genuine communication projects. Teachers can develop checklists of grammar and usage skills to teach at a particular grade level, or they can list errors they observe in students' writing. Then teachers observe students as they write and examine their compositions to note errors, plan and teach minilessons based on students' needs, note further errors, plan and teach other minilessons, and so on. As teachers identify grammar and usage problems, they should plan minilessons to call students' attention to the problems that make a bigger difference in writing (Pooley, 1974). For example, in the sentences "Mom leave me go outside" and "I fell off of my bike," the use of *leave* for *let* is a more important problem than the redundant use of *of*.

Review

Spelling, handwriting, and grammar are language tools, and through instruction in all three areas, students learn to communicate more effectively. During the elementary grades, students learn to spell conventionally, develop legible and fluent handwriting, and learn a variety of ways to arrange words in sentences. The key concepts discussed in this chapter are:

1. Students move from using scribbles and single letters to represent words through a series of stages that lead to conventional spelling.
2. The five stages of invented spelling are precommunicative, semiphonetic, phonetic, transitional, and conventional.

3. Spelling instruction includes opportunities to read and write and mini-lessons about spelling procedures, concepts, and strategies and skills.
4. Weekly spelling tests, when they are used, should be individualized so that students learn to spell words they do not already know how to spell.
5. The two traditional handwriting forms are manuscript and cursive, and a newer, transitional form is D'Nealian.
6. The six elements of handwriting are letter formation, size and proportion, spacing, slant, alignment, and line quality.
7. Handwriting instruction must be linked with writing at all grade levels, even in kindergarten.
8. Grammar is the structure of language, while usage is the socially accepted way of using words in sentences.
9. Parts of speech, parts of sentences, sentence types, and usage are the four components of grammar instruction.
10. Students use sentences from books they are reading and sentences from their own writing for grammar instruction.

Extensions

1. Observe how spelling is taught in an elementary classroom. How is the spelling program organized? Which components described in this chapter are used in this classroom?
2. Collect samples of a primary-grade student's writing and analyze the spelling errors as shown in Figure 12–3 to determine the student's stage of spelling development.
3. Interview a middle- or upper-grade student about spelling. Ask questions such as these:

   * Are you a good speller? Why? Why not?
   * What do you do when you don't know how to spell a word?
   * How would you help a classmate who didn't know how to spell a word?
   * Are some words harder for you to spell than other words? Which words?
   * What rules about how to spell words have you learned?
   * Do you use a dictionary to look up the spelling of words you don't know how to spell?

4. Help students proofread their writing and identify possible misspelled words. Watch what strategies students use to identify and correct misspelled words.
5. Practice forming the manuscript and cursive letters shown in Figures 12–6 and 12–7 until your handwriting approximates the models. Practicing these handwriting forms will prepare you for working with elementary students. Be sure to take note

of the handwriting charts displayed in the classroom before beginning to work with students, because several different handwriting programs are available today. The programs are similar, but students are quick to point out when you are not forming a letter correctly!

6. Observe in a primary-grade classroom where the D'Nealian handwriting program is used. Talk with teachers and students about this innovative form. How do the students like it? Do the teachers believe that it alleviates some of the problems with manuscript handwriting and the transition to cursive, as the developer claims?
7. Observe a left-handed writer and compare this student to right-handed writers in the same classroom. How does the left-handed student's handwriting differ from right-handed students'? What types of special adaptations has the teacher made for teaching the left-handed student?
8. Plan and teach a grammar lesson using one of the minilesson topics (e.g., sentence slotting, combining sentences) described in this chapter. Choose sentences for the activity from a book that students are reading.
9. Read and analyze a set of stories, reports, or journals written by a class of middle- or upper-grade students and identify five possible grammar and usage topics for minilessons. Choose one of the topics and create a lesson plan for teaching a series of minilessons.

PRO-File
Becoming Literate in a Bilingual Classroom

PROCEDURE

Two-thirds of my first graders are Spanish speakers, and the other one-third are English speakers. I speak both languages, and it's natural for me to use them both in my classroom. I have signs and messages written in both languages. Our calendar is labeled in both English and Spanish, and our bulletin board displays are labeled in both languages.

I have both Spanish and English books in the class library. I used to have trouble finding Spanish versions of the books, but now more books are available in Spanish. I try to have Spanish and English versions of the same book. For example, I have *Doctor De Soto* (Steig, 1982), *Frog and Toad Are Friends* (Lobel, 1970), *Corduroy* (Freeman, 1968), *Where the Wild Things Are* (Sendak, 1963), and *The True Story of the Three Little Pigs!* (Scieszka, 1989) in both languages. My first graders really like the Robert Munsch books, including *Mortimer* (1985), and I'm glad that these books are available in both languages.

I have only one or two copies of most books, but I have sets (10 in Spanish and 5 in English) of our focus books. I spend approximately one week on each book, and my students read these books, talk and write about them, and work on art projects and other related activities.

Each week I teach students to read a new poem and hang the English and Spanish versions in the Poetry Center. I have two racks with pocket charts. I write each line of the poem on sentence strips using one color marking pen for the English version and a different color for the Spanish version. Groups of students sort and sequence the strips in the pocket charts, and they reread the poem using choral reading techniques.

My students also write in journals every day. They write about events in their own lives, books we are reading, or things we are studying. My aide works with students at the Writing Center. She encourages them to use invented spelling and helps them sound out words as they write. She also writes back to students. If the student writes in Spanish, she responds in Spanish, and if the student writes in English, she uses English. One of Jessica's

> **❝** My goal is for every student to learn to read and write. Some students use Spanish; others use English. Both languages are valued in my classroom, and the processes of reading and writing are the same in Spanish and English. **❞**
>
> **Paula Schiefer**
> *First Grade Bilingual Teacher*
> *Washington School*

journal entries is shown in the accompanying figure. Jessica is learning to read and write in Spanish. At the top of the entry she writes "Today is Tuesday." Along the left side of the paper she has written "I like the stars in the sky." Jessica's spelling is almost entirely conventional, but she began the word *cielo* (sky) with an *s* instead of a *c* because she concentrated on the /s/ sound at the beginning of the word. My aide did not correct Jessica; instead, she complimented her on how easy her writing was to read and encouraged her to write more. Later my aide responded in Spanish on the right side of the entry, "Jessica, I also really like the stars."

My students spend two hours each morning involved in reading, writing, listening, and talking activities. My schedule is:

8:30–9:00—*Class Meeting*
I introduce students to the focus book of the week. Later they will reread the book with me. I also present the poems for the poetry center and teach minilessons.

9:00–10:00—*Students Work at Centers*
They reread the focus book with me at the Reading Center, write in journals at the Writing Center, and also work on projects, listen to books at the Listening Center, read independently at the Library Center, and read the poem at the Poetry Center.

10:00–10:15—*Recess*
10:15–10:45—*Read Aloud*

I read aloud books related to the literature focus unit, and we talk about the book in grand conversations or do quickdraws.

ASSESSMENT

I think it's my job to listen and watch students as they work. I track my students' development in writing, for example, by noting the topics they choose, their invented spellings, and the length and complexity of their writing. For reading, I listen to my students read orally, examine their responses to books, and watch them read independently at the Library Center.

ADAPTATIONS

I think that children learn to read and write by reading and writing—in a safe, supportive environment, so I don't change my program very much for individual students. I do provide more individual attention and support for any student who is not off to a smooth start. My aide and I read and write more often with this student. I encourage students who are off to a strong start to select challenging books to read, and I involve them in writing books and other projects.

REFLECTIONS

Teaching a bilingual class isn't any more difficult than teaching a monolingual class. I teach my students to respect each other and to value their own language and culture. Both my Spanish and English speakers learn to read and write. That's success!

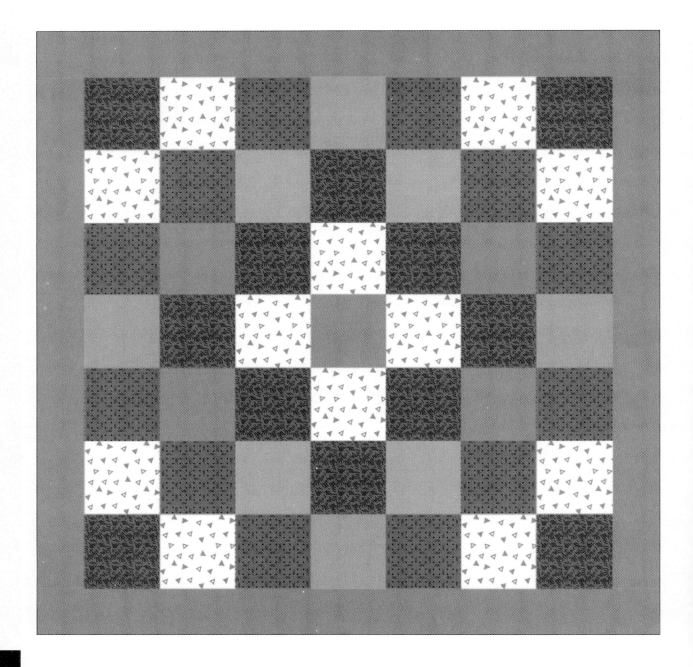

E ileen Boland's middle school students who are learning English as a second language made this quilt, "We Give Thanks to Mother Earth," based on
Giving Thanks: A Native American Good Morning Message (Swamp, 1995),
available in both English and Spanish versions. The students brainstormed a list
of natural things they were thankful for and drew pictures and wrote sentences
on fabric (in either English or Spanish). One student wrote: "I am thankful for
Elder Brother Sun because he chases away the clouds." The design of quilt
square on the opposite page is called "Around the World."

eachers face many challenges as they design their instructional programs. First and foremost, they consider their students, and in classrooms today, students represent a range of linguistic and cultural groups. Multiculturalism should permeate the classroom. Teachers provide equal educational opportunities for all students, introduce cultural alternatives, and promote tolerance for and an appreciation of ethnic diversity. Multicultural literature is an important vehicle for helping students value cultural differences and recognize ethnic similarities. Reading a book like *Roll of Thunder, Hear My Cry* (Taylor, 1976) presents students with the opportunity to "walk a mile" in an African-American's shoes, or to step into a recent immigrant's shoes in *How Many Days to America? A Thanksgiving Story* (Bunting, 1988).

Next, teachers think about how to create a community of learners in their classrooms and plan the block of time allocated for language arts instruction. They also think about how the language arts are used as tools for learning and decide how to incorporate language arts across the curriculum. The three instructional approaches are literature focus units, reading and writing workshop, and theme cycles. Teachers choose one or two of these approaches or adapt all three to meet the needs of their students.

Teachers often search for the "one best way" to develop units or design language arts instruction, but there is no one best way. Instead, teachers pick and choose from thousands of books, activities, and assignments as they plan literature focus units, reading and writing workshop, and theme cycles. In this text, you've read about these components of language arts instruction:

- Creating a community of learners
- The reading and writing processes
- Language arts procedures, concepts, skills, and strategies
- Word walls and vocabulary activities
- Journals and other ways to use writing as a learning tool
- Three purposes for listening
- Grand conversations and other talk and drama activities
- Language arts centers
- Reading and writing stories and learning about the structure of stories
- Reading and writing information and learning about expository text structure
- Reading and writing poetry and learning about poetic forms and stylistic devices
- Spelling, handwriting, and grammar

Teachers pick and choose among these components as they plan for instruction. Choosing to have students write in reading logs or create a story quilt is not necessarily better than having students write sequels or collect sentences from a book to examine sentence structure. Teachers begin with frameworks for the three instructional approaches and then choose the literature, activities, and assignments based on their instructional goals and beliefs about how children learn.

As teachers gain experience developing units, they often go beyond the "What shall I do with this book?" or "What shall I teach in this unit?" questions to think about the choices they make as they plan instruction and teach (McGee & Tompkins, 1995). Teachers need to think about why students should choose many of the books they read and why skill and strategy instruction should be taught in context. Through this reflection, teachers realize how theories about how children learn, along with their instructional goals, provide the foundation for language arts instruction (Zarrillo, 1989).

As you continue reading, think about how you will organize for language arts instruction and how you will design literature focus units, reading and writing workshop, and theme cycles. Consider these key points:

- How can teachers incorporate multicultural literature in the language arts program?
- How do teachers develop literature focus units?
- How do teachers set up reading and writing workshop?
- How do teachers develop theme cycles?

MULTICULTURAL LITERATURE

"Literature that represents any distinct cultural group through accurate portrayal and rich detail" is known as multicultural literature (Yokota, 1993, p. 157). Multicultural literature is a vehicle for fostering cultural awareness and appreciation. It affirms the cultural identity of students of diverse backgrounds and develops all students' understanding of and appreciation for other cultures. Students explore and expand their cultural values and beliefs as they read multicultural literature (Rasinski & Padak, 1990). They vicariously experience other cultures, and these experiences influence the way they interact with people in our culturally pluralistic world (Yokota, 1993). Check *Kaleidoscope: A Multicultural Booklist for Grades K–8* (Bishop, 1994) for an extensive annotated list of multicultural books.

Culturally Conscious Literature

Educators recommend selecting multicultural literature that is culturally conscious (Sims, 1982), that is to say, literature that accurately reflects a group's culture, language, history, and values without perpetuating stereotypes. Such literature often deals with issues of prejudice, discrimination, and human dignity. According to Yokota (1993), these books should be rich in cultural details with authentic dialogue and should present cultural issues in enough depth that readers can think and talk about them. Inclusion of cultural group members should be purposeful. They should be distinct individuals whose lives are rooted in the culture, never simply added to fulfill a quota.

Multicultural literature includes six types of literature, and each type offers a different perspective on the lives and contributions of each cultural group. The six types are:

1. Folktales and other traditional stories.   Traditional stories—including folktales, legends, and myths—are a part of every culture, and a wide variety of these stories are available for children. Cinderella stories, for example, come from many different cultures and include *Mufaro's Beautiful Daughters: An African Tale* (Steptoe, 1987), *Yeh-Shen: A Cinderella Story From China* (Louie, 1982), *The Egyptian Cinderella* (Climo, 1989), and *The Rough Face Girl* (Martin, 1992), an Algonquin Indian version.

2. Historical fiction.   These books describe the immigration of different cultural groups to the United States and their assimilation into American life. Two stories about the struggles of Jewish immigrants from Russia set in the late 1880s are *Immigrant Girl: Becky of Eldridge Street* (Harvey, 1987) and *Molly's Pilgrim* (Cohen, 1983).

3. Contemporary realistic fiction.   These contemporary stories focus on the experiences of culturally diverse people, and they take place in America. Two stories that show the difficulties in adjusting to life in the United States are *I Hate English!* (Levine, 1989), in which Mei Mei moves to New York from Hong Kong and has difficulty learning to speak English, and *Hello, My Name is Scrambled Eggs* (Gilson, 1985), which is about a Vietnamese refugee who is overwhelmed by iced tea, hair dryers, escalators, and other unfamiliar aspects of American life.

4. Biographies.   These books detail the contributions of people from various cultural groups. Some biographies—such as *Escape From Slavery: The Boyhood of Frederick Douglass in His Own Words* (McCurdy, 1994)— detail the lives of historical figures; others highlight contemporary persons.

5. Poetry.   There are a few collections of poems, songs, and chants written by people of various cultural groups that are available for children. In *Good Luck Gold and Other Poems* (1994), for example, Janet S. Wong shares her experience of growing up as an Asian American, and Gary Soto shares his Mexican American childhood experiences in *Neighborhood Odes* (1992) and *Canto Familiar* (1995). Other collections of multicultural poetry include *Pass It On: African-American Poetry for Children* (Hudson, 1993) and *The Trees Stand Shining: Poetry of the North American Indians* (Jones, 1993).

6. Informational books.   Other books provide information about various cultures, including information about holidays and rituals, language, cooking, and the arts, as well as information about the country in which the culture originated. Two informational books about Mexican Americans are *Hector Lives in the United States Now: The Story of a Mexican American Child* (Hewett, 1990) and *The Mexicans in America* (Pinchot, 1989).

Multicultural literature must meet the criteria for good literature as well as for cultural consciousness. One example is *The Gold Cadillac* (Taylor, 1987), a story about the harsh realities of racial discrimination that an African-American family encounters as they travel from Ohio to Mississippi in their new Cadillac during World War II. The story is well written, and the details are both historically and culturally accurate (Yokota, 1993).

Until recently, most books about Native Americans, Hispanic Americans, and other cultural groups have been written by European-American authors who, because of their own ethnicity, represent an "outside" viewpoint (Bishop, 1992b). An inside perspective is more likely to give an authentic view of what members of the cultural group believe to be true about themselves, while an outside perspective describes how others see that group's beliefs and behaviors. The difference in perspective means that there is a difference in what the authors say and how they say it, as well as a difference in their purpose for writing (Reimer, 1992). Some authors, however, do successfully write about another culture. Byrd Baylor and Paul Goble are notable examples. They have a sensitivity learned through research about and participation in differ-

Teachers include a wide variety of books, including culturally conscious literature, in their classroom libraries.

ent cultural groups. Today more people within each cultural group are writing about their own cultures and are providing more authentic "inside" viewpoints in multicultural literature.

There are many reasons to use multicultural literature in elementary classrooms, whether students represent diverse cultures or not. First, multicultural literature is good literature. Students enjoy reading these stories, informational books, and poems; through reading they learn more about what it means to be human, and they discover that people of all cultural groups are real people with similar emotions, needs, and dreams. Allen Say's *El Chino* (1990), for example, tells about a Chinese American who realizes his dream of becoming a great athlete, and the book provides a model for children and adults of all ethnic groups.

Second, students learn about the wealth of diversity in the United States through multicultural books, and they develop sensitivity to and appreciation for people of other cultural groups (Walker-Dalhouse, 1992). *Teammates* (Golenbock, 1990), for example, tells about the friendship between baseball greats Jackie Robinson and Pee Wee Reese, and it teaches a valuable lesson in tolerance and respect for fellow human beings. Multicultural literature also challenges racial and ethnic stereotypes by providing an inside view of a culture.

Third, students broaden their knowledge of geography and learn different views of history through multicultural literature. They read about the countries that minority groups left as they immigrated to America, and they gain nonmainstream perspectives about historical events. For example, Yoshiko

Uchida tells of her experiences in Japanese-American internment camps in the United States during World War II in *The Bracelet* (1993) and *Journey to Topaz* (1971). Through reading and responding to multicultural books, students challenge traditional assumptions about the history of America and gain a more balanced view of historical events and the contributions of people from various cultural groups. They learn that traditional historical accounts have emphasized the contributions of European Americans, and particularly those made by men.

Fourth, multicultural literature raises issues of social injustice—prejudice, racism, discrimination, segregation, colonization, anti-Semitism, and genocide. Two books that describe the discrimination and mistreatment of Chinese Americans during the 1800s, as well as their contributions to the settlement of the western United States, are *Chang's Paper Pony* (Coerr, 1988), a story set during the California gold rush, and *Ten Mile Day and the Building of the Transcontinental Railroad* (Fraser, 1993), a factual account of the race to complete the first railroad across North America.

Using multicultural literature has additional benefits for nonmainstream students. When students read books about their own cultural group, they develop pride in their cultural heritage and learn that their culture has made important contributions to the United States and to the rest of the world (Harris, 1992a, 1992b). In addition, students often become more interested in reading because they identify with the characters and events.

Literature About African Americans. More books are available about African Americans than about other cultural groups, and books published after 1970 do not seem to perpetuate stereotypes as much as those written earlier. Some books—such as *Follow the Drinking Gourd* (Winter, 1988), which describes the Underground Railroad, and *Roll of Thunder, Hear My Cry* (Taylor, 1976), which is about discrimination in the South during the 1930s—document events in the history of African Americans. Other books focus on contemporary events, such as *Tar Beach* (Ringgold, 1991), which is about a family who spends hot summer nights on the roof of their city apartment building. African-American authors have written collections of poems, such as Eloise Greenfield's *Night on Neighborhood Street* (1991) and *Nathaniel Talking* (1988). Also, many biographies of African-American personalities—athletes and political figures in particular—have been published.

Some of the best-known African-American authors are Eloise Greenfield, Virginia Hamilton, Walter Dean Myers, Mildred Taylor, and Patricia McKissack; books by these authors and others who write about the African-American experience are presented in Figure 13–1. Themes of these books include survival through the love and help of extended families, factors that mold a person's character, and the value of cultural traditions. Some books about African Americans use nonstandard language forms.

Literature About Asian Americans. Multicultural books about Asian Americans should deal with a specific Asian-American group, the characters should go beyond common stereotypes, and the books should correct historical errors and omissions. Asian-American authors who write books for children and adolescents include Allen Say, Yoshiko Uchida, Taro Yashima, Paul Yee, Laurence Yep, and Ed Young.

Figure 13–1   *Literature About the African-American Experience*

Crews, D. (1991). *Bigmama's.* New York: Greenwillow. (P–M)

Flournoy, C. (1985). *The patchwork quilt.* New York: Dial. (M)

Fox, P. (1973). *Slave dancer.* New York: Bradbury. (U)

Freedman, F. B. (1990). *Two tickets to freedom: The true story of Ellen and William Craft, fugitive slaves.* New York: Bedrick. (M–U)

Greenfield, E. (1975). *Paul Robeson.* New York: Crowell. (M–U)

Greenfield, E. (1989). *Nathaniel talking.* New York: Black Butterfly Children's Books. (P–M)

Greenfield, E. (1991). *Night on Neighborhood Street.* New York: Dial. (P–M)

Hamilton, V. (1967). *Zeely.* New York: Macmillan. (U)

Hamilton, V. (1974). *M. C. Higgins, the Great.* New York: Macmillan. (M–U)

Hamilton, V. (1985). *The people could fly: American black folktales.* New York: Knopf. (M–U)

Hamilton, V. (1988). *Anthony Burns: The defeat and triumph of a fugitive slave.* New York: Knopf. (U)

Hamilton, V. (1992). *Drylongso.* San Diego: Harcourt Brace Jovanovich. (M)

Hoffman, M. (1991). *Amazing Grace.* New York: Dial. (P–M)

Howard, E. F. (1991). *Aunt Flossie's hats (and crab cakes later).* New York: Clarion. (P–M)

Lester, J. (1987). *The tales of Uncle Remus: The adventures of Brer Rabbit.* New York: Dial. (M)

Mathis, S. B. (1975). *The hundred penny box.* New York: Viking. (M)

McKissack, P. (1988). *Mirandy and brother wind.* New York: Knopf. (M)

McKissack, P., & McKissack, F. (1989). *A long hard journey: The story of the Pullman Porter Walker.* New York: Walker. (U)

Meltzer, M. (1984). *The black Americans: A history in their own words, 1619–1983.* New York: Crowell. (U)

Myers, W. D. (1988). *Scorpions.* New York: Harper & Row. (U)

Parks, R., with J. Haskins. (1992). *Rosa Parks, my story.* New York: Dial. (M)

Rappaport, D. (1991). *Escape from slavery.* New York: HarperCollins. (M–U)

Ringgold, F. (1991). *Tar beach.* New York: Crown. (P–M)   *Own*

Ringgold, F. (1992). *Aunt Harriet's underground railroad in the sky.* New York: Crown. (M)

Slote, A. (1991). *Finding Buck McHenry.* New York: HarperCollins. (U)

Stolz, M. (1991). *Go fish.* New York: HarperCollins. (M–U)

Taylor, M. (1976). *Roll of thunder, hear my cry.* New York: Dial. (U)   *Own*

Taylor, M. (1981). *Let the circle be unbroken.* New York: Dial. (U)

Taylor, M. (1987). *The gold cadillac.* New York: Dial. (M)

Taylor, M. (1990). *Mississippi bridge.* New York: Dial. (M–U)

Williams, S. A. (1992). *Working cotton.* San Diego: Harcourt Brace Jovanovich. (P–M)

Yarbrough, C. (1979). *Cornrows.* New York: Coward-McCann. (M)

P = primary grades (K–2); M = middle grades (3–5); U = upper grades (6–8).

A list of books about the Asian experience in America is presented in Figure 13–2. Many of the books have been written by Asian Americans and are about their own assimilation experiences or remembrances as children in the United States. For example, *Angel Child, Dragon Child* (Surat, 1983) is the story of a Vietnamese-American child who adjusts to life in the United States, and *Baseball Saved Us* (Mochizuki, 1993) tells of a Japanese-American boy's experiences in a concentration camp in the United States during World War II.

Literature About Hispanic Americans.   Fewer books about Hispanic Americans are available than for other cultural groups, despite the fact that Hispanic Americans are one of the largest minority groups in the United States. Two authors who are making a significant contribution are Nicholasa Mohr, who writes short stories and novels about life in the Puerto Rican–American

Figure 13–2   *Literature About the Asian-American Experience*

Ashley, B. (1991). *Cleversticks.* New York: Crown. (P) (Chinese American)

Chiemroum, S. (1992). *Dara's Cambodian new year.* New York: Scholastic. (P–M)

Choi, S. N. (1991). *The year of impossible goodbyes.* Boston: Houghton Mifflin. (U) (Korean American)

Coerr, E. (1985). *Chang's paper pony.* New York: Harper & Row. (M) (Chinese American)

Crew, L. (1989). *Children of the river.* New York: Dell. (U) (Cambodian American)

Fraser, M. A. (1993). *Ten mile day and the building of the transcontinental railroad.* New York: Henry Holt. (M–U) (Chinese American)

Gilson, J. (1985). *Hello, my name is scrambled eggs.* New York: Morrow. (U) (Vietnamese American)

Graff, N. P. (1993). *Where the river runs: A portrait of a refugee family.* Boston: Little, Brown. (M–U) (Cambodian American)

Hamanaka, S. (1990). *The journey: Japanese Americans, racism, and renewal.* New York: Orchard. (U)

Ho, M. (1992). *The clay marble.* New York: Farrar, Straus & Giroux. (U)

Hoyt-Goldsmith, D. (1992). *Hoang Anh: A Vietnamese American boy.* New York: Holiday House. (M)

Kraus, J. (1992). *Tall boy's journey.* Minneapolis: Carolrhoda. (M–U) (Korean American)

Leathers, N. L. (1991). *The Japanese in America.* Minneapolis: Lerner. (M–U)

Lee, M. G. (1993). *If it hadn't been for Yoon Jun.* Boston: Houghton Mifflin. (M–U) (Korean American)

Lehrer, B. (1988). *The Korean Americans.* New York: Chelsea House. (M–U)

Lord, B. (1984). *In the year of the boar and Jackie Robinson.* New York: Harper & Row. (M–U) (Chinese American)

Martin, A. M. (1988). *Yours turly* [sic], *Shirley.* New York: Harper & Row. (U) (Vietnamese American)

Nhuong, H. Q. (1982). *The land I lost: Adventures of a boy in Vietnam.* New York: Harper & Row. (M–U)

Pettit, J. (1992). *My name is San Ho.* New York: Scholastic. (U) (Vietnamese American)

Say, A. (1991). *Tree of cranes.* Boston: Houghton Mifflin. (M) (Japanese American)

Say, A. (1993). *Grandfather's journey.* Boston: Houghton Mifflin. (M) (Japanese American)

Toff, N. (1990). *The Filipino Americans.* New York: Chelsea House. (M–U)

Uchida, Y. (1971). *Journey to Topaz.* Berkeley, CA: Creative Arts. (U) (Japanese American)

Uchida, Y. (1978). *Journey home.* New York: Atheneum. (U) (Japanese American)

Uchida, Y. (1991). *The invisible thread.* New York: Messner. (U) (Japanese American)

Uchida, Y. (1993). *The bracelet.* New York: Philomel. (P-M) (Japanese American)

Waters, K. (1990). *Lion dancer: Ernie Wan's Chinese new year.* New York: Scholastic. (M)

Winter, F. H. (1988). *The Filipinos in America.* Minneapolis: Lerner. (M–U)

Yee, P. (1989). *Tales from Gold Mountain.* New York: Macmillan. (M–U) (Chinese American)

Yep, L. (1975). *Dragonwings.* New York: Harper & Row. (U) (Chinese American)

Yep, L. (1977). *Child of the owl.* New York: Harper & Row. (M–U) (Chinese American)

Yep, L. (1991). *The star fisher.* New York: Morrow. (U) (Chinese American)

Yep, L. (Ed.). (1993). *American dragons: 25 Asian American voices.* New York: HarperCollins. (U)

community in New York, and Gary Soto, who writes poems and stories about life in the Mexican-American community in California. Both writers bring first-hand knowledge of life in a barrio to make their writing authentic (Soto, 1992; Zarnowski, 1991). In addition, Arthur Dorros has written *Abuela* (1991) and its sequel *Isla* (1995), fantastical flying stories about a little girl and her *abuela* (grandmother). A list of books about Hispanic Americans is presented in Figure 13–3. The themes in these books emphasize the richness of life in the barrio, as well as the importance of maintaining cultural identity, the struggles and triumphs of everyday life, and surviving oppression (Harris, 1992a).

Literature About Native Americans. Many books are available about Native Americans, but very few were written by Native American authors.

Figure 13–3 *Literature About the Hispanic-American Experience*

Anzaldua, G. (1993). *Friends from the other side/ Amigos del otro lado.* San Francisco: Children's Book Press. (P–M) (Mexican American)

Behrens, J. (1978). *Fiesta!* Chicago: Childrens Press. (M)

Brimmer, L. D. (1992). *Migrant family.* Minneapolis: Lerner. (M–U) (Mexican American)

Cazet, D. (1993). *Born in the gravy.* New York: Orchard. (P)

Cisneros, S. (1983). *The house on Mango Street.* Houston: Arte Publico. (U)

Concord, B. W. (1992). *Cesar Chavez.* New York: Chelsea House. (M–U)

Delacre, L. (1989). *Arroz con leche.* New York: Scholastic. (P)

Dorros, A. (1991). *Abuela.* New York: Dutton. (P)

Garza, C. L. (1990). *Family pictures.* San Francisco: Children's Book Press. (P) (Mexican American)

Hewett, J. (1990). *Hector lives in the United States now: The story of a Mexican-American child.* New York: Lippincott. (M–U)

Larsen, R. J. (1989). *The Puerto Ricans in America.* Minneapolis: Lerner. (M–U)

Metzer, M. (1982). *The Hispanic Americans.* New York: Crowell. (M–U)

Mohr, N. (1979). *Felita.* New York: Dial. (M) (Puerto Rican American)

Mohr, N. (1986). *El Bronx remembered.* Houston: Arte Publico. (U) (Puerto Rican American)

Mohr, N. (1986). *Nilda.* Houston: Arte Publico. (U) (Puerto Rican American)

Mohr, N. (1988). *In Nueva York.* Houston: Arte Publico. (U) (Puerto Rican American)

Mora, P. (1992). *A birthday present for Tia.* New York: Macmillan. (P) (Mexican American)

O'Dell, S. (1979). *The captive.* Boston: Houghton Mifflin. (U) (Mexican American)

O'Dell, S. (1981). *Carlota.* Boston: Houghton Mifflin. (U) (Mexican American)

O'Dell, S. (1983). *The amethyst ring.* Boston: Houghton Mifflin. (U) (Mexican American)

Pinchot, J. (1989). *The Mexicans in America.* Minneapolis: Lerner. (M–U)

Politi, L. (1949). *Song of the swallows.* New York: Scribner. (P–M) (Mexican American)

Politi, L. (1976). *Three stalks of corn.* New York: Scribner. (P–M) (Mexican American)

Soto, G. (1986). *Small faces.* New York: Dell. (U) (Mexican American)

Soto, G. (1990). *Baseball in April and other stories.* Orlando: Harcourt Brace Jovanovich. (M–U) (Mexican American)

Soto, G. (1990). *A fire in my hands.* New York: Scholastic. (U) (Mexican American)

Soto, G. (1992). *Neighborhood odes.* Orlando: Harcourt Brace Jovanovich. (U) (Mexican American)

Soto, G. (1992). *Pacific crossing.* Orlando: Harcourt Brace Jovanovich. (U) (Mexican American)

Soto, G. (1993). *Too many tamales.* Orlando: Harcourt Brace Jovanovich. (P–M) (Mexican American)

Stanek, M. (1989). *I speak English for my mom.* New York: Whitman. (M)

Williams, V. B. (1982). *A chair for my mother.* New York: Mulberry. (P)

Authors who have written sensitively about Native American topics are Byrd Baylor, Jamake Highwater, and Paul Goble. Most books about Native Americans are retellings of traditional folktales, myths, and legends, such as *The Legend of the Indian Paintbrush* (de Paola, 1988) and *Iktomi and the Boulder* (Goble, 1988). A number of biographies about Indian chiefs are also available. Other books describe Indian rituals and ceremonies, such as *Totem Pole* (Hoyt-Goldsmith, 1990), in which a contemporary Indian boy describes how his father carved a totem pole. A list of books about Native Americans is presented in Figure 13–4. The themes in these books include passing on rituals and stories to the next generation, mistreatment and injustice that Native Americans have suffered at the hands of Europeans and European Americans, and a reverence for living things and the earth.

Literature About Other American Cultural Groups. In addition to the four cultural groups already discussed, there are distinct regional and religious

Figure 13–4   *Literature About the Native American Experience*

Aliki. (1976). *Corn is maize: The gift of the Indians.* New York: Crowell. (P–M)

Ancona, G. (1993). *Powwow.* Orlando: Harcourt Brace. (M–U)

Baylor, B. (1975). *The desert is theirs.* New York: Scribner. (P–M)

Baylor, B. (1978). *The other way to listen.* New York: Scribner. (P–M)

Bierhorst, J. (1983). *The sacred path: Spells, prayers, and power songs of the American Indians.* New York: Morrow. (P–M–U)

Cohen, C. L. (1988). *The mud pony.* New York: Scholastic. (M)

Freedman, R. (1987). *Indian chiefs.* New York: Holiday House. (U)

Freedman, R. (1988). *Buffalo hunt.* New York: Holiday House. (U)

Freedman, R. (1992). *An Indian winter.* New York: Holiday House. (M–U)

Fritz, J. (1983). *The double life of Pocahontas.* New York: Putnam. (M–U)

George, J. C. (1972). *Julie of the wolves.* New York: Harper & Row. (U) (Eskimo)

George, J. C. (1983). *The talking earth.* New York: Harper & Row. (U)

Highwater, J. (1977). *Anpao: An American Indian odyssey.* New York: Lippincott. (U)

Hoyt-Goldsmith, D. (1990). *Totem pole.* New York: Holiday House. (M)

Hoyt-Goldsmith, D. (1992). *Arctic hunter.* New York: Holiday House. (M)

Jones, H. (1993). *The trees stand shining: Poetry of the North American Indians.* New York: Dial. (P–M–U)

Keegan, M. (1991). *Pueblo boy: Growing up in two worlds.* New York: Cobblehill Books. (P–M)

Locker, T. (1991). *The land of gray wolf.* New York: Dial. (M–U)

Luenn, N. (1990). *Nessa's fish.* New York: Atheneum. (P–M) (Eskimo)

Martin, B., & Archambault, J. (1987). *Knots on a counting rope.* New York: Holt, Rinehart & Winston. (P–M)

Medearis, A. S. (1991). *Dancing with the Indians.* New York: Holiday House. (M)

O'Dell, S. (1970). *Sing down the moon.* Boston: Houghton Mifflin. (U)

O'Dell, S. (1988). *Black star, bright dawn.* Boston: Houghton Mifflin. (U)

O'Dell, S., & Hall, E. (1992). *Thunder rolling in the mountains.* Boston: Houghton Mifflin. (U)

Paulsen, G. (1988). *Dogsong.* New York: Bradbury Press. (U)

Regguinti, G. (1992). *The sacred harvest: Ojibway wild rice gathering.* Minneapolis: Lerner. (M)

Seattle, C. (1991). *Brother eagle, sister sky.* New York: Dial. (P–M–U)

Sneve, V. D. H. (1972). *Jimmy yellow hawk.* New York: Holiday House. (M)

Sneve, V. D. H. (1974). *When thunder spoke.* New York: Holiday House. (M–U)

Sneve, V. D. H. (1989). *Dancing teepees: Poems of American Indian youth.* New York: Holiday House. (P–M–U)

Speare, E. G. (1983). *The sign of the beaver.* Boston: Houghton Mifflin. (M–U)

cultures in the United States, including Jewish, Amish, Cajun, and Appalachian groups. One book set in Appalachia is *Amber on the Mountain* (Johnston, 1994), the story of a determined girl, isolated in the mountains, who teaches herself to write. As the majority culture, European Americans are sometimes ignored in discussions of cultural groups, but to ignore them denies the distinct cultures of many Americans (Yokoto, 1993). Within the European-American umbrella category are a variety of groups, including German Americans, Italian Americans, Swedish Americans, and Russian Americans. Patricia Polacco's *Thunder Cake* (1990), the story of a grandmother who calms her granddaughter's fear of thunderstorms by making a "thunder cake," is a popular book featuring Russian Americans.

Teaching About Cultural Diversity

Some teachers periodically share books of multicultural literature with their students, while other teachers include multicultural components in lessons they teach and teach literature focus units and theme cycles to raise students' awareness of racism, inequality, and other social issues. I encourage teachers to develop units and theme cycles using multicultural literature. According to Zarillo (1994), the characteristics of multicultural literature focus units and theme cycles are that they:

- Celebrate cultural diversity in the United States
- Increase cultural understanding and respect
- Provide opportunities to use all six language arts
- Provide opportunities for students who are learning English to use language in meaningful ways
- Incorporate aesthetic reading and response-to-literature activities
- Use books that accurately portray cultural groups

Rasinski and Padak (1990) have identified four approaches for incorporating multicultural literature into literature focus units and theme cycles. These approaches are based on Banks's (1994b) multicultural curriculum model and differ in the extent to which multicultural issues become a central part of the curriculum.

1. The contributions approach. This approach focuses on lessons taught in connection with a holiday or other special occasions (Rasinski & Padak, 1990). The purpose of activities is to familiarize students with holidays, specific customs, or the contributions of important people, but these activities do not teach cultural values or challenge students to reexamine their beliefs. Single lessons might focus on reading *Seven Candles for Kwanzaa* (Pinkney, 1993), a story about Kwanzaa, an African-American holiday celebrated from December 16 to January 1, or reading *How My Parents Learned to Eat* (Friedman, 1984), a story about an American sailor who courts a young Japanese woman after World War II. In the latter book, the young woman learns to eat with a knife and fork to surprise the sailor, and the sailor learns to eat with chopsticks to surprise the woman. Or, teachers might read *A Picture Book of Martin Luther King, Jr.* (Adler, 1989) to celebrate the Civil Rights leader's birthday. This approach is an easy way to include a multicultural component in the curriculum, but students gain only a superficial understanding of cultural diversity.

2. The additive approach. In this second approach, lessons using multicultural literature are added to the existing curriculum (Rasinski & Padak, 1990). In a genre unit on folktales, for example, *Mufaro's Beautiful Daughters: An African Tale* (Steptoe, 1987), *Yeh-Shen: A Cinderella Story From China* (Louie, 1982), and *The Egyptian Cinderella* (Climo, 1989) might be added as international versions of the Cinderella story. Or, for a literature focus unit, an upper-grade teacher might choose a multicultural chapter book such as *Year of Impossible Goodbyes* (Choi, 1991), the story of a Korean girl who is forced to immigrate to America after enduring the cruelties of the Japanese military force occupying her country at the end of World War II. The teacher would choose to read this book because it is a powerful, well-written book and one that the students would enjoy. This approach is similar to the contributions approach because the curriculum is based in the European-American perspective. Information about cultural diversity is added to the curriculum, but not woven through it.

3. The transformation approach. Literature focus units and theme cycles are modified in this approach to promote the study of historical events and contemporary issues from the viewpoint of culturally diverse groups (Rasinski & Padak, 1990). Primary-grade students, for instance, might read *A Chair for My Mother* (Williams, 1982), *Everybody Cooks Rice* (Dooley, 1991), and *Bigmama's* (Crews, 1991) as part of a unit on families and then talk about the common features of families from diverse cultural groups. Or, during a theme cycle on World War II, upper-grade students might read *Journey to Topaz* (Uchida, 1971) to learn about the Japanese-American viewpoint about the war and their unfair internment. These literature experiences and response activities allow students to see the interconnectedness of various ethnic groups within American society and the ways that diverse cultural groups have shaped American history.

4. The social action approach.   In this fourth approach, students study important social issues and take action to solve problems through theme cycles (Rasinski & Padak, 1990). Students read culturally conscious literature in order to gain an "inside" view on social issues. For example, students might study immigration and begin by reading *How Many Days to America? A Thanksgiving Story* (Bunting, 1988) to learn about modern-day refugees who risk their lives coming to America. Afterwards they can talk about their own attitudes toward immigrant groups and research how and when their families came to America. Another book they might read is *Who Belongs Here? An American Story* (Knight, 1993). The question "Who belongs here?" might direct their study and lead them to find ways to encourage tolerance and assist with refugee programs in their community. In this approach, students read, do research, think deeply about social issues, and apply what they are learning in their own communities.

LITERATURE FOCUS UNITS

Teachers plan literature focus units featuring popular and award-winning stories for children and adolescents. Some literature focus units feature a single book, either a picture book or a chapter book, while others feature a text set of books for a genre unit or an author study unit. Figure 13–5 presents a list of trade books, genres, and authors recommended for literature focus units for kindergarten through eighth grade. During these units, students move through the five stages of the reading process as they read and respond to stories, learn reading and writing skills and strategies, and engage in language arts activities.

How to Develop a Literature Focus Unit

Teachers develop a literature focus unit through an eight-step series of activities, beginning with choosing the literature for the unit, continuing to identify

Books	Genres	Authors and Illustrators

Primary Grades (K–2)

Books	Genres	Authors and Illustrators
Blume, J. (1971). *Freckle juice.* New York: Bradbury Press.	Number books	Jan Brett
Brett, J. (1989). *The mitten.* New York: Putnam.	Folk tales	Eric Carle
Carle, E. (1970). *The very hungry caterpillar.* New York: Viking.	Pattern stories	Donald Crews
Dorros, A. (1991). *Abuela.* New York: Dutton.	Alphabet books	Tomie de Paola
Galdone, P. (1972). *The three bears.* New York: Clarion.	Fairy tales	Dr. Seuss
Henkes, K. (1991). *Chrysanthemum.* New York: Greenwillow.	Biographies	Lois Ehlert
Hutchins, P. (1968). *Rosie's walk.* New York: Macmillan.		Mem Fox
Lester, H. (1988). *Tacky the penguin.* Boston: Houghton Mifflin.		Tana Hoban
Lionni, L. (1969). *Alexander and the wind-up mouse.* New York: Knopf.		Steven Kellogg
Most, B. (1978). *If the dinosaurs came back.* San Diego: Harcourt Brace.		James Marshall
Noble, T. H. (1980). *The day Jimmy's boa ate the wash.* New York: Dial.		Bill Martin and John Archambault
Numeroff, L. (1985). *If you give a mouse a cookie.* New York: Harper & Row.		Patricia and Frederick McKissack
Rylant, C. (1985). *The relatives came.* New York: Bradbury Press.		Bernard Most
		Bernard Waber
		Audrey and Don Wood

Middle Grades (3–5)

Books	Genres	Authors and Illustrators
Barrett, J. (1978). *Cloudy with a chance of meatballs.* New York: Macmillan.	Biography	Byrd Baylor
Blume, J. (1972). *Tales of a fourth grade nothing.* New York: Dutton.	Fables	Beverly Cleary
Cleary, B. (1981). *Ramona Quimby, age 8.* New York: Morrow.	Native American myths	Jean Fritz
Coerr, E. (1977). *Sadako and the thousand paper cranes.* New York: Putnam.	Poetry	Paul Goble
Cohen, B. (1983). *Molly's pilgrim.* New York: Morrow.	Tall tales	Eloise Greenfield
Gardiner, J. R. (1980). *Stone Fox.* New York: Harper & Row.	Wordplay books	Patricia MacLachlan
Lowry, L. (1989). *Number the stars.* Boston: Houghton Mifflin.		Ann Martin
MacLachlan, P. (1985). *Sarah, plain and tall.* New York: Harper & Row.		Patricia Polacco
Naylor, P. R. (1991). *Shiloh.* New York: Macmillan.		Jack Prelutsky
Paterson, K. (1977). *Bridge to Terabithia.* New York: Crowell.		Cynthia Rylant
Speare, E. G. (1983). *The sign of the beaver.* Boston: Houghton Mifflin.		William Steig
White, E. B. (1952). *Charlotte's web.* New York: Harper & Row.		R. L. Stine
		Marvin Terban
		Chris Van Allsburg
		Jane Yolen

Figure 13–5 continued

Books	Genres	Authors and Illustrators
Upper Grades (6–8)		
Avi. (1991). *Nothing but the truth.* New York: Orchard.	Science fiction	Lloyd Alexander
Babbitt, N. (1975). *Tuck everlasting.* New York: Farrar, Straus & Giroux.	Myths	Avi
Fox, L. (1984). *One-eyed cat.* New York: Bradbury Press.	Poetry	Paula Danziger
George, J. C. (1972). *Julie of the wolves.* New York: Harper & Row.		Russell Freedman
Hamilton, V. (1967). *Zeely.* New York: Macmillan.		Virginia Hamilton
Hinton, S. E. (1967). *The outsiders.* New York: Viking.		David Macaulay
L'Engle, M. (1962). *A wrinkle in time.* New York: Farrar, Straus & Giroux.		Walter Dean Myers
Lewis, C. S. (1950). *The lion, the witch and the wardrobe.* New York: Macmillan.		Scott O'Dell
Lowry, L. (1993). *The giver.* Boston: Houghton Mifflin.		Katherine Paterson
Paulsen, G. (1987). *The hatchet.* New York: Viking.		Gary Paulsen
Peck, R. (1972). *A day no pigs would die.* New York: Knopf.		Richard Peck
Taylor, M. (1976). *Roll of thunder, hear my cry.* New York: Dial.		Jerry Spinelli
Voigt, C. (1982). *Dicey's song.* New York:		Yoshiko Uchida
		Laurence Yep
		Paul Zindel

and schedule activities, and ending with deciding how to assess students' learning. Whether teachers are using trade books or textbook selections, they develop a unit using these steps to meet the needs of their students. Effective teachers do not simply follow directions in basal reader teachers' manuals and literature focus unit planning guides that are available for purchase in school supply stores. Teachers need to make the plans themselves because they are the ones who best know their students, the reading materials they have available, the time available for the unit, the skills and strategies they want to teach, and the language arts activities they want to use.

Usually literature focus units featuring a picture book are completed in one week, and units featuring a chapter book are completed in two, three, or four weeks. Genre and author units may last two, three or four weeks. Rarely, if ever, do literature focus units continue for more than a month. When teachers drag out a unit for six weeks, two months, or longer they risk killing students' interest in this particular book or, worse yet, their love of literature.

Step 1: Select the Literature. Teachers begin by selecting the reading material for the literature focus unit. The literature may be a story in a picture book format, a chapter book, or a story selected from a basal reading textbook. The reading materials should be high-quality literature and should often include multicultural selections. Sometimes teachers select several related stories—books representing the same genre, books written by the same author for an author study, or books illustrated by same artist for an illustrator study. Teachers collect multiple copies of the book or books for the literature focus unit. When teachers use trade books, they have to collect class sets of the books for the unit. In some school districts, class sets of selected books are available for teachers. However, in other school districts, teachers have to request that administrators purchase multiple copies of books or buy them themselves through book clubs. When teachers use picture books, students can share books so only half as many books as students are needed.

Once the book (or books) is selected, teachers collect related books for the text set. Books for the text set include:

- other versions of the same story
- other books written by the same author
- other books illustrated by the same artist
- books with the same theme
- books with similar settings
- books in the same genre
- informational books on a related topic
- books of poetry on a related topic

Teachers collect one or two copies of 10, 20, 30, or more books for the text set, which they add to the classroom library during the focus unit. Books for the text set are placed on a special shelf or in a crate in the library center. At the beginning of the unit, teachers do a book talk to introduce the books in the text set, and then students read them during independent reading time.

Step 2: Develop a Unit Plan. Teachers read or reread the selected book or books and then think about the focus they will use for the unit. Sometimes teachers focus on an element of story structure, the historical setting, wordplay, the author or genre, or a concept or topic related to the book, such as weather or life in the desert.

After determining the focus, teachers think about which activities they will use at each of the five stages of the reading process. For each stage, teachers ask themselves these questions:

1. Preparing

- What background knowledge do students need before reading?
- What key concepts and vocabulary should I teach before reading?
- How will I introduce the story and stimulate students' interest for reading?

2. Reading

- How will students read this story?
- What reading strategies and skills will I model or ask students to use?
- How can I make it more accessible for less capable readers and students learning English as a second language?

3. Responding

- Will students write in reading logs? How often?
- Will students participate in grand conversations? How often?
- What scenes from the book will students want or need to dramatize?

■ *See Chapter 3, "The Reading and Writing Processes," pp. 90–108, to review the stages of the reading process.*

4. Exploring

- What words might be added to the word wall?
- What vocabulary activities might be used?
- Will students reread the story?
- What skill and strategy minilessons might be taught?
- How can I focus students' attention on words and sentences in the book?
- How will books from the text set be used?
- What can I share about the author, illustrator or genre?

5. Extending

- What projects might students choose to pursue?
- How will books from the text set be used?
- How will students share projects?

Teachers often jot notes on a chart divided into sections for each stage. Then they use the ideas they have brainstormed as they plan the unit. Usually not all of the brainstormed activities will be used in the literature focus unit, but teachers select the most important ones according to their focus and the available time. Teachers do not omit any of the stages, however, in an attempt to make more time available for activities during any one stage.

■ *To read more about the language arts strategies, check Chapter 1, "Learning and the Language Arts," pp. 31–34. Also, check the lists of minilesson topics in Chapters 3–12.*

Step 3: Identify Language Arts Strategies and Skills to Teach During the Unit. Teachers decide which strategies and skills to teach using the book. Their choice is dependent on the students' observed needs, opportunities afforded by the book, and school district requirements. Sometimes teachers plan minilessons to directly teach skills and strategies, and at other times they plan to model how to use the skills and strategies as they read aloud or to ask students to share how they use the skills and strategies during grand conversations.

Step 4: Locate Multimedia Materials Related to the Unit. Teachers locate multimedia materials to use in the unit, including film, CD-ROM, and video versions of stories for students to view and compare to the book version, audiotapes of stories to use at listening centers, story boards made from paperback versions of the story for students to sequence, and author information and interviews on videotapes and audiotapes. Teachers also plan how they will use computers for writing and researching activities and cameras for photographic essays related to the unit.

■ *For more informa-tion on the six lan-guage arts, see Chapter 1, "Learning and the Language Arts," pp. 23–26.*

Step 5: Incorporate Activities Representing All Six Language Arts. Teachers review the plans they are developing to make sure that students have opportunities to engage in listening, talking, reading, writing, viewing, and visually representing activities during the literature focus unit. Of course, not all six language arts fit into every unit, but for most units they do. Figure 13–6 lists many of the activities discussed in this book, according to the lan-guage art they illustrate.

Step 6: Coordinate Grouping Patterns With Activities. Teachers think about how to incorporate whole-class, small-group, buddy, and individual activities into their unit plans. It is important that students have opportunities to read and write independently as well as to work with small groups and to

Figure 13–6 *Activities Illustrating the Six Language Arts*

Listening

Listen to books at listening centers
Listen to teacher read aloud
Listen to classmates' comments during conversations about literature
Listen to choral readings and readers theatre performances
Listen to classmates retell stories
Listen to classmates read their books from the author's chair
Listen to oral reports and debates

Talking

Participate in conversations about literature
Retell and tell stories
Do book talks
Present oral reports
Interview community members
Participate in debates
Talk with classmates about their rough drafts
Share projects and writings

Reading

Read stories, informational books, and poems
Read books independently
Read books with a buddy
Participate in readers theatre and choral reading activities
Read words on the word wall
Proofread rough drafts
Read books from the author's chair
Reread favorite stories
Participate in a read-around

Writing

Write entries in reading logs and other journals
Do quickwrites
Write friendly letters, business letters, and letters to authors
Write stories, retellings of familiar stories, and innovations
Write "All About . . ." books, reports, and other books
Write poems
Write words and sentences on word walls, charts, and story quilts

---

Viewing

Present oral reports
Sequence story boards
Watch classmates dramatize and retell stories
Compare book and video versions of stories
View videos on topics related to literature focus units and theme cycles
View filmstrips and videos about authors and illustrators
View posters and other projects classmates create

Visually Representing

Make diagrams about elements of story structure
Make puppets
Create posters, Venn diagrams, semantic feature analysis, and other charts
Make clusters during prewriting
Design story quilts
Draw open-mind portraits
Present puppet shows and dramatizations of stories

---

come together as a class. If the piece of literature that students are reading will be read together as a class, then students need opportunities to reread it with a buddy or independently, or to read related books independently. These grouping patterns should be alternated during various activities in the unit. Teachers often go back to their planning sheet and highlight activities with colored markers according to grouping patterns.

Step 7: Create a Time Schedule. Teachers create a time schedule that allows students sufficient time to move through the five stages of the reading process and to complete the activities planned for the focus unit. Literature-based reading programs require large blocks of time, at least two hours in length, in which students read, listen, talk, and write about the literature they are reading.

Using this block of time, teachers complete weekly lesson plans, and the activities they include represent each of the five stages of the reading process. The stages are not clearly separated and they overlap, but preparing, reading, responding, exploring, and extending activities are included in the lesson plan.

■ *Turn to Chapter 2, "Teaching Language Arts," pp. 70–84, to read more about assessing students' learning.*

Step 8: Plan for the Assessment of the Literature Focus Unit. Teachers often distribute unit folders for students to use. They keep all work, reading logs, reading materials, and related materials in the folder. Then at the end of the unit, students turn in their completed folders for teachers to evaluate. Keeping all the materials together makes the unit easier for both students and teachers to manage.

Teachers also plan ways to document students' learning and assign grades. One form of record keeping is an assignment checklist. This sheet is developed with students and distributed at the beginning of the literature focus unit. Students keep track of their work during the unit and sometimes negotiate to change the sheet as the unit evolves. Students keep the lists in unit folders, and they mark off each item as it is completed. At the end of the unit, students turn in their completed assignment checklist and other completed work. An assignment checklist for an upper-grade literature focus unit on *The Giver* (Lowry, 1993), a story about a "perfect" community that isn't, is presented in Figure 13–7. While this list does not include every activity students were involved in, it does list the activities and other assignments that the teacher holds students accountable for. Students complete the checklist on the left side of the sheet and add titles of books and other requested information. Teachers award points (up to the number listed in parentheses) on the lines on the right side of the sheet, and total the number of points on the bottom of the page. Then the total score can be translated into a letter grade or other type of grade.

A Primary-Grade Literature Focus Unit on The Mitten

■ *To read more about literature focus units, turn to Chapter 3, pp. 106–110 and 127–128, Chapter 9, pp. 367–372 and 376–380, and Chapter 11, pp. 445–449 and 469–470.*

Jan Brett's *The Mitten* (1989), a cumulative picture book story about a series of animals who climb into a mitten that a little boy has dropped in the snow on a cold winter day, is the featured selection in literature focus units taught in many primary-grade classrooms. A planning cluster for a literature focus unit on *The Mitten* is shown in Figure 13–8. Teachers use the big book version of *The Mitten* to introduce the unit and to examine Brett's innovative use of borders. Students use the teacher's collection of stuffed animals and puppets representing the animals in the story—a mole, a rabbit, a hedgehog, an owl, a badger, a fox, a bear, and a mouse—as they retell the story. Students read the story several times—in small groups with the teacher, with partners, and independently. The teacher also reads aloud several other versions of the story, including *The Woodcutter's Mitten* (Koopmans, 1990) and *The Mitten* (Tresselt, 1964), and students make a chart to compare the versions. The teacher presents minilessons on phonemic awareness and phonics skills, creates a word wall, and involves students in word-study activities. Students participate in sequencing and writing activities, and learn about knitting from a parent volunteer. The teacher also sets out a text set of other books by Jan

Figure 13–7   An Upper-Grade Assignment Checklist

The Giver

Name _____

Student's Check		Teacher's Check

Student's Check _____   1. Read *The Giver*.   Teacher's Check _____

_____   2. Write at least 10 entries in your reading log. Use a double-entry format with quotes and your connections. (20)   _____

_____   3. Participate in small-group grand conversations.   _____

_____   4. Create a story board. Chapter # _____ (10)   _____

_____   5. Make an open-mind portrait of Jonas with four mind pages. (10)   _____

_____   6. Write an essay about the theme of the book. (10)   _____

_____   7. Choose and analyze 10 words from the word wall according to prefix, root word, and suffix. (10)   _____

_____   8. Read one book from the text set. Write a brief summary in your reading log and compare what you learned about societies with *The Giver*. (10)   _____

Title _____
Author _____

_____   9. Make a square for the class story quilt. (5)   _____

_____   10. Create a project and share it with the class. (25)   _____

Project _____
Date shared _____

Total _____

Brett and reads some of the books aloud to students. As their extension project, students divide into small groups to research one of the animals mentioned in the story. Fifth graders work with the primary-grade students as they research the animals and share what they learn on large posters.

A Middle-Grade Literature Focus Unit on Eve Bunting and Her Books

Students begin the unit by reading *Smoky Night* (Bunting, 1994) together as a class. This Caldecott Medal story tells how the riots in Los Angeles brought together people of different cultures. After students read this book together, they read other books by Eve Bunting in small groups and independently. Teachers focus on strategies and skills, teaching both by modeling and through planned minilessons. Students keep reading logs in which they write after reading each of the books. They participate in a variety of visually representing activities, including making open-mind portraits of favorite characters, and learn about story structure. Many of Bunting's stories focus on theme, and students have opportunities to think deeply about the meanings of the stories. Students learn about Eve Bunting and read her autobiography,

Word Wall

Nicki	grandmother
Baba	mitten
glove	mole
cozy	tunneling along
snowshoe rabbit	big kickers
hedgehog	prickles
owl	commotion
swooped down	glinty talons
badger	diggers
fox	trotted
drowsy	muzzle
bear	lumbered by
swelled	stretched
meadow mouse	acorn
wriggled	bear's nose
whiskers	enormous sneeze
yarn	knitted
wool	sheep
Ukraine	borders

Word-Study Activities

- Word posters
- Word sorts
- Individual word cards
- Semantic feature analysis to compare animals

Maps and Globes

- Mark Massachusetts—the state Jan Brett lives in—on a U.S. map.
- Locate the Ukraine setting for this book on a map or globe.

Phonemic Awareness and Phonics

- Collect rhyming objects and pictures related to the story for students to match (e.g., mitten–kitten, fox–box, bear–hair–pear–chair, mouse–house).
- Have students "stretch" these words from the story: *mole, snow, owl, mouse, cozy, nose.*
- Focus on a consonant sound: /m/ for *mitten,* /y/ for *yarn,* or /n/ for *Nicki.*
- Teach the *r*-controlled vowel sound using *yarn.*
- Focus on a vowel sound: short *i* for *mitten,* long *o* for *snow.*

Illustration Techniques

- Examine Brett's use of borders in many of her books, and encourage students to create borders in the books they write.
- Also, note the side mitten panels with looking back and looking forward scenes on each page of *The Mitten.*

Compare Versions of the Story

Read these versions and make a chart to compare them with Brett's version:

Koopmans, L. (1990). *The woodcutter's mitten.* New York: Crocodile Books.

Tresselt, A. (1964). *The mitten.* New York: Lothrop, Lee & Shepard.

Big Book

Introduce the story using the big book version of the book (published by Scholastic) and shared reading.

Research

- Research one of the animals—mole, rabbit, hedgehog, owl, badger, fox, bear, mouse—mentioned in the story and create a class book about the animal.
- Research sheep, wool, and yarn using these books:

Fowler, A. (1993). *Wooly sheep and hungry goats.* Chicago: Childrens Press.

Mitgutsch, A. (1975). *From sheep to scarf.* Minneapolis: Carolrhoda.

The Mitten

Sequencing Activities

- Sequence events using story boards cut from two copies of the book, backed with cardboard and laminated.
- Dramatize the story with puppets or stuffed animals.
- Create a circle diagram of the story. Have students draw pictures of each event and post them in a circle, beginning and ending with the grandmother.

Other Books by Jan Brett

(1985). *Annie and the wild animals.* Boston: Houghton Mifflin.

(1987). *Goldilocks and the three bears.* New York: Putnam.

(1991). *Berlioz the bear.* New York: Putnam.

(1991). *The owl and the pussycat.* New York: Putnam.

(1992). *Trouble with trolls.* New York: Putnam.

(1994). *Town mouse, country mouse.* New York: Putnam.

(1995). *Armadillo rodeo.* New York: Putnam.

Writing Activities

- Write a reading log entry.
- Write a class collaboration retelling of the story.
- Create a found poem using words and phases from the book.
- Write letters to the author.
- Create a story quilt with a mitten design on each square and a sentence about the book.

Other Activities

- Compare mittens and gloves
- Examine types of yarn
- Have a parent demonstrate how to knit a mitten
- Experiment with stretching a mitten.

Figure 13–8 A Planning Cluster for a Primary-Guide Unit on The Mitten

Author Study

- Learn about author Eve Bunting using brochures available from her publisher and her picture autobiography *Once Upon a Time* (1995), published by Richard C. Owen.
- Have students make a poster with information about the author to hang in the library center near the text set of books.

Types of Reading

- Read books together as a class.
- Read books in small literature study groups.
- Read books in small groups with the teacher using guided reading.
- Read books with a buddy.
- Read books individually.
- Listen to books read aloud at the listening center.

Visually Representing Activities

- Create a graph with photocopies of the covers of each of Bunting's books at the top of each column. Have students choose their favorite books and color in a square in that column.
- Make a story quilt, and for each square students draw a picture and select a sentence from their favorite Eve Bunting book.
- Have students make open-mind portraits to examine the characters.
- Have students make Venn diagrams to compare two books or two characters in a story.

Strategies and Skills

- Focus on connecting to personal experiences, visualization, generalizing themes, and monitoring strategies.
- Encourage students to use meaning-making skills (e.g., summarizing, noting details) and decoding skills (e.g., peeling off affixes, dividing words into syllables).

Talk and Drama

- Have students dress up as one of the characters from a book written by Eve Bunting and be interviewed by the class.
- Write a "I Am" poem from the viewpoint of one character and read it aloud to the class.
- Have a small group of students dramatize a scene from one of her books and tell why that scene was chosen.

Eve Bunting and Her Books

Reading Logs

- Have students write a reading log entry for each of Eve Bunting's books.
- Have students keep a double-entry journal by copying one or two quotes from a book and writing their connections or reactions to the quote.
- Have students create a dialogue journal and write back and forth to classmates and the teacher.

Projects

- Have students together as a class select a social action or community project.
- Have students create other individual projects about favorite books.

Books by Eve Bunting

(1984). *The man who could call down owls.* New York: Macmillan.
(1987). *Ghost's hour, spook's hour.* New York: Clarion.
(1988). *How many days to America? A Thanksgiving story.* New York: Clarion.
(1989). *The Wednesday surprise.* New York: Clarion.
(1990). *The wall.* New York: Clarion.
(1991). *Fly away home.* New York: Clarion.
(1993). *Someday a tree.* New York: Clarion.
(1993). *Red fox running.* New York: Clarion.
(1994). *A day's work.* New York: Clarion.
(1994). *Smoky night.* San Diego: Harcourt Brace.
(1995). *Cheyenne again.* New York: Clarion.
(1995). *Dandelions.* San Diego: Harcourt Brace.

Story Structure

- Focus on the theme. Ask students to identify the theme—honesty, freedom, neighborliness—and then have them expand on the concept.
- Ask students to reflect on why Bunting uses a contemporary setting for most books.

Word Wall

Smoky Night	Los Angeles
riots	destroy
collage	angry
smashing	smoke drifts
stealing	staggering
Mrs. Kim	Daniel
Jasmine	crowds
hooligans	Loco the parrot
Mrs. Ramirez	shelter
hazy orange	carrot-colored cat
broken glass	empty cartons
yowling	screeching
Gena	Caldecott Medal
smashed streetlights	

Figure 13–9   A Planning Cluster for a Middle-Grade Unit on Eve Bunting and Her Books

Introducing the Book

- Read the book when studying ancient civilizations and focus on the traits of a civilization.
- Discuss the problems in American society, and ask students to create a "perfect" society.
- Create a world with no colors
- Share objects from a book box including an apple, a bicycle, a sled, the number 19, a stuffed bear "comfort object," and a kaleidescope of colors.

Story Structure Activities

- Create a set of story boards, one for each chapter, with a picture representing the chapter and a summarizing paragraph.
- Analyze the theme of the book.
- Create a plot diagram to graph the highs and lows of the book.
- Make an open-mind portrait with several "mind" pages to track Jonas's thinking through the book.
- Draw a setting map with the locations mentioned in the books.

Word Wall

Chapter 1	Chapter 2
Jonas	Gabriel
bicycle	broken rules
citizens	Elders
loudspeakers	The Receiver
obediently	assignment
Lily	volunteer hours
frightened	Hall of Records
released	recreation hours
punishment	comfort object
Asher	stuffed elephant
community	bear
palpable	
public apology	Chapter 3
rumpled tunic	pale eyes
apprehensive	birthmother
ritual	hippo
Nurturer	Laborers
gender	humiliation
family unit	hoarded
Ceremony of Twelve	bewilderment
	apple

Strategies and Skills

- Model monitoring and revising meaning strategies. Ask students to reflect on their use of strategies when reading.
- Focus on decoding longer words by peeling off affixes and breaking words into syllables. Some words from the first two chapters to use: *obediently, inconveniencing, distraught, apprehensive, sympathetically, bewilderment.*

Grand Conversations

Hold grand conversations after reading 2, 3, or 4 chapters. Begin grand conversations in small groups and then come together for a whole-class discussion.

Choral Reading

To celebrate colors, have students prepare and present choral readings of color poems in Mary O'Neill's *Hailstones and Halibut Bones* (1989), published by Doubleday.

The Giver

Author Information

- Collect information about Lois Lowry, including "Newbery Acceptance" by Lois Lowry, published in the July/August 1994 issue of *Horn Book* (pp. 414–422).
- Write letters to the author.

Comparing Societies

Students read a book about American democratic society and compare it to the "perfect" society in *The Giver*.

Cowman, P. (1995). *Strike! The bitter struggle of American workers from colonial times to the present.* New York: Millbrook.

Fleming, R. (1995). Rescuing a neighborhood: *The Bedford-Stuyvesant Volunteer Ambulance Corps.* New York: Walker.

Haskins, J. (1993). *The march on Washington.* New York: HarperCollins.

Hoose, P. (1993). *It's our world, too! Stories of young people who are making a difference.* New York: Joy Street.

Meltzer, M. (1990). *Crime in America.* New York: Morrow.

Word-Study Activities

- Create word clusters.
- Sort a set of words.
- Play the duck game with a secret word of the day.
- Collect powerful sentences and write them on posters.

Reading Log

- Keep a simulated journal, written from Jonas's viewpoint after reading each chapter.
- Write a double-entry journal with quotes from the story in one column and personal connections or predictions in the other column.

Writing Projects

- Write a sequel.
- Write found poems, "I Am" poems, or other poems.
- Write an essay comparing Jonas's society with ours.
- Write a reaction to this quote: "The greatest freedom is the freedom of choice."

Figure 13–10 *A Planning Cluster for an Upper-Grade Unit on* The Giver

Once Upon a Time (1995), and they may choose to write letters to the author as a project. Students create a graph to determine their favorite book written by Eve Bunting and pursue group and individual projects. A planning cluster for this unit is presented in Figure 13–9.

An Upper-Grade Literature Focus Unit on The Giver

Upper-grade students spend three or four weeks reading, responding to, exploring, and extending their understanding of Lois Lowry's Newbery Medal book, *The Giver* (1993). Lowry creates a "perfect" community in which the people are secure but regulated. Jonas, the main character, is chosen to be a leader in the community, but he rebels against the society and escapes. To introduce this book, teachers might connect the book to the United States Constitution and the Bill of Rights, or discuss the problems in American society today and ask students to create a "perfect" society. Or, students might think about how their lives would be different in a world without colors, like Jonas's.

Students can read the story together as a class, in small groups with the teacher or in literature study groups, with buddies, or independently. Students come together to discuss the story in grand conversations and deal with the complex issues presented in the book in both small groups and whole-class discussions. They also write in reading logs. Teachers identify skills and strategies to model during reading and teach in minilessons. Students write important words from the story on the word wall and engage in a variety of word-study activities. Students also learn about the author and examine the story structure in the book. After reading, they can do a choral reading, create a story quilt, compare American society with the society described in the book, and create other projects. Figure 13–10 shows a planning cluster for *The Giver*. Only words from the first three chapters are listed in the cluster due to space limitations.

READING AND WRITING WORKSHOP

■ To read more about reading and writing workshop, see Chapter 3, pp. 109–111 and 128–129, Chapter 9, pp. 372–374 and 380–381, and Chapter 11, pp. 445 and 467–469.

Nancie Atwell (1987) introduced reading workshop as an alternative to traditional reading instruction. In reading workshop, students read books that they choose themselves and respond to books through writing in reading logs and conferencing with teachers and classmates. This approach represents a change in what we believe about how children learn and how literature is used in the classroom. Atwell developed reading workshop with her middle-school students, but it has been adapted and used successfully at every grade level, first through eighth (Hornsby, Sukarna, & Parry, 1986; McWhirter, 1990). There are several versions of reading workshop, but they usually contain these components: reading, sharing, minilessons, and reading aloud to students.

Writing workshop is similar to reading workshop, except that the focus is on writing. Students write on topics that they choose themselves, and they assume ownership of their writing and learning (Atwell, 1987; Calkins, 1994; Graves, 1994; Hornsby et al., 1986). At the same time, the teacher's role changes from being a provider of knowledge to serving as a facilitator and guide. The classroom becomes a community of writers who write and share their writing. There is a spirit of pride and acceptance in the classroom.

Writing workshop is 60- to 90-minute period scheduled each day. During this time students are involved in three components: writing, sharing, and minilessons. Sometimes a fourth activity, reading aloud to students, is added to writing workshop when it is not used in conjunction with reading workshop.

Establishing a Workshop Environment

Teachers begin to establish the workshop environment in their classroom from the first day of the school year by providing students with choices, time to read and write, and opportunities for response. Through their interactions with students, the respect they show to students, and the way they model reading and writing, teachers establish the classroom as a community of learners.

Teachers develop a schedule for reading and writing workshop with time allocated for each component, or they alternate between the two types of workshop. In their schedules, teachers allot as much time as possible for students to read and write. After developing the schedule, teachers post it in the classroom and talk with students about the activities and discuss their expectations with students. Teachers teach the workshop procedures and continue to model the procedures as students become comfortable with the routines. As students share what they are reading and writing at the end of workshop sessions, their enthusiasm grows and the workshop approaches are successful.

Students keep two folders—one for reading workshop and one for writing workshop. In the reading workshop folder, students keep a list of books they have read, notes from minilessons, reading logs, and other materials. In the writing workshop folder, they keep all rough drafts and other compositions. They also keep a list of all compositions, topics for future pieces, and notes from minilessons. They also keep language arts notebooks in which they jot down images, impressions, dialogue, and experiences that they can build upon for writing projects (Calkins, 1991).

Teachers use a classroom chart to monitor students' work on a daily basis. At the beginning of reading workshop, students or the teacher record what book they are reading or if they are writing in a reading log. For writing workshop, students identify the writing project they are involved in or the stage of the writing process they are at. A sample writing workshop chart is shown in Figure 13–11. Teachers can also use the chart to award weekly "effort" grades, to have students indicate their need to conference with the teacher, or to have students announce that they are ready to share the book they have read or publish their writing. Atwell (1987) calls this chart "the state of the class." Teachers can review students' progress and note which students need to meet with the teacher or receive additional attention. When students fill in the chart themselves, they develop responsibility for their actions and a stronger desire to accomplish tasks they set for themselves.

To monitor primary-grade students, teachers often use a pocket chart and have students place a card in their pocket, indicating whether they are reading or responding during reading workshop or at which stage of the writing process they are working during writing workshop.

Teachers take time during reading and writing workshop to observe students as they interact and work together in small groups. Researchers who have observed in reading and writing workshop classrooms report that some students, even as young as first graders, are excluded from group activities

■ *Check Chapter 2, "Teaching Language Arts," pp. 64–66, for more information about creating a community of learners and a language-rich environment.*

Writing Workshop Chart

Names	Dates 10/18	10/19	10/20	10/21	10/22	10/25	10/26	10/27
Antonio	4 5	5	5	6	7	8	8	8 9
Bella	2	2	2 3	2	2	4	5	6
Charles	8 9 1	3 1	1	2	2 3	4	5	6 7
Dina	6	6	6	7 8	8	9 1	1	2 3
Dustin	7 8	8	8	8	8	8	9 1	1
Eddie	2 3	2	2 4	5 6	8	9 1	1 2	2 3
Elizabeth	7	6	7	8	8	8	9	1 2
Elsa	2	3	4 5	5 6	6 7	8	8	9 1

Code:
1 = Prewrite *4 = Writing Group* *7 = Conference*
2 = Draft *5 = Revise* *8 = Make Final Copy*
3 = Conference *6 = Edit* *9 = Publish*

Figure 13–11   *"State of the Class" Chart*

because of gender, ethnicity, or socioeconomic status (Henkin, 1995; Lensmire, 1992). The socialization patterns in elementary classrooms seem to reflect society's. Henkin recommends that teachers be alert to the possibility that boys might only share books with other boys or that some students won't find anyone willing to be their editing partner. If teachers see instances of discrimination in their classrooms, they should confront it directly and work to foster a classroom environment where students treat each other equitably.

How to Set Up a Reading Workshop

Teachers move through a series of steps are they set up their classroom, prepare students to work independently in the classroom, and provide instruction. The six steps are:

Step by Step

1. **Collect books for reading workshop.**   Students read all sorts of books during reading workshop, including stories, informational books, biographies, and books of poetry. They also read magazines. Most of their reading materials are selected from the classroom library, but students also bring books from home and borrow books from the public library, the school library, and classmates. Students read many award-winning books during reading workshop, but they also read series of popular books and technical books related to their hobbies and special interests. These books are not necessarily the same ones that teachers use for literature focus units, but students often choose to reread books they read earlier in the school year or during the previous year in literature studies.

K-1ˢᵗ

SU

genre pp 370-373 - a category

Teachers need to have literally hundreds of books in their class libraries, including books written at a range of reading levels, in order to have enough books so that every student can read during reading workshop. Primary teachers often worry about finding books that their emerging readers can handle independently. Wordless picture books in which the story is told entirely through pictures, alphabet and number books, pattern and predictable books, and books the teacher has read aloud several times are often the most accessible for kindergartners and first graders. Primary-grade children often read and reread easy-to-read books such as books in the Scholastic Bookshelf series and the Wright Group's Story Box kits.

Teachers introduce students—especially reluctant readers—to the books in the classroom library so that they can more effectively choose books to read during reading workshop. The best way to preview books is using a very brief book talk to interest students in the book. In book talks, teachers tell students a little about the book, show the cover, and perhaps read the first paragraph or two (Prill, 1994/1995). Teachers also give book talks to introduce text sets of books, and students give book talks as they share books they have read with the class during the sharing part of reading workshop.

2. **Teach students *reading workshop procedures*.** Students need to learn how to choose books, write responses to books they are reading, share books they have finished reading, and conference with the teacher, as well as other procedures related to reading workshop. Some of these procedures need to be taught before students begin reading workshop, and others can be introduced and reviewed as minilessons during reading workshop.

3. **Identify topics for minilessons.** Minilessons are an important part of reading workshop because the workshop approach is more than reading practice. Instruction is important, and minilessons are the "teaching" step. Teachers present minilessons on reading workshop procedures and on reading concepts, strategies, and skills. Teachers identify topics for minilessons based on what they observe students doing during reading workshop, the questions students ask, and the skills and strategies teachers are expected to introduce, practice, or review at their grade levels. Teachers use examples from books students are reading, and students are often asked to reflect on their own reading processes. These minilessons can be taught to the whole class, small groups, or individual students, depending on which students need the instruction.

4. **Choose books to read aloud to students in conjunction with reading workshop.** When teachers include the reading aloud component with reading workshop, they carefully choose the books they will read. These books may be more difficult than that those students can read independently or may be chosen in order to introduce students to a genre, an author, or a literary element. Sometimes teachers read the first book in a series aloud to students and then invite students to continue reading the sequels themselves. Whatever the reason, teachers choose books to read aloud for specific instructional purposes.

■ *To learn more about reading aloud to students, turn to Chapter 7, "Listening to Learn," pp. 268–270.*

5. **Design a schedule for reading workshop.** Teachers examine their daily schedule, consider the other language arts activities in which their students are involved, decide how much time is available for reading workshop, and allocate time to each of the reading workshop components. Some teachers make reading and writing workshop their entire language arts program. They begin by reading

aloud a book, chapter by chapter, to the class and talking about the book in a grand conversation for the first 30 minutes of reading workshop. During this time, teachers focus on modeling reading strategies and talking about elements of story structure during the grand conversations. For the next 45 to 50 minutes, students read self-selected books independently. The teacher conferences with small groups of students as they read and presents minilessons to small groups of students as needed. Then students spend the next 15 to 20 minutes writing in reading logs about their reading. Often teachers have students keep double-entry journals in which students record quotes from the story in one column and react to the quotes in the second column. Sharing is held during the last 15 minutes, and students do book talks about books they have finished reading.

■ To read more about double-entry journals, turn to Chapter 6, "Writing in Journals," pp. 231–233.

Other teachers coordinate reading workshop with literature focus units. For example, they decide to allocate one hour to reading workshop at the beginning of their language arts block. Students begin with 30 minutes of independent reading and then use the next 10 minutes to share books they have finished reading with the class. The last 20 minutes are used for a minilesson. Then students move into a literature focus unit for the next 90 minutes. In some classrooms, teachers alternate reading and writing workshop, either month by month or grading period by grading period.

6. **Plan for conferencing.**   During reading workshop, students are reading independently and teachers must find ways to monitor students' progress. Many teachers begin each reading period by moving around the classroom to check that students have chosen books and are reading purposefully, and then use the rest of the reading period for individual and small-group conferences. Teachers create conference schedules and meet with students on a regular basis, usually once a week, to talk about their reading and reading skills and strategies, listen to them read excerpts aloud, and make plans for the next book. Teachers take notes in folders they keep for each student during these conferences.

Variations of Reading Workshop

Teachers sometimes integrate reading workshop into literature focus units or across-the-curriculum themes. In one adaptation, students choose and read books from a special themed text set. Text sets may focus on a social studies or science theme such as the ocean or ancient Egypt, or the books may be written by one author or represent one genre, such as tall tales or time warp stories.

Another variation is literature circles (Daniels, 1994), also called literature study groups (Peterson & Eeds, 1990) and book clubs (Raphael & McMahon, 1994), in which students read in small groups. Students divide into small groups to read one of five or six related books. For example, first graders might choose and read Dr. Seuss stories in small groups, third graders might read different versions of a fairy tale, such as "The Three Little Pigs," and sixth graders might read survival stories. A list of suggested text sets for literature circles is presented in Figure 13–12.

In a literature circle, small groups of students read a book and write in reading logs. They also participate in one or more grand conversations about the book, depending on the length of the book. Students often make only one

Figure 13–12   Text Sets for Literature Circles

Primary Grades

Dr. Seuss Stories

Dr. Seuss. (1960). *Green eggs and ham.* New York: Random House.
Dr. Seuss. (1960). *One fish, two fish, red fish, blue fish.* New York: Random House.
Dr. Seuss. (1963). *Hop on pop.* New York: Random House.
Dr. Seuss. (1967). *The cat in the hat.* New York: Random House.
Dr. Seuss. (1968). *The foot book.* New York: Random House.

Frog and Toad Books

Clarke, B. (1990). *Amazing frogs and toads.* New York: Knopf.
Lobel, A. (1970). *Frog and Toad are friends.* New York: Harper & Row.
Mayer, M., & Mayer, M. (1975). *One frog too many.* New York: Dial.
Pallotta, J. (1990). *The frog alphabet book.* Watertown, MA: Charlesbridge.
Yolen, J. (1980). *Commander Toad in space.* New York: Coward-McCann.

Versions of "The Three Little Pigs"

Bishop, G. (1989). *The three little pigs.* New York: Scholastic Hardcover.
Lowell, S. (1992). *The three little javelinas.* Flagstaff, AZ: Northland.
Marshall, J. (1989). *The three little pigs.* New York: Dial.
Scieszka, J. (1989). *The true story of the three little pigs!* New York: Viking.
Trivizas, E. (1993). *The three little wolves and the big bad pig.* New York: McElderry Books.

Middle Grades

Magic School Bus Books

Cole, J. (1987). *The magic school bus inside the earth.* New York: Scholastic.
Cole, J. (1989). *The magic school bus inside the human body.* New York: Scholastic.
Cole, J. (1990). *The magic school bus lost in the solar system.* New York: Scholastic.
Cole, J. (1992). *The magic school bus on the ocean floor.* New York: Scholastic.
Cole, J. (1994). *The magic school bus in the time of the dinosaurs.* New York: Scholastic.

Tall Tales

Kellogg, S. (1984). *Paul Bunyan.* New York: Morrow.
Kellogg, S. (1986). *Pecos Bill.* New York: Morrow.
Kellogg, S. (1992). *Mike Fink.* New York: Morrow.
Lester, J. (1994). *John Henry.* New York: Dial.
Isaacs, A. (1994). *Swamp angel.* New York: Dutton.

Bevery Cleary Books

Cleary, B. (1954). *Henry and Ribsy.* New York: Morrow.
Cleary, B. (1965). *The mouse and the motorcycle.* New York: Morrow.
Cleary, B. (1975). *Ramona and her father.* New York: Morrow.
Cleary, B. (1981). *Ramona Quimby, age 8.* New York: Morrow.
Cleary, B. (1983). *Dear Mr. Henshaw.* New York: Morrow.

Upper Grades

Arthurian Legends

Andronik, C. M. (1989). *Quest for a king: Searching for the real King Arthur.* New York: Atheneum.
Pyle, H. (1984). *The story of King Arthur and his knights.* New York: Scribner.
Riordan, J. (1982). *Tales of King Arthur.* New York: Macmillan.
Sutcliff, R. (1980). *The light beyond the forest: The quest for the Holy Grail.* New York: Dutton.
Tennyson, A. L. (1986). *The lady of Shalott.* Oxford, England: Oxford University Press.

Survival Stories

George, J. C. (1972). *Julie of the wolves.* New York: Harper & Row.
Hamilton, V. (1971). *The planet of Junior Brown.* New York: Macmillan.
Lowry, L. (1993). *The giver.* Boston: Houghton Mifflin.
Paulsen, G. (1987). *Hatchet.* New York: Viking.
Sperry, A. (1940). *Call it courage.* New York: Macmillan.

Ancient Egypt

Bradshaw, G. (1991). *The dragon and the thief.* New York: Greenwillow.
Carter, D. S. (1987). *His majesty, Queen Hatshepsut.* New York: HarperCollins.
Dexter, C. (1992). *The gilded cat.* New York: Morrow.
McMullan, K. (1992). *Under the mummy's spell.* New York: Farrar, Straus & Giroux.
Snyder, Z. K. (1967). *The Egypt game.* New York: Atheneum.

entry when reading a picture book, but they make entries after reading every chapter or periodically in longer books. They also participate in grand conversations in which they talk about the book and their reflections. Writing in reading logs and talking about the book replace traditional workbook activities.

Teachers design text sets for literature circles with five, six, or seven related titles and collect six copies of each book. Then the teacher gives a book talk about each book, and students sign up for the book they want to read. One way to do this is to set each book on the chalk tray and have students sign their names on the chalkboard above the book they want to read. Or, teachers can set the books on a table and place a sign-up sheet beside each book. Students take time to preview the books, and then they select the book they want to read. Once in a while, students don't get to read their first-choice book, but they can always read it later during reading workshop.

The books in the text set often vary in length and difficulty, but students are not placed in groups according to reading level. Students choose the books they want to read, and as they preview the books they consider how good a "fit" the book is, but that is not their only consideration. They often choose to read the book they find most interesting or the book their best friend has chosen. Students can usually manage whatever book they choose because of support and assistance from their group or through determination. Once in a while, teachers counsel students to choose another book or provide an additional copy of the book to practice at home or with a tutor at school.

Students use reading workshop time to read the book. Teachers set a time schedule for students to follow as they read, respond to the book, and participate in grand conversations. As students read, the teacher moves around the classroom, meeting with each group. During group meetings, the teacher may read along with students, read their reading log entries, or participate in grand conversations. While the teacher is meeting with one group, the other groups read independently or participate in other activities. They write in reading logs. Sometimes students write entries in their logs after each chapter, and at other times they write once a week.

Since everyone in the group is reading the same book, students talk about the book in a grand conversation. Sometimes teachers participate in the conversations and sometimes they don't. When the teachers are participants, they participate as fellow readers who share joys and difficulties, insights and speculations. They also help students develop literary insights by providing information, asking insightful questions, and guiding students to make comments. Eeds and Peterson (1991) advise that teachers need to listen carefully to what students say as they talk about a book, and label what students are talking about when appropriate.

Students talk about the characters, the plot, the theme—all the important issues in a story. They also make connections between the story and their own lives and the story and other stories they have read. They also notice literary language and read memorable passages aloud.

For years teachers have devoted 10, 20, or 30 minutes a day for silent reading in the classroom. Lyman Hunt (1970) called it Uninterrupted Sustained Silent Reading (USSR), the McCrackens (1972) called it Sustained

Silent Reading, and teachers have created their own acronyms, such as DEAR (Drop Everything and Read) Time. Students read self-selected library books during these practice periods. The idea behind these programs is that students need lots of reading practice in addition to the regular reading instruction. These add-on programs were very innovative when they were developed because research showed that children had few opportunities to transfer the skills and strategies they were learning to more genuine reading activities and to read for sustained periods in school. However, it is important to note that these practice programs are not the same as reading workshop, because they lack instructional components.

How to Set Up a Writing Workshop

As teachers set up a writing workshop classroom, they collect writing supplies and materials for making books for the writing center. Teachers set out different kinds of paper—some lined and some unlined—and various writing instruments, including pencils and red and blue pens. Bookmaking supplies include cardboard, contact paper, cloth, and wallpaper for book covers, stencils, stamps, art supplies, and a saddleback stapler and other equipment for binding books. Teachers also set up a bank of computers with word-processing programs and printers or arrange for students to have access to the school's computer lab. Teachers also encourage students to use the classroom library, and many times students' writing grows out of favorite books they have read.

Teachers also think about the classroom arrangement. Students sit at desks or tables arranged in small groups as they write. The teacher circulates around the classroom, conferencing briefly with students, and the classroom atmosphere is free enough that students converse quietly with classmates and move around the classroom to collect materials at the writing center, assist classmates, or share ideas. There is space for students to meet together for writing groups, and often a sign-up sheet for writing groups is posted in the classroom. A table is available for the teacher to meet with individual students or small groups for conferences, writing groups, proofreading, and minilessons.

In addition to collecting supplies and arranging the classroom, teachers need to prepare students for writing workshop and make plans for the instruction. Six steps are:

Step by Step

1. **Teach the stages of the writing process.** Teachers often begin writing workshop by teaching or reviewing the five stages of the writing process, setting guidelines for writing workshop, and taking students through one writing activity together. A set of guidelines for writing workshop that one seventh-grade class developed is presented in Figure 13–13.

2. **Teach writing workshop procedures.** Teachers need to explain how students will meet in groups to revise their writing, how to sign up for a conference with the teacher, how to proofread, how to use the publishing center, and other procedures used in writing workshop.

Figure 13–13 *A Seventh–Grade Class's Guidelines for Writing Workshop*

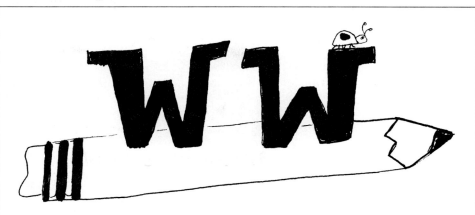

Ten Writing Workshop Rules

1. Keep everything in your writing folder.
2. Write rough drafts in pencil.
3. Double-space all rough drafts so you will have space to revise, and only write on one side of a page.
4. Revise in blue ink.
5. Edit in red ink.
6. Show your thinking and never erase except on the final copy.
7. Don't throw anything away—keep everything.
8. Date every piece of writing.
9. Keep a record of the compositions you write in your writing folder.
10. Work hard!

■ *To review the steps in the writing process, check Chapter 3, "The Reading and Writing Processes," pp. 111–126.*

3. Identify topics for minilessons. As with reading workshop, teachers teach minilessons during writing workshop. Teachers present minilessons on procedures related to writing workshop and writing concepts, skills, and strategies that students can apply in their own writing. Some topics for minilessons come from teachers' observations of students as they write, questions students ask, and topics identified in grade-level curriculum guides.

Teachers also share information about authors and how they write during minilessons. In order for students to think of themselves as writers, they need to know what writers do. Each year there are more autobiographies written by authors. Eve Bunting, author of *Smoky Night* (1994), has written an autobiography called *Once Upon a Time* (1995) in which she reflects on her writing processes and why she writes about contemporary issues. Some of the other books in the "Meet the Author" series are *Firetalking* by Patricia Polacco (1994), *Hau Kola/Hello Friend* by Paul Goble (1994), and *Surprising Myself* by Jean Fritz (1992). Filmstrip and video productions about authors and illustrators are also available. For example, in the 27-minute video *Eric Carle: Picture Writer* (1993),

Teachers establish procedures, such as where to keep writing folders, in order for writing workshop to operate smoothly.

Eric Carle demonstrates how he uses paint and collage to create the illustrations for his popular picture books.

4. **Design a writing workshop schedule.**   An important instructional decision that teachers make is how to organize their daily schedule and what portion of the language arts block to allocate to reading and writing workshop. Some teachers make reading and writing workshop the focus of their language arts program. During the writing workshop portion, students move through the writing process as they write on self-selected topics for 45 or 50 minutes. The teacher meets with small groups of students or individual students as they draft, revise, and edit their compositions during this writing time. Next, teachers use a 15- to 30-minute block of time for minilessons, and they present minilessons on writing workshop procedures and writing concepts, skills, and strategies to the whole class, small groups of students, or individual students as needed. Sharing is held during the last 15 minutes, and students do book talks about books they have finished reading.

Other teachers coordinate writing workshop with literature focus units. For example, they may allocate the last hour of their language arts block for reading and writing workshop, and alternate reading workshop and writing workshop month by month or grading period by grading period. Another way some teachers allocate time for writing workshop is during the last week of a literature focus unit when students are developing a writing project. For example, in the literature focus unit on *The Mitten* discussed earlier in this chapter, primary-grade students use a writing workshop approach as they research one of the animals mentioned in the story and create posters to share what they learn.

5. **Plan for conferencing.**   Teachers conference with students as they write. Many teachers prefer moving around the classroom to meet with students rather than having the students come to a table to meet with the teacher. Too often a line forms as students wait to meet with the teacher, and students lose precious writing time. Some teachers move around the classroom in a regular pattern, meeting with one-fifth of the students each day. In this way they can conference with every student during the week.

Other teachers spend the first 15 to 20 minutes of writing workshop stopping briefly to check on 10 or more students each day. Many use a zigzag pattern to get to all parts of the classroom each day. These teachers often kneel down beside each student, sit on the edge of the student's seat, or carry their own stool to each student's desk. During the one- or two-minute conference, teachers ask students what they are writing, listen to students read a paragraph or two, and then ask what they plan to do next. Then these teachers use the remaining time during writing workshop to more formally conference with students who are revising and editing their compositions. Students often sign up for these conferences. The teachers make comments to find strengths, ask questions, and discover possibilities during these revising conferences. Some teachers like to read the pieces themselves, while others like to listen to students read their papers aloud. As they interact with students, teachers model the kinds of responses that students are learning to give to each other.

As students meet together to share their writing during revising and editing, they continue to develop their sense of community. They share their rough drafts with classmates in writing groups composed of four or five students. In some classrooms, teachers join in the writing groups whenever they can, but students normally run the groups themselves. They take turns reading their rough drafts to each other and listen as their classmates offer compliments and suggestions for revision. In contrast, students usually work with one partner to edit their writing, and they often use red pens.

After proofreading their drafts with a classmate and then meeting with the teacher for a final editing, students make the final copy of their writings. Students often want to put their writings on the computer so that their final copies will appear professional. Many times students compile their final copies to make books during writing workshop, but sometimes they attach their writing to artwork, make posters, write letters that are mailed, or perform scripts as skits or puppet shows. Not every piece is necessarily published, however. Sometimes students decide not to continue with a piece of writing. They file the piece in their writing folders and start something new.

6. **Include sharing.**   For the last 10 to 15 minutes of writing workshop, the class gathers together to share their new publications and make other related announcements. Younger students often sit in a circle or gather together on a rug for sharing time. If an author's chair is available, each student sits in the special chair to read his or her composition. After reading, classmates clap and offer compliments. They may also make other comments and suggestions, but the focus is on celebrating completed writing projects, not on revising the composi-

tion to make it better. Classmates help celebrate after the child shares by clapping, and perhaps the best praise is having a classmate ask to read the newly published book.

Variations of Writing Workshop

Sometimes teachers set up writing workshop for a limited period of time when their students are working on a project and need lengthy periods of time for writing. For example, as third graders write weather reports after reading *Cloudy With a Chance of Meatballs* (Barrett, 1978), or as upper-grade students write simulated journals or reports about the Civil War, they may participate in writing workshop for a week or two. During these project-oriented writing workshops, teachers sometimes teach minilessons on topics related to the assignment, but usually all of the writing workshop time is used for writing and then for sharing when students complete their projects.

■ *Check Chapter 11, "Reading and Writing Poetry," pp. 464–469, to read more about teaching poetry.*

After students learn about various poetic forms, they often choose to write poems during writing workshop. They write poems about favorite topics or to express their strong feelings. They also experiment with forms that have been introduced during recent minilessons. Students who especially like to write poems publish collections of their poems during writing workshop and share them with their classmates. This sharing often stimulates other students to write poetry.

Teachers can use this combined reading-writing workshop format when studying any literary genre. Students can read and write biographies, read and write tall tales or pourquoi tales, or read and write collections of letters or journals.

THEME CYCLES

■ *To read more about theme cycles, see Chapter 3, pp. 109 and 128, Chapter 9, pp. 374–375 and 380, and Chapter 11, pp. 449–451 and 470–471.*

Theme cycles are interdisciplinary units that integrate reading and writing with social studies, science, math, and other curricular areas (Altwerger & Flores, 1994; Kucer, Silva, & Delgado-Larocco, 1995). Sometimes they focus on one curricular area, such as a theme cycle on insects or the Revolutionary War, and at other times they extend across most or all of the school day and students are involved in planning the direction for the theme. Topics for these extended theme cycles are broad and encompass many possible directions for exploration, such as houses and homes and people who have changed the world.

Students are involved in planning the theme cycles and identifying some of the questions they want to explore and activities that interest them. Students are involved in authentic and meaningful learning activities, not reading chapters in content-area textbooks in order to answer the questions at the end of the chapter. Textbooks might be used as a resource, but only as one of many available resources. Students explore topics that interest them and research answers to questions they have posed and are genuinely interested in answering. Students share their learning at the end of the theme cycle and are assessed on what they have learned as well as the processes they used in learning and working in the classroom.

How to Develop a Theme Cycle

To begin planning a theme cycle, teachers choose the general topic and then identify three or four key concepts that they want to develop through the theme. The goal of a theme cycle is not to teach a collection of facts but to help students grapple with several big understandings (Tunnell & Ammon, 1993). Next, teachers identify the resources that they have available for the theme and develop their teaching plan. Ten important considerations in developing a theme cycle are:

1. Collect a text set of stories, informational books, and poems. Teachers collect stories, poems, informational books, magazines, newspaper articles, and reference books for the text set related to the theme. The text set is placed in the special area for materials related to the theme in the classroom library. Teachers plan to read aloud some books to students, some will be read independently, and others students will read together as shared or guided reading. These materials can also be used for minilessons—to teach students, for example, about reading strategies and expository text structures. Other books can be used as models or patterns for writing projects. Teachers also write the poems on charts to share with students or arrange a bulletin board display of the poems.

2. Set up a listening center. Teachers select tapes to accompany stories or informational books or create their own tapes so that absent students can catch up on a book being read aloud day by day, or the tapes can be used to provide additional reading experiences for students who listen to a tape when they read or reread a story or informational book.

3. Coordinate content-area textbook readings. Teachers can teach theme cycles without textbooks; however, when information is available in a literature or content-area textbook, it can be used. Upper-grade students, in particular, read and discuss concepts presented in textbooks or use them as a reference for further study.

4. Locate multimedia materials. Teachers plan the films, videotapes, filmstrips, CD-ROM, charts, timelines, maps, models, posters, and other displays to be used in connection with the theme cycle. Children view films and videos to provide background knowledge about the theme, and other materials are used in teaching the key concepts. They can be viewed or displayed in the classroom, and students can make other materials during the theme.

■ *To read more about word walls, see Chapter 5, "Looking Closely at Words," pp. 202–204.*

5. Identify potential words for the word wall. Teachers preview books in the text set and identify potential words for the word wall. This list of potential words is useful in planning vocabulary activities, but teachers do not simply use their word lists for the classroom word wall. Students and the teacher develop the classroom word wall together as they read and discuss the key concepts and other information related to the theme.

■ To review learning logs, see Chapter 6, "Writing in Journals," pp. 233–237.

6. Plan how students will use learning logs. Teachers plan for students to keep learning logs in which students take notes, write questions, make observations, clarify their thinking, and write reactions to what they are learning during theme cycles (Tompkins, 1994). They also write quickwrites and makes clusters to explore what they are learning.

7. Identify literacy skills and strategies to teach during the theme. Teachers plan minilessons to teach literacy skills and strategies, such as expository text structures, how to use an index, skimming and scanning, how to write an alphabet book, and interviewing techniques. Minilessons are taught using a whole-part-whole approach so that students can apply what they are learning in reading and writing activities.

8. Plan talk and visually representing activities related to the theme. Students use talk and visually representing to learn during the theme cycle and to demonstrate their learning (Erickson, 1988; Nelson, 1988; San Jose, 1988). These are possible activities:

• Give oral reports.
• Interview someone with special expertise on the theme.
• Participate in a debate related to the theme.
• Create charts and diagrams to display information.
• Role-play a historical event.
• Assume the role of a historical figure.
• Participate in a readers theatre presentation of a story or poem.
• Tell or retell a story, biography, or event.
• Use a puppet show to tell a story, biography, or event.
• Make a quilt with information or vocabulary related to the theme.
• Write and perform a skit or play.

■ Check Chapter 3, "The Reading and Writing Processes," pp. 107–108, for more information about projects.

9. Brainstorm possible projects students may create to extend their learning. Teachers think about possible projects students may choose to develop to extend and personalize their learning during theme cycles. This advance planning makes it possible for teachers to collect needed supplies and to have suggestions ready to offer to students who need assistance in choosing a project. Students work on projects independently or in small groups and then share the projects with the class at the end of the theme. Projects involve one or more of the six language arts. Some suggestions are:

• Read a biography related to the theme cycle.
• Create a poster to illustrate a key concept.
• Write and mail a letter to get information related to the theme.
• Write a story related to the theme.
• Perform a readers theatre production, puppet show, or other dramatization.
• Write a poem, song, or rap related to the theme.
• Write an "All About . . ." book or report about one of the key concepts.
• Create a commercial or advertisement related to the theme.
• Create a tabletop display or diorama about the theme.

10. Plan for the assessment of the theme. Teachers consider how they will assess students' learning as they make plans for activities and

Figure 13–14   An Assignment Checklist for a Primary-Grade Theme Cycle

Money Unit

Name _____

☐   1. Make a money journal with 8 pages.

☐   2. Make 10 word cards and read them.

☐   3. Write an "All About Money" book with 5 pages.

☐   4. Make a poster about coins and bills.

☐   5. Name the coins and tell their value.

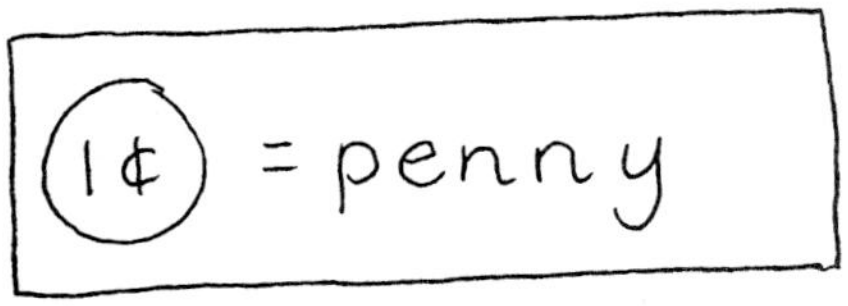

assignments. In this way, teachers can explain to students how they will be assessed at the beginning of the theme cycle and check that their assessment will emphasize students' learning of the key concepts and important ideas. An assignment checklist for a theme cycle about money for primary-grade students is shown in Figure 13–14.

Teacher's Notebook
Guidelines for Using Content-Area Textbooks

1. **Comprehension Aids**

   Teach students how to use the comprehension aids in content-area textbooks, including chapter overviews; headings that outline the chapter; helpful graphics, such as maps, charts, tables, graphs, diagrams, photos, and drawings; technical words defined in the text; end-of-chapter summaries; and review questions.

2. **Questions**

   Divide the reading of a chapter into sections. Before reading each section, have students turn the section heading into a question and read to find the answer to the question. As they read, have students take notes about the section and then answer the question they created using the section heading after reading.

3. **Expository Text Structures**

   Teach students about expository text structures and assist students in identifying the patterns used in the reading assignment, especially cause-and-effect or problem-and-solution, before reading.

4. **Vocabulary**

   Introduce only the key terms as part of an introductory presentation or discussion before students read the textbook assignment. Present other vocabulary during reading, if needed, and after reading develop a word wall with all important words.

5. **Key Concepts**

   Have students focus on key concepts or the big ideas instead of trying to remember all the facts or other information.

6. **Content-Area Reading Techniques**

   Use content-area reading techniques, such as PReP, exclusion brainstorming, or anticipation guides, to help students identify and remember main ideas and details after reading.

7. **Headings**

   Encourage students to use headings and subheadings to select and organize relevant information. The headings can be used to create a semantic map, and students add details as they read.

8. **Listen-Read-Discuss Format**

   Use a listen-read-discuss format. First the teacher presents the key concepts orally, and then the students read and discuss the chapter. Or, have students read the chapter as a review activity rather than as the introductory activity.

Teachers consider the resources they have available, brainstorm possible activities, and then develop clusters to guide their planning. The goal in developing plans for a theme cycle is to consider a wide variety of resources that integrate listening, talking, reading, writing, viewing, and visually representing with the content of the theme (Pappas, Kiefer, & Levstik, 1995).

Why Aren't Content-Area Textbooks Enough?

Sometimes content-area textbooks are used as the entire instructional program in social studies or science, and that's not a good idea. Textbooks typically only survey topics; other instructional materials are needed to provide the depth and understanding. Students need to read, write, and discuss topics. It is most effective to use the reading process and then extend students' learning with projects. Developing theme cycles and using content-area textbooks as one resource is a much better idea.

Using Content-Area Textbooks

Content-area textbooks are often difficult for students to read—more difficult, in fact, than many informational books. One reason textbooks are difficult is that they briefly mention many topics without developing any of them. A second reason is that content-area textbooks are read differently than stories. Teachers need to show students how to approach content-area textbooks, and teach students how to use specific expository text reading strategies and procedures to make comprehension easier. The Teacher's Notebook on page 570 presents guidelines for using content-area textbooks.

Teachers can make content-area textbooks more readable and show students ways to remember what they have read. Some activities are used before reading and others after reading. The before-reading activities are used to help students activate prior knowledge, set purposes for reading, or build background knowledge. The after-reading activities help students identify and remember main ideas and details. Other activities are used when students want to locate specific information. Seven activities to make content-area textbooks more readable are:

1. *Preview.* Teachers introduce the reading assignment by asking students to note main headings in the chapter and then skim or rapidly read the chapter to get a general idea about the topics covered in the reading assignment.
2. *Prereading plan (PReP).* Teachers introduce a key concept discussed in the reading assignment and ask students to brainstorm words and ideas related to the concept before reading (Langer, 1981).
3. *Anticipation guides.* Teachers present a set of statements on the topic to be read. Students agree or disagree with each statement and then read the assignment to see if they were right (Head & Readence, 1986).
4. *Exclusion brainstorming.* Teachers distribute a list of words, most of which are related to the key concepts to be presented in the reading assignment. Teachers ask students to circle the words that are related to a key concept and then read the assignment to see if they circled the right words (Johns, Van Leirsburg, & Davis, 1994).

■ Turn to Chapter 7, "Listening to Learn," pp. 280–282, for more information about note-taking.

5. *Clusters.* Teachers distribute a cluster, map, or other graphic organizer with main ideas marked. Students complete the graphic organizer by adding details after reading each section.
6. *Note-taking.* Students develop an outline by writing the headers and then take notes after reading each section.
7. *Scanning.* Students reread quickly to locate specific information.

Students in the upper grades also need to learn how to use the SQ3R study strategy, a five-step technique in which students survey, question, read, recite, and review as they read a content-area reading assignment. This study strategy was devised in the 1930s and has been researched and thoroughly documented as a very effective technique when used properly (T. H. Anderson & Armbruster, 1984; Caverly & Orlando, 1991). Teachers introduce the SQ3R study strategy and provide opportunities for students to practice each step. At first, students can work together as a class as they use the technique with a text the teacher is reading to students. Then students can work with partners and in small groups before using it independently. Teachers need to emphasize that if students simply begin reading the first page of the assignment without doing the first two steps, they won't be able to remember as much of what they read. Also, when students are in a hurry and skip some of the steps, the technique will not be as successful.

No longer are content-area texts viewed as the only source for learning, but they continue to be useful tools for learning across the curriculum and are available in most classrooms. Tierney and Pearson (1992) recommend that teachers shift from teaching *from* textbooks to teaching *with* textbooks and incorporate other types of reading materials and other types of activities into theme cycles.

A Primary-Grade Theme Cycle on Money

Teachers connect math, social studies, and language arts in a theme cycle on money. Students read stories such as *Pigs Will Be Pigs* (Axelrod, 1994) and informational books including *The Story of Money* (Maestro, 1993) and *If You Made a Million* (Schwartz, 1989) as part of the theme cycle. They learn to read money-related words, write in journals, make posters and charts about money, and write money story problems. Students investigate how people use money through field trips and literacy centers, examine money from other countries, and learn how early peoples bartered for goods and services and used shells and beads for money. A planning cluster for a primary-grade theme cycle on money is presented in Figure 13–15.

A Middle-Grade Theme Cycle on Birds

Middle-grade students connect science and language arts in a theme cycle on birds. To begin the theme, students and the teacher create a K-W-L chart and students write facts about birds and identify questions they will investigate. The teacher sets out a text set of stories, poems, and informational books about birds that students will read during the theme. Some of the books are on tape, and students can listen to them at the listening center. Students write words about birds on a word wall and participate in a variety of word-study

Stories

Axelrod, A. (1994). *Pigs will be pigs.* New York: Four Winds Press.

Baylor, B. (1994). *The table where the rich people sit.* New York: Scribners.

Kimmel, E. (1990). *Four dollars and fifty cents.* New York: Holiday House.

McPhail, D. (1990). *Pig Pig gets a job.* New York: Dutton.

Precek, K. W. (1989). *Penny in the road.* New York: Macmillan.

Smith, M. (1994). *Argo, you lucky dog.* New York: Lothrop, Lee & Shepard.

Zimelman, N. (1992). *How the second grade got $8,205.50 to visit the Statue of Liberty.* New York: Whitman.

Field Trips and Interviews

- Tour a bank and interview a teller to learn about that job.
- Take a walking field trip around the community and take photos of people using money.

Writing Projects

- Write a class collaboration book about money, and have each child contribute one page to the book.
- Have children write individual books about things they would like to buy and how much the things cost.
- Have children write individual books about an amount of money, such as $1.00, and on each page draw a combination of coins and/or bills to equal that amount of money.
- Have students write riddles about money. The riddles can be compiled into a book. For example, "What is worth 4 quarters and has a picture of George Washington on it? A $1.00 bill."

Informational Books

Kain, C. (1993). *The story of money.* New York: Troll.

Leedy, L. (1992). *The monster money book.* New York: Holiday.

Maestro, B. (1993). *The story of money.* New York: Clarion.

Schwartz, D. M. (1989). *If you made a million.* New York: Lothrop, Lee & Shepard.

Money Journal

- Have students keep a money journal in which they paste pictures of the coins and bills and write information about money.
- Write story problems about money. Students can use newspaper ads and coupons.

Money

Timeline

- Create a timeline to document the history of money, beginning with bartering, the use of coins, introduction of paper money, Indian wampum, and money and credit cards used today.

Skills and Strategies

- Teach students how to write dollar ($) and cents (¢) symbols.
- Connect names of coins with their values (e.g., a dime is 10¢).

Literacy Centers

- Create a restaurant center with menus, pads for taking orders, and a cash register.
- Set up a store (grocery store, toy store, shoe store, etc.) center with objects with prices for students to "buy," play money, and a cash register.
- Create a bank center so students can practice writing checks and depositing and withdrawing money.

Visually Representing

- Make posters about each of the common U.S. coins and bills, and include information about the images on the front and back of each one.
- Create a display with examples of money from countries around the world.
- Make charts showing different coins that total 10¢, 25¢, 50¢, $1, $5, and $10.

Word Wall

money	coins
bills	round and metal
paper money	penny
1 dollar bill	nickel
5 dollar bill	dime
10 dollar bill	quarter
20 dollar bill	half dollar
50 dollar bill	trading
100 dollar bill	barter
$ = dollar	salt
¢ = cents	shells
silver	blankets
gold	wampum
US mint	bucks
Fort Knox, KY	serial numbers
presidents	landmarks
Baht	Rupee
Pesos	Yen
Pounds	Francs
credit cards	checks
banks	debit cards
money orders	bankrupt
automated teller machines	

Figure 13–15   *A Planning Cluster for a Primary-Grade Theme Cycle on Money*

Word Wall

Aves	molting
flyers	domesticated
flightless	pets
flippers	pests
swimmers	range
waders	migration
predators	flyways
fowl	divers
songbirds	preening
symbols	songs
8,600 kinds	incubation
protective coloration	penguin
hummingbird	owl
ostrich	turkey
Dodo	swan
vulture	flamingo
blue jay	goldfinch
kiwi	goose
duck	pelican
robin	parrot
toucan	woodpecker
gull	dove
cardinal	puffin
eagle	peacock
Baltimore oriole	hatch
quail	vertebrates
hawk	beak
red-winged blackbird	bill
eggs	urban birds
nests	tropical birds
warm blooded	wading birds
bird watching	extinct

Listening Center

• Have students read books about birds at the listening center.

Visually Representing

• Draw diagrams of birds, labeling their body parts.
• Make charts to compare birds' bills, wings, or feet.
• Create papier-mâché birds.
• Design a poster about a bird, with information about the bird's life cycle, habitat, diet, and enemies.
• Mark the habits of birds on U.S. or world maps.

Word-Study Activity

Collect words and phrases related to birds and investigate the meanings of the words, including *bird-brained, to duck one's head, eagle-eyed, aviation, owlet.*

Symbols of Birds

Investigate the symbols people associate with birds: eagle—power, dove—peace, owl—wisdom.

Birds

Stories

Andersen, H. C. (1965). *The nightingale.* New York: HarperCollins.
Cauley, L. B. (1979). *The ugly duckling.* San Diego: Harcourt Brace.
Paterson, K. (1990). *The tale of the Mandarin ducks.* New York: Dutton.
Polacco, P. (1988). *Rechenka's eggs.* New York: Philomel.
Yolen, J. (1987). *Owl moon.* New York: Philomel.
Yolen, J. (1991). *Wings.* San Diego: Harcourt Brace.

Poetry

Fleischman, P. (1985). *I am phoenix: Poems for two voices.* New York: Harper & Row.
Yolen, J. (1990). *Bird watch.* New York: Philomel.

Learning Logs

Have students keep learning logs with notes, drawings, maps, diagrams, lists of books read, and other information.

Talk Activities

• Have students present oral reports about birds.
• Have students interview a zoo keeper who cares for birds, a birdwatcher, or other person interested in birds.

Research

• Divide students into small groups to study particular birds, such as penguins, owls, eagles, robins, geese, peacocks, parrots, and woodpeckers.
• Have students research bird habitats, such as urban places, woodlands, grasslands, deserts, marshes, and seacoasts.

Writing Projects

• Create a class alphabet book.
• Write individual or small group reports about birds.

Informational Books

Arnold, C. (1993). *On the brink of extinction: The California Condor.* San Diego: Gulliver.
Arnosky, J. (1995). *All about owls.* New York: Scholastic.
Bash, B. (1990). *Urban roosts: Where birds nest in the city.* Boston: Sierra Club Books and Little, Brown.
Ehlert, L. (1990). *Feathers for lunch.* San Diego: Harcourt Brace.
Gibbons, G. (1991). *The puffins are back.* New York: HarperCollins.
Hirschi, R. (1989). *The mountain bluebird.* Bergenfield, NJ: Cobblehill Books.

Johnson, S. (1995). *Raptor rescue! An eagle flies free.* New York: Dutton.
Markle, S. (1994). *Outside and inside birds.* New York: Bradbury Press.
Patent, D. H. (1993). *Looking at penguins.* New York: Holiday House.
Patent, D. H. (1992). *Pelicans.* New York: Clarion.
Tyrrell, E. Q. (1992). *Hummingbirds: Jewels in the sky.* New York: Crown.

Figure 13–16 A Planning Cluster for a Middle-Grade Theme Cycle on Birds

Talk

- Have students give brief oral reports in which they describe an invention and explain how it benefited people.
- Have students present brief talks based on compare-contrast, cause-effect, or problem-solution essays they have written.
- Have students dramatize scenes from the industrial revolution, including working conditions in factories, life in tenements, and the vast wealth of industrialists.
- Have students debate issues related to the industrial revolution, including whether the industrialization of the United States was actually a "revolution" or whether industrialization has ultimately been more beneficial or harmful.

K-W-L Chart

Have students brainstorm what they already know about the industrial revolution at the beginning of the theme cycle and add questions to the middle column during the theme. At the end, finish the "L: What We Learned" section.

Stories

Collier, J. L. (1989). *The Winchesters.* New York: Avon.
McCully, E. A. (1996). *The bobbin girl.* New York: Dial.
Paterson, L. (1991). *Lyddie.* New York: Lodestar Books.
Skurzynshi, G. (1992). *Good-bye, Billy Radish.* New York: Bradbury Press.

Literature Study Groups

In small groups, students read and respond to *Lyddie* (Paterson, 1991) or another story set during the industrial revolution.

Industrial Revolution

Learning Logs

Have students take notes, write quickwrites, draw diagrams, and list important events on timelines in learning logs.

Informational Books

Clare, J. E. (1994). *Industrial revolution.* San Diego: Gulliver.
Colman, P. (1995). *Strike! The bitter struggle of American workers from colonial times to the present.* New York: Millbrook.
Fischer, L. E. (1992). *Tracks across America: The story of the American railroad.* New York: Holiday.
Freedman, R. (1991). *The Wright brothers: How they invented the airplane.* New York: Holiday House.
Freedman, R. (1994). *Kids at work: Lewis Hine and the crusade against child labor.* New York: Clarion.

Haskins, J. (1991). *Outward dreams: Black inventors and their inventions.* New York: Walker.
Isherow, W. (1995) *The Triangle Factory fire.* New York: Millbrook.
Langly, A. (1994). *The industrial revolution.* New York: Viking.
Macaulay, D. (1983). *Mill.* Boston: Houghton Mifflin.
Richards, N. (1984). *Dreamers and doers: Inventors who changed the world.* New York: Atheneum.
Towle, W. (1993). *The real McCoy: The life of an African American inventor.* New York: Scholastic.

Timelines, Lifelines, and Other Crafts

- Create timelines noting significant events of the industrial revolution.
- Draw a lifeline for an inventor.
- Make a Venn diagram comparing the domestic system and the industrial system.

Writing

- Create a class book comparing life for laborers, the middle class, and the wealthy during the industrial revolution.
- Make a cube, exploring six dimensions of the industrial revolution.
- Write compare-contrast, cause-effect, or problem-solution essays about events and outcomes of the industrial revolution.

Word Wall

standard of living	factory
manufacture	machines
middle class	upper class
laborers	unsanitary
working conditions	pollution
entrepreneurs	textiles
industrial revolution	guilds
industrialization	coal mining
capitalists	iron
domestic system	merchants
cottage industries	unskilled
apprentices	steel
mass production	inventions
steamships	banks
labor unions	telegraphs
working class	tenements
transportation	petroleum
rail network	clothing
transcontental railroad	immigrants
Triangle Shirtwaist Factory	

Word-Study Activites

- Examine etymologies of words such as *textiles, factory, manufacturing, laborers, telegraph,* and *unsanitary.*
- Have students sort words related to textiles, transportation, communication, agriculture, and mining and minerals.

Figure 13–17   A Planning Cluster for an Upper-Grade Theme Cycle on the Industrial Revolution

■ To read about K-W-L charts, turn to Chapter 8, "Sustaining Talk in the Classroom," pp. 319–321.

activities, including doing a word sort or making a semantic feature analysis chart. Students keep learning logs, research particular birds, and present oral reports or prepare written reports to share what they learn. They make diagrams, charts, and posters, and write poems about birds. A planning cluster for a theme cycle on birds is presented in Figure 13–16.

An Upper-Grade Theme on the Industrial Revolution

As they study the industrial revolution, students learn social studies and science concepts and use the language arts as tools for learning. Teachers often use a K-W-L chart to begin the theme. Students read stories set during the industrial revolution and read informational books and biographies to learn more about the historical period. Sometimes students form literature study groups to read *Lyddie* (Paterson, 1991) or another story set in this period. Students keep learning logs and post important words on the word wall. They research inventors and inventions of the period, and share what they learn in oral and written reports. Students participate in a variety of talk activities, including reports, debates, and dramatizations. They develop individual and class projects and share their individual projects with classmates at the end of the theme. Students often create a variety of visually representing activities, including timelines, posters, clusters, and Venn diagrams. They also make cubes to explore six dimensions of the industrial revolution; they describe, compare, analyze, associate, apply, and argue for or against industrialization. Figure 13–17 presents a planning cluster for an upper-grade theme cycle on the industrial revolution.

■ See Chapter 6, "Writing in Journals," pp. 248–250, to read more about cubing.

Review

Designing language arts instruction that reflects the theory and research about language and how children learn is an important responsibility. Teachers use socially conscious multicultural literature to help students learn about the cultural groups in the United States. Multicultural literature should be chosen as featured selections in literature focus units and included in classroom libraries for reading workshop and in text sets for theme cycles. Ten key concepts presented in this chapter are:

1. Multicultural literature helps students to understand the viewpoints of minority groups and encourages greater appreciation for other cultures.
2. Teachers should select culturally conscious literature for literature focus units and theme cycles.
3. The three instructional approaches are literature focus units, reading and writing workshop, and theme cycles.
4. Students use all six language arts in literature focus units and theme cycles.
5. Teachers incorporate activities from all five stages of the reading process in literature focus units.
6. Teachers organize reading and writing workshop with plenty of time for reading and writing, and present minilessons on procedures, skills, and strategies.

7. Teachers can adapt and combine literature focus units, reading and writing workshop, and theme cycles to fit the needs of their students and their curriculum.
8. Teachers focus on several key concepts as they develop theme cycles.
9. Content-area textbooks can be used as one resource in theme cycles, but they should never be the only resource.
10. Teachers design assignment checklists for all three instructional approaches that students complete as part of the unit.

Extensions

1. Read a collection of multicultural books and create an annotated reading list or card file.
2. Plan a literature focus unit featuring a picture book or a chapter book. Draw a planning cluster and make a lesson plan. Incorporate activities involving all six language arts and create an assignment checklist.
3. Observe in a classroom using the reading and writing workshop approach. Write journal entries about your observations and note how the teacher manages the routine and conferences with students.

4. Plan a theme cycle incorporating language arts and one or more areas of the curriculum. Draw a planning cluster and make a lesson plan. Compile a text set of ten or more books, including stories, informational books, and poems. Also design an assignment checklist.
5. Teach a lesson using a content-area textbook and follow the guidelines presented in the Teacher's Notebook on page 570.

References

Professional References

Adams, M. J. (1990). *Beginning to read: Thinking and learning about print.* Cambridge, MA: MIT Press.

Alexander, H. (1962). *The story of our language.* Garden City, NY: Doubleday.

Allen, V. A. (1991). Teaching bilingual and ESL children. In J. Flood, J. M. Jensen, D. Lapp, & J. R. Squire (Eds.), *Handbook of research on teaching the English language arts* (pp. 356–364). Upper Saddle River, NJ: Prentice Hall/Merrill.

Altwerger, B., & Flores, B. (1994). Theme cycles: Creating communities of learners. *Primary Voices K–6, 2,* 2–6.

Anderson, H. (1949). Teaching the art of listening. *School Review, 57,* 63–67.

Anderson, K. F. (1985). The development of spelling ability and linguistic strategies. *The Reading Teacher, 39,* 140–147.

Anderson, T. H., & Armbruster, B. B. (1984). Studying. In P. D. Pearson, R. Barr, M. L. Kamil, & P. Mosenthal (Eds.), *Handbook of reading research* (pp. 657–679). New York: Longman.

Anderson-Inman, L., Horney, M. A., Chen, D. T., & Lewin, L. (1994). Hypertext literacy: Observations from the Electotext project. *Language Arts, 71,* 279–287.

Applebee, A. N. (1978). *The child's concept of story: Ages 2 to 17.* Chicago: University of Chicago Press.

Applebee, A. N., & Langer, J. A. (1983). Instructional scaffolding: Reading and writing and natural language activities. *Language Arts, 60,* 168–175.

Applebee, A. N., Langer, J. A., & Mullis, I. V. S. (1987). *Grammar, punctuation, and spelling: Controlling the conventions of written English at ages 9, 13, and 17* (Report No. 15-W-03). Princeton, NJ: Educational Testing Service.

Apseloff, M. (1979). Old wine in new bottles: Adult poetry for children. *Children's Literature in Education, 10,* 194–202.

Ashton-Warner, S. (1965). *Teacher.* New York: Simon & Schuster.

Askov, E., & Greff, K. N. (1975). Handwriting: Copying versus tracing as the most effective type of practice. *Journal of Educational Research, 69,* 96–98.

Atwell, N. (1987). *In the middle: Writing, reading, and learning with adolescents.* Portsmouth, NH: Heinemann.

Au, K. H. (1992). Constructing the theme of a story. *Language Arts, 69,* 106–111.

Baghban, M. J. M. (1984). *Our daughter learns to read and write: A case study from birth to three.* Newark, DE: International Reading Association.

Ball, E., & Blachman, B. (1991). Does phoneme segmentation training in kindergarten make a difference in early word recognition and developmental spelling? *Reading Research Quarterly, 26,* 49–86.

Banks, J. A. (1994a). *An introduction to multicultural education.* Boston: Allyn & Bacon.

Banks, J. A. (1994b). *Multiethnic education: Theory and practice* (3rd ed.). Boston: Allyn & Bacon.

Barbe, W. B., & Milone, M. N., Jr. (1980). *Why manuscript writing should come before cursive writing* (Zaner-Bloser Professional Pamphlet No. 11). Columbus, OH: Zaner-Bloser.

Barone, D. (1990). The written responses of young children: Beyond comprehension to story understanding. *The New Advocate, 3,* 49–56.

Baskwill, J., & Whitman, P. (1988). *Evaluation: Whole language, whole child.* New York: Scholastic.

Baugh, A. C., & Cable, T. (1978). *The history of the English language* (3rd ed.). Upper Saddle River, NJ: Prentice Hall.

Baumann, J. F. (1987). Direct instruction reconsidered. *Journal of Reading, 31,* 712–718.

Bear, D. R., Templeton, S., Invernizzi, M., & Johnston, F. (1996). *Words their way: Word study for phonics, vocabulary, and spelling instruction.* Upper Saddle River, NJ: Prentice Hall/Merrill.

Beaver, J. M. (1982). Say it! over and over. *Language Arts, 59,* 143–148.

Beers, J. W., & Henderson, E. H. (1977). A study of developing orthographic concepts among first graders. *Research in the Teaching of English, 11,* 133–148.

Berthoff, A. E. (1981). *The making of meaning.* Montclair, NJ: Boynton/Cook.

Bishop, R. S. (1992a). Extending multicultural understanding. In B. Cullinan (Ed.), *Invitation to read: More children's literature in the reading program* (pp. 80–91). Newark, DE: International Reading Association.

Bishop, R. S. (1992b). Multicultural literature for children: Making informed choices. In V. J. Harris (Ed.), *Teaching multicultural literature in grades K–8* (pp. 37–54). Norwood, MA: Christopher-Gordon.

Bishop, R. S. (Ed.). (1994). *Kaleidoscope: A multicultural booklist for grades K–8.* Urbana, IL: National Council of Teachers of English.

Blachowicz, C., & Fisher, P. (1996). *Teaching vocabulary in all classrooms.* Upper Saddle River, NJ: Prentice Hall/Merrill.

Blachowicz, C. L. Z., & Lee, J. J. (1991). Vocabulary development in the whole literacy classroom. *The Reading Teacher, 45,* 188–195.

Blackburn, E. (1985). Stories never end. In J. Hansen, J. Newkirk, & D. Graves (Eds.), *Breaking ground: Teachers relate reading and writing in the elementary school* (pp. 3–13). Portsmouth, NH: Heinemann.

Blanchard, J. S., & Rottenberg, C. J. (1990). Hypertext and hypermedia: Discovering and creating meaningful learning environments. *The Reading Teacher, 43,* 656–661.

Blanton, W. E., Wood, K. D., & Moorman, G. B. (1990). The role of purpose in reading instruction. *The Reading Teacher, 43,* 486–493.

Bode, B. A. (1989). Dialogue journal writing. *The Reading Teacher, 42,* 568–571.

Bonin, S. (1988). Beyond storyland: Young writers can tell it other ways. In T. Newkirk & N. Atwell (Eds.), *Understanding writing* (2nd ed.) (pp. 47–51). Portsmouth, NH: Heinemann.

Booth, D. (1985). "Imaginary gardens with real toads?": Reading and drama in education. *Theory into Practice, 24,* 193–198.

Bowser, J. (1993). Structuring the middle-school classroom for spoken language. *English Journal, 82,* 38–41.

Braddock, R., Lloyd-Jones, R., & Schoer, L. (1963). *Research in written composition.* Champaign, IL: National Council of Teachers of English.

Brent, R., & Anderson, P. (1993). Developing children's classroom listening strategies. *The Reading Teacher, 47,* 122–126.

Britton, J., Burgess, T., Martin, N., McLeod, A., & Rosen, H. (1975). *The development of writing abilities, 11–18.* London: Schools Council Publications.

Bromley, K. D. (1991). *Webbing with literature: Creating story maps with children's books.* Boston: Allyn & Bacon.

Bromley, K. D. (1996). *Webbing with literature: Creating story maps with children's books* (2nd ed.). Boston: Allyn & Bacon.

Brooks, C. K. (Ed.). (1985). *Tapping potential: English and language arts for the black learner.* Urbana, IL: National Council of Teachers of English.

Bruner, J. (1986). *Actual minds, possible worlds.* Cambridge, MA: Harvard University Press.

Busching, B. A. (1981). Readers theatre: An education for language and life. *Language Arts, 58,* 330–338.

Butler, A., & Turbill, J. (1984). *Towards a reading-writing classroom.* Portsmouth, NH: Heinemann.

Butler, S., & Cox, B. (1992). Writing with a computer in grade one: A study in collaboration. *Language Arts, 69,* 633–640.

Button, K., Johnson, M. J., & Furgerson, P. (1996). Interactive writing in a primary classroom. *The Reading Teacher, 49,* 446–454.

Cairney, T. (1990). Intertextuality: Infectious echoes from the past. *The Reading Teacher, 43,* 478–484.

Cairney, T. (1992). Fostering and building students' intertextual histories. *Language Arts, 69,* 502–507.

Calkins, L. M. (1980). When children want to punctuate: Basic skills belong in context. *Language Arts, 57,* 567–573.

Calkins, L. M. (1991). *Living between the lines.* Portsmouth, NH: Heinemann.

Calkins, L. M. (1994). *The art of teaching writing* (2nd ed.). Portsmouth, NH: Heinemann.

Cambourne, B., & Turbill, J. (1987). *Coping with chaos.* Rozelle, New South Wales, Australia: Primary English Teaching Association.

Camp, D. J. (1987). *Language functions used by four middle grade students.* Unpublished doctoral dissertation, Norman, University of Oklahoma.

Camp, D. J., & Tompkins, G. E. (1990). Show-and-tell in middle school? *Middle School Journal, 21,* 18–20.

Carr, E., & Wixon, K. K. (1986). Guidelines for evaluating vocabulary instruction. *Journal of Reading, 29,* 588–595.

Caserta-Henry, C. (1996). Reading buddies: A first-grade intervention program. *The Reading Teacher, 49,* 500–503.

Caverly, D. C., & Orlando, V. P. (1991). Textbook study strategies. In D. C. Caverly & V. P. Orlando (Eds.), *Teaching reading and study strategies at the college level* (pp. 86–165). Newark, DE: International Reading Association.

Cazden, C. D. (1988). *Classroom discourse: The language of teaching and learning.* Portsmouth, NH: Heinemann.

Cecil, N. L. (1994). *For the love of language: Poetry for every learner.* Winnipeg, Canada: Peguis.

Cheng, L. R. (1987). *Assessing Asian language performance.* Rockville, MD: Aspen.

Cintorino, M. A. (1993). Getting together, getting along, getting to the business of teaching and learning. *English Journal, 82,* 23–32.

Clay, M. M. (1967). The reading behavior of five-year-old children: A research report. *New Zealand Journal of Education Studies,* 11–31.

Clay, M. M. (1985). *The early detection of reading difficulties* (3rd ed.). Portsmouth, NH: Heinemann.

Clay, M. M. (1991). *Becoming literate: The construction of inner control.* Portsmouth, NH: Heinemann.

Cleary, L. M. (1993). Hobbes: "I press rewind through the pictures in my head." In S. Hudson-Ross, L. M. Cleary, & M. Casey (Eds.), *Children's voices: Children talk about literacy* (pp. 136–143). Portsmouth, NH: Heinemann.

Clemmons, J., Lasse, L., Cooper, D., Areglado, N., & Dill, M. (1993). *Portfolios in the classroom: A teacher's sourcebook.* New York: Scholastic.

Clymer, T. (1996). The utility of phonic generalizations in the primary grades. *The Reading Teacher, 50,* 182–187.

Cochran-Smith, M. (1984). *The making of a reader.* Norwood, NJ: Ablex.

Copeland, J. S. (1993). *Speaking of poets: Interviews with poets who write for children and young adults.* Urbana, IL: National Council of Teachers of English.

Copeland, J. S., & Copeland, V. L. (1994). *Speaking of poets 2: Interview with poets who write for children and young adults.* Urbana, IL: National Council of Teachers of English.

Corcoran, B. (1987). Teachers creating readers. In B. Corcoran & E. Evans (Eds.), *Readers, texts, teachers* (pp. 41–74). Upper Montclair, NJ: Boynton/Cook.

Cox, C. (1985). Filmmaking as a composing process. *Language Arts, 62,* 60–69.

Cox, C., & Many, J. E. (1992). Toward an understanding of the aesthetic response to literature. *Language Arts, 69,* 28–33.

Crafton, L. K. (1996). *Standards in practice, K–2.* Urbana, IL: National Council of Teachers of English.

Cullinan, B. E. (1987). Inviting readers to literature. In B. E. Cullinan (Ed.), *Children's literature in the reading program* (pp. 2–14). Newark, DE: International Reading Association.

Cullinan, B. E., Jaggar, A., & Strickland, D. (1974). Oral language expansion in the primary grades. In B. Cullinan (Ed.), *Black dialects and reading.* Urbana, IL: National Council of Teachers of English.

Cullinan, B. E., Scala, M. C., & Schroder, V. C. (1995). *Three voices: An invitation to poetry across the curriculum.* York, ME: Stenhouse.

Cummins, J. (1981). *Schooling and minority students: A theoretical framework.* Sacramento: California State Department of Education.

Cummins, J. (1989). *Empowering minority students.* Sacramento: California Association for Bilingual Education.

Cunningham, P. M. (1995). *Phonics they use: Words for reading and writing* (2nd ed.). New York: HarperCollins.

Cunningham, P. M., & Cunningham, J. W. (1992). Making words: Enhancing the invented spelling-decoding connection. *The Reading Teacher, 46,* 106–115.

Dale, E., & O'Rourke, J. (1971). *Techniques of teaching vocabulary.* Palo Alto, CA: Field Educational Publications.

Daniels, H. (1994). *Literature circles: Voice and choice in the student-centered classroom.* York, ME: Stenhouse.

D'Aoust, C. (1992). Portfolios: Process for students and teachers. In K. B. Yancy (Ed.), *Portfolios in the writing classroom* (pp. 39–48). Urbana, IL: National Council of Teachers of English.

de Beaugrande, R. (1980). *Text, discourse and process.* Norwood, NJ: Ablex.

De Fina, A. A. (1992). *Portfolio assessment: Getting started.* New York: Scholastic.

De Ford, D. (1981). Literacy: Reading, writing, and other essentials. *Language Arts, 58,* 652–658.

DeGroff, L. (1990). Is there a place for computers in whole language classrooms? *The Reading Teacher, 43,* 568–572.

Dekker, M. M. (1991). Books, reading, and response: A teacher-researcher tells a story. *The New Advocate, 4,* 37–46.

Devine, T. G. (1978). Listening: What do we know after fifty years of theorizing? *Journal of Reading, 21,* 296–304.

Devine, T. G. (1981). *Teaching study skills: A guide for teachers.* Boston: Allyn & Bacon.

Devine, T. G. (1982). *Listening skills schoolwide: Activities and programs.* Urbana, IL: ERIC Clearinghouse on Reading and Communication Skills and the National Council of Teachers of English.

Dickinson, D. K. (1986). Cooperation, collaboration, and a computer: Integrating a computer into a first-second grade writing program. *Research in the Teaching of English, 20,* 357–378.

Dixon-Krauss, L. (1996). *Vygotsky in the classroom: Mediated literacy instruction and assessment.* White Plains, NY: Longman.

Downing, J. (1971–1972). Children's developing concepts of spoken and written language. *Journal of Reading Behavior, 4,* 1–19.

Downing, J., & Oliver, P. (1973–1974). The child's conception of "a word." *Reading Research Quarterly, 9,* 568–582.

Dressel, J. H. (1990). The effects of listening to and discussing different qualities of children's literature on the narrative writing of fifth graders. *Research in the Teaching of English, 24,* 397–414.

Dunning, S., & Stafford, W. (1992). *Getting the knack: 20 poetry writing exercises.* Urbana, IL: National Council of Teachers of English.

Durkin, D. (1966). *Children who read early.* New York: Teachers College Press.

Duthie, C. (1994). Nonfiction: A genre study for the primary classroom. *Language Arts, 71,* 588–595.

Duthie, C., & Zimet, E. K. (1992). "Poetry is like directions for your imagination!" *The Reading Teacher, 46,* 14–24.

Dweck, C. S. (1986). Motivational processes affecting learning. *American Psychologist, 41,* 1040–1048.

Dwyer, J. (Ed.). (1991). *"A sea of talk."* Portsmouth, NH: Heineman.

Dyson, A. H. (1984). "N spells my grandmama": Fostering early thinking about print. *The Reading Teacher, 38,* 262–271.

Dyson, A. H. (1985). Second graders sharing writing: The multiple social realities of a literacy event. *Written Communication, 2,* 189–215.

Dyson, A. H. (1986). The imaginary worlds of childhood: A multimedia presentation. *Language Arts, 63,* 799–808.

Dyson, A. H. (1993). *Social worlds of children learning to write in an urban primary school.* New York: Teachers College Press.

Eckhoff, B. (1983). How reading affects children's writing. *Language Arts, 60,* 607–616.

Edelsky, C. (1989). Putting language variation to work for you. In P. Rigg & V. G. Allen (Eds.), *When they don't all speak English: Integrating the ESL student into the regular classroom* (pp. 96–107). Urbana, IL: National Council of Teachers of English.

Eeds, M., & Peterson, R. (1991). Teacher as curator: Learning to talk about literature. *The Reading Teacher, 45,* 118–126.

Eeds, M., & Peterson, R. L. (1995). What teachers need to know about the literary craft. In N. L. Roser & M. G. Martinez (Eds.), *Book talk and beyond: Children and teachers respond to literature* (pp. 10–23). Newark, DE: International Reading Association.

Eeds, M., & Wells, D. (1989). Grand conversations: An exploration of meaning construction in literature study groups. *Research in the Teaching of English, 23,* 4–29.

Egawa, K. (1990). Harnessing the power of language: First graders' literature engagement with *Owl moon*. *Language Arts, 67,* 582–588.

Elbow, P. (1973). *Writing without teachers.* London: Oxford University Press.

Erickson, A. (1985). Listening leads to reading. *Reading Today, 2,* 13.

Erickson, K. L. (1988). Building castles in the classroom. *Language Arts, 65,* 14–19.

Ernst, K. (1993). *Picturing learning.* Portsmouth, NH: Heinemann.

Faigley, L., & Witte, S. (1981). Analyzing revision. *College Composition and Communication, 32,* 400–410.

Faltis, C. J. (1993). *Joinfostering: Adapting teaching strategies for the multilingual classroom.* Upper Saddle River, NJ: Prentice Hall/Merrill.

Farr, R., & Tone, B. (1994). *Portfolio and performance assessment.* Orlando: Harcourt & Brace.

Fennessey, S. (1995). Living history through drama and literature. *The Reading Teacher, 49,* 16–19.

Fine, E. S. (1987). Marbles lost, marbles found. Collaborative production of text. *Language Arts, 64,* 474–487.

Fisher, B. (1991). *Joyful learning: A whole language kindergarten.* Portsmouth, NH: Heinemann.

Fisher, C. J., & Natarella, M. A. (1982). Young children's preferences in poetry: A national survey of first, second, and third graders. *Research in the Teaching of English, 16,* 339–354.

Fitzgerald, J. (1989). Enhancing two related thought processes: Revision in writing and critical thinking. *The Reading Teacher, 43,* 42–48.

Five, C. L. (1986). Fifth graders respond to a changed reading program. *Harvard Educational Review, 56,* 395–405.

Five, C. L. (1988). From workbook to workshop: Increasing children's involvement in the reading process. *The New Advocate, 1,* 103–113.

Flavell, J. H. (1985). *Cognitive development* (2nd ed.). Upper Saddle River, NJ: Prentice Hall.

Fleming, M. (1985). Writing assignments focusing on autobiographical and biographical topics. In M. Fleming & J. McGinnis (Eds.), *Portraits: Biography and autobiography in the secondary school* (pp. 95–97). Urbana, IL: National Council of Teachers of English.

Fleming, M., & McGinnis J. (Eds.). (1985). *Portraits: Biography and autobiography in the secondary school.* Urbana, IL: National Council of Teachers of English.

Flexner, S. B. (1993). *The Random House dictionary of the English language* (3rd ed.). New York: Random House.

Flood, J., Lapp, D., & Farnan, N. (1986). A reading-writing procedure that teaches expository paragraph structure. *The Reading Teacher, 39,* 556–562.

Flower, L., & Hayes, J. R. (1994). The cognition of discovery: Defining a rhetorical problem. In S. Perl (Ed.), *Landmark essays on writing process* (pp. 63–74). Davis, CA: Heragoras Press.

Foulke, E. (1968). Listening comprehension as a function of word rate. *Journal of Communication, 18,* 198–206.

Fountas, I. C., & Pinnell, G. S. (1996). *Guided reading: Good first teaching for all children.* Portsmouth, NH: Heinemann.

Fraser, I. S., & Hodson, L. M. (1978). Twenty-one kicks at the grammar horse. *English Journal, 67,* 49–53.

Freedman, R. (1992). Fact or fiction? In Freeman, E. B., & Person, D. G. (Eds.), *Using nonfiction tradebooks in the elementary classroom: From ants to zeppelins* (pp. 2–10). Urbana IL: National Council of Teachers of English.

Freeman, D. E., & Freeman, Y. S. (1993). Strategies for promoting the primary languages of all students. *The Reading Teacher, 46,* 552–558.

Freeman, E. B. (1991). Informational books: Models for student report writing. *Language Arts, 68,* 470–473.

Freeman, E. B., & Person, D. G. (Eds.). (1992). *Using nonfiction trade books in the elementary classroom: From ants to zeppelins.* Urbana, IL: National Council of Teachers of English.

Freeman, Y. S., & Freeman, D. E. (1992). *Whole language for second language learners.* Portsmouth, NH: Heinemann.

Freppon, P. A., & Dahl, K. L. (1991). Learning about phonics in a whole language classroom. *Language Arts, 68,* 190–197.

Frith, U. (Ed.). (1980). *Cognitive processes in learning to spell.* London: Academic Press.

Fulwiler, M. (1986). Still writing and learning, grade 10. *Language Arts, 63,* 809–812.

Fulwiler, T. (1985a). Research writing. In M. Schwartz (Ed.), *Writing for many roles* (pp. 207–230). Upper Montclair, NJ: Boynton/Cook.

Fulwiler, T. (1985b). Writing and learning, grade 3. *Language Arts, 62,* 55–59.

Fulwiler, T. (1987). *The journal book.* Portsmouth, NH: Boynton/Cook.

Furner, B. A. (1969). Recommended instructional procedures in a method emphasizing the perceptual-motor nature of learning in handwriting. *Elementary English, 46,* 1021–1030.

Gambrell, L. B. (1985). Dialogue journals: Reading-writing interaction. *The Reading Teacher, 38,* 512–515.

Gardner, H. (1993). *Frames of mind: The theory of multiple intelligences.* New York: Basic Books/HarperCollins.

Geller, L. G. (1981). Riddling: A playful way to explore language. *Language Arts, 58,* 669–674.

Geller, L. G. (1985). *Word play and language learning for children.* Urbana, IL: National Council of Teachers of English.

Gentry, J. R. (1981). Learning to spell developmentally. *The Reading Teacher, 34,* 378–381.

Gentry, J. R. (1982). Developmental spelling: Assessment. *Diagnostique, 8,* 52–61.

Gentry, J. R. (1987). *Spel . . . is a four-letter word.* Portsmouth, NH: Heinemann.

Gentry, J. R. (1996, November). *Fourteen ways to teach spelling with the three little pigs (or your favorite story).* Paper presented at the 1996 convention of the National Council of Teachers of English, Chicago.

Gentry, J. R., & Gillet, J. W. (1993). *Teaching kids to spell.* Portsmouth, NH: Heinemann.

Gere, A. R., & Abbott, R. D. (1985). Talking about writing: The language of writing groups. *Research in the Teaching of English, 19,* 362–381.

Gibbons, P. (1991). *Learning to learn in a second language.* Portsmouth, NH: Heinemann.

Golden, J. M. (1984). Children's concept of story in reading and writing. *The Reading Teacher, 37,* 578–584.

Golden, J. M., Meiners, A., & Lewis, S. (1992). The growth of story meaning. *Language Arts, 69,* 22–27.

Goodman, K. S. (1965). A linguistic study of cues and miscues in reading. *Elementary English, 42,* 639–643.

Goodman, K. S. (1993). *Phonics phacts.* Portsmouth, NH: Heinemann.

Goodman, K. S., Goodman, Y. M., & Hood, W. J. (Eds.). (1989). *The whole language evaluation book.* Portsmouth, NH: Heinemann.

Goodman, Y. M. (1978). Kid watching: An alternative to testing. *National Elementary Principals Journal, 57,* 41–45.

Goodman, Y. M., Watson, D. J., & Burke, C. L. (1987). *Reading miscue inventory: Alternative procedures.* Katonah, NY: Richard C. Owen.

Grabe, M., & Grabe, C. (1985). The microcomputer and the language experience approach. *The Reading Teacher, 38,* 508–511.

Graham, S. (1992). Issues in handwriting instruction. *Focus on Exceptional Children, 25,* 1–14.

Graves, D. H. (1976). Let's get rid of the welfare mess in the teaching of writing. *Language Arts, 53,* 645–651.

Graves, D. H. (1983). *Writing: Teachers and children at work.* Portsmouth, NH: Heinemann.

Graves, D. H. (1989). *Experiment with fiction.* Portsmouth, NH: Heinemann.

Graves, D. H. (1991). *Build a literate classroom.* Portsmouth, NH: Heinemann.

Graves, D. H. (1992). *Explore poetry.* Portsmouth, NH: Heinemann.

Graves, D. H. (1994). *A fresh look at writing.* Portsmouth, NH: Heinemann.

Graves, D. H., & Hansen, J. (1983). The author's chair. *Language Arts, 60,* 176–183.

Graves, D. H., & Sunstein, B. S. (Eds.). (1992). *Portfolio portraits.* Portsmouth, NH: Heinemann.

Graves, M. (1985). *A word is a word . . . or is it?* Portsmouth, NH: Heinemann.

Green, D. H. (1989). Beyond books: Literature on the small screen. In M. K. Rudman (Ed.), *Children's literature: Resources for the classroom* (pp. 207–217). Norwood, MA: Christopher-Gordon.

Greenlee, M. E., Hiebert, E. H., Bridge, C. A., & Winograd, P. N. (1986). The effects of different audiences on young writers' letter writing. In J. A. Niles & R. V. Lalik (Eds.), *Solving problems in literacy: Learners, teachers, and researchers* (pp. 281–289). Rochester, NY: National Reading Conference.

Griffith, F., & Olson, M. (1992). Phonemic awareness helps beginning readers break the code. *The Reading Teacher, 45,* 516–523.

Groff, P. J. (1963). Who writes faster? *Education, 83,* 367–369.

Hackney, C. (1993). *Handwriting: A way to self-expression.* Columbus, OH: Zaner-Bloser.

Hakuta, K., & Garcia, E. (1989). Bilingualism and education. *American Psychologist, 44,* 374–379.

Haley-James, S. M., & Hobson, C. D. (1980). Interviewing: A means of encouraging the drive to communicate. *Language Arts, 57,* 497–502.

Halliday, M. A. K. (1973). *Explorations in the functions of language.* London: Edward Arnold.

Halliday, M. A. K. (1975). *Learning how to mean: Explorations in the development of language.* London: Edward Arnold.

Halliday, M. A. K. (1978). *Language as social semiotic: The social interpretation of language and meaning.* Baltimore: University Park Press.

Hancock, M. R. (1992). Literature response journals: Insights beyond the printed page. *Language Arts, 61,* 141–150.

Hancock, M. R. (1993). Exploring and extending personal response through literature journals. *The Reading Teacher, 46,* 466–474.

Hanna, P. R., Hanna, J. S., Hodges, R. E., & Rudorf, E. H. (1966). *Phoneme-grapheme correspondences as cues to spelling improvement.* Washington, DC: US Government Printing Office.

Hansen, J. (1987). *When writers read.* Portsmouth, NH: Heinemann.

Harris, V. J. (1992a). Multiethnic children's literature. In K. D. Wood & A. Moss (Eds.), *Exploring literature in the classroom: Content and methods* (pp. 169–201). Norwood, MA: Christopher-Gordon.

Harris, V. J. (Ed.). (1992b). *Teaching multicultural literature in grades K–8.* Norwood, MA: Christopher-Gordon.

Harrison, S. (1981). Open letter from a left-handed teacher: Some sinistral ideas on the teaching of handwriting. *Teaching Exceptional Children, 13,* 116–120.

Harste, J. (1990). Jerry Harste speaks on reading and writing. *The Reading Teacher, 43,* 316–318.

Harste, J. (1993, April). Inquiry-based instruction. *Primary Voices K–6, 1,* 2–5.

Harste, J. C., Short, K. G., Burke, C. (1988). *Creating classrooms for authors: The reading-writing connection.* Portsmouth, NH: Heinemann.

Harste, J. C., Woodward, V. A., & Burke, C. L. (1984a). Examining our assumptions: A transactional view of literacy and learning. *Research in the Teaching of English, 18,* 84–108.

Harste, J. C., Woodward, V. A., & Burke, C. L. (1984b). *Language stories and literacy lessons.* Portsmouth, NH: Heinemann.

Harwayne, S. (1992). *Lasting impressions: Weaving literature into writing workshop.* Portsmouth, NH: Heinemann.

Hayes, J. R., & Flower, L. S. (1980). Identifying the organization of writing processes. In L. W. Gregg & E. R. Steinberg (Eds.), *Cognitive processes in writing* (pp. 3–30). Hillsdale, NJ: Erlbaum.

Head, M. H., & Readence, J. E. (1986). Anticipation guides: Meaning through prediction. In E. K. Dishner, T. W. Bean, J. E. Readence, & D. W. Moore (Eds.), *Reading in the content areas* (2nd ed.) (pp. 229–234). Dubuque, IA: Kendall/Hunt.

Heald-Taylor, G. (1987). How to use predictable books for K–2 language arts instruction. *The Reading Teacher, 40,* 656–661.

Heard, G. (1989). *For the good of the earth and sun: Teaching poetry.* Portsmouth, NH: Heinemann.

Heath, S. B. (1983a). Research currents: A lot of talk about nothing. *Language Arts, 60,* 999–1007.

Heath, S. B. (1983b). *Ways with words: Language, life, and work in communities and classrooms.* Cambridge: Cambridge University Press.

Henderson, E. H. (1980). Word knowledge and reading disability. In E. H. Henderson & J. W. Beers (Eds.), *Developmental and cognitive aspects of learning to spell: A reflection of word knowledge* (pp. 138–148). Newark, DE: International Reading Association.

Henkin, R. (1995). Insiders and outsiders in first-grade writing workshops: Gender and equity issues. *Language Arts, 72,* 429–434.

Hepler, S. (1991). Talking our way to literacy in the classroom community. *The New Advocate, 4,* 179–191.

Hickman, J. (1995). Not by chance. In N. L. Roser & M. G. Martinez (Eds.), *Book talk and beyond: Children and teachers respond to literature* (pp. 3–9). Newark, DE: International Reading Association.

Hidi, S., & Hildyard, A. (1983). The comparison of oral and written productions in two discourse modes. *Discourse Processes, 6,* 91–105.

Hildreth, G. (1960). Manuscript writing after sixty years. *Elementary English, 37,* 3–13.

Hillerich, R. L. (1977). Let's teach spelling—not phonetic misspelling. *Language Arts, 54,* 301–307.

Hillocks, G., Jr. (1987). *Research on written composition: New directions for teaching.* Urbana, IL: National Conference on Research in English and the ERIC Clearinghouse on Reading and Communication Skills.

Hillocks, G., Jr., & Smith, M. W. (1991). Grammar and usage. In J. Flood, J. M. Jensen, D. Lapp, & J. R. Squire (Eds.), *Handbook of research on teaching the English language arts* (pp. 591–603). Upper Saddle River, NJ: Prentice Hall/Merrill.

Hipple, M. L. (1985). Journal writing in kindergarten. *Language Arts, 62,* 255–261.

Hirsch, E., & Niedermeyer, F. C. (1973). The effects of tracing prompts and discrimination training on kindergarten handwriting performance. *Journal of Educational Research, 67,* 81–83.

Hitchcock, M. E. (1989). *Elementary students' invented spellings at the correct stage of spelling development.* Unpublished doctoral dissertation, Norman, University of Oklahoma.

Holdaway, D. (1979). *The foundations of literacy.* Portsmouth, NH: Heinemann.

Hook, J. N. (1975). *History of the English language.* New York: Ronald Press.

Hopkins, L. B. (1987). *Pass the poetry, please!* New York: Harper & Row.

Horn, E. (1926). *A basic writing vocabulary.* Iowa City: University of Iowa Press.

Horn, E. (1947). The effect of the corrected test on learning to spell. *Elementary School Journal, 47,* 277–285.

Horn, E. (1957). Phonetics and spelling. *Elementary School Journal, 57,* 425–432.

Hornsby, D., Sukarna, D., & Parry, J. (1986). *Read on: A conference approach to reading.* Portsmouth, NH: Heinemann.

Hoskisson, K. (1975a). The many facets of assisted reading. *Elementary English, 52,* 312–315.

Hoskisson, K. (1975b). Successive approximation and beginning reading. *Elementary School Journal, 75,* 442–451.

Howell, H. (1978). Write on, you sinistrals! *Language Arts, 55,* 852–856.

Hudson, B. A. (1980). Moving language around: Helping students become aware of language structure. *Language Arts, 57,* 614–620.

Hunt, L. C., Jr. (1970). The effect of self selection, interest and motivation upon independent, instructional, and frustration levels. *The Reading Teacher, 24,* 416.

Jackson, A. D. (1971). A comparison of speed of legibility of manuscript and cursive handwriting of intermediate grade pupils. Unpublished doctoral dissertation, University of Arizona. *Dissertation Abstracts, 31,* 4384A.

Jackson, L. A., Tway, E., & Frager, A. (1987). Dear teacher, Johnny copied. *The Reading Teacher, 41,* 22–25.

Jaggar, A. (1980). Allowing for language differences. In G. S. Pinnell (Ed.), *Discovering language with children* (pp. 25–28). Urbana, IL: National Council of Teachers of English.

Jalongo, M. R. (1991). *Strategies for developing children's listening skills* (Phi Delta Kappan Fastback Series #314). Bloomington, IN: Phi Delta Kappa Educational Foundation.

Jipson, J., & Paley, N. (1991). The selective tradition in teachers' choice of children's literature: Does it exist in the elementary classroom? *English Education, 23,* 148–159.

Johns, J. L., Van Leirsburg, P., & Davis, S. J. (1994). *Improving reading: A handbook of strategies.* Dubuque, IA: Kendall/Hunt.

Johnson, T. D., Langford, K. G., & Quorn, K. C. (1981). Characteristics of an effective spelling program. *Language Arts, 58,* 581–588.

Johnson, T. D., & Louis, D. R. (1987). *Literacy through literature.* Portsmouth, NH: Heinemann.

Johnston, P., & Winograd, P. (1985). Passive failure in reading. *Journal of Reading Behavior, 17,* 279–301.

Juel, C. (1991). Beginning reading. In R. Barr, M. L. Kamil, P. Mosenthal, & P. D. Pearson (Eds.), *Handbook of reading research* (Vol. 2, pp. 759–788). New York: Longman.

Juel, C., Griffith, P. L., & Gough, P. B. (1986). Acquisition of literacy: A longitudinal study of children in first and second grade. *Journal of Educational Psychology, 78,* 243–255.

Kardash, C. A. M., & Wright, L. (1987, Winter). Does creative drama benefit elementary school students: A meta-analysis. *Youth Theater Journal,* 11–18.

Karelitz, E. B. (1993). *The author's chair and beyond: Language and literacy in a primary classroom.* Portsmouth, NH: Heinemann.

Kawakami-Arakaki, A., Oshiro, M., & Farnan, S. (1989). Research to practice: Integrating reading and writing in a kindergarten curriculum. In J. Mason (Ed.), *Reading and writing connections* (pp. 199–218). Boston: Allyn & Bacon.

Kiefer, B. Z. (1994). The potential of picturebooks: From visual literacy to aesthetic understanding. Upper Saddle River, NJ: Prentice Hall/Merrill.

Kiefer, B. Z. (1995). Responding to literature as art in picture books. In N. L. Roser & M. G. Martinez (Eds.), *Book talk and beyond: Children and teachers respond to literature* (pp. 191–200). Newark, DE: International Reading Association.

King, L., & Stovall, D. (1992). *Classroom publishing*. Hillsboro, OR: Blue Heron.

King, M. (1985). Proofreading is not reading. *Teaching English in the two-year college, 12,* 108–112.

Kingore, B. W. (1982). Storytelling: A bridge from the university to the elementary school to the home. *Language Arts, 59,* 28–32.

Kitagawa, M. M. (1989). Observing Carlos: One day of language use in school. In G. S. Pinnell & M. L. Matlin (Eds.), *Teachers and research: Language learning in the classroom* (pp. 3–7). Newark, DE: International Reading Association.

Klein, A., & Schickedanz, J. (1980). Preschoolers write messages and receive their favorite books. *Language Arts, 57,* 742–749.

Klein, M. L. (1988). *Teaching reading comprehension and vocabulary: A guide for teachers.* Upper Saddle River, NJ: Prentice Hall/Merrill.

Klesius, J. P., Griffith, P. L., & Zielonka, P. (1991). A whole language and traditional instruction comparison: Overall effectiveness and development of the alphabetic principle. *Reading Research and Instruction, 30,* 47–61.

Koch, K. (1980). *Wishes, lies, and dreams.* New York: Vintage.

Koch, K. (1990). *Rose, where did you get that red?* New York: Vintage.

Koskinen, P. S., Wilson, R. M., Gambrell, L. B., & Neuman, S. B. (1993). Captioned video and vocabulary learning: An innovative practice in literacy instruction. *The Reading Teacher, 47,* 36–43.

Krashan, S. (1985). *The input hypothesis: Issues and implications.* London: Longman.

Krashen, S. (1982). *Principles and practices of second language acquisition.* Oxford: Pergamon Press.

Kreeft, J. (1984). Dialogue writing—Bridge from talk to essay writing. *Language Arts, 61,* 141–150.

Krogness, M. M. (1987). Folklore: A matter of the heart and the heart of the matter. *Language Arts, 64,* 808–818.

Kucer, S. B. (1991). Authenticity as the basis for instruction. *Language Arts, 68,* 532–540.

Kucer, S. B., Silva, C., & Delgado-Larocco, E. L. (1995). *Curricular conversations: Themes in multilingual and monolingual classrooms.* York, ME: Stenhouse.

Kukla, K. (1987). David Booth: Drama as a way of knowing. *Language Arts, 64,* 73–78.

Kutiper, K. (1985). *A survey of the poetry preferences of seventh, eighth, and ninth graders.* Unpublished doctoral dissertation, University of Houston.

Kutiper, K., & Wilson, P. (1993). Updating poetry preferences: A look at the poetry children really like. *The Reading Teacher, 47,* 28–35.

Labbo, L. D., & Teale, W. H. (1990). Cross-age reading: A strategy for helping poor readers. *The Reading Teacher, 43,* 362–369.

LaBerge, D., & Samuels, S. J. (1976). Toward a theory of automatic information processing in reading. In H. Singer & R. Ruddell (Eds.), *Theoretical models and processes of reading* (pp. 548–579). Newark, DE: International Reading Association.

Lacey, C. (1994). *Moving on in spelling: Strategies and activities for the whole language classroom.* New York: Scholastic.

Laminack, L. L., & Wood, K. (1996). *Spelling in use: Looking closely at spelling in whole language classrooms.* Urbana, IL: National Council of Teachers of English.

Lamme, L. L. (1979). Handwriting in an early childhood curriculum. *Young Children, 35,* 20–27.

Landry, D. (1969). The neglect of listening. *Elementary English, 46,* 599–605.

Lane, B. (1993). *After the end: Teaching and learning creative revision.* Portsmouth, NH: Heinemann.

Langer, J. A. (1981). From theory to practice: A prereading plan. *Journal of Reading, 25,* 152–157.

Langer, J. A. (1985). Children's sense of genre. *Written Communication, 2,* 157–187.

Langer, J. A. (1986). *Children reading and writing: Structures and strategies.* Norwood, NJ: Ablex.

Lapp, D., Flood, J., & Lungren, L. (1995). Strategies for gaining access to the information superhighway: Off the side street and on to the main road. *The Reading Teacher, 48,* 432–436.

Lara, S. G. M. (1989). Reading placement for code-switchers. *The Reading Teacher, 42,* 278–282.

Larrick, N. (1991). *Let's do a poem! Introducing poetry to children.* New York: Delacorte.

Laughlin, M. K., & Latrobe, K. H. (1989). *Readers theatre for children: Scripts and script development.* Englewood, CO: Libraries Unlimited.

Law, B., & Eckes, M. (1990). *The more than just surviving handbook: ESL for every classroom teacher.* Winnipeg, Canada: Peguis.

Lehr, S. S. (1991). *The child's developing sense of theme: Responses to literature.* New York: Teachers College Press.

Lensmire, T. (1992). *When children write.* New York: Teachers College Press.

Lewin, L. (1992). Integrating reading and writing strategies using an alternating teacher-led/student-selected instructional pattern. *The Reading Teacher, 45,* 586–591.

Lewis, M. E. (1991). Videodisc: Part of the classroom picture. *Language Arts, 68,* 333–336.

Lindfors, J. W. (1987). *Children's language and learning* (2nd ed.). Upper Saddle River, NJ: Prentice Hall.

Lindsay, G. A., & McLennan, D. (1983). Lined paper: Its effects on the legibility and creativity of young children's writing. *British Journal of Educational Psychology, 53,* 364–368.

Loban, W. (1976). *Language development: Kindergarten through grade twelve* (Research Report No. 18). Urbana, IL: National Council of Teachers of English.

Lomax, R. G., & McGee, L. M. (1987). Young children's concepts about print and meaning: Toward a model of word reading acquisition. *Reading Research Quarterly, 22,* 237–256.

Lukens, R. J. (1995). *A critical handbook of children's literature* (5th ed.). New York: HarperCollins.

Lundberg, I., Frost, J., & Petersen, O. (1988). Effects of an extensive program for stimulating phonological awareness in preschool children. *Reading Research Quarterly, 23,* 263–284.

Lundsteen, S. W. (1979). *Listening: Its impact on reading and the other language arts* (Rev. ed.). Urbana, IL: National Council of Teachers of English.

Lutz, W. (1989). *Doublespeak.* New York: HarperCollins.

Lutz, W. (1991). Notes toward a description of doublespeak (Revised). In W. Gibson & W. Lutz (Eds.), *Doublespeak: A brief history, definition, and bibliography, with a list of award winners, 1974–1990* (Concept Paper No. 2). Urbana, IL: National Council of Teachers of English.

Macon, J. M., Bewell, D., & Vogt, M. E. (1991). *Responses to literature, Grades K–8.* Newark, DE: International Reading Association.

Mallon, T. (1984). *A book of one's own: People and their diaries.* New York: Ticknor & Fields.

Mandler, J. M., & Johnson, N. S. (1977). Remembrance of things parsed: Story structure and recall. *Cognitive Psychology, 9,* 111–115.

Manna, A. L. (1984). Making language come alive through reading plays. *The Reading Teacher, 37,* 712–717.

Many, J. E. (1991). The effects of stance and age level on children's literary responses. *Journal of Reading Behavior, 23,* 61–85.

Marcus, S. (1990). Computers in the language arts: From pioneers to settlers. *Language Arts, 67,* 519–524.

Marinelli, S. (1996). Integrated spelling in the classroom. *Primary Voices K–6, 4,* 11–15.

Martin, N., D'Arcy, P., Newton, B., & Parker, R. (1976). *Writing and learning across the curriculum* (pp. 11–16). London: Schools Council Publications.

Martinez, M. G., & Roser, N. L. (1985). Read it again: The value of repeated readings during storytime. *The Reading Teacher, 38,* 782–786.

Martinez, M. G., & Roser, N. L. (1995). The books make a difference in story talk. In N. L. Roser & M. G. Martinez (Eds.), *Book talk and beyond: Children and teachers respond to literature* (pp. 32–41). Newark, DE: International Reading Association.

Martinez, M., & Teale, W. H. (1988). Reading in a kindergarten classroom library. *The Reading Teacher, 41,* 568–572.

McCracken, R. A., & McCracken, M. J. (1972). *Reading is only the tiger's tail.* San Rafael, CA: Leswing Press.

McGee, L. M., & Richgels, D. J. (1985). Teaching expository text structure to elementary students. *The Reading Teacher, 38,* 739–748.

McGee, L. M., & Richgels, D. J. (1996). *Literacy's beginnings: Supporting young readers and writers* (2nd ed.). Boston: Allyn & Bacon.

McGee, L. M., & Tompkins, G. E. (1995). Literature-based reading instruction: What's guiding the instruction? *Language Arts, 72,* 405–414.

McGonegal, P. (1987). Fifth-grade journals: Results and surprises. In T. Fulwiler (Ed.), *The journal book* (pp. 201–209). Portsmouth, NH: Boynton/Cook.

McKenzie, G. R. (1979). Data charts: A crutch for helping pupils organize reports. *Language Arts, 56,* 784–788.

McWhirter, A. M. (1990). Whole language in the middle school. *The Reading Teacher, 43,* 562–565.

Meyer, B. J., & Freedle, R. O. (1984). Effects of discourse type on recall. *American Educational Research Journal, 21,* 121–143.

Mills, H., O'Keefe, T., & Stephens, D. (1992). *Looking closely: Exploring the role of phonics in one whole language classroom.* Urbana, IL: National Council of Teachers of English.

Mohr, M. M. (1984). *Revision: The rhythm of meaning.* Upper Montclair, NJ: Boynton/Cook.

Moore, M. A. (1991). Electronic dialoguing: An avenue to literacy. *The Reading Teacher, 45,* 280–287.

Morrice, C., & Simmons, M. (1991). Beyond reading buddies: A whole language cross-age program. *The Reading Teacher, 44,* 572–578.

Morrow, L. M. (1979). Exciting children about literature through creative storytelling techniques. *Language Arts, 56,* 236–243.

Morrow, L. M. (1985). Reading and retelling stories: Strategies for emergent readers. *The Reading Teacher, 38,* 870–875.

Morrow, L. M. (1989). Designing the classroom to promote literacy development. In D. S. Strickland & L. M. Morrow (Eds.), *Emerging literacy: Young children learn to read and write.* Newark, DE: International Reading Association.

Morrow, L. M. (1996). *Motivating reading and writing in diverse classrooms* (NCTE Research Report No. 28). Urbana, IL: National Council of Teachers of English.

Moss, B. (1995). Using children's tradebooks as read-alouds. *Language Arts, 72,* 122–126

Muhammad, R. J. (1993). Mario: "It's mostly after I read a book that I write." In S. Hudson-Ross, L. M. Cleary, & M. Casey (Eds.), *Children's voices: Children talk about literacy* (pp. 92–99). Portsmouth, NH: Heinemann.

Mulligan, P. A., & Gore, K. (1992). Telecommunications: Education's missing link? *Language Arts, 69,* 379–384.

Murray, D. H. (1982). *Learning by teaching.* Montclair, NJ: Boynton/Cook.

Nagy, W. E. (1988). *Teaching vocabulary to improve reading comprehension.* Urbana, IL: ERIC Clearinghouse on Reading and Communication Skills and the National Council of Teachers of English and the International Reading Association.

Nagy, W. E., & Herman, P. (1985). Incidental vs. instructional approaches to increasing reading vocabulary. *Educational Perspectives, 23,* 16–21.

Nash, M. F. (1995). "Leading from behind": Dialogue response journals. In N. L. Roser & M. G. Martinez

(Eds.), *Book talk and beyond: Children and teachers respond to literature* (pp. 217–225). Newark, DE: International Reading Association.

Nathan, R. (1987). I have a loose tooth and other unphotographic events: Tales from a first grade journal. In T. Fulwiler (Ed.), *The journal book* (pp. 187–192). Portsmouth, NH: Boynton/Cook.

Nathenson-Mejia, S. (1989). Writing in a second language: Negotiating meaning through invented spelling. *Language Arts, 66,* 516–526.

NCTE Elementary Section Steering Committee. (1996). Exploring language arts standards within a cycle of learning. *Language Arts, 73,* 10–13.

Neeld, E. C. (1986). *Writing* (2nd ed.). Glenview, IL: Scott Foresman.

Nelson, P. A. (1988). Drama, doorway to the past. *Language Arts, 65,* 20–25.

Newkirk, T., & McLure, P. (1992). *Listening in: Children talk about books (and other things).* Portsmouth, NH: Heinemann.

Niles, O. S. (1974). Organization perceived. In H. L. Herber (Ed.), *Perspectives in reading: Developing study skills in secondary schools.* Newark, DE: International Reading Association.

Noguchi, R. R. (1991). *Grammar and the teaching of writing: Limits and possibilities.* Urbana, IL: National Council of Teachers of English.

Noyce, R. M., & Christie, J. F. (1983). Effects of an integrated approach to grammar instruction on third graders' reading and writing. *Elementary School Journal, 84,* 63–69.

Nystrand, M., Gamoran, A., & Heck, M. J. (1993). Using small groups for response to and thinking about literature. *English Journal, 82,* 14–22.

Ogle, D. M. (1986). K-W-L: A teaching model that develops active reading of expository text. *The Reading Teacher, 39,* 564–570.

Ogle, D. M. (1989). The know, want to know, learn strategy. In K. D. Muth (Ed.), *Children's comprehension of text: Research into practice* (pp. 205–223). Newark, DE: International Reading Association.

Ohlhausen, M. M., & Jepsen, M. (1992). Lessons from Goldilocks: "Somebody's been choosing my books but I can make my own choices now!" *The New Advocate, 5,* 31–46.

Oldfather, P. (1995). Commentary: What's needed to maintain and extend motivation for literacy in the middle grades? *Journal of Reading, 38,* 420–422.

Opie, I., & Opie, P. (1959). *The lore and language of school children.* Oxford: Oxford University Press.

Papandropoulou, I., & Sinclair, H. (1974). What is a word? Experimental study of children's ideas on grammar. *Human Development, 17,* 241–258.

Pappas, C. C. (1991). Fostering full access to literacy by including information books. *Language Arts, 68,* 449–462.

Pappas, C. C. (1993). Is narrative "primary"? Some insights from kindergartners' pretend readings of stories and information books. *Journal of Reading Behavior, 25,* 97–129.

Pappas, C. C., & Brown, E. (1987). Learning to read by reading: Learning how to extend the functional potential of language. *Research in the Teaching of English, 21,* 160–184.

Pappas, C. C., Kiefer, B. Z., & Levstik, L. S. (1995). *An integrated language perspective in the elementary school: Theory into action* (2nd ed.). New York: Longman.

Paris, S. G., & Jacobs, J. E. (1984). The benefits of informed instruction for children's reading awareness and comprehension skills. *Child Development, 55,* 2083–2093.

Paris, S. G., Wasik, B. A., & Turner, J. C. (1991). The development of strategic readers. In R. Barr, M. L. Kamil, P. B. Mosenthal, & P. D. Pearson (Eds.), *Handbook of reading research* (Vol. 2, pp. 609–640). New York: Longman.

Parry, J., & Hornsby, D. (1985). *Write on: A conference approach to writing.* Portsmouth, NH: Heinemann.

Pearson, P. D. (1993). Teaching and learning reading: A research perspective. *Language Arts, 70,* 502–511.

Pearson, P. D., & Fielding, L. (1982). Research update: Listening comprehension. *Language Arts, 59,* 617–629.

Perfitti, C., Beck, I., Bell, L., & Hughes, C. (1987). Phonemic knowledge and learning to read are reciprocal: A longitudinal study of first grade children. *Merrill-Palmer Quarterly, 33,* 283–319.

Perl, S. (1994). Understanding composing. In S. Perl (Ed.), *Landmark essays on writing process* (pp. 99–106). Davis, CA: Heragoras Press.

Peterson, R., & Eeds, M. (1990). *Grand conversations: Literature groups in action.* New York: Scholastic.

Peyton, J. K., & Seyoum, M. (1989). The effect of teacher strategies on students' interactive writing: The case of dialogue journals. *Research in the Teaching of English, 23,* 310–334.

Phenix, J., & Hannan, E. (1984). Word processing in the grade one classroom. *Language Arts, 61,* 804–812.

Piaget, J. (1969). *The psychology of intelligence.* NJ: Littlefield, Adams.

Piaget, J. (1975). *The development of thought: Equilibration of cognitive structures.* New York: Viking.

Piccolo, J. A. (1987). Expository text structures: Teaching and learning strategies. *The Reading Teacher, 40,* 838–847.

Pinnell, G. S. (1975). Language in primary classrooms. *Theory into Practice, 14,* 318–327.

Pinnell, G. S., & Jaggar, A. M. (1991). Oral language: Speaking and listening in the classroom. In. J. Flood, J. M. Jensen, D. Lapp, & J. R. Squire (Eds.), *Handbook of research on the teaching of the English language arts* (pp. 691–742). New York: Macmillan.

Pinnell, G. S., & McCarrier, A. (1994). Interactive writing: A transition tool for assisting children in learning to read and write. In E. Hiebert & B. Taylor (Eds.), *Getting reading right from the start: Effective early literacy interventions* (pp. 149–170). Needham, MA: Allyn & Bacon.

Pitcher, E. G., & Prelinger, E. (1963). *Children tell stories: An analysis of fantasy.* New York: International Universities Press.

Pittelman, S. D., Heimlich, J. E., Berglund, R. L., & French, M. P. (1991). *Semantic feature analysis: Classroom applications.* Newark, DE: International Reading Association.

Pooley, R. C. (1974). *The teaching of English usage.* Urbana, IL: National Council of Teachers of English.

Porter, C., & Cleland, J. (1995). *The portfolio as a learning strategy.* Portsmouth, NH: Heinemann.

Pressley, M. (1992). Encouraging mindful use of prior knowledge: Attempting to construct explanatory answers facilitates learning. *Educational Psychologist, 27,* 91–109.

Prill, P. (1994/1995). Helping children use the classroom library. *The Reading Teacher, 48,* 363–364.

Queenan, M. (1986). Finding grain in the marble. *Language Arts, 63,* 666–673.

Rankin, P. R. (1926). The importance of listening ability. *English Journal, 17,* 623–640.

Raphael, T. E., Englert, C. S., & Kirschner, B. W. (1989). Acquisition of expository writing skills. In J. M. Mason (Ed.), *Reading and writing connections* (pp. 261–290). Boston: Allyn & Bacon.

Raphael, T. E., & McMahon, S. I. (1994). Book club: An alternative framework for reading instruction. *The Reading Teacher, 48,* 102–116.

Rasinski, T. V., & Padak, N. D. (1990). Multicultural learning through children's literature. *Language Arts, 67,* 576–580.

Read, C. (1975). *Children's categorization of speech sounds in English* (NCTE Research Report No. 17). Urbana, IL: National Council of Teachers of English.

Read, C. (1986). *Children's creative spelling.* London: Routledge & Kegan Paul.

Reimer, K. M. (1992). Multiethnic literature: Holding fast to dreams. *Language Arts, 69,* 14–21.

Reutzel, D. R., & Fawson, P. C. (1990). Traveling tales: Connecting parents and children in writing. *The Reading Teacher, 44,* 222–227.

Reyes, M. de la Luz. (1991). A process approach to literacy using dialogue journals and literature logs with second language learners. *Research in the Teaching of English, 25,* 291–313.

Rhodes, L. K., & Dudley-Marling, C. (1988). *Readers and writers with a difference: A holistic approach to teaching learning disabled and remedial students.* Portsmouth, NH: Heinemann.

Rhodes, L. K., & Nathenson-Mejia, S. (1992). Anecdotal records: A powerful tool for ongoing literacy assessment. *The Reading Teacher, 45,* 502–511.

Rico, G. L. (1983). *Writing the natural way.* Los Angeles: Tarcher.

Roop, P. (1992). Nonfiction books in the primary classroom: Soaring with the swans. In Freeman, E. B., & Person, D. G. (Eds.), *Using nonfiction tradebooks in the elementary classroom: From ants to zeppelins* (pp. 106–112). Urbana, IL: National Council of Teachers of English.

Roop, P. (1995). Keep the reading lights burning. In M. Sorensen & B. Lehman (Eds.), *Teaching with children's books: Paths to literature-based instruction* (pp. 197–202). Urbana, IL: National Council of Teachers of English.

Rose, D. H., & Meyer, A. (1994). The role of technology in language arts instruction. *Language Arts, 71,* 290–294.

Rosenblatt, L. M. (1978). *The reader, the text, the poem: The transactional theory of the literary work.* Carbondale: Southern Illinois University Press.

Rosenblatt, L. M. (1983). *Literature as exploration* (4th ed.). New York: Modern Language Association.

Rosenblatt, L. M. (1985a). The transactional theory of the literary work: Implications for research. In C. R. Cooper (Ed.), *Researching response to literature and the teaching of literature* (pp. 33–53). Norwood, NJ: Ablex.

Rosenblatt, L. M. (1985b). Viewpoints: Transaction versus interaction—A terminological rescue operation. *Research in the Teaching of English, 19,* 98–107.

Rosenblatt, L. M. (1991). Literature—S.O.S.! *Language Arts, 68,* 444–448.

Routman, R. (1996). *Literacy at the crossroads: Crucial talk about reading, writing, and other teaching dilemmas.* Portsmouth, NH: Heinemann.

Rudasill, L. (1986). Advertising gimmicks: Teaching critical thinking. In J. Golub (Ed.), *Activities to promote critical thinking* (Classroom practices in teaching English) (pp. 127–129). Urbana, IL: National Council of Teachers of English.

Rumelhart, D. (1975). Notes on a schema for stories. In D. G. Bobrow (Ed.), *Representation and understanding: Studies in cognitive science* (pp. 99–135). New York: Academic Press.

Salem, J. (1982). Using writing in teaching mathematics. In M. Barr, P. D'Arcy, & M. K. Healy (Eds.), *What's going on? Language/learning episodes in British and American classrooms, grades 4–13* (pp. 123–134). Montclair, NJ: Boynton/Cook.

Samway, K. D., Whang, G., Cade, C., Gamil, M., Lubandina, M. A., & Phommachanh, K. (1991). Reading the skeleton, the heart, and the brain of a book: Students' perspectives on literature study circles. *The Reading Teacher, 45,* 196–205.

San Jose, C. (1988). Story drama in the content areas. *Language Arts, 65,* 26–33.

Scarcella, R. (1990). *Teaching language minority students in the multicultural classroom.* Upper Saddle River, NJ: Prentice Hall/Merrill.

Schickedanz, J. A. (1990). *Adam's righting revolutions: One child's literacy development from infancy through grade one.* Portsmouth, NH: Heinemann.

Schmitt, M. C. (1990). A questionnaire to measure children's awareness of strategic reading processes. *The Reading Teacher, 43,* 454–461.

Schubert, B. (1987). Mathematics journals: Fourth grade. In T. Fulwiler (Ed.), *The journal book* (pp. 348–358). Portsmouth, NJ: Boynton/Cook.

Shafer, K. (1993). Talk in the middle: Two conversational skills for friendship. *English Journal, 82,* 53–55.

Shanahan, T. (1988). The reading-writing relationship: Seven instructional principles. *The Reading Teacher, 41,* 636–647.

Shanahan, T., & Knight, L. (1991). *Guidelines for judging and selecting language arts textbooks: A modest proposal* (NCTE Concept Paper No. 1). Urbana, IL: National Council of Teachers of English.

Shannon, P. (1986). Hidden within the pages: A study of social perspective in young children's favorite books. *The Reading Teacher, 39,* 656–661.

Shefelbine, J. (1995). *Learning and using phonics in beginning reading* (Literacy research paper; volume 10). New York: Scholastic.

Shuy, R. W. (1987). Research currents: Dialogue as the heart of learning. *Language Arts, 64,* 890–897.

Siegler, R. S. (1986). *Children's thinking.* Upper Saddle River, NJ: Prentice Hall.

Siemens, L. (1996). "Walking through the time of kids": Going places with poetry. *Language Arts, 73,* 234–240.

Sierra-Perry, M. (1996). *Standards in practice, grades 3–5.* Urbana, IL: National Council of Teachers of English.

Sims, R. B. (1982). *Shadow and substance.* Urbana, IL: National Council of Teachers of English.

Slaughter, H. (1988). Indirect and direct teaching in a whole language program. *The Reading Teacher, 41,* 30–34.

Slaughter, J. P. (1993). *Beyond storybooks: Young children and the shared book experience.* Newark, DE: International Reading Association.

Smith, F. (1975). *Comprehension and learning.* New York: Holt, Rinehart & Winston.

Smith, F. (1982). *Writing and the writer.* New York: Holt, Rinehart & Winston.

Smith, F. (1988). *Joining the literacy club: Further essays into education.* Portsmouth, NH: Heinemann.

Smith, J. (1991). Goin' wild in hypercard. *Language Arts, 68,* 674–680.

Smith, N. J. (1985). The word processing approach to language experience. *The Reading Teacher, 38,* 556–559.

Smith, P. L., & Tompkins, G. E. (1988). Structured note-taking: A strategy for content area readers. *Journal of Reading, 32,* 46–53.

Sommers, N. (1994). Revision strategies of student writers and experienced adult writers. In S. Perl (Ed.), *Landmark essays on writing process* (pp. 75–84). Davis, CA: Heragoras Press.

Sorenson, M. (1993). Teach each other: Connecting talking and writing. *English Journal, 82,* 42–47.

Soto, G. (1992). Author for a day: Glitter and rainbows. *The Reading Teacher, 46,* 200–202.

Sowers, S. (1985). The story and the "all about" book. In J. Hansen, T. Newkirk, & D. Graves (Eds.), *Breaking ground: Teachers relate reading and writing in the elementary school* (pp. 73–82). Portsmouth, NH: Heinemann.

Spangenberg-Urbschat, K., & Pritchard, R. (Eds.). (1994). *Kids come in all languages: Reading instruction for ESL students.* Newark, DE: International Reading Association.

Speaker, R. B., Jr., & Speaker, P. R. (1991). Sentence collecting: Authentic literacy events in the classroom. *Journal of Reading, 35,* 92–95.

Standards for the English Language Arts. (1996). Urbana, IL: National Council of Teachers of English and the International Reading Association.

Stanford, B. (1988). Writing reflectively. *Language Arts, 65,* 652–658.

Stanovich, K. (1980). Toward an interactive-compensatory model of individual differences in the development of reading fluency. *Reading Research Quarterly, 16,* 37–71.

Staton, J. (1980). Writing and counseling: Using a dialogue journal. *Language Arts, 57,* 514–518.

Staton, J. (1987). The power of responding in dialogue journals. In T. Fulwiler (Ed.), *The journal book* (pp. 47–63). Portsmouth, NH: Boynton/Cook.

Stauffer, R. G. (1970). *The language experience approach to the teaching of reading.* New York: Harper & Row.

Stauffer, R. G. (1975). *Directing the reading-thinking process.* New York: Harper & Row.

Stein, N. L., & Glenn, C. G. (1979). An analysis of story comprehension in elementary school children. In R. O. Freedle (Ed.), *New Directions in Discourse Processing* (pp. 53–120). Norwood, NJ: Ablex.

Steinbergh, J. W. (1993). Chandra: "To live a life of no secrecy." In S. Hudson-Ross, L. M. Cleary, & M. Casey (Eds.), *Children's voices: Children talk about literacy* (pp. 202–214). Portsmouth, NH: Heinemann.

Stennett, R. G., Smithe, P. C., & Hardy, M. (1972). Developmental trends in letter-printing skill. *Perceptual and Motor Skills, 34,* 183–186.

Stewig, J. W. (1981). Choral speaking: Who has the time? Why take the time? *Childhood Education, 57,* 25–29.

Stewig, J. W. (1983). *Informal drama in the elementary language arts program.* New York: Teachers College Press.

Stewig, J. W. (1987). Students' spelling errors. *Clearing House, 61,* 34–37.

Sticht, T. G., & James, J. H. (1984). Listening and reading. In P. D. Pearson (Ed.), *Handbook of reading research* (pp. 293–318). New York: Longman.

Stires, S. (1991a). Thinking through the process: Self-evaluation in writing. In B. M. Power & R. Hubbard (Eds.), *The Heinemann reader: Literacy in process* (pp. 295–310). Portsmouth, NH: Heinemann.

Stires, S. (Ed.). (1991b). *With promise: Redefining reading and writing for "special" students.* Portsmouth, NH: Heinemann.

Strong, W. (1996). *Writer's toolbox: A sentence-combining workshop.* New York: McGraw-Hill.

Strother, D. B. (1987). Practical applications of research: On listening. *Phi Delta Kappan, 68,* 625–628.

Sulzby, E. (1985a). Children's emergent reading of favorite storybooks: A developmental study. *Reading Research Quarterly, 20,* 458–481.

Sulzby, E. (1985b). Kindergartners as readers and writers. In M. Farr (Ed.), *Advances in writing research, vol. 1: Children's early writing development* (pp. 127–199). Norwood, NJ: Ablex.

Sumara, D., & Walker, L. (1991). The teacher's role in whole language. *Language Arts, 68,* 276–285.

Swift, K. (1993). Try reading workshop in your classroom. *The Reading Teacher, 46,* 366–371.

Taylor, D. (1983). *Family literacy: Young children learning to read and write.* Exeter, NH: Heinemann.

Taylor, D. (1993). *From the child's point of view.* Portsmouth, NH: Heinemann.

Taylor, D., & Dorsey-Gaines, C. (1987). *Growing up literate: Learning from inner-city families.* Portsmouth, NH: Heinemann.

Taylor, K. K., & Kidder, E. B. (1988). The development of spelling skills: From first grade through eighth grade. *Written Communication, 5,* 222–244.

Teale, W. H. (1982). Toward a theory of how children learn to read and write. *Language Arts, 59,* 555–570.

Teale, W. H., & Sulzby, E. (1989). Emerging literacy: New perspectives. In D. S. Strickland & L. M. Morrow (Eds.), *Emerging literacy: Young children learn to read and write* (pp. 1–15). Newark, DE: International Reading Association.

Temple, C. (1992). Lots of plots: Patterns, meanings, and children's literature. In C. Temple & P. Collins (Eds.), *Stories and readers: New perspectives on literature in the elementary classroom* (pp. 3–13). Norwood, MA: Christopher-Gordon.

Temple, C., Nathan, R., Burris, N., & Temple, F. (1988). *The beginnings of writing.* Boston: Allyn & Bacon.

Templeton, S. (1979). Spelling first, sound later: The relationship between orthography and higher order phonological knowledge in older students. *Research in the Teaching of English, 13,* 255–265.

Templeton, S. (1980). Young children invent words: Developing concepts of "word-ness." *The Reading Teacher, 33,* 454–459.

Templeton, S., & Spivey, E. (1980). The concept of word in young children as a function of level of cognitive development. *Research in the Teaching of English, 14,* 265–278.

Terry, A. (1974). *Children's poetry preferences: A national survey of upper elementary grades* (NCTE Research Report No. 16). Urbana, IL: National Council of Teachers of English.

Thurber, D. N. (1987). *D'Nealian handwriting* (Grades K–8). Glenview, IL: Scott, Foresman.

Tiedt, I. (1970). Exploring poetry patterns. *Elementary English, 45,* 1082–1084.

Tierney, R. J. (1983). Writer-reader transactions: Defining the dimensions of negotiation. In P. L. Stock (Ed.), *Forum: Essays on theory and practice in the teaching of writing* (pp. 147–151). Upper Montclair, NJ: Boynton/Cook.

Tierney, R. J., & Pearson, P. D. (1983). Toward a composing model of reading. *Language Arts, 60,* 568–580.

Tierney, R. J., & Pearson, P. D. (1992). Learning to learn from text: A framework for improving classroom practice. In E. K. Dishner, T. W. Bean, J. E. Readence, & D. W. Moore (Eds.), *Reading in the content areas: Improving classroom instruction* (pp. 85–99). Dubuque, IA: Kendall-Hunt.

Tompkins, G. E. (1994). *Teaching writing: Balancing process and product* (2nd ed.). Upper Saddle River, NJ: Prentice Hall/Merrill.

Tompkins, G. E. (1995). Hear ye, hear ye, and learn the lesson well: Fifth graders read and write about the American Revolution. In M. Sorensen & B. Lehman (Eds.), *Teaching with children's books: Paths to literature-based*

instruction (pp. 171–187). Urbana, IL: National Council of Teachers of English.

Tompkins, G. E., Friend, M., & Smith, P. L. (1987). Strategies for more effective listening. In C. R. Personke & D. D. Johnson (Eds.), *Language arts and the beginning teacher* (Chapter 3). Upper Saddle River, NJ: Prentice Hall.

Tompkins, G. E., & McGee, L. M. (1983). Launching non-standard speakers into Standard English. *Language Arts, 60,* 463–469.

Tompkins, G. E., & McGee, L. M. (1993). *Teaching reading with literature: Case studies to action plans.* Upper Saddle River, NJ: Prentice Hall/Merrill.

Tompkins, G. E., Smith, P. L., & Hitchcock, M. E. (1987). *Elementary students' use of expository text structures in report writing.* Paper presented at the National Reading Conference, St. Petersburg Beach, FL.

Tompkins, G. E., & Webeler, M. B. (1983). What will happen next? Using predictable books with young children. *The Reading Teacher, 36,* 498–502.

Tompkins, G. E., & Yaden, D. B., Jr. (1986). *Answering students' questions about words.* Urbana, IL: ERIC Clearinghouse on Communication Skills and the National Council of Teachers of English.

Trachtenburg, R., & Ferruggia, A. (1989). Big books from little voices: Reaching high risk beginning readers. *The Reading Teacher, 42,* 284–289.

Traxel, J. (1983). The American Revolution in children's fiction. *Research in the Teaching of English, 17,* 61–83.

Treiman, R. (1985). Phonemic analysis, spelling, and reading. In T. H. Carr (Ed.), *The development of reading skills* (pp. 5–18). San Francisco: Jossey-Bass.

Trelease, J. (1995). *The new read-aloud handbook* (4th ed.). New York: Penguin.

Troika, R. C. (1981). Synthesis of research on bilingual education. *Educational Leadership, 38,* 498–504.

True, J. (1979). Round robin reading is for the birds. *Language Arts, 56,* 918–921.

Tunnell, M. O., & Ammon, R. (Eds.). (1993). *The story of ourselves: Teaching history through children's literature.* Portsmouth, NH: Heinemann.

Tunmer, W., & Nesdale, A. (1985). Phonemic segmentation skill and beginning reading. *Journal of Educational Psychology, 77,* 417–427.

Tutolo, D. (1981). Critical listening/reading of advertisements. *Language Arts, 58,* 679–683.

Tway, E. (1980). How to find and encourage the nuggets in children's writing. *Language Arts, 57,* 299–304.

Urzua, C. (1980). Doing what comes naturally: Recent research in second language acquisition. In G. S. Pinnell (Ed.), *Discovering language with children* (pp. 33–38). Urbana, IL: National Council of Teachers of English.

Urzua, C. (1992). Faith in learners through literature studies. *Language Arts, 69,* 492–501.

Valencia, S. W., Hiebert, E. H., & Afflerbach, P. P. (1994). *Authentic reading assessment: Practices and possibilities.* Newark, DE: International Reading Association.

Valentine, S. L. (1986). Beginning poets dig for poems. *Language Arts, 63,* 246–252.

Vardell, S. M. (1991). A new "picture of the world": The NCTE Orbis Pictus Award for outstanding nonfiction for children. *Language Arts, 68,* 474–479.

Vardell, S. M. (1996). The language of facts: Using nonfiction books to support language growth. In A. A. McClure & J. V. Kristo (Eds.), *Books that invite talk, wonder, and play* (pp. 59–77). Urbana, IL: National Council of Teachers of English.

Vardell, S. M., & Copeland, K. A. (1992). Reading aloud and responding to nonfiction: Let's talk about it. In E. B. Freeman & D. G. Person (Eds.), *Using nonfiction trade books in the elementary classroom: From ants to zeppelins* (pp. 76–85). Urbana, IL: National Council of Teachers of English.

Venezky, R. L. (1970). *The structure of English orthography.* The Hague: Mouton.

Vygotsky, L. S. (1978). *Mind in society.* Cambridge, MA: Harvard University Press.

Vygotsky, L. S. (1986). *Thought and language.* Cambridge, MA: MIT Press.

Wagner, B. J. (1976). *Dorothy Heathcote: Drama as a learning medium.* Washington, DC: National Education Association.

Wagner, B. J. (1983). The expanding circle of informal classroom drama. In B. A. Busching and J. I. Schwartz (Eds.), *Integrating the language arts in the elementary school* (pp. 155–163). Urbana, IL: National Council of Teachers of English.

Wagner, B. J. (1988). Research currents: Does classroom drama affect the arts of language? *Language Arts, 65,* 46–55.

Walker-Dalhouse, D. 1992). Using African-American literature to increase ethnic understanding. *The Reading Teacher, 45,* 416–422.

Weaver, C. (1979). *Grammar for teachers: Perspectives and definitions.* Urbana, IL: National Council of Teachers of English.

Weaver, C. (1994a). *Reading process and practice: From socio-psycholinguistics to whole language* (2nd ed.). Portsmouth, NH: Heinemann.

Weaver, C. (Ed.). (1994b). *Success at last! Helping students with AD(H)D achieve their potential.* Portsmouth, NH: Heinemann.

Weaver, C. (1996). *Teaching grammar in context.* Portsmouth, NH: Heinemann.

Wells, G. (1986). *The meaning makers: Children learning language and using language to learn.* Portsmouth, NH: Heinemann.

Wells, G., & Chang-Wells, G. L. (1992). *Constructing knowledge together: Classrooms as centers of inquiry and literacy.* Portsmouth, NH: Heinemann.

Werner, E. K. (1975). *A study of communication time.* Unpublished master's thesis, University of Maryland, College Park.

White, T. G., Sowell, J., & Yanagihara, A. (1989). Teaching elementary students to use word-part clues. *The Reading Teacher, 42,* 302–308.

Whitin, D. J., & Wilde, S. (1992). *Read any good math lately? Children's books for mathematical learning, K–6.* Portsmouth, NH: Heinemann.

Whitin, P. E. (1994). Opening potential: Visual response to literature. *Language Arts, 71,* 101–107.

Whitin, P. E. (1996a). Exploring visual response to literature. *Research in the Teaching of English, 30,* 114–140.

Whitin, P. E. (1996b). *Sketching stories, stretching minds.* Portsmouth, NH: Heinemann.

Wilde, S. (1993). *You kan red this! Spelling and punctuation for whole language classrooms, K–6.* Portsmouth, NH: Heinemann.

Wilde, S. (1996). A speller's bill of rights. *Primary Voices K–6, 4,* 7–10.

Wilen, W. W. (1986). *Questioning skills for teachers* (2nd ed.). Washington, DC: National Education Association.

Wilhelm, J. D. (1996). *Standards in practice, grades 6–8.* Urbana, IL: National Council of Teachers of English.

Wilkinson, L. C. (1984). Research currents: Peer group talk in elementary school. *Language Arts, 61,* 164–169.

Wilson, L. (1994). *Write me a poem: Reading, writing, and performing poetry.* Portsmouth, NH: Heinemann.

Wilt, M. E. (1950). A study of teacher awareness of listening as a factor in elementary education. *Journal of Educational Research, 43,* 626–636.

Wittrock, M. C., & Alesandrini, K. (1990). Generation of summaries and analogies and analytic and holistic abilities. *American Research Journal, 27,* 489–502.

Wollman-Bonilla, J. E. (1989). Reading journals: Invitations to participate in literature. *The Reading Teacher, 43,* 112–120.

Wolvin, A. D., & Coakley, C. G. (1979). *Listening instruction* (TRIP Booklet). Urbana, IL: ERIC Clearinghouse on Reading and Communication Skills and the Speech Communication Association.

Wolvin, A. D., & Coakley, C. G. (1985). *Listening* (2nd ed.). Dubuque, IA: William C. Brown.

Wong-Fillmore, L. (1985). When does teacher talk work as input? In S. M. Gass & C. G. Madden (Eds.), *Input in second language acquisition* (pp. 17–50). Rowley, MA: Newbury House.

Wood, J. W. (1993). *Mainstreaming: A practical approach for teachers* (2nd ed.). Upper Saddle River, NJ: Prentice Hall/Merrill.

The World Almanac and book of facts 1997. (1996). Mahwah, NJ: World Almanac Books.

Wright, C. D., & Wright, J. P. (1980). Handwriting: The effectiveness of copying from moving versus still models. *Journal of Educational Research, 74,* 95–98.

Wylie, R. E., & Durrell, D. D. (1970). Teaching vowels through phonograms. *Elementary English, 47,* 787–791.

Yaden, D. B., Jr. (1988). Understanding stories through repeated read-alouds: How many does it take? *The Reading Teacher, 41,* 556–560.

Yaden, D. B., Jr., & Templeton, S. (Eds.). (1986). *Metalinguistic awareness and beginning literacy: Conceptualizing what it means to read and write.* Portsmouth, NH: Heinemann.

Yokota, J. (1993). Issues in selecting multicultural children's literature. *Language Arts, 70,* 156–167.

Yopp, H. K. (1988). The validity and reliability of phonemic awareness tests. *Reading Research Quarterly, 23,* 159–177.

Yopp, H. K. (1992). Developing phonemic awareness in young children. *The Reading Teacher, 45,* 696–703.

Yopp, H. K. (1995). Read-aloud books for developing phonemic awareness: An annotated bibliography. *The Reading Teacher, 48,* 538–542.

Yopp, H. K., & Yopp, R. H. (1996). *Literature-based reading activities* (2nd ed.). Boston: Allyn & Bacon.

Young, T., & Vardell, S. M. (1993). Weaving readers theater and nonfiction into the curriculum. *The Reading Teacher, 46,* 396–409.

Zarnowski, M. (1991). An interview with author Nicholasa Mohr. *The Reading Teacher, 45,* 100–106.

Zarnowski, M. (1988, February). The middle school student as biographer. *Middle School Journal, 19,* 25–27.

Zarrillo, J. (1989). Teachers' interpretations of literature-based reading. *The Reading Teacher, 43,* 22–28.

Zarrillo, J. (1994). *Multicultural literature, multicultural teaching: Units for the elementary grades.* Fort Worth, TX: Harcourt Brace.

Zebroski, J. T. (1994). *Thinking through theory: Vygotskian perspectives on the teaching of writing.* Portsmouth, NH: Boynton/Cook.

Zutell, J. (1979). Spelling strategies of primary school children and their relationship to Piaget's concept of decentration. *Research in the Teaching of English, 13,* 69–79.

Children's Books

Abbett, L. (1996). *Freebies for kids.* Chicago: Contemporary Books.

Adler, D. A. (1989). *A picture book of Martin Luther King, Jr.* New York: Holiday House.

Adler, D. A. (1990). *A picture book of Helen Keller.* New York: Holiday House.

Adler, D. A. (1995). *A picture book of Patrick Henry.* New York: Holiday House.

Ahlberg, J., & Ahlberg, A. (1986). *The jolly postman, or other people's letters.* Boston: Little, Brown.

Aker, S. (1990). *What comes in 2's, 3's, and 4's?* New York: Simon & Schuster.

Aliki. (1979). *Mummies made in Egypt.* New York: HarperCollins.

Aliki. (1995). *Tabby: A story in pictures.* New York: HarperCollins.

The American Heritage children's dictionary. (1994). Boston: Houghton Mifflin.

The American Heritage picture dictionary. (1989). Boston: Houghton Mifflin.

The American Heritage student dictionary. (1994). Boston: Houghton Mifflin.

Ancona, G. (1992). *Man and mustang.* New York: Macmillan.

Anno, M. (1983). *Anno's U.S.A.* New York: Philomel.

Archambault, J. & Martin, B. Jr. (1994). *A beautiful feast for a big king cat.* New York: HarperCollins.

Arnold, C. (1993). *Dinosaurs all around: An artist's view of the prehistoric world.* New York: Clarion.

Arnosky, J. (1995). *I see animals hiding.* New York: Scholastic.

Avi. (1984). *The fighting ground.* New York: HarperCollins.

Avi. (1991). *Nothing but the truth.* New York: Orchard.

Axelrod, A. (1994). *Pigs will be pigs.* New York: Four Winds Press.

Babbitt, N. (1975). *Tuck everlasting.* New York: Farrar, Straus & Giroux.

Baker, K. (1991). *Hide and snake.* Orlando: Harcourt Brace.

Baron, A. (1996). *Red fox dances.* Cambridge, MA: Candlewick.

Barracca, D., & Barracca, S. (1990). *The adventures of taxi dog.* New York: Dial.

Barrett, J. (1978). *Cloudy with a chance of meatballs.* New York: Atheneum.

Barrett, J. (1983). *A snake is totally tail.* New York: Atheneum.

Bates, K. L. (1993). *America the beautiful.* New York: Atheneum.

Bayer, J. (1984). *A my name is Alice.* New York: Dial.

Baylor, B. (1981). *Desert voices.* New York: Scribner.

Baylor, B., & Parnall, P. (1981). *Desert voices.* New York: Scribner.

Beatty, P. (1987). *Charley Skedaddle.* New York: Morrow.

Behn, H. (1964). *Cricket songs.* New York: Harcourt Brace Jovanovich.

Behn, H. (1971). *More cricket songs.* New York: Harcourt Brace Jovanovich.

Blume, J. (1972). *Tales of a fourth grade nothing.* New York: Dutton.

Bonners, S. (1981). *A penguin year.* New York: Delacorte.

Bonsall, C. (1996). *Mine's the best.* New York: HarperCollins.

Bowen, G. (1994). *Stranded at Plimoth plantation, 1626.* New York: HarperCollins.

Brett, J. (1989). *The mitten.* New York: Putnam.

Brown, M. (1983). *What do you call a dumb bunny? And other rabbit riddles, games, jokes, and cartoons.* Boston: Little, Brown.

Browne, P. (1996). *A gaggle of geese: The collective names of the animal kingdom.* New York: Atheneum.

Bunting, E. (1984). *The man who could call down owls.* New York: Macmillan.

Bunting, E. (1988). *How many days to America? A Thanksgiving story.* New York: Clarion.

Bunting, E. (1990). *The wall.* New York: Clarion.

Bunting, E. (1991). *Fly away home.* New York: Clarion.

Bunting, E. (1994). *A day's work.* New York: Clarion.

Bunting, E. (1994). *Smoky night.* San Diego: Harcourt Brace.

Bunting, E. (1995). *Once upon a time.* Katowah, NY: Richard C. Owen.

Bunting, E. (1996). *The blue and the gray.* New York: Scholastic.

Burningham, J. (1985). *Opposites*. New York: Crown Books.

Byars, B. (1968). *The midnight fox*. New York: Viking.

Carle, E. (1969). *The very hungry caterpillar*. Cleveland: Collins-World.

Carle, E. (1984). *The very busy spider*. New York: Philomel.

Carle, E. (1986). *The grouchy ladybug*. New York: Harper & Row.

Carle, E. (1987). *A house for hermit crab*. Saxonville, MA: Picture Book Studio.

Carle, E. (1989). *Animals, animals*. New York: Philomel.

Carle, E. (1990). *The very quiet cricket*. New York: Philomel.

Carrick, C. (1989). *Aladdin and the wonderful lamp*. New York: Scholastic.

Cauley, L. B. (1984). *The town mouse and the country mouse*. New York: Putnam.

Cherry, L. (1992). *A river ran wild*. Orlando: Harcourt Brace.

Chester, J. (1995). *A for Antarctica*. New York: Tricycle.

Choi, S. N. (1991). *Year of impossible goodbyes*. Boston: Houghton Mifflin.

Cleary, B. (1981). *Ramona Quimby, age 8*. New York: Morrow.

Cleary, B. (1983). *Dear Mr. Henshaw*. New York: Morrow.

Cleary, B. (1990). *Muggie Maggie*. New York: Morrow.

Climo, S. (1989). *The Egyptian Cinderella*. New York: Crowell.

Coerr, E. (1986). *The Josefina story quilt*. New York: Harper & Row.

Coerr, E. (1988). *Chang's paper pony*. New York: Harper & Row.

Coerr, E. (1995). *Buffalo Bill and the Pony Express*. New York: HarperCollins.

Cohen, B. (1983). *Molly's pilgrim*. New York: Lothrop, Lee & Shepard.

Cole, H. (1995). *Jack's garden*. New York: Greenwillow.

Cole, J. (1981). *A snake's body*. New York: Morrow.

Cole, J. (1989). *The magic school bus inside the human body*. New York: Scholastic.

Cole, J. (1994). *The magic school bus in the time of the dinosaurs*. New York: Scholastic.

Cole, J. (1995). *The magic school bus inside a hurricane*. New York: Scholastic.

Cole, J. (1996). *On the bus with Joanna Cole: A creative auto-biography*. Portsmouth, NH: Heinemann.

Colman, P. (1994). *Toilets, bathtubs, sinks, and sewers: A history of the bathroom*. New York: Atheneum.

Colman, P. (1995). *Rosie the riveter: Women working on the home front in World War II*. New York: Crown.

Conrad, P. (1989). *The tub people*. New York: Harper & Row.

Conrad, P. (1991). *Pedro's journal: A voyage with Christopher Columbus, August 3, 1492–February 14, 1493*. Honedale, PA: Boyds Mill Press.

Cooper, F. (1996). *Mandela: From the life of the South African statesman*. New York: Philomel.

Corville, B. (1991). *Jeremy Thatcher, dragon hatcher*. San Diego: Harcourt Brace.

Cowcher, H. (1990). *Antarctica*. New York: Farrar, Straus & Giroux.

Cox, J. A. (1980). *Put your foot in your mouth and other silly sayings*. New York: Random House.

Crews, D. (1991). *Bigmama's*. New York: Greenwillow.

Cullinan, B. E. (Ed.). (1996). *A jar of tiny stars: Poems by NCTE award-winning poets*. Honesdale, PA: Boyds Mill Press.

Cushman, K. (1994). *Catherine, called Birdy*. New York: HarperCollins.

Cushman, K. (1996). *The ballad of Lucy Whipple*. New York: Clarion.

Dahl, R. (1961). *James and the giant peach*. New York: Knopf.

Dahl, R. (1964). *Charlie and the chocolate factory*. New York: Knopf.

Danziger, P. (1994). *Amber Brown is not a crayon*. New York: Putnam.

de Gasztold, C. B. (1992). *Prayers from the ark*. New York: Viking.

Degen, B. (1983). *Jamberry*. New York: Harper & Row.

Degen, B. (1996). *Sailaway home*. New York: Scholastic.

Denenberg, B. (1996). *When will this cruel war be over? The Civil War diary of Emma Simpson*. New York: Scholastic.

de Paola, T. (1978). *Pancakes for breakfast*. New York: Harcourt Brace Jovanovich.

de Paola, T. (1988). *The legend of the Indian paintbrush*. New York: Putnam.

Donnelly, J. (1991). *A wall of names: The story of the Vietnam Veterans Memorial*. New York: Random House.

Dooley, N. (1991). *Everybody cooks rice*. Minneapolis: Carolrhoda.

Dorros, A. (1991). *Abuela*. New York: Dutton.

Dorros, A. (1995). *Isla*. New York: Dutton.

Dunphy, M. (1995). *Here is the southwestern desert*. New York: Hyperion.

Ehlert, L. (1987). *Growing vegetable soup*. San Diego: Harcourt Brace Jovanovich.

Ehlert, L. (1989). *Color zoo*. New York: Lippincott.

Ehlert, L. (1990). *Feathers for lunch*. Orlando: Harcourt Brace.

Ehlert, L. (1994). *Eating the alphabet: Fruits and vegetables from A to Z*. San Diego: Harcourt Brace.

Ehlert, L. (1994). *Mole's hill*. Orlando: Harcourt Brace.

Ehlert, L. (1996). *Under my nose*. Katonah, NY: Richard C. Owen.

Elkin, B. (1983). *Money*. Chicago: Childrens Press.

Eric Carle: Picture writer. (1993). New York: Philomel.

Ernst, L. C. (1983). *Sam Johnson and the blue ribbon quilt*. New York: Mulberry Books.

Feelings, M. (1971). *Moja means one: Swahili counting book*. New York: Dial.

Fitzhugh, L. (1964). *Harriet the spy*. New York: Harper & Row.

Fleischman, P. (1985). *I am phoenix: Poems for two voices*. New York: Harper & Row.

Fleischman, P. (1988). *Joyful noise: Poems for two voices*. New York: Harper & Row.

Fleischman, P. (1991). *Bull Run*. New York: HarperCollins.

Fleming, D. (1994). *Barnyard banter*. New York: Henry Holt.

Flournoy, V. (1985). *The patchwork quilt*. New York: Dial.

Forbes, E. (1970). *Johnny Tremain: A story of Boston in revolt*. Boston: Houghton Mifflin.

Fowler, A. (1990). *It's a good thing there are insects.* Chicago: Childrens Press.

Fowler, A. (1992). *It could still be water.* Chicago: Childrens Press.

Fox, M. (1988). *Wilfred Gordon McDonald Partridge.* New York: Kane-Miller.

Fox, P. (1973). *The slave dancer.* New York: Bradbury.

Fraser, M. A. (1993). *Ten mile day and the building of the transcontinental railroad.* New York: Henry Holt.

Freedman, R. (1987). *Lincoln: A photobiography.* New York: Clarion.

Freedman, R. (1988). *Buffalo hunt.* New York: Holiday House.

Freedman, R. (1993). *Eleanor Roosevelt: A life of discovery.* New York: Clarion.

Freedman, R. (1996). *The life and death of Crazy Horse.* New York: Holiday House.

Freeman, D. (1968). *Corduroy.* New York: Viking.

Freeman, D. (1972). *A pocket for Corduroy.* New York: Viking.

Friedman, I. R. (1984). *How my parents learned to eat.* Boston: Houghton Mifflin.

Fritz, J. (1976). *Will you sign here, John Hancock?* New York: Coward-McCann.

Fritz, J. (1983). *The double life of Pocahontas.* New York: Putnam.

Fritz, J. (1987). *Brady.* New York: Penguin.

Fritz, J. (1989). *The great little Madison.* New York: Putnam.

Fritz, J. (1992). *Surprising myself.* Katonah, NY: Richard C. Owen.

Fritz, J. (1995). *You want women to vote, Lizzie Stanton?* New York: Putnam.

Froman, R. (1974). *Seeing things: A book of poems.* New York: Crowell.

Galdone, P. (1970). *The three little pigs.* New York: Seabury.

Galdone, P. (1972). *The three bears.* New York: Houghton Mifflin.

Galdone, P. (1973). *The little red hen.* New York: Seabury.

Galdone, P. (1975). *The gingerbread boy.* New York: Seabury.

Galdone, P. (1978). *Cinderella.* New York: McGraw-Hill.

Gardiner, J. R. (1980). *Stone Fox.* New York: Harper & Row.

George, J. C. (1972). *Julie of the wolves.* New York: Harper & Row.

George, R. E. (1976). *Roald Dahl's Charlie and the chocolate factory.* New York: Knopf.

George, R. E. (1982). *Roald Dahl's James and the giant peach.* New York: Knopf.

Gibbons, G. (1991). *Surrounded by sea: Life on a New England fishing island.* Boston: Little, Brown.

Gibbons, G. (1992). *Spiders.* New York: Holiday House.

Giblin, J. C. (1990). *The riddle of the Rosetta stone: Key to ancient Egypt.* New York: Crowell.

Giff, P. R. (1995). *Ronald Morgan goes to camp.* New York: Viking.

Gilson, J. (1985). *Hello, my name is scrambled eggs.* New York: Morrow.

Goble, P. (1988). *Iktomi and the boulder.* New York: Orchard.

Goble, P. (1994). *Hau kola/Hello friend.* Katonah, NY: Richard C. Owen.

Goldstein, B. S. (Ed.). (1992). *Inner chimes: Poems on poetry.* Honesdale, PA: Wordsong.

Golenbock, P. (1990). *Teammates.* San Diego: Harcourt Brace Jovanovich.

Goodall, J. S. (1986). *The story of a castle.* New York: Macmillan.

Graham, J. B. (1994). *Splish splash: Poems.* New York: Ticknor.

Greenfield, E. (1988). *Nathaniel talking.* New York: Black Butterfly Children's Books.

Greenfield, E. (1991). *Night on Neighborhood Street.* New York: Dial.

Gregory, K. (1996). *The winter of red snow: The Revolutionary War diary of Abigail Jane Stewart.* New York: Scholastic.

Guiberson, B. Z. (1991). *Cactus hotel.* New York: Henry Holt.

Gwynne, F. (1970). *The king who rained.* New York: Windmill Books.

Gwynne, F. (1976). *A chocolate moose for dinner.* New York: Windmill Books.

Gwynne, F. (1980). *The sixteen hand horse.* New York: Prentice Hall.

Gwynne, F. (1988). *A little pigeon toad.* New York: Simon & Schuster.

Hadley, E., & Hadley, T. (1983). *Legends of the sun and moon.* Cambridge: Cambridge University Press.

Hague, M. (1985). *Aesop's fables.* New York: Holt, Rinehart & Winston.

Hall, D. (1994). *I am the dog/I am the cat.* New York: Dial.

Hall, R. (1985). *Sniglets for kids.* Yellow Springs, OH: Antioch.

Hamilton, V. (1968). *The house of Dies Drear.* New York: Macmillan.

Hamilton, V. (1992). *Drylongso.* Orlando: Harcourt Brace.

Harter, P. (1994). *Shadow play: Night haiku.* New York: Simon & Schuster.

Hartman, G. (1991). *As the crow flies: A first book of maps.* New York: Bradbury Press.

Harvey, B. (1987). *Immigrant girl: Becky of Eldridge Street.* New York: Holiday House.

Harvey, B. (1988). *Cassie's journey: Going west in the 1860s.* New York: Holiday House.

Heller, R. (1983). *The reason for a flower.* New York: Putnam.

Heller, R. (1987). *A cache of jewels and other collective nouns.* New York: Grosset & Dunlap.

Heller, R. (1990). *Merry-go-round: A book about nouns.* New York: Grosset & Dunlap.

Heller, R. (1991). *Up, up and away: A book about adverbs.* New York: Grosset & Dunlap.

Heller, R. (1995). *Behind the mask: A book of prepositions.* New York: Grosset & Dunlap.

Henkes, K. (1991). *Chrysanthemum.* New York: Greenwillow.

Henry, M. (1963). *Misty of Chincoteague.* Chicago: Rand McNally.

Hewett, J. (1990). *Hector lives in the United States now: The story of a Mexican American child.* New York: Lippincott.

Hirschi, R. (1992). *Desert.* New York: Bantam.

Hoban, T. (1987). *26 letters and 99 cents.* New York: Greenwillow.

Hopkins, L. B. (1984). *Surprises.* New York: Harper & Row.

Hopkins, L. B. (1987). *Dinosaurs.* San Diego: Harcourt Brace Jovanovich.

Hopkins, L. B. (1992). *Questions: Poems.* New York: HarperCollins.

Hopkins, L. B. (1994). *Hand in hand: An American history through poetry.* New York: Simon & Schuster.

Hopkins, L. B. (1994). *Weather.* New York: HarperCollins.

Hopkins, L. B. (1995). *Blast off! Poems about space.* New York: HarperCollins.

Hopkinson, D. (1993). *Sweet Clara and the freedom quilt.* New York: Knopf.

Howard, E. F. (1991). *Aunt Flossie's hats (and crab cakes later).* New York: Clarion.

Howe, D., & Howe, J. (1979). *Bunnicula: A rabbit-tale of mystery.* New York: Atheneum.

Howe, J. (1982). *Howliday Inn.* New York: Atheneum.

Howe, J. (1983). *The celery stalks at midnight.* New York: Atheneum.

Howe, J. (1987). *Nighty-nightmare.* New York: Atheneum.

Howe, J. (1989). *The fright before Christmas.* New York: Atheneum.

Howe, J. (1989). *Scared silly.* New York: Atheneum.

Howe, J. (1990). *Hot fudge.* New York: Atheneum.

Howe, J. (1992). *Return to Howliday Inn.* New York: Atheneum.

Hoyt-Goldsmith, D. (1990). *Totem pole.* New York: Holiday House.

Hudson, W. (1993). *Pass it on: African-American poetry for children.* New York: Scholastic.

Hunt, I. (1987). *Across five Aprils.* New York: Berkley.

Hunt, J. (1989). *Illuminations.* New York: Bradbury.

Hutchins, P. (1968). *Rosie's walk.* New York: Macmillan.

Hutchins, P. (1976). *Don't forget the bacon!* New York: Mulberry.

Hutchins, P. (1987). *Rosie's walk* (big book edition). New York: Scholastic.

Hyman, T. S. (1983). *Little Red Riding Hood.* New York: Holiday House.

Isaacs, A. (1994). *Swamp Angel.* New York: Dutton.

Janeczko, P. B. (1994). *Poetry from A to Z: A guide for young writers.* New York: Bradbury.

Janeczko, P. B. (1995). *Wherever home begins: 100 contemporary poems.* New York: Orchard/Jackson.

Jeffers, S. (1991). *Brother eagle, sister sky: A message from Chief Seattle.* New York: Dial.

Johnston, T. (1985). *The quilt story.* New York: Putnam.

Johnston, T. (1994). *Amber on the mountain.* New York: Dial.

Jonas, A. (1984). *The quilt.* New York: Greenwillow.

Jones, H. (1993). *The trees stand shining: Poetry of the North American Indians.* New York: Dial.

Kalan, R. (1995). *Jump, frog, jump.* New York: Greenwillow.

Kellogg, S. (1973). *The island of the Skog.* New York: Dial.

Kellogg, S. (1987). *Aster Aardvark's alphabet adventures.* New York: Morrow.

Kellogg, S. (1988). *Johnny Appleseed.* New York: Morrow.

Kennedy, X. J., & Kennedy, D. M. (1982). *Knock at a star: A child's introduction to poetry.* Boston: Little, Brown.

Knight, A. S. (1993). *The way west: Journal of a pioneer woman.* New York: Simon & Schuster.

Knight, M. B. (1993). *Who belongs here? An American story.* Gardiner, ME: Tulbury House.

Koopmans, L. (1990). *The woodcutter's mitten.* New York: Crocodile Books.

Langstaff, J. (1974). *Oh, a-hunting we will go.* New York: Atheneum.

Lansky, B. (1996). *Free stuff for kids.* New York: Simon & Schuster.

Larrick, N. (1988). *Cats are cats.* New York: Philomel.

Lasky, K. (1983). *Sugaring time.* New York: Macmillan.

Lasky, K. (1996). *A journey to the new world: The diary of Remember Patience Whipple.* New York: Scholastic.

Lasky, K. (1996). *Surtsey: The newest place on earth.* New York: Hyperion.

Lauber, P. (1990). *Seeing earth from space.* New York: Orchard.

Lauber, P. (1995). *Who eats what? Food chains and food webs.* New York: HarperCollins.

Lear, E. (1995). *Daffy down dillies: Silly limericks by Edward Lear.* Honesdale, PA: Wordsong.

L'Engle, M. (1962). *A wrinkle in time.* New York: Farrar, Straus & Giroux.

Lester, H. (1988). *Tacky the penguin.* Boston: Houghton Mifflin.

Levine, E. (1986). *. . . If you traveled west in a covered wagon.* New York: Scholastic.

Levine, E. (1989). *I hate English!* New York: Scholastic.

Lewis, C. S. (1950). *The lion, the witch and the wardrobe.* New York: Macmillan.

Lewis, J. P. (1995). *Black swan/white crow.* New York: Atheneum.

Lewis, R. (Ed.). (1965). *In a spring garden.* New York: Dial.

Lionni, L. (1969). *Alexander and the wind-up mouse.* New York: Pantheon.

Lionni, L. (1985). *Frederick's fables.* New York: Pantheon.

Livingston, M. C. (Sel.). (1991). *Lots of limericks.* New York: McElderry Books.

Lobel, A. (1970). *Frog and Toad are friends.* New York: Harper & Row.

Lobel, A. (1972). *Frog and Toad together.* New York: Harper & Row.

Lobel, A. (1972). *Mouse tales.* New York: Harper & Row.

Lobel, A. (1980). *Fables.* New York: Harper & Row.

Lobel, A. (1983). *Pigericks: A book of pig limericks.* New York: Harper & Row.

Lobel, A. (1990). *Alison's zinnia.* New York: Greenwillow.

Longfellow, H. W. (1990). *Paul Revere's ride.* New York: Dutton.

Louie, A. (1982). *Yeh-Shen: A Cinderella story from China.* New York: Philomel.

Lowell, S. (1992). *The three little javelinas.* Flagstaff, AZ: Northland.

Lowry, L. (1979). *Anastasia Krupnik.* Boston: Houghton Mifflin.

Lowry, L. (1989). *Number the stars*. Boston: Houghton Mifflin.

Lowry, L. (1993). *The giver*. Boston: Houghton Mifflin.

Macaulay, D. (1977). *Castle*. Boston: Houghton Mifflin.

Macaulay, D. (1990). *Black and white*. Boston: Houghton Mifflin.

MacLachlan, P. (1985). *Sarah, plain and tall*. New York: Harper & Row.

Maestro, B. (1992). *How do apples grow?* New York: HarperCollins.

Maestro, B. (1993). *The story of money*. New York: Clarion.

Maestro, G. (1984). *What's a frank Frank? Tasty homograph riddles*. New York: Clarion Books.

Martin, B., Jr. (1983). *Brown bear, brown bear, what do you see?* New York: Holt, Rinehart & Winston.

Martin, B., Jr. (1992). *Polar bear, polar bear, what do you hear?* New York: Holt, Rinehart & Winston.

Martin, B., Jr., & Archambault, J. (1985). *The ghost-eye tree*. New York: Holt, Rinehart & Winston.

Martin, B., Jr., & Archambault, J. (1986). *White Dynamite and Curly Kidd*. New York: Henry Holt.

Martin, F. (1992). *The rough face girl*. New York: Putnam.

Mayer, M. (1974). *Frog goes to dinner*. New York: Dial.

Mayer, M. (1978). *Beauty and the beast*. New York: Macmillan.

Mayer, M. (1987). *The ugly duckling*. New York: Macmillan.

McCloskey, R. (1969). *Make way for ducklings*. New York: Viking.

McCully, E. A. (1984). *Picnic*. New York: Harper & Row.

McCurdy, M. (Ed.). (1994). *Escape from slavery: The boyhood of Frederick Douglass in his own words*. New York: Knopf.

McKissack, P. C. (1986). *Flossie and the fox*. New York: Dial.

McKissack, P. C. (1988). *Mirandy and Brother Wind*. New York: Knopf.

McKissack, P. C. (1997). *A picture of freedom: The diary of Clotee, a slave girl*. New York: Scholastic.

McKissack, P. C., & McKissack, F. (1995). *Red-tail angels: The story of the Tuskegee airmen of World War II*. New York: Walker.

McMillan, B. (1989). *Super, super, superwords*. New York: Lothrop, Lee & Shepard.

McMillan, B. (1995). *Summer ice: Life along the Antarctic peninsula*. Boston: Houghton Mifflin.

Merriam, E. (1966). *It doesn't always have to rhyme*. New York: Atheneum.

Mills, L. (1991). *The rag coat*. Boston: Little, Brown.

Milne, A. A. (1956). *The house at Pooh Corner*. New York: Dutton.

Mochizuki, K. (1993). *Baseball saved us*. New York: Lee & Lothrop.

Morimoto, J. (1987). *My Hiroshima*. New York: Puffin.

Moss, L. (1995). *Zin! Zin! Zin! A violin*. New York: Simon & Schuster.

Munsch, R. (1985). *Mortimer*. Toronto: Annick Press.

Myers, W. D. (1988). *Scorpions*. New York: Harper & Row.

Naylor, P. R. (1991). *Shiloh*. New York: Atheneum.

Ness, E. (1966). *Sam, Bangs, and moonshine*. New York: Holt, Rinehart & Winston.

Newton, P. (1990). *The stonecutter*. New York: Putnam.

Nixon, J. L. (1987). *A family apart*. New York: Bantam Books.

Noble, T. H. (1980). *The day Jimmy's boa ate the wash*. New York: Dial.

Numeroff, L. J. (1985). *If you give a mouse a cookie*. New York: Harper & Row.

Numeroff, L. J. (1991). *If you give a moose a muffin*. New York: HarperCollins.

Numeroff, L. J. (1993). *Dogs don't wear sneakers*. New York: Simon & Schuster.

Numeroff, L. J. (1995). *Chimps don't wear glasses*. New York: Simon & Schuster.

Obligado, L. (1983). *Faint frogs feeling feverish and other terrifically tantalizing tongue twisters*. New York: Puffin.

O'Dell, S. (1976). *The 290*. Boston: Houghton Mifflin.

O'Neill, M. (1989). *Hailstones and halibut bones: Adventures in color*. Garden City, NJ: Doubleday.

Pallotta, J. (1988). *The flower alphabet book*. Watertown, MA: Charlesbridge.

Pallotta, J. (1991). *The underwater alphabet book*. Watertown, MA: Charlesbridge.

Parish, P. (1963). *Amelia Bedelia*. New York: Harper & Row.

Paterson, K. (1977). *Bridge to Terabithia*. New York: Crowell.

Paterson, K. (1991). *Lyddie*. New York: Viking.

Paulsen, G. (1987). *Hatchet*. New York: Viking.

Paulsen, G. (1993). *Nightjohn*. New York: Delacorte.

Peek, M. (1985). *Mary wore her red dress*. New York: Clarion.

Pinchot, J. (1989). *The Mexicans in America*. Minneapolis: Lerner.

Pinkney, A. (1993). *Seven candles for Kwanzaa*. New York: Dial.

Polacco, P. (1988). *The keeping quilt*. New York: Simon & Schuster.

Polacco, P. (1988). *Rechenka's eggs*. New York: Philomel.

Polacco, P. (1990). *Thunder cake*. New York: Philomel.

Polacco, P. (1994). *Firetalking*. Katonah, NY: Richard C. Owen.

Polacco, P. (1994). *Pink and Say*. New York: Philomel.

Potter, B. (1902). *The tale of Peter Rabbit*. New York: Warne.

Potter, B. (1995). *Dear Peter Rabbit*. New York: Warne.

Prelutsky, J. (1982). *The baby uggs are hatching*. New York: Mulberry.

Prelutsky, J. (Sel.). (1983). *The Random House book of poetry for children*. New York: Random House.

Prelutsky, J. (1984). *The new kid on the block*. New York: Greenwillow.

Prelutsky, J. (1988). *Tyrannosaurus was a beast*. New York: Greenwillow.

Prelutsky, J. (1993). *The dragons are singing tonight*. New York: Greenwillow.

Prelutsky, J. (1996). *A pizza the size of the sun*. New York: Greenwillow.

Pryor, B. (1987). *The house on Maple Street*. New York: Morrow.

Ransome, A. (1968). *The fool of the world and the flying ship*. New York: Farrar, Straus & Giroux.

Rathmann, P. (1995). *Officer Buckle and Gloria*. New York: Putnam.

Rauzon, M. J. (1993). *Horns, antlers, fangs, and tusks.* New York: Lothrop, Lee & Shepard.

Ringgold, F. (1991). *Tar beach.* New York: Crown.

Ringgold, F. (1992). *Aunt Harriet's underground railroad in the sky.* New York: Crown.

Roop, P., & Roop, C. (1990). *I Columbus: My journal 1492–1493.* New York: Walker.

Roop, P., & Roop, C. (1993). *Off the map: The journals of Lewis and Clark.* New York: Walker.

Roth, S. L. (1992). *Marco Polo: His notebook.* New York: Doubleday.

Rotner, S. (1996). *Action alphabet.* New York: Atheneum.

Rowland, D. (1991). *Little Red Riding Hood/The wolf's tale.* New York: Birch Lane Press.

Rylant, C. (1985). *The relatives came.* New York: Bradbury Press.

Say, A. (1990). *El chino.* Boston: Houghton Mifflin.

Schwartz, D. M. (1989). *If you made a million.* New York: Lothrop, Lee & Shepard.

Schwartz, D. M. (1994). *How much is a million?* New York: Morrow.

Scieszka, J. (1989). *The true story of the three little pigs!* New York: Viking.

Scott, A. H. (1990). *One good horse: A cowpuncher's counting book.* New York: Greenwillow.

Sendak, M. (1963). *Where the wild things are.* New York: Harper & Row.

Seuss, Dr. (1963). *Hop on Pop.* New York: Random House.

Seuss, Dr. (1965). *Fox in socks.* New York: Random House.

Seuss, Dr. (1979). *Oh say can you say?* New York: Beginner Books.

Seuss, Dr. (1985). *The cat in the hat.* New York: Random House.

Seuss, Dr. (1988). *Green eggs and ham.* New York: Random House.

Shannon, C. (1996). *Spring: A haiku story.* New York: Greenwillow.

Shaw, N. (1992). *Sheep out to eat.* Boston: Houghton Mifflin.

Shea, P. D. (1995). *The whispering cloth: A refugee's story.* Honesdale, PA: Boyds Mill Press.

Sherman, I. (1980). *Walking talking words.* New York: Harcourt Brace Jovanovich.

Showers, P. (1985). *What happens to a hamburger?* New York: Harper & Row.

Siebert, D. (1988). *Mojave.* New York: HarperCollins.

Siebert, D. (1991). *Sierra.* New York: HarperCollins.

Silverman, E. (1994). *Don't fidget a feather!* New York: Simon & Schuster.

Silverstein, S. (1974). *Where the sidewalk ends.* New York: Harper & Row.

Silverstein, S. (1981). *A light in the attic.* New York: Harper & Row.

Simon, S. (1989). *Whales.* New York: Crowell.

Simon, S. (1992). *Wolves.* New York: HarperCollins.

Simon, S. (1993). *Mercury.* New York: Morrow.

Smith, J. (1988). *The show-and-tell war.* New York: Harper & Row.

Smucker, B. (1996). *Selina and the bear paw quilt.* New York: Crown.

Soto, G. (1992). *Neighborhood odes.* Orlando: Harcourt Brace.

Soto, G. (1995). *Canto familiar.* Orlando: Harcourt Brace.

Soto, G. (1995). *Chato's kitchen.* New York: Putnam.

Speare, E. G. (1958). *The witch of Blackbird Pond.* Boston: Houghton Mifflin.

Speare, E. G. (1983). *The sign of the beaver.* Boston: Houghton Mifflin.

Spier, P. (1971). *Gobble growl grunt.* New York: Doubleday.

Spier, P. (1972). *Crash! Bang! Boom!* New York: Doubleday.

Spinelli, J. (1990). *Maniac Magee.* Boston: Little, Brown.

Stanley, D. (1983). *The conversation club.* New York: Macmillan.

Stanley, D., & Vennema, P. (1994). *Cleopatra.* New York: Morrow Junior Books.

Steig, W. (1969). *Sylvester and the magic pebble.* New York: Simon & Schuster.

Steig, W. (1971). *Amos and Boris.* New York: Farrar, Straus & Giroux.

Steig, W. (1982). *Doctor De Soto.* New York: Farrar, Straus & Giroux.

Steig, W. (1986). *Brave Irene.* New York: Farrar, Straus & Giroux.

Steptoe, J. (1987). *Mufaro's beautiful daughters: An African tale.* New York: Lothrop, Lee & Shepard.

Sterne, N. (1979). *Tyrannosaurus wrecks: A book of dinosaur riddles.* New York: Crowell.

Stevens, J. (1987). *The three billy goats Gruff.* San Diego: Harcourt Brace Jovanovich.

Stevenson, J. (1995). *Sweet corn: Poems.* New York: Greenwillow.

Surat, M. M. (1983). *Angel child, dragon child.* Milwaukee: Raintree.

Swamp, Chief J. (1995). *Giving thanks: A Native American good morning message.* New York: Lee & Low.

Taylor, B. (1992). *Desert life.* New York: Dorling Kindersley.

Taylor, M. D. (1976). *Roll of thunder, hear my cry.* New York: Dial.

Taylor, M. D. (1987). *The gold Cadillac.* New York: Dial.

Taylor, M. D. (1990). *Mississippi bridge.* New York: Dial.

Terban, M. (1982). *Eight ate: A feast of homonym riddles.* New York: Clarion.

Terban, M. (1983). *In a pickle and other funny idioms.* New York: Clarion Books.

Terban, M. (1989). *Superdupers! Really funny real words.* New York: Clarion.

Terban, M. (1990). *Punching the clock: Funny action idioms.* New York: Clarion Books.

Terban, M. (1991). *Hey, hay! A wagonful of funny homonym riddles.* New York: Clarion Books.

Terban, M. (1993). *It figures! Fun figures of speech.* New York: Clarion.

Terkel, S. (1974). *Working.* New York: Pantheon.

Thomson, P. (1995). *Katie Henio: Navajo sheep herder.* New York: Cobblehill.

Tresselt, A. (1964). *The mitten.* New York: Lothrop, Lee & Shepard.

Turner, A. (1987). *Nettie's trip south.* New York: Macmillan.

Uchida, Y. (1971). *Journey to Topaz.* Berkeley: Creative Arts Book Company.

Uchida, Y. (1993). *The bracelet.* New York: Philomel.

Van Allsburg, C. (1979). *The garden of Abdul Gasazi.* Boston: Houghton Mifflin.

Van Allsburg, C. (1981). *Jumanji.* Boston: Houghton Mifflin.

Van Allsburg, C. (1984). *The mysteries of Harris Burdick.* Boston: Houghton Mifflin.

Van Allsburg, C. (1985). *The polar express.* Boston: Houghton Mifflin.

Van Allsburg, C. (1987). *The Z was zapped.* Boston: Houghton Mifflin.

Van Allsburg, C. (1993). *The sweetest fig.* Boston: Houghton Mifflin.

Van Allsburg, C. (1995). *Bad day at Riverbend.* Boston: Houghton Mifflin.

Viorst, J. (1977). *Alexander and the terrible, horrible, no good, very bad day.* New York: Atheneum.

Viorst, J. (1981). *If I were in charge of the world and other worries.* New York: Atheneum.

Waber, B. (1972). *Ira sleeps over.* Boston: Houghton Mifflin.

Waber, B. (1995). *Do you see a mouse?* Boston: Houghton Mifflin.

Wadsworth, G. (1995). *Giant sequoia trees.* Minneapolis: Lerner.

Waggoner, K. (1995). *Partners.* New York: Simon & Schuster.

Waters, K. (1989). *Sarah Morton's day: A day in the life of a pilgrim girl.* New York: Scholastic.

Watts, B. (1987). *Ladybug.* Morristown, NJ: Silver Burdett.

Westcott, N. B. (1989). *Skip to my Lou.* Boston: Little, Brown.

Westcott, N. B. (1994). *Never take a pig to lunch: And other poems about the fun of eating.* New York: Orchard.

White, E. B. (1980). *Charlotte's web.* New York: Harper-Collins.

Wiesner, D. (1991). *Tuesday.* New York: Clarion.

Williams, S. (1989). *I went walking.* San Diego: Harcourt Brace Jovanovich.

Williams, S. A. (1992). *Working cotton.* San Diego: Harcourt Brace Jovanovich.

Williams, V. B. (1982). *A chair for my mother.* New York: Mulberry.

Winter, J. (1988). *Follow the drinking gourd.* New York: Knopf.

Wittels, H., & Greisman, J. (1985). *A first thesaurus.* Racine, WI: Western.

Wong, J. S. (1994). *Good luck gold and other poems.* New York: McElderry Books.

Wood, A. (1982). *Quick as a cricket.* London: Child's Play.

Yolen, J. (1980). *Commander Toad in space.* New York: Coward McCann.

Yolen, J. (1986). *The sleeping beauty.* New York: Knopf.

Yolen, J. (1987). *Owl moon.* New York: Philomel.

Yolen, J. (1992). *Encounter.* Orlando: Harcourt Brace.

Yolen, J. (1992). *A letter from Phoenix Farm.* Katonah, NY: Richard C. Owen.

Yolen, J. (1993). *Welcome to the green house.* New York: Putnam.

Young, E. (1979). *The lion and the mouse.* New York: Putnam.

Zemach, M. (1983). *The little red hen.* New York: Farrar, Straus & Giroux.

Ziefert, H. (1986). *A new coat for Anna.* New York: Knopf.

Zolotow, C. (1992). *This quiet lady.* New York: Greenwillow.

APPENDIX A

Award-Winning Books for Children

Caldecott Medal Books

The Caldecott Medal is named in honor of Randolph Caldecott (1846–86), a British illustrator of children's books. The award is presented by the American Library Association each year to "the artist of the most distinguished American picture book for children" published during the preceding year. The award was first given in 1938 and is awarded annually. The winning book receives the Caldecott Medal, and one or more runners-up are also recognized as "Honor" books.

1997 *Golem,* David Wisniewski (Clarion). **Honor books:** *Hush! A Thai Lullaby,* Minfong Ho, illustrated by Holly Meade (Orchard); *The Graphic Alphabet,* David Pelletier (Orchard); *The Paperboy,* Dav Pilkey (Orchard); *Starry Messenger,* Peter Sis (Farrar, Straus & Giroux).

1996 *Officer Buckle and Gloria,* Peggy Rathmann (Putnam). **Honor books:** *Alphabet city,* Stephen T. Johnson (Viking); *Zin! Zin! Zin! A violin,* Lloyd Moss, illustrated by Marjorie Priceman (Simon & Schuster); *The faithful friend,* Robert D. San Souci, illustrated by Brian Pinkney (Simon & Schuster); *Tops and bottoms,* Janet Stevens (Harcourt & Brace).

1995 *Smoky night,* Eve Bunting, illustrated by David Diaz (Harcourt & Brace). **Honor books:** *Swamp angel,* Anne Isaacs, illustrated by Paul O. Zelinsky (Dutton); *John Henry,* Julius Lester (Dial); *Time flies,* Eric Rohmann (Crown).

1994 *Grandfather's journey,* Allen Say (Houghton Mifflin). **Honor books:** *Peppe the lamplighter,* Elisa Bartone (Lothrop); *In the small, small pond,* Denis Fleming (Holt); *Owen,* Kevin Henkes (Greenwillow); *Raven: A trickster tale from the Pacific northwest,* Gerald McDermott (Harcourt Brace Jovanovich); *Yo! Yes?* Chris Raschak (Orchard).

1993 *Mirette on the high wire,* Emily McCully (Putnam). **Honor books:** *Seven blind mice,* Ed Young (Philomel); *The stinky cheese man and other fairly stupid tales,* Jon Scieszka, illustrated by Lane Smith (Viking); *Working cotton,* Sherley Anne Williams, illustrated by Carole Byard (Harcourt Brace Jovanovich).

1992 *Tuesday,* David Wiesner (Clarion). **Honor book:** *Tar beach,* Faith Ringgold (Crown).

1991 *Black and white,* David Macaulay (Houghton Mifflin). **Honor books:** *Puss in boots,* Charles Perrault, illustrated by Fred Marcellino (Farrar, Straus & Giroux); *"More, more, more" said the baby,* Vera B. Williams (Morrow).

1990 *Lon Po Po, A Red Riding Hood story from China,* Ed Young (Philomel). **Honor books:** *Bill Peet: An autobiography,* William Peet (Houghton Mifflin); *Color zoo,* Lois Ehlert (Lippincott); *Herschel and the Hanukkah goblins,* Eric A. Kimmel, illustrated by Trina Schart Hyman (Holiday House); *The talking eggs,* Robert D. San Souci, illustrated by Jerry Pickney (Dial).

1989 *Song and dance man,* Jane Ackerman, illustrated by Stephen Gammel (Knopf). **Honor books:** *Goldilocks,* James Marshall (Dial); *The boy of the three-year nap,* Diane Snyder, illustrated by Allen Say (Houghton Mifflin); *Mirandy and Brother Wind,* Patricia McKissack, illustrated by Jerry Pickney (Knopf); *Free Fall,* David Wiesner (Lothrop).

1988 *Owl moon,* Jane Yolen, illustrated by John Schoenherr (Philomel). **Honor book:** *Mufaro's beautiful daughters: An African tale,* John Steptoe (Morrow).

1987 *Hey, Al,* Arthur Yorinks, illustrated by Richard Egielski (Farrah, Straus & Giroux). **Honor books:** *Alphabatics,* Suse MacDonald (Bradbury); *Rumplestiltskin,* Paul O. Zelinsky (E. P. Dutton); *The village of round and square houses,* Ann Grifalconi (Little, Brown).

1986 *The polar express,* Chris Van Allsburg (Houghton Mifflin). **Honor books:** *King Bidgood's in the bathtub,* Audrey Wood (Harcourt Brace Jovanovich); *The relatives came,* Cynthia Rylant (Bradbury).

1985 *Saint George and the dragon,* Margaret Hodges, illustrated by Trina Schart Hyman (Little, Brown). **Honor books:** *Hansel and Gretel,* Rika Lesser, illustrated by Paul O. Zelinsky (Dodd, Mead); *Have you seen my duckling?* Nancy Tafuri (Greenwillow); *The story of jumping mouse,* John Steptoe (Lothrop, Lee & Shepard).

1984 *The glorious flight: Across the channel with Louis Bleriot,* Alice and Martin Provensen (Viking). **Honor books:** *Little red riding hood,* Trina Schart Hyman (Holiday); *Ten, nine, eight,* Molly Bang (Greenwillow).

1983 *Shadow,* Blaise Cendrars, translated and illustrated by Marcia Brown (Scribner). **Honor books:** *A chair for my mother,* Vera B. Williams (Greenwillow); *When I was young in the mountains,* Cynthia Rylant, illustrated by Diane Goode (E. P. Dutton).

1982 *Jumanji,* Chris Van Allsburg (Houghton Mifflin). **Honor books:** *On Market Street,* Arnold Lobel, illustrated by Anita Lobel (Greenwillow); *Outside over there,* Maurice Sendak (Harper & Row); *A visit to William Blake's inn: Poems for innocent and experienced travelers,*

Nancy Willard, illustrated by Alice and Martin Provensen (Harcourt Brace Jovanovich); *Where the buffaloes begin,* Olaf Baker, illustrated by Stephen Gammell (Warne).

1981 *Fables,* Arnold Lobel (Harper & Row). **Honor books:** *The Bremen-Town musicians,* Ilse Plume (Doubleday); *The gray lady and the strawberry snatcher,* Molly Bang (Four Winds); *Mice twice,* Joseph Low (Atheneum); *Truck,* Donald Crews (Greenwillow).

1980 *Ox-cart man,* Donald Hall, illustrated by Barbara Cooney (Viking); **Honor books:** *Ben's trumpet,* Rachel Isadora (Greenwillow); *The garden of Abdul Gasazi,* Chris Van Allsburg (Houghton Mifflin); *The treasure,* Uri Shulevitz (Farrar, Straus & Giroux).

1979 *The girl who loved wild horses,* Paul Goble (Bradbury). **Honor books:** *Freight train,* Donald Crews (Greenwillow); *The way to start a day,* Byrd Baylor, illustrated by Peter Parnall (Scribner).

1978 *Noah's ark: The story of the flood,* Peter Spier (Doubleday), **Honor books:** *Castle,* David Macaulay (Houghton Mifflin); *It could always be worse,* Margot Zemach (Farrar, Straus & Giroux).

1977 *Ashanti to Zulu,* Margaret Musgrove, illustrated by Leo and Diane Dillon (Dial). **Honor books:** *The amazing bone,* William Steig (Farrar, Straus & Giroux); *The contest,* Nonny Hogrogian (Greenwillow); *Fish for supper,* M. B. Goffstein (Dial); *The Golem: A Jewish legend,* Beverly Brodsky McDermott (J. B. Lippincott); *Hawk, I'm your brother,* Byrd Baylor, illustrated by Peter Parnall (Scribner).

1976 *Why mosquitoes buzz in people's ears,* Verna Aardema, illustrated by Leo and Diane Dillon (Dial). **Honor books:** *The desert is theirs,* Byrd Baylor (Scribner), illustrated by Peter Parnall; *Strega Nona,* Tomie de Paola (Prentice-Hall).

1975 *Arrow to the sun,* Gerald McDermott (Viking). **Honor book:** *Jambo means hello: A Swahili alphabet book,* Muriel Feelings, illustrated by Tom Feelings (Dial).

1974 *Duffy and the devil,* Harve and Margo Zemach (Farrar, Straus & Giroux). **Honor books:** *Cathedral: The story of its construction,* David Macaulay (Houghton Mifflin); *The three jovial huntsmen,* Susan Jeffers (Bradbury).

1973 *The funny little woman,* Arlen Mosel, illustrated by Blair Lent (E. P. Dutton). **Honor books:** *Hosie's alphabet,* Hosea, Tobias, and Lisa Baskin, illustrated by Leonard Baskin (Viking); *Snow-White and the seven dwarfs,* translated by Randall Jarrell from the Brothers Grimm, illustrated by Nancy Ekholm Burkert (Farrar, Straus & Giroux); *When clay sings,* Byrd Baylor, illustrated by Tom Bahti (Scribner).

1972 *One fine day,* Nonny A. Hogrogian (Macmillan). **Honor books:** *Hildilid's night,* Cheli Duran Ryan, illustrated by Arnold Lobel (Macmillan); *If all the seas were one sea,* Janina Domanska (Macmillan); *Moja means one: Swahili counting book,* Muriel Feelings, illustrated by Tom Feelings (Dial).

1971 *A story, a story.* Gail E. Haley (Atheneum). **Honor books:** *The angry moon,* William Sleator, illustrated by

Blair Lent (Atlantic-Little); *Frog and Toad are friends,* Arnold Lobel (Harper & Row); *In the night kitchen,* Maurice Sendak (Harper & Row).

1970 *Sylvester and the magic pebble,* William Steig (Windmill/Simon & Schuster). **Honor books:** *Alexander and the wind-up mouse,* Leo Lionni (Pantheon); *Goggles!* Ezra Jack Keats (Macmillan); *The judge: An untrue tale,* Harve Zemach, illustrated by Margot Zemach (Farrar, Straus & Giroux); *Pop Corn and Ma Goodness,* Edna Mitchell Preston, illustrated by Robert Andrew Parker (Viking); *Thy friend, Obadiah,* Brinton Turkle (Viking).

1969 *The fool of the world and the flying ship,* Arthur Ransome, illustrated by Uri Shulevitz (Farrar, Straus & Giroux). **Honor book:** *Why the sun and the moon live in the sky: An African folktale,* Elphinstone Dayrell, illustrated by Blair Lent (Houghton Mifflin).

1968 *Drummer Hoff,* Barbara Emberley, illustrated by Ed Emberley (Prentice-Hall). **Honor books:** *Frederick,* Leo Lionni (Pantheon); *Seashore story,* Taro Yashima (Viking); *The emperor and the kite,* Jane Yolen, illustrated by Ed Young (Harcourt Brace Jovanovich).

1967 *Sam, Bangs & Moonshine,* Evaline Ness (Holt, Rinehart & Winston). **Honor book:** *One wide river to cross,* Barbara Emberley, illustrated by Ed Emberley (Prentice-Hall).

1966 *Always room for one more,* Sorche Nic Leodhas, illustrated by Nonny Hogrogian (Holt). **Honor books:** *Hide and seek fog,* Alvin Tresselt, illustrated by Roger Duvoisin (Lothrop); *Just me,* Marie Hall Ets (Viking); *Tom tit tot,* Evaline Ness (Scribner).

1965 *May I bring a friend?* Beatrice Schenk de Regniers, illustrated by Beni Montresor (Atheneum). **Honor books:** *Rain makes applesauce,* Julian Scheer, illustrated by Marvin Bileck (Holiday House; *The wave,* Margaret Hodges, illustrated by Blair Lent (Houghton Mifflin); *A pocketful of cricket,* Rebecca Caudill, illustrated by Evaline Ness (Holt).

1964 *Where the wild things are,* Maurice Sendak (Harper & Row). **Honor books:** *Swimmy,* Leo Lionni (Pantheon); *All in the morning early,* Sorche Nic Leodhas, illustrated by Evaline Ness (Holt); *Mother Goose and nursery rhymes,* illustrated by Philip Reed (Atheneum).

1963 *The snow day,* Ezra Jack Keats (Viking). **Honor books:** *The sun is a golden earring,* Natalia M. Belting, illustrated by Bernarda Bryson (Holt); *Mr. Rabbit and the lovely present,* Charlotte Zolotow, illustrated by Maurice Sendak (Harper & Row).

1962 *Once a mouse . . . ,* Marcia Brown (Scribner). **Honor books:** *The fox went out on a chilly night: An old song,* Peter Spier (Doubleday); *Little bear's visit,* Else Holmelund Minarik, illustrated by Maurice Sendak (Harper & Row); *The day we saw the sun come up,* Alice E. Goudey, illustrated by Adrienne Adams (Scribner).

1961 *Baboushka and the three kings,* Ruth Robbins, illustrated by Nicolas Sidjakov (Parnassus). **Honor book:** *Inch by inch,* Leo Lionni (Obolensky).

1960 *Nine days to Christmas,* Marie Hall Ets & Aurora Labastida, illustrated by Marie Hall Ets (Viking). **Honor**

books: *Houses from the sea*, Alice E. Goudey, illustrated by Adrienne Adams (Scribner); *The moon jumpers*, Janice May Udry, illustrated by Maurice Sendak (Harper & Row).

Newbery Medal Books

The Newbery Medal is named in honor of John Newbery (1713–67), a British publisher and bookseller in the 1700s. Newbery is known as the "father of children's literature" because he was the first to propose publishing books specifically for children. The award is presented each year by the American Library Association to "the author of the most distinguished contribution to American literature for children" published during the preceding year. The award was first given in 1922 and is awarded annually. The winning book receives the Newbery Medal, and one or more runners-up are also recognized as "Honor" books.

1997 *View from Saturday*, E. L. Konigsburg (Atheneum). **Honor books:** *A Girl Named Disaster*, Nancy Farmer (Orchard); *Moorchild*, Eloise McGraw (McElderry); *The Thief*, Megan Whalen Turner (Greenwillow); *Belle Prater's Boy*, Ruth White (Farrar, Straus & Giroux).

1996 *The midwife's apprentice*, Karen Cushman (Clarion). **Honor books:** *What Jamie saw*, Carolyn Coman (Front Street); *The Watsons go to Birmingham—1963*, Christopher Paul Curtis (Delacorte); *Yolanda's genius*, Carol Fenner (McElderry); *The great fire*, Jim Murphy (Scholastic).

1995 *Walk two moons*, Sharon Creech (HarperCollins). **Honor books:** *Catherine called Birdy*, Karen Cushman (Clarion); *The ear, the eye and the arm*, Nancy Farmer (Orchard).

1994 *The giver*, Lois Lowry (Houghton Mifflin). **Honor books:** *Crazy Lady!*, Jane Leslie Conly (HarperCollins); *Dragon's gate*, Laurence Yep (HarperCollins); *Eleanor Roosevelt: A life of discovery*, Russell Freedman (Clarion).

1993 *Missing May*, Cynthia Rylant (Orchard). **Honor books:** *The dark-thirty: Southern tales of the supernatural*, Patricia McKissack (Knopf); *Somewhere in the darkness*, Walter Dean Myers (Scholastic); *What hearts*, Bruce Books (HarperCollins).

1992 *Shiloh*, Phyllis Reynolds Naylor (Atheneum). **Honor books:** *Nothing but the truth*, Avi (Orchard); *The Wright brothers: How they invented the airplane*, Russell Freedman (Holiday).

1991 *Maniac Magee*, Jerry Spinelli (Little, Brown). **Honor book:** *The true confessions of Charlotte Doyle*, Avi (Orchard).

1990 *Number the stars*, Lois Lowry (Houghton Mifflin). **Honor books:** *Afternoon of the elves*, Janet Taylor Lisel (Orchard); *Shabanu, daughter of the wind*, Susan Fisher Staples (Knopf); *The winter room*, Gary Paulsen (Orchard).

1989 *Joyful noise: Poems for two voices*, Paul Fleishman (Harper & Row). **Honor books:** *In the beginning*, Virginia Hamilton (Harcourt Brace Jovanovich); *Scorpions*, Walter Dean Myers (Harper & Row).

1988 *Lincoln: A photobiography*, Russell Freedman (Clarion). **Honor books:** *After the rain*, Norma Fox Mazer (Morrow); *Hatchet*, Gary Paulsen (Bradbury).

1987 *The whipping boy*, Sid Fleischman (Greenwillow). **Honor books:** *A fine white dust*, Cynthia Rylant (Bradbury); *On my honor*, Marion Dane Bauer (Clarion); *Volcano: The eruption and healing of Mount St. Helen's*, Patricia Lauber (Bradbury).

1986 *Sarah, plain and tall*, Patricia MacLachlan (Harper & Row). **Honor books:** *Commodore Perry in the land of the Shogun*, Rhoda Blumberg (Lothrop, Lee & Shepard); *Dog song*, Gary Paulsen (Bradbury).

1985 *The hero and the crown*, Robin McKinley (Greenwillow). **Honor books:** *Like Jake and me*, Mavis Jukes (Alfred A. Knopf); *The moves make the man*, Bruce Brooks (Harper & Row); *One-eyed cat*, Paula Fox (Bradbury).

1984 *Dear Mr. Henshaw*, Beverly Clearly (Morrow). **Honor books:** *The sign of the beaver*, Elizabeth George Speare (Houghton Mifflin); *A solitary blue*, Cynthia Voigt (Atheneum); *Sugaring time*, Kathryn Lasky (Macmillan); *The wish giver*, Bill Brittain (Harper & Row).

1983 *Dicey's song*, Cynthia Voigt (Atheneum). **Honor books:** *The blue sword*, Robin McKinley (Greenwillow); *Doctor DeSoto*, William Steig (Farrar, Straus & Giroux); *Graven images*, Paul Fleischman (Harper & Row); *Homesick: My own story*, Jean Fritz (Putnam); *Sweet Whispers, Brother Rush*, Virginia Hamilton (Philomel).

1982 *A visit to William Blake's inn: Poems for innocent and experienced travelers*, Nancy Willard (Harcourt Brace Jovanovich). **Honor books:** *Ramona Quimby, age 8*, Beverly Clearly (Morrow); *Upon the head of the goat: A childhood in Hungary, 1939–1944*, Aranka Siegal (Farrar, Straus & Giroux).

1981 *Jacob have I loved*, Katherine Paterson (Crowell). **Honor books:** *The fledgling*, Jane Langton (Harper & Row); *A ring of endless light*, Madeleine L'Engle (Farrar, Straus & Giroux).

1980 *A gathering of days: A New England girl's journal, 1830–1832*, Joan W. Blos (Scribner). **Honor book:** *The road from home: The story of an Armenian girl*, David Kerdian (Greenwillow).

1979 *The westing game*, Ellen Raskin (Dutton). **Honor book:** *The great Gilly Hopkins*, Katherine Paterson (Crowell).

1978 *Bridge to Terabithia*, Katherine Paterson (Crowell). **Honor books:** *Anpao: An American Indian odyssey*, Jamake Highwater (Lippincott); *Ramona and her father*, Beverly Clearly (Morrow).

1977 *Roll of thunder, hear my cry*, Mildred Taylor (Dial). **Honor books:** *Abel's Island*, William Steig (Farrar, Straus & Giroux); *A string in the harp*, Nancy Bond (Atheneum).

1976 *The grey king*, Susan Cooper (Atheneum). **Honor books:** *Dragonwings*, Laurence Yep (Harper & Row); *The hundred penny box*, Sharon Bell Mathis (Viking).

1975 *M. C. Higgins, the great*, Virginia Hamilton (Macmillan). **Honor books:** *Figgs and phantoms*, Ellen Raskin (E. P. Dutton); *My brother Sam is dead*, James Lincoln

Collier and Christopher Collier (Four Winds); *The perilous guard*, Elizabeth Marie Pope (Houghton Mifflin); *Philip Hall likes me, I reckon maybe*, Bette Green (Dial).

1974   *The slave dancer*, Paula Fox (Bradbury). **Honor book:** *The dark is rising*, Susan Cooper (Atheneum).

1973   *Julie of the wolves*, Jean C. George (Harper & Row). **Honor books:** *Frog and Toad together*, Arnold Lobel (Harper & Row); *The upstairs room*, Johanna Reiss (Crowell); *The witches of worm*, Zilpha Keatley Snyder (Atheneum).

1972   *Mrs. Frisby and the rats of NIMH*, Robert C. O'Brien (Atheneum). **Honor books:** *Annie and the old one*, Miska Miles (Atlantic-Little); *The headless cupid*, Zilpha Keatley Snyder (Atheneum); *Incident at Hawk's Hill*, Allan W. Eckert (Little, Brown); *The planet of Junior Brown*, Virginia Hamilton (Macmillan); *The tombs of Atuan*, Ursula K. LeGuin (Atheneum).

1971   *The summer of the swans*, Betsy Byars (Viking). **Honor books:** *Enchantress from the stars*, Sylvia Louise Engdahl (Atheneum); *Kneeknock rise*, Natalie Babbitt (Farrar, Straus & Giroux); *Sing down the moon*, Scott O'Dell (Houghton Mifflin).

1970   *Sounder*, William Armstrong (Harper & Row). **Honor books:** *Journey outside*, Mary Q. Steele (Viking); *Our Eddie*, Sulamith Ish-Kishor (Pantheon); *The many ways of seeing, An introduction to the pleasures of art*, Janet Gaylord Moore (Harcourt Brace Jovanovich).

1969   *The high king*, Lloyd Alexander (Holt, Rinehart & Winston). **Honor books:** *To be a slave*, Julius Lester (Dial); *When Shlemiel went to Warsaw and other stories*, Isaac Bashevis Singer (Farrar, Straus & Giroux).

1968   *From the mixed-up files of Mrs. Basil E. Frankweiler*, E. L. Konigsburg (Atheneum). **Honor books:** *The black pearl*, Scott O'Dell (Houghton Mifflin); *The Egypt game*, Zilpha Keatley Snyder (Atheneum); *The fearsome inn*, Isaac Bashevis Singer (Scribner); *Jennifer, Hecate, Macbeth, William McKinley, and me, Elizabeth*, E. L. Konigsburg (Atheneum).

1967   *Up a road slowly*, Irene Hunt (Follett). **Honor books:** *The jazz man*, Mary Hays Weik (Atheneum); *The King's Fifth*, Scott O'Dell (Houghton Mifflin); *Zlateh the goat and other stories*, Isaac Bashevis Singer (Harper & Row).

1966   *I, Juan de Pareja*, Elizabeth Borton de Trevino (Farrar, Straus & Giroux). **Honor books:** *The animal family*, Randall Jarrell (Pantheon); *The black cauldron*, Lloyd Alexander (Holt, Rinehart & Winston); *The noonday friends*, Mary Stolz (Harper & Row).

1965   *Shadow of a bull*, Maia Wojciechowska (Atheneum). **Honor book:** *Across five Aprils*, Irene Hunt (Follett).

1964   *It's like this, cat*, Emily Neville (Harper & Row). **Honor books:** *The loner*, Ester Wier (McKay); *Rascal*, Sterling North (E. P. Dutton).

1963   *A wrinkle in time*, Madeleine L'Engle (Farrar, Straus & Giroux). **Honor books:** *Thistle and thyme: Tales and Legends from Scotland*, Sorche Nic Leodhas (Holt); *Men of Athens*, Olivia Coolidge (Houghton Mifflin).

1962   *The bronze bow*, Elizabeth George Speare (Houghton Mifflin). **Honor books:** *Frontier living*, Edwin Tunis (World); *The golden goblet*, Eloise McGraw (Coward); *Belling the tiger*, Mary Stolz (Harper & Row).

1961   *Island of the blue dolphins*, Scott O'Dell (Houghton Mifflin). **Honor books:** *America moves forward*, Gerald W. Johnson (Morrow); *Old Ramon*, Jack Schaefer (Houghton Mifflin); *The cricket in Times Square*, George Selden (Farrar, Straus & Giroux).

1960   *Onion John*, Joseph Krumgold (Crowell). **Honor books:** *My side of the mountain*, Jean Craighead George (Dutton); *America is born*, Gerald W. Johnson (Morrow); *The gammage cup*, Carol Kendall (Harcourt Brace Jovanovich).

APPENDIX B

Resources About Authors and Illustrators

Books About Authors and Illustrators

Aardema, Verna Aardema, V. (1992). *A bookworm who hatched.* Katonah, NY: Richard C. Owen (P–M)*

Andersen, Hans Christian Greene, C. (1991). *Hans Christian Andersen: Prince of storytellers.* Chicago: Childrens Press. (P–M)

Asch, Frank Asch, F. (1997). *One man show.* Katonah, NY: Richard C. Owen. (P–M)

Blegvad, Erik Blegvad, E. (1979). *Self-portrait: Erik Blegvad.* Reading, MA: Addison-Wesley, (P–M–U)

Brown, Margaret Wise Brown, M. W. (1994). *The days before now.* New York: Simon & Schuster. (P–M) Greene, C. (1993). *Margaret Wise Brown: Author of Goodnight Moon.* Chicago: Childrens Press. (P–M)

Bunting, Eve Bunting, E. (1995). *Once upon a time.* Katonah, NY: Richard C. Owen. (P–M)

Burnett, Frances Hodgson Carpenter, A. S., & Shirley, J. (1990). *Frances Hodgson Burnett: Beyond the secret garden.* Minneapolis: Lerner Books. (U)

Byars, Betsy Byars, B. (1991). *The moon and I.* New York: Messner. (M–U)

Carson, Rachel Wadsworth, G. (1991). *Rachel Carson: Voice for the earth.* Minneapolis: Lerner Books. (U)

Cleary, Beverly Cleary, B. (1988). *A girl from Yamhill: A memoir.* New York: Morrow (M–U)

Cole, Joanna Cole, J. (1996). *On the bus with Joanna Cole.* Portsmouth, NH: Heinemann. (M–U)

Cowley, Joy Cowley, J. (1988). *Seventy kilometres from ice cream: A letter from Joy Cowley.* Katonah, NY: Richard C. Owen. (P)

Dahl, Roald Dahl, R. (1984). *Boy: Tales of childhood.* New York: Farrar, Straus & Giroux. (M–U)

de Paola, Tomie de Paola, T. (1989). *The art lesson.* New York: Putnam. (P)

Dillon, Leo and Diane Preiss, B. (1981). *The art of Leo and Diane Dillon.* New York: Ballantine. (M–U)

Dr. Seuss Weidt, M. N. (1994). *Oh, the places he went: A story about Dr. Seuss—Theodor Seuss Geisel.* Minneapolis: Carolrhoda. (M)

Duncan, Lois Duncan, L. (1982). *Chapters: My growth as a writer.* Boston: Little, Brown. (U)

Ehlert, Lois Ehlert, L. (1996). *Under my nose.* Katonah, NY: Richard C. Owen. (P–M)

Fritz, Jean Fritz, J. (1982). *Homesick: My own story.* New York: Putnam (M–U); Fritz, J. (1992). *Surprising myself.* Katonah, NY: Richard C. Owen. (M)

Goble, Paul Goble, P. (1994). *Hau kola/ Hello friend.* Katonah, NY: Richard C. Owen. (M)

Goodall, John Goodall, J. S. (1981). *Before the war, 1908–1939. An autobiography in pictures.* New York: Atheneum. (M–U)

Heller, Ruth Heller, R. (1996). *Fine lines.* Katonah, NY: Richard C. Owen. (P–M)

Henry, Marguerite Henry, M. (1980). *The illustrated Marguerite Henry.* Chicago: Rand McNally. (M–U)

Hinton, S. E. Daly, J. (1989). *Presenting S. E. Hinton.* Boston: Twayne. (U)

Hopkins, Lee Bennett Hopkins, L. B. (1992). *The writing bug.* Katonah, NY: Richard C. Owen. (M)

Howe, James Howe, J. (1994). *Playing with words.* Katonah, NY: Richard C. Owen. (M)

Hughes, Langston Cooper, F. (1994). *Coming home: From the life of Langston Hughes.* New York: Philomel. (M–U)

Hyman, Trina Schart Hyman, T. S. (1981). *Self-portrait: Trina Schart Hyman.* Reading, MA: Addison-Wesley. (P–M–U).

Kuskin, Karla Kuskin, K. (1995). *Thoughts, pictures, and words.* Katonah, NY: Richard C. Owen. (M)

Lester, Helen Lester, H. (1997). *Author: A true story.* Boston: Houghton Mifflin. (P–M)

Lewis, C. S. Lewis, C. S. (1985). *Letters to children.* New York: Macmillan. (M–U)

Lyon, George Ella Lyon, G. E. (1996). *A wordful child.* Katonah, NY: Richard C. Owen. (P–M)

Mahy, Margaret Mahy, M. (1995). *My mysterious world.* Katonah, NY: Richard C. Owen. (M)

McKissack, Patricia McKissack, P. (1997). *Can you imagine?* Katonah, NY: Richard C. Owen. (P–M)

McPhail, David McPhail, D. (1996). *In flight with David McPhail.* Portsmouth, NH: Heinemann. (P–M)

Meltzer, Milton Meltzer, M. (1988). *Starting from home: A writer's beginnings.* NY: Viking. (U)

Mohr, Nicholasa Mohr, N. (1994). *Nicholasa Mohr: Growing up inside the sanctuary of my imagination.* New York: Messner. (U)

Naylor, Phyllis Naylor, P. R. (1978). *How I came to be a writer.* New York: Atheneum. (U)

Pallotta, Jerry. Ryan, P. (1993). *Chasing the alphabet: The story of children's author Jerry Pallotta.* Boston, MA: Shining Sea Press. (M)

---

*P = primary grades (K–2); M = middle grades (3–5); U = upper grades (6–8).

Peck, Richard   Peck, R. (1991). *Anonymously yours.* New York: Messner. (U)

Peet, Bill   Peet, B. (1989). *Bill Peet: An autobiography.* Boston: Houghton Mifflin. (M–U)

Polacco, Patricia   Polacco, P. (1994). *Fire talking.* Katonah, NY: Richard C. Owen. (M)

Potter, Beatrix   Aldis, D. (1969). *Nothing is impossible: The story of Beatrix Potter.* New York: Atheneum. (M); Collins, D. R. (1989). *The country artist: A story about Beatrix Potter.* Minneapolis: Carolrhoda. (M)

Rylant, Cynthia   Rylant, C. (1992). *Best wishes.* Katonah, NY: Richard C. Owen. (P–M)

Singer, Isaac Bashevis   Singer, I. B. (1969). *A day of pleasure: Stories of a boy growing up in Warsaw.* New York: Farrar, Straus & Giroux. (U)

Stevens, Janet   Stevens, J. (1995). *From pictures to words: A book about making a book.* New York: Holiday House. (P–M)

Uchida, Yoshiko   Uchida, U. (1991). *The invisible thread.* New York: Messner. (U)

Wilder, Laura Ingalls   Blair, G. (1981). *Laura Ingalls Wilder.* New York: Putnam. (P–M); Greene, C. (1990). *Laura Ingalls Wilder: Author of the Little House books.* Chicago: Childrens Press. (P–M)

Yep, Laurence   Yep, L. (1991). *The lost garden: A memoir.* New York: Messner. (U)

Yolen, Jane   Yolen, J. (1992). *A letter from Phoenix Farm.* Katonah, NY: Richard C. Owen. (P–M–U)

Zemach, Margot   Zemach, M. (1978). *Self-portrait: Margot Zemach.* Reading, MA: Addison-Wesley. (P–M–U)

Individual Articles Profiling Authors and Illustrators

Adoff, Arnold   White, M. L. (1988). Profile: Arnold Adoff. *Language Arts, 65,* 584–591.

Alexander, Lloyd   Greenlaw, M. J. (1984). Profile: Lloyd Alexander. *Language Arts, 61,* 406–413; Tunnell, M. O. (1989). An interview with Lloyd Alexander. *The New Advocate, 2,* 83–96.

Anno, Mitsumasa   Aoki, H. (1983). A conversation with Mitsumasa Anno. *Horn Book Magazine, 59,* 132–145; Swinger, A. K. (1987). Profile: Mitsumasa Anno's journey. *Language Arts, 64,* 762–766.

Baker, Keith   Baker, K. (1993). "Have you ever been dead?" Questions and letters from children. *The Reading Teacher, 46,* 372–375.

Baylor, Byrd   Bosma, B. (1987). Profile: Byrd Baylor. *Language Arts, 64,* 315–318.

Brett, Jan   Raymond, A. (April, 1992). Jan Brett: Making it look easy. *Teaching PreK–8, 22,* 38–40.

Brown, Marcia   Brown, M. (1983). Caldecott Medal Acceptance. *Horn Book Magazine, 59,* 414–422.

Brown, Margaret Wise   Hurd, C. (1983). Remembering Margaret Wise Brown. *Horn Book Magazine, 59,* 553–560.

Browne, Anthony   Marantz, S., & Marantz, K. (1985). An interview with Anthony Browne. *Horn Book Magazine, 61,* 696–704.

Bryan, Ashley   Marantz, S., & Marantz, K. (1988). Interview with Ashley Bryan. *Horn Book Magazine, 64,* 173–179; Swinger, A. K. (1984). Profile: Ashley Bryan. *Language Arts, 61,* 305–311.

Bunting, Eve   Raymond, A. (October, 1986). Eve Bunting: From Ireland with love. *Teaching PreK–8, 17,* 38–40.

Byars, Betsy   Robertson, I. (1980). Profile: Betsy Byars—Writer for today's child. *Language Arts, 57,* 328–334.

Carle, Eric   Yolen, J. (1988). In the artist's studio: Eric Carle. *The New Advocate, 1,* 148–154.

Ciardi, John   Odland, N. (1982). Profile: John Ciardi. *Language Arts, 59,* 872–876.

Cleary, Beverly   Cleary, B. (1984). Newbery Medal acceptance. *Horn Book Magazine, 50,* 429–438; Reuter, D. (1984). Beverly Cleary, *Horn Book Magazine, 50,* 439–443.

Clifton, Lucille   Sims, R. (1982). Profile: Lucille Clifton. *Language Arts, 59,* 160–167.

Collier, James and Christopher   Raymond, A. (January, 1988). Meet James and Christopher Collier. *Teaching PreK–8, 18,* 35–38.

Conrad, Pam   Raymond, A. (November/December, 1990). Pam Conrad: She said to herself, "Now what?" *Teaching PreK–8, 21,* 38–40.

Creech, Sharon   An interview with Sharon Creech, 1995 Newbery Medal winner. (1996). *The Reading Teacher, 49,* 380–382.

Degan, Bruce   Elliot, I. (October, 1991). Bruce Degan: Doing what he likes best. *Teaching PreK–8, 21,* 44–47.

Diaz, David   Conversation with a winner—David Diaz talks about *Smoky Night.* (1996). *The Reading Teacher, 49,* 386–388.

Dillon, Leo and Diane   Cummings, P. (1992). *Talking with artists* (pp. 22–29). New York: Bradbury Press.

Dr. Seuss   Roth, R. (1989). On beyond zebra with Dr. Seuss. *The New Advocate, 2,* 213–226.

Egielski, Richard   Cummings, P. (1992). *Talking with artists* (pp. 30–35). New York: Bradbury Press; Egielski, R. (1987). Caldecott Medal acceptance. *Horn Book Magazine, 63,* 433–435; Yorinks, A. (1987). Richard Egielski. *Horn Book Magazine, 63,* 436–438.

Ehlert, Lois   Cummings, P. (1992). *Talking with artists* (pp. 36–41). New York: Bradbury Press.

Feelings, Tom   Feelings, T. (1985). The artist at work: Technique and the artist's vision. *Horn Book Magazine, 61,* 685–695.

Fleischman, Sid   Fleischman, P. (1987). Sid Fleischman. *Horn Book Magazine, 63,* 429–432; Fleischman, S. (1987). Newbery Medal acceptance. *Horn Book Magazine, 63,* 423–438; Johnson, E. R. (1982). Profile: Sid Fleischman. *Language Arts, 59,* 754–759.

Fox, Mem   Manning, M., & Manning, G. (March, 1990). Mem Fox: Mem's the word in down under? *Teaching PreK–8, 20,* 29–31; Phelan, C. (1993, May). Talking with Mem Fox, *Book Links,* 29–32.

Freedman, Russell   Dempsey, F. J. (1988). Russell Freedman. *Horn Book Magazine, 64,* 452–456; Freedman, R. (1988). Newbery Medal acceptance. *Horn Book Magazine, 64,* 444–451.

Fritz, Jean Ammon, R. (1983). Profile: Jean Fritz, *Language Arts, 60,* 365–369; Fritz, J. (1985). Turning history inside out. *Horn Book Magazine, 61,* 29–34; Heins, E. L. (1986). Presentation of the Laura Ingalls Wilder Medal. *Horn Book Magazine, 62,* 430–431.

Gerstein, Mordicai Yolen, J. (1990). In the artist's studio: Mordicai Gerstein. *The New Advocate, 3,* 25–28.

Giff, Patricia Reilly Raymond, A. (April, 1987). Patricia Reilly Giff: A writer who believes in reading. *Teaching PreK–8, 17,* 34–37.

Gilson, Jamie Johnson, R. (1983). Profile: Jamie Gilson. *Language Arts, 60,* 661–667.

Goble, Paul Stott, J. C. (1984). Profile: Paul Goble. *Language Arts, 61,* 867–873.

Goffstein, M. B. Marantz, S., & Marantz, K. (1986). M. B. Goffstein: An interview. *Horn Book Magazine, 62,* 688–694; Shannon, G. (1983). Goffstein and friends. *Horn Book Magazine, 59,* 88–95.

Greenfield, Eloise Kiah, R. B. (1980). Profile: Eloise Greenfield. *Language Arts, 57,* 653–659.

Haley, Gail E. Haley, G. E. (1990). Of mermaids, myths, and meaning: A sea tale. *The New Advocate, 3,* 1–12.

Hamilton, Virginia Hamilton, V. (1986). Coretta Scott King Award acceptance. *Horn Book Magazine, 62,* 683–687; Garret J. (1993, January). Virginia Hamilton: 1992 Andersen winner, *Book Links,* 22–25.

Henkes, Kevin Elliot, I. (January, 1989). Meet Kevin Henkes: Young man on a roll. *Teaching PreK–8, 19,* 43–45.

Hoover, H. M. Porter, E. J. (1982). Provile: H. M. Hoover. *Language Arts, 59,* 609–613.

Howe, James Raymond, A. (February, 1987). James Howe: Corn, ham and punster cheese. *Teaching PreK–8, 17,* 32–34.

Hyman, Trina Schart Hyman, K. (1985). Trina Schart Hyman. *Horn Book Magazine, 61,* 422–425; Hyman, T. S. (1985). Caldecott Medal acceptance. *Horn Book Magazine, 61,* 410–421; Saul, W. (1988). Once-upon-a-time artist in the land of now: An interview with Trina Schart Hyman. *The New Advocate, 1,* 8–17; White, D. E. (1983). Profile: Trina Schart Hyman. *Language Arts, 60,* 782–792.

Jonas, Ann Marantz, S., & Marantz, K. (1987). Interview with Ann Jonas. *Horn Book Magazine, 63,* 308–313; Raymond, A. (December, 1987). Ann Jonas: Reflections 1987. *Teaching PreK–8, 18,* 44–46.

Keats, Ezra Jack Lanes, S. G. (1984). Ezra Jack Keats: In memoriam. *Horn Book Magazine, 60,* 551–558; Pope, M., & Pope, L. (1990). Ezra Jack Keats: A childhood revisited. *The New Advocate, 3,* 13–24.

Kellogg, Steven Cummings, P. (1992). *Talking with artists* (pp. 54–59). New York: Bradbury Press.

Konigsburg, E. L. Jones, L. T. (1986). Profile: Elaine Konigsburg. *Language Arts, 63,* 177–184.

Lasky, Kathryn Lasky, K. (1990). The fiction of history: Or, what did Miss Kitty really do? *The New Advocate, 3,* 157–166.

L'Engle, Madeleine Raymond, A. (May, 1991). Madeleine L'Engle: Getting the last laugh. *Teaching PreK–8, 21,* 34–36; Samuels, L. A. (1981). Profile: Madeleine L'Engle. *Language Arts, 58,* 704–712.

Lester, Julius Lester, J. (1988). The storyteller's voice: Reflections on the rewriting of Uncle Remus. *The New Advocate, 1,* 137–142.

Livingston, Myra Cohn Porter, E. J. (1980). Profile: Myra Cohn Livingston. *Language Arts, 57,* 901–905.

Lobel, Anita Raymond, A. (November/December, 1989). Anita Lobel: Up from the crossroad. *Teaching PreK–8, 20,* 52–55.

Lobel, Arnold Lobel, A. (1981). Caldecott Medal acceptance. *Horn Book Magazine, 57,* 400–404; Lobel, A. (1981). Arnold at home. *Horn Book Magazine, 57,* 405–410; White, D. E. (1988). Profile: Arnold Lobel. *Language Arts, 65,* 489–494.

Lowry, Lois Lowry, L. (1988). Rabble Starkey. *Horn Book Magazine, 64,* 29–31; Lowry, L. (1990). *Number the stars:* Lois Lowry's journey to the Newbery Award. *The Reading Teacher, 44,* 98–101; Raymond, A. (October, 1987). "Anastasia, " and then some. *Teaching PreK–8, 18,* 44–46; An interview with Lois Lowry, 1994 Newbery Medal winner. (1994–1995). *The Reading Teacher, 48,* 308–309.

Macaulay, David Ammon, R. (1982). Profile: David Macaulay. *Language Arts, 59,* 374–378.

MacLachlan, Patricia Babbitt, N. (1986). Patricia MacLachlan: The biography. *Horn Book Magazine, 62,* 414–416; Courtney, A. (1985). Profile: Patricia MacLachlan. *Language Arts, 62,* 783–787; MacLachlan, P. (1986). Newbery Medal acceptance. *Horn Book Magazine, 62,* 407–413; MacLachlan, R. (1986). A hypothetical dilemma. *Horn Book Magazine, 62,* 416–419; Raymond, A. (May, 1989). Patricia MacLachlan: An advocate of "Bare boning." *Teaching PreK–8, 19,* 46–48.

Martin, Bill, Jr. Larrick, N. (1982). Profile: Bill Martin, Jr. *Language Arts, 59,* 490–494.

Mayer, Marianna Raymond, A. (January, 1991). Marianna Mayer: Myths, legends, and folklore. *Teaching PreK–8, 21,* 42–44.

McCloskey, Robert Mandel, E. (1991, May). *Make way for ducklings* by Robert McCloskey. *Book Links,* 38–42.

McDermott, Gerald McDermott, G. (1988). Sky father, earth mother: An artist interprets myth. *The New Advocate, 1,* 1–7; White D. E. (1982). Profile: Gerald McDermott. *Language Arts, 59,* 273–279.

McKinley, Robin McKinley, R. (1985). Newbery Medal acceptance. *Horn Book Magazine, 61,* 395–405; Winding, T. (1985). Robin McKinley. *Horn Book Magazine, 61,* 406–409.

McKissack, Patricia Bishop, R. S. (1992). A conversation with Patricia McKissack. *Language Arts, 69,* 69–74.

Merriam, Eve Cox, S. T. (1989). A word or two with Eve Merriam: Talking about poetry. *The New Advocate, 2,* 139–150; Sloan, G. (1981). Profile: Eve Merriam. *Language Arts, 58,* 957–964.

Mikolaycak, Charles White, D. E. (1981). Profile: Charles Mikolaycak. *Language Arts, 58,* 850–857.

Mohr, Nicholasa   Zarnowski, M. (1991). An interview with author Nicholasa Mohr. *The Reading Teacher, 45,* 100–107.

Montresor, Beni   Raymond, A. (April, 1990). Beni Montresor: Carmen, Cannes and Caldecott. *Teaching PreK–8, 20,* 31–33.

Moser, Barry   Moser, B. (1987). Artist at work: Illustrating the classics. *Horn Book Magazine, 63,* 703–709; Moser, B. (1991). Family photographs, gathered fragments. *The New Advocate, 4,* 1–10.

Munsch, Robert   Jenkinson, D. (1989). Profile: Robert Munsch, *Language Arts, 66,* 665–675.

Myers, Walter Dean   Bishop, R. S. (1990). Profile: Walter Dean Myers. *Language Arts, 67,* 862–866.

Naylor, Phyllis Reynolds   Naylor, P. R. (1992). The writing of *Shiloh. The Reading Teacher, 46,* 10–13.

O'Dell, Scott   Roop, P. (1984). Profile: Scott O'Dell. *Language Arts, 61,* 750–752.

Parker, Nancy Winslow   Raymond, A. (May, 1990). Nancy Winslow Parker: "I knew it would happen." *Teaching PreK–8, 20,* 34–36.

Paterson, Katherine   Jones, L. T. (1981). Profile: Katherine Paterson. *Language Arts, 58,* 189–196; Namovic, G. I. (1981). Katherine Paterson. *Horn Book Magazine, 57,* 394–399; Paterson, K. (1981). Newbery Medal acceptance. *Horn Book Magazine, 57,* 385–393.

Pinkney, Jerry   Cummings, P. (1992). *Talking with artists* (pp. 60–65). New York: Bradbury Press.

Prelutsky, Jack   Raymond, A. (November/December, 1986). Jack Prelutsky . . . Man of many talents. *Teaching PreK–8, 17,* 38–42; Vardell, S. (1991). An interview with Jack Prelutsky. *The New Advocate, 4,* 101–112.

Provensen, Alice and Martin   Provensen, A., & Provensen, M. (1984). Caldecott Medal acceptance. *Horn Book Magazine, 50,* 444–448; Willard, N. (1984). Alice and Martin Provensen. *Horn Book Magazine, 50,* 449–452.

Rice, Eve   Raymond, A. (April, 1989). Meet Eve Rice: Author/artist/doctor (doctor?). *Teaching PreK–8, 19,* 40–42.

Rylant, Cynthia   Silvey, A. (1987). An interview with Cynthia Rylant. *Horn Book Magazine, 63,* 695–702.

Say, Allen   An interview with Allen Say, 1994 Caldecott Award winner. (1994–1995). *The Reading Teacher, 48,* 304–306.

Schoenherr, John   Gauch, P. L. (1988). John Schoenherr. *Horn Book Magazine, 64,* 460–463; Schoenherr, J. (1988). Caldecott Medal acceptance. *Horn Book Magazine, 64,* 457–459.

Schwartz, Alvin   Vardell, S. M. (1987). Profile: Alvin Schwartz. *Language Arts, 64,* 426–432.

Schwartz, Amy   Cummings, P. (1992). *Talking with artists* (pp. 66–71). New York: Bradbury Press.

Scieszka, Jon   Raymond, A. (1992, May). Jon Scieszka: Telling the *true story. Teaching PreK–8, 22,* 38–40.

Sendak, Maurice   Sendak, M. (1983). Laura Ingalls Wilder Award acceptance. *Horn Book Magazine, 59,* 474–477.

Sewall, Marcia   Sewall, M. (1988). *The pilgrims of Plimoth, Horn Book Magazine, 64,* 32–34.

Shulevitz, Uri   Raymond, A. (January, 1992). Uri Shulevitz: For children of all ages. *Teaching PreK–8, 21,* 38–40.

Smith, Lane   Cummings, P. (1992). *Talking with artists* (pp. 72–77). New York: Bradbury Press.

Soto, Gary   Soto, G. (1992). Author for a day: Glitter and rainbows. *The Reading Teacher, 46,* 200–203.

Speare, Elizabeth George   Hassler, P. J. (1993, May). The books of Elizabeth George Speare. *Book Links,* 14–20.

Spinelli, Jerry   Spinelli, J. (1991). Capturing Maniac Magee. *The Reading Teacher, 45,* 174–177.

Steig, Bill   Raymond, A. (August/September, 1991). Jeanne and Bill Steig: It adds up to magic. *Teaching PreK–8, 21,* 52–54.

Steptoe, John   Bradley, D. H. (1991). John Steptoe: Retrospective of an imagemaker. *The New Advocate, 4,* 11–24.

Tafuri, Nancy   Raymond, A. (January, 1987). Nancy Tafuri . . . Nature, picturebooks, and joy. *Teaching PreK–8, 17,* 34–36.

Taylor, Mildred D.   Dussel, S. L. (1981). Profile: Mildred D. Taylor. *Language Arts, 58,* 599–604.

Taylor, Theodore   Bagnall, N. (1980). Profile: Theodore Taylor: His models of self-reliance. *Language Arts, 57,* 86–91.

Uchida, Yoshiko   Chang, C. E. S. (1984). Profile: Yoshiko Uchida. *Language Arts, 61,* 189–194.

Van Allsburg, Chris   Cummings, P. (1992). *Talking with artists* (pp. 78–83). New York: Bradbury Press; Keifer, B. (1987). Profile: Chris Van Allsburg in three dimensions. *Language Arts, 64,* 664–671; Macaulay, D. (1986). Chris Van Allsburg. *Horn Book Magazine, 62,* 424–426; McKee, B. (1986). Van Allsburg: From a different perspective. *Horn Book Magazine, 62,* 556–571; Van Allsburg, C. (1982). Caldecott Medal acceptance. *Horn Book Magazine, 58,* 380–383; Van Allsburg, C. (1986). Caldecott Medal acceptance, *Horn Book Magazine, 62,* 420–424.

Voigt, Cynthia   Kauffman, D. (1985). Profile: Cynthia Voigt. *Language Arts, 62,* 876–880; Voigt, C. (1983). Newbery Medal acceptance. *Horn Book Magazine, 59,* 401–409.

Weisner, David   Cummings, P. (1992). *Talking with artists* (pp. 84–89). New York: Bradbury Press.

White, E. B.   Hopkins, L. B. (1986). Profile: In memoriam: E. B. White. *Language Arts, 63,* 491–494; Newmeyer, P. F. (1985). The creation of E. B. White's *The Trumpet of the Swans:* The manuscripts. *Horn Book Magazine, 61,* 17–28; Newmeyer, P. F. (1987). E. B. White: Aspects of style. *Horn Book Magazine, 63,* 586–591.

Wiesner, David   Caroff, S. F., & Moje, E. B. (1992–1993). A conversation with David Wiesner: 1992 Caldecott Medal winner. *The Reading Teacher, 46,* 284–289.

Willard, Nancy   Lucas, B. (1982). Nancy Willard. *Horn Book Magazine, 58,* 374–379; Willard, N. (1982). Newbery Medal acceptance. *Horn Book Magazine, 58,* 369–373.

Williams, Vera B.   Raymond A. (October, 1988). Vera B. Williams: Postcards and peace vigils. *Teaching PreK–8, 19,* 40–42.

Worth, Valerie   Hopkins, L. B. (1991). Profile: Valerie Worth. *Language Arts, 68,* 499–501.

Yolen, Jane   White, D. E. (1983). Profile: Jane Yolen. *Language Arts, 60,* 652–660; Yolen, J. (1989). On silent wings: The making of *Owl moon. The New Advocate, 2,* 199–212; Yolen, J. (1991). The route to story. *The New Advocate, 4,* 143–149; Yolen J. (1992). Past time: The writing of the picture book *Encounter. The New Advocate, 5,* 235–239.

Yorinks, Arthur   Raymond, A. (November/December, 1991). Arthur Yorinks: Talent in abundance. *Teaching PreK–8, 21,* 51–53.

Zalben, Jane Breskin   Yolen, J. (1990). In the artist's studio: Jane Breskin Zalben. *The New Advocate, 3,* 175–178.

Audiovisual Materials Profiling Authors and Illustrators

Alexander, Lloyd   "Meet the Newbery author: Lloyd Alexander," American School Publishers (sound filmstrip). (U)

Andersen, Hans Christian   "Meet the author: Hans Christian Andersen," American School Publishers (sound filmstrip or video). (M)

Armstrong, William H.   "Meet the Newbery author: William H. Armstrong," American School Publishers (sound filmstrip). (M–U)

Babbitt, Natalie   "Meet the Newbery author: Natalie Babbitt," American School Publishers (sound film-strip). (U)

Berenstain, Stan and Jan   "Meet Stan and Jan Berenstain," American School Publishers (sound film-strip). (P)

Blume, Judy   "First choice: Authors and books—Judy Blume," Pied Piper (sound filmstrip). (M–U)

Brown, Marc   "Meet Marc Brown," American School Publishers (video). (P–M)

Byars, Betsy   "Meet the Newbery author: Betsy Byars," American School Publishers (sound filmstrip). (M–U)

Carle, Eric   "Eric Carle: Picture writer," Philomel (video). (P–M)

Cherry, Lynne   "Get to know Lynne Cherry," Harcourt Brace (video). (M)

Cleary, Beverly   "First choice: Authors and books—Beverly Cleary," Pied Piper (sound filmstrip). (M); "Meet the Newbery author: Beverly Cleary," American School Publishers (sound filmstrip). (M)

Collier, James Lincoln and Christopher   "Meet the Newbery authors: James Lincoln Collier and Christopher Collier," American School Publishers (sound filmstrip). (U)

Cooper, Susan   "Meet the Newbery author: Susan Cooper," American School Publishers (sound film-strip). (U)

Crews, Donald   "Trumpet video visits Donald Crews," Trumpet Book Club (video). (P–M)

Dahl, Roald   "The author's eye: Roald Dahl," American School Publishers (kit with video). (M–U)

Fleischman, Sid   "First choice: Authors and books—Sid Fleischman," Pied Piper (sound filmstrip). (M–U)

Fritz, Jean   "Homesick: My own story," American School Publishers (sound filmstrip). (M–U)

George, Jean Craighead   "Meet the Newbery author: Jean Craighead George," American School Publishers (sound filmstrip). (U)

Giovanni, Nikki   "First choice: Poets and poetry—Nikki Giovanni," Pied Piper (sound filmstrip). (M–U)

Greene, Bette   "Meet the Newbery author: Bette Greene," American School Publishers (sound film-strip). (M–U)

Haley, Gail E.   "Tracing a legend: The story of the green man by Gail E. Haley," Weston Woods (sound filmstrip). (M); "Creating Jack and the bean tree: Tradition and technique," Weston Woods (sound filmstrip). (M)

Hamilton, Virginia   "First choice: Authors and books—Virginia Hamilton," Pied Piper (sound filmstrip). (U); "Meet the Newbery author: Virginia Hamilton," American School Publishers (sound filmstrip). (U)

Henry, Marguerite   "First choice: Authors and books—Marguerite Henry," Pied Piper (sound filmstrip). (M–U); "Meet the Newbery author: Marguerite Henry," American School Publishers (sound filmstrip). (M)

Highwater, Jamake   "Meet the Newbery author: Jamake Highwater," American School Publishers (sound film-strip). (M–U)

Keats, Ezra Jack   "Ezra Jack Keats," Weston Woods (film). (P)

Kellogg, Steven   "How a picture book is made," Weston Woods (video). (P–M); "Trumpet video visits Steven Kellogg," Trumpet Book Club (video). (P–M)

Konigsburg, E. L.   "First choice: Authors and books—E. L. Konigsburg," Pied Piper (sound filmstrip). (M–U)

Kuskin, Karla   "First choice: Poets and poetry—Karla Kuskin," Pied Piper (sound filmstrip). (M–U); "Poetry explained by Karla Kuskin," Weston Woods (sound film-strip). (M–U)

L'Engle, Madeleine   "Meet the Newbery author: Madeleine L'Engle," American School Publishers (sound filmstrip). (U)

Livingston, Myra Cohn   "First choice: Poets and poetry—Myra Cohn Livingston," Pied Piper (sound filmstrip). (M–U)

Lobel, Arnold   "Meet the Newbery author: Arnold Lobel," American School Publishers (sound filmstrip). (P–M)

Macaulay, David   "David Macaulay in his studio," Houghton Mifflin (video). (M–U)

McCloskey, Robert   "Robert McCloskey," Weston Woods (film). (P–M)

McCord, David   "First choice: Poets and poetry—David McCord," Pied Piper (sound filmstrip). (M–U)

McDermott, Gerald   "Evolution of a graphic concept: The stonecutter," Weston Woods (sound filmstrip). (P–M)

Merriam, Eve   "First choice: Poets and poetry—Eve Merriam," Pied Piper (sound filmstrip). (M–U)

Milne, A. A.   "Meet the author: A. A. Milne (and Pooh)," American School Publishers (sound filmstrip or video). (P)

Most, B.   "Get to know Bernard Most," Harcourt Brace (video). (P–M)

O'Dell, Scott   "Meet the Newbery author: Scott O'Dell," American School Publishers (sound filmstrip). (U); "A visit with Scott O'Dell," Houghton Mifflin (video). (U)

Paterson, Katherine   "The author's eye: Katherine Paterson," American School Publishers (kit with video).

(M–U); "Meet the Newbery author: Katherine Paterson," American School Publishers (sound filmstrip). (M–U)

Paulsen, Gary   "Trumpet video visits Gary Paulsen," Trumpet Book Club (video). (U)

Peet, Bill   "Bill Peet in his studio," Houghton Mifflin (video). (M)

Pinkney, Jerry   "Meet the Caldecott illustrator: Jerry Pinkney," American School Publishers (video). (P–M)

Potter, Beatrix   "Beatrix Potter had a pet named Peter," American School Publishers (sound filmstrip or video). (P)

Rylant, Cynthia   "Meet the Newbery author: Cynthia Rylant," American School Publishers (sound filmstrip or video). (M–U); "Meet the picture book author: Cynthia Rylant," American School Publishers (video). (P–M)

Sendak, Maurice   "Sendak," Weston Woods (film). (P–M)

Seuss, Dr.   "Who's Dr. Seuss?: Meet Ted Geisel," American School Publishers (sound filmstrip). (P–M)

Singer, Issac Bashevis   "Meet the Newbery author: Isaac Bashevis Singer," American School Publishers (sound filmstrip). (U)

Sobol, Donald J.   "The case of the Model-A Ford and the man in the snorkel under the hood: Donald J. Sobol," American School Publishers (sound filmstrip). (M)

White, E. B.   "Meet the Newbery author: E. B. White," American School Publishers (sound filmstrip). (M–U)

Wilder, Laura Ingalls   "Meet the Newbery author: Laura Ingalls Wilder," American School Publishers (sound filmstrip). (M–U)

Willard, Nancy   "Meet the Newbery author: Nancy Willard," American School Publishers (sound filmstrip). (M–U)

Yep, Laurence   "Meet the Newbery author: Laurence Yep," American School Publishers (sound filmstrip). (U)

Zolotow, Charlotte   "Charlotte Zolotow: The grower," American School Publishers (sound filmstrip). (P–M)

Addresses for Audiovisual Manufacturers

American School
  Publishers
P.O. Box 408
Hightstown, NJ 08520

Houghton Mifflin
2 Park Street
Boston, MA 02108

Pied Piper
P.O. Box 320
Verdugo City, CA 91046

Trumpet Book Club
P.O. Box 604
Holmes, PA 19043

Weston Woods
Weston, CT 06883

Author Index

Subject Index